GOING TO THE WARS

GOING TO THE WARS

The Experience of the English Civil Wars
1638–1651

Charles Carlton

BCA
LONDON · NEW YORK · SYDNEY · TORONTO

To the memory of my father, Colonel Charles
Hope Carlton, M.C., Royal Army Medical
Corps, who as a surgeon in two world wars knew
only too well the actuality of battle,
and
to my children, and their posterity,
in the hope that they may never know the
reality of what I am trying to describe.

This edition
published 1992
by BCA by arrangement
with Routledge
11 New Fetter Lane, London EC4P 4EE

Simultaneously published in the USA and Canada
by Routledge
a division of Routledge, Chapman and Hall, Inc.
29 West 35th Street, New York, NY 10001

© 1992 Charles Carlton
Typeset in 10 on 12 point Garamond by Intype Ltd, London
Printed in Great Britain by T. J. Press (Padstow) Ltd,
Padstow, Cornwall

CN 6862

CONTENTS

List of illustrations   vi
Foreword by John Keegan   viii
Acknowledgments   xi

1 THE ACTUALITIES OF WAR   1

2 THE DRUM'S DISCORDANT SOUND   7

3 A SIGHT – THE SADDEST THAT EYES CAN SEE   31

4 NAMING OF PARTS   66

5 A SOLDIER'S LIFE IS TERRIBLE HARD   89

6 THE EPITOME OF WAR   113

7 THE MISERABLE EFFECTS OF WAR   150

8 TRADESMEN OF KILLING . . . MANAGERS OF VIOLENCE   180

9 TO SLAY AND TO BE SLAIN   201

10 WHEN THE HURLYBURLY'S DONE   230

11 MORE TO SPOIL THAN TO SERVE   265

12 I DON'T WANT TO GO TO WAR   289

13 THEN WE STARTED ALL OVER AGAIN   310

14 DOES IT MATTER?   339

Notes   351
Index   410

ILLUSTRATIONS

between pages 276 and 277

1 'And when did you last see your father?', painting by W. F. Yeames. Walker Art Gallery, Liverpool

2 'De militia equestri antiqua et nova', 1630.

3 'Militarie instructions for the cavallrie', 1632.

4 Battle of Naseby, 1645. Illustration from Joshua Sprigge's *Anglia Rediviva*. E. T. Archive

5 Another contemporary plan of the Battle of Naseby, 1645, exaggerating the strength of the Royalist army. E. T. Archive

6 A 1642 caricature of a pillaging soldier. British Library

7 'The Parliament of Women', 1646. British Library

8 Prince Rupert's dog Boy, painted by his sister Princess Louise. National Trust; photograph Courtauld Institute

9 'A dog's elegy', from a contemporary satirical pamphlet, 1644, on the death of Prince Rupert's pet dog. British Library

10 Hugh Peters, parliamentary army chaplain

11 'The Loyall Sacrifice'. British Museum

12 Scene from 'Les Misères et les malheurs de la guerre', showing the hanging of thieves. Etching by Jacques Callot, 1633. E. T. Archive

13 The Siege of Basing House, 1645, in its final stages, with the principal tower destroyed. British Museum

14 An engraving of the Battle of Dunbar, commissioned by Parliament in 1651. Ashmolean Museum, Oxford

15 Atrocities in Ireland, 1641. Fotomas Index

16 Irish massacre scenes. Fotomas Index

17 A page from William Barriffe's Drill Book, 1639.

18 'A great and bloody fight at Colchester', 1648. Fotomas Index

19 The Siege of Oxford by Jan de Wyck. E. T. Archive

20 Sir Edward Walker and Charles I by unknown artist. National Portrait Gallery

21 Portrait of John 1st Lord Byron by William Dobson. Tabley House Collection, University of Manchester; photograph Courtauld Institute

22 Colonel Thomas St Aubyn, by Popham. Private collection; photograph Courtauld Institute

FOREWORD

Military history has undergone a great change in the last thirty years. Even in the two decades after the Second World War it remained what it had traditionally been, a record of events and decisions rather than of personal experience. The war inspired a great deal of personal reminiscence, yet historians – even those who were themselves veterans – made little attempt to integrate any of it with their narrative. The development of social history had already influenced political and economic historians; the social history of warfare continued to remain neglected long after historians in other disciplines had begun to realize the importance of admitting the personal dimension into their writing.

Signs of change appeared slowly. In 1943 Irvin Bell Wiley published his remarkable *The Life of Johnny Reb* and in 1952 followed it with a companion volume, *The Life of Billy Yank*. The two books attempted to portray, with considerable success, what the material circumstances of campaign were for the common soldier on each side in the American Civil War. He did not, however, deal at length with the experience of the soldier on the battlefield. In 1947 the American combat historian, S. L. A. Marshall, published a short but seminal work, *Men Against Fire*, which argued that the battlefield experience was a social one; his theme was that social and cultural factors went far to determine how men did – or did not – fight.

These approaches began to bear fruit in the 1970s. In 1976 I published a book, *The Face of Battle*, which drew upon the methods of both Marshall and Wiley. It attracted considerable attention, was translated into seven languages and remains in print to this day. It was, however, experimental in method and limited in scope. More recently specialist scholars have applied the social history method to particular wars or periods of military history with a more rigorous attention to sources than I had attempted. Victor Hanson, an American classical scholar, re-interpreted hoplite warfare in fifth-century Greece through careful assessment of city-state social history in the texts. Geoffrey Parker had already reconstructed the social dimension of the Eighty Years' War in great detail from the records of the Spanish army in the Netherlands.

Parker confined his treatment, however, to the routines of the Spanish army, while Hanson had been more interested in the battlefield experience. Though each had achieved noteworthy scholarly advances, they had been made on a single axis rather than across the whole front. Charles Carlton, in this admirable and original book, shows how our knowledge and understanding of a much-studied war can be transformed by integrating the social history of both campaign and battle into a single whole.

By meticulous re-sifting of the texts, using testimony overlooked or rejected by earlier historians, he has made the English Civil War – and its satellite conflicts in Scotland and Ireland – a comprehensible, convincing and moving human event. It is difficult to think of any of its aspects he has neglected. Death, wounds, hunger, hardship, fatigue, want of shelter, absence from home and of loved ones, lack of news – all the ordeals, fears and anxieties which form the real and daily experience of the soldier in battle or on campaign are here, richly documented from letters, contemporary pamphlets and official records. So, too, are the inducements and consolations of going to the wars – loot, travel, freedom from the daily grind, jolly company, chance encounters with the opposite sex. He recognizes and records the ordeals that the war threw on women; but also the emancipation that it brought some of them, obliged to run families or manage estates in the absence of their menfolk. His passages on the anguish that separation brought to couples united by heartfelt affection supply an important corrective to the view propagated by many early modern historians that marriage in the pre-Romantic age was a 'businesslike' arrangement. His emphasis on the deep affront to their Christian morality felt by many challenged to take sides – even when they did so – is a corrective, too, to the approach of those historians who represent seventeenth-century religion as a cloak for material interest.

Historians of battle – who think, as I do, that battle is what war is ultimately about – will be particularly impressed by his unflinching analysis of what happened when pike and shot drew to killing range on the small – but surprisingly numerous – fields of the war's engagements. Carlton's civil war is war in all its dimensions. His book is a magnificent book. It will be read, used, quoted and admired by historians of the English Civil War, and by military historians in general, for decades to come. As an example of how the history of a single war may be written in the round, it will put the historical community on its mettle.

ACKNOWLEDGMENTS

In writing this book I have incurred many obligations, which it is my most pleasant duty to acknowledge. First and foremost I am extremely grateful to the Harry F. Guggenheim Foundation for awarding me a fellowship for two years during which I was able to do the bulk of the research and writing. My own university generously supplemented this grant. I am grateful to the Folger Shakespeare Library, and to the Cambridge University Library for their help and many kindnesses. Staff from my own university library, particularly from the inter-library loan department, are a tribute to the outstanding work of North Carolina State University's unsung heroines – and heroes. At Cambridge University I enjoyed the hospitality of Wolfson College, and the intellectual stimulation of Professor Collinson's and Dr Morrill's seminars. I am grateful to the members of the latter, as well as to audiences at the Pacific Coast Conference of British Studies, the North American Conference of British Studies, the American Military Institute, and Triangle Strategic Studies Seminar, for many helpful comments.

I am particularly delighted that John Keegan has written the foreword to this book for it was he who – perhaps unknowingly – planted the seed from which it has grown. About ten years ago I was invited to an after-dinner talk given by a Sandhurst lecturer at Cambridge to a small group of senior army officers on what had historically made the British soldier fight. Drugs – especially alcohol – and plunder, Mr Keegan argued with compelling evidence, were the main reasons. As colonels fumed and brigadiers turned puce, I thought this was a brilliant insight. It prompted me to read Mr Keegan's work which has been the inspiration not just for this book but for a generation of 'new military historians'.

I am grateful to my niece and nephew, Sophie and Ralph Bostock, for the patience (doubtless augmented by the promise of a trip to MacDonalds) they displayed when I dragged them around Edgehill and Cropredy. Hally Philips hosted my visits to Carisbrook, while Alan Turton showed me Basing, letting me try on his armour and port his pike. Visiting battlefields has been one of the more pleasant tasks, from striding across Naseby in the rain, getting my legs torn in the hedgerows of Newbury, getting lost in the bocage of Lostwithiel, and picnicking near the (disgracefully neglected) Queen's Sconce at Newark.

While researching and writing this book I was fortunate to be invited to teach during the early summers of 1988 and 1989 at Liaoning University, Shenyang, China, where friends – who had better remain nameless – taught me a lot about revolutions and the memory of civil war. Even though my course on the English Revolution, scheduled a couple of weeks before Tiananmen Square, was cancelled by the Chinese one, those exhilarating days taught me much about the tumultuous 1640s. Reading about them in the quiet of a library or the security of one's study one can too easily forget how emotionally draining such times can be. Then ordinary men can be great, powerful people can turn craven, and all have to live with their consciences. As the regicide Thomas Harrison said about Charles I's trial and execution, 'It was not a thing done in a corner.'* Seeing Shenyang's students march off to protest against a corrupt regime must have been like watching, say, the London Trained Bands depart for Gloucester. Being the only westerner on a train hijacked by radicals gave me some idea of the chaos and fear that ideas in action can engender. Sitting with a quarter of a million people outside the provincial communist party headquarters, the world seemed about to be turned upside down. And a few days later when the experience of defeat came to Tiananmen Square, I cried: but then so did many cavaliers on 30 January, 1649.

In another respect, at least, writing a book is similar to fighting a war: in both what keeps one going – more than anything else – is the friendship and advice of others. Among the many people who have helped me far more than they can ever realize and I can ever acknowledge with a mere alphabetical list are: G. R. Aylmer, Joe Caddel, Anthony Clayton, Esther Cope, Barbara Donagan, Christopher Duffy, G. R. Elton, Mark Fissell, Edward Furgol, Ian Gentles, Don Higginbotham, Joe Hobbs, Richard Holmes, J. R. Kenyon, Clark McCauley, Alistair Menzies, John Morrill, Jane Ohlmeyer, Geoffrey Parker, Linda Peck, Paul Seaver, Joe Slavin, Lawrence Stone and Andrew Wheatcroft. Last, and never least, to Caroline my greatest debt is due, for always being there whenever I came back from the wars.

5 August 1991
Raleigh, North Carolina

* Quoted by C. V. Wedgwood, *The Trial of Charles I* (1964), 252.

1

THE ACTUALITIES OF WAR

If I had time and anything like your ability to study war, I think I should concentrate almost entirely on 'the actualities of war' – the effects of tiredness, hunger, fear, lack of sleep, weather . . . it is the actualities which make war so complicated and difficult, and are usually so neglected by historians.

> Field Marshal Wavell to Basil Liddell-Hart

In the summer of 1639 Richard Lovelace had everything a young man of 20 could wish for, 'being then accounted', wrote the contemporary historian, Anthony Wood, 'the most amiable and beautiful person that eye ever beheld . . . much adored and admired by the female sex'.[1] Lovelace was the eldest son of a large, wealthy and ancient Kentish family. Both his father and grandfather had been distinguished soldiers. He had the double blessing of a Cambridge education and an Oxford MA, while his excellent connections at court obtained him an ensign's commission in the First Bishops' War and a captain's in the Second. In the well-known lines Lovelace explained to his Lucasta the excitement that he – like so many other innocent young men before and since – felt about going to the wars:

> Tell me not, Sweet, I am unkind
> That from the nunnery
> Of thy chaste breast and quiet mind,
> To war and arms I flee.

Over the years much has been written about the wars to which Lovelace went, because historians as distinguished as G. M. Trevelyan have argued that the cataclysm which engulfed the British Isles in the middle of the seventeenth century was the most important happening in our history. At the time Edward Hyde, the Earl of Clarendon, described it as the Great Rebellion in which a few extremists duped the mass of decent moderate men. While this view prevailed during the eighteenth century, in the first half of the nineteenth Thomas Babington Macaulay challenged it by arguing that the civil wars were essentially a Herculean struggle between liberty

1

and despotism, which the former won, thus making possible the glories of Victorian England. Towards the end of the century S. R. Gardiner portrayed the turmoil as a Puritan Revolution, in which Godly Protestants resisted the counter reformation of pseudo-catholic royalists. In more recent times Karl Marx and his followers have interpreted the crisis of mid-seventeenth-century England as the first great Bourgeois Revolution. During this period the gentry supposedly rose – or at least the mere gentry came to the top – as the aristocracy experienced a crisis. Others have turned this thesis on its head by arguing that the aristocracy was behind the revolution all the time. Recently revisionist historians have stressed the short-term, even accidental nature of events, in which the acts of individuals played a more important role than the seemingly inevitable and impersonal forces that the reformation set in motion a century before. John Morrill, for instance, has suggested that the civil wars were essentially Wars of Religion.[2]

Whatever these events may have been, of two things there can be no doubt. First that the debate over the causes and nature of the crisis that engulfed the British Isles during the middle of the seventeenth century will continue, and second that they were a complex series of wars, in which men and women killed and were killed, had their bodies maimed, and had to endure some of the most traumatic experiences any human being can face. While these wars may have had different causes, may have been waged for widely varying goals, and may have employed different techniques, they share a commonality which is only just beginning to be recognized.[3] The appellation 'the Wars of the Three Kingdoms' is rather a mouthful (which anyway ignores the Principality of Wales). Perhaps they could be better called 'The British Civil Wars' if only because this is more succinct, and may be used to include Ireland as part of the British Isles.[4] Without doubt contemporaries recognized the conflict's complex nature, the first use of the term 'civil wars' being in a pamphlet of 1643.[5]

There is no shortage of excellent books on the civil wars. J. R. Kenyon's *The Civil Wars of England* (New York, 1988) is the best recent survey that combines military and political history. *The English Civil Wars: A Military History of the Three Civil Wars, 1642–51* (1974) by P. Young and R. Holmes is an excellent introduction. Austin Woolrych's *Battles of the English Civil War* (1961) and A. H. Burne's *The Battlefields of England* (1951) deal with the confrontations between armies, while Brigadier Peter Young, the doyen of civil-war historians, has covered individual battles in his many books and articles.[6]

The supply of local studies is just as rich. County histories as those by Mary Coate on Cornwall, R. W. Ketton-Cremer on Norfolk, A. C. Wood on Nottinghamshire, David Underdown on Somerset, Anthony Fletcher on Sussex, Alan Everitt on Kent, Anne Hughes on Warwickshire, and Valerie Pearl on London, spring to mind.[7] So do regional studies, such as

Clive Holmes's *The Eastern Association during the English Civil War* (Cambridge, 1974), John Morrill's *The Revolt of the Provinces* (1976), and David Stevenson's *The Scottish Revolution, 1637–44* (Newton Abbot, 1973), and *Revolution and Counter Revolution in Scotland* (1977). The list of biographical studies of participants in the war, ranging from major figures, such as Charles I and Cromwell, to minor players, such as Sir Richard Grenville or Ralph Josselin, is too long to mention. C. H. Firth and Godfrey Davis have written widely on the parliamentary forces.[8] Mark Kishlansky has contributed a provocative interpretation in *The Rise of the New Model Army* (Cambridge, 1979), while the work of Ronald Hutton, Peter Newman, Ian Roy and Joyce Malcolm have done much to shed light on the royalist armed forces.[9] Last, and far from least, there are numerous investigations of the wars' political background, of which those by J. H. Hexter, Blair Worden and Brian Manning are especially noteworthy.[10]

This book will not try to duplicate such works. Instead it will look at the war as a war, as an experience in which violence – real or threatened – affected the lives of the inhabitants of the British Isles. Since there was little fighting at sea, the main effect of the navy, which parliament controlled, being to prevent foreign intervention, this book will examine the 'actualities of war' on land.

'If I had time and anything like your ability to study war,' wrote Field Marshal Wavell, the Second World War British Commander, to Sir Basil Liddell-Hart, another equally distinguished writer on military matters,

> I think that I should concentrate almost entirely on the 'actualities of war' – the effects of tiredness, hunger, fear, lack of sleep, weather. . . .
> The principles of strategy and tactics, and the logistics of war are really absurdly simple: it is the actualities that make war so complicated and so difficult, and are usually so neglected by historians.

Wavell was reiterating a point that Leo Tolstoy had made nearly a century before. The Russian novelist, who had seen action in the Caucasus and Crimea, admitted that he was fascinated with 'the reality of war, the actual killing. I was more interested to know in what way and under the influence of what feeling one soldier kills another than to know how the armies were arranged at Austerlitz and Borodino.' Professor Geoffrey Elton, the distinguished Cambridge historian, who also fought as an infantryman in the British Army in Italy, agrees that professional historians have neglected the realities of war, since 'astonishingly few' of them have addressed this topic.[11]

At one level the reasons for this neglect are simple: at another they are extraordinarily complex.

Surviving records dictate the sort of history which may be written. Ordnance, for instance, always creates large amounts of paperwork, if only because 'bumpf' is a hedge against the misappropriation of material. For much the same reason armies usually create good pay and muster rolls. Thus it is far easier to write a history of the raising of an army than on how that army fought. Again, because headquarters units are safely away from combat, it is much simpler to write on strategy, showing how divisions and regiments moved cleanly like pins on a map, than it is to show tactically how platoons, squads, individuals, scrabbled frantically on the ground.

Training manuals, military codes of conduct usually survive as records of how things should be done. Unit diaries or ships' logs may record a version of what might have happened. Yet even logs or diaries, sometimes written during the heat of battle, usually eschew the actualities of war, for the banalities of hard facts, such as the text of orders rather than whether they were, or could have been carried out. During battle men are often too busy or too frightened to create records, and when they do so are often surprised by the banality of what they produce. For instance, the recording of RAF crew intercom conversations or the chatter of US gunship helicopter pilots in Vietnam during intense combat frequently sound like a parody of a bad war film.

The reason is simple: human beings often try to hide behind banality in order to escape the extraordinary.

Without doubt war is the most horrible, most catastrophic, and most immoral event known to man. It is, to quote Tolstoy again, 'the vilest thing in life'. Such a conclusion contradicts the assumptions of human progress inherent in the Whig view of history. For Marxist historians war is in itself irrelevant since the long-term results are inevitable. Because all too often military history has been used to glorify war, or else to train officers to win bigger and bloodier battles, it has gained a less than savoury reputation. But as Clausewitz, the nineteenth-century Prussian who founded the modern study of war warned, 'it is of no purpose, it is even against one's better interests to turn away from the consideration of the real nature of the affair, because the horror of its elements excites repugnance.'[12] At the individual level war threatens death or horrid wounds, noises, sights and fears that those innocent of battle cannot imagine, and those who have survived cannot forget. War is so obscene that it is pornographic.

And yet war, like pornography, exerts a profound fascination. If, as General William T. Sherman insisted, war is hell, then, as artists from Dante to Hieronymous Bosch have recognized, many people find looking at the experience of hell, as opposed to actually going there, far more interesting than heaven. 'As long as war is regarded as wicked, it will have its fascination', Oscar Wilde observed. Norman Davies took this point a stage further when he wrote that 'The popularity of books and films dealing with war and violence, like that for pornography . . . attests to the pleasure provided by the vicarious satisfaction of frustrated drives.' The links between male sexuality and violence are nigh universal, having been charted in some 112 different societies. They do not appear to have changed much over time, having been recognized long before Sigmund Freud delineated them. During the American Revolution, for instance, Dr Samuel Johnson noted that 'every man thinks meanly of himself for not having been a soldier'. More recently during the Falklands campaign an officer in the Parachute Regiment observed 'The only real test of a man is when the firing starts.'[13]

It is as if having experienced battle was as much a criterion for full masculinity as having had sex. Indeed the links between being a warrior and being a man have always been strong. Bulstrode Whitelocke, who took part in the civil war, recalled that in September 1643 at the First Battle of Newbury 'both sides performed then with good manhood and animosity'.[14] The ability of a soldier's uniform to attract women has always helped persuade young men to take the Queen's shilling. Just as US Marine Corps recruiters used to promise 'to build men', so Captain Abraham Stanton, a veteran of the English civil war, avowed that as a result of military training 'Myriads of men now bear arms that bore nothing but only shapes of men before.'[15] Troops innocent of battle are called virgin soldiers, waiting for the baptism of fire, which is seen as an important an event – although hopefully a far less pleasant one – in their lives, as losing their virginity.[16] Thus Edward Hyde, the civil wars' most distinguished contemporary historian, called Lord Somerset, the duke whom Charles I made a general notwithstanding his complete lack of military experience, 'a virgin soldier'.[17]

Having never seen combat – although having served as a part-time soldier – I am all too aware of the problems faced in trying to write about an experience of which I am innocent. They are a little like those faced by a lifelong celibate trying to draft a sex manual. Both activities are so personal, so intense that no amount of reading other people's experiences can fully compensate for the lack of one's own.

On the other hand, because they are so intensely personal, one's own experiences can cloud other people's. One tends to see all military events in egotistical terms. Having combat experience may lock one into a view of battle from which it is very difficult to escape. For instance, a Vietnam veteran, even one who believes in God, may find it hard to credit the role religion played in combat in the English civil war: he would credit his survival to our artillery support, their bad shooting, or pure luck, rather than the direct personal intervention of the Almighty. As Sir Basil Liddell-Hart observed, the historian who fought during the defeat of Dunkirk might find the elation felt by the victorious cavalry at Naseby far harder to comprehend than if he had never left the secure confines of his study.[18]

'We have shared the incommunicable experience of war', wrote Oliver

Wendell Holmes of his service in the Union Army. Battle is so traumatic an experience that even today survivors are loath to talk about it, particularly those who were on the losing side. When they do so they often hide in formulas or clichés, which seem to act as salve for mental wounds that may never heal. Such was even more true in the seventeenth century, for which records of close introspection about all matters (except religious salvation) were extremely rare.[19] The few autobiographies or diaries from the period do not convey a very strong sense of self. When seventeenth-century men did write about their wartime experiences they invariably used the third person. Just because those veterans did not talk so openly about fear, violence, elation and despair, as men do today, it does not necessarily follow that they did not experience them as intensely. Thus whenever possible I have quoted extensively from the records so the survivors of the civil wars may speak for themselves. If the subject of my book is war and the pity of war, then the people best able to explain it are those others who have known it at first hand.

To overcome the chasm between his own experience and the experiences about which he is writing the military historian must use all the tools of his trade. While the experience of battle changes over time, as General Sir John Hackett has recently argued 'the essential soldier remains the same. Whether he is handling a sling shot weapon on Hadrian's Wall, or whether he is in a main battle tank today, he is essentially the same.' As the pop singer Donovan described 'The Universal Soldier':[20]

> He's four foot two, and he's six foot four
> He fights with muscles and with spears.
> He's all of thirty one and he's only seventeen
> He's been a soldier for a thousand years.

Perhaps historians have focused too much on change rather than continuity. We may be able to learn more about the experience of war in the British Isles three centuries ago by also examining it in more recent times, when interviews, even statistical surveys, the starkness of film, the frankness of novelists and the writers of memoirs, and the work of military sociologists have done much to shed light on its reality.

But come to think of it there is little difference between this and other historical endeavours. Few political historians have served as kings or presidents: hardly a business historian has headed a major corporation. So going to the British civil wars is in many respects much like embarking on any other historical journey. To discover the actualities of war the historian must first immerse himself in the surviving records, and then with caution and imagination combine his own experiences with those of others to make that leap into the dark that is the past.

2

THE DRUM'S DISCORDANT
SOUND

I hate the Drum's Discordant Sound,
Parading round and round and round.
To thoughtless youth it pleasure yields
And lures from cities and from fields.
John Scot of Amwell (1730–83)

In 1628 Sir Edward Cecil, Viscount Wimbledon, a veteran of the continental wars, complained that 'This Kingdom hath been too long at peace.'
Perhaps he was trying to justify the failure of the expedition to Cadiz
which he had led with a degree of incompetence noteworthy even for
early seventeenth-century English generals, for he continued, 'our old
commanders, both by sea and by land are worn out, and few men are
bred in their places, for the knowledge of war, and almost the thought of
war is extinguished.'[1]

Others – at home and abroad – agreed with Cecil. In the Spanish
Netherlands most people thought the English had become 'effeminate,
unable to endure the fatigations and travails of a war: delicate, well-fed,
given to tobaccos, wine, strong drink, feather beds; undisciplined,
unarmed, unfurnished with money and munitions'.[2] Englishmen agreed.
'What hath effeminated our English, but a long disuse of arms?' asked
Richard Johnson in 1631.[3] Seven years later James Wemyss, Master Gunner
of England, wrote to Charles I, who was contemplating going to war
against the Scots, that the realm was woefully unprepared: there were, for
instance, only four men in the land who knew how to fire a mortar.[4] The
situation in the Ordnance Office was even worse. According to Sir John
Haydon, the surveyor was ill, the chief clerk was in prison, two other
clerks had absconded, a third was out of town, the yeoman and his gunner
were absent without leave, while the master gunner was dead.[5]

In spite of such dire warnings, and contrary to the advice of John
Stewart, Earl of Traquair and Lord Treasurer of Scotland, that it would
take a standing army of at least forty thousand English troops to make
the Scots use the new prayer book just issued in the king's name, Charles

insisted on a war.[6] The preparations reflected England's pacific traditions. 'Out of curiosity to see the spectacle of our public death, I went to Bramham Moor to see the training of our light horse', wrote Sir Henry Slingsby, a Yorkshire gentleman. His diary entry continued: 'These are a strange spectacle to this nation in this age that have lived this long peaceable, without noise of shot or drum, and we have stood neutral and in peace whilst all the world beside hath been in arms and wasted with it.'[7]

The contrast between the bumbling light cavalry which Slingsby saw playing on Bramham Moor, and the reality of continental combat could not have been more marked. Seventeenth-century Europe was extremely warlike. 'This is the century of the soldier', observed the Italian poet, Falvio Testir, in 1641.[8] There were only three years of peace during the whole of the seventeenth century: its wars were more frequent and widespread, lasted longer, and killed many more people, both civilians and combatants, than before. As Sir George Clark has written, 'war was not a mere succession of occurrences, but an institution, a regular and settled mode of action, for which provision was made through the ordering of social life.'[9] So profound was this change that several historians have talked of a 'Military Revolution'. Armies became bigger, soldiers were better trained, the state grew more powerful. Europe was approaching the modern age when, to use Clausewitz's dictum, 'War is a mere continuation of policy by other means.'[10]

The ways by which wars are continued are many. The causes of wars may be complex, and although not fully understood at the time can become a matter of acrimonious debate for historians ever since. To fight a war, taxes must be levied, soldiers must be recruited and trained, officers appointed, plans made, and supplies supplied. All these changes took place in the British Isles during the 1640s when the military revolution touched all the three kingdoms, transforming the British Isles from a military backwater to the forefront of European affairs. All over the land large armies were raised, modern tactics were introduced, and millions were touched by war and its violence. So profound was this change that war became the norm. Instead of the demand for demobilization which has usually followed great wars, such as the Napoleonic War, or the World Wars of our own century, soldiers – at least on the winning side – wanted to remain with the colours. Thus a standing army came into being.[11]

Even though the Restoration did much to curb the power of the military, by turning the commonwealth into a horrid example of what happens when jumped-up major generals take over, Britain continued to maintain a strong military presence, primarily at sea. Just as parliament changed from being an occasion into an institution, so did the conduct of war. Such should not be surprising, for a main function of the former has always been to pay for the latter.

It has always been the individual soldier, sailor or airman who has paid war's final price, and has been the ultimate means by which it has been prosecuted. It is they who answer the drum's discordant sound: they are the ones who must bridge that chasm from peace and living to killing and death.

John Evelyn experienced this transition when on coming down from Oxford he volunteered to join the king's army. The drunkenness, swearing and fornication of the soldiery upset him so much that he retreated quite literally to cultivate his garden. When England became too dangerous even for that harmless hobby, Evelyn fled to the continent.

Of course nothing can fully prepare one for the realities of war, and yet the British Isles went to civil war during the middle of the seventeenth century with a surprising ease. Five influences greased the skids. First, the varying degree of violence present in different parts of the British Isles. Second, the previous experiences and folk memories of war. Third, the military institutions which already existed. Fourth, the mental mechanisms that facilitated going to war. And fifth, the baptism of fire that most individuals faced. The first three influences will be discussed in this chapter, and the last two in the next.

Several historians have argued that early modern England was a pretty violent place, where men frequently carried weapons which they used at the least provocation. 'This was a rough, superstitious, excitable and volatile society', Geoffrey Elton wrote about Henrician England.[12] According to A. L. Rowse things had, if anything, got worse by Good Queen Bess's Glorious Days. 'One cannot exaggerate the violence latent in society', he wrote,

> the violence of men's impulses was, as often as not, uninhibited and released ... stealing and robbery were endemic ... murder and manslaughter were frequent, there were constant fights and affrays, ending in wounding or death. ... Life in a world where pestilence and famine were regular, was indeed very cheap.

This image of an England which apparently combined the nastiest features of Matt Dillon's Dodge City with those of Ian Paisley's Belfast, carried over into the early seventeenth century, when, according to Carl Bridenbaugh, the 'daily life in England' was 'crowned with crimes of violence'.[13] The authorities then responsible for law and order agreed. They instituted vicious public punishments for violent crimes, and ordered that the official homily against 'Contention and Brawling' be read frequently in every church on Sunday.[14]

A statistical analysis (albeit a rudimentary one), does not support the view that early modern England was an especially violent place. Between 1588–90 and 1630–9 a peer's chances of being involved in a fray fell threefold.[15] In seventeenth-century Myddle, the Shropshire village chronicled by Richard Gough, there were only two executions: one, a civil war soldier, hanged for horse stealing, and the other a common murderer. Between 1560 and 1750 in Earls Colne, a larger village in Essex, there were three homicide convictions. In the county of Essex, between 1620 and 1630, there were some 190 accusations of murder – a rarely undiscovered crime.[16] These killings owed as much to alcohol as to pre-meditation, one-third being committed during or immediately after a drinking bout. Then, as now, drink was an important narcotic in releasing men's inhibitions against violence. While the comparative scarcity of fire-arms, which accounted for 11.6 per cent of the homicides, would lessen fatalities from brawls, rudimentary medical care meant that a far higher proportion of those wounded during them died.

Figures from Westmorland in the second half of the seventeenth century show even lower levels of violent crimes. There were very few assaults, or rapes, or even cattle rustling in the county, particularly when compared to non-violent crimes such as coin clipping, burglary and theft. In the whole of Westmorland, a border county where one might anticipate much mayhem, during the last half of the century there were only half a dozen murders. Perhaps this was due to a shortage of firearms. In Kirkby Lonsdale in the 1620s only 5 per cent and in the 1630s 7 per cent of households possessed weapons, as compared to 17 per cent in the 1640s.[17]

Levels of violence are, of course, relative. Yet compared to other societies seventeenth-century England was surprisingly peaceful. In late Elizabethan and early Stuart England, when one monograph alleges that rural artisans lived 'in contempt of all authority', there were some forty food riots. Yet during the eighteenth century – that Age of the Aristocracy when deference seemingly prevailed – the rate was three times higher.[18] Stuart England lacked the casual and common, official and private violence of Bourbon France. Compared to seventeenth-century rural China, where murder, mutilations, revenge killings, organized crime, bandits and blood feuds, were mundane, it was a veritable oasis of tranquillity.[19] Using the figures for reported murders, and cases ruled as murder after they had been brought to trial, we can calculate a homicide rate per hundred thousand inhabitants of 1.42 and 0.83 for Essex. The figure for Westmorland was lower at 0.04: that for Kent higher at 4.2. The equivalent figures for England and the United States today are 4 and 9.4. So the problems of obtaining and interpreting statistics notwithstanding, seventeenth-century England seems to have been a reasonably peaceful society.[20]

Of course, the relationship between a society's level of violence and its capability to go to war is a tenuous one. For instance it would be hard – and perilous – to compare the fighting records of British Army regiments which recruit from vicious slums, with those who draw from bucolic shires. While the American South has a record of personal violence, it would be foolish to suggest that its long-standing military traditions have given it a pronounced superiority on the battlefield as compared to other parts of the United States. On the other hand inhibitions against war, such of those of various Indian ethnic groups as compared to, say, the Sikhs, Gurkhas or Rajputs, can inhibit a group's readiness to fight.

In the dozen years before the outbreak of the British civil wars official royal propaganda extolled the blessings of peace. 'Look up', Ben Jonson advised people as they entered the Banqueting Hall at Whitehall, 'to read the king in all his actions.' Above them they would see Rubens' master-piece, one of whose three great central panels acclaimed James I as a peace-maker.[21] More obvious was the message in Rubens' 'Saint George and the Dragon', a painting which so pleased the king that he gave the artist a diamond ring. In it he painted Charles as St George, England's patron saint, who has just rescued a maiden (who bears an uncanny resemblance to Queen Henrietta Maria) from the Dragon of War. On the left two women support a third who has apparently just survived a fate worse than death. In the foreground are corpses, and civilians begging for mercy. All of them are symbolic victims of the Thirty Years' War, from which happy England has been spared, as demonstrated by the idyllic rural background and the heavenly choir of cherubs fluttering above.[22]

Painting was not the only form of court-sponsored art which celebrated the advantages of peace. Poets identified the king with peace:

> Welcome Great Sir, and with all the joy that's due,
> To the return of Peace and You.

Thus wrote Abraham Cowley on Charles's return from a state visit to Scotland in 1633.[23] Masques such as *The Triumph of Peace* (1633) were dedicated:

> To you, Great King and Queen, whose
> Smile doth scatter blessings through the Isle.

Thomas Carew joined in the chorus:[24]

> But let us that in Myrtyle bowers sit
> Under secure shields, use the benefit
> Of peace and plenty, which the blessed hand
> Of our good king gives this obdurate land.

And if England did have problems then they were due to a surfeit of peace. *Salmacida Spolia*, the Twelfth Night Masque for 1640, opens with a Fury fomenting a storm over England:

> And I do stir the humours that increase,
> In thy full body, overgrown with peace.

This conceit, together with the masque's main message that the love of king and queen will bring harmony to a land where by early 1640 Charles's

Scots policy had failed, his army had refused to fight, and his personal rule was in tatters, was clearly absurd.

Notwithstanding the work of officially sponsored artists, poets and playwrights, Charles I's commitment to peace was a little thicker than the paint upon the ceiling of the Banqueting Hall. The king would have loved to bow to public pressure and join the Thirty Years' War, and thus restore his sister Elizabeth and her husband Frederick to the German Palatine whence they had been driven in 1618. Ballads urged:

> The true religion to maintain
> Come let us to the wars again.

But going to the wars meant going to parliament for taxes, and parliament inevitably meant a renewal of the constitutional crisis that had bedevilled the 1620s.

Levels of violence in Ireland and Scotland seemed to have been much higher than those in England. During the sixteenth century, as Elizabeth ruled a peaceful land, James VI had to quell his discordant nobility. In the Highlands and Western Islands 'periodic violence was an essential and honourable part of life'.[25] The warrior was the hero: loyalty unto death to one's clan chief the supreme virtue. Such blood feuds, which often degenerated into massacres, were in part the product of pastoral farming that forced clans to compete for grazing. Cultural, religious and linguistic differences engendered tensions between the Highlands and the Lowlands. In Ireland, where several groups such as the Irish, Old and New English competed against each other, religion was the main cause of violence (as it still is today). A survey of 4,255 adult males in Ulster in 1630 revealed that 2.3 per cent owned guns, while 56.7 per cent had swords or pikes, a far higher level of weapons ownership than in England.[26] Thus while comparative statistics on levels of violence in early seventeenth-century Scotland and Ireland with those in England are flawed, it seems safe to assume that they were far higher in the Celtic fringes. Scotland and Ireland went to war before England, without much debate, and with – it cannot be argued – a far greater degree of ferocity.

Even though a very high proportion of English adult males, and a fair number of Scotsmen, had gone off to fight in the Elizabethan conquest of Ireland (which obviously affected most of that island's inhabitants), by the late 1630s few veterans were still alive, and all were too old to unsheath their swords once more. Nonetheless the collective memory of the Elizabethan campaigns was still powerful. Fathers and grandfathers told young men of their experiences, engendering the tradition that each generation had to fight its own war – if only to satisfy the Oedipal urge of sons to prove that they are as good as their fathers. For instance, Charles and Buckingham attacked Cadiz in 1625 to emulate Sir Francis Drake's epic raid, even though their basic objective was the restoration of the Palatine a thousand miles away in Germany.

The remembrances of Tudor rebellions and previous civil wars figured far more prominently in early Stuart mentalities than did the conquest of Ireland.[27] Sir Thomas More estimated that the Wars of the Roses had cost more English lives than the campaigns in France, while towards the end of the sixteenth century Thomas Craig put the casualties at a hundred thousand. Shakespeare portrayed the Wars of the Roses as an unmitigated disaster:

> I and ten thousand in this luckless realm
> Had left no mourning widows for our death

So declared Lord John Clifford in *Henry VI* (II, vi, 14). In *Richard II* (iv, i, 144) the Bishop of Carlisle warned of the horrifying consequences of rebellion and the deposition of kings:

> The blood of English shall manure the ground
> And future Ages groan for this foul act. . . .
> Disorder, Horror, Fear and Mutiny
> Shall here inhabit, and the land be call'd
> The Field of Golgotha and dead men's skulls.

Even though collective memories greatly exaggerated the horrors of the Wars of the Roses – and by implication the benefits of living under a stable Tudor monarchy – the memory of rebellion was not half as dangerous as its contemplation. The printer dared not include the Bishop of Carlisle's speech until 1608. Perhaps he remembered how close the Bard and his players came in 1601 to being committed to the Tower after they staged *Richard II* the evening before the Earl of Essex's abortive coup against the queen.[28] Shakespeare and his company had good cause for fear because the Tudors ruthlessly punished those even remotely connected with rebellion. Although a couple of people died fighting during the Pilgrimage of Grace of 1536, one hundred and seventy rebels were executed afterwards. In comparison 'Bloody Mary Tudor' was positively indulgent: after Wyatt's rebellion of 1554, between sixty to seventy people were hung, about the same number as died in combat. Even though only six Englishmen were killed during the Northern Rising of 1567, between two to three hundred were executed afterwards.[29] Perhaps such ferocious punishments worked, for a surprising feature of early Stuart English life was the absence of rebellions. Unlike Elizabeth, Charles I never used the rack to root out subversives, nor executed a single aristocrat for rebellion.[30]

Indeed there was a marked drop in the number of aristocrats taking part in wars of any sort. While in Henry VIII's reign practically every able-bodied peer had seen active duty, by the 1620s only one in five had done so.[31] Without doubt the actions in which British forces were engaged during that decade were so inglorious that they were hardly worth the view.

One such débâcle was the expedition that left England in early 1624 under the command of Count Ernest von Mansfeld, a freebooter whom the Spanish Ambassador called 'an infamous man that had long wasted the empire by his spoils and robberies'.[32] The illegitimate son of the Governor of Luxembourg, who felt the stigma so bitterly that he became one of those bully boys who bloomed during the Thirty Years' War. As liable to plunder his own employer as he was the enemy or neutrals, Mansfeld raised a rag-tag expeditionary force, which rendezvoused in late December at Dover. While most Englishmen were only too eager to ring bells, light bonfires, and even cheer the departing troops, few were willing to pay taxes to support them, and even fewer volunteered to join their adventures. To dodge the draft men gouged out their eyes, or hacked off fingers; a few committed suicide; many deserted. Mansfeld's army was poorly armed and worse disciplined: indeed had they been better equipped with anything more lethal than cudgels they might have killed more of their officers whom they beat up.

At the end of January the Mansfeld expedition set sail from Dover, much to the relief of the Mayor and citizens, without much idea of where they were headed. When the French refused to let them land at Calais, they sailed aimlessly around for several days, before finally going ashore near Breda. Lacking rations, warm clothing and ready cash they could not survive a winter in the Rhine Delta (an experience which decimated the far better disciplined and equipped allied troops in 1944–5). 'We die like dogs,' wrote one commander from his regimental headquarters (a pig-sty the tenancy of which he had most likely obtained by consuming the previous occupant), 'and in the face of an enemy we could not suffer as we now do.'[33] Within six months only six hundred of Mansfeld's twelve thousand men were left.

The record of the next expedition was even more catastrophic. It was commanded by Lord Wimbledon, 'the general', wrote a contemporary, 'from whom as little could be expected as he performed'.[34] Chosen for his court connections, rather than any military experience or competency, Wimbledon sailed at the van of some eighty-five ships out of Portsmouth Harbour on 2 October 1626. Then they anchored for a council of war which decided to attack Cadiz. When the English bombarded the port on the 20th, to avoid getting hit they opened fire beyond the range of the enemy's cannon. Since the range of their cannon was equally limited the Royal Navy accorded the enemy a similar convenience. Two days later some two thousand British infantry landed on the dunes a few miles south of the castle guarding the entrance to Cadiz Harbour. Having forgotten to fill their water bottles just outside the castle they were delighted to stumble across a warehouse containing 600 tunns of wine. 'No words of exhortation, nor blows of correction would restrain them,' one of their officers wrote,

> but breaking with violence into the rooms where the wine were, crying that they were King Charles's men and fought for him, caring for no man else, they claimed the wine their own . . . till in effect the whole army, except the commanders, were drunken and in common confusion.[35]

Seeing the opportunity the Spanish sallied out to clobber the plastered English troops. 'I must confess', reported Wimbledon, displaying that *sang froid* so characteristic of British commanders after a débâcle, 'that it put me to some trouble.' But he excused the incident by saying that even when sober the troops were 'incapable of order', and never obeyed him.[36]

As the expedition sailed home in defeat and disgrace, Lord Delaware, one of its leaders, confessed to a friend, 'Never an army went out, continued, and returned with so much disorder as this.'[37]

Delaware's forecast that the record of the Cadiz expedition for incompetence could never be beaten lasted less than two years. Charles and his chief adviser, the Duke of Buckingham, learned nothing from their mistakes, except, perhaps, not to let minions make them for them. Thus in June 1627 Buckingham personally led a fleet of a hundred ships from Portsmouth to capture the Isle of Ré, just off La Rochelle, where Louis XIII was besieging his rebellious Protestant subjects, the Huguenots. The landings on 12 July went well, some two thousand men wading ashore.[38] Five days later the British started to besiege the main French position at St Martins. By September it seemed as if the French would surrender. The St Martins' garrison was down to a couple of days' rations. On the night of the 28th, however, the French managed to break through using the small fort of La Prée on the mainland side of the island that Buckingham had neglected to take in the initial landing. The mistake cost the British dear. The besiegers became the besieged. 'Our army grows everyday weaker,' an officer wrote home, 'our victuals waste, our purses are empty, ammunition consumed, winter grows.'[39] On 27 October the British made one last desperate effort to take St Martins. They failed, largely because the scaling ladders were 5 feet too short – an inexcusable piece of negligence considering the fact that the besiegers had been staring at the walls for over three months during which they had had plenty of time to measure them.

Two days later two thousand French troops sallied out of La Prée, forcing the British to pull back. Thanks to Buckingham's decision to place the rearguard on the wrong side of the bridge to the small island from which the main evacuation took place, the retreat turned into a rout. A few weeks later the jubilant French king and his victorious officers heard a *Te Deum* sung in Notre Dame, Paris, beneath some forty captured British colours hung from the cathedral walls.

Had not John Felton, an army lieutenant deranged at being denied promotion, assassinated Buckingham in August 1628, the duke would have surely led the second expedition to relieve the Huguenots at La Rochelle. Under the command of Robert Bertie, Earl of Lindsay, the fleet sailed from Portsmouth the following month, arriving off La Rochelle on the 10th. They found the entrance into the horseshoe-shaped harbour blocked by a boom of large tree trunks chained to one another. A captain tried to blow it up, but instead blasted himself to smithereens. Five days later the English attacked, losing six men. Even more faint-hearted was the next day's assault, in which neither side suffered a single fatality. Several days afterwards, as the anchored fleet watched through their telescopes, the four thousand surviving members of La Rochelle's original garrison of fifteen thousand surrendered to the French king, having eaten all of the city's horses, dogs, cats, and most of its rats. On 1 November Lindsey's ships departed for home.

For sheer incompetence it would be hard to find such a quartet as the expeditions which left England during the 1620s. Admittedly amphibious operations are extremely difficult to mount and prone to disaster. Yet if such was the case why then were the six most senior officers on the Cadiz raid all soldiers? Without doubt bad weather played a crucial role in all of the expeditions, but bad planning meant that they set out far too late in the year, many troops having hung around billets in England since the spring, untrained and undisciplined. For their limited objectives, most of the expeditions were too large, and thus took too long to assemble: Mansfeld took 12,000 men to the Rhine Delta, 16,399 sailed for Cadiz. True the English lacked the one quality which Napoleon demanded that all his generals possess – luck. The Spanish treasure fleet replete with gold and silver from the Americas sailed into Cadiz a few days after the English had left. Soon after Lindsey's fleet headed home a Biscay storm broke the boom at La Rochelle.

Nonetheless the reasons for the failure are obvious. Leadership was poor. Command was fractured. Goals were poorly defined. Senior commanders issued orders that made those given the Light Brigade seem like models of clarity. Intelligence – both in the psychological and military sense of that word – was in short supply, none of the four targets, for instance, having been adequately reconnoitered. Even though equipment was old and lacking, surely someone could have issued water before landing at Cadiz, measured the height of the walls at St Martins, or fabricated a waterproof charge to blow up the boom at La Rochelle?

By the late 1620s most Englishmen were convinced they knew the answers to these and a host of other questions. At first the loss of men did not cause much of a public outcry. His draftees were, admitted

Mansfeld, 'a rabble of raw and poor rascals'. They conformed to the Elizabethan stereotype of pressed men; 'we disburden the prisons of them, we rob the taverns and ale houses of tosspots and ruffians, we scour both town and county of rogues and vagabonds.'[40] Their neighbours – if not their friends – were more than happy to see them go. Village constables readily forked out to pay, equip and march draftees off to the appointed rendezvous.[41] In Great Waltham, Essex, the Rev. Thomas Barnes preached that it was far better to have 'those straggling vagrants . . . which do swarm amongst us', and those 'loitering and lewd livers' conscripted to fight abroad, than 'tippling in tap houses' at home.[42] And if most of the twelve thousand Mansfeld took away failed to return home, few of them were missed.

As the demand for men increased, and the supply of ne'r-do-wells ran out, the authorities started to draft local worthies, and the size of expeditions decreased.[43] While over sixteen thousand sailed to Cadiz, only five thousand went to La Rochelle. Casualties were horrendous: 83 per cent on the Mansfeld expedition, 65 per cent in the Cadiz disaster.

Public reaction became shriller after each failure. While few lamented the loss of those who went to the Rhine Delta, in his diary John Rous described the Cadiz expedition as a 'shameful return'. He was even more caustic about the expedition to Ré, which he prophesied 'will breed but evil blood'.[44] Rous was right. Ré caused an outrage. One letter-writer called it 'the greatest and shamefulest overthrow the English have received since we lost Normandy'.[45] A poetaster prayed of the expedition's leader, the Duke of Buckingham:[46]

> And now, Just God! I humbly pray,
> That thou wilt take that slime away.

The political consequences of these military disasters are well known. They produced the constitutional crisis of Charles's first three parliaments that climaxed with the Petition of Right of June 1628. Two months later John Felton took that slime away by assassinating Buckingham, and within six months the king dissolved parliament to rule on his own for eleven years.

The impact these expeditions had on the coming of the civil war is, however, harder to chart. They could have associated military ventures in many men's minds with absolutism and incompetence.[47] Even though during the 1630s the bellicose demanded that England intervene in what they saw as a great Protestant crusade, the Thirty Years' War, the memories of the 1620s made many people as reluctant to get involved in another war, as did, say, those of the First World War, or Vietnam. Perhaps as few as thirteen thousand of the fifty thousand English troops drafted to fight overseas in the 1620s made it home again.[48] Since many of the survivors were broken in health, and others were reluctant conscripts determined never again to go to the wars, these expeditions did not create a significant pool of veterans for the civil wars. Far more important in this process was the Thirty Years' War, which attracted those restless young men, eager to fight, no matter how doleful the immediate experience of the past.

Although the Thirty Years' War started in 1618 after James I's son-in-law, Frederick, upset the religious balance of Europe by accepting the Bohemian throne, Britain never formally joined the conflict. The war was a confused struggle, fought basically between the Protestant states of northern Europe and the Catholic Holy Roman Empire. The first phase involved the expulsion of Frederick and his wife Elizabeth from both Bohemia (roughly modern Czechoslovakia) and the Palatine, their ancestral territories on the Rhine and Danube. The second phase centred on Denmark, to which the English Royal family was linked by ties of marriage. In the third phase Gustavus Adolphus swept south from Sweden conquering all in his path until he was killed in 1632 at the Battle of Lutzen. And in the last, longest, and perhaps bloodiest period until the war ended in 1648 the Catholic French intervened to try to curb the power of the Hapsburg Holy Roman Emperor.

The Thirty Years' War caused a staggering amount of damage. 'I could never have believed a land could have been so despoiled had I not see it with my own eyes', wrote one traveller in post-war Germany. The population of Germany as a whole declined from about twenty million to fifteen to sixteen million (in relative terms a far greater loss than during the Second World War). In some places the loss of life was even greater: Marburg fell to half, and Chemnitz to a fifth of their pre-war size. The number of Bohemian villages tumbled from thirty-five thousand to six thousand, while some thirty-five thousand people were slaughtered in 1631 at the sack of Magdeburg alone.[49]

Naturally the inhabitants of the British Isles were keenly interested in the monstrous struggle going on across the North Sea. In the early 1630s large numbers of newsbooks appeared detailing the achievements of that great Protestant hero, Gustavus Adolphus. The Swedish king's death in battle was mourned as though an English monarch had perished. Newsbooks reported a war of unmatched brutality, in which promiscuous plunder, rape, sackings and atrocities, led to famine, disease, cannibalism, and untold miseries (see plate 12). For instance, *A True Representation of the Miserable Estate of Germany* (1638) illustrated the horrors with crude woodcuts that can still sicken modern stomachs hardened by photographs of Dachau or Cambodia. One woodcut showed soldiers using a minister's library of rate books to roast him alive. In another they had just torn a baby from its mother's breast and tossed it the air, to be caught on a pike. A third illustrated troopers stripping a victim's muscles from his hands. The caption to a fourth reads 'Men's guts pulled out of their mouths.'[50] No wonder after looking at such material Nehemiah Walling-ton, the London artisan, wrote how lucky he was to live in England and not famine-torn Germany, where 'they did boil whole pots and kettles of frogs and did eat them with their entrails'.[51]

Equally horrible news of the Thirty Years' War reached the British Isles through private correspondence. 'The whole army', wrote Sydenham Poyntz of the Swedish capture of Wurzburg, 'in a fury breaking in the Town pillaged it, Cloisters and Abbies, committing great disorders, using such tyranny towards the clergymen, cutting off their members, and deflowering the nuns.'[52] Writing to his uncle and aunt back home in England from Maastricht, Amias Steynings, an officer in Lord Vane's Regiment, lamented, 'We have passed through great miseries both by sea and land since we left England, and are now in great want for victuals.' So bad were conditions that gentlemen had to dig trenches under cannon fire like common labourers, trying to get by on only a couple of hours' sleep a night.[53]

Poyntz was one of many of Charles's subjects who volunteered for the Thirty Years' War. Ten to fifteen thousand Englishmen saw continental service, as did perhaps as many, if not more, Irish. There were, for instance, several Hibernian regiments in the Spanish and Austrian armies, and seven in the French. Although between 1624 and 1637 the crown issued warrants authorizing the recruitment of 41,400 Scots for service overseas, it is unlikely that these targets were met. Yet some 25,000 Scots, or 10 per cent of the nation's adult males, fought abroad.[54] Some volunteers left the British Isles in officially sanctioned groups, such as the expedition-ary force which the Earl of Hamilton raised with royal sponsorship in 1631 to fight for Gustavus Adolphus. (They were such a sorry lot that after a year the Swedish king sent them home.) Others went to fight abroad on their own initiative.

A minister's son, James Turner was educated at the University of Glas-gow from which he graduated with an MA in 1631 at the age of 16. Defying his father's wishes that he enter the kirk, the following year Turner volunteered to serve Gustavus Adolphus. He landed in Denmark in 1632 and after marching to Meckleburg 'fell grievously sick'. It was five weeks before he was able to walk. Turner took part in the Siege of Nurenburg, in which four thousand were killed and six thousand wounded, and fought at Hamelin, where nine thousand imperial soldiers perished. In his memoirs he recalled the horrors of war. 'After the battles I saw a great many killed in cold blood by the Finns, who professed to give no quarter.' Campaigning was nearly as bad. 'My best entertainment was bread and water', he wrote, adding with the dry humour that has kept many a soldier going that he had 'abundance of the last, but not so the first'. After a couple of years' service he had become a seasoned campaigner so capable of fending for himself under all circumstances that

'I wanted nothing – horses, clothes, meat nor monies.' Thomas Raymond, an English veteran, concurred that 'so long as money lasted we had a merry life'.[55]

In all Turner became an effective infantry officer, reaching the rank of captain. Some of his memories were of Mars. He recalled how he led fifty musketeers who winkled out a group of snipers hiding in hedgerows near Hessich 'with great loss to them and only three or four of our men'. Other recollections were of Venus. In early 1634 he was billeted with a widow and her widowed daughter at Olendorpe. 'She was very handsome, witty and discrete [sic] . . . I became very enamoured.' Most of his experiences were harrowing. He remembered seeing burnt-out towns, inhabited by people who had lost everything – goods, families, friends. After briefly returning home in 1634, following his father's death, Turner found that he could not settle down in civilian life, and returned to the Thirty Years' War. He left Sweden in 1640 to continue his trade at home.

The tens of thousands of veterans who took part in the Thirty Years' War and then returned to fight in the British civil wars had a profound impact.

It was one that many Englishmen dreaded. As one sardonically wrote in 1640 about Alexander Leslie, the veteran of Swedish service where he had reached the rank of field marshal, who returned to command the Scots Army, 'he took up the trade of killing men abroad, and now is returned to kill, for Christ's sake, men at home'.[56] In July 1642 *The Manifold Miseries of Civil War* used stories of starvation, cannibalism, and torture from the continent to warn what might happen if civil war broke out at home – all arguments which Thomas Morton repeated the following month in *Englands Warning-Piece*.

Leaders on both sides were especially worried about the effect of introducing mercenaries who had learned their trade abroad. While admitting to Lord Ruthven, the continental veteran, that he was 'a better soldier', Edward Somerset, Marquis of Worcester opposed letting him fight for the king since as 'a soldier of fortune' he was 'here today and God knows where tomorrow'. On the other side Baron Brooke, the Lord Lieutenant of Warwickshire, agreed about excluding mercenaries.[57] Addressing the officers of the county militia in late 1642 he explained that 'In Germany they fought only for spoil, rapine, and destruction. Merely money it was and hope of gain.' Parliament was fighting, he continued, for higher causes, and wanted men who were committed to more than their pay. Mercenaries would inevitably prolong the war for as long as possible to continue earning a good living. Another problem with employing mercenaries was that they were liable to introduce into England the horrors of total war which had decimated the continent. 'I shall therefore speak my conscience,' concluded Brooke, 'I had rather a thousand honest citizens who can handle their arms, whose hearts go with their hands, than thousands of mercenary soldiers that boast of foreign experience.'

All too soon, however, the gentlemen realized war was not cricket and that they needed the players: not thousands of veterans bragging about brutalities abroad, but a small cadre distributed throughout the armies to train recruits, reassure raw troops, and to provide a leaven of experienced leadership at every level. They taught both sides the latest techniques. One of Prince Rupert's first services to his uncle's cause was to show the king's sappers how to use a petard to blow in castle gates. The mercenaries helped professionalize armies, a process which took about two and a half years (about the same time it took the British Army in the Second World War). All of the field army commanders in the civil wars were veterans of foreign wars, except Charles, Cromwell, and the Earls of Manchester and Newcastle.[58] In only one of the twenty-nine Scots regiments that invaded England in January 1644 were all three of the senior officers without continental experience: in other words fifty-three out of eighty-seven field officers were veterans. Later that year three out of the four most senior generals at Cropredy Bridge had seen foreign service.[59] Of a sample of 76 civil war leaders, 31 (40.8 per cent) had fought on the continent, 6 (9.2 per cent) in the Bishops' Wars, making a total of 37 (48.7 per cent). Of the 35 parliamentarians, 10 (28.6 per cent) were veterans, as compared to 27 (60 per cent) of the 41 royalists.[60]

In addition to British veterans, foreign mercenaries fought in the civil wars. Although the king may have had some French units, by and large Frenchmen served as individual advisers who brought badly needed military skills. Two engineers, Bernard de Gomme and Leca Roche, came with Prince Rupert, while parliament paid John Rosworme, a German, to supervise the construction of Manchester's defences. At Edgehill, the war's first major battle where expertise was sorely lacking, two Dutchmen, Hans Behre and Philibert de Boyne, advised the Earls of Bedford and Peterborough, while Captain Fanton, a flamboyantly polymath Croatian, who spoke some thirteen languages, helped the Earl of Essex.[61]

While before the civil war Scotland lacked an organized militia – apart from a few ceremonial units in the Royal Burghs – for most Englishmen the militia was their main pre-war experience of things military.[62] By custom all able-bodied males were required to serve to defend their counties, attending musters when ordered, and providing equipment commensurate to their rank in society. The idea that all the king's subjects had a duty to protect the kingdom went back to the Anglo-Saxon fyrd. By Tudor times the militia was the responsibility of the lord lieutenant, the county's leading aristocrat, who through deputies and a muster master was supposed to organize and train its civilian soldiers.

On paper the militia could be a formidable body. A muster roll of February 1638 for England and Wales listed 93,718 infantry and 5,239 cavalry, ranging from 130 soldiers for Rutland to 12,641 from Yorkshire.[63] Many believed the militia was far less impressive in reality that it was on paper. Like 'Dad's Army', these 'weekend warriors' frightened few foreigners, and impressed fewer Englishmen. John Dryden wrote:

> The country rings around with loud alarms,
> And raw in field the rude militia swarms;
> Mouths without hands: maintained at vast expense,
> In peace a charge; in war a weak defence;
> Stout once a month they march, a blustering band,
> And ever, but in times of need, at hand.

Professional soldiers could be just as caustic as poets. John Corbet, who fought in the Siege of Gloucester of 1643, described the county's militia as 'effeminate in courage and incapable of discipline'.[64] Lieutenant Colonel William Barriffe started his widely read training manual by lamenting that the trained bands are 'called forth to exercise their postures and motions every four to five years. Whose fault it is I know not, but I pray God it will be amended.'[65] Colonel Ward described what he maintained was a typical pre-war summer field day. 'After a little casual hurrying over their postures' the militia men would load their muskets, 'to give their captain a brave volley of shot at his entrance into his inn, where after having solaced themselves for a while after this brave service every man repairs home, and that which is not well taught them is easily forgotten.'[66] The tensions between the professional and amateurs (like that between RN and RNVR officers) continued well into the war. For instance in 1644 a court martial found Sergeant West, a regular from Colonel Baker's regiment, guilty of using 'scandalous and reproachful language' to the Tower Hamlets' militia.[67]

The central government shared these reservations about the quality of the militia. Soon after becoming king, Charles ordered their standards improved by using the brief *Instructions for Musters and Armes and their use* that the Privy Council had issued three years earlier. Far more significant was the cadre of eighty-nine sergeants, all veterans of the Thirty Years' War, whom the crown dispatched to the counties to train the militia. The presence of seasoned soldiers did much to expose civilians to military realities, particularly those who served in the infantry. Cavalry soldiers, who provided their own horses, and thus came from gentry or richer yeomen families, tended to be less amenable to the advice of vulgar veterans. The king had to cancel the regional musters that he scheduled for cavalry regiments during the summer of 1630 because their training was not up to this fairly simple operation.

Charles's attempts to create what he called 'a perfect' or 'exact' militia were doomed to failure. They were symptomatic of his propensity for grandious objectives that exceeded both his resources and his attention span. The king's plans were most conservative. He deplored the introduction of a newfangled continental style of marching, issuing a warrant in 1632 to retain the traditional English march, as 'the best of all marches'. He urged the militia to revive the use of the longbow, a weapon which had seen its glory days two centuries earlier in the Hundred Years' War. While the longbow was superior to the match-fired musket, it required constant training – far more than the militia was prepared to do.[68]

After all, during the 1630s there was no obvious threat from abroad to stimulate enthusiastic practice, or to prompt local governments into spending vast sums of money on defence. With the repeal in 1603 of the Tudor militia legislation the crown's right to compel subjects to attend musters fully equipped at their own expense rested on custom and the prerogative, not the firmer bases of statute. In 1635 the Mayor and Aldermen of Norwich contested the king's right to raise a militia. More important than legal challenges was the refusal to attend. 'There is not law to enforce him', explained John Bishe of Brighton for having skipped musters for three decades.[69] Magistrates were less inclined to prosecute the recalcitrant, especially if they were also friends. During the 1630s, as the government demanded more and more in unpaid services from local elites, it became harder to find volunteers to serve as company officers. One muster master, Gervase Markham, complained that he never got any respect, having to put up with contempt and rudeness from those he tried to train. In addition muster masters often had to wait for years for their wages: the only way that Somerset could pay Captain Carne was from the county's maimed soldiers' fund. By the end of the personal rule the Somerset militia was in such bad shape that even if it had wanted to fight it would have been incapable of doing so. The Sussex trained bands were in a similarly sorry state.[70]

But there were exceptions to the norm. In 1633 Captain Thelwell reported that Lancashire's forces were 'reasonably well exercised . . . and able bodied', the county having spent £10,000 over fifteen years to produce a fairly exact militia.[71] Two years later Lieutenant Hammond watched the 'ready exercised and well disciplined' Isle of Wight militia skirmishing along the River Medina; 'A brave show there is, and good service performed', he concluded.[72] Captain de Eugaine, a continental veteran, hired to train the Yarmouth militia, reported after their 1638 field day that 'although I have seen good service in the Netherlands and other places, yet never I saw a better thing.'[73]

Without doubt the best-trained militia was London's. There permanent officers were regularly paid and young men enthusiastically marched off on weekends and in the evenings to the Artillery Ground to drill and fire their weapons. Indeed the trained bands were so widely supported in the capital that when Beaumont and Fletcher satirized them in *The Knight of the Burning Pestle* (1613), the audience hissed the play from the stage.[74]

Like all militias (such as the Territorial Army or National Guard), the trained bands combined the strengths and weaknesses of both civilians and soldiers. They attracted the ambivalence that the former feels towards the latter: dressing up, going off with one's mates for the weekend, for some drill, target practice, and a few beers, was as much fun and as ridiculous then as it is today. To civilians 'weekend warriors' seemed braggarts, worthy of scorn at worst and ribaldry at best. To regular soldiers they appeared dangerously rank amateurs who affronted their own hard-won professionalism. The militia reflected the civilian communities from which they were drawn. For instance, Sir Robert Phelips's refusal to let the sergeants the central government had dispatched to the counties train the regiment he commanded was not the result of a military decision, but the continuation of a county based civilian quarrel.

Notwithstanding their weaknesses, the militia exposed a very high proportion of the king's subjects to military matters. As the officers drilled, perhaps with little enthusiasm, and afterwards as they drank, with certainly far more, they got to know each other better, and the bonds of civilian life were strengthened into comradeship.

By and large the militia was a reasonable enough foundation for an army. Mobilized, given full-time training, fortified by a veteran or two, and stimulated by the coming of war, it could be licked into an effective force. In 1642 John Pym was told that the Boston militia consisted of 'A Hundred VOLUNTEERS, handsome young men, well armed and every way well appointed', their target practice displaying 'much readiness in the use of arms'. In contrast a few months earlier it was reported that for 'want of exercise' the Pembrokeshire militia was 'not fit for sudden service'.[75] Sometimes the trained bands could be of value: other times – as the two Bishops' Wars demonstrated – they were worse than useless.

The Bishops' Wars, fought between England and Scotland in 1639 and 1640, were far more important politically than militarily because both sides shied from fighting, and when they came to unwelcome blows, sparred with great restraint and little enthusiasm.

Charles's plans for the First Bishops' War were ambitious. A force of Irish Catholics was to land near Carlisle, while their fellows in Ulster were to harass the province's Scots settlers. With an expeditionary force of five thousand troops James, Duke of Hamilton, managed to land in the Firth of Forth region, but failed to prevent the covenanters either from taking Aberdeen and Edinburgh Castle, or from sending the royalists packing at the 'Trot of Tariff'. Next the Scots turned their attention south to the border, where on 30 May Charles joined his army of some twenty thousand men. Neither side wanted to fight: few Englishmen were willing to hazard their lives for a cause in which they did not believe: most Scots shrank from actually using force against their divinely anointed sovereign. On 4 June the Earl of Holland led a mixed force of a thousand cavalry

24

and three thousand infantry on a reconnaissance into Scotland. Since the former could move faster than the latter, who on a hot summer's day were hampered by the lack of water bottles, the cavalry were on their own by the time they came across Alexander Leslie's men at Kelso. Unable to attack, Holland retreated. This pusillanimous episode shattered the morale of the English forces. Before Kelso an English officer boasted, 'here is a gallant company of cavaliers as brave in courage as in clothes'. Afterwards a captain quaked 'The Scots are very strong . . . our army is very weak.'[76] Negotiations opened on 10 June, and a week later both sides agreed to start demobilizing within forty-eight hours.

The chief political effect of the First Bishops' War was the end of personal rule. In December Charles decided to call a parliament, the first for eleven years. But as the Venetian secretary noted, 'the long rusted gates of parliament cannot be opened without difficulty'.[77] Nonetheless expectations ran high on 13 April 1640 when the king opened the new session. Balladeers cheerfully sang:

> We may be assured of this,
> If anything hath been amiss,
> Our king and state will all redress,
> In this good parliament.

Hopes that England and Scotland could solve their problems peacefully came crashing down within less than a month. At a hastily called dawn meeting of the Privy Council on 5 May, Charles dismissed the gathering which posterity called the Short, and contemporaries the 'still-born', parliament. The reasons for the king's fatally precipitous decision are obscure. He might have believed that the negotiations he was having with three Spanish ambassadors to exchange Royal Naval protection of their convoys in the Channel for the services of Spanish soldiers, backed up by papal gold, would enable him to crush the Scots without going cap in hand to parliament for money. Anyway the abrupt dismissal of an assembly on which so many had pinned their hopes – let alone the prospect of Spanish intervention in Britain's domestic affairs – was deeply disturbing. After taking part in the First Bishops' War, Thomas Carew, went to rest at the Earl of Kent's house, West Park in Bedfordshire. He contrasted the blessings of peace, as epitomized by England's great country houses and simple rustic foods, with the next war, which was as inevitable as the morrow's hunt:[78]

> Thus I enjoy myself and taste the fruit
> Of Blessed peace, whilst toiled in the pursuit
> Of Bucks and Stags, the emblems of war, you strive
> To keep the memory of our arms alive.

Thomas Peyton found the thought of renewed hostilities so appalling that he wrote from London to his friend Henry Oxinden in Norfolk, 'Death's harbinger, the sword, famine and other plagues that hang over us are ready to swallow up the wicked age.'[79]

Even though the Second Bishops' War was not the holocaust that Thomas Peyton feared, it was bad enough. On 20 August 1640 Charles left London to join his Northern Army. The same evening the Scots crossed the Tweed at Coldstream and advanced towards Newcastle. Even though the king had at least twenty-five thousand men arrayed on the border they were barely trained; 'we were never disciplined, nor mustered', one wrote in his diary.[80] Sir Edward Conway could only collect three thousand infantry and fifteen hundred cavalry to march the 4 miles from Newcastle to Newburn to try to stop the invaders from crossing the Tweed. Like most battles that of Newburn began on 28 August in a haphazard way. Each side was on one bank of the river, waiting for the tide to go out so they could cross. John Rushworth recalled seeing a Scots officer sporting a black feather in his cap, emerge from his billet, a thatched house in Newburn, and ride to the Tyne to water his horse, a splendid beast.[81] Even though troops on both sides had been moving around unmolested for the whole day, under one of those unspoken agreements to 'live and let live' that soldiers often reach, an English trooper, annoyed by the arrogant way in which a Scots officer stared at him, opened fire, wounding the fellow. Angry, the covenanters waded the river and easily drove the English back to Newcastle, which they abandoned the following week.

Zachary Boyd, a minister from Glasgow, portentously celebrated the triumph:[82]

> In Squadrons came like fire and thunder,
> Men's hearts and heads both to pierce and plunder
> Their errand was (when it was understood)
> To bathe men's bosoms in a scarlet flood.

In fact the Battle of Newburn, the first significant Scots victory over the English since Bannockburn, was more a walk-over than a wipe-out, because one side refused to fight. Thus the king had to make a treaty at Ripon that allowed the Scots to occupy Northumberland and Durham, and paid them £806 per day for the privilege. This meant Charles was once more forced to call parliament.

Support in Scotland for resisting the king's new prayer book by force of arms was both intense and widespread. The Scots swore a covenant refusing to accept the new liturgy, as well as the institution of bishops. Like the Declaration of Independence, the covenant turned a rebellion into a just war in defence of long-held rights. Some Scots could not have enough of the compact. 'Give me a thousand Covenants, I'll subscribe them all,' promised the poet, William Drummond, 'or more, if more you can contrive.'[83] It was far easier to get people to agree on what they were against (be it George III or a new prayer book), than about what they were for. And most Scots were against Bishops, whom one Edinburgh shoemaker called 'the Firebrands of Hell, the Panders of the Whore of Babylon, and the instruments of the Devil'.[84] By adopting a covenant the Scots associated themselves (in their own eyes at least) with God's chosen people, and turned their cause into a crusade. 'Zeal of Religion transports men beyond themselves', wrote one correspondent from Edinburgh. Another added, 'We are busy preaching, praying and drilling.'[85]

The experience of the ordinary soldier was, as always, far less lofty. John Livingston was conscripted by his presbyter to join the Earl of Carlisle's regiment, with whom he marched to Newcastle. 'I had a little trench tent and a bed hung between two leager chests, and having lain several nights with my clothes on, I being wearied for want of sleep did lie one night with my clothes off.' He got so stiff that he could not move: unable to get dressed, Livingston had to ride Godiva-like to Dunse where he was thawed out in a bed surrounded by pots of boiling water.[86]

During the Bishops' Wars the gap between propaganda and reality was even wider on the English side. Edward Waller imagined the aristocracy leading the royal army to the Border:[87]

> Brave Holland leads, and with him Falkland goes
> Who hears this told, and does not straight suppose
> We send the braves and the Muses forth,
> To Civilize and instruct the North.

As he celebrated Lord Falkland's decision to go and fight the Scots, Abraham Cowley also recognized that war would provide opportunities for some unsavoury characters:[88]

> And this great prince of knowledge is by Fate,
> Thrust into the noise and business of a state.
> He is too good for war, and ought to be
> As far from danger, as from fear he's free.
> Those men alone (and they are useful too),
> Whose valour is the only art they know
> Were for sad wars and bloody battles born,
> Let them the state defend, and he adorn.

In fact in both Bishops' Wars hardly anyone was willing to play the hero. Colonel Garrard, an impetuous young volunteer in Lord Goring's horse, shed the first blood by crossing the Tweed alone and without orders, and thus precipitated the ruinous raid on Kelso.[89] The only heroes of the Second Bishops' War were a couple of Welsh soldiers who stood and fought to the death as their English comrades took French leave for Newcastle.[90]

The reasons for the failure of the English forces are obvious. Although ever since 1323 before each war kings had called parliaments to vote taxes, Charles did not do so in 1638. Although he did so in May 1640, the king dismissed the Short Parliament before it could vote a penny. Charles did not like parliaments, likening them to obstreperous cats 'who ever grow cussed with age'.[91] Having tried – and failed – to rule on its own for eleven years, an unpopular government was now asking people to fight and die for it – something people are loath to do even for the finest of causes. And the king's cause, as a Scots versifier noted, was far from the best:[92]

> What will you fight, for a Book of Common Prayer?
> What will you fight, for a Court of High Commission?
> What will you fight, for a mitre gilded fair?
> Or to maintain the prelates proud ambition?
> What will you get? Your yoke will be lighter
> For when we're slain, the rod comes to your breech.

Many Englishmen did all they could to avoid fighting the Scots. Henry Oxinden, a Kentish gentleman, managed to get two of his tenants exempted from the draft, one pressed man hung himself, while in Lincolnshire and Essex conscripts cut off their big toes so they could not march north.[93]

Those troops that did so were poorly led. The king appointed the Earl of Arundel as commander-in-chief. Edward Hyde, who as the Earl of Clarendon was to advise King Charles II, as well as write the great *History of the Rebellion and Civil Wars in England*, observed that Arundel 'had nothing martial about him but his presence and looks'.[94] The king gave senior appointments to the Earls of Holland and Newport because they were friends of his wife (who had just lost a baby). The Marquis of Hamilton, commander of the amphibious attack on the east coast, did not want to go to Scotland, telling the king 'next to hell I hate this place'. He became even more loath to fight after his mother vowed personally to shoot him if he ever landed in their native land.[95]

The royal army was as poorly equipped as it was led. No bakeries or brew houses were provided. Unlike the Scots, only senior officers had tents, leaving the men to sleep out on the ground. Many of the pistols issued to the soldiers had broken butts, or ones that had been poorly glued together. In theory this made them far more lethal to the firer than the target: in practice, since the firing mechanisms rarely functioned and many pistols lacked touch holes, the point was often moot. To be sure some pistols actually worked. One belonging to a trooper in the Earl of Holland's regiment accidentally went off, killing a gentleman's son from Lincolnshire. When soldiers pay was docked to cover the cost of repairing the deficiencies in their weapons, many of them mutinied, for which two were hanged. Other forms of protest were more efficacious. 'Our soldiers are so disorderly that they shoot bullets through our own tents', an officer wrote home, 'the king's tent was shot through once.'[96]

The only exception to this dismal performance were the Welsh levies, who were not infected by the insubordination that permeated the English troops. In August 1640, Captain Herbert, a Welshman sent specially with his cavalry troop, forestalled a mutiny in Sir Jacob Astley's English regiment.[97]

Bad recruiting produced soldiers whom one officer curtly called 'most of them beggarly fellows'. Some were signed up from the militia, who could with hard work be turned into decent troops. But by custom, unlike conscripts, militiamen were not obliged to serve outside their counties. So (rather like the US National Guard in the Vietnam War) local worthies managed to wangle a safe billet in the militia, while those at the bottom of society got drafted for the war. Thus the royal army had 'the fewest volunteers that I ever saw in any army', wrote Lord Poulet from Berwick. Hardly any of the pressed men had received any training. Hamilton reported that only two hundred of his five thousand soldiers had actually fired a musket. Sir Edmund Verney summed up the situation by telling his son that 'Our men are very raw, our victuals scarce and provisions for horses worse. I daresay there was never so raw, so unskilful and so unwilling an army brought to fight.' Lord Conway agreed that the troops were 'more fit for Bedlam or Bridewell' than the king's service.[98]

At times it seemed as if a madness swept the land during the Bishops' Wars. The most disturbing thing about the English troops was not their poor fighting ability but the crimes they committed, which, thought Sir Jacob Astley, proved they were 'all the archknaves in the kingdom'.[99] The troops' abuses went well beyond those normally expected from poor recruits. Almost daily in Selby, Yorkshire, soldiers perpetrated infamies on both civilians and their own officers. In Derbyshire they tore down enclosures. They broke jails open in Malborough, Wakefield, Derby, London, and Cirencester, freeing their comrades and those who had refused to pay taxes to fight the Scots. In Essex levies murdered a pregnant woman and plundered several houses. They rioted in Royston, Beccles and Cambridge. Pressed men from Staffordshire chopped up fences around a game park in Uttoxeter for firewood.[100] Troops beat up Oxford undergraduates, whom they despised both as draft dodgers and as privileged members of that bastion of Laudian superstition.

The religious context of many outrages were obvious. In Suffolk conscripts started wearing white sheets to parody bishops' surplices. In churches in Hertfordshire and Essex troops axed for firewood the altar rails just installed on Archbishop Laud's command. Captain Edmund Ayle and seven troopers barged into Rickmansworth church in the middle of Sunday morning service in the summer of 1640, to smash in the altar and its rails. That evening, over his cups in the local tavern, the gallant captain boasted that it was his seventeenth such visitation.

The most notorious outrages were the murder of officers whom conscripts suspected of being Catholics. At Wellington recruits beat their officer to death, convinced he was a papist since he refused to attend divine service. At Farringdon recruits, outraged at Lieutenant Eures for allegedly cutting off a drummer's hand after the lad hit him with his stick, attacked the officer when he was upstairs in a tavern having dinner. They forced him to crawl out on the beam from which the inn sign hung, beating and stoning him until he fell to the ground. Convinced he was dead, they tossed him into a dung heap. Barely alive Eures crawled out. Discovering he was still alive, the soldiers cudgelled in their officer's brains, and dragged his corpse through the town to stick it in the pillory. The only way that Francis Windebanke, scion of a distinguished Catholic family, could persuade his new company that he was a Protestant, and get them to obey him, was to order them to kneel, and sing psalms, before issuing them with drink and 'stinking tobacco'. And thus were the Godly convinced that he was such a jolly good fellow that he could not possibly be a papist.

Many ordinary folk protested vehemently. 'We find ourselves oppressed with the billeting of unseemly soldiers, whose speeches and actions tend to the burning of our villages,' declared a Yorkshire petition, 'as we cannot say that we possess our wives, children and estates in safety.' Anticipating the Clubmen movement some civilians struck back. So scared was one company of recruits of being waylaid by latter-day Robin Hoods as they marched north through Sherwood Forest, that they doubled their guard.[101]

By forcing the king to call the Short and Long Parliaments, the importance of the Bishops' Wars was far greater constitutionally than it was militarily. Unlike, say, the Thirty Years' War, they were not nurseries that produced cadres of battle-hardened veterans. Indifference, indiscipline, indecision, and pure cowardice all lessened their significance as wars. Indeed the act of war that – more than anything else – changed attitudes towards violence was the outbreak of a rebellion in Ireland in October 1641.

3

A SIGHT – THE SADDEST THAT
EYES CAN SEE

One noonday, at my window in the town
I saw a sight – the saddest that eyes can see –
Young soldiers marching hastily
Unto the wars.
    Herman Melville, on watching Union troops
      moving up to the Battle of Ball's Bluff,
                   October 1861

In June 1642, during a last summer of peace that for many seemed, in retrospect at least, as halcyon as would be the summer of 1914 for a later generation, Christopher Browne sent a letter to 'My Beloved Daughter'. His chief concern was not the rapidly deteriorating political situation, the frantic collection of arms by all sides, nor the flood of pamphlets that grew more vituperative and numerous by the day. Far from it. Christopher Browne was worried about finding a 'skilful preserver' who could take advantage of his large strawberry crop and the 'abundantly cheap' supply of sugar, to make a good stock of jam.[1] Unlike posterity, Christopher Browne did not know what the future would bring. All he could do was lay in provisions for the morrow.

Notwithstanding the bias of hindsight there is no doubt that the letters, diaries, even public speeches of men and women in the three or four years before the formal declaration of the English civil war on 22 August 1642 were full of fears about the dangers and horrors of strife.

The immediate run-up to the war started twenty months earlier when Charles called another parliament. The auguries were ominous. On 2 November 1640, as Thomas Trenchard and his family were seated for dinner at Wullick, their manor house in Dorset, they were startled when the sceptre, the symbol of royal authority, inexplicably fell out of the hand of the king's statue in the hall, smashing in pieces on the floor.[2]

In London the next day Charles opened the Long Parliament. 'I saw his Majesty ride in pomp', John Evelyn wrote in his diary that evening, 'with all the Marks of a happy Peace.' But once again the euphoria did

not last. Led by John Pym, the Commons purged the king's chief ministers, throwing Archbishop Laud into the Tower and condemning Strafford
to death by an act of attainder. 'We hear rumours of war again with the
Scots,' Ann Bampfield wrote to her father from Cornwall, 'let the
Almighty avert us from those apparent dangers which the times threaten.'[3]
The public execution of the king's leading adviser, the Earl of Strafford,
was immensely popular: a hundred thousand folk came to see him die on
Tower Hill. Although some hoped that the earl's end would usher in a
new beginning, many feared that it could lead to hostilities. On 28 May,
less than a fortnight after the execution, William Dave voiced his apprehen-
sions to his friend John Willoughby:[4]

> I hope that under colour of preserving the king's prerogatives, we
> shall not destroy one another, whilst we protest on all sides to make
> the king glorious and the kingdom happy. We have all protested to
> maintain the king and privileges of Parliament, and we cannot better
> perform our vows than keeping the peace.

During the early summer of 1641 it seemed that peace would be as
well preserved as Christopher Browne's strawberries. Charles wooed his
opponents, appointing moderates, such as the Earl of Essex and Lord
Hertford, to positions within the royal household. He attempted to buy
off the radical peer Lord Saye and Sele with the mastership of the court
of wards – probably the most lucrative sinecure in the land. While publicly
declaring 'I never had any design but to win the affections of my people',
Charles privately intrigued to make an alliance with the Scots so as to
teach his English subjects a lesson.[5] In August he went to Edinburgh to
try to win Scottish support: but after three months he failed to do so and
had to return to London.

The king's entry into his capital on 25 November was, according to
one observer, 'the greatest acclamation of joy that had been known on
any occasion'.[6] The Lord Mayor, Aldermen, and some five hundred digni-
taries, met Charles outside the city walls to escort him to St James'
Palace, as church bells pealed and fountains flowed with wine. Two forces
produced the jubilation. First, the fear on the part of moderates that
radicals within parliament had gone too far: London merchants were
particularly disturbed by outbreaks of mob violence. Second, nearly all
Englishmen were terrified by the news that the previous month Ireland's
Catholics had risen in rebellion, massacring Protestant settlers in ways and
numbers that grew in magnitude and horror with every telling. The atrocities convinced most people that England must raise an army to be sent
to Ireland to put down this cruel and unchristian rebellion.

At one level the causes for the Irish troubles then – and for hundreds
of years to come – were deceptively simple. 'I see plainly,' explained
Thomas Wentworth, Earl of Strafford, Charles I's Lord Lieutenant of

Ireland, 'that so long as this kingdom continues popish, they are not a people for the crown of England to appear confident of.'[7] Barely a generation earlier the English had completed the conquest of their Catholic neighbour with the surrender of Ulster in 1603. They settled the province with loyal Calvinists from Scotland, displacing many of the indigenous inhabitants. During Wentworth's Lord Lieutenancy (1633–9), English rule became far harsher because he believed that 'Ireland was a conquered territory, and the king could do with it as he liked.'[8] An unlikeable man, Wentworth alienated almost everyone as he tried to play off the various segments of society against each other.

In the short run, dividing enabled the English to rule: in the long term it brought them catastrophe. After Strafford was recalled to deal with the Prayer Book Rebellion and was executed in May 1641, the prestige of England's administration in Ireland naturally suffered. The earl's successor, Sir Christopher Wandesford, was an ineffectual governor, who died suddenly in December 1640. The Protestants who dominated the Dublin parliament blocked the succession of the Earl of Ormonde, an able and loyal magnate, in preference for two ciphers, Sir John Borlase and Sir William Parsons. Parliament demanded and received further concessions from the king during the summer of 1641, whilst he dickered with the Irish for support against the Commons. Fearful that Charles was losing influence both in Dublin and London, as well as – after the Bishops' Wars – in Edinburgh, to radical Protestants who were more likely to attack them than the king, Ireland's Catholics launched a pre-emptive strike.[9]

It came on 23 October 1641 as a terrible surprise. Even though an informer had betrayed the plot to seize Dublin Castle, the headquarters of the English administration, all over the land men and women rose in revolt with that spontaneous heroism that has always been the glorious tragedy of Ireland's quest for freedom. 'The crisis burst upon us with the suddenness of a violent torrent', wrote Sir William Temple as he cowered inside Dublin Castle: he added that the rebels, inflamed by Jesuits, 'march on furiously destroying all the English, sparing neither sex nor age, most barbarously murdering them, and that with greater cruelty than was ever used amongst Turks or Infidels'. The Mayor of Londonderry was caught equally unawares, writing to his superiors,

> It cannot but seem incredible to your Lordships that so many British, and so many able for war . . . should by a base, rascally, contemptible and disorderly multitude be reduced upon the sudden to that extremity as to be forced to fly for their lives.

A terrified settler wrote to the king, 'all the papists in the kingdom are conspired against us. . . . We cannot resist such force.'[10]

Like all spontaneous risings against alien oppressors – from Nat Turner's Rebellion to Mau Mau – the Irish Rebellion was not without its excesses.

Settlers were murdered, or else cast out naked to die in the cold and rain of winter. 'I saw the miserable destruction of 120 men, women and children by sword, famine and many diseases, amongst whom fell my mother Elizabeth, and my youngest brother, Joseph', wrote a survivor who caught a boat from Ireland in the nick of time (only to be captured by Algerian pirates and sold into slavery).[11] Sir William Parsons, a Lord Justice of Ireland, had to hide in a hen house. The Bishop of Killala and his family were found barely alive, dressed in rags, cringing in a snow-drift. Babes were reported impaled on pikes, or cut from their mothers' wombs, children were roasted on spits, daughters were raped – all as parents and spouses were forced to watch. According to *Treason in Ireland for blowing up of the King's English Forces with 100 Barrels of Gunpowder* (1642, T2077) (a pamphlet whose title aroused memories of Guy Fawkes), at Rockoll, accompanied by bagpipes which 'they played exceedingly loud,' the rebels 'cruelly murdered' an English family. At Nassey they slew Henry Orell, his wife and daughter 'in the most barbarous manner that ever was known'. At Athy they hanged an English woman by her hair from her door, and boiled a maidservant alive in a vat of beer. At Kilkenny they raped Mrs Atkins, who was heavy with child, before ripping open her womb and tossing mother and child into a fire. In County Tyrone sixteen Scots children were purportedly hanged alive, and a fat Caledonian killed and rendered into candles. The rebels tied another victim to a tree, slit open his belly, pulled out his intestines to see if 'a dog's or Scotchman's guts were the longer'.[12]

Such atrocity stories lost nothing in the telling as they crossed the sea to England, particularly when they were brought by thousands of terrified refugees. Illustrated by cheap woodcuts they can still turn modern stomachs hardened by photographs of Belsen or Cambodia (see plates 15 and 16). Numbers of the dead were grossly exaggerated twenty, thirty, perhaps fortyfold. The Reverend Devereux Spratt, a clergyman from Tralee, thought that the papists had massacred a hundred and fifty thousand Protestants, while both Richard Baxter and Lucy Hutchinson put the figure at two hundred thousand.[13]

It would be hard to exaggerate the effect the Irish Rebellion had on opinion in the rest of the British Isles.[14] Four days after its outbreak, Secretary of State Nicholas wrote from London to the king that 'the alarm of popish plots amaze and fright the people here more than anything.'[15] 'O what fears and tears, cries and prayers, day and night, was there then in many places, and in my dear mother's house in particular!' remembered Joseph Lister of Bradford, 'I was about twelve or thirteen years old, and though I was afraid of being killed, yet I was weary of so much fasting and praying.'[16] Looking back, Richard Baxter agreed that 'the terrible massacres in Ireland, and the threatening of the rebels to invade England were the chief reasons why the nation moved to a state of war'.[17] Clarendon concurred that without the Irish rebellion the Great Rebellion would have been unthinkable.

Terrified Englishmen blamed every incident, every accident on Irish Catholics. In Derbyshire papists were reported storing weapons and powder for a surprise massacre. In Norwich a pamphlet revealed that they had deliberately set fire to a house on High Street in an attempt to burn down the whole town, rhetorically asking, 'O yee blood Thirsty Papists, What are your intents?'[18]

Mrs Hutchinson remembered that when her husband heard about the atrocities he went to his country estate to read all he could find about their intentions. After ploughing through the vast mass of material (nearly 40 per cent of the pamphlets which came pouring off the presses in April 1642 dealt with Ireland), John Hutchinson concluded that a rebellion against his sovereign was a just war.

In truth the war waged across the Irish Sea had little justice and even less humanity. It was fought with such ferocity that it had a brutalizing effect, and made killing in England and Scotland easier. According to an English defender who kept a diary during the Siege of Limerick, the combat started in 'the most civilized and humane fashion', but the behaviour of the English troops quickly degenerated.[19]

Charles told his forces in Ireland to 'prosecute the Rebels and Traitors with fire and sword'. The Lords of the Council instructed Ormonde 'to burn, spoil, waste, consume, destroy and demolish all the places, towns, and houses where the said rebels are . . . and to *kill and destroy all the men there inhabiting able to bear arms*.' The Earl, who had just hanged the defenders of Naas, had few scruples about obeying such commands, particularly as the rebels held his wife and children captive. When Secretary of State Conway ordered Colonel Crawford to send a punitive expedition to ravage Counties Wicklow and Kildare, he wrote, 'you are to kill, slay and destroy all the rebels you can there find'.[20]

The king's soldiers needed little official encouragement. One news report described their blood lust: 'so earnestly did they desire to have the killing of more of the rebels'. Another related that after the rebels called 'our men English dogs and Scotch dogs', they 'put them all to the sword'.[21] Neighbour fought neighbour to settle old festering scores. For instance, John Erwyn led a party of Scots soldiers next door to Mary Mullen's house. Grabbing her, he slashed her about the head and fingers with his sword as she screamed repeatedly, 'Dear John, do not kill me, for I have never offended you!' Then he thrust his sword under her right breast into her heart, stripped her naked, and to make sure she was dead placed a live coal on her forehead.[22]

The full horror of the fighting in Ireland, which British forces conducted with the casual cruelty characteristic of an SS Einsatzgruppe on the Russian Front, can be seen in a diary of an anonymous officer who took part in a search and destroy mission through County Wicklow in November 1641.[23] On the 28th they captured two spies, whom they hung on the castle wall at Newcastle. The next day 'were taken and hung some men and women', their numbers and offences the diarist apparently felt not worth recording. Later that day two more were hanged, and one shot for trying to stop the troops rustling his cattle. When they reached Wicklow on the morrow the troops hanged three people, including a pregnant woman. After being ambushed on their way to Bray, they killed eight prisoners, and casually shot and killed a peasant who was ploughing his fields. Such expeditions were the bloody norm. For instance the diary of a two-week foray against the rebels – which was published in England under the title *Welcome news from Ireland* – reported how 'we marched . . . burning and pillaging all the way'. The list of atrocities becomes tediously numbing. On every day but two the English burned villages and hanged rebels – two on 5 April, four on the 6th, eight on the 7th, fourteen on the 8th, and on the 12th 'We rested at Mariborough, and that night hanged 3 poor Rogues . . . all dying without any show of penitence.'

In many respects Ireland became one huge 'Free Fire Zone' in which, as the Earl of Clanricarde admitted, English troops murdered, plundered, mutilated, and ransomed to their hearts' content. Apart from an English lieutenant who was reported hanged for murdering a woman in May 1642, they did so virtually unchecked, and with an excess that horrified veterans of the Thirty Years' War, such as Sir James Turner. Such behaviour, both Turner and Clanricarde warned, was counter-productive because it encouraged further atrocities from the other side.[24]

Such pleas for humanity fell on deaf ears, for the fighting in Ireland had got out of control. In sum, it not only brutalized the conflict in England, but by being a running sore, maintained the intensity of feelings in the rest of the British Isles. For instance, the parliamentary practice of hanging the Irish they took prisoner in England, led to reprisals that heightened animosities on all sides.

In Ireland the enemy was defined in ways that made killing him – and her – far easier. Of course, for centuries the English had seen the Irish as savages, who only understood one sort of treatment. 'Withdraw the sword' warned John Hooker, who fought in the Elizabethan conquest, 'and as the dog to his vomit, and the sow to her dirt and puddle, they will return to their old and former insolence, rebellion and disobedience.'[25] In *A New Remonstrance from Ireland* (1642, E712), Thomas Emitee declared that the Irish were 'a people of no religion but heathen'. For seventeenth-century Protestants that meant that they were not really human beings. At the same time their religion, Roman Catholicism, somehow added to their lack of humanity, which made killing them as acceptable to God as it was to most Englishmen. After describing how he helped defeat some rebels on 15 February 1642, Captain William Tucker concluded, 'the hand of God is always with us, in all our actions against them'.[26] The author of *God Fighting for Us in Ireland* (1642) made his views obvious from the title of his pamphlet. Since Irish women often went bare-headed, a fashion used at home by prostitutes, English troops assumed they were whores beyond the chivalric pale.

Rather like the western view of the Japanese at the start of the Second World War, many Englishmen viewed the Irish as both sub-human beings and superhuman soldiers, whose treacheries ranged far and wide. 'The rebels they increase daily, like Hydra's heads,' reported a news-sheet, 'one is no sooner cut off, but there arise another in his place.' Early in 1642 *The True Relation of the Bloody Conspiracy of the Papists in Cheshire. Intended for the destruction of the whole country. Invented by the treacherous Lord Chomes and Henry Starkey, his Steward* graphically described how a single volley from fifty Catholics slew twenty-five of the county's trained band.[27] Considering that a 10 per cent hit rate was normal for trained regulars in Frederick the Great's Army, the 50 per cent rate for Chester's papists would qualify them for Olympic medals, as well as first place in any Hall of Protestant Paranoia.[28]

Parliamentarians tried hard to tar the king's English supporters with the brush of Irish papism. *A Most true and exact Relation of a Great Overthrow given to the Cavaliers* (1642, T2453B) described how after capturing Marlborough the enemy 'most cruelly pillaged the same, ravishing the women and maidens in a most barbarous manner, showing themselves to be the true sons of the rebels in Ireland'. The widely used *Soldier's Catechism: composed for the Parliamentary Army* defined the enemy as 'Papists and Atheists . . . for the most part inhuman, barbarous and cruel . . . the enemies of God'.[29] In July 1643 John Dod, a survivor of the Irish Rebellion, told a horrified Commons' committee how in the king's camp at Oxford 'he saw a great number of Irish Rebels whom he knew had a hand in the most barbarous actions of that rebellion, as the dashing of small infants and the ripping up of woman with child, and the like'.[30]

Both sides could play this game. At the start of the war the king told his army that the enemy were 'Traitors, most of them Brownists, Anabaptists and atheists'. Just before his regiment took up their positions at Edgehill, Sir James Ramsay informed them that the enemy were 'Papists, Atheists or Irreligious persons for the most part'. 'All men know the great numbers of Papists, which serve in their army', proclaimed the king, who called puritans 'papists' on the rather specious grounds that both were outside the established church.[31]

The immediate effect of the rebellion that broke out in Ireland in October 1641 was to push English moderates into the king's camp, and to encourage Charles to stage a counter-coup of his own. On 4 January 1642 at the head of a party of soldiers he marched into the House of

Commons to arrest the five members, whom he believed were the ring leaders of the opposition. Forewarned, they had left by a back door to seek refuge in the city of London, as the king walked into the front. Unable to see the gang of five from the Speaker's throne, Charles wryly observed 'all the birds have flown'.[32]

So too had any good prospect of a peaceful settlement with parliament. That next day Thomas Smith wrote to a friend, 'These violent proceedings of the king give much discontent, and we are daily in fear of uproar.'[33] Six days later the royal family impulsively left London for Windsor, their departure being so hurried that it was said that they all had to spend that night in one bed, the castle servants having not been warned of their arrival. That same day Lady Sussex wrote to Ralph Verney, 'these distracted times put us all in great disorder, but I hope we shall not be killed yet'. Others shared the view that the king's abortive coup had brought that prospect far closer. At the end of January Henry Oxinden wrote from London,

> I find here all full of fears and void of hopes. Parents and children, brothers, kindred, I and dear friends have the seed of difference and division abundantly sowed in them. . . . I have heard foul language and desperate quarrelling even between old and entire friends, and how we can thus stand and not fall, certainly God must needs work a miracle.

Bulstrode Whitelocke agreed, writing the following month that 'The times began to appear very dreadful, & all discourses were of the threatening Civil War.'[34]

The issue that everyone was debating was fundamental – who should control the gun barrels of the new army to be raised to put down the Irish rebellion. Both Charles and parliament believed that this is whence political power came, just as fervently as would Mao Zedong. Fearful that the monarch would first use this army to suppress opposition in England, the Commons passed a Militia Bill depriving him of his long-standing right to appoint army officers. Charles would have nothing of it. 'By God not for an hour', he angrily told a parliamentary deputation who begged him to sign the bill, 'You have asked of me that was never asked of a king and with which I would not trust my wife and children.'[35]

It was widely recognized that the control of the armed forces was so basic an issue that it might well be the fittest subject over which the nation could go to civil war. Yet the prospect of such a conflict was quite terrifying. All over the land men and women considered its appalling implications. They tried to reassure themselves that somehow war would not – it could not – happen. In March Robert Wynne of Gray's Inn wrote to a friend in Wales that things had got bad and would get worse, 'but I hope in God it will be otherwise, and we shall have peace'.[36] So astute an observer as Sir Thomas Roe could still maintain that civil war was imposs-ible. 'I can see no other hope', wrote the veteran diplomat,

> but when we shall come to join, they will remember that they are brethren, all Englishmen, and that the equality of the balance, and the uncertain chance of battle will raise both in due consideration, that it is too much that either part doth hazard.

John Taylor agreed. 'There is nothing', declared the water poet, 'more uncertain than the event of war, nor is there anything more unsure than the success of a battle.'[37]

The king had no such reservations. On 23 April 1642 he arrived before the gates of Hull to demand that the governor, Sir John Hotham, surrender the keys to the arsenal. In the first open act of military rebellion, Hotham refused, and due to ill luck and incompetence, Charles was unable to seize the large stock of weapons. The effect on public opinion was gloomy. 'We are in as many doubts about the issue of things here as you are there,' wrote Sir Francis Newport, MP, from London to his uncle Sir Richard Lewson at Trentham, Staffordshire, 'I hope God will give you a happy ending of them.'[38]

The awareness of the reality of civil strife was beginning to dawn upon more and more people. 'The first blows will wound deeply', warned Henry Knyvett, a Norfolk gentleman. In Buckinghamshire Mistress Eure worried that a war would give the Verney Family's tenants an excuse not to pay their rents, and then 'we shall be in a hard case'.[39] The Earl of Leicester confided to the Countess of Carlisle, 'I fear it is not so much a malignant party, as a malignant fate that awaits us.' The Earl of Pembroke told his fellow peers that 'we hear every fellow say in the streets as we pass by in our coaches, that they hope to see us on foot shortly, and be as good men as the Lords, and I think they will. . . . If we take this course.'[40] Common folk were equally fearful. Even though crowds cheered the king as he progressed through Lincolnshire many of them (at least according to a parliamentary pamphlet) had 'no courage to fight'. Paradoxi-cally some feared that this reluctance to take up arms would make any war even bloodier. After seeing the king on his summer tour of the North of England, Thomas Salisbury, a distinguished soldier from Denbighshire, grew sure that war was both inevitable and would be prolonged, because, he reasoned, those who would use force against the king were neither strong enough to win a short victory, nor weak enough to be speedily crushed, and thus they 'are like to embroil the kingdom in a perpetual war'.[41]

Writing to his wife that summer, Bulstrode Whitelocke ruminated about what such a war would be like. 'We must surrender up all our laws, liberties, properties and living into the hands of insolent Mercenaries, whose rage and violence will command us.' He was sure that amongst the first casualties would be 'reason, honour and justice'. The world that he and his wife had loved would be turned upside down, with base folk lording it over the noble, the profane usurping the pious. Fields would be laid waste, goods pillaged, the land would bleed itself to death. Whitelocke concluded that 'you will hear other sounds, beside those of drums and trumpets, the clattering of armour, the roaring of guns, the groans of wounded and dying men, the shriek of dishonoured women, the cries of widows and orphans'.[42]

Yet the credence that peace might somehow prevail lasted right up until – and even after – the formal declaration of hostilities. A fortnight before the king raised the royal standard at Nottingham on 22 August proclaiming his subjects in rebellion, using a ceremony so antiquated that the heralds were uncertain of its correct form, Stephen Charlton ended a description of Lord Goring's refusal (backed up by force of arms) to hand Portsmouth over to parliament's forces by hoping 'but for all this we are in good hopes for pacification before they come to blows'.[43]

So strong was this refusal to accept the possibility of the horrors of civil war that even after fighting started, many tried to deny the reality. 'We have already tasted the bitter, bloody Fruits of War', admitted Sir Benjamin Rudyerd to the Commons in February 1643, before trying to console them, 'There is yet some comfort left, that our miseries are not likely to last long, for we cannot fight here as they do in Germany.'[44]

The example of the brutal Thirty Years' War had made a profound impression on all sorts of Englishmen. 'Let us behold the miseries of Germany, a kingdom once as famous and flourishing as ours lately was', advised the author of the *Miseries of War* in 1643. A pamphlet luridly entitled *Syon's Calamity or England's Misery Hieroglyphically Delineated* warned:[45]

> Alas poor England! How thou art distressed
> With War! Which for a long time was so blessed
> With peace: that all thy neighbouring nations
> Admired thy glory, when all their stations
> Were filled with bloody wars and strife.

Another ballad was even more pessimistic:[46]

> Lament!
> And let thy tears run down,
> To see the rent,
> Between the robe and Crown. . . .
> War like a serpent, has its head got in,
> And will not end as soon as it did begin.

The fear of a civil war was so profound that many attempted to imagine what it would be like. 'Unhappy Civil War quite simply produced nothing but evil', wrote one pamphleteer. Another added, 'Tu Bellum causa malorum. War is a womb big with many miseries, when it travels it swells envy, quickens malice, begets jealousies, separates friends, undoes families and kingdom. Its anger is fierce.'[47] So horrible was civil war that Captain Edward Chisenhall described its outbreak in his own county of Lancashire in terms of the plague, the most lethal holocaust familiar to civilians. Like the Black Death 'this subtle poison had so wrought in that little body, that the whole country was swelled to one tumour, which by all symptoms had broke out in 3 days'.[48]

Apart from the danger, there was the discomfort of war. Thomas Raymond, an English veteran of the Thirty Years' War, recalled,

> I cannot but think that the life of the private or common soldier is the most miserable in the world, and that not so much because his life is in danger – that is little or nothing – but for the terrible miseries he endures in hunger and nakedness, in hard marches and bad quarters.[49]

An officer's life was just as hard. As Bulstrode Whitelocke told his wife, going to the wars meant that he had to 'leave a soft bed, close curtains, and a warm chamber to lodge *sub Deo* upon the hard and cold earth'. He would have to give up fine food and wines for scraps of coarse mouldy bread washed down with ditch-water, and – if he was lucky – a pipe of pungent tobacco. He would have to forsake the pleasant conversation and company of friends, wives and children 'for the dreadful whistling of bullets and bodies dropping dead at one's feet'.[50]

The fear of disorder was as disturbing as actual chaos. 'We have to punish tumults and riots', declared the king in the summer of 1642, 'to keep our towns, our forests and parks from violence'.[51] Many believed that a civil war would allow 'the many headed monster', who were the 'rabble . . . the greatest and most savage beast in the whole world', to rise up and destroy their betters.[52] So scared were the town governments of Colchester and Chester that 'our unruly multitude' would use conflict in some distant county as an excuse to 'work mischief by plundering' shops and houses, that they tried to stop parliament mobilizing the city's trained bands.[53]

Going to war meant having to kill one's fellow human beings, an act which most societies regard as akin to murder. In 'A Soldier Thinks of Sin', the covenanting trooper George Withers wrote:[54]

> Now in myself I notice take
> What life we soldiers lead.
> My hair stands up, my heart doth ache
> My soul is full of dread.

41

Defend me, Lord, from those misdeeds,
Which my profession shame,
And from a vengeance that succeeds,
When we are so to blame.

Even though the biblical commandments taught seventeenth-century Englishmen that thou shalt not kill, and the execution of murderers was a
public demonstration of its consequences, little attention was paid to
overcoming scruples about taking the lives of one's fellow creatures – let
alone one's fellow countrymen. Such is surprising, for today subduing this
taboo is a major goal of a soldier's basic training, in which NCOs urge
recruits to plunge bayonets into straw dummies, as they scream obscenities
and have obscenities screamed at them. In the civil war such conditioning
does not appear to have been very necessary. Rather than the raucous
shouts of sergeant-majors, obliterating the Sixth Commandment was left
to the quiet logic of preachers. The Reverend John Bond reassured Devonshire's trained bands who were about to leave for active service that 'God
bad them go up: their cause was his.' Thus, he continued, killing His
enemies was not murder, but a punishment rightly due to 'traitors, rav-
ishers, rebels and delinquents'. On the other side, Stephen Marshall justified killing parliament's enemies by using the text 'Cursed be he that
withheld his hand from blood.'[55]

One common way of overcoming guilt is to blame the victim. When
the royalists trapped three parliamentary regiments at Brentford in November 1642 the slaughter was terrible. 'It was heartrending to observe the
death and so miserable end of so many goodly men we slew', a royalist
trooper wrote home to his mother. But the same soldier went on to say
that the enemy had only themselves to fault: 'They ran into the Thames,
and about two hundred on them . . . drowned by themselves, and so were
guilty of their own deaths.'[56]

Most gentlemen were less concerned about killing in general, and slaying
the many-headed monster in particular, than they were about having to
kill their confreres, and social superiors. As Sir Hugh Cholmley, the
royalist Governor of Scarborough, lamented, 'I am forced to draw my
sword, not only against my countrymen, but my dear friends, and allies,
some of which I know to be well affected in religion and lovers of their
liberties.'[57]

Events proved such fears far from groundless. 'My affection to you is
unchangeable, that hostility itself cannot violate my friendship to your
person', wrote 'your most affectionate friend and faithful servant, William
Waller' to 'My noble friend Sir Ralph Hopton', as they prepared to fight
in 1643. Friends not merely led troops against each other, but actually
tried to kill one another. When Edmund Ludlow's roundhead cavalry
came across a troop of enemy horse just outside Winchester in July 1644

he saw his old school chum William Neale. 'I called to him telling him I was sorry to see him there, but since it was so I offered to exchange a shot.' They did. One round from Neale's double-shotted musket hit Ludlow's breastplate, the other killed his horse.

As England drifted into civil conflict during the summer of 1642, an aptly named pamphlet, *A Warning piece to warre* summed up the ambivalence many folk felt toward soldiers and their profession. Kipling recognized this contradiction when he wrote of how the public attitude towards Tommy Atkins of 'chuck him out, the brute', gave way to 'Saviour of 'is country when the guns begin to shoot'.[58] *A Warning piece to warre* pointed out that since the fall of Adam and Eve imperfect societies had always needed soldiers, who were invariably drawn from the margins of society. Sometimes they were misfits, who could not settle down into the humdrum round of peaceful life: or else they had committed some indiscretion, such as making a girl pregnant, that forced them to flee their civilian responsibilities. All too often soldiers were men who would not be missed, and would not miss the societies whence they came. And being armed they were always dangerous.

Society often tries to control such people by subjecting them to the strict authority of officers, drawn from its elite (such as the aristocracy), who are unlikely to upset the status quo. Before the civil wars the officer who exercised the greatest influence over the ordinary trooper, his company captain, was socially little better than they were. Thomas Nashe, the Elizabethan writer, castigated such officers as mercenaries who 'do wholly bestow themselves upon pleasure . . . gaming, the following of harlots, drinking and seeing a play'.[59]

Discipline attempts to restrain and direct the violence which is the essence of a soldier's trade. Frederick the Great once remarked that he wanted his men to be more afraid of him and their officers than they were of the enemy. Nonetheless the potential power of a soldier, armed with weapons of destruction, can be frightening, particularly in a nation that is sliding into civil war.

A fear of professional soldiers in part explains the public back-lash that followed the king's appointment of Colonel Thomas Lunsford as Lieutenant of the Tower of London in late 1641. Lunsford was an extremely violent fellow, 'who fears neither God nor man', thought his cousin the Earl of Dorset, 'having given himself over to all lewdness and dissoluteness'.[60] Charged with attempting to murder, after a Sunday morning service in 1633, a relative whose deer he had been poaching, Lunsford fled abroad to fight in the French Army. On his return home Charles not only pardoned, but promoted him. During the Bishops' Wars, as a captain responsible for marching conscripts north, Lunsford boasted of having shot a couple of mutineers out of hand. During the war both sides believed him guilty of cannibalism. He 'made children with *their* tongues run for't',

43

wrote Samuel Butler.[61] In sum, Lunsford was typical of the hard men who surrounded the king in growing numbers, and upon whom Charles increasingly relied, much to the consternation of moderate civilian opinion.

Donald Lupton, a veteran of the Thirty Years' War, tried to reassure civilian fears in his *Warre-Like Treatise of the Pike* (1642). No profession, he admits,

> hath been more disgraced with opprobrious language than this of a Soldier. For some have held it unlawful, others have held that all Soldiers are irreligious and perfidious because of many heinous abuses committed by Soldiers, as Sacrilege, Swearing, Murders, Rapes, Stealing, Pillaging, Firing of House, Drunkenness.

But surely it was unfair, Lupton continued, to blame all soldiers for the abuses of the few. Anyway commanders always punished those guilty of such crimes severely because 'an army is but a well governed Commonwealth in Arms'. Indeed because soldiers were often close to death they were far more concerned than civilians about the state of their souls, and thus were equally likely to live good lives.[62]

It is plausible that those who read Lupton's treatise when it first appeared in 1642 might have found it nearly as entertaining as the antics of Shakespeare's soldiers as they strutted about the London stage. Captains Fluellen and MacMorris, those Celtic comedians, debated martial matters with as much vigour as real soldiers attacked each other in military manuals.[63] The motley crew of Captain Sir John Falstaff, Ensign Bardolph, Corporal Nym *et al.*, were licentious braggarts. The dregs of society, they drank, fornicated, belched and boasted of their courage and cruelties, in a way that amused so long as it was confined to *The Globe*, and terrified once it escaped into the world outside.

Historians have spent much time and effort trying to discover why men chose sides during the civil wars. The act was complicated: unlike, say, voting, it was not a threefold choice between one side, the other, or abstaining, taken on a single day: it was instead a decision fraught with dangers, that could be undone or undo the actor. Moreover the options were not so clear cut at the time as they appear in retrospect. At the start of the war Colonel Goring, governor of the garrison besieged at Portsmouth, was groping for definitions when he 'declared himself to be for the king alone, and not for the king and Parliament: but for the king alone, against parliament'.[64]

In most civil wars there have been clear determinants of side, be they region (as in the American), sects (as in Ulster or Beruit) or ethnicity (as in Sri Lanka or Nigeria). While such determinates prevailed in the Irish and Scots civil wars, they were nowhere as clear cut in the English. Except for Middlesex, in no English county were all the MPs, including those who represented boroughs, on the same side. As Mrs Hutchinson recalled, 'Every County has the civil war, more or less, within itself.'[65] Without doubt religion was crucial in determining which side people chose, as was region, profession, one's network of friends, and, possibly, class. But just as important, and far less studied, as the motivation for choosing on which side to fight, were the forces which kept men fighting once they had joined the fray. Of course, motivations for choosing sides and for fighting could be similar, as with the case of religion or peer groups. Often they were disparate. As John Dolland, a survivor of the Spanish Civil War, wrote, 'Ideology functions *before* battle to get the man in: and *after* battle by blocking thoughts of escape.' But *during* battles the ideas which brought man into combat played no role. Robert Graves, spokesman for a generation who volunteered for King and Country during the First World War, was even more blunt: 'Patriotism in the trenches was too remote a sentiment, and at once rejected as fit only for civilians or prisoners.'[66]

The decision to take a fraught-ridden act such as going to war is usually made in an emotionally charged atmosphere. Looking back over the centuries, from the snug haven of a study or library, it is hard to realize how noisy and unsafe were such moments, how extreme were the oscillations of joy and despair, of trepidation and hope, of enthusiasm and dread. The approach of war 'caught us with a great fear and astonishment', reported a news writer, 'the like was never seen in Manchester'.[67] Richard Baxter recalled the hysteria which prevailed in Kidderminster at the start of the war. 'If a stranger moved in many places that has short hair and a civil habit, the rabble presently cried "Down with the roundheads", and some knocked down openly in the streets.'[68] Baxter, who was twice nearly lynched, had to flee his native county. 'I was glad to spur on and be gone', he recalled. His escape was not enough, however, to convince him of the rightness of parliament's cause. Baxter refused an offer from a then obscure gentleman from Huntingdon, Captain Oliver Cromwell, to be the chaplain of a cavalry troop he was raising. Instead Baxter sat out the war for three years before he was able to see his way to doing his bit.

Deciding to go to war is never an easy bit to do. Some men, such as John Hutchinson, read all they could before making up their minds. Other folk consulted astrologers. Many asked William Lilly as to whether the stars thought it 'best to adhere to King or Parliament'. Mr Whitely wanted to know if it were safe for his son to go to war, while Captain Willoughby wondered if he should stay in the service or seek civilian employment. Lilly's *A Prophesy of the White King* (1644, L2240) played on people's fears about the future. Purporting to be a translation of an ancient Welsh poem, this best-seller, which sold 1,800 copies in its first three days, used the stars to show that peace did not return to the land until after the

White King's death. So the royalists commissioned their astrologer to show that in fact the constellations favoured Charles I.[69]

Most people turned to prayer. 'When I put my hand to the Lord's Work in 1642,' recalled the parliamentary Captain John Hodgson, 'I did it not rashly, but had many an hour and night to seek God to know my way.' On the king's side Sir William Campion, a gentleman from Sussex, found the decision to fight equally difficult:[70]

> I did not rashly or unadvisedly put myself upon this service, for it was daily in my prayers for two or three months together to God to direct me in the right way, and besides I had conference with diverse able and honest men for advice, who confirmed me in my judgment.

The fact that both Hodgson and Campion unconsciously used the language of the marriage ceremony to explain that their commitment was neither rash nor without advice would suggest that they believed that, once taken, their choice was one with which they must live until death did them part.

Deciding to choose sides could be easier than deciding to fight. Take, for instance, the experience of mercenaries, whose choice of a professional career had already committed them to arms. When the option arose for practising their profession at home the choice of side was rarely taken with vexatious deliberations. Sir James Turner, the veteran who fought with Gustavus Adolphus, recalled that when he reached the harbour to board ship to return to Scotland there were two vessels, one carrying mercenaries to fight for the king, and the other for the covenant. He did not much care which one he boarded. 'I had swallowed without chewing in Germany a very dangerous maxim,' Turner explained, 'so long as we serve our master honestly, it is no matter which master we serve.' When in May 1639 the Royal Navy captured a vessel carrying twenty Scots veterans home to fight for the covenant, they all promptly agreed to serve the crown. Returning from the Thirty Years' War, Colonel Edward Massey went to York to seek a command in the King's service, but finding he lacked the connections rode on to London where there was more money and fewer officers, and he quickly obtained a colonelcy in the Earl of Stamford's Regiment.[71]

The reasons why men fight are complicated, and spring from deep within our psyches. Freud argued that violence is partly a product of sexual repression. Certainly to survive every society needs the willingness of its young and usually single males – who have the highest sex drives and little opportunity to satisfy them – to fight and die in war. While it might be hard to accept that aggression, cruelty and violence seem ingrained in human nature, it is undeniable that most cultures have, when necessary, been able to persuade practically every mother's son to kill and be killed.[72]

War is exciting: it is dramatic: at times it can be beautiful: often it provides an escape from the boredom of peace: always it allows individuals to indulge in the delights of destruction.[73] War provides the companionship of comrades – that intense love of men you may not personally like, but on whom your life may depend, and which all who have experienced can never forget. Surrendering oneself completely to the whole, produces a liberation from individual freedom. Sergeants tell soldiers that they did not join the army to think: armies give them a chance to feel. War provides a communal ecstasy that at times comes close to religion. In war those that die are called martyrs: in Christian wars they are soldiers who march onward to fight the good fight. Once taken, the commitment to war – as to religion – can move mountains, providing simple answers to complicated questions. War provides common, concrete and obtainable goals that are far more tangible than the uncertainties of compromise. Thus one royalist standard, captured at Marston Moor, portrayed a cavalier using a sword to cut a knot – presumably the Gordian Knot of peace.[74]

Sydenham Poyntz explained why as a lad of 17 he first decided to go to war. 'It is well known to most how near youth and rashness are', wrote the parliamentary colonel in his autobiography, 'to be bound apprentice I deemed little better than a dog's life and base. At last I resolved with myself thus: to live and die a soldier would be as noble a death as a life.'[75] Having hazarded one's self in combat, an experience which Dr Samuel Johnson admitted envying, was something of which Ben Jonson was extremely proud. As a young soldier he had killed a Spaniard in hand-to-hand combat in the Low Countries: as a middle-aged playwright he recalled the vocation of his youth:[76]

> I swear by your true friend, my muse, I love
> Your great profession, which I once did prove.
> And did not shame it with my actions then
> No more than I do now with my pen.

That there should be some hesitancy, camouflaged by irony, in Jonson's recollections should not surprise us for being a soldier touches on fundamental fears such as death, killing and masculinity. Today we stress masculinity so much in preparing young men for war (as we also do in advertising, family life, and in bed), that one feminist commentator has (without even a hint of humour) called misogyny 'The mother's milk of Militarism'.[77]

By comparison seventeenth-century appeals to machismo were infrequent. 'A manly presence' had been listed as a qualification for the Yeomen of the Guard.[78] Donald Lupton's *A Warre-like treatise on the Pike* (1642, L3946), linked 'Effeminacy and Cowardice'. In a sermon Simeon Ashe urged the London Trained Bands to 'quite ye like men' and 'play the men'. The following year William Bridge preached from the same biblical text to the trained bands from Norwich and Yarmouth: 'Be of good courage, and let us play the man for our people and for the cities of our God.'[79]

Soldiers were asked to consider what their wives and families would think of them if they failed to play the man. This 'What did you do in the War, Daddy?' argument has a long history. Shakespeare used it in *Henry V* (IV, iii, 45–6):

> He that shall live this day and see old age,
> Will yearly on the vigil feast his neighbours.

Less poetically General Patton assured his men that if they fought bravely they would never have to squirm as they confessed to their grandchildren that 'I shovelled crap in Louisiana.' Playing on the anticipation of future pride or shame Hugh Peters preached to the Ironsides after the Battle of Worcester that 'When your wives and children shall ask you where have you been . . . say you have been in Worcester.'[80]

Human beings feel ambivalent towards aggression. We laud the Victoria Cross winner, and loathe the mass murderer. Because societies must oft-times call upon their members to be aggressive and violent, they mute this risky invitation by claiming religion or self-defence as an excuse.[81] The Reverends Ashe and Bridge employed the former to prepare their audiences for battles. Like the Confederate who explained to the invading Yankees that he was shooting at them ''cos y're here', many seventeenth-century Britons saw their struggle in terms of a resistance to aggression from outside their localities so blatant that they had no alternative but to fight: it was so obvious, it was so simple; it needed no further discussion. James McDonnell explained why he and his friends had just joined the Catholic rebels in Ireland after hearing of a plot against them: 'I and all these gentlemen, with my wife and children, had been utterly destroyed' had they not taken up arms. William Chillingworth said that he and his fellow royalists had gone to war to 'defend our lives and livelihood, wives, children, houses and lands'.[82] 'They took arms against us', Richard Hubberthorn, a Lancashire yeoman (who later became a Quaker), explained his decision to enlist in the parliamentary army, 'we fought in a defensive way for our Rights and Liberties.'[83]

Many men went to war, and remained at war, because they were told to do so by superiors whom they were used to obeying. Recent experimental research has shown that people will 'inflict' electric shocks on innocent subjects with little compunction if ordered to do so by authority. Such compliance seems even more likely in a hierarchical society, such as early modern England, where the age-old habit of obedience was strong, being continually reinforced.[84]

Historians have long recognized that sermons were one of the most important source of ideas during the seventeenth century. Their impact, however, should not be exaggerated. Perhaps a thousand troops – many restless and bored – heard those given by the Reverends Ashe and Bridge, while twice as many might have read them in print. Perhaps as many would have read royalist polemics such as Thomas Jordan's *The Christian Soldier in Preparation for Battle* (1642, J1022).

The effect of the official homilies appointed to be read out aloud in church was far greater. Repeated time and time again, Sunday in and out, they entered the mentalities of most seventeenth-century Englishmen: a bit like a modern advertising slogan, they were nigh unrealized, yet unremitting. Such sermons were almost subliminal. 'God can work upon the hearts of man,' preached William Hussy in 1647, 'the work shall be done though they think not so.'[85] Thus when Shakespeare warned 'Take but degree away, untune that string/And hark what discord follows', it would have struck a familiar cord with the audience of *Troilus and Cressida*, all of whom must have heard the official homily, 'An exhortation to Obedience'. Indeed they most probably accepted the idea without thinking, for it resonated with a familiar and accepted note.

The homily on obedience started with the concept of a great chain of being, of a universe in which everything had a place, and in which everything should be in its place. If things were displaced then 'no house, no city, no commonwealth can continue and endure'. When kings, rulers and magistrates fail, anarchy will prevail, and no one's life, family or property would be safe. 'Let no man think that he can escape unpunished that committeth treason, conspiracy or rebellion against his sovereign Lord the King', the homily concluded, 'treason will out'.[86]

The government had long recognized the importance of such sermons. 'If the pulpits teach not obedience', Charles wrote, 'the king will have but small comfort of the militia.'[87] At the start of the war Charles and his moderate advisers took advantage of the centuries of tradition, reinforced a hundredfold in church, that supported their case. They tried to push men off the fence, sure that the habit of obedience would prompt many more to come down on their side, rather than that of rebellion.

'I am environed by such contradictions as I can neither get from them, nor reconcile them', wrote the Earl of Leicester to his sister-in-law, three days after Charles raised his standard. Parliament commanded him to join them, the king told him to await further orders. 'How soon I shall get out of the labyrinth I cannot tell.' When push came to shove, the earl joined the king at Oxford. Sir Thomas Knyvett's quandary was very similar. After parliament appointed him a company commander in the militia and the king sent him a commission of array authorizing him to raise troops, the Norfolk gentleman realized he was caught on the horns of an excruciating dilemma. 'Oh! sweet heart, I am now in a great straight what to do', he agonized to his wife. Forced to come off the fence, Knyvett landed on the king's side, staged an abortive coup at Lowestoft, was captured, imprisoned, and had his estates sequestered. As the epitaph on his tombstone suggests, for Knyvett – like so many other country gentlemen – royalism was associated with a lifelong respect for law and order:[88]

> Here lies loyal Knyvett, who hated anarchy,
> Lived a true Protestant and died with monarchy.

The thinking of some was even simpler – and like all simple ideas had profound effects. 'I do not like this quarrel, and do heartily wish the king would yield', declared Sir Edmund Verney, who had first served Charles in 1623 during his farcical trip to Madrid to woo the king of Spain's daughter, but

> my conscience is only concerned with honour and gratitude for to follow my master. I have eaten his bread and served him near thirty years, and will not do so base a thing as to forsake him, and choose rather to give my life – which I am sure I shall do.[89]

Such a simple conclusion, albeit taken reluctantly, was potent enough to make Verney give his life trying to save the royal standard at Edgehill. According to one story, to pry the flag away from its bearer the round-heads had to hack off Verney's hand, on which was also a small ring with a miniature portrait of his sovereign.

The equally ingenuous idea that the king was the father of his country whom all true Christians were commanded to obey was stalwart enough to sustain the royalist Lord Capel as he stood before a parliamentary firing squad. 'I die, I take it, for maintaining the Fifth Commandment.' Other concepts were as plain but as potent as the Flag is in America today. 'I cannot contain myself indoors, when the king of England's standard waves in the field', is how Sir Bevil Grenville explained his decision to enlist in the royal forces at York in 1642. Sir Henry Vane was not grovelling too obsequiously when he told the king in the First Bishops' War that his presence with the army was worth twenty thousand troops.[90]

The great chain of being was also a chain of command. Of course, it served the king far better than it did parliament, for his was an unbroken chain, a point illustrated by the case of Sir William, fifth Baron Paget. Since Paget had been a vocal opponent of royal policies, in 1642 parliament appointed him Lord Lieutenant for Buckinghamshire, usurping a prerogative that had been the king's for centuries. Paget replied:[91]

> It may seem strange that I, who with all zeal and earnestness have prosecuted in the legitimacy of this parliament, the reformation of all disorders in church and commonwealth, should not, in times of great distractions desert the cause . . . but when I found the preparation of arms against the king under the shadow of loyalty, I am rather resolved to obey a good conscience than particular ends, and am now

50

on my way to his Majesty, where I will throw myself down at his feet and die a loyal subject.

Yet the fact that tens of thousands of ordinary folk did what their betters told them by fighting against the king showed that the chain of being and of command could work for all sides. To be effective a society's military system cannot be independent of its social systems; rather it must be central to them. In other words waging war is a pivotal institution in any human society. Thus when the British Isles went to war in the middle of the seventeenth century they used many of the civilian institutions which had served them well in peace.

Ties of friendship, blood and tenancy were remarkably potent. Sir Roger Mostyn, who was only 18, having just inherited his father's Flintshire estate, employed them to raise fifteen hundred men for the king in seventeen hours in August 1642.[92] When Lord Strange asked 'my very good friend William ffarington' to recruit troops, he used the phrase 'good friend' twice more in a brief note.[93] 'Dear Cousin, I shall deem a favour', wrote Hugh Wyndham to George Trevelyan on 23 July 1643, 'that you will please to assist . . . to raise some men.'[94] The 1627 muster of Sir John Scudamore's militia company listed twenty-four of his household servants and thirty-eight retainers as well as his son, John.[95] Bulstrode Whitelocke rode to war 'with a gallant company of horse of my neighbours', while Sir William Russell's troop included 'twelve of his servants in scarlet cloaks, well horsed and armed'.[96] All but one of the officers in Colonel Thomas Fosters' royalist regiment were kin.[97] Colonel Edmund Ludlow went to war with Henry Coles, an old family retainer who had been his father's groom.[98]

All of them – Scudamore, Strange, Russell, Coles, Whitelocke, Mostyn – went to the wars blissfully ignorant of their reality. Afterwards some thought it had been fun – particularly those who had seen no fighting. 'I had but a short time being a soldier,' recalled Sir Henry Slingsby of his actionless experience of the First Bishops' War, 'and I liked it as a commendable way of breeding for a gentleman.' A couple of years later in 1642 many felt that the war would be short, and reasonably sweet. On the king's side, concluded Clarendon, over-confidence that a single battle would determine everything 'was the principal cause of this continuing of the war'. Once the war started Richard Baxter admitted that, 'so wise in matters of war was I, and all the county besides, that we commonly supposed that in a very few days or weeks one Battle would end the war'.[99]

At one level it would be easy to dismiss such wild optimism as the triumph of hope over experience, yet the news coming from Ireland supported the conclusion that victories could be won without much cost. John Balle reported seven hundred enemy dead at Cardoughee for three killed. Arnold Boate recounted that near Drogheda the English slew one hundred and fifty Irish for one dead, and the following day another hundred without a single loss. 'The rogues all ran away' was his constant refrain.[100] So when contrary to first expectations the rogues did not run away, and the war degenerated into a long and brutal blood-bath the shock was profound. As William Lilly (who as the century's leading astrologer should have foreseen better) ruefully concluded, 'The God of all glory and power, who hath created us, and given us now more war than we expected.'[101]

While many mentalities were common on all sides, others predominated on one side or the other.

Edward Symmons, Chaplain to the Prince of Wales's Lifeguard, explained the cavalier will to fight in *A Militarie Sermon . . . Preached at Shrewsbury . . . To His Majesty's Army* (1644, S6346):

> A complete Cavalier is a Child of Honour, a Gentleman well born and bred that loves his King for conscience sake, of a clearer countenance and bolder look than other men, because of a more loyal heart.

This view, which has been described as coming 'as near to what we might call grass roots Anglican-Cavalierism as any we can get', went much further than the traditional habit of obedience to the crown, or even the use of honour as a form of social control.[102] There was an intense, almost hallowed character to it. 'I beseech you to consider that majesty is sacred', Edmund Verney wrote, just before their father's death at Edgehill as he tried to persuade his brother Ralph to join the king's cause.[103] Royalism was in many respects a form of extended paternalism. Sir Thomas Wyndham's dying words to his five sons were 'to honour and obey your sovereign, and in all times to adhere to the crown'.[104]

Seeing one's leader as a father-figure not only accorded with the peacetime concept of the king as the *pater patriae* but as the *pater familias*. In combat – the most traumatic of all human ordeals – it enabled soldiers to return to the secure world of infancy where they could put their trust in a father-figure who would make everything all right. In addition he would shoulder the blame for the evil they did in his name. 'We know enough if we know we are the king's subjects', says Private Bates on the eve of the Battle of Agincourt in *Henry V* (IV, i, 138–9), 'Our obedience to the king wipes the crime of it out of us.' Thomas Swadlin repeated the rank and file's traditional excuse for killing in his widely used pamphlet, *The Soldiers Catechism composed for the King's Army* (1645). Edward Symmons used copious biblical examples to demonstrate that, lacking royal authority to kill, the enemy 'are therefore rank murderers'.[105]

The argument could be taken one stage further by saying that since the enemy were not observing the traditional military standards, they had

placed themselves beyond the professional pale. After the Earl of Northampton was killed at the Battle of Hopton Heath in 1644, Sir William
Brereton and Sir John Gell sent a trumpeter to the royalist camp offering
to return his body in return for some captured artillery pieces. A royalist
who heard the proposal was outraged at this breach of professional standards, which he concluded once more proved how right he was to fight
these 'Rogues' who were 'rebels both against God and man, and ignorant
of what belongs to the honour of a soldier'.[106]

Endymion Porter's reasons for pledging his faith to Charles were as
naïve as they were sincere. 'My duty and loyalty have taught me to follow
my King and Master', he wrote to his wife in January 1642, 'and by the
Grace of God nothing shall direct me from it.' Lord George Goring
explained, 'I had it all from his Majesty, and he hath it all again.' The
Duke of Newcastle professed, 'I have no other ambition than to live and
die a loyal subject of his Majesty.'[107] From the scaffold the Earl of Derby
declared in 1651, 'I was born in honour, have lived in honour, and hope
to die in honour.'[108] Sir Richard Bulstrode's decision to fight for the king
was based on a childhood memory. As a boy his father had taken him to
court, 'where we were all brought into the King's presence by the Lord
Chamberlain, and had the honour to kiss the King's hands, who took our
coming very kindly'. William Beau explained that he left Oxford to join
the king's army 'animated by his presence'.[109] The day before the Battle
of Edgehill Richard Shuckburgh was out hunting, oblivious to the great
events unfolding around him. Chancing across the king, he asked Charles
why he was leading his army into battle. 'I am going to fight for my
crown and dignity', was Charles's simple reply. On the spot Shuckburgh
marched with his monarch off to battle.

Within the cavalier ethos there was an inherent sense of social and
sexual superiority that gave its possessor a degree of self-confidence in
battle that might provide the edge for victory. Not only were they better
gentlemen, but better men who could out-fight and out-roger any roundhead any day (and night) of the week. Such was the claim made by a
1642 ballad, delightfully entitled 'The London Cuckold: or, an Antient
Citizen's Head well fit with a flouring pair of Fashionable Horns, by his
Buxome Young Wife, who was well bucked by a Coltish spark, in the
time of her Husband's Absence at the Campaign on Hounslow Heath.'[110]

Because the cavalier ethos appealed to gentlemen, and their sons (and
to those who wished to become gentlemen, and were not quite really
there) it helped the king raise cavalry, the key arm during the civil war.
On the other hand, this sense of social superiority could degenerate into
snobbery, especially among those swordsmen born on the margins of
gentility, who became an increasingly important part of the royalist officer
corps as the war went on. All too often royalist propaganda mocked
the humble origins of the king's opponents. John Taylor dismissed the

parliamentary commanders as 'Tradesmen broken, grown rich with plunder, late scarce worth a token, some cobbling Preachers, some perfidious nobles.'[111] One flyer described the purple uniformed soldiers of Lord Brooke's regiment as 'all butchers and dyers'. Another called a roundhead general 'Faggot-Monger' Browne, because he had once sold firewood in London. In its description of the Second Battle of Newbury in 1644, the influential royalist newspaper, *Mercurius Aulicus*, sneered that 'since the Lord Brooke was found peeping out at a Casement, we confess we did not meet one Rt. Honourable Rebel'. Sir James Turner described the roundhead captain, a glover in civilian life, who accepted his surrender in 1648 as having 'both the mind and manners of a mechanic'.[112]

One would expect such gibes to have discouraged the low-born from fighting for snobbish officers. Strangely it did not do so. As the Brigade of Guards has proved, the British Army has rarely found this to be much of a problem. To the contrary. During the civil war those who fought fiercest for the crown were often outsiders, provincials on the Celtic fringes. 'There were the very best foot I ever saw for marching and fighting', wrote Captain Atkyns of the Cornish troops. Such has been the case in many armies. The deprived, the rejected, the unemployed, the evicted, those scorned by the establishment, will often fight for the powers that be with the utmost bravery. For instance, during the Second World War the most decorated unit in the United States Army, the 445th Regimental Combat Team, was composed of Japanese Americans, who had been interned after Pearl Harbor. In much the same fashion after the Battle of Culloden, and the evictions, no regiments fought harder for the British Empire than those recruited from the Scots Highlanders. What Erich Fromm has called 'group narcissism' might help explain this paradox.[113] Outsiders compensate for a lack of satisfaction in their lot by excessive loyalty to those insiders whose kismet is far better than theirs, to give their lives some meaning.

To the end of his life Charles pinned his hopes on the loyalty of Irish Catholics.[114] The Scots Highlanders, led by the Earl of Montrose, posed one of the major threats to the covenanting cause. Cornwall provided regiments of excellent soldiers for the king. No troops fought as long, as loyally and as well, as did the king's Welsh soldiers, who since the Hundred Years' War have been the finest infantry in the British Army.[115]

Although the Welsh fought well during the Bishops' Wars their infantry did badly at Edgehill, the first major battle. An eyewitness to the engagement called them 'poor Welsh vermins, the off-scourings of the nation'.[116] To be fair they were poorly armed, some with no more than scythes – which explains why they broke and ran. But as far as Sir Thomas Salisbury of Denbighshire was concerned that did not absolve them. Four weeks later, just before the Battle of Brentford, he addressed his regiment from North Wales: 'Gentlemen, you lost your honour at Edgehill. I hope you will regain it here.' And regain it they did. The Welsh acquitted themselves most creditably (the language implies paying off a debt). After a long hard fight, which Captain John Lilburne, whom they took prisoner, described as 'to the sword point and to the butt end', they drove three crack regiments, Holles's, Hampden's and Brooke's, into the Thames, drowning many roundheads and capturing the survivors.[117]

The Welsh fought well because they wanted to wipe out the shame of defeat, which, if Erich Fromm is correct, would be even harder for outsiders to bear.[118] Roundheads in particular regarded Wales as well beyond the pale. John Corbet, the governor of Gloucester, talked of ' blind Wales, and other dark corners of the land'. A member of the Rump Parliament wondered if one could find a place with more ignorance, and hatred of God's people 'than in Merionethshire?' Parliament never made much of an effort to obtain Cymric support. It did not publish a single pamphlet in Welsh, even though the Principality was enjoying a linguistic revival.[119] So Wales became, to quote Sir Arthur Trevor, 'the nursery of the King's infantry'. Poverty as well as patriotism prompted many Welshmen into joining the armed forces. Indeed so many did so from Caernarvonshire that the Justices of the Peace had to offer a 10-shilling bounty for killing foxes, hunting them having ceased due to the war.[120]

The Welsh were formidable soldiers, especially when led by their own officers, many of whom were younger sons of the local gentry who had learned their trade in the Thirty Years' War. Indeed the Welsh disliked serving under English officers. 'If your Highness will be pleased to command me to the Turk or Jew or Gentile, I will go on my bare feet to serve you', protested Thomas Darbridgecourt to Prince Rupert on learning he was to be posted from Bristol to Ludlow, 'but from the Welsh, good Lord, deliver me . . . '.

Because the Welsh were outsiders they had both a clannish sense of self-confidence, and (as Shakespeare recognized with Fluellen) displayed a particularly prickly sense of self-esteem. Sir Thomas Salisbury played upon these two slightly contradictory forces when he told his regiment that they had to redeem their honour after Edgehill. Yet the idea of honour was far more complicated, and much more powerful in persuading royalist gentlemen, the insiders, to fight.

Of the civil wars' many appeals to honour the best known is that of Richard Lovelace to his Lucasta:

> True a new mistress now I chase,
> The First foe in the field;
> And with a stronger faith embrace
> A sword, a horse, a shield.
>
> Yet this inconstancy is such,
> As you too shall adore:

> I could not love thee, Dear, so much,
> Loved I not honour more.

Doggerel echoed poetry:[121]

> Fair Fidelia, tempt me no more,
> I may no more this beauty adore,
> Nor offer to thy shrine
> I serve one more divine,
> And far more great than you.
> I must go,
> Least the Foe
> Gain the cause and win the day.

In 'The Soldier going to the Field', Sir William D'Avenant qualified his advice to 'preserve thy sighs, unthrifty girl', with characteristic cavalier irony:[122]

> For I must go where lazy Peace
> Will hide her drowsy head,
> And, for the sport of Kings, increase
> The number of the dead.

Alexander Brome assured 'His Mistress Affrighted in the Wars':[123]

> Come sigh no more but kiss again,
> These troubles shall never trouble me. . . .
> Let Cannons keep roaring
> And bullets still fly,
> While I am adoring
> Thee, my deity.

Lord Henry Spenser, Earl of Sunderland, told his wife that the only reason why he remained at the king's encampment was 'to save the punctillo of honour'. Sir Thomas Peyton wrote to the sequestration committee for Kent, who were trying to confiscate his lands for his loyalty to the crown, 'this I shall willingly give up and yet be happy', so long as they left him with his honour. A year later, in 1645, Lord Napier, who had been imprisoned for his loyalty, declared that 'my honour and reputation' meant more to him than his 'life and fortune'.[124] Looking back on his experiences during the civil war, Captain Thomas Venn concluded that honour was far more important than pay in making men fight: 'It is blood and not gold that hath been the price of honour.'[125]

Considerations of honour applied to ladies as well as to gentlemen. The Countess of Derby answered the roundhead demand to surrender Lathom House that 'she would neither tamely give up her honour, nor purchase her peace with the loss of her honour'.[126] Professional soldiers claimed not to be inveigled by the siren song of honour. 'It is a life of honour', Prince Rupert admitted about his trade, 'but a dog would not lead it.'[127] Yet their pride in doing a job well done was in itself a form of honour.

Honour derived from the feudal concepts of knighthood and chivalry. During the reformation Humanism tried to civilize honour, as monarchs, who were becoming more powerful, attempted to co-opt it by claiming to be the fount of all honour. In 1562 Gerald Legh defined honour as 'glory got by courage of manhood'.[128] Joseph Bampfield, the cavalier colonel, re-echoed this ideal when he declared that 'to abandon my honour' would be an act of 'womanish modesty'.[129] But in those pre-Freudian days honour was less connected with machismo insecurity, but more with birth and breeding, and the good opinion of one's fellows.

Honour was gained from one's lineage. It was something one's family accumulated over generations, endowing its possessors with pride and potency. Maintaining one's dynastic honour was an obligation as compelling as making good marriages for one's children, and helping kin. While the drive to obtain honour was internal, the award of honour was external. 'Honour is not in his head who is honoured', wrote James Cleland in *Propaideia, or the Institution of a Young Nobleman* (1607), 'but in the hearts and opinions of other men.' While a gentleman could not earn honour in the same way as a merchant could grub for money, he could lose it in a single act far more precipitously than a townsman could go bankrupt. As Iago pointed out:[130]

Who steals my purse steals trash – tis something, nothing; . . .
But he that filches from me my good name
Robs me of that which not enriches him
And makes me poor indeed.

In battle men usually stay and fight because they have no choice, or else the consequences of flight are even more painful than staying. One obvious repercussion is being shot for cowardice.[131] But far more certain than a firing squad is the scorn of brave comrades. If a unit was recruited from the same area, sometimes the same streets, a coward could not escape his shame by going home. 'That craven, that milk sop, who did run away', thought Simeon Ashe, an army chaplain, should be humiliated by his comrades as surely as he would by God on the Day of Judgement.

More than any other influence it is the respect of one's immediate peers – one's mates, oppos, buddies – which motivates men in battle. For the cavalier gentleman honour was the bench-mark of respect in which his fellows held him. If he lost honour he lost his caste. When Edward, First Baron Montagu was being taken to the Tower of London in 1642 (where he was imprisoned and eventually died for his loyalty to the crown), he met the Earl of Essex.[132] The recently appointed commander of the parliamentary army stopped his coach, intending to go and see the old gentleman. Montagu refused, saying 'this is no time for compliments'. As far as the baron was concerned the rebellious earl had lost his caste, and was no longer worthy of an introduction. Without honour a gentleman was no longer a gentleman for he had dishonoured his lineage. He had failed to fulfil both the biblical injunction to honour his forefathers, as well as the biological obligation to hand on to his children a birthright which most gentlemen regarded as essential as food, clothing and shelter.

While common soldiers might be able to atone for lack of honour by fighting with exemplary courage (as did Sir Thomas Salisbury's Welsh regiment), gentlemen found it next to impossible to redeem themselves as easily – which made the loss of honour an even more painful consequence than staying to fight.[133] For surrendering Reading in 1643, Colonel Richard Fielding was court-martialled and sentenced to death. Even though the rank and file demanded that he be shot, Charles commuted the verdict. Sir Richard had to fight as a private soldier, and although he did so with great bravery, could never redeem his honour. On the parliamentary side, Nathaniel Fiennes received a similar sentence for yielding Bristol. Even though his death sentence was commuted, he was cashiered, and 'the shame of it persuaded him to leave the kingdom'.[134] Following the defeat of the king's forces at Marston Moor the Duke of Newcastle felt that he had no alternative but to go into exile.

While such gestures were examples of the extravagant romanticism of the cavalier ethos, which even Charles sometimes thought went too far, the mentality which kept the royalist gentlemen in battle long after all reasonable chance of victory was gone had a less celibate side. When Lovelace explained 'To Lucasta from Prison' why he must stay at the wars it seems that he loved – or at least lusted after – something more tangible than her honour:[135]

> When I lie, tangled in her hair
> And fettered to her eye.
> The birds that wanton in the Air,
> Know no such liberty.

Men have relied on erotic day-dreams to escape unpleasant reality nearly as frequently as they have resorted to alcohol. At first glance the stereotype of the cavalier with a tankard in one hand, a wench on his knee, and a jest on his lips can be an attractive one. On closer examination it reveals a bitter misogynist, who may have been lurking beneath a romantic veneer until exposed by defeat.[136]

Without doubt a sardonic sense of humour kept many of the king's troops going in the face of battle. One suspects that those Devonshire royalists who marched off to fight under a standard which showed a cannon firing, surrounded by the biblical text 'O Lord open thou my lips, and my mouth shall show forth thy praise', did so with an added spring to their steps.[137] And, as Lovelace recognized, when humour failed and bravery was not enough, when defeat seemed inevitable, and honour no longer worked, there was always booze:

> Now is there such a trifle
> As honour, the fools quest?
> What is there left to rifle,
> When war makes all parts pliant?
> Let others glory follow,
> In their false riches wallow,
> And in their grief be merry,
> Leave me but love and sherry.

The cavalier propensity for the bottle was more than the figment of prurient puritan propaganda. 'Honour is dog cheap now', maintained a parliamentary playwright in 1644, 'and if any man can swear and swagger, and cry God damn me, I am for the king, he is in the road way to be knighted.'[138] Tales of royalist whoremongering, looting and drunkenness, began immediately the war started. In September 1642 the king's inebriated troops were reported abusing the sober folk at Oxford, and having murdered an eight-month pregnant woman in Leicester.[139] The following month a parliamentary propagandist called them 'those malignant and blood-sucking Cannibals'. Nehemiah Wallington, the London artisan, expressed a widely held image of the cavaliers in his commonplace book: 'When they are in their cups they swagger, roar, swear, and domineer, plundering, pillaging, and doing all other kind of wrong.' One parliamentary pamphlet alleged that the enemy could 'out swear the French, out-drink the Dutch, and out paramour the Turk'.[140] This view became prevalent enough to worry William Chillingworth. After bravely fighting as a sapper during the Siege of Gloucester, he returned to Oxford, where he preached a sermon before the king (which Charles ordered to be printed), expressing the fear that 'the goodness of our cause may sink under the burden of our sins'.[141] When 'a sober friend of mine' raised this point Sir Philip Warwick admitted, 'thou sayest true: for in our army we have the sins of men (drinking and wenching), but in yours you have those of devils, spiritual pride and rebellion.'[142]

The mentality which prompted parliamentarians to fight was far more complicated than that which predominated amongst the cavaliers. It took longer to develop, although, once reached, was a far more radical and potent ideology.

   At first the rebels used honour to make men fight, nearly as much as the royalists. Parliament appointed aristocrats to command its forces, less for their ability and more for their birth, which would, it hoped, persuade men to join its army. Roundheads were not above the occasional bit of snobbery. Sir Samuel Luke, the governor of Newport Pagnell, described an opponent as 'Captain Pudding, alias Jack Pudding, the rope dancer', while a parliamentary news report described Major Langley, a royalist captured near Basing, as 'more like a Tinker than a gentleman'.[143]

If parliament had to – as it must – cut the great chain of being, it preferred to sever it as close to the top link as possible. After all, puritans held firmly to the concept of a hierarchical society. The day before John Winthrop landed in Massachusetts – which was, perhaps, the most puritan moment of all – he preached that 'God Almighty in his most holy and wise providence hath so disposed of the condition of mankind, as in all times some must be rich, some poor, some high and eminent in power and dignity, others mean and in subjection.'[144] Acting on this assumption, parliament initially appointed magnates, such as the Earls of Manchester or Essex, to command its forces in the hope that their rank would recruit men to their cause if only by giving it a little bit of respectability. Royalists were not impressed, invariably calling Lord General Essex 'The Great Cuckold', as if his wife's affair with the Earl of Rochester, and subsequent divorce on the grounds of his alleged impotence, had robbed him of caste, command and masculinity.[145] Boozy cavaliers boasted:[146]

> Come fill my cup full,
> Here's to the taking of Hull
> To the Men that shall bring
> The Great Cuckold to the King.

Cavalier propaganda crudely punned that Essex was not the only round-head (or rather 'Ramhead') to qualify for the cuckold's horns.[147] Lord Brooke, another general parliament appointed more for his pedigree than any proven proficiency, rejected the assistance of mercenaries from the Thirty Years' War partly on account of their humble social origins. Indeed there was something archaic about this aristocrat who was in many respects the spiritual heir of Sir Philip Sydney, the exemplar of Elizabethan honour, when he offered to settle the Siege of Warwick Castle man-to-man 'by Lordly combat'.[148] Had he not been such a snob, Brooke might not have been killed in action a few days later.

There was nothing old-fogeyish about Cromwell's observation concerning the differences between the two sides and their motivations. 'Your troopers are most of them old decayed serving men, and tapsters,' he told John Hampden soon after the Battle of Edgehill, 'and their troopers are gentlemen's sons, younger sons, and persons of quality . . . that have honour and courage and resolution in them.'[149]

Unlike the royalists, who had the tradition of legitimacy behind them, parliament found it very hard, nigh impossible, to justify fighting against the king. How could they 'commit Treason, Felony, Rapine and Sacrilege in the fear of God?' demanded Peter Heylyn, the royalist divine.[150]

'Nothing is more frequent with these Agents of Rebellion than to fasten their Treasons on God and Religion', chimed in *The Round-Head's Remembrancer* (Oxford, 1643, R2009). The pamphlet called them brazen for claiming 'to shoot at the king and to say that it is to save his own life'. After parliament asserted that they were really fighting to protect the king from his wicked advisers (which was so patently false that once the army finally realized its absurdity in 1648 they immediately decided to execute Charles), William Cartwright wrote a poem celebrating the Queen's survival of the parliamentary naval bombardment at Bridlington Bay on 22 February 1643. Sarcastically the poet wondered if the round-heads had cannonaded Her Majesty *'for the King's own good?'*[151]

The author of *A Spiritual Snapsacke for the Parliamentary Soldier* (1643, P3348), was at least honest enough to admit that some might think his exhortation that the roundheads were fighting not just for Jesus, and the Holy Ghost, but for the king 'a paradox, a riddle, a lie'. The Earl of Manchester recognized the intellectual difficulties of trying to justify fighting against his sovereign, when he exclaimed after the Second Battle of Newbury, 'If we beat the king nine and ninety times, he is king still.' To this Cromwell angrily replied, 'My Lord, if this be so, why then did we take up arms first?'[152]

The king's opponents eventually found the answer to this question – as they did to most – in religion.

War has always posed a dilemma for Christians.[153] The earliest followers of Jesus were pacifists, as were the Anabaptists of the sixteenth century and Quakers in more recent times. After Christianity became the state religion following the conversion of Constantine, theologians co-opted the Roman idea of the just war. According to Cicero a war was just so long as it was fought to repel an invasion, avenge a wrong, or recover something unlawfully seized. St Augustine took this theory one stage further by arguing that a war was just so long as the ruler had authorized it. Even though medieval theologians argued that wars against heretics and infidels were *ipso facto* just, the criterion that the ruler should approve them remained paramount. When Machiavelli wrote that 'war is just when it is necessary', he left the determination of necessity to the prince.

Protestants adopted this view. Luther wrote that 'war is as necessary as eating, drinking or any other business', and that once war had been formally declared the soldier had as little responsibility for the justness of his killing as the public executioner had for carrying out the sentences of the courts. The problem with this argument was that it lent itself far better to the royalist cause than the parliamentary. The polemics of people such as Henry Parker and William Prynne who argued that they were fighting against the king in self-defence, and had as much right to draw their swords against him as they would have had if they had caught Guy Fawkes *in flagrante* underneath parliament, carried little water. Like the

61

modern distinction between terrorism and state-sanctioned acts of war, the royalist used the far more effective argument that only the sovereign could legitimize the taking of life: anyone doing so without that authority 'commits murder'.[154]

The dilemma for those who opposed the sovereign was obvious. It was one with which puritan thinkers wrestled during the 1620s, when James I refused to go to war with Catholic Spain. Using Ludovick Lloyd's assertion that 'the whole bible, is a book of the battles of the Lord', preachers such as William Gouge, Alexander Leighton and John Davenport concluded that if the cause was just enough it did not need the magistrate's sanction.[155] In other words, because a war against Spain was quite clearly a war against Satan, then it was too important a matter to be left to the judgment of the king, but should be decided by the internal determination of the individual. A war thus sanctioned by conscience was obviously a crusade with such noble goals that it must also have been declared by God, and by God alone. In a sermon given to the Honourable Artillery Company in September 1641 Calybute Downing, Vicar of Hackney, used biblical quotations to justify war, without once resorting to royal authority. 'If the Lord please to beat up the Drum,' Simeon Ashe preached to the London Trained Bands in 1642, 'if the Lord please to bid them arm and come aboard, His call is sufficient.'[156] And so if the king refused to heed His call, then he must be a tyrant.

Puritans found the concept of war as a crusade congenial because it meshed with their view of life as a battle. This notion was not confined to 'the Godly sort', of course. 'Gracious Father', Charles prayed, 'the life of man being a warfare upon earth & his life invaded with diverse dangers'.[157] The king was echoing a commonplace. 'This life', preached Thomas Taylor, 'is the time of warfare.' 'The time of our life', agreed William Gouge, is 'a time of war'. John Downame's pamphlet, *The Christian Warfare*, which ran to seven editions between 1604 and 1638, described the Christian life in terms of military images. Thomas Taylor repeated these themes in *Christ's Combate and Conquest* (1618) and *Christ's Victory over the Dragon* (1633), as did Richard Bernard, in *The Bible-Battal, or the Sacred Art Military* (1629).

Underpinning, and complementing, this concept of the civil war as a crusade was the idea of being a chosen people, who had sworn a covenant with God. The Scots covenanters had, of course, done so literally in 1638, and in 1643 signed the Solemn League and Covenant with parliament. Yet these documents probably had less effect on the roundhead mentalities than the experience of battle. Afterward the survivors attributed their survival to the Almighty, who had obviously chosen them for some purpose.

Soldiers also used Him to try and improve the image of their profession. Even though there was a wide chasm between the reality and the ideal, in *The Theorike and Practike of Modern Warres* (1598) Robert Barret described the perfect warrior as 'diligent careful, vigilant and obedient . . . sober, quiet, friendly . . . no blasphemer, nor swearer' – all virtues to which puritans aspired.[158] Thus it became possible for Thomas Sutton to declare that God 'above all creatures loves soldiers'. He concluded his sermon *The Good Fight of Faith* (1624) with 'the life of every Christian man is a continual battle and bloody skirmish against the devil'.[159] During the civil war parliamentarians were able to fuse these ideas into a common, yet potent, bond. 'To be a soldier is a lawful calling', preached Robert Ram to Colonel Rossiter's regiment during the Siege of Newark, ''tis a necessary calling . . . a very honourable calling.' Ram began his *Soldiers' Catechism*, which he claimed was intended 'especially for the common soldier', and which went to seven editions between 1644 and 1645, by asking:[160]

> Question: What profession are you?
> Answer: I am a Christian and a soldier.
> Question: Is it lawful for a Christian to be a soldier?
> Answer: Yes, doubtless.

Parliamentary theorists combined the link between the soldier and Christianity with that between his unit and the church. For instance, Richard Baxter described the troop of cavalry that Oliver Cromwell first raised as 'a gathered church'.[161] Thus puritans bolstered the small unit for which most men fight, by portraying it as a spiritual as well as a military entity.

Such a view helped men fight in another fashion. It has been argued that Protestantism, and later puritanism, appealed to people such as merchants whose lives were especially insecure. If such was the case, then its appeal to those faced with the much greater anxiety of battle would have been even greater.

The efficacy of the belief that a war is in fact a crusade must not, however, be exaggerated. Many troops saw the Second World War in similar terms, General Dwight D. Eisenhower even called his military memoirs *Crusade in Europe*. None of the soldiers who liberated the concentration camps could doubt that they were fighting a just war against a monstrous evil. Yet it did not make them fight with any greater crusading zeal. If anything it increased atrocities against the enemy, and made them more cautious, so as to survive a war that all realized was nearly over. In much the same fashion as the civil war dragged on puritan troops became both less and more motivated by religion. Whilst some soldiers, notably the elite roundhead cavalry units, grew more Godly, the ranks of the infantry became filled with 'ignorant men, of little religion', who, observed Richard Baxter, 'had been taken prisoners, or turned out of Garrisons under the king, and had been soldiers in his army'.[162]

Soldiers are rarely intellectuals but pragmatic creatures, being conditioned by their immediate situation. One of the most important seventeenth-century writers on the idea of a just war was the Dutch theologian Hugo Grotius, who was imprisoned in Lovestyne for his ideas. In his autobiography, Thomas Raymond, a well-read Englishman, who 'trailed a pike' in the Thirty Years' War, recalled campaigning nearby. He was very interested in Grotius, and with great pleasure described how the philosopher managed to escape hidden in a hamper of his books. Raymond obviously admired Grotius, calling him 'a person of prodigious learning' and 'a great admirer of the Anglican Church'. Yet never once did the soldier mention the philosopher's work on a just war.[163]

Be they just or unjust, for most individuals wars simply happen, coming nigh unnoticed and forcing them to act, often without much previous thought, and usually more from reflex than careful contemplation. Such was the case for most men when blood was first shed. In July 1642 Bulstrode Whitelocke wrote to his wife:[164]

> It is strange to note how we have insensible slid into the beginnings of a civil war, by one unexpected accident after another, as waves of the sea, which have brought us thus far, and scarce we know how, but from paper combats, by declarations, remonstrances, protestations, votes, messages, answers and replies, we are now come to the question of raising forces.

If at the time people hardly realized how they had slid imperceptibly to the point of killing, few had any illusions about the effect of shedding blood. 'If blood once again begins to touch blood, we shall presently fall into a certain misery and must attend an uncertain success', Benjamin Rudyerd warned the House of Commons in July 1642, 'Blood is a crying sin, it pollutes the land.'[165]

In England at least, the first bloody pollution came as often as not over the recruitment of soldiers, or the requisition of horses.[166]

For instance, on 9 August 1642, two weeks before the king raised his standard, Captain John Smith (who was to recapture that standard at Edgehill), led a troop of royalist cavalry into the village of Kilsby in Northamptonshire. It was dawn, and raining. Seeing a crowd armed with muskets and pitchforks, they stopped Thomas Winkles, and asked him whom he was for. When he answered 'for the king and parliament', one of the cavaliers shot him dead. His friend, Thomas Marriot, protested, and received a large number of sword blows about the head, being shot as he tried to run away. As they searched the village for arms the soldiers also speared John White with his pitchfork. By now the troops were getting panicky. Crammed together, they were hardly able to move in the village's crowded street. A growing mob started to surround them. Armed men appeared at upstairs windows. Although Captain Smith ordered everyone not to shoot, some of the villagers did, and his men returned fire, killing three or four of the locals. The crowd ran, 'all except an old man [probably Henry Barefoot] that with his pitchfork ran at Captain Smith, whom he hit without much effect, heedless of warnings to desist, 'till a pistol quieted him'.[167]

Not just in Kilsby, but all over the land, nothing would be the same. For instance, after describing the outbreak of violence in his own county a catholic gentleman concluded a letter to a friend, 'The face of things in Cheshire is strangely altered . . . God in his mercy prevent the effusion of innocent blood.'[168]

Innocent blood was first shed in similarly unforeseen incidents. Often they got out of control because – like innocent country folk caught by a mugger in a big city street – people such as Henry Barefoot had yet to learn how to handle violence. When Sir William Brereton marched into Chester on 8 August 1642 provocatively beating a drum to raise recruits for parliament, the mob nearly lynched him. When the Earl of Bath entered Exeter to read the commission of array that the king had issued him to recruit men, 'the common sort of the town fell in a great rage', vowing to stop him even 'if they were all hanged for it'.[169] Lord Chandos provoked a similar reaction when he tried to raise men in Gloucester. Even though he had a bodyguard of some thirty men with drawn swords, 'being in a great fear' the Earl agreed to leave town surreptitiously. Afterwards the mob vented their anger by dragging his empty coach to the market-place and tearing it to pieces.[170] The only reason why Lord Hastings' attempt to read his commission of array in Leicester did not result in bloodshed was the weather. Captain Worsley ordered his troops to open fire at Hastings' party (which tactlessly included some twenty-four ministers wearing their surplices) but the rain extinguished the match, preventing the weapons from firing. Hastings held his pistol at Worsley's head, but again the wet caused a misfire.[171]

Sometimes events did not end so felicitously. On 1 August Sir Ralph Hopton rode into Shepton Mallet to recruit men for the king. An 'unruly rabble' of about a thousand managed to stop him, and as a result both sides retired to muster the men they had already raised. They met three days later at Marshall's Elm, where the royalists routed the parliamentary troops, killing twenty-seven of them and taking sixty prisoners. Compared with later battles it was a minor event, remembered by few. But for those who were first blooded at Marshall's Elm the fracas was a decisive personal experience. 'And thus', Hopton recalled, 'innocently began this cursed war.'[172]

4

NAMING OF PARTS

> To-day we have naming of parts. Yesterday
> We had daily cleaning, and tomorrow morning
> We shall have what to do after firing. But to-day,
> Today we have naming of parts.
>
>   Henry Reed, 'Naming of Parts' (1946)

Much of a soldier's life is spent in training. Sometimes of the mind-numbing sort, in which the speed is set so as not to tax the moronic: occasionally it is rushed at the last moment to throw raw troops into battle. Training fulfils a number of functions. At its simplest it teaches men how to use and maintain their weapons, and helps turn civilians into soldiers. Training imparts the codes that soldiers need, and through lessons and punishments, the penalties exacted for failing to follow them. Like apprentices, recruits are taught the symbols of what Stephen Crane called 'that mysterious fraternity'. They must learn its peculiar language, traditions and hierarchy. Training can be akin to a conversion experience that plays on the novice's emotions as much as it does on his mind, teaching him to feel as well as act in new ways. Training does far more than create individual soldiers (who anyway on their own are not much use in winning battles). Through drill, living together, sharing similar experiences – sometimes the same women, more often the same bottle – training fuses small units – the building blocks of any army, in which, and for which, most men fight, kill and die.

For those happy warriors who go willingly to the wars training can be a pleasure. 'For my part I go with joy and comfort to venture my life in so good a cause, and with a good company as every Englishman', declared Sir Bevil Grenville.[1] Natural soldiers took to training as ducks to water. A friend described Sir Simon Harcourt, who had first joined the army at the age of 16 as a lieutenant and died two decades later in Ireland, as a man 'who loved always to be in action'.[2] Many enjoyed the civil wars for their freedom, opportunities and comradeship. For both Charles I and Oliver Cromwell they were a liberation from the frustrations of civilian circumscription. Sir John Gell, Sir William Brereton, Sir Richard Grenville and Sir Anthony Weldon all had 'good wars'. Sir Thomas Birch recalled that several of his comrades enjoyed theirs so much that they tried to prolong hostilities.

Other young men joined up in search of adventure. William St Lawrence and John Gandy, two schoolboys, ran away from Bury St Edmunds 'to the intolerable grief of their parents' to enlist in Waller's army; William apparently died, while John survived, being fined £28 by the Committee for Compounding.[3] Many of those who flocked to the colours were the naturally restless. Richard Baxter commented how much quieter things were in Kidderminster after royal recruiting sergeants had enlisted all the town's rowdies. A parliamentary pamphlet explained one yokel's reasons for doing his bit for the Crown:[4]

> I will sell my chest and eke my plough
> And get a sword if I know how,
> And each man means to be right
> I will swear and drink and roar,
> And (Gallant like), I will keep a whore.

Most men were, to some degree or other, coerced into enlisting. Samuel Priestly acknowledged that unemployment in the Halifax cloth trade made him volunteer for the parliamentary army.[5] The same reasons would explain why in Devonshire disproportionately far more artisans than agricultural labourers enlisted with the king. Adam Martindale could hardly be described as an enthusiastic volunteer. He became a teacher near Wigan to avoid the draft, but finding the children impossible, and having failed to pass himself off as a crypto-cavalier 'by swearing and debauching', he enlisted as a company clerk in a parliamentary infantry regiment. Here he kept the rolls, and spent his evenings in 'godly discourse', hoping all along to escape combat.[6] 'I did run up and down the country to save myself from being a soldier', Leonard Wheatcroft wrote in his autobiography, 'but at last I was forced to take up arms, and was a soldier for the space of 8 or 9 years.'[7]

Popular magnates could raise and train men fairly easily. 'I caused my drum to be beaten up at York and other places, and there came to me to be enlisted', recalled Sir Henry Slingsby, 'up to the number of 200.' But when Sir Paul Harris, a landowner (whom the locals thought 'a proud imperious person'), aided by Robert Moore and Matthew Bayle, ('the veriest knaves in Pimhill Hundred'), tried to do the same in Myddle, they were chased out of the village.[8] In Lancashire Colonel Tildsley summoned all his tenants, and forced them to march with him to Edgehill 'whence most of them never returned'.[9] The county's lord lieutenant, the Earl of Derby, ordered men to report for duty 'on pain of death', and stationed a sergeant behind them with orders to shoot stragglers as they marched off to war. It was alleged that 'Sir Bevil Grenville hath been a tyrant, especially to his tenants, threatening to thrust them out of house and home, if they will not assist him'.[10] In Somerset, another royalist, Lord Poulett, was accused of evicting any tenant who did not agree with him. Sometimes tenants, such as Sir William Davenport's, resisted pressure: in September 1642 they petitioned their landlord as he was having dinner that they would not 'venture our lives in causes that our hearts and consciences do persuade us are not good or lawful'.[11]

While many troops who were trained for the civil war were ostensibly volunteers, others were conscripts. Both sides used the county authorities and village constables to draft men. 'Have an especial care', advised Norfolk's High Constable, 'to take idle servingmen, and such other able bodied persons who live dissolutely or idly.'[12] The first to go were the unemployed and misfits. The authorities at Coggeshall, Essex, were delighted to be able to draft William Yorke straight out of jail. He had a long record of theft, receiving stolen goods, and riot that went back to 1625. Parliament exempted the clergy, students, the sons of esquires, and those assessed for taxes as having more than £5 in goods, or £3 on hand. Constables tried to shanghai those whom the community would not miss, or better still, were strangers who might be missed by someone else. When Thomas Browne went from Boston to marry a Bristol girl, he was drafted into the king's forces, and in addition to losing his bride, was eventually fined £260 by parliament.[13]

The draft was as unsuccessful as it was unpopular. In August 1643, for instance, it provoked riots in London that killed five people. The following year diplomats reported that recruits were being virtually kidnapped in the streets of the capital 'with barbarous violence', and were sent to the rendezvous at Maidenhead by barge so they could not escape.[14] At Upwell, Cambridgeshire, the local witch cast spells upon the constable and his assistants for taking her son. (Those local worthies were probably less worried by the threat of sorcery than by the County Committee's policy of drafting officials who did not fill their quota of recruits.) The quality of conscripts was so bad that the Earl of Essex had to dismiss those men whose impressment had provoked the London riots. As a senior officer in charge of the Suffolk draft, Oliver Cromwell was concerned that the mutinous conscripts would slit his throat. 'Most counties press the Scum of all their Inhabitants,' thought Colonel Venn, 'men taken out of prison, Tinkers, Peddlers and Vagrants that have no dwelling and such as whom no account can be given; it is no marvel if such run away.'[15] And desert they did: of drafts of 334 men from Berkshire and 209 from Cambridge-shire, only 121 (36 per cent) and 75 (36 per cent) respectively reached the army for training.

Once they arrived at the army – be it willing, or coerced – it had to turn civilians into soldiers. 'No man is born a soldier, nor can attain to any excellency in the Art Military without practice, but by practice is gained knowledge, knowledge begets courage and confidence', were the opening words of William Barriffe's best selling training manual (plate 17).[16]

Not even the trained bands were really trained. John Corbet thought that Gloucester's volunteers were 'like a cake not turned, a kind of soldiers not wholly drawn off from the plough or domestic contentment'. According to Sir Thomas Fairfax, at the start of the war, parliament's recruits were as impatient to fight as they were ignorant of how to do so. Sir Ralph Hopton's West Country royalists had the same problem, treating mobilization as 'a great fair'. Hopton continued that 'They were so transported by the jollity of the thing that no man was capable of the labour and care of discipline.' As a result Hopton's men were thrashed. Realizing that defeat was the reward of the ill-trained, the Earl of Essex instituted a short sharp refresher course for his troops, which made them 'so valiant and hardy' that they had no trouble capturing Plymouth in February 1644.[17]

According to Edward Cooke's *The Perspective Glasse of Warre, shewing you a glimpse of Warres Mysteries* (1623), the ideal recruit should be alert, straight necked, broad breasted, wide shouldered, with strong fingers and long arms. He should have a taut belly, slender legs and muscular calves. The finest trainees were smiths, carpenters and butchers, the latter being used to the sight of blood.[18]

The material with whom professional soldiers usually had to work was very different. 'I am teaching cart horses to manage, and men that are fit for Bedlam or Bridewell, the ten commandments', fulminated Lord Conway. Sir Arthur Trevor described the inhabitants of Oxford as a bunch of 'foggy Burghers' who needed a good kick in the arse to wake them up.[19] When Sir Hugh Cholmley was training recruits for the Second Bishops' War on Paxton Moor, one Hallden, 'a stubborn fellow' was marched before him for refusing to obey his captain. After the defaulter used 'some unhandsome language' to his commanding officer, Cholmley hit him with his cane, knocking him to the ground. Hallden claimed that the blow had hurt him so badly that he could no longer serve, and requested his discharge – something Cholmley was only too happy to grant. Sir Arthur Aston was scathing in his comments to Prince Rupert about turning English civilians into soldiers:[20]

> I am so extremely abjected at this business that I do wish with all my heart that either I had some German soldiers to command, or that I could find some German courage in them, for the English soldiers are so poor and base that I could never have a greater affliction light on me than to be put in command of them.

But well trained, British civilians could become soldiers second to none. With proper tutelage the Gloucester Regiment – whom John Corbet described as half-baked – defended their city with the same tenacity their namesakes displayed three centuries later at the Imjim River.

Other volunteers did equally as well. For instance, the undergraduates at Oxford University sided with the king almost to a man. At the outbreak of war they paraded and drilled on August 18th, 20th and 25th, with great enthusiasm, quickly learning how to handle a pike. Soon afterwards a correspondent praised 'the magnificent valour of the scholars ... completely armed ... with the title of heroic cavaliers'. He added that the five hundred recruits were better off now than they had been as undergraduates when 'their whole time was spent in whoring, drinking and swearing'. As a bonus, the correspondent continued, the students had actually put some backbone into the dons by persuading many of them to enlist.[21] As a boy Anthony Wood saw the scholars drilling in New College Quadrangle. 'Some of them were so besotted with their training and activity, and gaiety', he recalled, 'that they would never be brought to their books again.'[22] After two years studying at Balliol College, Richard Atkyns confessed that he could no longer 'read a Greek or Latin author with pleasure', and so joined the king's service, becoming a captain. Anthony Cowper described his military career in verse:[23]

> When first to Oxford, fully there intent
> To study learned science there I went,
> Instead of logic, physick, school converse
> I did attend the armed troop of Mars,
> Instead of books, I sword, horse, pistols bought,
> My young head not amounted full eighteen,
> Till I am in the field wounded three times had been,
> Three times in sieges close had been immured,
> Three times imprisonments restraints endured.

The eager Oxford scholars did not fight as units, but acted as leaven for the rest of the king's army. In contrast the Londoners who went off to fight did so as members of the trained bands, units which had been preparing to defend the city for decades.

Henry VIII granted a charter to the Fraternity of St George in 1537 permitting them to hold drills, and thus founded the British Army's oldest regiment, the Honourable Artillery Company. Londoners took to drilling with great enthusiasm; two years after the king issued the charter he reviewed some sixteen thousand soldiers in a march past. The City authorities approved of training as a way of keeping apprentices occupied and out of stews and ale-houses. Preaching to the Honourable Artillery Company in 1629, John Davenport begged the troops to 'abandon your caviling, dicing, chambering, wantonness, dalliance, scurrilous discourses, and vain reveling' in favour of extra square-bashing.[24] To protect the independence of their militia, the corporation refused to accept Charles's appointment of Captain John Fisher as their muster master in 1630.

Apprentices seemed keen to train, turning out sometimes as often as once a week to practise in the Artillery Yard at Spitalfields. 'Well I say, their grave Artillery Yard', wrote Ben Jonson, became 'their seed plot of the War'. In 1642 Londoners responded to 'The General Cry of all is arm, arm, fight, fight' with the same enthusiasm a later generation of young men showed to the invitation to join Kitchener's Army.[25] The standing orders Colonel Denzil Holles issued for his regiment on 25 August laid down that every soldier should report at six every morning to his company colours. In the first three months of the war the trained bands tripled from six to eighteen thousand men, organized in six regiments. According to the *Declaration of the valiant . . . Famous apprentices of London* (1642, D774) there were some eight thousand 'brave spirited young men', who were 'with much alacrity and cheerfulness, resolved, to the utmost hazard of their lives, to oppose and resist the Malignant army'. Parliament passed an ordnance that all apprentices who joined its forces should not suffer any penalties, such as the forfeiture of bonds, but be guaranteed their old jobs back at the end of hostilities. Amongst the first to enlist were 71 dyers, 88 butchers, 186 weavers, 157 tanners, 124 shoemakers, 88 bakers and 49 saddlers, all from trades skilled enough to readily learn the arts of Mars.[26]

In addition to being well trained, the London militia was fortunate to have as its commander Major General Philip Skippon, a veteran of the Thirty Years' War, and to have first-rate officers, who had learned their skills in the Honourable Artillery Company, which was (as it is now) partially an officer training unit. Such men were selected for their abilities, not their previous professions. By 1643 the colonel of the Southwark Regiment was 'a Distiller of Strong Waters' while his sergeant-major (or second in command) had been a soap boiler. Captain Hook of the Tower Hamlets Regiment was listed as 'a vinegar man' – presumably a reference to his civilian trade rather than his disposition.[27]

When it seemed likely that they would have to learn how to become officers responsible for leading men in a civil war, many gentlemen purchased training manuals. Of course, the need to train the militia had always provided a market for such works: between 1600 and 1634, some sixty of them were published in England. With the outbreak of hostilities the demand greatly increased, thirty-five appearing in the next seven years.[28] In March 1642 Colonel Edward Harley spent £2 10s 0d on eleven manuals. Such works were well used, being carried in battle.[29] Sir John Gell's copy of Thomas Styward's, *The Pathwaie to Martiall Discipline* is much worn, being stained with human blood, presumably from the wounds Gell suffered at Hopton Heath.[30]

Some of the manuals were next to useless. Gervase Markham's, *The*

71

Souldier's Exercise (1639, STC 17390), was a very complicated text, written by a hack who specialized in 'how to' books based on a quick read of the literature. Much of its information was irrelevant, including the concluding section, a complex battle plan called 'the windmill' that required the deployment of some fifty thousand troops. Edward Cooke's *The Character of Warre* (1626, reissued 1640), and his *The Perspective Glasse of Warre* (1628), were equally complicated and impractical. They included some forty-four commands for loading and firing a musket, and the suggestion that soldiers learn how to swim because bridges might not be available – a piece of advice that could prove catastrophic to heavily armoured troops. Captain Henry Hexham's *The Principles of the Art Militarie* (which appeared in two volumes in 1637, being reissued in 1642) was a highly complicated and thorough manual, with some thirty-two orders for the musket and thirty-three for the pike. Based on Hexham's twenty-six years' service in the Dutch Army – in which he had fought 'in many hot engagements, yet the enemy had never drawn one drop of blood from him' – its comprehensive advice on such matters as field kitchens does not appear to have been much heeded in the British civil wars. Even though it was based on his twenty-six years' experience as a veteran in the Low Countries and muster master of the Kent militia, Thomas Fisher's *The Warlike Directions* (first published in 1633, and reissued in 1643 in a pocket version), was much too complicated, with some forty-eight musket orders, and sixty-five for the pike. Published in 1609 'for the young or inexpert', Jacob de Gheyn's *The Exercise of Armes* tried to convey the complexity of officially sanctioned drill movements by supplementing its four pages of text with 119 pages of woodcuts. It sold far better than John Raynsford's *The Young Soldier* (1642, 132), a very basic five-page manual, perhaps because those who went off to the war assumed that something longer was more likely to help them survive as soldiers.

The best-selling works of John Cruso (a fellow of Caius College, Cambridge) and William Barriffe lend credence to this speculation.[31] The former's *Militarie instructions for the cavallrie* (first printed in Cambridge in 1632, and reissued in 1644) was the most important textbook on handling what turned out to be the civil wars' decisive arm (see plate 3). William Barriffe's *Military Discipline* (first published in 1635, and reissued six times in the next twenty-six years), was the most influential drill manual. Clearly laid out, it provided practical information that all sides widely used.

Regular soldiers did not find writing manuals for civilians easy. As William Barriffe admitted, 'I can better manage the Pike than the Pen.' Finding it hard to address their social superiors the rough veteran captains would often fill the prefaces to their manuals with long and fulsome testimonials from the gentry and nobility, and crammed them with classical illusions. Indeed John Cruso, the author of the best-selling cavalry manual, also translated and published *The Complete Captain*, an abridged edition of Caesar, in the hope that knowing how to fight the Gallic wars might somehow help his readers win the civil ones.[32]

For over a century, at least, military theorists had argued that tactics and strategy had never really changed, and that the key to victory was understanding the eternal truths the ancients had first discovered. The problem with this view, which laid down that all one could possibly need to know about, say, handling the pike could be learned from the Spartans, was that it tended to ossify tactics. Thus for the first two or three years of the civil war there were too many pikemen in a foot regiment, until practical experience demonstrated the need for a higher ratio of musketeers.

Most manuals made military manoeuvres so complicated, admitted one Elizabethan author, that they could only be accomplished in the heat of battle by veterans with at least seven years of service.[33] Captain Thomas Venn's manual laid down three styles of marching, and contained a series of highly complicated orders. One doubts if a sergeant had much chance of being heard – let alone obeyed – during the cacophony of combat as he barked out the commands, 'half double your front to the right and files double your depth to the left', or 'bringer up stand, the rest pass through to your left and place yourself behind your bringer up'.[34] The stand to which Venn referred was used to rest a musket. Yet when he wrote his *Military Observations* in 1672, based on his civil war experiences, the musket stand had fallen out of use. Could he have mentioned it so as to make the profession of arms seem more complicated than it really was, and thus to enhance the status of those captains such as himself, who tried to teach it to civilians?

Unquestionably many thought that the professionals were making their training manuals far too complicated. Sir James Turner, the Scots veteran, admitted that 'It is my private opinion that there be many superfluous works in the exercises.' Lord General Essex told his officers not to burden recruits with involved and mainly ceremonial drills. Even before the war the Privy Council had recognized this problem, issuing an abbreviated set of military orders to the militia, which contained, for instance, only ten pike movements.[35] Modern re-enactment groups have shown that a musketeer can cut corners by, for instance, sharply tapping the butt of his weapon on the ground rather than using a ramrod to tamp down the bullet. He can get by with three basic commands – 'make ready, present, fire' – greatly increasing his rate of fire albeit at the expense of accuracy. A reasonably competent pikeman can be trained in six sessions. At the start of the war an enterprising printer put out a one-page sheet that used ditties to teach even the stupidest recruit the rudiments of formation drill:[36]

> In March, in motion, troop or stand
> Observe both leaders and Right Hand.

With silence note in what degree
You in the Godly place be.
That so you may without more trouble,
Know when to stand, and when to double.

Even though his *Military Discipline*, the most widely used manual, dealt with everything a soldier could ever need to know, William Barriffe devised a six-day training programme theoretically intended as a refresher for experienced troops, but surely used to train recruits.[37] On the first day, for example, soldiers were drilled at the company level to respond to the drum call to rendezvous at the colours, fall in with their officers and NCOs, dress rank, do left and right turns, double march, about turn and wheel. By the end of the week the men were ready enough for battle.

In the middle ages it took far longer to produce a fully trained archer than it did a seventeenth-century musketeer. Not only had archers to spend years learning how to aim and fire the longbow, but they had to develop the muscle power and co-ordination to draw their devastating weapon. In many respects the longbow was a far superior arm than the muzzle-loading musket. With a firing rate six times faster than that of the standard civil war musket (and twice that of 'the brown Bess' of the eighteenth century), and having a lethal range of 400 yards, the longbow was not exceeded as a standard infantry weapon until the introduction of the bolt-action rifle during the second half of the nineteenth century. Even though Charles tried to get the students of Oxford University to raise a company of a hundred archers, the bow was not used in the civil war (except to fire message arrows). There was not enough time to produce effective archers.[38]

'He that will be a complete soldier must first begin to learn the use of his arms', began Lieutenant Colonel Richard Elton's *The Compleat Body of the Art Military* (1659, E654). To produce complete soldiers both sides desperately needed experienced NCOs. Early in the war Sir William Brereton begged for 'some old soldiers for sergeants', while Joshua Sprigge, the parliamentary chaplain, ascribed the early royalist victories to their cadre of 'old soldiers'. A veteran sergeant managed to steady the parliamentary forces at Powick Bridge, preventing their first defeat from degenerating into a rout.[39] Old sweats could quickly teach recruits how to stand with the pike, and how to fire their muskets. Indeed neither action was very complicated. Muskets had to be kept clean, and not double shotted so they did not blow up, while a little oil was all that was needed to maintain a pikeman and his armour.

The rub came in teaching individuals how to use their weapons as members of units. The origins of drill go back thousands of years. Two thousand years before the birth of Christ, Egyptian armies stepped off marching with the left foot, as has every army since. Drill turns individuals into groups, who by moving together become as one. It helps overcome fear in battle, hesitation in obeying orders, and thought while enduring the unthinkable. During the early seventeenth century Prince Maurice of the Netherlands developed drills that enabled pikemen to form ranks and wheel, so as to protect the musketeers. The latter stood in rows, usually six deep. The first rank fired, then fell back to reload while the next rank moved forward to repeat the process. Such skills needed extensive training and constant practice. Although Sir John Meldrum told the House of Commons that 'long and continuous practice in warlike actions' was vital to produce effective troops, the surviving records say surprisingly little about time spent in drill. It is unthinkable, however, that most soldiers did not pass many, if not most of the hours, square-bashing, both to keep them out of idle mischief, and to teach them automatic movements, which would both win battles and prevent them from running away.[40]

For cavalry, training was far less formal and routine. Before the war there had been much emphasis on the graceful, ritualized drill of the great cavalry horse, known as the *manège*, both Charles and the Duke of Newcastle being exponents of this complicated style. Once the war began small horses, of no more than 15 hands, were commonly used. Instead of riding up to the enemy, firing pistols or carbines, before retiring to reload, cavalry charged broken units, to hack it out with swords, or else chased routed infantry. In such actions peacetime sports, such as fencing and hunting, were a useful background that the gentry, the backbone of mounted regiments, had all learned as young men before the war.

The skills needed to produce good gunners were far harder to find in civilian life. So poor was the civilian level of maths – a crucial skill for an artilleryman – that John Aubrey declared that 'a bar-boy at an ale house will reckon better and readier than a Master of Arts at the University'.[41] A shortage of trained gunners had become all too obvious during the Irish rebellion. Because none of the English attackers at the Siege of Limerick in 1642 knew how to blow up some houses the enemy were using as cover, artillery had to be used. Overloaded, a cannon blew up, killing Master Gunner Beech and his mates.[42] To remedy the shortage, manuals such as Thomas Eldred's *The Gunner's Glass* (1647, E332) were published, with complete and highly technical instructions.

Training, no matter how complicated, always involves having a group of men work, eat and sleep together. As they learn new skills, they become small cohesive units that fight together effectively.

Asked why his regiment had fought so tenaciously during the defence of Calais in 1940, the adjutant of the First Battalion of the Rifle Brigade answered quite simply, 'we were with friends'.[43] After closely observing American troops in action during the European campaign of 1944–5, General S. L. A. Marshal concluded: 'I hold it to be one of the simplest truths of war that the thing which enables an infantry soldier to keep going with his weapons is the near presence or perceived presence of a comrade.' Three centuries earlier Robert Monro, the veteran of a 'worthy Scotch regiment', made much the same point: 'Nothing therefore is, in my opinion, more worthy to be kept next unto Faith, than this kind of friendship, grown up with education, conformed by familiarity, in frequenting the danger of war.' Richard Baxter expressed this feeling even more eloquently when he remembered the men with whom he served in Colonel Whalley's regiment:[44]

> Many of my dearest friends were there, whose society had formerly been delightful to me, and whose welfare I was tender of, being men that had a deeper interest in my affections than any in the world had before those times. . . . It was they that stuck to me, and I to them. . . . I would not forsake them . . . my faithful people that purposedly went through with me . . . so many wars and dangers.

Ralph Josselin, another parliamentary chaplain, wrote in his diary after his regiment mustered at Saffron Walden in June 1645, 'The Colonel was pleased to honour me to be his comrade. I shall never forget his great love and respect.'[45] Amias Steynings, a veteran of the Thirty Years' War, was convinced that it was comradeship that made fighting possible. From Lord Vere's camp in Maastricht he wrote to his uncle and aunt, 'If one man or two should endure alone, and not thousands, there would be no wars.'[46]

Simply knowing each other, and having been together for some time, helps produce intense comradeship. At the start of the war especially, regiments were raised locally, which, as the Earl of Manchester explained, 'made the soldiers more united amongst themselves'.[47] Crack units often had a regional foundation. Raising his first regiment from the Fen Country, Oliver Cromwell appointed relatives as troop commanders: Edward Whalley, a cousin, Valentine Walton, a nephew, and his son Oliver. All but one of the officers in Sir Bevil Grenville's regiment came from north-west Cornwall, while eight of Sir John Trevanneon's officers hailed from a small area around his father's estates in the south-central part of the county.[48]

Locally recruited units not only tended to fight better but were easier to raise. For instance, in August 1642 the king sent Lord Paget a commission of array authorizing him to recruit an infantry regiment. He focused his efforts in the eastern part of Staffordshire, where the bulk of his estates were located, and in the southern part of the county, where he was able to use the influence of the Dyott family. Although he entrusted training to Captains Bolle and D'Ewes, veterans from outside the county, all his officers were local men, with close links to the villages from which their companies were drawn. Within a month this ramshackle system had raised over a thousand men, and Lord Paget was using it to do the same in North Wales.[49] If officers were removed from men they had known in civilian life they could become deeply upset. On learning of his transfer from the company he had recruited in Holsworthy, Devon, for Sir William Rolle's regiment, Robert Bennet wrote in his diary for 22 August 1642, 'I took some small disrellish and left.'[50]

Although no civil war regiment could flaunt a proud historical tradition of battle honours embroidered on its colours that traced its roots back centuries, most of them had an effective short-term continuity. Of the twenty-seven royalist regiments to fight at Cropredy on 29 June 1644, two were founded in 1640, none in 1641, fourteen in 1642, nine in 1643, and none in 1644. Ten of the regiments had fought at Edgehill two years earlier. The twenty-three royalist regiments that saw action at Marston Moor four days later, showed a similar pattern: six were raised in 1640, none in 1641, six in 1642, nine in 1643, and one in 1644.[51] Elite New Model Army units evinced even greater continuity. For instance, at the end of the second civil war in one troop in Colonel Whalley's regiment fifty men had at least six years' service, in another there were sixty-five such veterans, while in Whalley's own company, the largest, there were eighty-seven. Of a total of 726 men listed, 402 had first seen service in Manchester's army and 205 in the New Model.[52]

Training was intended to produce an intense loyalty towards 'us', as well as deep antipathy against 'them' – the enemy. And there was no shortage of scribblers anxious to portray the other side in the most obnoxious light.

Perhaps the most effective such writer was John Berkenhead, a man of vitriolic humour, able to craft a cruelly witty phrase. He edited *Mercurius Aulicus*, which he published weekly in Oxford and distributed, often secretly by carters, throughout the land. The penny paper was so sought after that some parliamentarians were prepared to pay 1s 6d for it – three days' wages for a foot soldier. At times Berkenhead's barbs were worth every penny. In May 1643 he replied to exaggerated parliamentary claims of royalist casualties by printing the announcement that 'Sir Jacob Astley, lately slain at Gloucester, desires to know was he slain with a musket or cannon bullet.' At other times Berkenhead's humour was downright taste-less. He described how a Presbyterian elder purportedly had his dog sodomize a serving girl.[53]

> An Elder's maid near Temple Bar,
> Ah what a Queen was she
> Did Take an Ugly Mastiff Cur
> Where Christians used to be.

The other side could be just as nasty. One puritan propagandist implied that Prince Rupert was having sex with his pet monkey. When William Harrington's wife gave birth to a stillborn hermaphrodite child 'which had no head, but yet having two ears, two eyes and a mouth in the breast', deformed hands, and a cleft back, John Vicars attributed this to Harrington's support for the king's cause. (According to royalist hacks Mrs Harrington replied that giving birth to a child with no head was better than bringing forth a roundhead.)[54]

Without doubt the most ludicrous propaganda piece was *The Wicked Resolution of the Cavaliers* (1642, W2080), which described a drunken conversation between two royalists.[55] They explained how much they were looking forward to the rape, loot and plunder, which they assured the reader was the main reason why they and their mates fought for King and Country. Once they captured London, they were particularly interested in ravishing the wives of the Goldsmiths in order to force their husbands to reveal where they had hidden their money, boasting that 'We will force them to hold up their wives' smocks, and after this they shall kneel down and thank us.' Next the cavaliers planned to cut off the heads of the merchant tailors to use as tennis balls, and to grind up the bones of old crones to make gunpowder. For a finale *The Wicked Resolution of the Cavaliers* assured its presumably no longer gentle readers that the cavaliers intended violating all the good-looking women, before turning their skins into gloves, as they cooked the master bakers alive in their ovens.

While such patent nonsense might frighten civilians, such as the London artisan, Nehemiah Wallington, it had little effect on the troops in the field, whose view of the enemy was largely determined by the military circumstances of the moment.

Soldiers tended to accept the basic stereotype of the other side, perhaps because it was a projection of the guilt they were loath to see within themselves. Thus after a particular fierce fight a survivor could say of the foe, 'They were devils, not men.' Cavaliers blamed the roundheads (so called because of their brief fad for short hair), for trying to destroy the good old ways of the good old days.[56] When Shakespeare chided Malvolio 'Dost thou think, because thou art virtuous there shall be no more cakes and ale', he anticipated the message of Matthew Parker's highly influential royalist ballad:[57]

> Let's hope for a peace
> For the wars will not cease,
> Till the King enjoys his own again.

Just as Vera Lynn's sadly hopeful songs, with their wistful promises 'till we meet again', kept people going during the Second World War, so the image of the good old days became, for cavaliers at least, an inspiration that they would overcome some day, somewhere. 'And in this pleasant Island Peace did dwell/No noise of war, or sad tale it could tell', remembered Margaret Cavendish, Duchess of Newcastle. A little like a seventeenth-century J. B. Priestley, during the war Peter Hausted, an

Oxford don, waxed lyrical about the virtues of traditional English country life, where a man could eat his wife's cherry pie without some 'grim saucy trooper' plundering his goods. Royalists, from the king down, said a fervent amen to Hausted's conclusion, 'O those were golden days!' Edward Hyde, Lord Falkand, Thomas Crew all used the phrase 'Halcyon days' to describe a happy time when, as a street ballad put it:[58]

> With an old song, made by an old ancient pate
> Of an old worshipful gentleman, who had a great estate.
> Which kept an old house at a beautiful rate,
> And an old porter to relieve the poor at his gate.

If royalists sneered at Malvolio, parliamentarians mocked Sir Toby Belch, that swaggering Shakespearian braggart, for the split that divided England was as much a cultural one as anything else. The name 'cavalier' alluded to the Spanish cavalry, who were notorious for committing atrocities against good Protestants in the Thirty Years' War. All this contrasted with their own self-image. 'Our soldiers from first to the last had prayers and singing of Psalms daily,' declared one of the parliamentary defenders of Manchester, 'being religious men, of a civil and inoffensive conversation.' The convenanters could be just as sanctimonious: 'There was nothing to be heard almost through the whole army but singing of psalms, prayer and reading of Scriptures by the soldiers', reported Chaplain Livingstone.[59]

Front-line troops tended to have a grudging respect for each other. While they traded insults across the lines – 'Papist dogs', 'rebel rogues', 'sons of a puritan bitch', 'Essex's bastards' and 'go preach in a crab tree' being especially popular – they rarely expressed a deep hatred: rather the common soldiers voiced a profound scepticism of official propaganda.[60] 'By experience we find that many are too lavish of their Pen, and instead of verity, publish their own Fancies', maintained a trooper in Sir William Waller's army. A satire had one of the king's soldiers declare that the royalist newspaper, *Mercurius Aulicus*, 'kills more in a sheet in a week than we can kill in many months in the field'.[61] Fighting cavaliers agreed, singing:[62]

> To give the rebel dogs their due
> When the roaring shot poured through and hot
> They were stalwart men and true.

Roundheads returned the compliment. 'And as for the enemy the truth is that they behaved themselves with more valour and resolution then ever man saw coincident with a bad cause', admitted 'Captain W. H.', a survivor of Marston Moor.[63] Another parliamentary veteran found it hard to explain why bad men fought so well. 'You cannot imagine the courage, spirit and resolution that was taken up on both sides', he wrote, before sanctimoniously consoling himself with the thought that while there were 'in their Army the cream of all the papists in England', his own side contained 'such as hath the greatest antipathy to Popery and Tyranny'.[64]

Religious differences, as well as brutal fighting, could destroy normal restraints. Just before the final assault on Basing House in September 1645, William Beech preached a sulphur and brimstone sermon to the parliamentary troops. He called the royalists 'open enemies of God . . . bloody Papists . . . vermin', who deserved the fate the Lord of Hosts had justly meted out to Sodom and Gomorrah.[65] The assault was successful, and the sack of Basing and its defenders was appalling. The brutality, however, could have been due more to the terrifying nature of a siege and storm, which tends to destroy all regard for the other side, than to the fire of Beech's sermon.

In order to control their men in the heat of battle, as well as during the boredom of camp and campaigning, all sides issued articles and ordinances of war that officers read out aloud before their troops at regular intervals, and which laid down how soldiers were to behave, and the punishments for military crimes. As Captain William Clark observed, 'An army without rule a tumult is.'[66] Veteran generals usually copied those used in their previous service. Thus Alexander Leslie, who had been a Field Marshal in Gustavus Adolphus's employ, used the Swedish version when he drafted the *Articles and Ordinances of War for the . . . Army of . . . Scotland* (1644).[67] In the same fashion Lords Ormonde and Castlehaven borrowed Spanish models for the articles they issued to Irish troops in 1641 and 1643. In England the parliamentary and cavalier articles were very similar. Both laid down punishments for desertion, attacking officers, plundering, sounding false alarms, and duelling. Even though the royalist articles prescribed boring through the tongue with a red-hot iron for blasphemers, they tended to be more lenient than the parliamentarian, with only thirteen compared to twenty-eight capital offences. In keeping with their self-image, the cavalier articles were more indulgent to officers who got drunk and duelled.

In practice, however, the strict punishments for a myriad of offences were rarely enforced. While soldiers were usually hung for rape or murder (as were civilians), common military crimes such as plunder, striking a superior or desertion, rarely received the ultimate punishment.[68] Since the articles of military conduct on all sides were very similar, the difference in behaviour was due in part to enforcement, and, in greater part to leadership, and the provision of pay.

Of course, coercion still played a significant part in making men fight. In his *Treatise of Modern War* (1640) John Cruso argued that no profession needed strict discipline more than the military. The pay was poor, and without punishments soldiers could quickly degenerate into 'pillaging rogues'. Citing classical precedents, Cruso favoured the Roman practice of sentencing all found guilty to death, and later choosing by lot those actually executed. In one of the century's most perceptive analysis of battle, General George Monck observed that men fight for two reasons: 'the first is Emulation of Honour, the next is the hopes they have by License to do evil'.[69] Thus severe punishments were vital to curb the evil that war releases in us all.

Sir Ralph Hopton agreed: 'pay well, command well, hang well', he insisted. The gallows impressed some. After seeing a trooper executed, John Aston called the noose 'a bridle to base minds only awed with fear of punishment'. Others thought that carrots were more effective than sticks in motivating soldiers. Before Marston Moor General Fairfax wrote to the Committee of Both Kingdoms: 'with my want of money my men are likely to run away, for I cannot in justice punish having nothing to pay them with all.' A few weeks later Lord Robartes told the same committee that his 'ill paid' troops 'are low in courage, but loud in complaints'.[70]

Pay was an important reward. 'The soldier is encouraged with nothing but money, or hopes of it', thought the Duke of Newcastle.[71] Even though lack of pay was the major reason for mutiny, such actions mainly took place after the war, and were more strikes rather than a refusal to fight in the face of an enemy. Occasionally soldiers were promised a bonus for an especially dangerous job. Fairfax gave 6 shillings (in advance) to the spearhead that assaulted Bristol in 1645, while later that year Cromwell gave 5 bob to the privates who survived the storm of Winchester.[72] A royalist officer, charged with providing recruits for the defence of the city, acknowledged that 'new clothes . . . hath been the chiefest allurement' in persuading them to enlist.[73] But (as we will see in chapter 11) for most troops the hope of plunder was a far more tangible, lucrative and certain reward than the promise of pay.

Promotion was a relatively cheap and effective way of rewarding officers, particularly those cavaliers who were motivated by an intense sense of personal honour. At the suggestion (and at the expense) of Thomas Bushell, Master of the Oxford mint, Charles ordered gold medals struck to reward those taking part in dangerous assaults.[74] John Staynings was presented with two captured colours for his bravery during the attack on Malborough in December 1642.[75] Between 1643 and 1645 the king created thirty-seven new peers, including Sir Edward Lake. Wounded sixteen times he kept on fighting at Edgehill by holding his horse's reins in his teeth so he could use his remaining good hand to wield his sword.[76] During the first civil war the king dubbed sixty-six men as knights, many of them for bravery on the field of battle.[77] Captain John Smith was made Sir John for recapturing the royal standard at Edgehill. For leading the King's Lifeguard in a crucial charge at the same battle Charles not only dubbed Lieutenant Troilus Turbeville a knight, but had Oxford University make him a Doctor of Civil Laws. The king ordered the university to promote Richard Rallingson of Queen's College from a Bachelor to a

Master of Arts for his work in designing the city's fortifications. So common did this abuse of the academic process become that in February 1643, after awarding 140 Master of Arts degrees on the king's command, the University objected, and Charles agreed to stop the practice. Only once did the other side follow suit.[78] In May 1649, Oxford had to make Colonel Sir John Okey, an Anabaptist no less, a Master of Arts for signing the king's death warrant and for helping Cromwell crush the Leveller mutiny at Burford.[79] Five years after Laud's death, and five months after Charles's, so far had that proud bastion of Anglican royalism sunk!

One of the most important mechanisms (and surely the one most ignored by historians), in persuading men to fight as they stare battle in the face, has been drugs, usually alcohol. Excessive drinking was (and still is) a crucial part of the male bonding that produces an effective small unit. In addition it anaesthetizes fear and post-combat stress. Reports of soldiers flushed with Dutch courage were legion. One reason for the failure of the king's forces to take St John's, Worcester in 1646 was that they were 'half drunk'.[80] Two years later Sir John Gell gave his roundheads £40 to get well and truly smashed, after capturing Belvoir Castle. According to a parlimanetary prisoner taken during the Siege of Gloucester in 1643, the governor always plied his raiding parties with 'as much wine and strong waters as they desired'. This was 'the only means to make them stand', sneered the royalist newspaper *Mercurius Aulicus*, and 'to pour out their blood in the act of rebellion'.[81] The following year a cavalier officer remembered taking a gunner at Lostwithiel 'who was pitifully drunk, having shot off his cannon but once'. In March 1645 two hundred of the king's men got so smashed in Winchester that for a lark they decided to capture the nearby enemy position at Marwell Hall. They continued drinking as they galloped towards the enemy, shooting a sentry who challenged them. Alerted, the roundheads returned fire, hitting Sir Thomas Phillips in the head, which sobered his comrades fast enough to persuade them to ride post-haste back home. At Preston four years later, Captain Hodgson recalled, 'we got a pint of strong waters amongst several of us', to encourage them to pursue the broken Scots. In 1650 Charles II gave his cavalry 2 shillings apiece to buy drinks before sending them into their first battle.[82]

Ritual has an important role in all armies. Soldiers take oaths, revere totems, such as their regimental colours, salute their superiors and wear marks signifying their rank. While such rituals were not as marked in civil war armies as they are today, they still played a significant part in persuading men to fight.

The formal declaration of war was a ritual. The ceremony took place in Nottingham on 22 August 1642. Before a guard of honour of three troops of horse and six hundred foot, the royal standard was marched out of the castle to a nearby park, to be formally raised in the king's presence, as a herald read out the proclamation declaring the Earl of Essex and his followers rebels. The standard was a large flag bearing the royal coat of arms and the motto 'Give Caesar his due.'[83]

Battle standards were important symbols in persuading men to fight, often defining the cause for which they were asked to give their lives. Sometimes they did so graphically. The Earl of Carnarvon's showed six dogs baiting the royal lion, while Lieutenant Colonel Caryll Molyneux's mocked Essex's cuckoldry, by portraying a reindeer (with large horns), supported by five hands (the five Members of Parliament who started the rebellion). More often the standard's message was verbal. 'Monarchy the best of Governments', and 'Ruin is the Fate of Discord', proclaimed two cavalier flags. Parliamentary standards stressed religion and law: 'For Reformation', 'If God be with us who can be against us', 'The Supreme Law is the Welfare of the Country', 'Not against the King I fight, but for the King and Commons' Right'. Battle cries reiterated these messages. At Naseby the royalists shouted 'God and Queen Mary', at Newark they yelled 'King and Queen', while the roundheads bellowed back 'Religion'. When it was discovered during the Battle of Cheriton that both sides had chosen 'God with us', the parliamentarians promptly changed their war cry to 'Jesus with us'.[84]

Soldiers attached great importance to battle-cries and standards. With loving detail Lieutenant Richard Symonds recorded in his notebook all the flags of the London trained bands.[85] They were prized possessions, symbols of the unit, as well as rallying points in the chaos of battle. Colours were especially significant when many units lacked uniforms or centuries-old identities, and needed some common symbol around which they could group, both during training and in the mêlée of battle, when it was hard to tell friend from foe. An ensign, the most junior officer, carried the standard into combat. He and his bodyguard of sergeants were expected to protect it with their lives. 'Indeed a Greater act of Cowardice cannot be found', thought Captain Thomas Venn, 'than to suffer the Colours to be lost.' When the Prince of Wales's troop surrendered their standard at Hopton Heath on 19 March 1643 they could not carry another until they had redeemed their honour as a unit by capturing one from the enemy – which they did three months later at Chalgrove.

As they marched into battle parliamentary soldiers often chanted psalms. Occasionally this lessened their effectiveness. At Powick Bridge, one of the war's first skirmishes, Captain Sandys caught the roundheads unawares as they were singing a psalm, routing them. Mostly psalm-singing was, to quote John Vicars, the puritan chaplain, 'a blessed badge'.[86] Lord Brooke's troops stormed Lichfield cathedral chanting the 149th Psalm:

Let the saints be joyful in glory . . .

Let the high praises of God be in their mouth, and the two edged
  sword in their hand . . .
To bind their kings with chains and their nobles with fetters of iron.

Whether his Lordship approved of the bit about nobles and fetters of iron
is not known. Without doubt Chaplain Vicars applauded the mien of his
troops at the Battle of Winceby: 'So soon as our men had knowledge of
the Enemy's coming, they were very full of joy and resolution', he recorded, 'our men went on in several bodies singing Psalms.'[87] Sir Edward
Walker recalled seeing the enemy advance against his position singing
hymns at the Second Battle of Newbury. Psalm singing made the difference
between victory and defeat for the parliamentary forces that assaulted
Leeds on 23 June 1644. Sergeant-Major Forbes led a frontal incursion
against the cannon the rebels had placed to cover the bridge at Beeston, but
failed. So Fairfax infiltrated some musketeers across the water meadows, to
provide enfilading fire at the artillerymen. Forbes and his men once more
attacked the enemy trenches, as the Reverend Jonathan Scholefield, minister of Croston Chapel in Halifax, led the rest of the troops against the
cannon, singing the 68th Psalm, 'Let God arise, let his enemies be scattered: let them also that hate him flee before him.' And flee His enemies
did. After killing the gunners, Scholefield's troopers, many of whom had
only been recruited the previous Saturday, waged a fierce house-to-house
fight to take the town.[88]

  Writers of civil war training manuals agreed on one thing – that the
primary purpose of training was not just to teach men military skills, but
to steel them for the ordeal of war. In other words its function was, to
use the modern jargon, 'battle-proofing'. As the motto of the British
Army's Parachute Training School puts it 'knowledge dispels fear'. (It
didn't work in the author's case.) John Raynford affirmed in *The Young
Soldier* (1642, Y132) that 'By practice is gained knowledge, knowledge
begets confidence and courage.' In his *Military Observations* (1672, V192)
Thomas Venn concurred that 'knowledge in all things belonging to war
giveth courage'. 'Knowledge of war', wrote Edward Cooke, would make
soldiers 'the more bold to fight'.[89]

  Training also taught the civilians who formed the civil war armies that
war is a serious business.

> Methinks the proverb should not be forgot
> That wars are sweet to them that know them not.

So observed John Taylor in the summer of 1642. About the same time
Donald Lupton, a veteran of the Thirty Years' War, wrote *A Warre-like
Treatise of the Pike* (1642, L3496) reminding civilians of the harsh realities
of his profession. 'Soldiers are not for sport and joust, but for earnest.

Neither is war to be accounted a May-game, or a Morris dance, but as a Plague and Scourge.'[90]

Veterans reiterated this point. In some of the finest verse to come out of the experience of the civil war, Captain Sam Jervis warned:[91]

> Till now we did but butcher victories
> And were but sloven Death's men. What our eyes
> Were wanting to our hands, we fell upon
> A Miscellaneous Execution.
> We that grieved the slain, that they must die
> Without method and disorderly,
> But now we have obtained the handsome skill,
> By order, method, and by rule to kill.

Those who did not learn this lesson, or were not taught it, or forgot it, too often paid the ultimate price. Even though Captain John Gwynne was an experienced drill master, having exercised the king's children, he had only a day or two to prepare his soldiers before marching them off to the Battle of Brentford. It was not long enough. When a powder barge full of men blew up, Gwynne recalled, 'the fearful crash it gave, and the sad aspect of it, struck such a terror unto the rest of the recruits that they all vanished.' The Scots troops whom James Turner noted as 'lusty, well clothed, and well monied, but raw, untrained and undisciplined, their officers for the most part young and inexperienced', were repulsed with great loss during a night attack on Newcastle in 1644.[92] The Westminster Trained Bands who assaulted Basing House in November 1643 were in fact a pretty scratch lot – the more experienced troops having been allowed to go home. Thrown into one of the war's most desperate actions, they opened fire out of range, and instead of doing so by rank, shot all together. As a result those in the rear ranks hit many of their comrades in the front. Seeing the snafu the royalists showered them with grapeshot, and the parliamentary troops ran. 'Some on both sides did well, and others did ill and deserved to be hanged', concluded one of their officers, trying to make the best of a bad job.[93]

Of course, training can never really proof you for battle. As a veteran of the 1944 Burma campaign put it, 'Nothing, I believe, can prepare a man for the experience of being fired upon.' The differences between a soldier's preconceptions of combat and the reality of fighting, plays a great part in determining his ability to survive his baptism of fire. Thus modern training works hard to get him used to the noise of weapons being fired, the sights and sounds of explosions, the tiredness of marching, and, through such ordeals as parachute training and 'death slides', overcoming, or at least becoming familiar with, the experience of fear.[94] During the seventeenth century a greater reluctance to admit to fear may have facilitated this process. Today troops will readily confess to being afraid. 'War scares the hell out of me', admitted the American correspondent, Ernie Pyle, just before he was killed in the Pacific campaign. 'I was', confessed Michael Herr about Vietnam, 'scared every fucking minute.' But soldiers in the British civil wars (like those in the American) rarely talked about being afraid in combat, not, I suspect, because they were braver, but because their culture prevented them from making what they believed was a dishonourable admission.[95]

Unlike modern soldiers, those in the British civil wars rarely relied on personal rituals or talismans, such as rabbits' feet or lucky charms, to try to control fear. Sir Lewis Dyve, the royalist sergeant-major, was unusual in that he used to carry around his neck a bent gold piece that had stopped a bullet, saving his life. John Hampden's totem was less efficacious: the silver locket he wore about his neck inscribed 'Against my king I never fight/But for my king and country's right', did not save him from being fatally wounded at Chalgrove.[96] Contemporary reports do not mention the nervous pre-battle cleaning of already immaculate weapons or sharpening razor-honed bayonets, that is common before combat today. Indeed because the weapons on all sides were basically identical, soldiers could not pin their hopes of survival on the superiority of their arms.

Wherever possible soldiers were eased into combat by stages, new units being first sent to a quiet sector of the front. Thomas Raymond recalled how he was first exposed to war in Dutch service, besieging the Spanish. 'At my first coming my courage began to fail me', for he was convinced that every enemy cannon was aimed directly at his hat, in which he sported an Orange feather, the colour of the Dutch ruling house. After a few days, having survived shell and shot, 'I took myself to be a very gallant fellow, and had no more dread of danger than if I had been in a fair.'[97]

As the rout of the Westminster Trained Bands at Basing House suggests, there is, however, little indication that such battle-proofing was a deliberate part of civil war training and planning. In the seventeenth century men preferred to put their trust in God. Such should not be surprising, for while the modern cliché that there are no atheists in fox-holes may be true, three hundred and fifty years ago there were very few atheists anywhere in the British Isles.

A good sermon could whip up martial ardour. 'The Lord's Day we spent in preaching and prayer, whilst our gunners were battering', recalled Hugh Peters, that grating puritan chaplain, of the Siege of Winchester (see plate 10). Just before the New Model Army attacked Bridgwater on 20 July 1645 'Mr Peters preached a preparatory sermon to encourage the soldiers to go on', remembered Joshua Sprigge. Then after another homily from the Reverend Bowle, the drums beat, the troops attacked, and with 'fresh exhortation to do their duties with undaunted courage and resolution' from indefatigable Mr Peters, the roundheads took the town.

When John Sedgwick preached before the parliamentary soldiers at Malborough one of the congregation recalled that he 'thrashed such a sweating sermon that he put off his doublet'.[98] His brother, Obadiah, was an equally passionate preacher, who in Taunton church roused the troops to such a fury that they seized the prayer books, ripped out the prayers for the bishops, clergy and royal family, and smashed up the organ (which had just been bought for £400). In a very different tone (but with its humour and macho references equally effective), Dr Grossmede's sermon to the royalist defenders of Gloucester was 'a very gross one, wherein he called women meddlers, open Arses, with much ribaldry'.[99]

During war prayer became even more important than it had been in peace. Philip Skippon, the commanding general of the London Trained Bands, composed *A Salve for Every Sore* (1643, S3951), a devotional work which he admitted 'cost me no small labour'. He explained: 'I am not a scholar, I desire to be a Christian.' Both sides composed prayer manuals for their troops. Parliament put out *The Soldiers' Catechism* (1644, S4420). Thomas Swadlin replied with *The Soldier's Catechism composed for the King's Army* (1645, S6224). 'W. C.', the chaplain who wrote *A manual of prayers collected for the use of Sir Ralph Dutton's Regiment* (1643, C158), began by explaining why his were so brief, 'for soldiers are not at leisure for long prayers'. The chaplain's invocation was just as practical:

O Lord, that art the sun and shield in all that trust in thee, and who in times of danger hast ordained the calling of soldiers, to which thou wast pleased to move me, thy servant; put upon me, I beseech thee, thy whole armour, and give me courage against my Ghostly and bodily enemies.

The manual included prayers for the king, for peace, for and against the enemy, for one's officers, against swearing, for a successful raid, for thanks in victory, and 'for a good end'.

Bibles – usually in cheap abbreviated versions that troops could easily carry on the march – were equally popular. The most widely used was *The Souldier's Pocket Bible* (1643, S4428). It contained prayers as well as pertinent extracts dealing with matters such as courage, temptation, battle, God's concern for men in combat, and the reassurance that He will bring His people to final victory. Not surprisingly all but seven of its 125 extracts were from the Old Testament. Although such works were not issued free to soldiers, they were so common, and efficacious, that Chaplain Richard Baxter recalled that 'the marvelous preservation' of soldiers' pocket Bibles stopping bullets was so frequent an example of divine providence that 'I will not mention them'.

When the training was over, and all the parts had been named, the soldier set out on campaign to face the actuality of war. 'I would have such know', wrote that distinguished general, George Monck, 'that soldiers go into the field to Conquer and not to be killed.'[100]

5

A SOLDIER'S LIFE IS TERRIBLE HARD

They're changing guard at Buckingham Palace –
Christopher Robin went down with Alice.
Alice is marrying one of the Guard.
'A soldier's life is terrible hard'
Says Alice.
    A. A. Milne, *When We were Very Young* (1924)

In a letter home Amias Steynings described how terrible hard was a soldier's life during a campaign. Noting that '[we] are in great want for lack of victuals', he wrote how depressing he found the destruction of the lush countryside and prosperous cities. Conditions were so bad that to stay alive even senior officers had to dig fortifications and forage for themselves. Worse still the weather was wretchedly cold and wet: often he was lucky to get a couple of hours' sleep every twenty-four. 'Good Uncle,' Steynings concluded, 'it is a great deal of misery that a soldier doth endure, besides danger, every minute of his life.'[1]

Even though he was describing his experiences during the Thirty Years' War, they would have been just as familiar to any veteran of the British civil wars. Unlike garrison troops, who tended to stay put as they tried to control the surrounding countryside, soldiers who served in field armies usually followed a pattern the seasons determined. During the seventeenth century 87 per cent of the battles were fought between April and November.[2] In the English civil wars 64 per cent of the actions were fought during these months, although all of the major battles with over a thousand dead took place in this season. Table 1 shows how fighting followed the seasons of the year. The surprising point is that the peak during the summer and autumn was not as high as might have been thought, and that a fair level of fighting continued throughout the year. (For more on these figures see chapter 9, tables 3 and 4).

'My Lord, the King's business begins to settle', Arthur Trevor wrote to the Earl of Ormonde in December 1643, describing the annual round, 'The army is drawing into their winter quarters and disposed themselves at as great a distance as they can with security, which I suppose is done for the care of the counties.' After describing a similar hibernation of parliament's forces, one newspaper called Newport Pagnell, one of their main depots, a 'warm nest for a soldier in winter'.[3]

Table 1: Killed and prisoner by month in England

Month	Parliament killed	Parliament prisoner	Royalist killed	Royalist prisoner	Total incidents
January	1,110	390	1,347	6,015	39
February	1,673	1,521	1,907	2,620	30
March	3,273	3,261	1,655	5,831	56
April	2,690	2,148	1,646	5,583	53
May	2,856	2,685	4,560	6,853	63
June	3,475	2,893	5,377	5,195	68
July	4,816	4,402	8,756	6,300	69
August	3,023	3,999	5,796	7,645	53
September	2,545	2,350	5,520	19,425	26
October	2,783	1,640	3,447	3,562	43
November	1,235	1,430	1,110	2,115	25
December	1,571	2,166	2,332	2,180	53
Not known	3,080	3,938	7,247	10,143	67
Total	34,130	32,823	50,700	83,467	645

The winter weather made fighting very hard. Apart from cold, which contributed to illness, the wet rendered poor roads nigh impassable. Difficult transportation, as well as the shortage of forage for horses, meant that only small groups could be supplied once they had left their depots. So on all sides the armies retreated back to their bases, where they spent the time, as Charles explained to his men, 'for their better refreshing and recovering that they might be speedily ready to receive our command for the coming campaign'.[4]

During the winter many soldiers left the army, with or without leave, to go home to see their families, passing the frigid season in more comfortable quarters: some returned when they were needed once more in the spring. Of the 64 men who mustered in Major James Castle's Warwickshire company in November 1643, only 26 (41 per cent) were on the books in the following May, although the size of the company had increased to 68. A similar pattern could be seen for the following winter when 43 per cent of the soldiers remained with the company. Wastage was not as bad during the winter of 1645–6, when the muster roll fell from 72 to 45 (63 per cent): after a court martial cashiered six men at the end of December, only one soldier deserted.[5] A similar pattern may be seen for Captain Harvey's company in Hobart's regiment. Of the 107 troops mustered on 30 March 1645, 66 (62 per cent) were still on the books on May 25, 47

(43 per cent) on 19 September, 29 (27 per cent) on 13 December and 27 (25 per cent) the following 3 January.[6]

Some troops, particularly officers and senior NCOs, were given extended furloughs during the winter. When Cromwell's regiment, a crack unit, was sent to the West Country with hardly any warning in March 1645 many of the officers and NCOs had left for home or to visit friends, and had to rejoin at a special rendezvous.[7] During the winter of 1642–3 Sergeant William Preece, a veteran of the continental wars, was allowed to visit his family who lived in Myddle, Shropshire. Unfortunately a parliamentary patrol captured him and took him to the gaol at Wem, from which he managed to escape, making it back to his regiment at Shrewsbury. Preece was killed fighting at Ercal. During the winters of 1642–3 and 1643–4 the king sent Lord Belasyse back to his native county to rest, and to recruit men in Yorkshire, which he did from the ranks of AWOL soldiers he found milling about. Sir Henry Slingsby spent November 1645 on leave from the parliamentary base at Newark, at his home in Yorkshire; he had to travel heavily disguised, and passed most of his time hiding in his house, unknown to all but closest family.[8]

Other parliamentarians followed a similar winter pattern. Since their armies tended to be more dispersed, or were based in London, many men were fairly close to home so they were given shorter furloughs. Chaplains were an exception. They rarely stayed with their regiments during the winter, returning instead to their own parishioners.[9] Apparently they felt that when the weather got bad, God's work at home was more important than His work abroad.

The main royalist field armies tended to be concentrated around Oxford. Apart from the troops in the university city, there were surrounding garrisons at Reading, Wallingford, Abingdon and Brill, protected by cavalry patrols. Since the cavalry needed a fair amount of fodder for their animals, and were not as useful guarding the city's defences as infantry or gunners, they tended to be billeted in the countryside nearby. There were no barracks and hardly any hutted encampments, so most soldiers lived with civilians, who were required to support and feed them in return for an allotment that was always insufficient, usually late, and more often unpaid. The closest that troops came to a modern camp was at Oxford, where the colleges provided good accommodation for many men, while the surrounding houses were crammed with families and camp-followers, courtiers and courtesans. In St Aldgates, for instance, 408 strangers were billeted in 74 small, two- or four-roomed houses, in addition to their normal inhabitants.[10]

Wartime Oxford was an exciting place. Raucous sergeants replaced contemplative dons. The handful of students left lived in 'a dark nasty room' in New College. When the scholars complained about their conditions, hardly anyone listened, for most of the undergraduates had joined up.

Cavalry patrols jangled through the streets trying to catch the eye of those pretty girls who seemed to flock wherever the court met. Attracted by the sound of their drums, one afternoon Lady Anne Fanshawe strolled over to St John's College Garden, and leaning against a tree watched the soldiers drill. The commander, a family friend, 'in compliment gave us a volley of shot'. He did not realize that instead of blanks one of his musketeers had loaded a brace of bullets that pierced the bark a couple of feet above Anne's head.

Such near escapes did not deter women from waving, and children from running alongside the columns of infantry as they marched through the streets, their step light as they set out, their pace heavy as they returned. The colleges were used as barracks or warehouses. Magdalen became an artillery park, the Great Quad at Christ Church was a cattle pen. In the music and astronomy schools tailors stitched uniforms from cloth captured at Cirencester. The Schools of Law and Logic were granaries, that of Rhetoric a workshop for portable bridges. A powder mill was set up at Osney Abbey and a sword factory at Wolvercote. At New Inn Hall a mint turned college plate into coins, as well as striking medals for brave soldiers. All over town printing presses churned out propaganda that carters smuggled throughout the land. When the members of parliament who were still loyal to the Crown, having refused to join their colleagues at Westminster, came to Oxford in early 1644, the Commons sat in the Great Convocation House, and the Lords in the Upper Schools. The castle was turned into a prison camp that became as notorious as a Dartmoor, Colditz or Changi.

At the centre of this garrison town was, of course, the king. He lodged in Christ Church, while the queen, who spent several months at Oxford, had rooms in Merton. Once or twice a week Charles would rise early to ride about the town inspecting its defences; his majesty was so punctual in his rounds that a sniper could set his watch by them. In the afternoons the king and queen and their children, surrounded by courtiers, walked their dogs through the college gardens. Afterwards Charles attended chapel, had dinner, and then wrote letters, talked, played tennis or chess. The court tried to carry on as if it were still the halcyon days of peace. The House of Lords in Westminster gave permission for a pack of beagles to be sent to Oxford. The Master of the Revels doggedly produced entertainments. William Davenant continued writing verse. William Dobson painted portraits that were better than ever (plate 21).

The transformation of Oxford from a peaceful university city to a vibrant garrison was not without its problems. By and large the townsfolk did not support the king. When the occupation began in 1642 royalist troops disarmed the citizens and imprisoned the recorder, as well as one of Oxford's members of parliament, John Whistler. The citizens resented being forced on pain of a shilling a day fine to work from six in the morning to six at night (even though they got a fairly generous two hours off for lunch), building Oxford's defences. So scarce was labour, and so unproductive were those forced to perform it, that a proclamation of 21 July 1643 extended the draft to women.

In this crowded, tension-racked society, conflict was endemic. Even though another proclamation limited brewers to producing a weak beer, and wine and liquor were in short supply, troops got drunk, revealing a mean reality beneath the romantic veneer. In 1644 Lord Capel described the cavaliers at Oxford as 'neat enough and gay in their appearance, and yet they were very nasty and beastly . . . vain, empty and careless, rude whoremongers'.[11] Crowded conditions produced disease and accidents. In a single year some ninety soldiers were buried in St Martin's, Carfax. In 1644 a trooper, who was roasting a stolen pig in his billet in George Street, started a fire that burnt down property worth £30,000. Soldiers resented the civilians, especially the rump of the university, which tried to carry on as before. One trooper rushed into the hall where Dr Ralph Kettel, President of Trinity, was teaching, smashing the hour-glass he used to time his lectures.[12]

The authorities tried to maintain discipline. 'We have to our great Grief and High displeasure observed a General Liberty taken by all sorts of Officers and soldiers in our army', began a royal proclamation of 12 June 1643. It went on to order the severe punishment of all guilty of swearing, blaspheming, drunkenness and whoring. The proclamation also com-manded all chaplains to say services in front of the troops twice a day, to preach to them every Sunday morning, and on the first Sabbath of the month to celebrate communion which all officers and men had to attend. If the word of God failed, resort was made to that of man: on the second Sunday of each month chaplains were ordered to read out aloud the *Military Orders and Articles Established by His Majesty for the Better Governing of his Majesty's Army* (1643).[13] In April 1644 the king issued another proclamation for the better observation of prayer and divine service, and forbidding swearing and cursing on pain of a shilling fine for each offence.[14]

Had the penalties been collected it would have done much to resolve the financial problems which helped defeat His Majesty's forces, whose promiscuity was notorious. 'Prince Rupert is much given to his ease and pleasure', complained Arthur Trevor about the cavalier general, adding that his winter base, 'the city of Bristol, is but a great house of bawdy, and will ruin the king'.[15]

The winter was not just a time for rest, relaxation and fornication. It was also a season when the soldiers prepared to campaign, and the politicians negotiated in the hope of averting further bloodshed. Peace talks were held at Oxford in February 1643 and at Uxbridge twelve months later. When the parliamentary commissioners ventured to Oxford tensions were inevitable. One of the negotiators, Bulstrode Whitelocke, recalled that on arriving in the royalist headquarters in February 1643 he dined at Merton College with his old friend, Dr James Turner. Soon afterwards he fell ill. Dr Turner treated him, calling Whitelocke 'a rebel and a traitor, and do deserve to die,' before adding 'yet you art the gallantest of rebels that ever were'. Other royalists were not as charitable. After Whitelocke recovered, he was accosted by a group of cavaliers while walking on an Oxford street. He showed them his safe-conduct signed by the king, adding that as a parliamentary commissioner he was not prepared to tolerate their insults. 'Dam me and sink me', a rowdy replied, gabbling that parliament was a nest of traitors. The hooligans might well have attacked Whitelocke with their blades had not his brother-in-law, Sir Humphrey Bennet, appeared on the scene, telling them that 'he would thrust his sword into that party's guts', if they did not desist. Then Bennet escorted Whitelocke back to his lodgings in Merton.[16]

During their stay in winter quarters armies built up supplies of food and equipment, renewed their military organizations, and collected money to pay their men during the coming campaign season. As Edward Cooke noted in *The Perspective Glasse of Warre* (1628, STC 5670), 'Victuals is the Soul of an Army: Money but the sinews. Without the first your Army cannot fight, without the second but indifferently. But with both admirably well.'

Samuel Luke, the governor of the parliamentary depot at Newport Pagnell, warned the Earl of Essex that if paid his troops would fight, and if not they would most likely mutiny. In theory, at least, pay scales were generous. An infantry private received 4 to 6 shillings a week, about as much as an agricultural labourer, while dragoons got 12s. 6d. and cavalry 17s. 6d., from which they were expected to feed their mounts. The colonel of a royalist infantry regiment was supposed to receive £15 15s. 0d. a week, a major £8 5s. 0d. and a lieutenant £1 8s. 0d. In practice these amounts were rarely paid in full. In 1644 the Eastern Association's cavalry received 126 days' pay, its infantry got 252 days' worth, while Waller's army was paid for 77 days, and Essex's for 98. Royalist troops fared even worse, notably during the closing stages of the war.[17]

A few rich troopers did not need the money. The King's Lifeguard, commanded by Lord Berners, were reputed to be worth £100,000 a year, and able to buy out the House of Commons had they wished: one ensign was such a swell that it was said he shaved in sack. But for most soldiers lack of money was a problem. Constantly they complained about a shortage of cash, and the hardship that this inflicted on their dependants. In his diary Colonel Robert Bennet worried about the financial burden of volunteering to fight for the king: 'received not a penny', and 'not a penny had I', being a frequent refrain.[18]

The importance of food and drink in helping produce victory has long been recognized. Armies, Napoleon observed, march upon their stomachs. Brigadier Bernard Ferguson, the Chindit leader, noted that 'lack of food constitutes the biggest single assault on morale'. Lieutenant Elias Archer noted that after his regiment has been repulsed three times with heavy losses at the Siege of Basing House 'much provision of Victuals and strong waters' restored their confidence.[19] Apart from the physical need for nutrition, food plays an important psychological part in a soldier's life. The regular provision of meals gives certainty in the uncertain environment of war. Eating together enhances the cohesion of small units, improving communications and building loyalty amongst their members. It is no accident that the ranks of commissioned and non-commissioned officers in the British armed forces are defined in terms of their messes – their eating groups.

The official daily ration in the cavalier army was 2 lb of bread, 1 lb of meat and two bottles of beer. This provided about 4,500 calories, sufficient for a soldier involved in heavy exercise. Bread was baked in winter garrisons, particularly at Oxford, and sent out to surrounding units. Units that were a long way from a depot had to fend for themselves. Colonel Robert Bennet's Devonshire regiment had four bakers on its pay roll.[20] Because parliament controlled the fishing ports, Charles issued a proclamation in February 1643 suspending the statutes against consuming meat during Lent, so his men could obtain sufficient protein.[21]

In winter quarters, or in garrisons, troops usually got enough to eat. For instance, between January and June 1645 the parliamentary garrison of Chalfield House, Wiltshire, which averaged about two hundred men, consumed 40,000 lb of beef, 1,600 lb of bacon, 580 lb of pork, 1,900 lb of mutton, and 64 lb of veal, which would provide each man with 1.2 lb of meat per diem. The meat ration was even higher in Lyme Regis garrisons, where, it was reported, 'every man has two pounds of beef a day'. At Chalfield the garrison also consumed 15,000 pints of wheat, 27,000 pints of oats, 20,000 pints of malt, 5,000 pints of beans and 5,000 pints of peas, which was enough to provide each man with a daily ration of 9 oz. of grain and pulses, and (including 20,000 pints purchased elsewhere), 2.5 pints of beer. The provision of dairy products was less generous – about 2.5 oz. of cheese, and less than 0.5 oz. of butter a day. The garrison consumed 5,300 lb of cheese, 400 lb of butter and 5,500 lb of salt.[22] The typical daily ration served in a central mess hall to the Chalfield garrison consisted of 1 lb of meat, 8 oz. of bread, 12 oz. of oatmeal, 4 oz. of peas or beans, 2.5 oz. of cheese and 2.5 pints of beer.

Even though the diet lacked roughage, few troops complained. Their grub was much better than most of them had known in civilian life, when they had been lucky to eat meat once or twice a week.

Because of transportation difficulties, soldiers on the march rarely fared as well. Wherever possible armies tried to live off the land, or bring their meat with them on the hoof. When the Earl of Essex sallied to relieve Gloucester, in one of the war's most crucial movements, the thousand sheep and sixty cattle his column drove slowed them down. In August 1643 the average daily ration issued to Colonel Popham's regiment on campaign consisted of 10.5 oz. of biscuits, 3 oz. of peas, 5 oz. of meat or cheese, and half a pint of beer. Since this fairly typical issue provided less than half the calories needed for active service, soldiers had to supplement their diet, either from their own resources or through purchase, barter, requisitioning or outright plunder. Such private augmentations were far easier if done by small messes of friends, especially when units were dispersed on the march.[23]

Scrounging food was a daily preoccupation. Richard Coe's diary of his marches with Waller's Army constantly mentions it. Sometimes he and his comrades were lucky. On 17 May the royalist captain recorded that at Bagshot there 'was plenty of mutton, veal, lamb, some venison, good water, but neither bread nor beer for money'. At other times troops went hungry. 'Our supper was a hard egg and tough cheese', Ralph Josselin, the parliamentary padre, noted in his diary, adding 'Blessed be to God we had anything.' After their victory at Taunton in 1644 the roundheads were so hungry that they stopped chasing the enemy to plunder houses for food. Seizing the main chance, the royalists counter-attacked, dispatching some of the guzzlers 'with bread in their mouths'.[24] On 3 September 1644 a parliamentary trooper campaigning in the West Country wrote 'we lay in the open fields, that night being a bitter rainy night', and the next day they were so hungry that 'a penny loaf would have sold for half a crown and many thanks besides'.[25] During an attack on Basing House, Hampshire, which saw some of the most brutal combat in the civil war, Lieutenant Elias Archer of the London Trained Bands recalled that some of his men captured the great barn containing 'much provision of bread, beer, beef, pork, milk, cream, peas, and such like'. Even though the barn's thatched roof was ablaze, and they were under heavy sniper and cannon fire, the hungry soldiers gave up their assault to eat, drink and loot. They became so merry that the attack failed, and many of them were slaughtered.[26]

Clothing could be in just as short supply as food. In winter bases and in garrisons troops tended to fare better than on the march. Even though enlistees were supposed to be kitted out with a set of clothing and pair of shoes, often they did not receive the entitlement, especially if they had been drafted. When Silius Titus took command of a company from Hertfordshire he found the conscripts 'extremely ill provided for a march, without shoes, stockings, coats . . . they wanted nothing but all'.[27] 'I never saw worse tattered soldiers', wrote William Harlakenden about parliament's Cambridgeshire levies. As the winter of 1644 was drawing near

General William Waller bemoaned, 'our poor dragoons go naked this weather'.[28] Sometimes the supply system failed even troops in winter bases. Sir Samuel Luke complained that his men were so short of clothing that a couple had to share a single pair of trousers: so for decency's sake when one was on duty the other had to stay abed.[29]

Marching and fighting quickly wore out clothes and shoes. Then infantry men did not have strong boots, but shoes made from brown cowhide, which if they were lucky might last two or three months on the poor roads. Since many apprentice cobblers from Northampton volunteered to join the parliamentary army, the supply of shoes declined as demand increased. Being cut from the same pattern, having neither left nor right shapes, seventeenth-century footwear could hardly have been very comfortable, especially when being broken in.[30] One of the most useful pieces of booty Prince Rupert ever captured was some four thousand pairs of shoes taken at York in 1644. Fighting troops needed adequate clothing so desperately that victors invariably stripped corpses and prisoners of war of almost all they wore.

Problems such as a shortage of food, pay, and clothing were all too common to both sides during a seventeenth-century war. In a civil war, in which friend and foe invariably come from the same military traditions, they usually have similar weapons and organizations.

In theory both royalist and parliamentary cavalry regiments were commanded by a colonel or lieutenant-colonel, with six troops of seventy men. Each troop consisted of a major, a captain or lieutenant, one cornet, three corporals, two trumpeters and sixty troopers. In practice most troops were lucky to have forty members. The expansion of cavalry, as well as the needs of supply trains, created a tremendous demand for chargers and cart-horses. Even though domestic breeding satisfied the demand fairly well, prices for horses rose to levels that were not exceeded until the early eighteenth century. Surprisingly little evidence has survived of any deep affections between rider and mount. The only case found of someone mourning his horse was Arthur Trevor's brother, who was most upset after 'his jewel Bay Squire' was killed in Montgomery.[31]

On paper an infantry regiment (which would correspond to a modern British battalion) had 1,200 men, organized into ten companies. Unlike modern units the regimental officers also commanded companies. The colonel's company had 200 men, the lieutenant-colonel's 160, the major's 140, while the six captains had a hundred apiece. Each captain's company had one lieutenant, one ensign, one gentleman, two sergeants and three corporals, and a mixture of pikemen and musketeers. Regimental headquarters included a quartermaster, a provost, the surgeon and his mate, a carriage master, drum major, and the chaplain. The payroll for Colonel Robert Bennet's regiment of foot for 6 July 1646 shows a total of 30 officers and 984 other ranks.[32] Most units, primarily in the king's army, were rarely as close to full strength. Three hundred was a typical muster. The paper strength of a regiment of dragoons (mounted infantry used as scouts and skirmishers), was a thousand men, divided into ten equally sized companies. Because, as John Lilburne recalled, 'I and my regiment of dragoons were constantly quartered in the van of the army', losses meant that they seldom fought at full strength.[33]

Artillery trains had no standard sizes, consisting instead of what was available and needed. From the start of the war parliament had an advantage in artillery, which was only partially remedied after the king captured forty-nine pieces at Lostwithiel. Nonetheless by the war's end the New Model Army's artillery train had some fifty-six weapons, not including siege mortars which needed some 1,038 horses for transport and two companies of musketeers for protection.

By the end of the war both sides suffered from a shortage of infantry. Although pre-war military theorists had suggested an ideal ration of horse to foot of between 1 : 3 and 1 : 5, according to the 1638 muster of the trained bands this was as high as 1 : 19. Once the fighting started and men began to die, necessity displaced niggardliness: at Edgehill the ratio was 1 : 2.5, at Marston Moor 1 : 1.6 and at Naseby 1 : 1.25. The royalists suffered from a surfeit of cavalry, having more horse than foot in 27 out of 57 battles surveyed, as compared to the roundheads 1 out of 17.[34]

The advantages to being a horse soldier were obvious. In addition to getting paid more, having greater social cachet, and the mobility to forage more effectively on the march, a cavalryman was far safer. In the New Model Army infantry officers were killed 4.38 times more frequently than those in the cavalry.[35] In victory a man on horseback could cut down the enemy with brutal ease; in defeat, with four rather than two legs, he could run away much faster. Three and a half thousand of the king's four thousand infantry were killed or taken prisoner at the Battle of Naseby, while most of the cavalry managed to escape. 'The horse knew well how to save themselves,' Joshua Moore bitterly observed, 'though not their honour.'[36]

The purpose of military organization was, of course, to bring armed soldiers into combat in an orderly fashion. The weapons they carried were crucial: they were both the soldier's totom and the tool of his trade. As General George Monck put it, 'Arms are the security of your own soldier, the terror of the enemy, and the assured ordinary means of victory.'

Since perhaps as few as one household in fifteen possessed a firearm in pre-war England, the first weapons issued to troops were of poor quality. Sir George Greseley, who served in Sir John Gell's regiment, records that when they were raised in October 1642 the City of Sheffield lent them some 'old calivers with rotten stocks and rusty barrels, useless to them and of little service to us'.[37] Through imports and the rapid development of domestic production, the supply of arms gradually improved, and, as men learned how to look after their weapons, complaints about the quality and quantity of arms became unusual.

The simplest weapon of all was the pike. Supposedly 16.5 to 18 feet long it was made out of seasoned ash with an iron tip. The first four feet were sometimes covered with iron plates to stop the enemy from hacking them off with their swords. For protection pikemen wore a heavy armour with a helmet, breastplate and leg guards, which weighed 24 lb. They also carried swords. In theory these were for hand-to-hand combat, but in practice they used them for chopping firewood, blunting and often snapping the shoddy weapons. George Monck and Sir James Turner both suggested issuing all foot soldiers with axes. During 'long and quick marches in hot summer weather', one veteran recalled, carrying all this equipment, as well as food and spare clothing 'cannot but be wonderfully burdensome'.[38] The pike was not only heavy, but when held horizontally in the middle, the ends tended to vibrate uncomfortably up and down on the march. Thus it is not surprising that some pikemen succumbed to the temptation of cutting a couple of feet off their cumbersome weapon. This shortcut could have disastrous results, as the Scots discovered at Benburb in 1646, when their pikes were two feet shorter than those pushed at – and all too often into – them by Owen Roe's Irish infantry.

Even though some commentators claimed that a pike could hold off cavalry, and all agreed that it was 'the most honorable of weapons', as the war progressed the ratio of pikemen to musketeers reversed itself, until by the wars' end in the New Model Army's infantry the latter predominated two to one.[39] The British were slow to learn the lesson of the Thirty Years' War, that heavily armoured pikemen were vulnerable to musket fire. With mass production the cost of equipping a musketeer fell to £1 19s. 6d. as opposed to £2 7s. 4d. for a heavily armed pikeman.[40]

Civil war infantry soldiers – be they pikemen or musketeers – had to carry as much weight as their modern counterparts, even though they were not as heavily built and did not have the advantage of webbing equipment to spread the load efficiently about their bodies. They lugged 50–60 lb of armour, helmets, swords and knapsacks. Musketeers had to port a cumbersome weapon, which, unlike a modern rifle, could not be slung over the shoulder. In addition, at the start of the war at least, they had to cause their other hand to tote the musket rest, which on the march they often employed as a walking stick, moving it in a circular movement in front of them, a little like an eighteenth-century dandy. But unlike a dandy around a musketeer's neck hung a bandoleer of gunpowder charges. These rattled in the wind, got entangled with the rest of his equipment, and threatened to turn him into a live Roman candle if burning match cord or powder flash from other weapons set them alight.

Since match cord burnt fairly quickly, and was in short supply, musketeers only lit it immediately before battle, or when troops expected action. This limited their ability to respond to a surprise attack, while the glowing cord made them highly visible targets at night. For this reason Colonel Reinking ordered his men to have no more than two burning matches per company as they marched through the night of 20–21 February 1646 to capture Shrewsbury. It took 15 minutes for the light to be distributed amongst all the musketeers before they were ready to attack.[41]

While a musket ball could kill up to 400 yards, its effective range was the far shorter one at which the whites of the enemy's eyes could readily be seen. In theory muskets fired a 1.25 oz. ball, but when lead was scarce this was reduced to 1.12 oz., which meant that the smaller ball was liable to roll out of the barrel in the heat of combat. Muskets had a massive kick, and tended to fire high, especially in the hands of raw troops. A thankful Captain John Hodgson scornfully described coming under fire from raw Scots levies in the Preston campaign of 1648: 'they shot at the skies'.[42] The musket was an unreliable weapon. As the battle got hotter (or the weather wetter) the rate of misfires increased from 12 per cent to 18 per cent. All too often muskets went off by accident, killing one's own side.[43]

One major problem was the weapon's firing mechanism, a piece of burning cord held in a metal fork. Pulling the trigger moved it forward, igniting the powder in a flash pan, which through a blow hole set off the coarser grained powder inside the barrel. Attempts were made to overcome this problem by using a wheel-lock, in which a trigger released a wound spring that used a flint and metal to shower sparks at the flash pan. This system was so expensive that it was confined to officers' pistols, cavalry carbines, and a few elite troopers known as firelocks. 'I was forced to trust to my sword for the keeping down of the enemy', wrote Edmund Ludlow, after he had to fight his way out of a roundhead attack during the Siege of Wardour, 'My pistols being wheelocks and wound up all night, I could not get to fire.'[44]

As the proportion of musketeers – and thus the chances of being hit by a bullet – increased, troops tended to discard their armour. In his *Treatise of Modern War* (1640), John Cruso noted that most soldiers were reluctant to wear armour, which was not just uncomfortably heavy, but which they regarded as a sign of cowardice. He urged officers to stop this bad habit.

While body armour would protect against sword and pike cuts (which anyway were rarely fatal), its flat surfaces could not stop the standard musket ball from entering, frequently with lethal results. A full suit of armour, worn by cuirassiers, was expensive, costing £4 or £5. Worse still, heavy armour greatly hampered one's mobility in combat. After their first experience in battle most of Colonel Hutchinson's regiment discarded their armour. Edmund Ludlow wore a full suit at Edgehill, but on being dismounted found it so hard to regain his horse that for the rest of the war he only wore the helmet. The curved sides of steel helmets deflected pistol and musket balls, as well as pike and sword thrusts, from the body's most vulnerable parts. During bitter house-to-house fighting in Bristol in 1643 a bullet hit Colonel Moyle's helmet, richocheting off to wound his captain (not fatally) in the arm.[45]

Knowing all too well that if the Almighty willed, nothing could save a soldier from the holocaust of the coming campaign season, Randolph Crewe wrote, 'I moan and groan to think of it. God for his mercies sake look upon our miseries!' 'Now the armies march, and both sides prepare to undo the kingdom and be undone', bewailed Sir Thomas Roe. 'I wish myself in the Indies,' continued the veteran diplomat, who had served as British Ambassador to the Mogul Emperor, 'anywhere out of the noise.' All over the land captains raised men. 'The drums are gathering recruits in every corner of the city', reported the Venetian secretary. On both sides moderates realized that time for a negotiated peace was running out. *The Weekly Accompt* for 29 February 1644 compared the peace talks to the glories of the spring flowers. Yet like those flowers, hopes for peace will 'fade away so soon . . . . Since our more obstinate sins have condemned us to more winters of affliction, and the horror of a preserving war.'[46]

Many soldiers were reluctant to leave their home bases, because this would render their families and estates vulnerable to attack. Of the Lancashire gentry 71 out of 178 royalists (40 per cent) and 14 of 84 parliamentarians (17 per cent), never fought outside the county.[47] Troops from East Anglia, Yorkshire and Cornwall were similarly loath to quit their counties, although when persuaded to do so fought with outstanding courage. Such parochialism infuriated their commanders. Joseph Jane was livid when his Cornish royalists mutinied – twice – as he tried to march them to Devon. 'Nothing is more repugnant to the opinion and sense of this house, and dangerous to the kingdom', declared the Commons, 'than the unwillingess of their forces to march out of their several counties.'[48]

Troops often marched out to the applause of friends and neighbours. Such might help explain the fighting spirit of London's Trained Bands. As they strode forth to stop the cavaliers at Turnham Green in November 1642, cheering citizens plied them with food and drink. In addition to the victuals and plaudits, the troops who set off to relieve Gloucester the following year had poets wish them Godspeed.[49]

> Their Only sons the frantic women send
> Earnest, as if in Labour for their end
> The wives (what! that alas), the maidens too,
> The Maids themselves bid their own dear ones go.

Such euphoria (which Abraham Cowley satirized), lasted little beyond the suburbs. Poor roads, bad weather and heavy loads made marching an ordeal. In theory crack troops led the column, as outriders protected its flanks. These dangerous and arduous duties were rotated among units. Since companies were supposed to march with a 100-pace gap between them, and the distance between pikemen was 6 paces, the line of column quickly became strung out. Because pikemen, at least, did not march very close to each other they failed to get much of that sense of moving as a whole in a rhythm that helps the desperately tired and weighed-down infantryman to put one foot in front of the other.

Music was used to maintain morale and keep weary men moving. By the start of the civil war bagpipes had fallen out of favour in England. Fifes and drums replaced them, making their first recorded appearance in 1638 at the Honourable Artillery Company's production of *Mars and His Triumph* at the Merchant Taylors' Hall. Even though bandsmen were paid less than private soldiers – and did not, as today, act as stretcher bearers – their music was welcome. They dedicated some of the more popular tunes to leading generals such as Rupert, Montrose and Monck.[50]

Soldiers marched in tertia of about two thousand men commanded by a general officer. The horse tended to lead, followed by the foot, and then the headquarters section, followed by the general's bodyguard. After them came a column of foot, followed by the baggage train, who were protected on either side by troops armed with wheel-locks, the smoking matches of standard-issue muskets being too dangerous with all that powder around. Two hours before the morning rendezvous, reveille sounded for soldiers to fall in. They kept their places until the evening, when on falling out they would be shown to the houses and barns which the quartermaster's staff, sent on ahead, had selected as their billets. Soldiers spent the evening foraging, cooking, and repairing equipment.

Since only field rank officers were provided with tents, rather than sleep out in the open, the rank and file preferred the hospitality of someone else's home. All too often they demanded the finest from their reluctant hosts. In September 1644 a Somersetshire yokel offered a royalist quartermaster (who, being responsible for selecting billets, had presumably chosen the nicest for himself) some boiled meat and broth. The cavalier shouted, 'You old rogue, do you give us hog's wash? We will have roast beef!'[51]

The lack of tents added to sickness, especially in sparsely populated areas where there was little accommodation to be requisitioned. Sir James Turner thought the weather in Ulster in May 1642 was as bad if not worse than anything he had ever encountered on the continent during the Thirty Years' War. Without tents Cromwell's army which invaded Scotland in 1650 lost four and a half thousand men to sickness.[52]

In practice few armies moved as cohesive formations, but as gaggles of men, wagons and followers, who straggled from one designated rendezvous area to another.

Behind the soldiers came the baggage train, preferably drawn by horses, sometimes by oxen. In addition to pulling supplies needed for the fighting men, these animals had to haul their own food. One ox could drag the equivalent of what it would eat in eight days. Carters looked after the needs of beasts. Hordes of camp-followers looked after those of the men, which puritans thought could also be pretty beastly. 'They carried along with them many strumpets, which they termed "Leaguer Ladies". These they made use of in places where they lay in a very uncivil and unbecoming way', wrote one roundhead of Rupert's marching columns.[53] In fact most of the womenfolk were wives, or had a long-term relationship with a man, for whom they cooked, acting as nurses after a battle or during sickness. The number of camp-followers and the piles of baggage that officers took on campaign 'groweth in the twinkling of an eye' warned John Cruso, who advised generals to control this abuse.[54]

Roads were appallingly bad. Before the war it was reported that all the roads in Feckenham, Worcestershire 'are in a very great decay, and very dangerous for the King's liege people and cattle to pass over'. The Vicar of Alvechurch felt that the roads in his parish were so hazardous that it was not worth risking them to collect tithes.[55] The war, with its incessant movements and lack of money for maintenance, made roads even worse. Frequently troops cut across fields rather than march on what was supposed to be a highway.

Bridges were of crucial importance, for few armies had ferryng equipment or portable bridges, which, anyway, were hard to transport. Even the narrowest river crossings could be tactically crucial. Upton Bridge, on the road between Worcester and Gloucester, saw as much skirmishing as any place in the land. Close by there was fighting to control bridges at Twyford, Evesham, Pershore and Tewkesbury. The wars' first and last battles, Powick Bridge in September 1642, and Worcester, nine years later, were fought to control bridges.

Shortages of maps made marching all the more difficult. Whenever possible commanders employed local guides, ideally their own soldiers, who could be trusted to show them the best route and not lead them into an ambush. Locals were usually willing to tell troops of the same nationality the way when asked. Scots were sullen if requested directions by invading English forces (and vice versa), while in Ireland the locals soon learned that the English were as liable to hang them as solicit the way. So they took to their heels. In 1644 Wenceslaus Hollar published *The Kingdom of England and Principality of Wales exactly described . . . in six maps . . . portable for everyman's pocket*. Drawn at 5 miles to the inch (a fifth of the modern military norm) they showed only the main roads, had no information on fords and little on bridges. With pictures of hills rather than contour lines, these maps were of limited value, but being pocket-sized, and selling at 2 to 3 shillings, officers could buy them for active service.

Men often got lost. 'On Sunday morning, intending to march back to Stow,' wrote Richard Coe in his diary, 'we lost our way, and went backward and forward within a mile of where we lay before.' The movements of its own soldiers became so confused that in exasperation the Stafford Committee declared that they were traipsing all over the place like 'ducks in a pond'.[56] From the king's headquarters in October 1642 William Smith complained that even though they were under marching orders he had not the foggiest idea of when and where they were going.[57]

On the march, however, many troops were fascinated by what they saw. Having spent most of their lives within a few parishes of where they had been born, the war exposed hundreds of thousands of people to other parts of the British Isles. In their letters and diaries soldiers recorded the novel sights with the enthusiasm of modern tourists. 'You should have seen the Londoners run to see what manner of things cows were', Robert Harley wrote to his brother about the City's Trained Bands. 'We marched through Rutlandshire,' noted one trooper, 'a pleasant little county.' On his way to the First Bishops' War John Aston recorded details about church architecture, and that the further north he went 'the price of drink increases'. He was most fascinated to see the Highlanders dressed in their 'fastastique habits'.[58] The diary of Richard Symmonds, a captain in the king's army, reads a little like a travelogue. He wrote down practically every architectural and heraldic detail of the churches he marched past. Some places he hated, calling Crediton, Devon, 'a great lousy town': others he found fascinating, taking time during the Lostwithiel campaign to record words in the Cornish language.[59]

During the civil wars the weather in the British Isles was even worse than usual. Time and time again people complained about the seemingly incessant cold and wet. 'The severe weather', reported the Venetian Secretary (always desperate for the sunny climes of home) 'is worse than usual.' 'God alter the weather, and amend our lives', agreed Sir Humphrey Mildmay. 'We were quartered under a hedge for 3 to 4 hours, it rained extremely as it had done for the most part since our advance', noted Captain Coe. Rarely did combatants complain that it was too hot and dry. During the Battle of Langport, on 10 July 1645, Richard Baxter recorded that the dust greatly reduced visibility.[60]

Apart from making life difficult, weather might affect the outcome of a military operation. A sudden icy rainstorm turned back an assault by Waller's men against Basing House in November 1643. The cold and rain hindered parliament's efforts to take Bristol in early May 1645. It was hard carrying equipment through the mud; many horses died of the cold. When the weather improved, 'our soldiers, being refreshed by the warm beams of the sun, were impatient of falling in', capturing the city on the 12th.[61] Occasionally the cold could be a help. A severe frost that hardened the ruts in the road enabled Sir Ralph Hopton to move his troops so quickly to Arundel in 1644 that the defenders were caught unprepared. They surrendered within three days.[62] Incessant rain flooded the mines during the sieges of York and Gloucester, and contributed to the king's failure to capture the latter, which was a turning point in the war. Afterwards the rains severely affected his dispirited soldiers. 'When we drew off it proved to be the most miserable, tempestuous rainy weather, that few or none could take little or no rest', recalled Captain John Gwynne, 'and the creasing winds the next morning soon dried up our thorough wet clothes we lay pickled in all night.'[63]

Gwynne went on to describe how the retreat so exhausted some 'Kentish men, and newly raised' that they were captured in their sleep. 'We were like to drop every step we made for want of sleep, yet not withstanding we marched on still.'[64] Soldiers are invariably tired. In an *Enchiridion of Fortification* (1645, S573), Nicholas Stone called a good night's rest 'the whetstone' of military success. Lack of sleep can add to combat fatigue, destroying morale: on the other hand it numbs men from the horrors they must endure. Richard Atkyns described the nightmare of fatigue he suffered in July 1643 during the royalist retreat from Devizes to Oxford:[65]

> My horse had cast two shoes and I was forced to stay behind to set them at Lambourn, when leaning on a post I was so sleepy that I fell down like a log of wood, and could not be awakened for half an hour. 'Twas impossible to overtake them [the rest of his unit], so I went to Farringdon, being not able to reach Oxford that night. I fell off my horse twice upon the Downs, before I came to Farringdon, where I reeled upon my horse so extremely that the people took me as to be dead drunk. When I came to my house . . . I . . . desired my wife's aunt to provide a bed for me. The good woman took me to be drunk too, and provided a bed for me presently, where I slept for at least fourteen hours together without waking.

In his description of the ghastly retreat from Gloucester, Richard Gwynne displayed the weapon that soldiers invariably use to help them through such ordeals – a sardonic, usually self-mocking sense of humour. After reporting how the cold wind dried out the sodden clothes in which they had tried to sleep the previous night, he added that this was the best bath they had enjoyed since coming out of the trenches. In much the same wry fashion, Captain William Smith described the winter rains of West Wales as 'no invitation for a soldier to be in the fields'.[66] In June 1643 a parliamentary soldier derisively wrote about their stalled attack on Reading, 'In general our condition is not so good as our friends would have it, nor neither so ill as our enemies report it.'[67] During a march near Bridgnorth, Lord Capel, who was a member of the king's Lifeguard, turned down an offer to sleep in a feather bed in a requisitioned house, so as to spend the night in a barn sharing the straw with a hundred other troops. The next morning, the dishevelled peer met the king.

'My Lord, how did you like your bed last night?'

'Very well,' replied Capel, who was over 6 feet tall, 'for since I came with Your Majesty from York, I never before met with a bed large enough for me.'[68]

By permitting soldiers to mock the antics of the other side, laughter could also raise morale – as Lord Capel was to discover to his cost. In May 1643 at the head of fifteen hundred troops he approached Nantwich, Cheshire, which he bombarded. The enemy replied with musket fire killing several of his men. The following day, Capel's troops advanced towards the city's defences, but after killing a calf, and nothing else, withdrew. A wag recorded their heroism:[69]

> Lord Capel with a thousand and a half,
> Came to Barton's Cross and there killed calf.
> And staying there until the break of day,
> They took their heels and fast they ran way.

Laughter is an excellent way to control fear. Jeremy Taylor told the story of the trooper who panicked during a night attack and tried to harness a comrade instead of his horse. After leading his men on a sally out of Pembroke in April 1644 Sir Henry Stephen came across a herd of bullocks in the dark. Panic-stricken they all ran back to the Castle shouting 'God's Wounds! The roundhead dogs were coming.'[70] During the Siege of Devizes a message arrow struck the ground just in front of Sir Jacob Astley, slicing past his genitalia. 'You rogues,' he quipped, pulling it out of the earth, 'you missed your aim.'[71] To amuse and reassure raw recruits Sir James Turner often recounted how during the Thirty Years' War his old regiment, with the colonel zealously in the van, retreated in good order, without the loss of a single man, even though 'there was not as much as a foot boy pursuing them'.[72]

Some snafus ended humorously. One night in early 1643 a company of a hundred recruits under Captain Wathen were marching toward Monmouth. They were tired, having nearly finished climbing a mile-long hill, when from the other said they heard the jingle of harnesses. Just as they were about to run away in abject terror, over the hill came a party of charcoal burners and their pack animals. Relieved, the soldiers collapsed in hysterical laughter.[73]

All too often such encounters turned out less felicitously. When Captain Mollineux and his troopers came across some strangers near Bedminster 'they rode up to them and asked them who they were for. They swore, God dam them, for the king, and shot at us.' The parliamentarians returned fire with their pistols, and eventually captured Sir Bernard Ashely, who died a few days later from his wounds.

Such chance encounters could be quite terrifying, and needed a cool head to survive. At eight in the evening of 30 October 1644, Quartermaster Roe was riding in the moonlight with his CO, Colonel Birch, from Hungerford to Newbury, when they heard men and coaches approaching. 'Whatever you see me do, let the like be done by you', Birch ordered, promptly ducking into a lane. Birch counted ninety-one cavaliers, three carts, one coach and thirty horses pass by. Poor Roe was paralysed, admitting 'I was at the time in too great a fear to do anything.' Birch followed the party until they came across a straggler, about 40 paces behind the rest. Putting his pistol to the fellow's head, the colonel 'bid him hold his peace and turn back . . . or else he was a dead man'.

When the prisoner told Birch that the party consisted of the Earl of Forth's baggage train, as well as his wife, the colonel immediately rode back to report to Lord Manchester. The general was so tired that Birch could not get much sense out of him, so with the promise of the Earl's loot, he raised forty-seven volunteers. They galloped after the royalists and after 16 miles were challenged, 'What rogue is there?' Birch crept up to the sentry and putting his hand around his mouth and his rapier against his side, promised to 'make such a hole in his skin as brought a groan in him'. At this point another royalist soldier came out of the dark (for by now the moon had set), and asked what was happening. Birch's pretence that he was a traveller, innocently going about his business on the king's highway, gave his troop time enough to assemble. The trumpeter sounded the charge, and the cavaliers were soon killed or taken.

The main body of the royalists, plus the baggage train, were still ahead. As dawn broke Birch entered a village that was full of Lord Ruthven's troops. He straightaway ordered an attack, that afterwards he claimed killed forty cavaliers. The Earl of Forth's valuable coach, however, managed to escape. Birch and his men gave hot pursuit. Pell-mell they rode for 4 or 5 miles until they arrived in a village in which a considerable part of the Queen's Regiment were billeted. Recognizing that they were in deep trouble Birch pretended to be the billeting officer for a large and powerful parliamentary force. 'Lay out quarters in this town presently for my Lord Manchester's regiment', he ordered in a voice loud enough for the enemy to hear, 'Quartermaster, in the next village let Sir William Waller's regiment quarter.' Fearing the immediate arrival of two crack units of the New Model Army, to a man the Queen's Regiment spontaneously decided that they had urgent business elsewhere, leaving the Earl's coach behind.[74]

In another similar display of initiative on 25 June 1643 Colonel John Hurry's regiment made a surprise night attack on a troop of roundhead horse and an infantry company, whom they encountered asleep near West Wickham. The enemy were not a cohesive unit but a holding group for stragglers waiting to return to their regiments. This may explain why when caught unawares, they rushed terrified about in the dark, some naked, others without their trousers, shoes or socks. Although only two parliamentarians were killed, and twenty taken prisoner (several of whom promptly escaped in the confusion), a cavalier crowed, "Twas a terribliest thing in the world to have an Enemy fall unto ones quarters by night, and nothing more resembles the last resurrection and judgment than to see so many people rise up together naked.'[75]

An ambush could be traumatic enough to provoke atrocities. On their way to relieve Gloucester some royalist snipers surprised a regiment of the London Trained Bands near Aldermaston. The roundheads charged the enemy, whom they captured, and badly shaken by the explosion of an ammunition cart, smashed in their brains. Later that year in Monmouthshire a patrol of an officer and three privates came across half a dozen cavaliers from the garrison at Raglan. 'Who are you for?' rang the challenge through the night. 'For the King, and devil take the parliament', came the reply, prompting the roundheads to rush the enemy, whom they slew. They also killed another fifteen found sleeping near by. The surviving royalists fled, and finding some comrades, returned to the scene of the ambush, where they found the body of a comrade, which they hung from a tree. Why they committed such an atrocity one cannot say. It could have been that they were trying to placate the villagers, who said the fellow had been a notorious plunderer, or else to placate the fates: without doubt the ambush had scared them almost literally out of their wits.[76]

Only the best troops could survive a surprise onslaught. 'They fell up our rear before we could begin to march', the parliamentarian Luke Lylold wrote home to his wife on 13 June 1644, soon after a skirmish at Lupton Heath, 'They assaulted us a quarter of a mile this side of the leager [overnight camp] with such fury that had not our men behaved themselves very gallantly we would have been utterly defeated.'[77]

Such an attack, which (in a curious anticipation of RAF slang) was called 'a beating up', took place without warning, sometimes at night. Often it was the first experience of combat for soldiers who were not trained to fight in the dark. The royalist Sir Richard Bulstrode remembered how on coming across Colonel Nathaniel Fiennes' troops at Powick Bridge, on 23 September 1642, he lost control of his own horse, which ran into the enemy, pushing them back to the bridge. In the 'hurly I lost my hat', concluded the shaken cavalier. Sir Richard Byron, the royalist Governor of Newark Castle, lost an even more personal piece of adornment when Sir John Gell's troops ambushed his men in November 1644, killing many and driving the rest into a brook where more drowned. Sir John confessed that he 'had such a do to save himself in running' that he left 'his periwig behind him on the ground'.[78]

Humour – making the other side look silly – was one way of overcoming the first shock of war. Another was talking to comrades. Captain

Hodgson recalled that the evening after his company had first seen action, a successful ambush of some royalists at Bradford, 'we spent our time upon the guards on telling what exploits had been done, and blessing God for his deliverance'.[79]

An analysis of diaries shows that during campaigns soldiers and their leaders were exposed to a fairly high level of violence, being constantly on the move.

For instance, between 9 April and 23 November 1644 Charles moved on 92 days, or 40 per cent of the time. On these days he rode 949 miles, the longest he stayed in one place being at Boconnoc, Cornwall, during the Lostwithiel campaign. Between 7 May and 5 November 1645 the king moved an average of 16 miles on 76 occasions (again 40 per cent of the days). In 1644 Charles was involved in three major battles, Lostwithiel, Cropredy and Second Newbury, while in the following year he was at Naseby and Rowton Heath.[80]

Prince Rupert's itinerary was even more arduous. Between 5 September 1642 and 27 September 1645 he moved location 152 times, marched all night on 9 occasions, slept out in the open on 7 nights, and was involved in 11 major battles and 62 skirmishes.[81]

Ordinary soldiers moved nearly as far and as frequently. General William Waller's parliamentary infantry marched on 36 (52 per cent) of the 69 days between 23 May and 31 July 1644, staying no longer than three nights in one place. On 21 (42 per cent) of those nights, during an appallingly wet summer, they slept out in the open without even the cover of tents or bivouacs. 'Our lodging', a soldier wrote home, 'having for several nights been, and still is, on God's cold earth.'[82] During the 1644 Scots' invasion of England, Robert Douglas, a covenanter, marched on 73 days and was involved directly or indirectly in 30 actions – he also heard 35 sermons. Between May and August of the previous year George Hancock, a company clerk in the parliamentary forces, took part in 9 actions, including the capture of York and the Battle of Marston Moor.[83] After Lieutenant Elias Archer left London with the Trained Bands on 16 October 1643 he was constantly on the move, fought in a couple of skirmishes, suffered as many false alarms, watched the hanging of deserters on two separate occasions, and led his men in four very fiercely contested assaults on Basing House. Unlike many of his comrades, Archer survived to come home for Christmas, being 'joyfully received and welcomed of our friends'.[84] 'There did hardly one week pass', Captain Atkyns recalled of his own experiences near Farnham at this time, 'in which there was not a battle or skirmish fought, or a beating up.'[85] Notwithstanding all this activity, armies moved very slowly, the average distance Chaplain Sprigge's regiment covered each day during the Naseby campaign being 8 miles.[86]

Such statistics do not convey the experience of campaigning as effectively as the letters of individuals such as Neremiah Wharton and Henry Foster, both members of the London Trained Bands.

Sergeant Wharton, who had been apprenticed to George Williamham, merchant of St Swithin's Lane, gaily strode out of the capital with his unit, Denzil Holles's regiment, on 16 August 1642.[87] His war started with an orgy of mutiny and plunder, punctuated by Godly sermons from their chaplain, Obadiah Sedgwick. Three days after leaving London they mutinied against their Lieutenant-Colonel, whom Wharton called 'a Goddam blade and doubtless hatched in hell'. Once they had got rid of this officer, the regiment stripped Uxbridge of everything they could find, tearing surplices for handkerchiefs. Afterwards they were most annoyed when they had to discard much of the loot, to carry a full issue of ammunition. Wharton found Buckinghamshire 'the sweetest country that I ever saw'. The troops had a fine old time at Wendover, drinking, and chopping up altar rails for firewood until their company commander, Captain John Francis, forgetting that his musket was loaded, 'shot a maid through the head, and she immediately died'. 'From hence', Wharton wrote back to his old master, 'we marched very sadly.'

By the end of August Wharton was experiencing that toughening all soldiers experience as they approach combat. He heard a sermon from a puritan minister who claimed the cavaliers had plundered him. Day after day he marched, growing ever tired in the cold, getting more alienated from the civilians and their comfortable lives. 'This is a very malignant town', he wrote of Southam, Warwickshire, 'we pillaged the minister.' Receiving intelligence of the approach of an enemy raiding party, the virgin soldiers boasted of eating 'a mess of cavaliers' for supper. In fact during their initiation of fire the Londoners acquitted themselves fairly well, claiming to have killed some fifty of the king's men. Sergeant Foster, who had not been in combat before, but had surely seen the hung, drawn and quartered remains of traitors displayed on pikes about the city of London, registered little feeling towards the enemy dead. Like a battle brutalized old sweat, he complained that the shirt he took from a slain drummer boy 'was very lousy'.

By the start of September the light-hearted mood with which the campaign had begun had evaporated. Describing soldiering as 'my pilgrimage', Wharton related that the troops were up at six every morning for arduous drill parades. Spontaneously he and his mates got rid of the camp-followers by placing them in the pillory, or ducking them in a river. Although Lord Brooke threatened to hang anyone caught plundering, Wharton boasted to his old master that now he ate venison as often as he had eaten beef as an apprentice. Worried by the lack of news from home, the sergeant complained about the want of pay, and that some royalist cavalry had pillaged him of £3 plus his sword. Towards the end of the month, as they moved from Northampton to Worcester, his spirits rose. Chaplain

Sedgwick delivered 'two heavenly sermons', and 'we had a supply of drink, which on the march is very rare and very welcome'. He was developing a clear view of the enemy as well as of his own side. Prince Rupert had already become the bogey man, reportedly having threatened to wash his hands in roundhead blood. The enemy were mutilating corpses, and killing the wounded. 'We are all enraged against them for their barbarousness, and shall show them little mercy.'

Even though at the end of September Wharton wrote 'we shortly expect a pitched battle, which if the cavaliers stand, will be very hot', in fact during the next three weeks things seemed to quieten down a bit. Based in Worcestershire, which he thought 'a pleasant, fruitful and rich county', he especially liked the county seat and its fine cathedral with the tombs of King John and Prince Arthur, Henry VIII's eldest son.

Soon after Wharton wrote his last surviving letter on 7 October 1642, he marched out of Worcester. He may have survived the Battle of Edgehill, where Rupert's horse smashed through Holles's regiment even though one observer maintained 'everyone fought like a lion'.[88] He would have been most fortunate to have survived Brentford unhurt. Here, on 12 November the royalists destroyed the rump of Holles's regiment so thoroughly, killing, capturing or drowning its panic-stricken members as they ran into the Thames, that it was never reformed.

The following year, Henry Foster, a sergeant in the Red Regiment of the London Trained Bands, marched out of the city to relieve Gloucester.[89] At first the troops found campaigning fun. Pretty girls cheered them: old men told them what fine fellows they were. Three days after leaving London the reality of war struck home. At Chalfont St Giles the accidental discharge of a musketeer killed a comrade.[90] The troops seemed subdued, and grateful for the billets they found next day at Cheshunt. 'Our whole regiment was quartered at Mr Cheyney's house', wrote Sergeant Foster, 'where we were well accommodated for beer, having great plenty, two or three hundred of us this night lying in a barn.'

To raise morale Lord General Essex reviewed his men at Bayard's Green, near Banbury, on 1 September. It took the fifteen thousand soldiers an hour to march past 'whereat there was great shouting and triumph', recorded Foster, 'it was a great and godly sight to see the whole army of horse and foot together'.

As Foster gradually realized, soldiers fight less from a sense of being part of a large group, such as an army or even a regiment, and more from loyalty to one's mates. The sergeant, who had almost certainly known his comrades from pre-war days as an apprentice, having spent weekends training with them in the Artillery Yard, expressed this feeling when he described how some stragglers from his regiment – although not his own company – got drunk, and were killed by the enemy. 'They are not much to be pitied', was Foster's conclusion.

111

He was experiencing the hardening, brutalizing process, common amongst soldiers as they move towards battle. A few days later Foster saw his first corpse, that of the Marquis de la Veil, a French mercenary in the king's service. 'I viewed his wounds, he received three shot in the body from us, one in the right pap, another in the shoulder, and a third in the face.'

Soon afterwards the sergeant underwent his own baptism of fire, when a party of cavaliers ambushed his unit in some narrow lanes near Aldermaston. The parliamentary soldiers initially panicked, but taking cover in some hedges, turned the tables and captured several of the enemy whose brains they smashed with musket butts.

The next six days, as the troops slogged on towards Gloucester, were full of hardship. The roads were so steep and muddy that wagons turned over, killing several horses. In the final six days the weather was appalling – continuous rain, unseasonable cold – as the men slept in the open.

Cold, fear, hunger, tiredness – they are all things soldiers experience as they move into battle, which both sap the will and numb the senses for the coming ordeal. Some crack, but most continue, as did Foster, confident that they will survive. 'Such straits and hardships our citizens formerly knew not,' concluded the sergeant, 'Yet the Lord that called us to his work enabled us to undergo such hardness as he brought to us.' What eventually happened to Foster we do not know. He managed to survive the Siege of Gloucester, and fought at the Battle of Newbury. Here he experienced battle, that zenith for which soldiers train and armies campaign: it was, Sergeant Foster recalled, 'somewhat dreadful when bowels and brains flew in our faces'.

6

THE EPITOME OF WAR

The Battlefield is the epitome of war. All else in war, when war is perfectly conducted, exists but to serve the force of the battlefield, and to assure success in the field.

S. L. A. Marshall, *Men against Fire* (1947)

Three centuries before the American historian, General S. L. A. Marshall, called the battlefield 'the epitome of war', another distinguished soldier, Roger Boyle, Earl of Orrery, wrote that 'Battles . . . are the most Glorious and commonly the most important Acts of War, wherein usually the moments to obtain the victory are so few.' In his *Treatise on Modern War* (1640), John Cruso, the best-selling military author, agreed that 'Of all the actions of war the most glorious and most important is to give battle.'[1]

While Edward Luttark may be right that 'Battle is no more characteristic of war than copulation 'is of marriage', nonetheless battles are as decisive in making war as sex is in making love. Although it has been suggested that 'the battles which were fought in the inns and secluded manor houses of England were to prove more decisive in deciding the outcome of the war than were most of the events of the battlefield', in fact it was those great clashes of armies, such as Edgehill, Marston Moor and Naseby – and to a lesser extent sieges such as Gloucester, Lyme and Basing – that ultimately determined the result.[2]

Just as it has recently been argued that the causes of the war were not the long-term, inevitable product of seemingly impersonal forces, so there was no economic inevitability about the results. At times – and at the time – the outcome of the civil wars must have seemed like 'the nearest run thing you ever saw in your life'. Wellington's judgment of Waterloo is apt, because it reminds us that those who take part in a battle are rarely certain of its outcome. Every soldier may be convinced his side will win, and, like Lord Lovat, the D-Day commando leader, tell himself that 'it was easier to believe that the sky would fall in, than any of us might one day be killed.' Yet in fact he can never be certain that the nearest run thing will not end with the ending of his life.[3]

Chance – as every gambler, and far too few historians – recognizes, plays a significant part in human affairs. For instance, when they sailed past Greenwich Palace in 1635 the crew of the inaptly named ship, *The Safety*, forgot to remove a cannon ball before firing a salute to the king. They missed. Had their weapon been pointed in a slightly different angle, smashing King Charles to a pulp, it is hard to envisage a series of civil wars engulfing the British Isles in the middle of the seventeenth century.[4]

As Clausewitz knew 'War is the province of chance. In no human activity is such a margin to be left for this intruder.'[5] Many examples of this axiom can be found for the civil wars: had the royalists followed up their victory at Edgehill, or not paused to sack Brentford in 1642, they could well have captured London, ending the rebellion almost before it had begun; had not Cromwell seized the critical moment at Marston Moor, parliament would have lost the North, the Scots might have gone home, and the Lord Protector would have amounted to little more than a once-promising lieutenant-general; and the following year, had Charles taken the initiative at Naseby by leading his cavalry reserves in one last desperate attack he might have died on the field of battle (not on a scaffold), or else won an honourable peace.

In retrospect the results of battles (like so many other historical events), seem inevitable. Thus looking back with twenty/twenty hindsight over three centuries it is easy for a historian to conclude, say, that the round-heads had to win the Battle of Naseby, because they were better trained, better equipped, had higher morale, outnumbered the king two to one, and believed more intensely in God – who, we all know, has always been on the side of the bigger battalions. Looking back at the battle immediately after it had been won, Oliver Cromwell – who was as close to God as any seventeenth-century Englishman – came to a very different conclusion. He wrote to William Lenthall, the Speaker of the House of Commons, that for the first three hours of fighting the outcome had been 'very doubtful'. Indeed it is the uncertainty of battle which made its outcome so sweet. 'After a doubtful battle,' exulted John Rushworth after Naseby, 'a most glorious victory.'[6]

Battles are decisive events because they are intended to render a decision. Usually they are deliberate occasions in which both sides agree to stand and fight.[7] In most societies battles possess rituals, ranging from the formality of the Tudor Battle of the Spurs to the eighteenth-century meetings, where the officers on one side invited the other to fire first. Indeed, it is possible for battles to become so ritualized, as with the Stone Age tribesmen of New Guinea, that no one gets killed unless by accident.

The purpose of most battles, including those of the British civil wars, was the killing of one's fellow creatures. Much in life is terrible and terrifying – plague, accident, tempests, fire, floods – but these are all acts of God, not of man. While the pain of sickness or an accident can be excruciating and prolonged, the psychological wounds felt by those who have, for instance, been tortured are deeper because fellow creatures deliberately and remorselessly inflicted them. At its worst, battle is somewhat similar. It can be a place almost without mercy, and utterly without pity, when the virtues that humanity cultivates and admires – gentleness, compassion, tolerance, amity – become vices. So great is the chasm between battle and normal human behaviour that William Manchester, who fought as a US Marine in the South Pacific, concluded 'No man in battle is really sane.'[8] Over three hundred years earlier Hugo Grotius, the Dutch theologian, agreed that, 'When arms have been taken up there is no longer any respect for law, divine or human: it is as if in accordance with a general decree, frenzy had been openly let loose for the committing of all crimes.'[9]

While men in battle may behave as if they have lost their sanity, battles themselves are usually fought for rational objectives. For instance, that of Edgehill was to capture London, of Marston Moor to control the North, of Naseby to threaten East Anglia. But battles amount to much more than the taking or preservation of territory, and the killing and wounding of enemy soldiers. Victory is not an end in itself: there are a lot of substitutes for victories that fail to destroy the enemy's will to fight. The king's greatest loss at Naseby was not just the five thousand troopers killed or taken (for he still had ten times as many soldiers serving in dispersed garrisons), but the capture of his private papers. When parliament published them, showing Charles's duplicity, support for the king eroded far faster than on any field of battle.[10]

While all wars are confused events, civil wars are especially chaotic – and those which afflicted the British Isles in the 1640s more than most. Although they started in 1638 with the First Bishops' War, and ended in 1689 with the Glorious Revolution, in a sense at their central hub were the conflicts that took place in England between 1642 and 1646, that are known as the First English Civil War. In all these civil wars it was usually hard to tell one side from the other, for men rarely wore uniforms that defined their army. While in Scotland and Ireland, clan, ethnic or religious memberships might determine sides, in England (with the exception of Catholics fighting for the crown), things were far more complicated. Enemies often spoke the same language, sometimes the same dialect. Men frequently changed sides with a surprising ease that belies the view that the war was fought for clear-cut ideological reasons. Some counties were relatively peaceful: others, such as Nottinghamshire, were scenes of continuous fighting.

There were no battle lines, delineated by red and blue crayon on a talc-map, across which neat symbols representing units moved in orderly array. The main struggle tended to take place in the Midlands, while there were peripheral theatres of operations in the North, Wales, the West, and the Highlands of Scotland. At a local level there could be small but intense fighting between neighbouring forces.

For those who had to navigate through these difficult times the way was far from clear. It was a path that many, if not most, did not want to take, because it might lead to death, defeat or economic ruin. It was a road littered by countless skirmishes, exhausting forced marches, hurried councils of war, hours of boredom and moments of abject terror. And serving as signposts, pointing the way ahead, were a series of decisive battles.

Although there was fighting in Yorkshire in July 1642, the first real confrontation of the first civil war took place at Marshall's Elm, Somersetshire, on 4 August, two and a half weeks before the king's formal declaration of hostilities. Sixty-five cavalry and fifteen dragoons under Sir John Stawell and Henry Lunsford confronted some six hundred rebels under John Pyne. Having posted his dragoons in some chalk pits, Lunsford let the enemy advance to 120 paces before opening fire. After three volleys, which killed several men and shattered what little cohesion the parliamentary forces enjoyed, Stawell recalled that he 'took that opportunity, and with all his horse charged them so sharply that they were quickly broken and routed'. The following month the local forces met again at Babylon Hill in an inconclusive cavalry clash: 'the truth is that in a very short time, all the horse on both sides were in a state of confusion', admitted a royalist commander.[11]

The effects of Marshall's Elm and Babylon Hill were – like those of so many skirmishes – local, being confined to the west of England. That of Powick Bridge, however, was national because it established the reputation of Prince Repert and his royalist cavalry. 'We let them come up very near', reported one of Captain Nathaniel Fiennes's troopers,

> so that their horses' noses almost touched those of our first rank, before our's gave fire, and then their's gave fire, and very well (to my way of thinking with their coolness). But all of a sudden we found all the troops on both sides of us melted away.[12]

Richard Baxter, a parliamentary sympathizer, whose curiosity had prompted him to go and watch the fighting, 'having never seen any part of an army', voiced a frequent psychological reaction to defeat: 'The Sight quickly told me the vanity of armies, and how little Confidence is to be placed in them.'[13]

Although preachers such as Baxter might be so sure that all armies were full of vanity that he rejected Captain Cromwell's invitation to join the troop he was raising, both sides had to put their trust in their forces when they met at Edgehill, Warwickshire, on 23 October 1642. The roundheads and cavaliers were evenly matched: the king had 2,800 cavalry, 10,500 infantry, 1,000 dragoons and 20 cannon; parliament fielded 2,150 horse, 12,000 foot, 720 dragoons, and between 30 to 37 artillery pieces.[14] Initially the royalists had the strongest position having drawn up the bulk of their forces at dawn on Edgehill Ridge. This long treeless escarpment, some 350 feet high, dominated the rolling country to the north-east where the rebel forces were assembling.

Because Lord General Essex refused to budge, the king (whom a short and ineffective roundhead bombardment could well have provoked), ordered his troops to move down the slope. Here they faced the enemy some thousand yards away. On both sides infantry were stationed in the middle, with the cavalry on the flanks, artillery between formations, and the few dragoons posted behind bushes as sharpshooters.

The royalists did not complete their move down the slope until about two in the afternoon, when the gunners opened fire at the massed ranks on the other side. They did comparatively little damage, especially to the roundheads, for the soft ground absorbed many balls. At about three Prince Rupert ordered his cavalry on the right flank to charge. They advanced at the trot for about 200 yards. Trumpeters sounded the gallop. The royalist horse swept through Ramsay's cavalry, hacking and slashing the fleeing enemy for 2 miles until they reached Kineton, where they stopped to plunder the enemy's baggage train. Much the same thing happened on the left flank, where Henry Wilmot's horse broke Balfour and Stapleton's cavalry, chasing them to Kineton, where they also joined in the plunder. By the time Rupert and Wilmot were able to regroup their men and return to Edgehill, it was too late for them to play any further part in the fighting.

With the parliamentary cavalry broken, and his own horse lost to looting, Sir Jacob Astley ordered the king's infantry to advance. They did so, remembered the future James II (who as a young boy watched the battle from the ridge), 'with a slow steady pace, and a daring resolution'. Seeing the ranks move towards them, Charles Essex's infantry brigade broke and ran. Lord Mandeville begged his soldiers to stay and fight, beating some of them with a cudgel, but to no avail. Only 6,400 foot remained to meet the advance of over 10,000 of the king's men.

The battle came to what contemporaries called 'push of pike'. As Clarendon recalled, 'the remaining foot on both sides stood their grounds with great courage'. Although many of the king's soldiers were armed only with cudgels, they remained in their rank, picking up the muskets from the dead and wounded. 'And the execution was great on both sides', reported Clarendon. Yet neither broke and ran. 'The floor being engaged in such warm and close service, it was reasonable to imagine that one side should run and be disordered,' James recalled, 'But it happened otherwise, for each side, as if only by mutual consent retired some paces.' What next occurred was, concluded the prince, 'A thing extraordinary'. Those few musketeers who had not expended their dozen or so rounds of ammunition continued firing in a desultory fashion. A few of the remaining parliamentary infantry broke and ran. But the rest stood. They gazed at one another, and did nothing. Like two punch-drunk pugilists the infantry had fought themselves to exhaustion.

Their burn-out was both physical (most men having been up marching since four or five that morning), as well as psychological. For the overwhelming majority who had taken part in the battle, Edgehill was their first experience of combat.

Edward Benlowes, the poet who later served the king as a captain, wrote:[15]

> Edgehill, with graves looked white
> With blood looked red
> Maz'd at the numbers of the dead.

All did gaze in deep amaze at the man-made disaster that every battle is. Edgehill ended about sunset. During the especially cold night the wounded shrieked in pain or cried out for their maker, or whimpered for their mothers. 'There was a great deal of fear and misery about that field that night', a trooper wrote home to his mother.[16] As the frost took its lethal toll of bodies already in shock from their wounds as well as the trauma of war, a terrible moaning prevailed across that Golgotha: it was a low rumbling sound, almost a deep bass humming that slowly died away into an awful silence. Dumb with horror and mute with relief the living could do nothing. Until the middle of the next day the two sides faced off each other, zombies barely able to move, until the rebels decamped, leaving the king to claim a moral victory from an empty field.

It took the royalists a fortnight to follow up their advantage. They marched towards the capital, stopping on 12 November to brush aside parliamentary forces at Brentford. The sack of the town – mild by continental standards, or even those set later in the war – so terrified Londoners that the following day the Trained Bands came out *en masse* to Turnham Green to protect their city. 'Remember the cause is for God and the defence of yourself and your children,' General Philip Skippon reminded them, 'Pray heartily and fight heartily.' That evening, after much praying and little fighting, both sides withdrew, the royalists having concluded that 'it had been madness' for them to try to take London.[17] Turnham Green was one of the decisive confrontations of the civil war – for it was not bloody enough to be called a battle. Here the king lost his best chance of capturing the capital and seizing the rebel's heartland. Thus both sides returned to their winter depots to rest, and to prepare for the coming campaign season.

118

In 1643 peripheral battles took place in the western theatre at Braddock Down, Stratton, Lansdown and Roundway Down, and in the northern theatre at Adwalton Moor, Winceby and Hull. The central campaign, however, revolved around Prince Rupert's capture of Bristol on 26 July. Inspecting this prize, England's second city, Charles learned that Colonel Sir George Massey, the Governor of Gloucester, 35 miles up the River Severn, was willing to yield the city so long as he salve his honour by doing so personally to his sovereign. When Charles arrived at Gloucester, Massey reneged. Determined to teach him a lesson, the king insisted on capturing the town. Essex responded by mobilizing his forces around London post-haste to relieve the key point which controlled the River Severn and access to South Wales.

Unable to take the city, Charles raised the siege on 5 September and pursued Essex back to London. Having slowed the parliamentary withdrawal at Aldbourne Chase on 18 September, the royalists managed to block their retreat at Newbury, some 50 miles west of the capital. The two sides were evenly matched, the king having 8,000 foot and 6,000 horse, and Essex 10,000 foot and 4,000 horse. Because the battle was fought in hedgerow country, the king's superiority in cavalry was not as advantageous as it would have been in open terrain such as at Edgehill. The battle started at seven in the morning, being fought for control of its central feature, Round Hill. It was an incoherent affair in which artillery played an unusually important role. When nightfall ended the fighting, there was no clear-cut winner. Having expended all his powder, his gunners having fired off eighty barrels alone (four times more than at Edgehill), Charles had to withdraw, permitting Essex to retire to the security of London.

During the first two rounds of the war neither side gained a knockout, but the king was the winner on points. So on 25 September 1643 parliament signed the Solemn League and Covenant in which the Scots agreed to enter the war in return for a subsidy of £30,000 a month plus the promise to establish presbyterianism in England and Ireland. As a result the focus of military activity during 1644 shifted away from the centre to the peripheral theatres, such as the North, the West Country and the Highlands.

The invasion of England by some twenty thousand Scots in January 1644 prompted Charles to tell Rupert to capture Newark so as to secure his lines of communication with his Northern Army under the Earl of Newcastle. On 14 June the king sent Rupert with an ambiguous set of orders to relieve York, which he did on the 21st, setting the stage for the war's largest battle.[18]

Some forty-six thousand soldiers met at Marston Moor, 5 miles west of York on 2 July 1644. A participant called the battlefield 'the fairest ground for such use as I have seen in England'. Marston Moor was set

119

in open country, with few natural defensive positions. The troops were drawn up in the usual fashion, with the infantry in the centre and the cavalry on the flanks. Between the two sides a road and a ditch gave cover for a line of royalist musketeers, known as the forlorn hope. Determined to force a confrontation, Rupert arrayed most of his troops by nine in the morning. The combined Scots and Parliamentary Army arrived much later. Indeed by early evening, sure that the enemy would not be ready until the next day, the prince withdrew for a meal, and Newcastle retired to his coach for a smoke. 'About half an hour after seven o'clock,' recalled Lion Watson, the parliamentary scoutmaster,

> we seeing the enemy would not charge, we resolved by the grace of God, to charge them, and so the sign being given we marched down to the charge. In which you would call the bravest sight in the world: two such disciplined armies marching to the charge. We came down the hill in the greatest order, and with the greatest resolution that was ever seen.[19]

After the allied army moved forward across the road, winkling the forlorn hope from their ditch, in three sectors events took place virtually at the same time and independent of each other.

On the west flank Cromwell's horse clashed with Rupert's. At first it seemed as if the prince had an advantage, particularly after Cromwell had to withdraw to have a superficial neck wound dressed. When General Leslie's Scots charged on their wiry little ponies, the balance swung towards the allies. Cromwell was able to rout Rupert's cavalry and (most important), by retaining control of his own troopers, regrouped so as to return to continue fighting.

Meanwhile on the eastern flank things were not going so well for the allies. Sir Thomas Fairfax's troops found the ditch before the enemy's position a serious obstacle. Although some four hundred of them managed to cross it, they could not break the enemy in hand-to-hand fighting that lasted for almost an hour. Instead George Goring used his reserves to rout the allies, who ran in panic and confusion.

All this time the main battle was taking place between the ranks of infantry in the centre. It was a chaotic, bloody shoving match. As General Crawford's English foot managed to gain the upper hand, Newcastle's infantry, aided by Sir William Blakeston's, managed to drive a wedge through the middle of the allied line. The battle hung in the balance. Suddenly, as night was about to fall, Cromwell's regrouped cavalry attacked the king's infantry in the rear. Many panicked: a few surrendered. For an hour or two in the moonlight three thousand of the Whitecoat Regiment fought on stubbornly, refusing quarter.

Marston Moor was, as Cromwell exalted, 'an absolute victory obtained by the Lord's blessing'. Some 1,500 allied soldiers had perished, as had

3,000 – perhaps as many as 4,000 – of the king's men. Except for the Whitecoats, the majority of those who fell were hacked to pieces as they broke and tried to escape from the field.

But a win in the West made up for a loss in the North.

On 29 March 1644 General Sir William Waller's army of 10,000 men had beaten Lord Forth and Hopton's 6,000 troops at Cheriton. Greatly encouraged by parliament's first real victory, Essex marched his field army from London towards Abingdon, which he captured on 26 May, threatening the king's main depot at Oxford. With only two weeks' food left, Charles withdrew his troops from Oxford west to Worceter. The roundheads followed in hot pursuit. Essex and Waller soon quarrelled and parted company. The former went to the West Country to fight Prince Maurice, Rupert's brother: the latter pursued the king, who had advanced on Buckingham, thus threatening the parliamentary heartland of East Anglia.

At this point Charles lost his nerve. Turning back, he brushed against Waller's army at Cropredy Bridge on 29 June, as they were marching almost parallel on either side of the River Cherwell. Militarily the battle was inconclusive: psychologically Waller's army was broken, allowing the king to pursue Essex's troops.

The Lostwithiel campaign of 1644 was Charles's most brilliant military achievement. Perhaps Cropredy had endowed him with enough self-confidence to eschew his habit of accepting the advice of the person who had last given it. Anyway, skilfully he co-ordinated his forces on a wide front, where thick hedges and sunken roads (similar to those that bogged the allies down in Normandy in 1944) rendered communications extremely difficult. Charles drove Essex's forces back through Devon and Cornwall. Taking Lostwithiel on 21 August, he trapped the enemy in the peninsula on the west bank of the River Fowey. The capture of Castle Dore on the 31st convinced Essex that he was beaten. It was, he admitted, 'the greatest blow we ever suffered'. That night, as his cavalry under Sir William Balfour slipped through the royalist lines, the lord general escaped on a fishing boat, leaving Sir Philip Skippon to negotiate a surrender.

Skippon managed to snatch survival out of the jaws of defeat. Charles lost his nerve, allowing the roundheads to lay down their arms and march away to fight again. They recovered with amazing speed, forcing the king to chase them back to London. Once again their paths crossed at Newbury.

Because parliament had combined its forces, they outnumbered the king's, 19,000 to 12,000. Manchester's roundheads blocked the king's advance on London, as Waller's men, having made a 15-mile flanking movement around the enemy, attacked their left flank on 27 October. The two forces failed to co-ordinate their assaults, and Cromwell, for some unexplained reason, did not charge with his usual *élan*. So that evening, after sunset ended the fighting, Charles extricated himself from a dangerous situation by a night march through a 1,500-yard gap in the enemy's lines. He reached the safety of Oxford on 1 November.

As royalists' fortunes fell south of the border they rose to the north largely due to the genius of one man. James Graham was a truly romantic paladin, whom Thomas Carlyle called 'The Hero-Cavalier'.[20] The scion of one of Scotland's leading families, Montrose had initially supported the covenant. By 1643 he was so disillusioned with the ambitions of the kirk that he sent the king an offer to raise the Highlands which Charles accepted after the covenanters invaded England. Montrose's first rising was a fiasco: he was lucky to escape to England with his life. In August 1644, in disguise, with a couple of companions and a silk royal standard hidden around his waist, he returned to the Highlands. This time he was far more successful. Clansmen flocked to the king's colour, and the following February at Inverlocky they destroyed the Campbells. In May, Montrose routed a covenanting army led by Colonel Hurry at Auldearn, while in July and August he defeated General William Baillie at Alford and Kilsyth.

Outnumbered and out-trained, the comet from the north could not lighten the royal sky for ever. Montrose's brilliant campaign ended on 19 September 1645 when the main covenanting army, which had returned from England, under General David Leslie, surprised and defeated his forces at Philiphaugh, putting the survivors to the sword.

Montrose was a born leader of men: energetic, an outstanding guerrilla, he inveigled the enemy into adverse terrain. Two-thirds of his men were veterans, either of the Ulster campaign of 1641–2 or the Thirty Years' War. Fighting in all weathers, they set the Highlands ablaze. The flames warmed the king's hopes, becoming, Charles declared 'one of the most essential parts in my affairs'. Sir John Trelawny, the Cornish royalist agreed, gloating, 'In Scotland the Lord Montrose hath lately well banged the rebels.'[21]

In essence Montrose's campaign was less a struggle between covenanting Lowlanders and free-spirited Highlanders, than it was a clan feud between the Earl of Argyll's Campbells, and the MacDonalds, many of whom were Ulstermen led by the Earl of Antrim.

This made war in Scotland far bloodier than it was south of the border. After routing the covenanters outside Perth, Montrose's men boasted that they could walk the 3 miles back to the town using the enemy dead as stepping stones without once touching the earth. An eyewitness of their plunder of Nairn 'saw no man in the street but was stripped naked to the skin'.[22] After accepting the surrender of some Campbells commanded by Zachary Malcolm at Lagganmore in Glen Euchar, the royalists locked them and their women in a barn and set it alight, roasting all but two alive. No wonder at Auldearn the covenanters stood their ground: unfortunately they did so on a bog and thus lost half their men. After the Battle of Inverlocky where casualties were just as high, the poet Ian Lom MacDonald surveyed the corpse-strewed field, and the loch bloody with floating carcasses:

> You remember the place called Tawney Field?
> It got a fine dose of manure
> Not the dung of sheep or goats,
> But Campbell blood well congealed.

Long-standing clan hatreds had deprived the bard of all pity:

> To Hell with you, if I cared for your plight
> As I listen to your children's distress
> Lamenting the band that went into battle
> The howling of the women of Argyll.

Alasdair MacColla, Montrose's second-in-command, was just as callous: jubilant at the slaughter of sixteen Campbell lairds, he lamented that their pregnant wives had been spared.[23]

Both sides committed atrocities north of the border. In 1645 the covenanters butchered a hundred of the garrison of Asiog Castle, Ayrshire, who surrendered on promise of quarter, saving the thirty-six officers to be hung at leisure later. A couple of years afterwards General Leslie meted out a similar fate on the defenders of Dunaverty Castle.[24]

The civil war in the Highlands was also a religious struggle. At Tibbermore the covenanters' battle-cry was 'Jesus and no Quarter!' Losing, they received what they offered.

Apart from prolonging the war, and being one of those straws to which Charles was all too inclined to clutch, the Highland campaign did not affect its outcome. That was determined by what Charles called 'the battle of all for all', the climax of the 1645 campaign which would be, he told the queen, 'the hottest for war of any that has been yet'.[25]

The mother of all battles occurred nearly five months later on 14 June at Naseby, about 18 miles south of Leicester. Soon after leaving Oxford on 7 May, Charles divided his forces, sending 3,000 under Lord George Goring to the West Country, retaining the remaining 8,000. To keep open communications with Ireland, he moved north to relieve Chester, which Sir William Brereton was besieging. On hearing that the Siege of Chester had been raised, and in order to thwart Fairfax who had just encircled Oxford, as well as to threaten East Anglia, Charles shifted east, capturing Leicester. This reverse forced Fairfax to leave Oxford and link up with Cromwell, to confront the royal army.

The New Model Army they led was a formidable force. After the passage of the Self-Denying Ordinance in April, its officers had been chosen for proven professional abilities rather than pedigrees of nobility or gentility, while its men, especially the horse troopers, were well trained, superbly led and highly motivated.

Forewarned, Charles was not forearmed. He was out hunting when he learned of the New Model's approach. Although outnumbered 7,500 to 13,600, the king had little choice but to stand and fight on a gentle ridge about a mile north of the village of Naseby, astride the modern road to Sibbertoft. The sun burnt off the morning mists by about nine to reveal both sides drawn up in the traditional formation, with infantry in the centre and cavalry on the flanks. Since the roundheads were in dead ground south of Broad Moor, at about ten or eleven (the accounts vary) the royalists moved forward. Soon the horse got too far ahead of the foot and had to wait for them to catch up, as the parliamentary troops, screened by a forlorn hope of musket men, moved over the rise, so they could look slightly downhill at the advancing foe.

Coming under fire from Colonel John Okey's dragoons on their right flank, Rupert's horse charged and broke Henry Ireton's cavalry. Once again the stag-hunting squires tally-hoed too fast and much too far. They did not stop until they reached the enemy baggage train a little to the north-west of Naseby, which they spent the rest of the battle plundering. On the left flank Cromwell advanced his cavalry at a steady pace, so as not to lose control of them on the difficult muddy ground. For about an hour they fought hand-to-hand with Sir Marmaduke Langdale's Northern Horse. Sensing that his cavalry was about to break, the first of the fear-stricken men having already galloped past him, the king wanted to lead his reserves into the affray. The war, however, was not to have a Holly-wood ending, with Charles and Cromwell fighting it out hand-to-hand. Grabbing his sovereign's bridle the Earl of Carnwath shouted, 'will you go unto your death?' The gesture, plus a nebulous order, panicked the reserves who rode hell for leather back to Leicester, leaving the infantry to their fate.[26]

All this time the foot had been slugging it out in the centre. At first it seemed as if the more experienced royalists, who included the king's superb Welsh infantry, would prevail over the larger numbers of the New Model Army. But after an hour, when Fairfax sent in his own fresh regiment of foot, and Cromwell's horse and Okey's dragoons attacked, the king's infantry disintegrated so precipitously that most of them were taken prisoner.

For parliament Naseby was a famous victory: five hundred enemy dead, ten times as many taken, three hundred wagon-loads of booty worth £100,000, plus – the gem of them all – the king's private correspondence. Admittedly the war dragged on for nearly another year. In July Goring lost the West at Langport. In September Rupert surrendered Bristol and at Rowton Heath Langdale lost Chester, the main entrepôt to Ireland. Not until the following May did the king leave Oxford, to wander around aimlessly in disguise for days, before giving himself up to the Scots and ordering his remaining garrisons to surrender. Yet after Naseby everything else was a mopping up. Clarendon was right to call it 'a battle for a crown'.[27]

While, of course, no battle is the same, and no man's experience in that battle similar to another's, the battles of the first civil war – particularly the three decisive ones of Edgehill, Marston Moor and Naseby – had enough in common to enable us to try to see what they were like.

Because battles were usually deliberate events, mutually agreed upon, troops often knew that they were about to take place. 'Both Armies meet tomorrow, and goeth on some design', Luke Lloyd wrote to his wife before Marston Moor. On the eve of Cropredy Bridge, William Waller thought that 'This day in all likelihood will prove a deciding day.'[28] Rarely did a major engagement come as a total surprise. Captain Nathaniel Fiennes was the exception when he confessed that he and his troop rode to Edgehill 'little dreaming of a battle the next day'.[29]

Most participants not only expected to fight, but looked forward to doing so, sure that they would win. Take, for instance, the royalist morale before Naseby, a battle where they were outnumbered. 'My affairs were never in so fair or hopeful a way', the king told the queen. 'Never had the king so good men', added Sir George Digby. 'This Day is yours great CHARLES! And in this War/Your Fate and Ours Victorious are', chipped in a poet, while an astrologer assured His Majesty's forces of victory.[30]

On the other side, Simeon Ashe, chaplain to the Earl of Manchester's regiment, described what went on in the minds of his troops as they approached Marston Moor. On hearing that the royalists had captured York 'truly many of our hearts were oppressed with heaviness', for the roundheads interpreted the reverse as a sign of God's displeasure. Three days later, when it seemed that He would at last allow them to fight, morale soared, only to be dashed on the morrow, 4 July, when it appeared that Prince Rupert would withdraw his troops back to York. 'Upon this sad and unexpected disappointment, our hearts generally were filled with sorrow, but yet, in the middle of our sadness, many of us did encourage each other unto a hopeful expectation of a comfortable issue.' Such came the next day, when the prospect of battle 'moved our Soldiers to return merrily'.

On being told that they were going to fight at Rowton Heath 'there was great joy in the camp'. As they faced off at Naseby, 'Both sides with mighty shouts expressed a hearty desire of fighting.' Robert Harley, a roundhead captain, told his brother that on the morning of Cheriton, 'I saw such cheerfulness in everyone's countenance that it promised either victory or a willingness rather to die than lose the field.' In sum, most men were happy to march into battle, not because they were desperately keen to kill, and certainly not because they wanted to be killed, but from relief that the waiting was at last over.[31]

Invariably they did so tired, dirty, hungry and dehydrated. Ashe's troops were so thirsty that they had to lap like dogs from muddy puddles at Long Marston, having but 'a penny loaf' in four days. August 5, 1647 was so stifling that at the Battle of Dungon's Hill Captain Gibbs, a roundhead, 'being overheated in the service, died of drinking ditch water'. Before the Battle of Lansdown the parliamentary horse had no food for twenty-four hours, while Henry Fouche's men had to fight at Selby in December 1642 without any for forty-eight.[32] Most men entered battle desperately fatigued: the royalist troops, who started fighting late in the autumn afternoon at Edgehill, had been up and marching long before dawn, the king having cancelled the Sabbath day of rest which he believed they needed badly. A desperately tired Captain Harley apologized for the short and disorganized description of Roundway Down he sent his father, explaining that he had not slept in a bed for twelve nights.

Notwithstanding the notorious British summer, few major battles took place in the rain, perhaps because the reduced visibility and muddy conditions would have made fighting nigh impossible. The heavy ground at Naseby almost prevented Cromwell's cavalry from charging. While campaigners continually complained about the wet and cold which hindered their marches and turned sieges into nightmares, battles took place in better weather. 'It was as fair a day as that season of the year could yield', remembered Clarendon of Edgehill, 'the sun clear, no wind or cloud appearing.'[33]

As men moved closer to a set-piece battle, they became more hemmed in. Discipline tightened. Foraging was less tolerated. Desertion dropped, if only because those who wanted to run away had already done so. Troops were imprisoned, as it were, in a moving box, enclosed by the iron laws of tradition, military justice and self-respect. Not only was this a psychological box, but a physical one, for as they moved closer into battle, soldiers literally closed ranks, to march as units on to the field of battle, where they stood in place, watching, waiting for their fate.

Unlike a modern soldier, who leaps out of a trench, armoured personnel carrier, plane or landing craft straight into combat, the seventeenth-century fighting man usually watched the scene of battle gradually enfold before his eyes. 'When I saw the enemy draw up and march in gallant order towards us', remembered Cromwell of Naseby, 'I could not (riding about my business) but smile to God in praises in assurance of Victory.' Cromwell might smile, because, unlike the rank and file, as an officer he had something to do to steady his nerves.

Those who went into a civil war battle rarely did so with a clearly defined set of objectives. Orders might be discussed in a rudimentary fashion just before battle commenced. At Edgehill, as the troops were deploying down the ridge, the royalist commanders had a bitter argument as to whether they should draw up the army in the Dutch or Swedish formation. A couple of hours before the fighting started at Marston Moor, Prince Rupert showed Lord Eythin a plan he had sketched for the deposition of the king's forces. 'By God Sir,' replied the veteran of the Thirty Years' War, 'it is very fine on the paper, but there is no such thing in the field.'[34]

As the field slowly revealed itself, men naturally turned to God for solace. Roundheads frequently chanted psalms, the religious for comfort, the profane for something to do, and all for the solace and sense of oneness that community singing can bring. Sir Jacob Astley's prayer before Edgehill was short and sweet. 'O Lord! Thou knowest how busy I must be this day. If I forget thee do not forget me.' The roundheads who attacked Reading the following April did so with the verbosity of a revival meeting. 'I could hear nothing but encouraging words from the soldiers one to another, saying "God fights for us", "God will preserve us", "God will make good his promise to us to cover our heads in the day of battle" etc.', recalled an officer in Lord Barclay's regiment.[35]

Chaplains were assiduous in stilling men's fears, and preventing them from running away, as they praised God and passed the ammunition of hope. 'Myself, with other ministers,' recalled Chaplain Ashe, 'did our duty, by prayer and exhortation, to prepare them for the expected battle.' During the Siege of Crowland in April 1643, Mr Stiles, the royalist chaplain, was also in charge of the western bulwark. 'When the bullets flew the thickest', a parliamentary prisoner of war recalled, the Reverend Stiles was constantly 'running from place to place' encouraging his men 'with fearful oaths' which he believed were in keeping with 'the character of a good soldier'.[36] Before Edgehill, wrote a puritan minister, 'I had discharged my duty as far as I was enabled, by passing from regiment to regiment, and troop to troop, to encourage them.' Chaplain Hugh Peters was seen riding 'from rank to rank with a bible in one hand, and a pistol in the other, exhorting men to do their duty'.[37]

Charles did the same by riding up in front of the ranks, wearing a black cloak, lined with crimson, so all his men could see their sovereign. Shouting out battle yells, especially the primordial cries of Highlanders, must have provided some mental relief, as did calling the other side rude names.

What went through men's minds before battle started is hard to say, for they were curiously silent on the subject. Perhaps they thought of wives and lovers, or else their families, homes or mothers. Sometimes – as so often happens during times of great moment – inconsequentials sprang to mind. Sir Gamuel Dudley, the royalist governor of Pontefract, admitted that when he first saw the enemy lined up to attack him he thought of elephants: they were the most dangerous beasts he could envisage.[38]

As troops waited for hours, deathly afraid, they must have left the ranks, or dismounted, to relieve themselves, whilst chivying sergeants urged them to hurry back and repair the gap in their formation. Perhaps the ubiquity of the performance of such bodily functions in the seventeenth century did not make their performance then as distressing as it is for modern soldiers. (It is hard to have a bowel movement, for instance, on a paratroop aircraft or tank.) In addition, unlike modern troops, those who waited to go into action during the civil wars rarely did so under artillery fire. On the other hand, since waiting troops were seldom allowed to lie down, sit, or take cover, they were denied the chance of resting or doing much to ameliorate the dangers they faced. 'You could hear no other word of command than "stand straight in your files"', remembered a survivor of Cheriton.[39] Basically, as men waited under fire for the fighting to begin, maintaining the integrity of a unit's formation was more important than saving the lives of a few and soothing the fears of all.

Lord Saye and Sele described troops drawn up at Marston Moor as 'standing like an Iron Wall, so that they were not easily broken'. The analogy, which was repeated by writers on the American Civil War, is an apt one. In truth by the time battle started most men were in effect locked in an iron box, as unyielding as a modern tank.[40] Pictures of civil war battles always show men in groups: the more junior the man, the larger the group in which he was placed (see plates 4 and 5). Unable to move more than a few feet or influence events, the result of which were fraught with horror and uncertainty, troops must have felt a terrible sense of dependence. Just before they were expected to play the man, they were treated like infants. Only the start of combat could relieve their *angst*. Many a civil war soldier must have had the same experience as did R. H. Tawney, the distinguished historian, who went over the top as a sergeant at the Somme, 'I had not gone ten yards, before I felt a load fall from me.'[41]

The unburdening brought by being at last able to fight can be seen by the other side of the coin – the frustrations engendered by being withdrawn from combat at the last moment. Bulstrode Whitelocke marched with John Hampden's regiment in November 1642 to meet the advancing royalists at Turnham Green. In full view of the enemy they moved forward for about a mile until Sir John Meyrick galloped up with orders to retreat. 'At which point we were exceedingly troubled', Whitelocke recalled. The troops lost confidence in their commanders, whom they were sure a fifth column had subverted.[42]

Had Hampden's regiment gone into the attack they would have done so with cool deliberation and wild yells. Roger Boyle, Lord Orrery, could remember only one action in the whole of the civil wars in which he had not heard men shout their battle-cries – official or otherwise.[43] At the Second Battle of Newbury a royalist wrote that 'they came singing of psalms'. Sir Bevil Grenville told his wife of the steadiness of the royalist attack at Braddock Down. 'I had the van, and so, after some prayers at the head of every division, I led my part away, who followed me with so great courage, both down one hill, and up the other, that it struck great terror in them [i.e. the enemy].' Simeon Ashe described the parliamentary attack at Marston Moor in similar terms: 'Our Army in several parts moving down the Hill, was like unto so many thick clouds . . . the enemy was amazed and daunted.'[44]

A civil war battle was in many respects a process in which united groups of men clashed, and started to break down into smaller and smaller units. This clash could be between similar arms, such as infantry against infantry, or cavalry fighting cavalry, or between different arms, as when horsemen charged men on foot. As the battle progressed and became all the more confused, the vital groups in which men tried to survive became smaller, while their mental and visual horizons shrank. Victory went to the side which destroyed the integrity of its opponents, thus turning a unit into a crowd. And when that took place, the killing of one man by another began in bloody earnest.

Describing the preliminaries to battle during which units took up positions is fairly easy. Making sense of what happens once they advanced into contact is far more difficult. Indeed it is almost impossible, for by this stage the historian is trying 'to make orderly and rational what is essentially chaotic and instinctive'.[45]

The Duke of Wellington realized as much. 'The History of a battle is not unlike the history of a ball!' he wrote after Waterloo, 'Some individuals may recollect all the little events of which the great result is the battle lost or won: but no individual can recollect the order in which, or the exact moment at which they occurred.'[46] Sir Richard Bulstrode came to the same conclusion when he tried to make sense of his own experiences at Edgehill:[47]

> There is always great difference in relations of battles, it is certain that in a battle, the next man can hardly make a true relation of the actions of him that is next to him; for in such a Hurry and smoke of a Set Field, a man takes notice of nothing but what relates to his own safety. So that no man can give a clear account of particular passages.

Sir Henry Foulis almost gave up trying to convey the reality of combat. In *An Exact and True Relation of a Bloody Fight . . . before . . . Selby* (1642), he concluded 'You cannot imagine what hot service it is.' Trying to describe the Battle of Cheriton in a letter to his brother, Robert Harley apologized for 'these scribbled lines' for being 'nothing else but a confused thing patched up by a short memory'.[48]

After the trauma of battle, men's memories become more selective than usual. In their accounts of Marston Moor, Lion Watson, Sir Hugh Cholmley and the Earl of Newcastle all skipped over episodes that their side lost and dwelt upon those which they won.[49] A similar process can be seen in two descriptions of the same event, the attack on Northgate Turnpike Gate at Chester at six in the morning of 27 January 1645. According to a royalist, 'The rebels came with scaling ladders to scale the wall, but they had so hot a breakfast as divers went with bullets for concoction, which hindered their drinking afterwards.' Having managed to place but two of their eight scaling ladders up against the wall, they were driven back, leaving behind two muskets, three swords, and a corselet which the defenders triumphantly put on display at High Cross. Sir William Brereton, the parliamentary commander described the same incident in very different terms: 'Before daybreak we prepared and attempted to storm the outworks of Chester, but we failed to enter: nevertheless we escaped without damage.'[50]

It would be tempting to attribute such selectivity to propaganda, to the cynical manipulation of the truth for partisan ends. But for the many who were guilty of it, such distortion was an innocent process. During the ordeal of combat memory plays more that its usual quota of tricks, because a bias is part of the mental process that makes the unbearable bearable. 'What my memory hath kept I will here present unto you', Captain Robert Harley began a letter to his brother Edward, describing his experiences at Cheriton, a fortnight earlier.[51]

Notwithstanding such warnings about the difficulty of trying to understand the confusion of battle from the accounts of those who survived it, their descriptions are worth quoting at some length if only because they were there.

Captain Richard Atkyns never forgot 5 June 1643, the day he fought for the king at Lansdown:[52]

> The air was so darkened with smoke of powder that for a quarter of an hour together (I dare say), there was no light seen, but what the fire of the volleys gave: and 'twas the greatest storm that I ever saw, in which I thought I knew not wither to go, nor what to do, my horse had two or three musket bullets in him, which made him tremble under me at that rate, and I could hardly with my spurs keep him from lying down, and he did me the service to carry me off to a led horse, and then died.

Pausing not for a moment to show any sympathy to the brave beast which had given its life to save his, Atkyns returned to the battle with another mount, which was immediately wounded in the neck.

The day after Marston Moor, 'W. H.', a Captain in Manchester's army, wrote to a friend:[53]

> Sir, by God's blessing I can tell you that I am alive. . . . Last night
> He showed us what the furies of its [i.e. the Church of God's]
> enemies could do, which was so powerful and performed with so
> much resolution and audacity, noise and terror, that you could not
> have thought that now at last we had moved to Hell's gates. But to
> proceed orderly, (for now I am recollected), having brushed off the
> dust and fury of war and fallen into a calm of gratitude of my
> Protector.

Having gathered his wits, the roundhead captain went on to describe the
clash between the masses of infantry in the centre of the field.

> The two main bodies joining made such a noise with shot and clamour
> of shouts that we lost our ears, and the smoke of power was so thick
> that we saw no light, but what proceeded from the mouth of guns.

Sir Henry Slingsby describes a similar experience as the two infantry
masses came into contact at Naseby.[54]

> The foot on either side hardly saw each other until they were within
> Carbine Shot, and then only made one volley; our's falling in with
> Sword and Butt end of the Musket did notable execution. So much
> I did see their Colours fall, and their Foot in great disorder. And
> had our left wing but at this time done half as well as either the Foot
> or Right Wing, We had got in a few minutes a glorious Victory.

From these graphic descriptions of battle four themes may be discerned:
battle was incredibly chaotic; it was unbelievably terrifying; it progress-
ively limited a man's horizons; and as time passed it increasingly became
a matter of individual survival.

Once joined, battles are intrinsically frenzied events in which those who
can apply the most order often determine the outcome. (Or to put that
in the graphic way used by the author's first platoon sergeant, 'Battles are
won by the side which is least fucked up.')

In modern battles co-ordination is particularly important because even
at the most basic level they are conducted with considerable inter-weapon
and inter-arm co-operation: an infantry squad employs fire and movement
between its parts, and may call in armour, artillery, naval and air support.
In a civil war battle there was a virtual absence of inter-arm co-operation,
except for the company-level dependence between pikemen and musketeers. This was rigidly fixed by their deployment before fighting started,
and hardly ever changed once it had begun.[55]

While the level of command communications during a civil war battle
was extremely limited, that between men was dominated by rumours. For
instance, stories about slain leaders were endemic at Cropredy Bridge.
After describing the incredible hearsay he heard during Edgehill, Captain

Nathaniel Fiennes (who at the time may have believed more of it than he cared afterwards to admit) concluded that it is 'strange that men will give credit to every idle fellow'.[56]

Because battle is inherently both a dangerous and wild activity it is not surprising that men were killed by their own side. At Crewkerne in May 1645 George Goring's cavaliers had a two-hour fire-fight with each other under the impression that they were firing at the enemy. At Northallerton one of Sir Henry Foulis's men was taken prisoner; cut off from his unit, he approached an enemy troop 'thinking they had been his friends'.[57] At Cropredy one of Waller's officers was dismounted and surrounded by the enemy. Taking him for a comrade, a cavalier gave the parliamentarian a fresh horse with the admonition to 'make haste and kill a roundhead'.[58]

Uniforms would have done something to avert such mistakes. At Edgehill the roundheads wore orange scarves, and the cavaliers red ones. At the First Battle of Newbury Essex had his men place greenery plucked from hedges in their hats to be recognized. The royalists tried to trick them by following suit and shouting 'Friends! Friends!' At Marston Moor Sir Thomas Fairfax turned the tables. Cut off from his men, he pulled out the white cloth which the parliamentary soldiers had placed in their hats for identification, to pass as a royalist through the enemy lines. Before they attacked Dundee in 1645 General George Monck ordered his men to let their shirt tails hang out, or tie a white cloth over their behinds, so as better to identify each other (as well as make cowards easier targets if they turned tail).[59]

For most of the war uniforms were a regimental matter. Indeed many regiments, such as the Whitecoats, were named after the colour of their clothes. The redcoat did not become the standard for the British Army until the formation of the New Model in 1645. It remained the uniform for two and a half centuries because of its colour, which camouflaged the blood stains. There is something instrinsically horrible about the sight of blood; observers invariably exaggerate the amount that is shed.

Loud noises were another distressing aspect of battle, especially for seventeenth-century soldiers. Deprived of such technological marvels as jet planes, juggernaut lorries and amplified rock and roll bands, they lived in a far quieter world than we. The sound of cannon or musket fire was disorienting, especially when a comrade in the rank behind fired with the end of his weapon a few inches from one's ear. As the two sides got closer the noise of firing gave way in part to the clash of swords and pikes against each other, the clang of steel hitting armour and helmets, and the exhausted grunts of brawling men, mingled with the screams of the wounded and groans of the dying. Since the wounded were rarely carried to the rear to expire out of sight and mind, and killing took place right before a soldier's eyes, the horrors of war were all too obvious. The ubiquitous white gunpowder smoke drifting in from cannon which continued to fire from the flanks, did nothing to hide the holocaust. To the contrary by reducing visibility it made it easier for men inadvertently to tread on the bodies and in the entrails of the dead and wounded.

Once two sides had joined in the pandemonium of hand-to-hand fighting, the battlefield became pockets of densely crowded groups of milling men, further lessening visibility. Frightened humans tend to bunch; it is part of our herd instinct. While today this is highly undesirable because it presents concentrated targets for machine-gun or artillery fire, then it had advantages. Soldiers could become so pressed together that they could not fall down; the scrum carried the wounded like broken flotsam as it heaved and hacked.[60] Hemmed in by friend and foe, neither cowards, heroes nor the hurt could escape the crowd as it flowed hither and thither (a little like football fans up and down the terraces), threatening all the time to trample them under foot.

Billowing gunpowder smoke, whose acrid sulphuric smell assaulted noses and eyes, did much to reduce men's horizons. As the fighting became more intense, most soldiers' ability to see any distance decreased. Smoke was such a problem that armies would manoeuvre to get up wind of each other. The royalists tried to do so at Marston Moor and Naseby. After parliamentary efforts failed at Rowton Heath, a chaplain consoled himself with the thought that while 'they had the Wind and Sun, we had God with us'.[61] Smoke plays tricks upon the eyes. Sometimes all a man could see was a dirty white bank penetrated by flashes of yellow and red, from which lines of enemy would suddenly emerge, appearing against the billowing background to be much taller and more intimidating.

Smoke was not the only thing to reduce a soldier's radius of visibility. If he were an infantryman he would be drawn up in a file one to two dozen men long, and perhaps as many as six deep. His helmet and weapon (especially a pike) limited his vision by making it hard to turn to see what was going on beside and behind him. Since helmets lacked modern liners, being metal pots worn over a woollen cap, they were extremely uncomfortable during the exertion of combat. They were confining, especially if they had a face guard that made them feel even more claustrophobic.

The spatial reference points a soldier used were rarely topographical features – which explains why it is sometimes hard to say for sure where a battle actually took place.[62]

Instead soldiers defined their place with reference to the colours their units carried to show them where they were and where they should be. Leaders sometimes fulfilled a similar role. Towards the end of the Second Battle of Newbury Sir Charles Lucas threw off his buff coat, which gave protection against sword and pike cuts, so his own regiment (as well as enemy sharpshooters) could see his white shirt in the dusk.

If a soldier's radius of visibility in such a fracas was limited, so too were the threats to his immediate survival. As men swung musket butts, and slashed with their swords, they could only kill or be killed at arm's length.

Close-order combat varied depending on whether it took place between infantry and cavalry, or between similarly armed groups.

For instance, when infantry attacked infantry one line would tend to stand their ground as the other advanced. Each would fire one volley, perhaps two if they had time, before colliding into each other. The impact of these volleys was limited. Assuming a 10–15 per cent chance of a hit at 100 yards (for perhaps as many as a third of the weapons might misfire), an equal number of men on both sides, and a fifty/fifty ratio of musketeers to pikemen, it is hard to envisage more than one man in fifteen on each side being hit.[63] 'We came after our shot was spent to push of pike, and fought very gallantly having no relief from our horse', recalled Lord Belasyse of Edgehill.[64] Sir William Brereton described what it was like at Rowton Heath to stand and receive the enemy, who attacked 'with great resolution and boldness, and in very good order'. Once the two sides had come into contact, recalled the parliamentary commander, 'they fought so long and so fiercely until all their powder and bullet was spent. Afterwards they joined and fell to it pell mell, one upon the other, with the stocks of their muskets.'[65]

This process, which was known as coming 'to push of pike' rarely took place in such a dramatic fashion. It was not as if two large bodies of pikemen, their weapons held out horizontally, cold bloodedly ran into each other, like two monstrous hedgehogs committing mutual *hara-kiri*. For one thing, large bodies of men, roughly equal in number, rarely smash into one another. For another, converse chest armour, rounded helmets, face visors, and even buff coats deflected the fatal impact of pike thrusts. Donald Lupton, the Thirty Years' War veteran, thought that not one pikeman in twenty was resolute and strong enough to be able to stand his ground and use his 16-foot weapon skilfully enough to damage the enemy in such an encounter. Contact was more usually made in the fashion that Sir Walter Slingsby saw at Cheriton:[66]

> The foot, keeping their ground in a close body, not firing till within two pikes length [32 feet], and then three ranks at a time, after turning the butt end of their muskets, charging the pikes, and standing close, preserved themselves, and slew many of the enemy.

In Scotland, and to a lesser extent in Ireland, the famous 'Highland Charge' made this process all the more dramatic. First used during the Ulster campaign of 1641–2, it reached its apogee in Montrose's three years later. Rather than advancing in rank abreast, Highlanders dashed forward in clusters of about fifteen men, many of whom were blood relatives. When they came within effective musket range of the enemy, 60–75 feet, they fired a volley. Then they threw down their firearms, drew their swords, and raced at the foe screaming ghastly Gaelic yells. If this was not enough to persuade the other side that they had urgent appointments elsewhere (as usually it was), on reaching their lines the Highlanders dropped to one knee. Protecting themselves with their small shields, they thrust their swords up into the opponents' guts. They charged in a wedge-shaped formation, concentrating pressure on the opposing line with a predominance of men that was usually enough to cut it, putting the foe to flight. Being on the receiving end of a highland charge was a truly terrible experience. One of the few survivors of the Battle of Knockanoss of November 1647 recalled how the enemy 'came routing down like a Torrent tempestuously on our foot'.[67]

Contact between cavalry and cavalry was similar. According to military manuals, horse soldiers were expected to charge *en masse*, as close to each other as possible, with each man's knee tucked in behind that of the man to his right, and so on down a line perhaps twenty or thirty men long.[68] At the start of the war both sides favoured advancing in the Swedish formation of files three deep, as opposed to the Dutch formation of six. Even though military theorists advised the use of cavalry in concentrated formations, in practice they required considerable room. Such Lord Byron discovered at the Battle of Nantwich: 'The ground was so enclosed the horse could do no service, and some of them, who were struck with a panic fear, so disordered the rest, that those that did not run away, yet it was impossible to make them charge.'[69]

Cavalry did not gallop straight into enemy lines, for no matter how fiercely spurred, at the last moment horses will stop, or shy away. In practice the troopers rode up to the other side, fired their pistols or carbines, before retiring to reload. Only when it seemed that the enemy line was opening up did the cavalry join in hand-to-hand combat. Lord Bernard described how this process took place at Edgehill:[70]

We were fain to charge them uphill and leap over some 5 or 6 hedges and ditches, they gave fire with the canon lined among their horse, dragoons, carbines and pistols, but finding nothing did dismay the king's horse ... when our men charged, they all began to turn head, and we followed an execution upon them four or five miles together.

Oliver Cromwell records how the enemy dissolved when his cavalry charged them resolutely near Grantham:[71]

We stood a little above musket shot the one body from the other and the dragooners having fired on both sides for the space of half an hour or more, they now advancing towards us, we agreed to charge them, and advancing the body after many shots on both sides, we came out with our troops a pretty round trot, they standing firm to receive us: and our men charging fiercely upon them by God's providence, they were immediately routed and ran all away.

In both these instances the defending cavalry broke and ran just before the attacking troops reached their positions. When they stood their ground, a mêlée of hand-to-hand fighting followed. Edmund Ludlow described this process at Marston Moor: 'The Horse on both sides behaved themselves with the utmost bravery; for having discharged their pistols, and flung them at each other, they fell to it with their swords.' Lord Saye and Sele tells how at the same battle, 'The Enemy's Horse, being many of them, if not the greatest part Gentlemen, stood very firm a long time coming to a close fight with the Sword.'[72] Colonel Parsons depicted 'a very sharp and gallant charge by both sides' at Rowton Heath: 'After pistols were discharged at half pike's distance [i.e. eight feet, point-blank range] they disputed the matter with their swords for a full quarter of an hour, neither giving ground to another, till at length the enemy were forced to retreat.'[73]

Such struggles often degenerated into groggy man-to-man mêlées. An observer described what happened after Colonel Atkinson's roundhead horse charged Lieutenant Colonel Norton's dragoons before November 1643:[74]

Atkinson missed with his pistol, the other pulled him off his horse with his sword belt. Both being on the ground Atkinson's soldiers came in, felled Norton into the ditch with the end of their muskets: in comes Norton's soldiers and beat down Atkinson, and with blows broke both his thigh bones, whereof he died.

A cavalier ballad purportedly composed after the First Battle of Newbury described the chaos of hand-to-hand combat between horsemen:

Then 'spur and sword' was the battle word, and we made the helmets ring
Shouting like madmen all the while 'for God and for the King!'
And though they snuffed psalms, to give the rebel dogs their due
When the roaring shot poured thick and hot, they were stalwart men and true.

Being dismounted during such a fracas was extremely dangerous. Many troopers tried to run from the fighting, dodging sword slashes from friend or foe alike, or, falling to the ground, lay doggo, petrified lest they be trampled or kicked by fear-crazed horses. A dismounted officer was especially vulnerable: his gaudy dress made him an attractive target; lightly armed he could do little to protect himself.

During the first charge at Hopton Heath, the Earl of Northampton had his horse shot from under him, and was immediately surrounded by enemy troopers. Even though equipped with only a pole-axe he managed to kill their colonel, and wound a captain and several other ranks, before being knocked on the head with a musket. 'Grievously wounded', the Earl refused their offer to surrender, retorting that 'he scorned to take quarter off such base rogues and Rebels as they were'. Taken at his word, the rebellious rogues cleaved open his head with a halbardier.[75] The Earl of Northampton perished not just because of aristocratic arrogance, and because 'he was often heard to say that if he had outlived these wars he was certain never to have found so noble a death', but because he did not have a bodyguard to protect his rear and bring him a new mount.

Sir Philip Monckton did not make the same mistake. 'I had my horse shot under me as I caracoled [turned round half way] at the head of the body I commanded', he recalled of the time he charged with Goring's cavalry at Marston Moor. Finding himself on his feet and unable to obtain a mount, he ran towards the enemy, as his men followed and his servant found him another horse. 'When I was mounted upon him, the wind driving the smoke so I could not see what was come of the body I commanded, which went in pursuit of the enemy.'[76]

Captain Richard Atkyns owed his life to his subaltern. While fighting 'hand to fist' on horseback at Roundway Down he was surrounded by roundheads, who were about to kill him. 'In this nick of time' Atkyns remembered, 'came up Cornet Holmes to my assistance', firing his pistol. Although he saw the ball glance off an enemy breastplate, without even wounding the fellow, the shock distracted him long enough to let Atkyns escape.[77] Mixed-up and horrible as the mêlée between cavalry might have been, it was not a particularly fatal time. The killing fields came later.

The knife edge between surviving and being massacred was most acute when cavalry charged infantry.

So long as they did not break ranks, infantry were comparatively safe from cavalry attacks.[78] Horses will not run into fixed objects, be they walls of men or of stone. Infantry could make the former more formidable by lining them with pikes, or by having musketeers pound metal-tipped stakes, known as 'swines' feathers', into the ground before them at an angle pointed to the enemy.

Even before infantry and cavalry clashed, the former had a distinct advantage. As we have seen theoretically, as two infantry formations of equal size moved towards one another, 10 per cent to 15 per cent of the men had a chance of being hit by musket fire. But when cavalry charged infantry the ratio shifted drastically in the latter's favour. When horsemen approached to shoot at infantry at pistol range, they did so on the move, with weapons that fired a comparatively light ball, after having been subject to murderous musket fire. All this significantly limited their effectiveness: indeed cavalry would have been lucky to hit 5 per cent of the other side, and kill even fewer.[79]

On the other hand the numbers favoured the foot over the horse. On a line of equal length there were many more of the former than the latter. Horse usually charged in ranks at least two rank deep, against as many as six of infantry. Even knee to knee, horsemen were at least twice as wide apart, and because their mounts were vulnerable, presented broad targets. Thus if on a 60-foot front 36 horsemen in two ranks charged 180 infantry (half of whom were musketeers), during the twenty seconds it would have taken them to trot 200 yards, each side would have been able to fire a single volley. Firing as they stood, sometimes with their weapons on rests, the infantry would have shot 2.5 heavy bullets at each horseman. On the other hand the cavalry on the move would have been able to discharge one light round at every five infantry men. Or to put that another way, the enemy to bullets fired ratio favoured the infantry 12.5 to one. If we had counted the relative weight of the rounds, and differences in accuracy expected between firing on horseback and on foot, the figure might have been twice as high.

Of course, for those involved in a civil war battle such calculations were at best academic. Horsemen have for years terrified those on foot. The two groups have traditionally hated each other. A Marxist might explain the animosity in class terms: the troopers of the New Model Army often did so in religious ones. More likely a sense of relative impotence prompted such savagery. Foot-sloggers often treated dismounted cavalry with the brutality their modern counterparts vent on pilots of planes shot down during a strafing run.

In both battles and skirmishes, it was not the impact of charging cavalry, but the sight of their fearsome approach that broke infantry, particularly those neophytes who had not been properly trained to stand and fight. At Ancaster on 11 April 1643 about two to three hundred royalist horse were ordered to charge two hundred parliamentary musketeers who had taken cover behind some breastworks. The attack was down a steep hill, without any cover, which gave the enemy, thought Captain Atkyns, 'as good a mark as they could have wished'. When the other ranks refused to attack, about a dozen officers did so. 'The charge was as seemingly desperate as any I was ever in', Atkyns continued, and 'the enemy, seeing our resolution, never fired at us, but ran away, and we (like young soldiers) after them, doing execution upon them.' In their enthusiasm to hack the roundheads down, Captain Manners rode ahead of the rest smack-bang into an ambush, which forced the royalists back. Unfortunately by now the other ranks, seeing their officers' success, had charged, colliding with the retreating leaders. This precipitated a general retreat, with the parliamentary horse in hot pursuit. It stopped a few miles away at Little Dean, where Major Leighton once again demonstrated how resolute infantry could halt cavalry. Stationing his men in a stone house, through the walls of which they knocked slits, he ordered them to fire over his own retreating horse (so closely that a round knocked off Atkyns's hat) which stopped the enemy in their tracks.[80]

To his shame Captain Fiennes never forgot seeing how 'Four other regiments ran away, and fought not at all, but cast away their colours', when Prince Rupert's cavalry began to charge them at Edgehill.[81] The only time horse soldiers could expect to break resolute infantry was when they suddenly attacked the rear or flanks of tired men already engaged in fighting other infantry. Such was the secret of the victory that Cromwell's Ironsides won at Naseby and Marston Moor.

There is no doubt that civil war artillery badly scared its targets. With their dreadful weapons, convoluted jargon of sakers, minions, and drakes and culverins, and complicated mathematical formulae, gunners were seen as a mystery of satanic arts.[82] 'The first shot for the devil', declared a gunner's axiom, 'the second for God, and the third for the king.' 'From the Devils arse did guns beget', wrote Ben Jonson, the soldier turned playwright. John Milton agreed, calling cannon 'a devilish machination to plague the Sons of men'. In keeping with the wicked image of artillery Sir John Meldrum's roundheads nicknamed their heaviest piece, a 32-pounder, 4 yards long, 'Sweet Lips' after a notorious whore from Hull.[83]

The Earl of Denbigh maintained, 'I would rather lose ten lives than one piece of my artillery.' Even though they played a slight role north of the border, George Lauder expressed the joy and horror of the destruction guns wrought in his poem, *The Scottish Soldier*:[84]

> Let me still hear the Cannons thundering Voice,
> In terror then run; that sweet noise
> Rings in my ears more pleasing that the sound
> Of any music consort that can be found . . .
> Then to see legs and arms torn ragged fly
> And bodies gasping all dismembered lie.

Far from being poetic licence, mention of ripped bodies and flying limbs was a commonplace in contemporary descriptions of the effect of cannon fire. An observer claimed that near Chester in 1643 a drake firing a 5-pound ball 'killed sixty of the king's party in one shot'.[85] At Rowton Heath a 29-pound round fired at a roundhead infantry regiment, 'made such a line through them that they had little mind to close again'.[86] Colonel Slingsby claimed to have seen 'legs and arms flying apace' when balls hit infantry at the point-blank range of 200 yards.[87] During the First Battle of Newbury (which with Langport was the only battle where cannon played a major role), Captain Gwynne saw 'A whole file of men, six deep, with their heads struck off with one cannon shot of ours'.[88] George Creighton, chaplain to Lord Ormonde's regiment, described the effect of artillery fire at the Battle of Ross, Wexford, in March 1647: 'I did see what terrible work the ordnance had made, what goodly men and houses lay there all torn, and their guts lying on the ground, arms cast away, and strewn all over the field.'[89]

Whether for their devilish arts, or the fiendish destruction their weapons inflicted, cavalry and infantry undoubtedly loathed gunners. Somehow their weapons – like those carried by flame-thrower men in the Second World War – were so horrible that they placed them beyond the normal rules of war. Thus when the parliamentary cavalry overran some of the king's light cannon at Edgehill they slaughtered the helpless gunners who had taken refuge beneath their weapons.[90]

In practice artillery fire seldom broke and scattered lines of infantry. According to a contemporary pamphlet when Sir William Brereton opened fire with his drakes at Nantwich the 5-pound balls 'caused more terror than execution' (i.e. casualties). Nonetheless, because many of the rounds hit the stony ground, sending lethal shards whistling through the air, the royalists broke, shouting 'Lets fly, for they have great ordnance'.[91] On the other hand royalist artillery fire was ineffectual. As Brereton recorded, they 'played full upon us with their cannon, but without any success at all, there being only one or two hurt, but not mortal'.[92]

By and large the practical effect of artillery in pitched battles was far less than one would expect. Long before the war Thomas Digges had observed that 'Great artillery seldom or never hurts'.[93] At both Edgehill and Naseby most rounds plunged into the wet ground, showering the enemy with nothing more lethal than mud. Richard Baxter noted that several hours of bombardment from Fairfax's artillery did more to frighten than damage Goring's troops. 'Their cannon did very small execution amongst us', Robert Harley assured his brother after Cheriton.[94] Because cannon were so heavy, and moved so slowly, the king had only eight pieces at Naseby, while Oliver Cromwell was able to crush the Scots at Preston in 1648 without a single gun.

Although civil war battles could be complex and were certainly confused, most shared a common objective – the disintegration of the cohesion of enemy units. Once this collapse took place, once formations became crowds of milling individuals, the encounter reached its climax. Battle involved an escalating tension between group and individual experiences. The maintenance of the former offered victory and survival: the collapse to the latter brought death and defeat. And it is for this reason the battlefield becomes, as S. L. A. Marshall put it, 'the lonesomest place which men share together'.[95]

In the seventeenth century this process of disintegration was called 'a panic fear'. According to an observer of the collapse of the parliamentary forces at Brentford, it took place when 'unnatural, shameful and strange cruelties send force a voice . . . so loud and piercing that it awakes even secure and sleepy manhood'.[96] Active soldiers, caught in its toils, described disintegration in more prosaic terms. An officer in Sir John Clotworthy's regiment revealed how his men broke at a skirmish in County London-derry:[97]

> The British seeing themselves overpowered, took discouragement in bad time, and before they came to push of pike, took the Retreat. At which point the Irish took heart and fell upon their rear, and put them to the run, and so most of them were killed.

Sir Bevil Grenville told his wife how the charge he led against the rebels at Braddock Down 'struck great terror in them'.[98] Holles and Ballard's regiments displayed a similar lack of resolution at Edgehill. 'Upon the first charge of the enemy they wheeled about, abandoned their muskets, and came running down with the Enemy's horse at their heels and amongst them pell-mell'.[99] 'Those that ran away showed themselves most basely', said James Lumsden, condemning the troops which broke on his right flank at Marston Moor. Even though the parliamentary commander tried to prevent them, 'those that fled never came to charge with the enemy, but were so possessed with any panic fear, that they ran'.[100]

Veterans could recognize when a unit was just about to disintegrate, and would do all they could to prevent the catastrophe. At Powick Bridge, 'an old soldier' tried to rally the parliamentary forces, but it was too late, and 'in the confused panic', they ran 'in a very dishonorable manner'.[101] Sensing the critical moment at Naseby, Charles tried to lead his reserves personally in a one last do-or-die charge.

On the other hand seasoned commanders tried to turn a crack in the enemy's dyke into a tidal wave of panic. On 15 April 1642 at Blackhole Heath, near Athy, an English column came into contact with some rebels, who stood their ground at the top of a hill for about a quarter of an hour. A hundred and fifty musketeers, with two hundred firelocks commanded by that ferocious Captain Thomas Sanford, advanced. According to a news report this 'struck the Rogues into such a fear that some of the Pikes began to retreat. At sight whereof a great sigh was heard in our Army of derision, crying O hone! O Hone! O hone! [Go home?]' Since an incipient panic fear had broken out only on the rebels' right flank, the English shifted their attention to the left, breaking the whole line, and killing five hundred of the enemy, four-fifths of them as they ran.[102]

Normally the more experience troops had, the longer they could fight before losing unit cohesion. At Marshall Elm, the first skirmish, after little waiting, and three sharp volleys at the rebels, 'the whole body began to stagger'. Recognizing that the enemy were starting to disintegrate, Sir John Stawell led the charge, scattering them to the four corners of Somerset. At Naseby, the rot set in after about a couple of hours' fighting.

In a crowded battlefield, where units were locked in push of pike, disintegration did not take place at the front of a body of men. It could not. The rout began at the rear, where men could see and hear enough of what their comrades were experiencing in the front in contact with the enemy, but had room enough to run. Sometimes an attack, or the imminent threat of an attack by enemy reserves from behind, would precipitate the collapse. Or else the erosion took place on the sides, where men were both exposed to enemy fire, and had space in which to escape. Lord Belasye described how this took place at Edgehill. After his troops had been fighting hand-to-hand with the enemy infantry for some time, Lord General Essex sent in his reserves who, 'following upon our flank and charging through when we were at push of pike, we were at last broken'.[103]

Once a unit started to break, it had a rippling effect. Panic became contagious. 'Away! Away! Everyman shift for his Life', Sergeant Foster remembered the cry as his unit was caught in a night ambush near Aldermaston in September 1643. Trapped in a narrow lane, not just men, but animals panicked. Horses tried to bolt, overturning wagons, their loads blocking the narrow road. A munitions wagon caught fire, blew up, killing ten men: it terrified the rest, and illuminated targets for the royalist snipers hiding in the hedgerows.[104]

The sudden, accidental explosion of a powder wagon or magazine broke units during the Battles of Lansdown and Torrington. 'Truly, Sir, I never saw God in any part of my life', a parliamentary trooper told a friend about the explosion of eighty barrels of powder stored in Torrington parish church, which killed at least two hundred men in a flash. Another called it 'the most terriblest sight that I ever beheld'.[105] The death of a leader at a critical moment could have a similar effect. The battle-cries of troops confident of victory could shatter men whose cohesion was beginning to crumble. Hand-to-hand combat is extremely tiring, especially for already exhausted, frightened and hungry men, at the end of their tether, hardly amenable to reason or discipline. 'The frightened soldier, as well as the hungry belly, has no ears', observed Roger Boyle. In sum, units broke when they could battle no more. Boyle continued, 'Whatsoever may cause fear in your enemy, ought not to be omitted by you, since Fear is truly said to be a Betrayer of that Succor which reason also might afford.'[106]

Ironically once men succumbed to fear the truly fearful time began.

'They stood not the first charge of foot, but fled in great disorder, and we chased them many miles', recalled Sir Bevil Grenville right after Braddock Down. On the other side, Lion Watson recounted mopping up after the royalists disintegrated at Marston Moor:[107]

> To conclude, about nine of the clock we had cleared the field of all enemies, and followed the chase of them within a mile of York, cutting them down so that their dead bodies lay three miles in length.

Robert Douglas noticed that flight was far more dangerous than sticking around. 'God did preserve them that stayed marvelously', the covenanter wrote in his diary of the rout at Marston Moor, 'the most part of them killed running away, few of them killed standing.' One of the survivors recalled the full horror of this rout. Even though it had taken place six days before, Sir Arthur Trevor was still in a state of shock, apologizing for 'the disorder and unhandsomeness of this dispatch', when he wrote to the Marquis of Ormonde:[108]

> In the fire, smoke and confusion of that day I knew not for my soul wither to incline. The runaways on both sides were so many, so breathless, so speechless, and so full of fears that I should not have taken them for men, but by their very motions which still served them well: not a man of them being able to give me the least hint where the Prince was to be found, both armies both mingled, both horse and foot, no side keeping to their posts.
>
> In this horrible distraction did I court the centre here meeting with a shoal of Scots crying out 'Weys us, we are all undone', and so full of lamentations and mourning, as if their day of doom had over taken them, and from which they knew not to fly.

Units turned into mobs of individuals in which it was every man for himself: men so frightened that they were no longer men: men so distracted that they moved like shoals of fish: men behaving as if it was their doomsday – as it would be, since for so many of them a rout became a killing frenzy. Perhaps it sprung from some primeval instinct, when as packs of hunters men ran down and slaughtered defenceless game – the helplessness of victims somehow arousing our lust for blood.

Several incidents after Naseby demonstrated this primordial process. Having broken through the king's lines the roundheads came across a party of women, whose faces they slashed, and some of whom they killed. According to one story the puritans assumed they were whores, to be mutilated to make the future plying of their profession unpleasant for all concerned. Another source has it that the roundheads assumed they were Irish (not being able to understand what they were saying – for in truth they were Welsh), and slew them as papists. But could not the very helplessness of the women have provoked the atrocity – which was the closest the civil wars came to a gang rape. Might not the women have been broken for being 'the weaker vessel'?

A similar submissiveness explained the slaughter of English-speaking males during the same pursuit. Missing the turn to Lubenham, a party of the king's horse rode down a cul-de-sac into Marston Trussell churchyard. Here the roundheads cornered them, butchering them all like game, and tossing their corpses into a clay pit.[109] After running for 30 miles, another survivor from the same battle tried to steal a loaf of bread from a farmhouse near Ravenstone. The soldier was so demoralized that a servant girl was able to kill him with the stick she was using to stir a laundry tub.[110]

After Edgehill villagers smashed in the brains of royalist survivors who left the ranks to beg for the food. Having been broken by battle these soldiers, who beforehand had plundered without let or a second thought, allowed themselves to be 'knocked on the head by the common folk'.[111]

Those who survived ran or rode without stopping until they could go no further. After Marston Moor Lord Leven did not pause until he reached Wetherby, 14 miles away. After Naseby few of the king's horsemen stopped until they reached Leicester, 16 miles distant: some even made the 30 miles to Newark.

The disintegration of their units rendered men incapable of further resistance. After the roundheads shattered the royalist cavalry at Marston Moor, Colonel Sir Philip Monckton spotted Sir John Hurry, and rode up to him suggesting that they must rally the dispersed troopers, even though none of them belonged to their regiments: if they could lead them back into the battle the field might not be lost. 'He told me', Monckton recalled, 'broken horse would not fight, and galloped from me to York.'[112] After the roundheads had killed three hundred and captured three thousand royalists at the Battle of Langport, Sir George Goring admitted 'there is so great a terror and dejection amongst our men, that I am confident, at this point they would not be brought to fight against half their number'.[113]

Physical circumstances made the wounds inflicted during pursuit far more often fatal than those sustained in the hurly-burly of hand-to-hand combat. During the latter there were few stab wounds: instead men instinctively slashed at each other with swords, inflicting gory yet superficial gashes. In hot pursuit, when cavalry chased terrified foot soldiers, swords sliced down, severing necks, or fatally snapped vertebrae. After Sir John Digby's horse broke the roundhead foot at Torrington in 1643 they chased them 'until their swords were blunted with the slaughter'. Two hundred were killed and two hundred taken prisoner, a very high ratio, which suggests that the cavaliers went berserk in an orgy of butchery. Of the survivors, a contemporary recorded, there was 'scarce a man without a cut over the head or face'.[114]

Following a panic fear the cavalry became a frightfully efficient exterminating machine. For instance, after the foot had broken the rebels' cohesion at Blackhole Heath, killing about a hundred of them, five hundred British horse chased them, slaughtering four hundred Irish, taking no prisoners. Proportionately the cavalry killed 248 times more of the enemy than did the infantry.[115]

The elation of hot pursuit, a lust for blood, as well as the prospect of plunder, all too often proved the cavalry's nemesis. After breaking the enemy's lines at Edgehill and Naseby, Prince Rupert's cavalry continued to charge for several miles, looting the enemy baggage train. By the time they were able to regroup and come back to the fray the fighting was over. Sir John Okey was convinced that had Rupert's horse not been so intent on pursuit and plunder at Naseby, they would have decimated his regiment of dragoons, thus preventing them from pouring enfilading fire into the king's infantry. Even if the royalist horse had returned sooner to Edgehill or Naseby, the thrill of the chase, and the rapture of rapine, broke all unit cohesion. A contemporary wrote 'the soldiers were so dispersed that there were not ten of any one troop together'.[116]

Cromwell's genius was his ability to control cavalry: by stopping them from hunting down broken troops in unbridled pursuit, he kept them on the field of battle.

An explanation for the success of Cromwell's cavalry, and the failure of Rupert's, may be seen in terms of sport. Long before the first square broke, the Gatling jammed and the colonel died, schoolboys have been playing the game, and war has been described in sporting idioms. In recent times General Montgomery talked of 'knocking the enemy for six' at El Alamein, and General Schwarzkopf described his flanking movement in the Gulf as a 'Hail Mary' play – both presumably to the delight of cricket and basketball fans.

War has been viewed as a sport: sport has been seen as a substitute for war. For hundreds of years the tournament blurred the line between the two. 'Hunting is a military exercise', Ludovick Lloyd wrote in 1604, 'the like stratagems are often invented and executed in war against soldiers as the hunter doth against diverse kinds of beasts.' The gentlemen who formed the backbone of the king's cavalry brought to war their peacetime experiences in the hunting field, where the chase was long, exhilarating, guilt free, safe (as least for the chasers) and ended with the satisfying slaughter of frightened and defenceless victims. On the other hand, Cromwell's troopers did not come from this tradition, and were well disciplined enough to leave the hunt to return to the real business in hand.

Some units never broke, but like the Whitecoats at Marston Moor fought on stolidly to the death. Experienced troops, who were able to negotiate at the informal, face-to-face level, could have their surrenders accepted with comparatively little loss. Such took place at Naseby, where after the king's infantry gave up, hardly any of them lost their lives.

The Duke of Wellington once observed that 'Nothing except a battle lost can be half so melancholy as a battle won.' For both winners and losers there was no sadder sight than the field where brother had slaughtered brother. 'It was a lamentable spectacle the next morning to behold what heaps of bodies and diversities of slaughters', reported an observer of the aftermath to the Second Battle of Newbury.[117] Another eyewitness of this 'long and terrible fight' estimated that even after the townsfolk had carted sixty loads of dead and wounded back to Newbury there were still five hundred bodies left lying on the ground, some with arms locked together in an embrace of *rigor mortis* made all the more macabre by their mingled congealed blood.[118] Perhaps the most dismal sound was 'such crying there was for surgeons as never was the like heard'. A few days later a royalist wrote to a friend on the other side, 'the sight of so many brought to Oxford, some dead, some wounded, would make any true English heart bleed'.

Similar horrors could be seen after every major battle. After Edgehill 'the field was covered with the dead, yet no one could tell to what party they belonged'. After Naseby an eyewitness wrote, 'I saw the field so bestrewed with carcasses of horses and men, the bodies lay slain about four miles in length, but most thick on the hill where the king stood.' After Cheriton an observer reported 'they fetched off cart loads of dead men'. After Marston Moor Simeon Ashe recalled 'In the morning there was a mortifying object to behold, when the naked bodies of thousands lay upon the ground and not altogether dead.'[119] Initially they lay in a relaxed fashion, as if sleeping, a little reminiscent of the photographed corpses of the American Civil War. By the next day, after the onset of *rigor mortis*, and they had been stripped and tossed aside, they resembled those pathetically white matchsticks seen on films of liberated concentration camps.

The ghouls who haunted battlefields, pillaging corpses, dispatching the dying, and breaking their fingers to strip them of rings, were the dregs of society. They not only preyed on the dead, but on the living as well, victimizing those relatives who searched the detritus for the remains of loved ones. As Mary, Colonel Charles Towenley's widow, was rummaging through Marston Moor for her husband's corpse, she met Oliver Cromwell. He asked what she was doing in that vale of tears. When she told him, he gave her a bodyguard.[120]

Battles usually ended at sundown, after which the dark hid the most hellish sights.

None was more dreadful than at Edgehill, where so many innocents learned how ugly the face of battle really was. It was a cold, unusually frosty night. The scant medical help had broken down. Survivors succumbed to the lethargy and indifference that follows all disasters. Soon after sunset a careless trooper using a glowing fuse to see how much powder was left in a barrel, exploded a powder wagon, killing many and further demoralizing more.[121] Men were too drained to help each other: most were too tired even to loot. On both sides hungry men had nothing to eat and precious little to drink. 'We almost starved with cold that bitter night', recalled Denzil Holles.[122] After being without food for so long Edmund Ludlow found some bread. 'I could scarce eat it, my jaws for want of use having almost lost their natural faculty', he recalled. The reason for Ludlow's inability to eat was not a lack of practice but the intense clenching of teeth that is a frequent symptom of post combat trauma.[123] Ludlow's problems were not over. Having entrusted his cloak before the battle to a servant, all that night he had to walk up and down trying to keep warm in his suit of armour. Even the king fared little better. Shocked by the sight of some sixty corpses piled where the royal standard had flown, he huddled over a fire made from a few twigs, unable to sleep for the cries and last groans of the wounded around him.

Dawn came to reveal two exhausted sides numbly facing each other. On its own initiative a small party of royalist horse captured four of the enemy's guns with little resistance, which suggests that had Charles followed up with a resolute attack he might have won a major – even decisive – victory. But, like most of his men, the king was too emotionally and physically drained for decisive action, preferring conciliation instead. He sent Sir William Le Neve, the Clarence King of Arms, to the enemy with a proclamation commanding them to surrender. Although the roundheads refused, threatening to hang Neve if he tried to read it out aloud to the troops, he reported seeing 'so much trouble and disorder in the faces of the Earl of Essex and the principal officers' that they were unable to do anything for half a dozen more hours. Then at last, at three in the afternoon, over twenty-four hours after battle had commenced, the parliamentarians departed Edgehill.

The victory that the king claimed was hollow. Edgehill left him and his army so physically and mentally drained that they could take no decisive action for several days. Even after he had become a veteran of a dozen or more fights, Charles still succumbed to post-combat lethargy. For three weeks after his defeat at Naseby the king relaxed at Raglan Castle, the Marquis of Worcester's seat, 'all lulled to sleep with sports and entertainments', wrote his secretary, 'as if no crown had been at stake'.[124]

Charles was not alone in his lassitude, which is an almost universal reaction to the first exposure to combat.[125] After Cropredy Bridge, related a royalist officer, 'we lay all night, looking one upon the other'.[126] The parliamentary commander William Waller apologized to his superiors, 'I would have written to you last night, but I was utterly tired by the labours of the day.' Four days after the Second Battle of Newbury Captain Richard Symonds wrote in his diary: 'Saturday, 2 November the army lay still – till Tuesday.' Oliver Cromwell was less laconic. On 7 November Simeon Ashe heard him shout to the Earl of Manchester, 'My Lord, your horses are so spent, so harassed out by hard duty, that they will fall down under their riders if you thus command them: you may have their skins, but you can have no service.'[127]

After every battle the survivors tried to explain to themselves – and to anyone else who would listen – their traumatic experience. Some tried to compose short descriptions, many wrote to friends, still more talked to their comrades. After Edgehill a group of parliamentary officers got together to try to work out what had happened. 'Some on both sides did extremely well,' they concluded, 'and others did ill and deserved to be hanged for deserting.'[128] Captain William Stewart's description of Marston Moor, written a couple of days after the fighting in which he took part, is still hazy, notably about episodes he did not personally witness.[129]

Many survivors felt guilty as they tried to explain to themselves, and to others, why they had lived, while so many about them had perished. The thing that most worried a royalist defender of Limerick Castle, which suffered heavy cannon and sniper fire during the siege of May–June 1642, was the randomness of death.[130] Puritans were more inclined to see the choice of the living and slain as part of some divine, rational plan. A parliamentary pamphlet reported that the only person killed when heavy cannon fire tore up roofs during the Siege of Manchester, sending tile shards like shrapnel through the defenders, was 'a wicked child having overrun his parents'.[131]

Few combatants were prepared to go this far in interpreting death in combat as the Almighty's punishment for breaching the Fifth Commandment. Some sounded resigned. 'Dear Mother', wrote the Earl of Northampton, after his father was killed at Hopton Heath, 'Casualties in this world will happen.'[132] Most were less sanguine. 'It was an infinite mercy of God we had not all been lost', Thomas Ellis told his brother after Cropredy.[133] Even though puritans tended to interpret their survival as part of the Almighty's cosmic course, they were often unsure why He had saved them in particular. 'Sir, this is none other but the hand of God', declared Cromwell after Naseby, 'and to Him alone belongs the glory.'[134] Surviving not only induces guilt, but a sense of pleasure that can be so exquisite that it can complete the circle by making the godly feel guilty. Thus when Cromwell concluded that 'to Him alone belongs the glory', he was also passing to the Almighty any forbidden joy.

Many others believed that He should also have the last word. Battles were the epitome of what was invariably described as 'these *unnatural* civil wars'. Thus it is not surprising that after them supernatural events were frequently reported. Even before fighting started people recounted seeing fully equipped musketeers and horsemen fighting in the skies above the Cotswolds, and angels clashing above the college roof-tops in Cambridge. After the wars' first major battle accounts of sightings peaked, surely a sign of peoples' concern. John Green heard several stories about heavenly hosts struggling above Edgehill, where on 23 December William Marshall and the Reverend Samuel Marshall claimed they saw phantom troops fighting, beating their drums, firing their weapons, and charging 'pell mell'. When the same apparitions appeared the next day the brothers fell to the ground begging God 'to defend them from these hellish and prodigious enemies'. Instead Charles sent two courtiers from Oxford to investigate the sightings.[135]

Such apparitions continued throughout the war: for hundreds of years tales were told of heavenly hosts contesting above Naseby, and many swore that they had seen 'Ghostly Troopers' dressed in full civil war battle dress riding the neighbouring lanes and river banks; at Newmarket three men were seen duelling in the heavens; at Thetford a sword and pike appeared to hover in the sky; a whole fleet, flags flying, was espied sailing across the skies at Brandon; drums and fifes were heard, but not seen, at Marshlands and in Suffolk. 'What all this doth portend, God only knoweth', wrote a pamphleter, but it 'doubtless is sign of his wrath for these civil wars.' John Milton tried to answer the same question in *Paradise Lost*:[136]

> And when, to warn proud cities, war appears
> Waged in the troubled sky, and armies rush
> To battle in the clouds: before each van
> Prick forth the aery knights, and couch their spears

The rush of armies to battle in the fields was terrifying enough to prompt dozens of supernatural reports. Yet – as we shall see – the siege of proud cities could be as bad, if not worse.

7

THE MISERABLE EFFECTS OF
WAR

Here the miserable effects of war appeared in a very melancholy
manner; for the enemy, to prevent a famine amongst themselves had
driven all useless mouths from among them. . . . These wretched came
flocking in great numbers to our camp, devouring all the filth they
could meet with. Our dead horses crawling with vermin, as the sun
had parched them, were delicious food to them; while their infants
sucked their carcasses with much eagerness, as if they were at their
mothers' breasts.
Robert Parker, eyewitness account of the Siege of Ballymore, 1690,
    in *Memories of the Most Memorable Military Transactions* (1746)

In the British civil wars – as in most conflicts – a large proportion of
soldiers were not involved in set-piece battles, or even campaigning, with
its inevitable skirmishes and ambushes. Instead they passed the war as
members of garrisons, often living and letting live peacefully with nearby
enemy troops. They tried to dominate the surrounding countryside, which
they used to maintain themselves in money and supplies, being eager to
avoid the horrors of war. For most of the time garrison life was peaceful.
Indeed its routines could be numbingly boring. But when the enemy
besieged a garrison the experience of war could be the most miserable and
melancholy a soldier could endure.

The situation in Britain was very similar to that on the continent. For
instance, in November 1632 Gustavus Adolphus had 183,000 men under
arms, of whom 52 per cent were on garrison duty in Sweden or Germany,
36 per cent served in independent armies, and only 11 per cent came
under the king's direct command.[1] In June 1645 Charles I had nearly forty
thousand soldiers in his army, of whom 25 per cent were at Naseby, 27
per cent served in Prince Maurice's field army in the West Country, while
the remaining 48 per cent were scattered among garrisons mostly in Wales,
the West and Midlands.

On both sides the numbers of garrisons grew as the war continued.
Before Marston Moor the Marquis of Newcastle had troops in thirty-two

garrisons north of the River Trent, while parliament had nine major garrisons and fifteen minor ones in the North Midlands alone. In the spring of 1645 a contemporary listed thirty-nine royalist and thirty-six parliamentary garrisons in the Midlands and Wales, while a more detailed study shows thirty in Shropshire alone.[2] As the royalists went on the defensive, their forces fragmented into smaller and smaller garrisons. Between Naseby in June 1645 and the loss of their last strong point, Harlech, in March 1647 some eighty-one royalist garrisons surrendered, containing about twenty-three thousand troops.[3]

Soliders, like all human beings, want stability and security, a warm safe harbour where they can escape the storms of their profession. Once they have found such a snuggery they are reluctant to leave. Since garrisons were fairly independent of field armies and central commanders, they could lose their military effectiveness, disintegrating into gangs of bandits. 'There is a great rabble of all sorts of people convened there', a contemporary described the parliamentary garrison at Lichfield, 'being neither disciplined nor armed.'[4]

On the other hand an almost civilian social life could develop in a garrison town. Wives and children joined husbands. Soldiers used extortion to become self-supporting, and to avoid dependence on the caprices of central supply and pay systems. In doing so, however, they could also damage their own cause, for nothing alienated local support faster than plunder. One pamphlet called the garrison at Banbury 'This Den of Thieves', for purportedly extracting goods worth £18,000 per week from Oxfordshire.[5] Sir John Meldrum warned the Committee of Both Kingdoms in November 1644 that parliament's policy of dispersing troops into garrisons (which was admittedly far less burdensome than the crown's), 'may rather ferment than finish a war'.[6] The following January John Greene came to the same conclusion, noting in his diary that the growth of garrisons on both sides must prolong hostilities. Troops spent more energy maintaining themselves through plunder and exactions, and far less seeking the major decisive battle. Badly weakened, Greene went on, the realm would be vulnerable to foreign invasion and starvation, for 'Famine is feared by many.'[7]

Typical of the garrisons which scared so many civilians was that at Chalfield, a manor house about 6 miles east of Bath.[8] The detachment consisted of a troop of cavalry and a couple of infantry companies, which at full strength could total as many as four hundred men. It averaged about two hundred and sixty. Although the troops spent their time building fairly extensive earth defenses, they were involved in very little combat. In September 1644 and April 1645 royalists may have attacked the garrison – one man is recorded as having died of wounds. In early 1645 soldiers from Chalfield blocked the retreat of Colonel Long's cavaliers, helping Cromwell capture most of them. In July a detachment from Chalfield under a major (which suggests that it was a small one) spent two weeks blockading the royalists at Lacock. Next September the garrison buried John Woodbridge, who died from a service-related illness, in the local churchyard. In all, Chalfield was, to use the modern idiom, 'a pretty cushy number'.

Boredom and having nothing to do were all too often the garrison soldiers' lot. Parliamentary commanders were especially concerned that idleness would do the devil's work. John Hutchinson, the Governor of Northampton, set up a table of fines for those who broke the Sabbath, drank to excess, or swore. Governor Samuel Luke desperately worried that Newport Pagnell was becoming a latter-day Sodom and Gomorrah: some of his men persuaded the local girls that sleeping with them did not count as adultery as there was a war on. Surprisingly the most lasting effect of the idle hours that Newport Pagnell's troopers enjoyed was not a quiverful of bastards but a pilgrim's progress. As a young soldier John Bunyan spent his months there arguing about religion and refining his radicalism.[9]

In theory one of a garrison's chief functions was to hold and control the surrounding countryside. While its troops could not stop field armies, they could harass enemy patrols, and make life difficult for civilians who supported the other side. In the spring of 1643 Edmund Ludlow led a party from Wardour Castle, Somersetshire, to capture half a dozen cavaliers reported visiting friends in Sutton. A few weeks later he chased a roundhead patrol that had plundered his father's country house, and took particular pleasure in recapturing half a dozen pasties baked from his own poached deer.[10] About the same time Lord Crawford requested permission to take a patrol from the royalist garrison at Farringdon to ambush a 150-strong enemy force who 'plunder all, and take away horses and men'.[11] Such actions supported the view, advanced by both sides in their propaganda, that they were fighting in self-defence. In truth garrisons spent much more energy being self-sufficient.

When told that they would have to fend for themselves some garrison commanders became indignant. 'What horrid crime have I committed, or what brand of cowardice lies upon me and my men, that we are not thought worthy of a subsistence', asked Richard Howard, captain of a royalist troop based at Camden House. This sense of being disowned, rather than having been given an independent command, was heightened when, to quote another commander 'Our troops are in extreme necessity, many of them having neither clothes to cover their nakedness, nor boots.'[12]

Each garrison was assigned several surrounding parishes from which they could levy assessments for their support, and which, in return, they were supposed to safeguard. In theory this was a tax: in practice it all too often became a protection racket. Colonel John Birch admitted that garrisons caused 'a large amount of public and private suffering'. Instead of shielding them 'from violence and rapine', complained some Somerset villagers, the Malmesbury garrison had 'continually plundered and spoiled your petititoners', in order to support their 'drinking, profane swearing, and vicious rioting living'.[13]

If villagers resisted, or did not pay their assessments, they would be plundered and their houses burned down. Such the good folk of Woburn discovered after they drove off some royalist raiders, killing their major. Reinforcements from Oxford returned to plunder them, set fire to eighteen houses, and did £3,869 7s. 0d. in damages. For a similar lack of co-operation, pillagers torched houses at Brampton, Somerset, Bishop's Castle, Shropshire, Whitby, Yorkshire and Gosport, Hampshire.[14] So folk quickly learned the wisdom of placating those who tried to shake them down with food, ale, soft beds and tobacco. The constable of Upton, Nottingham, frequently noted in his accounts 'Colonel Stanton and his men when they came for the Assessment in meat and drink . . . 1s. 4d.'[15]

When garrisons on either side tried to dominate the same area, life could become especially difficult for the locals caught in the middle. Richard Gough remembered an incident at Myddle, in Shropshire, 'which I saw when I was a schoolboy'. Cornet Collins, an Irishman from Shrawardine Castle, stopped in the village, which the royalists regarded as being part of their assessment territory, to have his horse shoed. By ill-chance a party of seven roundheads were also in Myddle trying to arrest Nat Owen for theft and desertion. They bumped into each other at Allen Chaloner's smithy. Collins jumped on his horse and galloped away, but was shot, toppling into the village pond. After firing at the rebels, killing one of their horses, his two troopers escaped. (Soon afterwards they were taken, and, being Irish, were hanged.) The villagers dragged Collins out of the pond, and carried him bleeding profusly to Allen Chaloner's house, where they dumped him on the floor. He begged for a feather mattress to relieve the pain. There was none, Mrs Chaloner replied: he had thrown it into the pond yesterday for spite, after plundering her house. Nonetheless she retrieved the tattered and still wet palliasse and slid it under the officer, before summoning the local minister. 'I went with him', recalled Richard Gough, 'and saw the Cornet lying on the bed, and much blood running along the floor.' That night a party took Collins back to Shrawardine, where he died the next day.[16]

It was this sort of incident, repeated time and time again in villages and hamlets throughout the land, that was typical of the daily nagging pain garrisons could inflict. At times – particularly in hotly disputed areas – things became nasty. In April 1645 Lieutenant Colonel Michael Jones led a roundhead raiding party through Herefordshire. They rustled, 'by the blessing of God', six thousand sheep and five hundred cows. They burned a gentleman's house near Holliwell for harbouring a sniper who killed a parliamentary trooper. Nearby they captured the Widow Hammer's house.

Since it had been a thorn in their side they set it afire. One of the arsonists noted gleefully, 'all that refused quarter, viz. 12, put to the sword, 9 whereof were roasted!'[17]

No wonder the locals lived in terror of raiders. A letter writer reported that in 1645 in Shropshire many of the inhabitants were afraid to sleep in their own houses for fear of being murdered in bed. Thomas Broome, Warden of Clun Hospital, hired a bodyguard at a shilling a day: yet that did not stop him from being taken to Ludlow gaol where he was forced to reveal where he had hidden the almshouse's assets.[18]

In part this viciousness towards civilians was an inevitable product of the strain of living in a disputed area. In November 1643 Sir Ralph Hopton reported, 'scarce a day passed without some action or other' between the royalist and roundhead garrisons posted 5 miles apart at Farnham and Odiham. 'We never want constantly alarms', wrote a member of the parliamentary garrison at Sudely, 'so that we have a hellish life.'[19]

Raids could be terrifying. Sir John Usury led three hundred men from Abingdon to West Wycombe where five hundred enemy recruits were reported. Attacking at two in the morning, they drove the startled rebels naked from their beds to grovel in the woods. Only two rebels stood and fought. Another similar raid against Thame a couple of years later surprised the enemy as they were eating poached venison pasties – an offence which always aroused cavalier danders. The king's men killed twenty-seven enemy officers and captured between two to three hundred horses. Very late on the night of 3 June 1645 the royalists attacked Newport Pagnell, killing eleven and taking eighty-four.

Roundheads could be equally aggressive. In October 1645 Colonel John Hutchinson boasted that one of his patrols had killed thirty royalists, while another had slain twenty. In a single night, two patrols sent out by Charles White slaughtered nearly forty of the enemy.[20]

Raids could produce an escalating cycle of violence. For instance on 10 April 1643 a cavalier patrol from the Whitchurch garrison plundered Moss House, Audlem, of horses, oxen and household goods belonging to Captain Massie, a roundhead. Getting intelligence of the raid, a party from Nantwich sallied out to cut off the king's men, but missed them by half an hour. Finding some stragglers they killed three, took fifteen prisoners, and recovered a dozen plundered oxen. The next day, learning that the royalists were going to return to Massie's house, presumably to recover the oxen, the parliamentarians ambushed them, killing five and taking three.[21] The shift in the ratios of dead to prisoners suggests that within twenty-four hours fighting had become far more vicious.

The casualties, exactions and horror inflicted by garrison-based raids were nothing when compared to sieges – the most brutal and prolonged experience of the British civil wars. Of some 645 military actions in England

154

during the three civil wars, 198 (31 per cent) of them were sieges. In them a total of 20,981 people lost their lives, of whom 9,890 (31 per cent) were parliamentarians and 11,091 were royalists. Sieges account for 24 per cent of the wars' total deaths, 9 per cent more than the major pitched battles. They proved more damaging to the parliamentarians, who took 31 per cent of the casualties in sieges, than to the royalists who took only 21 per cent. (For more on these figures see chapter 9, tables 2–4.)

Siege warfare is almost as ancient as organized war itself. The oldest fortifications discovered at Jericho go back to 9000 BC, predating the walls that tumbled down to the blast of the Israelites' horns by at least 7,500 years. When cornered the weak frequently hide, using natural features to overcome an enemy's strength. Thus during the civil wars royalists tended to be the besieged, especially towards the end, when they were losing. In a sample of twenty-five of the most important sieges, parliament defended on only five occasions: one in 1642, three in 1643, and one in 1644.[22]

On the Continent by the middle of the seventeenth century sieges were far more common and decisive than pitched battles – prompting Roger Boyle to complain how 'we make war more like foxes than lions'. But in the British Isles the effect of sieges was more limited and less direct.[23]

Perhaps the most important siege of the war was that of Gloucester, which forced the king to over-extend himself in the summer 1643.

> As Gloucester stood against the numerous Power
> Of the Besiegers, who with thunder-shower
> Charged her old ribs, but vanished like a storm
> With their own loss, and did no more perform.

According to a local legend, as the king withdrew, having failed to take Gloucester (which was down to its last three barrels of gunpowder), one of his sons asked if they were going home. 'We have no home', Charles mournfully replied, recognizing that this was the beginning of his end.[24] The following year the relief of York precipitated the Battle of Marston Moor. The three sieges of Newark, which the roundheads failed to take, kept open links between the royal base in Oxford, and the North. In 1645 the king's capture of Leicester helped bring about the confrontation at Naseby, while his decision to dispatch men to besiege Lyme Regis contributed to the defeat of his forces in the West Country.

Sieges, as the Chinese theorist Sun-Tzu recognized five centuries before the birth of Christ, are wasteful in men and time – and must be avoided. Unlike battles, which were over in half a day at the most, sieges went on for weeks – the average length in the first civil war being fifty-four days.[25] While push of pike in a battle might last fifteen minutes, at the Siege of Bristol it went on once for over two hours.

Siege fighting was extremely intense. Because there was time during a siege to bring up plenty of ammunition and to reload weapons, cannon and musket fire was particularly damaging. Shortage of food, the presence of civilians, the difficulty of taking prisoners made siege warfare very brutal. On one side attackers grew enraged because they had to assault an enemy safely ensconced behind walls and bastions: on the other defenders grew more desperate when they realized that as the siege progressed their chances of surviving or being taken alive deteriorated.

Even during quiet times sieges could be bloody affairs. 'There was nothing of any consequence,' reported one of the besiegers of York about the week of 19 June, 'though there were daily small skirmishes with losses on both sides.'[26] Fighting could readily erupt into volcanoes of violence. 'Their fire seem a continued blaze', a parliamentary defender at Lyme noted in his diary, 'So many men were slain that the water that served the town was coloured with Blood.' During this thirty-two-day siege a diarist recorded eleven days of heavy and four of moderate bombardment. The enemy attacked Lyme on six days, while the defenders countered on seven. The diarist noted no action on only six days, two of which were official truces called to recover and bury the dead.[27]

Sometimes feelings in sieges became so bitter that such cease-fires were impossible. At Limerick the royalists tortured a lad suspected of smuggling messages into a fifth column. The rebels subjected a girl who had been allowed to leave Ballyally Castle 'to much torture' to make her reveal all she knew about the defenders.[28] During the Siege of Wardour Castle the parliamentary defenders suspended a 13-year-old boy with a rope around his neck to make him confess to being a roundhead spy. Soon afterwards the royalists exploded a mine. Although it failed to breach the wall, it did much damage, burying a defender up to his neck. Governor Edmund Ludlow requested a truce to rescue him, but the enemy refused and for three days both sides had to listen to the dying man's whimpers for help.[29]

A Scot described the horrors of a full-blown siege, that of Newcastle in July 1644:[30]

> Truly it was more than admirable to behold the desperate courage both of the assailants and defendants, the thundering cannons roaring from our batteries without, and their's roaring from the castle within; the thousands of musket balls flying at each others' faces, like the driving hailstones from septentrion [northern] blasts; the clangor and carvings of naked and unsheathed swords; the pushing of untrailed pikes, crying for blood, and the pitiful clamour of heart-fainting women imploring for mercy for their husbands, themselves and their children . . . the carcasses of men to be like dead dogs upon the groaning streets, and man against man to be the object of homicidal and barbarous cruelty.

Such sights and sounds turned sieges into intensely personal and vicious events. During that of Hereford in August 1645 the royalist defenders tied lighted matches around dogs, cats and old horses, and threw them over the walls. The crazed beasts ran hither and thither, panicking the enemy to open fire at each other.[31] Watching the bombardment of Winchester, the Reverend Hugh Peters exalted when a mortar shell 'cut off a commissioner of their's in the thighs'.[32] The parliamentary governor of Tamworth, one Captain Hart, became so involved that he sent a challenge to the colonel commanding the roundheads at Lichfield: 'Bagot, thou son of an Egyptian whore, meet me . . . tomorrow . . . I will whip thee.'[33] (Bagot had sense enough not to turn up.) Soldiers readily believed the worst of the other side. For instance, the royalists who attacked Manchester were convinced that the enemy had 'hanged and quartered' one Johnson, a prisoner of war.[34]

Terrible living conditions and a lack of food made atrocity stories all the more credible. During the Siege of Oxford, Dr Edward Greaves observed that he had never known 'so much filth and nastiness of dirt, worse lodging, unshifted apparel . . . '[35] Lord Belasyse fell into a muddy moat at Newark, and had to be pulled out, 'so dirty that he was scarce known'. At Lathom one of the attackers rightly deduced from the vile 'smell and taste of their garments' that the defenders could not hold out for much longer.[36] At the Siege of Hopton Castle, Colonel Samuel More and his men were up most nights, and 'not out of their clothes for a fortnight's time'.[37] At Limerick a mortar blew the body of a babe in arms (whom it had killed the day before) clean out of its grave. The hundred defenders of Wardour Castle survived on 8 oz. of cereals a day, plus half a horse between them all, while in Carlisle the garrison stole horse flesh from starving civilians.[38] No more horrible conditions could be found than at Scarborough, where half the soldiers on either side died from the fighting or from scurvy. Few of the survivors could stand. They lacked the strength to bury corpses, which lay around for days, or to grind corn, further adding to the dead. When the defenders eventually surrendered in July 1645 only a third of them could walk out on their own. The women of the town were so angry they stoned the governor, Sir Hugh Cholmley.[39]

Plague ravaged crowded, hungry communities, exhausted from war. In Bristol a news-sheet reported 'the new disease is very hot . . . and near 200 die weekly thereof'. Out of a normal population of ten thousand, two thousand people died there from typhus between 1643 and 1644. During the sieges of Crediton, Devon, 514 inhabitants, about one-eighth of the total, died of disease, while in Plymouth 2,845, a quarter of the population, succumbed.[40]

Property damage was just as awful. The grand jury assessed the loss to Gloucester at £28,740, which included 256 houses and untold barns. Individual estimates were less actuarial.[41] 'When we came to Arundel we met with a most dismal sight', which even as an old woman Lady Mary

Springate never forgot: 'the town being depopulated and all the windows broken with the great guns, and the soldiers making stables of the shops and lower rooms.'[42] William Jessop reported that after the Siege of Lyme, 'there was scarce a house in the town that was not battered'.[43] During the siege one-third of Taunton was burned to the ground. Wartime conditions sparked major conflagrations at Diss, Lowestoft, Leighton Buzzard, Wrexham, Beaminster and Oxford. After seeing the havoc wrought by the mine explosion during the Siege of York, Simeon Ashe, a veteran, confessed that 'the sad fruits of wasting wars' had become almost too bitter to bear: 'Truly my heart sometimes is ready to break with what I see here.'[44]

To protect themselves, towns expended much money and effort building defences. On fortifications in 1642–3 Exeter spent £4,374 11s. 4d., nearly three times its annual income, while Bristol got so deeply into debt to its orphans that it took forty years for the account to recover. Then, as now, raw soldiers were reluctant to dig defensive positions, believing it both cowardly and undignified to skulk in a trench. Sometimes troops were paid a bonus to construct works under fire. More often cannon fire from the other side convinced them that they should be as 'willing to fight with the Spade as with the sword'.[45]

When the war started not even the veterans knew much about military engineering. Sydenham Poyntz, for instance, had to learn on the job, after coming back from the Continent. During the Siege of Gloucester William Chillingworth, the divine turned sapper, tried to make up for a lack of current expertise by borrowing from the Romans. He built shot-proof wooden towers, with ten musketeers inside, known as sows from the crew's legs which resembled a pig's teats, dangling down as they moved.[46]

Such arcane technology failed. To employ the latest techniques developed during the sieges of the Thirty Years' War, both sides relied on foreigners. The queen's connections meant that Frenchmen tended to serve the Crown, while parliament employed Protestant Dutch and German mercenaries. Continental experience demonstrated that the medieval vertical walls which surrounded most British towns were far less effective against cannon fire than sloping earthworks, which absorbed or deflected shot. Many towns were grateful to the foreigners who modernized their defences. 'God by his providence . . . had sent a German engineer', wrote a survivor of the Siege of Manchester, 'to whose skill, industry, faithfulness and valour we owe (under God) much of our late preservation.' Sometimes gratitude lasted only a little longer than the siege: for years Manchester and its saviour, John Rosworme, bickered bitterly over arrears of pay.[47]

When an enemy threatened, all citizens were summoned to defend their home. Sometimes they did so reluctantly, as at Oxford. But in London, where the overwhelming majority of the inhabitants were ardent parliamentarians (particularly after the sack of Brentford in November 1642 demonstrated what might happen to their wives and property) thousands enthusiastically built the city's massive defences. As many as twenty thousand a day laboured on the earth wall, 18 feet high, 11 miles in circumference, with a ditch in front, and straddled by fourteen forts. Many foreign experts believed the capital's defences impregnable.[48] The authorities did all they could to drum up enthusiasm for this project. A visiting Scot recalled seeing two bonfires of books written 'by the popish prelatical faction', burned to whip up zeal, before the volunteers marched out 'with roaring drums, flying colours, and girded swords,' as girls cheered, to dig the defences.[49] Women – even children – joined in.[50]

> From Ladies down to oyster wenches
> Laboured the pioneers in the trenches
> Fallen to pickaxes and tools
> And helped the men dig like Moles.

Royalist poets might sneer, but the fear of a siege, like a siege itself, could bring soldiers and civilians together.

While medieval stone walls were susceptible to mines that collapsed them down rather than blew them up, and explosive charges, known as petards, which blast open iron-studded gates, cannon were the only way to break a hole in well-constructed defences. Except for wood splinters or fragments of stone caused by ricocheting balls, cannon fire did little direct damage to defenders. Brampton Bryan Castle took its first casualty to artillery fire, a cook wounded in the left arm (it proved fatally gangrenous), on the twenty-sixth day of the siege.[51] Artillery killed only five defenders at Scarborough and eight at Pontefract. Indeed at the latter it proved far more deadly to the attackers. 'We shot off that Iron Gun into the hedge where they lay', noted Francis Drake, 'which caused them to make a great lamentation.'[52]

Being cannonaded was, however, not much fun. 'The balls were whistling about me in such a style that you may easily believe that I loved not such a noise', Henrietta Maria told her husband about being bombarded at Bridlington Bay. Mortar fire was especially terrifying. 'Eleven Huge Granadoes like so many tumbling demi phaetons threatened to set the city, if not the whole world on fire', noted a defender of Chester in his diary for 10 December 1645, adding 'This was a terrible night indeed, our houses like so many split vessels crash their supporters and burst themselves in sunder through the very violence of these descending fire brands.' Three months earlier, mortar fire turned some women trapped in Banbury Castle hysterical, making them 'lamentable shriek out'. Some of them wanted to leave the castle, but, one of the royalist defenders hard-heartedly added, 'we would not suffer them'. When a 60-pound shell fell in the street during the Siege of Gloucester, a quick-witted woman doused the fuse with a bucket of water. The defenders of Bridgwater were not so fortunate. In June 1645 a shell started a fire that broke the last straw of the garrison's resistance, persuading them to surrender to the New Model Army.[53] Mortar fire so badly shattered the nerve of the garrison of Lathom House that it seemed possible that they might give up. At an opportune moment 'one thing now happily lent more courage to our men: that one of their engineers mounting the ramparts to see the fall of their granadoes, was happily slain by a marks man from one of our towers.' Lathom never surrendered.[54]

Snipers greatly affected morale. There was little one could do about them: they fired without warning, usually killing officers. Gamekeepers, or wildfowlers, often used their own weapons during sieges. Sixteen defended Lathom House, working in pairs, one spotting, the other shooting, with devastating results.[55] During the Siege of Withenshaw House, a royalist base in Cheshire, a serving girl shot and killed Captain Adams.[56] An even more graphic example of how snipers could upset the social order came the following month when in March 1643 one 'Dymb Dyott', a deaf-mute since birth, killed Lord Brooke during the Siege of Lichfield Cathedral, greatly demoralizing the roundheads.[57]

Food was one of the main determinants of a garrison's frame of mind. After a three-week siege 'without any supply or any news' and seeing many ships sail by, Arthur Freke, a member of the garrison besieged in Rathbury Castle, noted in his diary for July 1642, 'we despaired much'.[58] 'The daily skirmishes were none of them for the defence of the wall,' wrote Isaac Tullie, who at 18 defended Carlisle during the siege of 1644–5, 'but about the fetching of cattle.' Often the two sides fought over the same food supplies. In June 1645 at the Siege of Pontefract Richard Styles, an apprentice lad, climbed down the walls to gather apples, daring the enemy to hit him. After missing on several occasions 'they presently shot the boy', noted a defender, adding that 'the boy is not likely to recover'.[59] When the enemy could not maintain what contemporaries called 'a close siege' the defenders frequently broke through to forage for food. So burdensome might such raids become, that tenants close to the Siege of Newark claimed that they had nothing left to pay their rent.[60]

Since food was so significant it frequently became part of the psychological warfare crucial to any siege. To dispel rumours that they were starving during the Siege of Worcester, the governor, Colonel Edward Whalley sent a buck to Colonel Henry Washington, the commander of the encircling cavaliers.[61] During the Siege of Arundel the royalist defenders offered to swap beef and mutton for sack, tobacco and cards, saying they wanted them to while away the time as they munched their copious rations. The ruse did not work: a week later the cavaliers surrendered, desperately short of food and water.[62] Local tradition has it that Colonel Richard Prater, governor of Nunney Castle in Wales, ordered their last pig tortured to death, so that its prolonged squeals would convince the enemy they were slaughtering a whole herd.[63]

During a siege defenders felt an acute sense of being isolated, of being left to fend for themselves. Cut off, they sometimes minted their own money. They hungered for news as much as for food.[64] Messengers smuggled coded letters into besieged Oxford (where the defenders were eating horse meat) wrapped in a lead bullet which they swallowed, and (in both senses of that word) passed on to the king. With his customary breeding Charles described this as an 'extraordinary means of conveyance'.[65] More comfortable was the technique used by Richard Clark, a Shropshire lad who carried messages for the parliamentary garrison at Wem. He put them in a hollowed stick, sealing the end with dirt. Whenever he came across a party of cavaliers he would play the simpleton, throwing his stick at a bird, to pick up after the enemy had gone. One of the defenders of Limerick called news from outside 'the first comfort we had'. Resistance depended first and foremost on news of relief. When the Limerick garrison learned that the rumour that two English ships had broken through the blockade was false and that the vessels had in fact been driven back, their 'joy was quickly turned to a cold blast'. Three days later Limerick surrendered.[66] The news that Bristol, the heavily fortified city only 30 miles away, had fallen to the king's fores decimated the morale of Gloucester's garrison. The intelligence 'which was almost beyond our fears, brought forth a dark gloomy day', noted the Reverend J. Corbet. The Minister of St Mary Crypt continued that 'the minds of the people were filled with amazement'.[67]

Raids were a most effective way of raising one's own morale and damaging the enemy's. 'To keep the enemy from the town,' Thomas Venn advised in his *Military and Maritime Discipline* (1672), 'sally frequently.' On 18 May 1644 a sudden foray caught the besiegers of Pontefract unawares, still basking in the glow of Sunday morning church. The royalists killed between fifty and sixty of the enemy, stripping their corpses of cash. They also brought back a couple of 'Leager Ladies' – the last folk one would expect to find in a puritan camp during divine worship![68] At the Siege of Farringdon the royalist defenders came under intense fire from some fifty musketeers in a pest-house, 300 yards from the wall, which they had reinforced with sods of earth. After a careful reconnaissance using a telescope, Captain Richard Gwynne led a raiding party who rushed the bunker, fired their muskets each loaded with three balls through the weapon slits, and took forty-five prisoners. The raid, as neat as any in the whole war, took less than three minutes.

Equally effective was the attack that Captain Chisenhall led from Lathom House at four in the morning of 26 April 1644. For weeks a large mortar had bombarded the royalists, damaging their morale far more than their defences. Eventually they became desperate, for as one of the raiding party put it, ''Tis a hard choice, either to kill or be killed.' Suddenly fifty musketeers sallied out, and after a quarter of an hour's hand-to-hand combat scattered the enemy guarding the mortar. They pulled down the defence works, spiked the guns, and tried to drag the mortar back to the house, but a counter-attack thwarted them. Dawn brought the defenders a welcome sight: 'the mortar piece, which had frightened them from their meat and sleep, like a dead lion quietly lying'. It was a turning point: a few days later the enemy gave up.[69]

To maintain their morale defenders resorted to a number of expedients, ranging from drink to humour, from prayer to music.

During the Siege of York William Lewis composed a dozen psalms or hymn tunes, one for each Sunday. They were performed in the Minster which was, remembered Thomas Mace, a clerk from Trinity College, Cambridge, always 'squeezing full of people'. He added that during the siege there was 'the very best Harmonical-Music that I ever heard', much better than that in college chapels, or other cathedrals.[70]

Humour was another way of relieving the stresses of a siege. During that of Limerick a spent musket ball got stuck in the mouth of a laughing lad – much to his mates' amusement.[71] A puritan sapper, who was being paid a shilling bonus a day for undermining the wall at Worcester (a particularly dangerous job), sardonically told Arthur Trevor that he and his Godly friends would have been quite happy to pull down the cathedral for nothing. In August 1643 the king sent Sir Philip Warwick to inspect the works the Earl of Newcastle was constructing before Hull. When Warwick suggested that they were being dug so slowly and so carelessly that he should not count on them to take the town, the Catholic marquis replied, 'You often hear us called the popish army; but you see we trust not in our good works.' Class, rather than religion, lay behind the jibe of the royalist sentry on the walls of Oxford. Hungry, and fed up with a surfeit of officers, he shouted down 'Roundhead, fling me up half a mutton, and I will fling thee down a lord.'[72] More bitter was the response of one of the defenders of Gloucester to the proposal from 'two pettifogging lawyers' by the name of Hill and Bell that they surrender. He rhymed:[73]

> All know too well
> That every bell
> Is useless till it be hanged.

Since sieges were long and anxious ordeals it is not surprising that tobacco and alcohol played an important part in keeping men going.

During the Siege of Rathbury Castle two parliamentary soldiers, Christopher Rosgill and one Tantulus, got so desperate for a smoke that they slipped over the walls, found some tobacco, and lit up. Nicotine was more than hazardous to their health. As they were contentedly lying on a grassy bank, puffing away, the rebels captured them, hanging Private Tantulus and spitting Rosgill on a pike. On hearing the news the latter's wife died of grief, leaving four young orphans.[74]

Drunkenness became such a probem during the Siege of Carlisle that the governor rationed the brewers to only 50 bushels of corn a week.[75] When they ran short of firewood for fermenting the beer, volunteer boozers sallied out from the safety of their walls to strip houses in the suburbs. Another raiding party got so drunk on 'a good store of sack' that they kept on falling off their horses, and were unable to rustle any cattle. At the Siege of Worcester the following year soldiers pulled down privies for firewood, which they sold for liquor.[76]

Alcohol fortified men for the bitter fighting of siege war. The party sent with a petard to blow open the main gate at Oswestry Castle were 'well lined with sack'. One of them, George Cranage, climbed the main gate, cutting the ropes that held up the drawbridge. At the time he must have been fighting drunk, for in later years Richard Gough remembered him as 'a painful, laborious man . . . peaceable and a good neighbour'.[77] The parliamentary commander spent £1 12s. 0d. 'for a firkin of hot waters for the soldiers' who unsuccessfully stormed Corfe Castle in August 1643.[78] Sir John Gell gave his assault troops £40 'to drink' after the successful attack on Belvoir Castle that killed eleven and captured twenty-seven cavaliers.[79] One night, late in the Siege of Worcester, Lieutenant Reynolds and his friend Captain Hodgkins (known to the rest of the defenders as 'wicked Will'), got so plastered that they decided to launch an impromptu raid against some thirty dragoons. Sallying out they scattered the enemy. Wounded and having lost his sword, Hodgkins repulsed a counter-attack with a musket butt, before Reynolds rescued him. Even though the captain 'was so loaded with drink . . . that he fell off by the way', the duo managed to return to Worcester with seven prisoners.[80]

The presence of civilians added to the tensions of a siege. No more than thirty of Bristol's two hundred leading merchants showed the slightest commitment to either side during the city's two sieges. Many of them agreed with Dr Plumtree who asked Colonel Hutchinson, the parliamentary governor of Nottingham, 'What use is the cause to me if my goods are lost?' After the capture of Southsea Castle in 1642 morale in Portsmouth collapsed. 'Being frightened more by their wives', a contemporary reported, the garrison 'did throw away their arms, and absolutely refused to do their duty.' 'The Welsh Howlings' of the women trapped in Oswestry Castle persuaded the Earl of Denbigh not to blow up the parliamentary stronghold, but accept its surrender instead. The sight of the corpses, 'meanly shrouded' of ten women and children who starved to death during the Siege of Limerick destroyed the garrison's resistance.[81] Pressure from townsfolk helped persuade Hull, Bridgwater, Taunton and Plymouth to surrender, while in Brecon the burghers pulled down the walls to forestall a siege in the first place.[82]

Thus governors tried to do all they could to control civilians trapped within their walls. In May 1646, at the start of the Siege of Worcester, Henry Washington made every one in the city swear an oath not to surrender.[83] Then he took a census that showed there were 5,696 civilians and 1,507 troops in the town. Washington collected all the food, tools, timber, fuel and supplies he could find. He expelled many of the civilians as surplus mouths to feed. After relieving the unfortunates of their valuables, including clothes, Colonel Whalley, the enemy commander, drove them back. As the food situation became critical Washington ordered the bakers to produce more bread. They explained that the two surviving horses that powered the mill could not grind enough corn. When one miller, who had plenty of flour, told the governor that he'll be damned if he helped cavaliers, Washington 'switched Smith, the baker . . . and swore to throw him from the walls'. Seeing the error of his ways, Smith returned to his oven.

Such open defiance was rare, and as Miller Smith could vouch, was easily overcome. In sieges – as in wars – most folk tried to carry on with their normal life as best they could. During the Siege of Basing House Dr Thomas Fuller worked on his *History of the Worthies of England*, in spite of the parliamentary bombardment which, he had to admit, disturbed his concentration. William Dugdale fared better, using the college libraries during quiet moments in the Siege of Oxford to research his *Baronage of England*. He even slipped through the enemy lines to Lichfield for a research trip, and took advantage of the city's surrender to go and work on the State Papers in the Tower.[84] The Countess of Derby calmed her nerves as she led the defence of Lathom House by embroidering an exquisite bed hanging.

Although sieges, like most wars, tended to lower crime rates, violence could spill over from military to civilian life. Francis Rouse was outraged when someone stole the hides a tanner had hung up as he tried to ply his trade, the Siege of Pontefract notwithstanding.[85] Trapped in a besieged town Mary Chiles's husband suggested in February 1645 that they murder the merchant billeted in their home for the £300 he carried on him, arguing 'that it was no matter for killing a man twas no crime in a time of war'. So they hit him over the head, threw the body into the sea, walked home, stoked up the fire, 'and then went both to bed'.[86]

Such dastardly behaviour was unusual. For every amoral murderess, sieges produced legions of Amazons. A sniper killed the brave woman who brought ale for the sappers toiling under fire to repair Pontefract's walls. During the Siege of Worcester four hundred 'ordinary sort of women out of every ward' worked daily, often during bombardments, on the defences. Cannon killed several, while others lost their lives while filling in as snipers as the men got some rest.[87] At Bristol Dorothy Hazard (an appropriate name) and her friends rushed in to seal the breach in the wall with sandbags. Then they stood behind the guns to see that the men fired grapeshot at any roundhead who dared poke his head through the gap.[88]

Some females played an even more active part in the fighting. Legend has it that during the Siege of Bridgwater Lady Wyndham took a pot-shot at Oliver Cromwell – she missed. At Chester a diarist recorded 'our women are all on fire, storming in a gallant emulation to out do our men', shooting from walls, windows and roof tops. At Leicester in 1645 they continued sniping long after the royalists had breached the defences.[89]

At Lyme – the Regis would come later for helping Charles II to escape – some four hundred women were assiduous in the parliamentary cause. They put out fires started by incendiary arrows fired over the walls. Women stood guard at night. They reloaded soldiers' muskets, and even fired at the attacking royalists. When the enemy abandoned the siege the enraged women rushed out with picks and shovels, levelling the earth-works in three days.[90] James Strong, a local poet, celebrated their courage:

> To most 'tis known
> The weaker vessels are the stronger grown.

Many women remained with their husbands during sieges. 'My dear wife endured much hardship', wrote Sir Hugh Cholmley, governor of Scarborough Castle, 'yet in the greatest danger would not be daunted but showed a courage even above her sex.'[91] Elizabeth Twysden nursed the wounded during the siege, as did Lucy Hutchinson, the wife of the parliamentary governor of Nottingham.

Even more famous were the heroines who defended their homes when their husbands were away.

Two months after the outbreak of the Irish rebellion Lady Elizabeth Dowdall raised a company of soldiers in Munster. When the rebels tried to plunder her fortified house, she seized their horses and hanged ten men. After some more of them surrounded her house, 'In the night I sent out my soldiers with grenades' to set fire to their quarters, burning the rebels alive. 'I skirmished with the enemy twice or thrice a week', she recorded. Richard Stephenson arrived with three thousand men and with drums beating and pipes wailing, to demand her surrender. 'But I sent him a shot in the head that made him bid the world good-night, and routed the whole army, we shot so hot', concluded the indomitable Lady Elizabeth Dowdall.[92]

Elizabeth, the widow of Maurice Cuffe, a merchant, held out Ballylally Castle for six weeks against the Irish rebels. When they demanded her surrender, she replied that 'by the help of God this castle should to the hazard of life be kept for the Kings Majesty's use'.[93] The Countess of

165

Portland vowed personally to fire the first cannon rather than surrender Carisbrook Castle. Lady Mary Winter's refusal to give up Lydney House did much to thwart parliament's attempts to control Gloucestershire. In the summer of 1643 Lady Mary Bankes defended Corfe Castle during the absence of her husband, Sir John, the Chief Justice of Common Pleas, who was serving the king at Oxford. When the roundheads, some of whom were freed felons, and all of whom were well lubricated with 'hot waters', assaulted the castle, her Ladyship, her daughters and serving women, plus five soldiers, threw burning embers and stones from the battlements with such effect that the enemy could not scale their ladders.[94]

'My Heart: Our Condition is at this time very desperate', wrote Lady Helen Neale to her husband on 9 May 1646 from Hawarden Castle, which was under siege. Although the rebels had brought up heavy cannon to batter down the Great Round Tower, Lady Neale vowed,[95]

> I am purposed to hold out as long as there is meat for man, for none of these eminent dangers shall ever frighten me from my loyalty, but in life and death I will be the king's faithful subject and thy constant loving wife and humble servant.

While royalists might even approve of such defiance, they could not understand Lady Brilliana Harley's refusal to surrender Brampton Castle. When this 'woman of great spirit' spurned the king's demand in August 1643 to surrender, he attributed her defiance to evil counsellors who had taken advantage of a female's weaker nature. Although Lady Harley replied with fitting humility that she could not possibly surrender without her husband's permission, for the castle was his 'by the law of the land', in private she was deeply concerned that he might not approve of her unladylike defiance. Tormented by doubt, she managed to hold out for three months, her modest scorn turning her into the puritan heroine *par excellence*.[96]

On the royalist side the Countess of Derby dramatically displayed the tension between behaving properly as the weaker vessel, and showing courage above one's sex by filling in for one's husband as the governor of men. The daughter of the Huguenot Duc de Thouars and the grand-daughter of William the Silent, courage flowed through Charlotte de Tremoille's veins. In February 1643 she refused to surrender Lathom House, her husband's ancestral home in Lancashire, while he was off fighting for the king in the Isle of Man. 'Though a woman, and a stranger, divorced from her friends, and robbed of her estate,' the countess declared 'she was ready to refuse their utmost violence, trusting in God for both protection and deliverance.'

Lathom House was a mighty fortress, with walls 6 feet thick, nine towers, and a moat 18 yards wide and a fathom deep. The siege was long and bitter. Cannon balls crashed through the windows of the countess's chamber: the garrison suffered dreadfully from a mortar that lobbed 80-pound shells. Confident of victory Colonel Rigby (who had specially invited his friends and neighbours along to see the fun) demanded Lady Derby's surrender. The countess told the herald that 'a due reward for his pains is to be hanged up at her gates, but thou art a foolish instrument of a traitorous pride'. Summoning the garrison, she swore to fight to the death rather than surrender. The pep-talk worked. Cheering troops vowed, 'We'll die for his Majesty and your honour – God save the King!' Emboldened by the countess's defiance two days later they rushed out, captured the mortar, and broke the enemy's will.[97]

Sieges could end in three main ways. The besiegers could abandon them, and move elsewhere, or a relief column could drive them off. Second, a surrender could be negotiated. Or else the defenders could be overcome, either through betrayal from inside, or by a storm. In a sample of twenty-five significant sieges the defenders won in twelve cases, being relieved in seven instances. The attackers prevailed in thirteen instances, in eleven of them through a negotiated surrender, and only twice by storm.

Sieges were played for extremely high stakes. A determined set of defenders could inflict damage way out of proportion to their numbers. 'I am very sorry that we should spend our time unprofitably', wrote Sir Thomas Fairfax in June 1645 about the Siege of Oxford. For this operation he requisitioned some 2,000 spades, 200 scaling ladders, 500 barrels of powder, 40 tons of match, 30 of bullets, 600 mortar shells, and 1,000 hand grenades. On the other side of the walls, George Digby told William Legge, the city's governor, that if Oxford could hold out six months he would 'deliver the kingdom this summer from all its misery'.[98] William Waller promised the garrison of Wardour Castle that 'if we held out for a fortnight longer, he would relieve us or lay his bones under our walls'.[99] Isolated and surrounded, with nowhere to run, the defence clung desperately to the hope of relief. The joy of being rescued was intense. 'This is indeed the day of our deliverance, a day to be remembered, and never to be forgot throughout our generations', wrote Lady Brilliana Harley to her husband, after the royalists lifted the Siege of Brampton Bryan. After a ghastly blockade, in which the defenders of Rathbarry Castle had to eat horse flesh, and the horses consumed their own dung, a relief column under Colonel Myn arrived, sounding their trumpets in jubilation. 'They appeared to us like the Angels of God', exulted Arthur Freke.[100]

The predicament of the besiegers could be as bad, if not worse. Only rarely, as at Gloucester, Newcastle or Shrewsbury, did they enjoy the luxury of living in huts, having mostly to sleep, eat and fight for weeks on end in the open, the other side having destroyed surrounding buildings.[101] 'We endured a long and tedious siege', reported Jacob Travers, a parliamentary soldier at Arundel, 'the weather was cold, the night was long, and the season of the year troubled us who lay in the field extremely with high winds and extraordinary showers of rain'. A defender explained why the roundheads abandoned the Siege of Manchester: 'By reason of cold, wet, hunger and thirst and labour, want of sleep, and a bitter welcome that we gave them, their hearts were discouraged mightily.' Military writers agreed that there was nothing more dangerous than digging zig-zag trenches towards a strongly defended position, or setting off a mine under a city. In sum, as George Monck put it, 'Long sieges ruin armies.'[102]

They could also ruin the defenders.

The trick was not to surrender too soon, for that could lead to a court-martial and the firing squad, nor too late, for the enemy might refuse quarter, massacre the garrison and pillage the town.

'To betray that Town into plunder and slaughter', Sir Barnabus Scudamore justified his surrender of Hereford after a brief siege, 'had been an act unchristian and most barbarous.'[103] Colonel Francis Windebanke surrendered Bletchingdon House to Oliver Cromwell in 1645 without a fight, because he was desperately worried about the safety of his new wife and her lady friends: the crown court-martialled him and shot him against a wall of Merton College. Captain Thomas Steele met the same fate for surrendering Beeston Castle 'wickedly and treacherously' to Captain Thomas Sanford, after he had infiltrated the castle with eight men through a small back opening. After a short stand-off, Steel invited Sanford to his lodgings, 'where they dined together, and much beer was sent up'.[104]

Other governors were lucky to escape with their lives – although without their honour. Although at first Colonel Nathaniel Fiennes publicly burned royal proclamations and vowed he would 'consent to be hanged' rather than yield Bristol to the king's forces, he surrendered in July 1643 after a brief siege. Widely denounced as 'that bloody Coward', Parliament had Fiennes court-martialled and sentenced to death, before pardoning him at the last moment.[105] After letting him be twice marched out before a firing squad, Charles commuted Colonel Richard Fielding's death sentence for prematurely surrendering Reading. But the king never forgave his nephew, and greatest general, for surrendering Bristol in September 1645. Rupert's decision was a rational one: he was outnumberd nine to one; the townsfolk did not support him; he had just lost Fort Prior, a key bastion, the roundheads having massacred its defenders; as a professional soldier Rupert knew only too well the fate of those who tardily surrendered.

Front-line troops have always had conventions about the proper time to surrender. 'Sorry chum, too late' was a catch-phrase British soldiers used during the Second World War to justify shooting enemy trying to give up after they had fought beyond a reasonable time.[106] During the civil wars troopers called this process 'stouting it out'. When the royalist garrison of Hopton Castle, Herefordshire, fought beyond a reasonable time in 1644, all but one of them were massacred.[107] Troops were fully aware of the dangers of surrendering too late. After holding out for thirty-four days, and seeing the relief ships beaten back, Captain Courtnay, the governor of Limerick, sent out a surrender offer. While waiting for a reply a member of the garrison wrote in his diary that 'Every hour begat in us new cause of fears, and we doubted to be assaulted before the next morning, which if they had done, we should have been undone.' The offer was made just in time, for after much debate the defenders received quarter for their lives and goods.[108] Two years later the defenders of Duncannon were less fortunate. Captain William Smith warned Lord Esmonde of the peril of holding out for too long: 'if the rebels take the fort (by storming it) undoubtedly they will put you all to the sword: which would be much lamented.' It was. Esmonde perished in the ensuing massacre.[109]

Governors, such as Edmund Ludlow, were all too aware of the dangers of finding a balance between surrendering too soon and too late. Captain Thomas Sanford was so effective in persuading garrisons to surrender that a contemporary described him as 'a man lavish in ink, and long words'. While, as we have seen, beer may have been more effective in persuading the cowardly Captain Steele to surrender Beeston Castle to him, Sanford usually resorted to cruder threats. 'I presume you know very well', the captain told one garrison, 'that I neither give nor take quarter . . . if you put me to the least trouble or loss of blood to force you,' Sanford warned the defenders of Nantwich, 'Let not your zeal in a bad cause dazzle your eyes any longer.' If his troops had to assault the town they would become uncontrollable 'to the terror of the Old and Females'. So convincing were such threats that General Byron, Sanford's senior officer, reassured Nantwich that the story that he intended showing them no mercy was a 'false and wicked slander'. But the townsfolk had good cause for concern. A few days earlier the royalists had killed the defenders of the nearby village of Barthomley as they tried to give up.[110]

During the Siege of Gloucester the forces fired message arrows over the walls telling the defenders 'your God, Waller, has forsaken you', and that they had repulsed the Earl of Essex's relief column. In addition to adding to the sense of isolation, of being forgotten, that all besieged troops feel, the cavaliers threatened 'no quarter for such obstinate traitorous rogues', if they had to storm the city. A bowman fired back the answer:[111]

> Waller's no God of ours, base rogues you lie,
> Our God survives for all eternity.
> Though Essex beaten, as you do say
> Rome's yoke we are resolved nere to obey.

Normally surrender negotiations were carried out in a far more gentle-manly fashion. 'I shall offer to your consideration the example of Liverpool, Basing and Lathom, which by their refusal of honourable terms when they were propounded, were not long after subjected to captivity and the sword', Sir William Brereton reminded Lord Byron, who in 1646 was governor of Chester. Written proposals and counters would pass across the walls. 'After a fortnight's siege, and much ink and little blood spilled', John Rushworth sardonically noted, Hawarden Castle 'was surrendered'.[112]

As a rule the first demand for capitulation came at the start of the siege, with additional ultimata as the attackers tightened the noose. The critical moment transpired just before the storm. If such was averted defenders would be spared: if the town had to be taken they were lucky to escape with their lives.

Surrender terms varied. At best a garrison marched out, drums booming, flags flying, carrying their weapons, with lighted matches. At worst they yielded without conditions.

All too often, however, surrender agreements broke down. For one thing defeated troops were pitifully vulnerable. 'I never saw so many weak and feeble creatures together in my life', recalled Sir Thomas Berkeley about the garrison of Arundel Castle, who marched out on 6 January 1644, 'for almost all the common soldiers were half starved, and many of them hardly able to set one foot before another.'[113] More often such pathetic sights stimulated aggression rather than compassion on the part of victors (similar to the lust for blood that emerged after a unit was broken and ran from battle). In both instances the winners felt that they had already suffered enough from the vanquished. After parliamentary forces surrendered at Bristol in 1643, and at Lostwithiel in 1644, royalists soldiers and outraged civilians ignored the terms that their commanders had conceded. They beat up and pillaged the enemy, notwithstanding the efforts of their officers to stop them with drawn swords.[114]

If surrender negotiations failed, the attackers had either to abandon the siege, resort to a storm, or persuade someone inside to betray the city.

Since it was so easy and they were so vulnerable, governors dealt harshly with those who tried to double-cross them. The royalists dangled several townsmen up from *HMS Reformation*'s yard-arm for scheming to sell out Weymouth. Parliament hanged two London merchants in 1643 before their own houses for planning to betray the city in the so-called 'Waller Plot'. Not even the king's personal intervention could save Alderman Robert Yeomans and George Bouchier, two leading Bristol merchants, from being strung up by Governor Fiennes for intriguing to open a city gate to Prince Rupert's forces. To justify his action Fiennes cited 'The law of Nature amongst all men, and the Law of Arms among all soldiers.' In January 1644 a court-martial sentenced Roger L'Estrange to the gallows for trying to betray King's Lynn to the king's forces. But when Charles and Prince Rupert intervened (and threatened possible reprisals), the sentence was commuted, and L'Estrange spent the next four years in Newgate

Gaol. Lord Byron blamed the loss of Liverpool on 'the treachery of the common soldiers', many of whom had gone over to parliament. 'Some few of them are since fallen into my hands, upon whom I have done justice', he concluded with ominous satisfaction.[115]

Such 'secret spies and conspirators' were harshly treated for sparing the enemy the cost of a storm. 'It cannot be but a bloody business', Robert Baillie wrote in trepidation of the assault on York set for 15 June 1644. He was right. Three hundred Scots lost their lives when the mine under St Mary's blew up prematurely, burying dozens alive. So demoralized were the Scots that Baillie had to admit that 'they could not be brought to storm any more'.[116]

Because mines usually exploded without warning, and in the dead of night, they could damage a garrison's morale as much as its walls. 'I was lifted up with it from the floor, with much dust suddenly about me', recalled Sir Edmund Ludlow of the sudden firing of an enemy mine at Wardour Castle, 'I found both the doors of my chamber blown open, and my window.' Barnabus Scudamore remembered what happened when his servant told him that the enemy had blown an opening in Hereford:[117]

I leapt up, commanded him to get me a horse, and slipping into my clothes I ran instantly down with my sword and pistol in my hand, to the fore gate towards the street, when the enemy's horse had already fired upon me, and shot my secretary in the belly.

Artillery was another way to take a town. Cannon balls chipped away at walls, making a gap through which troops could clamber.

Charging across open ground to reach that gap in the first place was a terrible ordeal. 'To adventure naked bodies against an Army defended with Stone-Walls, Strong-Works, and a Castle', wryly noted an eyewitness of the parliamentary assault on Bristol in August 1645, 'was an argument of little self respect.' A similar point was made after the roundhead assault on Derby: 'the enemies being in the works, nothing but their heads appearing, and the parliament's force being without defence in the open field.'[118]

The royalist veteran, Richard Atkyns, knew only too well the vulnerability of flesh and blood to lead and iron. He wrote, "Twould grieve one's heart, to see men drop like ripe fruit in a strong wind, and never see their enemy: for they had made loopholes through the wall, that has the full bodies of the assailants for their mark.' An eyewitness used similar language to describe the failure of the first parliamentary assault against Bolton on 28 May 1644: '[We] gave them about half an hour's sharp entertainment . . . and repulsed them bravely to the enemy's great loss and discouragement, and in retreat cut them down before them in great abundance, and they fell like leaves from a tree in a winter storm.'[119] Attacking troops not only suffered heavy casualties, but did so in a highly visible manner that demoralized while encouraging the enemy, who even when hit were well hidden behind their defences.

Troops often revenged themselves on those, innocent or not, whom they believed had put them to the peril of a storm. When they learned that the defenders of York had rejected a surrender offer the roundheads were reported 'mightily enraged, and I doubt not will be careful to distinguish persons', once they took the city. Defenders could be just as vengeful to those who tried and failed to take their positions. 'Our men killed eight', wrote a captain in the Lichfield garrison, 'and took one, which they hanged three yards from the wall, like a sign, and bid Prince Rupert shoot him down.' Since the officer was writing to his wife, apparently he felt no shame for the atrocity.[120] Defeated troops could become numb. After the assault troops were pushed back for the third time at Lyme, losing some four hundred men in a maelstrom of fire, smoke and noise, an observer reported 'an almost general silence'.[121]

No military action was bloodier and more brutal than a storm. A roundhead warned Sir John Byron that if he wanted to capture Nottingham Castle 'he must wade to it in blood'.[122] Richard Sandys and his roundheads took half an hour of bitter fighting 'at swords' point' before they reached the top of the defences at Shelford House. A fortnight later, on 21 November 1645, Sandys and his officers had to use their swords to drive their own men against the defences of Belvoir Castle, 'the strongest I have seen in England'. Afterwards the roundheads turned their blades against the enemy, slaughtering them all without quarter and without exception.[123] When they discovered two of their own comrades setting fires to thwart the storm of Taunton, the roundhead troopers lynched the traitors on the spot, also stringing up a woman who happened to be with them. The royalists took eight hours to force a way through the defences of Lyme, and might well have been repulsed had not the flag bearer leading the charge nonchalantly told a comrade after his hands had been shot off, 'Here take you the colours while I go to the surgeons to be dressed.'[124]

Sir Anthony Ashley Cooper's description of the assault on Abbotsbury in October 1644 is one of the most graphic descriptions of civil war combat:[125]

> The business was extreme hot for above six hours, we were forced to burn down an outgate to a court before we could get to the house, and then our men rushed in through the fire and got in to the hall porch where with furse faggots they set fire on it, and plied the windows so hard with small shot, that the enemy durst not appear in the low rooms. In the meantime one of our guns played on the other side of the house, and the gunners with fire balls and the grenadiers with scaling ladders endeavoured to fire the second story,

but that not taking effect our soldiers were forced to wrench open the window with iron balls, and forcing in faggots of furse fire, set the whole house in a flaming fire, so that it was not possible to be quenched. And then they cried for quarter, but having beat diverse men before it, and considering how many garrisons of the same nature we had to deal with, I gave command that there should be none given.

As the victors plundered the smoldering ruins, stripping the corpses of friend and foe alike, the powder magazine blew up, killing eighty of them. Afterwards, Cooper's troops were so battle-worn that they had to be withdrawn from active service for several weeks.

Resistance sometimes continued even after the defences had been breached, particularly in a city where buildings provided plenty of cover. An eyewitness recalled the hand-to-hand fighting which took place in February 1643 as the roundheads tried to dislodge the cavaliers from Preston, 'where there was such a thrashing as never was heard of before'. There is no doubt that they were as keen as mustard. Captain Both's and Captain Holland's companies raced one another to be the first through the breach. After clearing one house a pair of musket men tried to root the enemy from another. Three times the royalists drove them back, grabbing their muskets as they were about to fire, flaying at the enemy with anything at hand. Eventually Captain Ashurst led sixteen men behind the house, smashed down a wall, shot a volley, flushing out the survivors. In retaliation the royalists burned the houses, killing a woman and child in the cross-fire. A few months later, having easily broken through Reading's outer defences, the cavaliers lost many men to snipers who fired from houses inside the town. In revenge they burned down any building suspected of harbouring resistance, and promiscuously pillaged the property of friend and foe alike with a ferocity usually reserved for towns that had shown much greater resistance.[126]

Just as the critical moment in a battle took place when a unit disintegrated, in a siege it occurred when the defenders broke. In a siege this collapse could be an even more savage affair. Because it took longer to bring about, and because it was far harder to overcome men hiding behind earthworks (as opposed to standing in open battle order), disintegration in a siege was all too often followed by a blood-bath. From her experiences as the governor's wife during the Siege of Nottingham, Lucy Hutchinson described this process: 'the brave turn cowards, fear unnerves the most mighty, makes the generous base, and great men do those things that they blush to think on.'[127]

During such a killing frenzy all were victims. Of 1,200–1,500 people who perished when the royalists sacked Bolton in 1644, 700 were civilians, which was nearly half the town's peacetime population.[128]

A royalist described the disintegration of the enemy when he stormed Cirencester in 1643: 'They were at their wits' end, and stood like men amazed, fear bereft them of understanding and memory.'[129] The Welsh infantry were in an especially pitiless mood, perhaps because when they wavered their own cavalry had forced them at sword's point into the breach. Even though the cavaliers killed few defenders during the assault, they slew many afterwards, and 'without quarter killed all they overtook, which so enraged our men' that, according to a parliamentary observer, 'they fired upon them for nearly an hour'. After resistance completely broke, the rage of the royalists knew few bounds. So shattered were eleven hundred rebel survivors taken at Cirencester that all but sixteen of them volunteered to fight for the king.

After a four-day bombardment the roundheads breached the walls of Cardigan Castle. One of the attackers recalled that the sight of him and his comrades pouring through the gap turned the enemy into 'men bereft of all sense'. They could not even fire the cannon loaded with grape and already aimed at the breach, which could have repulsed the attack. Dropping the smoking linstocks, they craved for mercy: it was granted.[130]

When asked to surrender Berkeley Castle in February 1645, Governor Sir Charles Lucas retorted that 'he would eat horse-flesh before he would yield, and man's flesh when that was done'. The roundheads scaled the wall with ladders, killing forty cavaliers as they tried to surrender. This, Chaplain Sprigge noted, 'was such a terror and discouragement to the enemy' that even though they still held most of the castle, and had plenty of men and supplies left, and could thus have easily continued fighting, they threw down their arms.

An eyewitness recalled how royalist resistance evaporated once the Scots had breached Newcastle's defences and chased them to the market-place. Unable to run any further 'they presently called for quarter, and laying down their arms without assurances, some were taken, some were shaken, some stood still, and some fled away to hide their bleeding bodies in some secret shelter'.[131]

In May 1644 after the parliamentarians stormed Lincoln's outer wall the garrison collapsed equally precipitously. Taking to their heels, they ran not knowing which way to turn. One of their chastisers recalled that they 'cried out for quarter, saying that they were poor Array men [conscripts]. We slew fifty of them', and took seven hundred prisoner. So demoralized were they by defeat and disillusioned with the king's cause that 'all the common soldiers after they were taken did cheerfuly desire to serve the parliament'.[132]

Some of the seven hundred royalists captured at Lincoln might a year earlier have taken part in the successful Siege of Preston. After their first assault was repulsed with heavy casualties in March 1643, the survivors were in no mood to turn the other cheek, when – thanks to a traitor who let them in through a back gate – the second attack succeeded.[133] The leading troops had just endured the Siege of Lathom House, which made them all the more intent on revenge. A survivor recalled:

> Nothing was heard but 'Kill dead! Kill Dead!' was the word in the town, killing all before them without any respect . . . their horse men pursuing the poor amazed people, killing, stripping, and spoiling all they could meet with, nothing regarding the doleful cries of the women or children.

Some were slashed down, as they begged for quarter: others had their brains dashed out when they fell beneath the flaying hoofs of fear-crazed horses.[134]

Ever since the walls came tumbling down at Jericho, victorious soldiers have believed that they were entitled to a sack after taking a city. Because it was as much a psychological as an economic reward for enduring a storm, sacks were carried out with needless brutality.[135] 'Three hours plundering is the shortest rule of war', Marshall Tilly said of the Siege of Magdeburg in 1633, 'A soldier must have something for his toil and trouble.' In fact the sack of Magdeburg went on for three days; its population fell from 30,000 to 5,000.

Many compared the sack of Brentford in November 1642, the first of the English Civil War, to the worst atrocities of the Thirty Years' War. Although Brentford was a pretty tame affair, it scared the citizens of London so badly that a few days later they turned the king back at Turnham Green, so denying Charles his best chance of winning the war.

This reverse did not, however, lessen cavalier appetites for booty. When they took Cirencester the following February they 'fell to plundering, all that night, and the next day, and the following'. The crown carried off enough wool to make uniforms for much of its army. The allegation that many innocent men, women and children were murdered became so widely accepted that the royalists had to put out a circular denying it. Few believed Prince Rupert's statement that he could not understand why 'their pamphlets make such a noise' about a 'little cloth borrowed by our soldiers'.[136]

The sack of Birmingham two months later dispelled any lingering doubts about the rapacity of the prince's troopers. They bore a special grudge against the townsfolk, whom they believed had insulted the king the previous October. Even though the inhabitants did not put up much resistance to Charles's crack troopers, according to a contemporary pamphlet 'The Cavaliers rode into the town like so many furies of Bedlams.' They burned down some eighty buildings, including Robert Porter's mill which was making swords for parliament, and left three hundred and fifty people homeless. They fired at anyone they saw at a window. They swore. They 'hacked, hewed and pistolled all they met with'. Fifteen naked bodies were found mangled to death. They shot Mr Tillam, a surgeon, as he stood at his door welcoming them. They murdered one Whitehall, a lunatic, who claimed to be Jewish (a disillusion which had already earned him twenty years in Bridewell), mistaking him for the Reverend Roberts, a local puritan divine. Finally, alleged parliament's hacks, they raped many women, bragging 'how many they had ravished, glorying in the shame'. Even though rape was surprisingly rare during the civil war, and it was later suggested that French papist troops were mostly to blame, such stories were widely believed. 'I heard of the miserable destruction of Birmingham, which I much confess took the deepest apprehension with me', a gentleman from Walsall wrote to a friend in Oxford.[137]

News of the fate meted out to Birmingham so terrified some of Gloucester's merchants that in 1643 they offered the royalists a large sum of money if they could restrict their troops to plundering only the possessions of parliamentary sympathizers. Senior commanders disliked pillaging, less from the milk of human kindness but because they turned military units into gangs of undisciplined brutes. Thus after the capture of the Earl of Chesterfield's house at Bretby, Derbyshire, in late 1642, Sir John Gell's officers begged his wife to give each of their men half a crown to forestall a sack. When she refused, saying she had no money left, they even offered to lend it to her, but 'she willfully and refractory said she would not give them a penny: and then indeed the soldiers plundered her house'.[138]

There was more to plundering a vanquished enemy than the simple economic bargain which Gell's officers were trying to make with Lady Chesterfield. She was too proud to submit. The soldiers enjoyed the sense of power plundering gave them, as much, if not more, than any financial gain. After storming Sherborne Castle in 1645 Fairfax's troops started to massacre the defenders, and only stopped when they discovered 'a great store of treasure'. Afterwards an observer noted that 'five shillings gotten in the way of spoil from the enemy gives them more content than twenty shilling by way of reward'.[139]

If wages are the payment for work, then plunder is the perquisite of power. When they plunder, soldiers, who are usually drawn from the bottom of society, and are always ordered about by those at the top, can put the boot in as they wear it on the other foot. In more ways than one, as they rampaged through a captured city, still terrified by the sights and sounds of the storm they have barely survived, may victorious soldiers turn the world upside down.

For the victims the upheaval of a sack was an even more traumatic event. 'Oh what a night and morning was that in which Bradford was taken', recalled Joseph Lister, who was a teenager when the town fell to the king's forces in July 1643. Forced to flee the city for his life, afterwards he was surprised by how few people had actually perished in the sack: 'I think it not mercy than half a score were slain, and that was a wonder considering what hatred and rage they came with against us'.[140]

After losing thirty of their men in the breach the royalist infantry were fighting mad as they despoiled Leicester in May 1645. They hanged Mr Raynor, 'an honest religious gentleman'. They killed Mr Sawyer in cold blood. They massacred many prisoners of war, and they 'put diverse women inhumanly to the sword'. By nightfall, remembered Captain Richard Symonds, one of the attackers, there was 'scarce a cottage unplundered . . . and no quarter given to any in the heat'. Many of the assault troops were infantry from the poor mountainous counties of mid-Wales, who robbed with enthusiasm and without mercy. The parish registers, which show seven hundred and nine burials immediately after the siege, do not tell the full story of the horror. Robert Warburton, who had been apprenticed to his father, who was killed, lost not only a parent but time served. William Harvey, who with his wife and children had lost all their possessions, desperately sought admission to the Cordwainers' Company so as to restore his fortunes. John Stocker, a joiner, similarly ravaged, begged to be admitted to the Carpenters' Company. Poor William Summers lost his house, fruit trees, all his possessions, had his son killed, his wife driven mad with grief, and had to resort to working as a butcher.[141]

Just as fighting was more vicious in Scotland and Ireland, so too were sacks of captured cities. After the defenders of Aberdeen refused to surrender to Montrose in September 1644, murdering the drummer boy who brought the invitation to show their determination, Montrose sent in his Irish troops. Taking the town after a fairly easy two-hour fight they sacked Aberdeen with a ferocity that recalled the excesses of the Thirty Years' War. Over a thousand perished. Montrose's troops forced well-dressed men to strip naked before hacking them to death, lest the blood ruin the value of their plundered clothes, and killed or raped the wives who protested.

Such an untamed lust for rapine and plunder the Irish rebels turned to their own advantage during the siege of Duncannon in January 1645. They left a trunk just outside the gates as if it contained some precious goods, dropped by a refugee in a desperate hurry to flee the carnage. The defenders brought the chest inside, and opened it up. Booby trapped and full of gunpowder it exploded, killing several rebels.[142]

In England, at least, there was no bloodier storm nor more vicious sack than that at Basing House (plate 13). One parliamentary officer called it 'absolutely the strongest place in England'. Another thought it 'as large and spacious as the Tower of London'. Without doubt the Marquis of Winchester's ancestral home was an enormous place, covering 14.5 acres, strategically located west of London. It consisted of an Old House, surrounded by a Norman earthwork, as well as a New House of 380 rooms built during Henry VIII's reign. The whole area was protected by guard towers linked by a brick wall 8 feet thick, with an earth core strong enough to absorb the heaviest cannon balls. The River Loddon had most likely been dammed, making it an even more difficult obstacle.

In July 1643 the Marquis easily repulsed the first attempt by local troops led by Colonel Richard Norton to take Basing. The following November a second assault posed a much more dangerous threat. William Waller arrived with sixteen horse troops, eight dragoon companies, and thirty-six of infantry, including the London Trained Bands. They made three assaults, and although they captured some of the outer works, their 'hot and desperate charge' was beaten back, at times by women hurling down sticks and stones, 'which hurt some of our men'. The failure to storm Basing broke the Londoners' morale. Waller had to threaten to shoot any mutineers who made good their chant to go 'Home! Home!'

Realizing that they had little chance of storming such a well-defended bastion, in the summer of 1645 the parliamentarians decided to starve Basing into submission. They failed when a relief column from Oxford arrived with supplies. So in September the roundheads concluded that a bloody frontal assault was their only option. After weeks of artillery fire, which made two breaches, both wide enough to 'let a regiment pass', six thousand of Cromwell's Ironsides attacked, at six in the morning of 16 October. Screaming their war-cry, 'Down with the Papists! Down with the Papists!' it took them about forty-five minutes to get through the breach. Once inside the walls they tried to get into the buildings through windows, out of which the enemy threw down hand grenades, with murderous effect. Colonel Pickery led his regiment to capture the Old House, where the defenders fought to the last, defending every entrance with their swords. As one man fell, another immediately leapt into his place, desperate to stop the waves of attackers. A newspaper reported:[143]

> Our men in full bodies and with great resolution came on. The dispute was long and sharp, the enemy for aught I can learn, desired no quarter, and I believe had but little offered them. You must remember what they were. They were most of them Papists. Therefore our muskets and swords did show them little compassion.

After two hours all passion was spent. Many, including women, perished in the hot blood of the final assault. When Dr Griffith's daughter rushed to stop a roundhead from beating her father, the fellow smashed her brains in. When eight or nine gentlewomen tried to run away they 'were entertained by the common soldiers somewhat coarsely, yet not uncivilly', reported Hugh Peters, 'they left them with some clothes upon them . . . '. Some royalists were murdered in cold blood, including six priests. 'Cursed be he that doth the Lord's Work negligently', said Major Thomas Harrison as he shot Major Robinson (who had been a Drury Lane comedian in civil life). Harrison also killed Major Craffaud as he was trying to escape.

A hundred cavaliers died, and three times as many were taken prisoner, being plundered without mercy. Inigo Jones, the architect, was stripped naked, and had to be carried out wrapped in a blanket. The booty was worth over £200,000 – an immense sum – the furnishings in one room alone were valued at £1,300. The soldiers pillaged all night. One man found £130 in gold. Another discovered three bags of silver, which he flaunted, and his comrades stole, leaving him with but half a crown. As the victors picked through the ruins, the stately home caught fire, taking twenty hours to burn down to its bare walls and chimneys. Even they did not survive, for the roundheads encouraged the locals to cart the stones away to rebuild their own barns and cottages. 'We had little loss; many of the Enemy our men put to the sword, and some officers of quality', reported Cromwell, 'God exceedingly abounds in His Goodness to us'.[144]

And so, in many more ways than one, sieges changed the face of Britain during the civil wars.

8

TRADESMEN OF KILLING ... MANAGERS OF VIOLENCE

Soldiers are the tradesmen of killing, but officers are the managers of violence.

Harold D. Lasswell, quoted G. Dyer, *War*, 131

Military history has always focused on generals: they are the stars of the drama – indeed, in many armies stars are their badges of rank. Their strategic decisions are investigated: their personalities are publicized. But for most soldiers generals remain remote, even unimportant figures. They give orders which are transmitted down through a chain of command to their own officers, who are responsible at the shop floor level, as it were, for the day-to-day management of the trade of violence.

Effective generals must recognize and bridge this chasm by satisfying some important need in their men. Some try to do so through cheap ploys of public relations, be they two badges in their berets or pearl handled revolvers. A good general, wrote Roger Boyle, the seventeenth-century soldier and military theorist, should tell his men before battle that their cause is just, that the results of victory will be highly beneficial, and those of defeat fatal, and that they must not lose the honour they have accrued over years of distinguished service.[1]

Although generals have been giving pep talks for thousands of years, their impact is limited.[2] A much more effective way of getting the individual to identify with his general is to link them both as part of a few, a happy few, as a band of brothers. Before the Armada Elizabeth attempted to do so in terms of gender. 'I know I have the body of but a weak and feeble woman, but I have the heart and stomach of a king', she reassured her troops at Tilbury. 'Come my boys, my brave boys', General Philip Skippon promised before Turnham Green, 'I will run the same hazards with you.' Before setting out to subdue the Welsh in 1648 Oliver Cromwell addressed each regiment, saying 'that he had often times ventured his life with them, and they with him, against the common enemy of the kingdom'. When he promised 'to live and die with them ... all threw up their caps, giving a great shout'.[3]

180

One of the most effective ways of convincing those you are asking to die for you is by citing your own heroic record. Sending men to their deaths requires tremendous self-confidence. As Clarendon – a civilian if ever there was one – noted, 'generals are a strange kind of people'. The image of the heroic leader is still with us. Generals sport medal ribbons on their chest not as guarantees that they will give the right orders, but as validations that they have the moral authority to order men to their possible deaths in the first place. Since the beginnings of warfare the hero has been the model for generalship. Alexander the Great was a legendary leader who quite literally led his men where the fighting was fiercest and most critical.[4] No protagonist exercised a greater impact on Protestants in the British Isles at the start of the civil wars than Gustavus Adolphus, stories of whose fearless leadership had filled newsletters for half a dozen years.

Heroic leadership can run the risk of becoming *opera buffa*, especially if a general opts to eschew excitement by leading his army from behind. But in the civil wars such men were rare. In February 1644 at the Battle of Torrington, to give one of many possible examples, the royalist general, Sir Ralph Hopton, was wounded in the face and had his horse shot from under him. His opponent, Sir Thomas Fairfax, was nearly killed when eighty-four barrels of gunpowder blew up, showering flaming timbers, bricks, and molten lead down upon him. Like every successful leader, from corporal to general, Hopton and Fairfax shared the same risks as their men.

Doing so inspired untrained conscripts to contend like veterans during the extremely savage siege of Colchester in 1648. 'I never saw men fight with more gallant resolution and courage, than these men did, although raw country fellows', recalled Sergeant-Major Carter. He credited such extraordinary courage to the willingness of all leaders, from 'those honourable lords and gentleman' to 'the meanest and inferior of [non commissioned] officers to share the hazards of the private soldiers'.[5]

Soldiers will follow men they like, they respect, and with whom they can identify. A trooper praised General Waller for staying with his men after the royalists had repulsed their assault on Basing House. 'Although it grew dark, and the cold wind blew, yet was Sir William Waller so resolute and valorous that he would not depart the field.'[6] All too soon, however, Waller learnt that more than anything else soldiers want to fight for a winner because the victorious optimizes their own chances of survival. At the start of the war Waller's use of sudden night marches was so successful that he earned the nickname 'William the Conqueror'. After he started to lose battles, men began to drift away from his command until it was said that soldiers would prefer to serve under any general other than Waller for 'all the money in England'.[7]

In peace, the maintenance of economic power and kinship relations was crucial. In combat the bottom line was winning and surviving. As violence ground on, waxing ever more ruthless, everything else got less relevant.

Indeed victory and staying alive are closely connected. Although far more troops fought for parliament than for the king, 48 per cent more royalists died in combat in England, while proportionately twice as many of their leaders perished.[8]

At the start of the first English civil war both sides chose commanders for their social cachet: they were selected not because they would wage total and effective war, but because the war they would wage would not threaten the status quo. Charles picked grandees such as the Marquis of Newcastle or the Earl of Glamorgan, whose local influence enabled them to raise troops, while their national stature implied that the troops they recruited would be used to defend, not destroy the *ancien régime*. Parliament paradoxically did the same in choosing the Earls of Essex and Manchester. In much the same fashion soldiers preferred to serve under local officers, particularly at the start of the war. In October 1642 the local levies mutinied at Chelmsford rather than serve under English and Scots veterans of the Thirty Years' War. They did not accept the Earl of Warwick's argument that 'the present time doth require men bred in war', insisting that Henry Farr from Great Burstead be their commanding officer.[9]

But as the war went on, and as the stakes got greater, both sides turned to professionals – to those plain russet-coated captains who knew what they fought for and loved what they knew – as opposed to those who were gentlemen and were nothing more. The problem that Cromwell recognized was more serious for parliament because it lacked well-born leaders in the first place. 'The officers of the enemy's side were', complained Clarendon, 'for the most part of no better families than the common soldier.' In the New Model Army 'most of the colonels were tradesmen, brewers, tailors, goldsmiths, shoemakers and the like', agreed Denzil Holles, 'a notable dung hill'. In fact of the 37 generals and colonels of the New Model, only 7 (or 19 per cent) were not born gentlemen, 9 sprung from the nobility, and 21 from the gentry. Promotion in the New Model was, as Fairfax told his father, 'either by antiquity or merit', those having served outside its ranks having little chance of advancement.[10]

In addition to ability officers needed energy. 'My General hates idleness', wrote one of the Earl of Denbigh's officers, 'I must tell you that he lets us not rest night and day.' Simeon Ashe recorded that before Marston Moor General Leslie 'exercised his martial abilities with unceased activity and industry', placing every unit in its right place and encouraging each one of his Scots soldiers.[11]

Leading troops into battle was not a young man's game. The average age of a sample of 126 colonels in the Royalist Northern Army was 35, that in the cavalry being 30, and the foot 38, which suggests that the physical demands of mounted warfare were greater than in the infantry, where anyway commanding officers usually rode. Of the 226 Lancashire gentry who took part in the civil war, the median age for royalists was 34 and for parliamentarians 38. The age differential for a sample of 35 roundheads and 41 cavalier senior leaders was almost the same, the average for the two being 43.2 and 39.5 years. Since this was a fairly senior group, 25 of them became generals or admirals; on average they started fighting at the comparatively late age of 41, and their military service lasted 7.3 years (7.7 for the parliamentarians and 6.9 for the roundheads). As a group they saw a fair amount of combat, taking part in an average of 3.5 major battles and 1.37 significant sieges. Or to put that another way, only 3 of the 76 were *not* present at Edgehill, Marston Moor, Newbury or Naseby.[12]

As the war continued both sides suffered from a surplus of officers. Between September 1644 and January 1645 the number of infantry in Manchester's parliamentary army fell 15 per cent, while the cost of its officer corps increased by 8 per cent.[13] This surplus of officers was a far more serious problem for the king than for parliament, especially as the war dragged on and he found it ever harder to recruit infantry.

At the start of the civil war Charles issued commissions of array authorizing a colonel to raise a regiment and appoint its officers. When that regiment lost men through attrition, instead of restoring it with replacements, the king issued a new commission of array to another colonel who would appoint a fresh set of officers, and find new recruits, or poach veterans from shattered units. Thus in twelve months in the middle of the first civil war Charles issued fresh commissions for forty-nine foot regiments, and forty of horse. At one stage the ratio of officers to common soldiers in the royalist garrison at Reading reached 1 : 2.4, as compared to 1 : 18.5 in the London Trained Bands. Surplus officers, known as reformadoes, were a serious problem. When amalgamated in special units to fight as common soldiers these gentlemen-rankers refused to act either as rankers or as gentlemen. Instead they degenerated into an expensive, quarrelsome and undisciplined 'rabble of gentility'. 'They could not agree on a leader', noted Isaac Tullie about the reformadoes with whom he fought at the Siege of Carlisle in 1644, 'so not embodying they were easily routed.'[14] The surplus of royalist officers was not due to a lack of courage on the field of battle (although being on horse, and having a retainer to serve as a bodyguard, enhanced an officer's chances of surviving), but because of the propensity of other ranks to desert. As a petition from a group of royalist officers admitted in March 1645, 'Many of our soldiers are wasted and do daily molder away.'[15]

Pundits agreed that high standards were mandatory for military command. Barnaby Rudge, the prolific Elizabethan writer on martial matters, laid down that a captain must possess experience, valour, authority, felicity, fortitude, prudence, justice and temperance. John Cruso thought that the ideal company commander should have served in the ranks to gain experience and understanding. To overcome the fear of death he should have a firm belief in God. He should know every one of his men by name to give them individual orders. Roger Boyle could not remember 'any famous Captain, who was not also a person of strong Judgment, and blessed with great Presence of mind in all emergencies'. He added that 'I very seldom saw the English soldiers flinch, if their officers were good.'[16]

The death of an outstanding leader in battle could be calamitous. When the roundheads attacked Farnham Church in November 1642 the fighting was extremely fierce. The defenders shot down into the assault troops, who became so crowded in the churchyard that as the forward ranks tried to retreat, they impaled themselves on the pikes of their comrades in the rear. They seemed doomed. But at the last moment the parliamentarians threw hand grenades into the church, killing the opposing commander, Colonel Birch. Abruptly the cavaliers collapsed. Most surrendered and received quarter: a few refused, being slaughtered on the spot. 'They fell on like mad men,' remembered a trooper who saw Colonel Needham's regiment wading into the enemy after they had killed their CO at Colchester on 13 June 1647, 'killing and slaying them in a terrible manner.'

If too many of officer rank were killed a unit could break. 'Their Common Soldiers', observed Sir William Brereton of the royalists he routed at Malpas on 26 April 1644, 'on the loss of so many of their Commanders, retreated.' The death of a single crucial or popular leader could destroy a regiment as a fighting unit. After John Hampden was fatally wounded in 1643 the strength of his regiment fell from 849 to 186 in ten months, largely through desertions, not combat, and it had to be disbanded. Incompetence could destroy a regiment even faster. So inept was their CO that in eight days of July 1651 the size of the Master of Caithness's regiment of foot fell from 644 to 7.[17]

The loss of a leader could affect victorious troops just as drastically. Having just taken Shrewsbury Castle, the Earl of Denbigh's men learned that their popular commander, Major Pinkney, had been fatally shot in the belly. They stopped taking prisoners.[18] When a sniper killed Sir Simon Harcourt during the assault on Carrick Castle in 1642, his regiment murdered all the prisoners in cold blood.[19] One of the qualifications for successful leadership in battle is the ability to convince one's troops that one's skill, and even luck, will guarantee their survival. Thus the death of such a man in combat is so traumatic a threat to a solidier's self-confidence that he may take it out on the other side.

Sometimes commanders followed the adage that there were no bad soldiers, only bad officers, by preventing the incompetent from being commissioned. Sir Samuel Luke, the parliamentary governor of Newport Pagnell, wrote of one candidate that he 'will never be a fit officer . . . for he looked more after himself than the cause and his own honour'.[20] Military command was one of the few professions for which most gentlemen were convinced that their birth – as opposed to mere ability or training – automatically qualified them. Thus many incompetents became commanders. During the Siege of Nottingham Sir John Meldrum, the veteran of the Thirty Years' War, complained that unlike the low-born mercenary captains with whom he had served overseas, his gentleman officers 'were so emulous of each other, and so refractory to commands' that they 'did not know how to obey orders'.[21]

The organizational structures within which such officers had to operate were not particularly helpful. Civil war training was skimpy, and lacked the standardized battle drills which today provide solutions for commanders during sudden crises. For instance, manuals provided little advice about what to do if caught in an ambush – or for that matter, how to stage one. There were no manuals of any value for field or general officers. Admittedly veterans handed down battle lore to novices, but many officers must have learned their lessons in the hard school of combat or, failing the course, paid with their own and their men's lives.

If training manuals provided little help, chains of command were equally rigid. In the standard infantry regiment ten companies reported to the commanding officer. He also commanded his own company which in theory numbered some 200 men, significantly larger and thus more difficult to lead than the 140-man companies commanded by each of his eight captains. Thus compared to a modern battalion C.O., a civil war colonel was overloaded with direct command responsibilities, and except for a quartermaster lacked a supporting staff.

The same was true at the company level. While today (on paper at least) a typical company of a hundred and twenty men has five officers, five sergeants and seven corporals, then a company of a hundred and forty had three officers, two sergeants and three corporals. In practice few units conformed to these theoretical manning levels. For example, the muster role for 6 July 1646 of Colonel Robert Bennet's parliamentary regiment of horse listed one hundred and forty men, with three officers, three sergeants and four corporals in the colonel's troop. The smallest troop commanded by a captain had sixty-five men, three officers, two sergeants and three corporals.[22] So a surplus of officers might not have been such a problem as has been suggested.

The quality of those officers was crucial. Sometimes soldiers praised the captains who led them into battle:

> Come along my valiant Soldiers
> Let us go unto the field
> O let us march after our Captain
> Unto the foe let us not yield.

Thus ran a parliamentary soldiers' song.[23] Captain John Stiles, who served in John Hampden's regiment, was fulsome about his commander:[24]

I have seen him,
In front of his regiment in green,
When Death about him did in ambush lie,
And whizzing shot, like showers of arrows, fly,
Wavering his conquering steel, as if that he
From Mars had got the sole monopoly
Of Never failing courage.

While Hampden was unlucky enough to die at Chalgrove in 1643, some officers survived many a bloody fight. Between January 1643 and October 1645 Captain Edward Place fought in four battles (including Marston Moor) and nine sieges, being taken prisoner twice. He also served in Cromwell's Scottish 1650 campaign, and fought at Worcester the following year.[25] Soldiers wanted to serve under such veterans because their experience and courage enhanced their own chances of survival. Take, for instance, the time that the royalists ambushed Colonel Popham's regiment just outside Salisbury. Seeing the colonel and his troop rush past in panic, Edmund Ludlow's men were about to follow suit. 'I put myself at the head of them,' Ludlow recalled, 'by which means I got my men to keep close together, which contributed much to their safety.' Ludlow's coolness saved his men's lives. Many of those who ran were 'killed in cold blood . . . after quarter given'. The enemy cut down a hundred more roundheads and wounded many more during the 22-mile rout back to the safety of Salisbury.[26]

The king's overwhelming advantage was that he was king. As the Earl of Manchester observed, 'If we beat the king nine & ninety times, yet he is king still.'[27] Moreover, as commander-in-chief, Charles had the opportunity of co-ordinating the royalist war effort. In this he failed (see plate 20). He also did a poor job of communicating to his men the mystique of the warrior king, a potent image that resonated of the Biblical David, or the Shakespearian Henry V.[28]

No one could question Charles's physical courage. During a reconnaissance near Beacon Hill in August 1644, the king came under cannon fire that smashed a sergeant near him to pulp. Charles did not flinch. When, a couple of months earlier, it seemed that the parliamentary army might capture him, Charles declared that 'possibly he might be found in the hand of the Earl of Essex, but that he would be dead first'.[29] At Naseby the king wanted to lead his cavalry reserves in one last desperate do-or-die charge. Charles also tried to identify himself with his common soldiers. He stayed all night on the field after Edgehill, listening to the cries and sobs of the wounded and dying. He was, alas, too restrained to go and dress their wounds, or order medical attention for them.

Such self-control, joined with a painful stutter, hampered the king's ability to communicate with the rank and file. After the victory of

Cropredy the royalists were in hot pursuit of the foe, when the king's carriage broke down during a thunderstorm. When his bodyguard offered to cut a gap in a hedge so he could shelter in an adjacent cottage, he told them not to bother. They congratulated him on his fortitude. Charles replied 'that as God has given him afflictions to exercise his patience, so he had given him patience to bear his afflictions'.[30] What a wonderful reply for a martyr! What a miserable rejoinder for a warrior! Leaders are not supposed to be passive but active. Rather than enduring suffering their job is to inflict pain on the other side.

Observers all agreed on the king's equanimity as a soldier. 'He showed a very great and exemplary temperance', recalled Sir Philip Warwick. 'I never observed any great severity in the king', added Sir Henry Slingsby.[31] The only time Slingsby remembered Charles losing his temper was at Wing, near Uppingham, when he ordered a soldier to be hanged on a signpost for stealing a chalice from a church.

Although the king's men continued to fight long after his cause was lost, surprisingly few of them displayed any direct personal affection for him. After being presented to Charles in 1643, Henry Verney, a cavalry major, whose father had died for the crown at Edgehill, wrote to his wife, 'The king's hand I have kissed. He looked earnestly upon me, but spoke not to me. In time, if the war goes on I hope to be known to him.'[32] Such icy restraint hardly helped produce the simple loyalty shown by a sentry at Magdelen Bridge, Oxford, who in 1643 refused a gold piece tip proffered by the parliamentary peace commissions. He said 'he would receive no money from such rebels, for he had the honour to serve a good master'. Delighted, the king sent him two gold pieces. Immediately after his troops had captured and sacked Leicester, Charles inspected the town. The soldiers called out to him to show him where a popular officer had been killed, and to tell him how gallantly he had died.[33] Significantly their loyalty was focused not on their commander-in-chief – a remote being – but on their own unit leader.

If the king failed to catch the attention of friend and foe, his nephew, Prince Rupert, became an epic figure who excited the fantasies of both sides.

Born in 1619, Rupert was an infant when his parents, Frederick and Elizabeth, were driven from Bohemia into exile in Holland. Aged but 14 he accompanied Frederick Henry, Prince of Orange, to the Siege of Rheinberg. Two years later he served with the Dutch Army during the invasion of Brabant. After visiting his Uncle Charles in 1636, he campaigned in Westphalia for two years before the French captured him. He used the three years he spent as their prisoner to read widely in military history and affairs.

When Rupert landed in England in 1642 to fight for his uncle, the royalists welcomed his arrival by publishing the paean *Joyful Newes From the Sea* (1642, J1144). Riding so hastily to join his uncle, he fell from his horse and sprained his arm (a village bone-setter was summoned to snap it back in place). Within a couple of hours the prince was on the road again. Charles made him general of his horse, a position which allowed Rupert ample scope to exercise both his genius and his fatal flaw. Without doubt he was a superb trainer of horsemen who managed to turn the gentry's hunting instincts into a force that smashed the enemy's line. Yet he could not stop their pell-mell pursuit and make them return to the field of battle.

The belief that a single cavalry charge was all that was needed to break the enemy began at Powick Bridge in September 1642. The king's first victory, the skirmish established Rupert's reputation and shattered the self-confidence of the parliamentary horse for nearly two years. 'His very name is half a conquest', boasted a royalist captain. Two months later at Brentford, Rupert showed his mettle as a tactical leader. The following year his personal bravery was decisive during the attack on Bristol. The royalist storm was about to fail. 'We lost many brave officers and soldiers', recalled Sir Bernard de Gomme. At the critical moment Rupert appeared. He rode up and down, oblivious of enemy fire, rallying the troops, to win the day. Soon after, when his forces walked into an ambush at Chalgrove, Rupert followed the classic tactic of turning the tables on the enemy. Shouting 'this insolency is not to be endured' he wheeled his horse, jumped a hedge, and with his bodyguard at his heels, scattered the parliamentary sharpshooters.[34]

Almost immediately this superb cavalry leader gained a larger than life reputation for invulnerability, which (like Rommel's in the Western Desert), cheered his friends and dismayed his foes. The parliamentary report of his death at Edgehill was the result of wishful thinking.[35] After the Prince was shown to be alive and kicking rebels, John Milton composed some verse that he pinned to his door as a talisman that would protect him.[36] Pamphlets such as *A True Relation of Prince Rupert's Barbarous Cruelty against the Town of Birmingham* (1643), and *Prince Rupert's Burning love to England discovered in Birmingham's Flames* (1643), described in graphic tones the fate of all who opposed the king's ferocious nephew. 'Prince Rupert is coming this way', wrote Colonel Thomas Mytton, governor of Oswestry, 'I will refer all to God, and defend the town to the utmost of my power.'[37] After inspecting the parliamentary defences of Dorchester in July 1643 a Mr Strode commented that 'those works may keep out the cavaliers about half an hour', adding that 'the king's soldiers made nothing of running up walls twenty feet high'.[38]

Rupert also won a reputation as a merciless plunderer. After Charles created his nephew the Duke of Cumberland, wags dubbed him 'Prince Robber, Duke of Plunderland'. Colonel Russell, the governor of Lichfield, declared that Rupert was not 'a gentleman, a Christian or an Englishman, much less a prince'.[39] A parliamentary pamphlet described him as 'an ungrateful viper', and asked 'How many towns hast thou fired? How many Virgins hast thou ruined? How many Godly ministers hast thou slain?' A horrifed House of Commons was informed that Rupert kept a hundred whores, including two dressed as boys.[40]

Stories soon started to circulate that Rupert went around in disguise to discover how ordinary folk really felt. One related how, dressed as a country gentleman, he fell into conversation with a widow who kept an inn just outside Worcester. As they talked about the war, he asked her what she thought of the king's nephew. 'A plague take Prince Rupert', she answered, 'he might have kept himself where he was born: the kingdom has been the worst since he landed.' Rupert gave the landlady three pieces of gold, more for her honesty than the quality of her food. In another story he came across a carter with a load of apples, and asked him why he had not joined the king's army. 'They are cavaliers and have a mad prince amongst them', the fellow explained. Rupert offered him 10 shillings for the use of his coat and cart, and spent the next day selling apples to his troops to assess their morale.[41]

Anecdotes about generals who disguise themselves to pass unnoticed amongst their men were familiar to seventeenth-century Englishmen. Shakespeare had Henry V do so before Agincourt. In the English civil war these tales focused not upon the king but on the prince, who took over much of the mystique of the heroic leader that traditionally belonged to the sovereign.

Tales about the warrior prince reached fantastic proportions. Rupert and his dog, Boy, were accused of possessing all manner of supernatural powers. It was reported that the animal could speak in a dialect supposed closely to resemble Hebrew, that its coat was stiletto-proof, and that it could catch musket bullets in its mouth. Worse still, Rupert had allegedly trained the four-footed succubus to perform sexual services of an unspecified nature. 'Is not this dog', asked a pamphlet, 'no dog, but a witch, a sorceress, and an Enemy to Parliament?' Thus when Rupert had to hide in a bean field to escape capture after Naseby, and a musketeer shot the infamous Boy, parliamentary propagandists had a field day. They portrayed a chastised prince lurking amongst the legumes, while his pooch lay dead on his back, all four paws pointing to the sky (plates 8 and 9).[42]

On the parliamentary side Sir Thomas Fairfax's ability to communicate his vision of leadership to his soldiers rested on his own personal courage, and modesty. Wounded four times, he fought in ten battles, three skirmishes and eleven sieges. Early in the war he won a reputation for personal courage at Sherborne when he led an attack against some royalists who had taken cover behind barricades. He charged their position, and although his horse had been wounded, leapt the defences, and with eight or nine troops in tow, scattered the enemy. The evening before Naseby, as commander of the New Model Army, Fairfax reconnoitered the battlefield. Returning in the dark, a sentry challenged him, demanding the password, which Fairfax could not remember. The sentry threatened to shoot him if he did not wait until he called for his officer. Having been identified, General Fairfax tipped the sentry for devotion to duty – his behaviour reminding one of the disguised prince.

The next day, however, there was nothing hidden nor unreal about the parliamentary commander. During the Battle of Naseby Fairfax rode up and down without his helmet so his troops could recognize him. During the final charge he killed an ensign whilst a trooper seized the enemy flag. Afterwards Colonel Charles D'Oyley, who saw the whole incident, reprimanded the trooper for claiming to have slain the bearer as well as grabbing his colour. Fairfax told him to desist: 'I have honour enough, let him take that to himself.'[43]

Without doubt the man best able to communicate his wishes, goals and personality to those who fought and died for him was Oliver Cromwell. Such an ability is an essential quality for a leader of genius: Napoleon had it, as did Alexander.[44]

After living a fairly normal – indeed disappointingly mundane – life as a modest country gentleman, the outbreak of the war came as something of a liberation. Cromwell revealed his genius in the speech he gave when he raised his first troop of horsemen in Huntingdon. He declared that he would not confuse them with any nonsense about fighting for 'king and parliament'. Their cause was so plain that if he came across His Majesty on the field of battle he 'would discharge his pistol at him as at any other person'. Years later, as a proven commander, he told his men before the Battle of Preston that their duty was simple – 'to engage the enemy to fight was our business'. But although Cromwell was direct, even to the point of bluntness, he was neither rude nor disobedient. He obeyed orders as cheerfully as he expected subordinates to carry out his own commands.[45]

Cromwell evinced frenetic energy as a troop or regimental commander. In 1643 he drove his men on a 40-mile ride overnight from Norwich to capture King's Lynn in a surprise dawn attack. A few days later he wrote to the county commissioners of Cambridge, 'The Lord give you, and us, zeal.' Oliver abhorred sloth. Addressing his letter 'haste, haste, post haste', he asked the Deputy Lord Lieutenants of Essex about the 'old pace' with which they were conducting parliament's business: 'Is this the way to save the kingdom?' His soldiers appreciated such energy: it could save their lives. 'Haste your horses', Cromwell told Sir William Springe and Maurice Barrow, 'a few hours may undo you if neglected.'[46]

Men followed Cromwell because he took them for what they were. He did not care what opinions they held, insisting instead that 'if they be willing to serve, that satisfies'. His secret was simple. 'If you chose Godly honest men to be captains of horse, honest men will follow them.'

And honest men did. He disciplined them firmly but fairly. Those who swore he fined twelve pence, those who got drunk he put in the stocks, those who insulted their comrades by calling them 'roundhead' he cashiered – well that, at least, is what parliamentary broadsheets would have us believe.[47] No one, however, can doubt that Cromwell was determined that his men were promptly paid. He apologized to the civilian authorities for his continual insistence that they find money to pay his troopers, because 'If we have not more money speedily they will be exceedingly discomposed.'[48]

Oliver loved his men. 'I have a lovely company', he wrote in 1643, 'they are honest, sober Christians: they expect to be used as men.' Time and time again he called his soldiers 'those honest men . . . those gallant men', and begged that 'they may not be forgotten'.[49]

In short, Cromwell enjoyed a fight. At Winceby in 1643 he led his regiment to rout at least eighty royalists in fifteen minutes, even though his horse was killed under him. An eyewitness recalled that before the Battle of Dunbar in 1650, he rode through his camp on a small Scottish pony 'biting his lips till the blood ran down his chin without his perceiving it'. After winning the battle, the most decisive of his career, 'he did laugh so excessively as if he had been drunk; his eyes sparkled with spirits'.[50]

Bravery is the quality which soldiers value more than any other in their leaders. The worse canard they can make about a commander is cowardice – as in 'Dugout Doug', the GIs' nickname for General MacArthur. Of a sample of 75 civil war military leaders, 42 (56 per cent) had performed at least one act of heroism on the field of battle.[51] Because courage can displace ability as the criterion for command the Duke of Wellington once noted that 'There is nothing on earth so stupid as a gallant officer.'[52] Acts of extreme bravery cannot only be stupid but resemble insanity, as evidenced by the phrase 'fighting mad'. Jeremy Taylor, who took part in the Siege of Cardigan Castle, recalled:[53]

> I have known a brave trooper fight in the confusion of a battle, and, being warm with heat and rage, receive from the sword of his enemy wounds open like a grave. But he felt them not. And when, by the streams of blood, he found himself masked with pain, he refused to consider then what he was to feel tomorrow, but when his rage hath cooled in the temper of a man, and clammy moisture hath checked the fiery emission of spirit, he wonders at his own boldness.

Sir Edward Lake behaved in such a fashion at Edgehill. Wounded six times, he had to hold his horse's bridle in his mouth so he could keep on slashing at the foe with his sword in his right hand. Taken prisoner, Lake, an attorney in civilian life, managed to escape. Charles called the hero to express personally his thanks and admiration – tempered by not a little incomprehension. 'For a lawyer, a professed lawyer, to throw off his gown to fight so heartily for me, I must need thank very well for it', declared the king.[54]

There was something almost suicidal about such bravery. Whether Viscount Falkland, the secretary of state, deliberately sought death when he charged the rebels at the First Battle of Newbury is a matter of conjecture. Torn between the dictates of conscience and loyalty, he became increasingly depressed. He disliked and distrusted the king, yet felt he was trapped into fighting for him. Falkland took unnecessary risks at the Siege of Gloucester, and laughed when friends warned him of his recklessness, saying that a leader must demonstrate his courage. Unable to sleep, he neglected his appearance. But on the morning of the First Battle of Newbury Falkland was unusually cheerful. Donning a clean shirt, he explained that if he was killed he would not want to be found wearing dirty linen. Then he volunteered for the front rank of Lord Byron's regiment. As they advanced against musketeers hidden in hedgerows, one hit Falkland in the stomach, toppling him from his horse. He was dead before he hit the ground.[55]

Friend and foe, soldier and civilian alike, prized such acts of courage. Forty years after the war, Mary Capel tried to find out all she could about her father, Arthur Lord Capel, who fought so hard for his monarch that he, like Charles I, was beheaded by parliament in 1649. Sir Henry Newton, who took part in an attack that Capel led against the roundheads at Loppington, Shropshire, told Mary that her father 'showed us great gallantry and skill', and in the vicious hand-to-hand combat 'was the busiest man amongst his soldiers'.[56]

While all these men were aristocrats, the first hero of the civil war was a commoner, who went by the ubiquitous name of John Smith, winning glory at Edgehill by saving the royal standard.

The king's colour bearer at the war's first battle was Sir Edmund Verney, who, like Falkland, could well have had a death wish. Perhaps it was the growing burden of his debts which made him reckless. Certainly it was his thirty years of service, which went back to Prince Charles's mad-cap trip to Madrid in 1623 to court the King of Spain's daughter, rather than a belief in the rightness of the king's cause, that prompted him to fight at Edgehill. A friend recalled that 'he would neither put on arms [armour] or buff coat the day of the battle the reason I know not'. Unprotected Verney deliberately sought out the hottest fighting. After his bodyguard and family retainer, Jason, was killed, leaving his rear open, Verney slew two of the enemy, before Ensign Arthur Young killed him and captured the king's standard.[57]

Rather than permit this disgrace, which might have dealt the king's cause a fatal blow, Captain John Smith charged into the mêlée to retrieve the royal standard. Charles was overjoyed. Immediately after the battle he knighted Smith, and, egging the custard, made him a baronet. Afterwards Charles presented Sir John with a large gold medal with his picture on one side and the royal standard on the other. The king continued giving gold medals for valour after Thomas Bushell, Master of the Royal Mint, offered to strike them at his own charge. Recipients were proud of the award, wearing the medals around their necks when they had their portraits painted.

Other common-born officers demonstrated a valour above and beyond the call of duty. There was Captain Hodgkins (known as 'Wicked Will' for his 'desperateness and valour'), who, drunk as a skunk, sallied forth from Worcester to rout the roundheads.[58] There was Captain Thomas Sanford who took Beeston Castle, and threatened to set his Irish firelocks loose on any other garrison that did not promptly yield. There was Captain Chisenhall who led raids from Lathom House to spike the round-head mortar.

Smith remained the royalist hero *par excellence*. He had first attracted public notice on 9 August 1642, two weeks before the king raised his standard, when he led a troop of royalist cavalry into the village of Kilsby in Northamptonshire, and shot Henry Barefoot for trying to stop him requisitioning horses.[59] In verse that was more a testament to his loyalty as a comrade, rather than any skill as a poet, Edward Walsingham praised the courageous captain:[60]

> Of one whose fame can never rust
> That noble, valiant, gallant knight
> Renowned Smith . . .

Smith was of middling stature, but strongly built. His hair was long, and ruddy, like his complexion. His appearance was so fierce and stern that it was, Walsingham tactfully put it, 'rather formed to command Armies than allure Ladies'. Indeed Smith lacked the characteristics of the arche-typical cavalier. He was no gallant. Short on charm and even shorter in words, Smith said little, and had even less time for those who spoke much. Generous to his troopers, he was as devout in his prayers as any round-head. According to a friend this perfect knight could not stand bullies. When Sir John came across one Wray, a roundhead notorious for beating up cavaliers taken prisoner at Hull, he thrashed the brute. When the citizens of Leicester complained about a billeting officer who was trying to extort money from them, Sir John threw the tin-pot Hitler into a dung heap.

Royalist sources record that Smith displayed all the knightly virtues after he was fatally wounded at Alresford. His first request was to be taken away from the field, lest the enemy capture him. The surgeons dressed his injuries, putting bandages on the two superficial ones, while failing to notice the fatal gunshot wound on his left side, under his armour (which must have driven metal and lead fragments into the chest cavity).

Evacuated to Wonston, a village north of Winchester, Smith slept a little. When he woke he asked after his men. Hearing that they had been defeated, he said that 'the conceit of our men running away did more trouble him by far than his wounds'. He spoke too soon. Realizing that the end was nigh, he asked Walsingham to tell 'his dear Mother that he died with a quiet conscience, and a resigned mind, hoping likewise that she would not take his death with so much heaviness, but rejoice that she had a son to shed his blood for his sovereign'. After a few more prayers the hero was no more.

All wars need heroes. They are both an inspiration and a shame to the mass of men, who have to overcome their own fears. Once they have done so, then they may despise those failures called cowards. Rarely do they forget them. For instance, about a decade after the shameful surrender, Captain John Gwynne had a long conversation with Lieutenant Harvey as they were whiling away the tedious hours of garrison duty in the Shetland Isles, about 'How Reading was betrayed by Fielding.' The two old soldiers concluded that they had never 'known so gross and shameful an undertaking'.[61]

While ministers such as the Reverend Robert Ram could fulminate that 'a coward degenerates from a man being of a base and ignoble nature', fighting soldiers recognized how close they could, and often did, come to panic. One of the defenders of Basing used the self-mocking vulgarity of the old sweat to describe how a bullet whizzed through the window while he was sleeping: 'he was so struck with fear that he leapt out of his bed and ran into another room without his britches.' Trouserless he could at least take comfort in the thought that he had not fouled them.

Leaders used humour to control their men's fears. Rarely was it of the thigh-slapping, belly-laughing sort: more often it was cruelly dry. A diarist described how he and his comrades ambushed and wiped out a party of cavaliers who had just looted a church near Brampton: 'We sent some of his Majesty's good subjects to Old Nick for their sacrilege.' Two years later, when John Gwynne surprised some of Wallers's men near Malborough quite literally asleep at noon, he ordered his men to sing 'a brisk lively tune' known as 'Up in the morning early' as they slaughtered the layabèd roundheads. In February of the same year Colonel William Reinking led his men in a surprise night attack on Shrewsbury. When a sentry challenged them 'who is there?' Colonel Reinking sardonically answered, 'you shall see presently'. And the sentry did, the colonel's words being the last he ever heard.[62]

All these leaders knew only too well they had to control panic, which could shatter even crack units. Captain Atkyns recalled that at the Battle of Caversham:[63]

I had much ado to keep them running away, having a lieutenant as fearful as any, which to prevent I was forced to cut some of them and threaten my lieutenant; with which we stuck together more like a flock of sheep than a party of horse.

Demoralized, they walked into an ambush and were scattered in every direction.

Roger Palmer, Earl of Castlemaine, described how Atkyns's troops must have reacted, claiming in his memoirs to have seen many a fight which should have been won but for fear:

> For though man in his reason be the most excellent of all creatures on earth, yet having lost it by passion of fear, is one of the least: and fear doth sometimes seize men, being in surprise to such a degree that they know not what to do.
>
> How many men in beating up quarters and routs are slain, not daring to turn their faces to make resistance: though the very same men being in their judgment, in diverse occasions had carried themselves formerly well enough.

Research on modern warfare has confirmed Roger Palmer's assertion that even in elite units, 'many men', during combat 'will not turn their faces to make resistance'. According to one highly regarded source only 15 per cent of US infantrymen actually fired their weapons in action during the Second World War.[64]

Fear and the confusion of battle could make a leader give the wrong order. At the Battle of Auldearn the MacDonalds suddenly charged Sir John Hurry's exposed flank. Captain Drummond panicked, ordering his men to wheel left instead of right, whence the enemy was coming. In the confusion the covenanter infantry and cavalry ran into each other, allowing the royalists to attack their rear, breaking their formation. Colonel Hurry court-martialled and shot the bewildered captain.[65]

Considering the strain of command, and the penalties for failure, it is not surprising that some officers turned to drink. As the royalist cause in the West Country collapsed during 1645 and 1646, it was reported that George Goring's fondness for the bottle had got so bad that he was up and sober for but an hour or two a day. A contemporary described Colonel John Poyer, who led the abortive royalist rising in West Wales in 1648, as 'A Man of two dispositions each day, in the morning sober and penitent, in the evening drunk and full of plots.'[66]

Some regiments, it must be admitted, were bad enough to drive a saint to drink. According to Clarendon, Wentworth's Horse was so worthless that their friends feared them, the enemy laughed at them, and they were 'only terrible in plunder and resolute in running away'. After the Basing House defenders thrashed the substitutes who had been paid to fill the London Trained Bands after the regulars' enlistments had expired, they deserted in droves. William – no longer the conqueror – Waller exclaimed 'Such men are only fit for a gallows here, and hell afterwards.'[67]

There has always been a distinct difference between desertion in the face of the enemy, and going absent without leave. While the latter may be a rational, carefully considered decision, the former is usually a spontaneous, almost uncontrollable reaction. Thus military discipline punishes battle desertions far more severely because they are more dangerous and highly infectious. Sir Arthur Trevor described how this process took place at the Battle of Montgomery in September 1644:

> In plain English our men ran shamefully, when they had no cause of so great fear. . . . All the Lancashire Horse ran without a blow struck, which disheartened the foot so infinitely that being in disorder with the pursuit of the enemy, they could not be persuaded to rally again, which the rebels did, and advanced and relieved the battle.

The cost of panic was heavy. Trevor reported that only a hundred of their two thousand infantry survived. A comparison of two regiments shows the fatal price of cowardice. During the Battle of Edgehill, Sir Henry Cholmley's regiment broke and ran, while Sir Thomas Ballard's stood and fought. Muster rolls show that between October and November 1642 the strength of Cholmley's regiment fell 55 per cent, while Ballard's decreased 43 per cent.[68] Of course battlefield attrition cannot completely explain the difference, because men are more likely to desert broken regiments than those which have proven their mettle.[69]

In a sense most civil war clashes ended in mass desertions, when units stampeded, and every man ran away, hopefully to live to fight another day. In such instances broken troops were rarely punished, and then only in special circumstances. In August 1644 four of the defenders of Basing House tried to climb out over the walls. One was apprehended and hanged on the spot. It worked. Even though the garrison was down to oats, peas and putrid water, desertion stopped.[70]

Most deserters were ordinary blokes who never wanted to be in the army in the first place. Of six hundred men from Hampshire pressed into royalist service in February 1645, a hundred immediately bolted, while two hundred escaped a heavy military guard before the column reached the rendezvous at Winchester.[71] Pressed men were just as loath to serve parliament. Eighty out of a hundred and fifty draftees for Bedfordshire ran before they were issued with clothes and weapons.[72] Once men joined the army, and experienced the bonding involved in belonging to a unit, desertion rates tended to drop, especially if they had participated in a successful military operation. Thus between June and October 1644 only 10 per cent of the members of five infantry companies in Manchester's army who had fought at Marston Moor, deserted.[73]

Deserters tended to come from the infantry, had few friends, had failed to integrate themselves within their units, and had a record of minor disciplinary infractions. Quiet simply most of them wanted to go home. 'They longed for nothing more than to see their own Chimneys', Waller said of the two thousand men who deserted his forces during the summer of 1644. The explanation of a deserter from Arlington, Sussex, was pathetically simple. He told a Justice of the Peace that all he wanted was to 'come home to his mother'.[74]

Those who stayed usually held quitters in contempt, particularly if they ran in the face of danger, and without good reason – such as a death in the family. 'A good riddance', wrote a royalist defender during the Siege of Chester, 'it's better such rotten members were out than in amongst us: far better to have an open foe than a treacherous friend.'[75]

Local authorities were required to round up and return deserters. Communities could be fined for sheltering them. Denied the opportunity to return home to their normal civilian employment, deserters were often forced into crime. For instance, in Bedfordshire in 1645 there was a large gang of AWOL soldiers, who hid in the woods and robbed folk along the highway, avowing that they were neither for king nor parliament.[76]

If apprehended it was unlikely that such men would have been hanged for desertion – although they could well have swung for highway robbery. Even though Charles issued a proclamation in November 1642 (which he renewed the following year), that all who deserted His Majesty's forces would suffer death, in practice the crown rarely carried out its threat. In March 1644 and in April 1645 the king signed proclamations promising a free pardon to everyone 'without exception' who had deserted his armies to serve parliament, so long as they straightaway returned to their first allegiance.[77]

In part, the royalists took this action because as the war continued it became harder for them to recruit, and they needed all the experienced soldiers they could find, without enquiring too closely how such experience had been gained. Such leniency also reflected Charles's own convictions that the truly penitent should be forgiven. One of the reasons why the king had Colonel Fielding court-martialled and sentenced to death for the surrender of Reading was a clause in the articles he had signed permitting Essex to hang any parliamentary deserters found among the royalist garrison. 'I had not known the king more offended than he was with that clause,' recalled Charles's adviser, Clarendon, 'he held the same most prejudicial to his service and derogatory to his honour.'[78]

So long as a prodigal was willing to admit the error of his ways Charles usually admitted him back into the fold. The king pardoned Fielding as he mounted the scaffold, then gave way to public protests, sending him back up again, before granting his son's entreaty to pardon the coward. In June 1643 the royalists captured Sergeant-Major James Chudleigh (a senior officer) at the Battle of Stratton, his halbard broken, his horse shot under him, and wounded in the head. After several long conversations with leading royalist officers, including Sir Ralph Hopton and Sir Richard Grenville, Chudleigh changed sides. Charged with treason by parliament, in *His Declaration to His Countrymen* the sergeant-major explained why he had turned his coat. He contended that 'evil counsels' had subverted the rebels, and added how the kindness and virtue of the king's army had impressed him. Three weeks later his father, Sir George, followed suit, telling the world, 'I have thrown myself at my Sovereign's feet, and embraced his gracious pardon.'[79]

Only rarely did the crown execute men for going over to the other side. The garrison of Romsey, Hampshire, which surrendered to Sir Ralph Hopton in March 1644, included six men who had once served in his own regiment. At the request of their erstwhile comrades they were court-martialled, and one, William Morris, hanged from the signpost of the Swan Inn.[80] Had he served in any regiment other than Hopton's, Morris surely would have been as lucky as the three deserters sentenced to be hanged at Carfax, Oxford. Marched out to the gallows, they were made to throw dice to see which one would die. At the last moment Prince Rupert intervened, pardoning the trio.[81]

Parliament was much less generous to those who deserted its forces to fight for the crown, particularly as the war continued and feelings on both sides became more bitter. They shot Colonel Hughes against Nantwich Church in January 1645 for fighting for the king after having taken the covenant.[82] In July 1643 they hanged Captain Arnold Howard at the High Cross in Barnstaple for deserting to the king and taking his whole troop with him. In retaliation Sir John Berkeley, the royalist governor of Exeter, carried out the sentence of death which Chief Justice Heath had imposed twelve months earlier on Captain Turpin, a sea captain, for blockade running. Outraged, parliament impeached Heath, who had to flee England to die a broken exile in Calais.[83]

Such a stern reaction may explain the end of royalist retaliation. Nothing happened after the hanging at Farnham in December 1643 of Captain Bartholomew Elliot, a butcher from Temple Bar, who deserted Essex's army, taking with him some of their payroll, as he tried to betray Aylesbury. An eyewitness reported that 'He died in a miserable condition, justifying himself', denying to the end that the king's army were a bunch of papists.[84]

Elliot at least died quickly, which if the royalist propagandist, Bruno Ryves, is to be believed, was a privilege refused the poor fellow who jilted parliament to fight for his king. Recaptured, he was hung at Thame. Instead of the usual slip knot that would break his neck, the rebels used a fixed one to strangle him, and held up his feet to prolong the agony.[85]

Court-martial papers provide a more accurate view of the treatment of deserters than such vignettes, as well as shedding light on military crime in general. Unfortunately only two sets of such records have survived, one for Waller's Army in August 1644, and another for Cromwell's forces in Dundee in 1651.[86] Thus considerable gaps in our knowledge do not explain, for instance, why the parish register of St Lawrence's Church, Reading, recorded the burial of 'A Parliamentary soldier executed' on 10 December 1642, followed two days later by that of 'Three of the King's Soldiers executed'.[87]

Between 22 April and 20 December 1644 court-martials tried thirty soldiers in Waller's army. Nine were charged with plunder or robbery, six with mutiny, five desertion, five neglect of duty, three murder, and two disobedience. Some of the offences were commonly squalid. David Rogers and Robert Baven stole a doublet and pair of breeches from a tailor in Woodstock, Henry Stone plundered a shirt and apron, while Thomas Dyer went around picking his comrades' pockets. Other crimes were more bizarre. Richard Allen, the surgeon to the artillery train, had a professional disagreement with Dr Pratt, physician to the army, about bleeding a patient, in the course of which he called his superior a 'fool, ass and cox comb'.

Sentences tended to be harsh. Eleven men were sentenced to be hanged, and one shot. Six were cashiered, eight suffered some physical humiliation, such as running the gauntlet or being tied head to toe. For one there was no record, while three were acquitted. Of the latter, two were officers charged with shooting men during the course of a mutiny, the court-martial being almost certainly assembled to investigate the fracas and clear the officers' names.

The crimes dealt with by court-martial in the Dundee area between September 1651 and January 1652 were less serious. The parliamentary forces had just won a campaign against the Scots, and were trying to build good relations with the local civilian population. There were sixteen cases of plunder or robbery, ten of neglect of duty, nine of desertion, eight of disobedience, six of a sexual nature, five of murder, and only one of mutiny.

Punishments reflected the change to a post-war, garrison mentality. Only two men were sentenced to death, while ten were reprimanded, two were cashiered, three imprisoned, two referred to higher authority, and eight acquitted. Twenty-eight, or half, received some physical punishment, the most common being the lash – fourteen soldiers being given an average of forty-one strokes.[88]

Of course there was a difference between sentences given and those carried out. Only about half of those the civilian courts condemned to death were actually executed.[89] The rate for military courts may have been higher. For instance, between December 1643 and May 1645 in Hampshire twenty soldiers were executed, ten by each side. While all those the crown killed were deserters, parliament executed two apiece for robbery, murder, and mutiny, and four for desertion. All these sentences were intended as ominous examples. Lieutenant Elias Archer recalled how his roundhead regiment was marched past a swinging mutineer's body on their way to storm Basing House. Before parliament hanged him in chains at Haslington for all to see, for murdering a comrade in a drunken rage, Private Parker confessed to Edward Burghall, the local vicar, that 'he had been a very great Sabbath breaker, & very disobedient to his Parents, and therefore the Hand of God was just upon him'.[90]

And, as we will see in the next chapter, during the British civil wars both directly and indirectly God laid the hand of death and the scourge of wounds and disease upon hundreds of thousands of men, women, and children.

9

TO SLAY AND TO BE SLAIN

And the raw astonished ranks stand fast
To slay and to be slain
By the men they knew in the kindly past
That shall never come again –

By the men they met at dance and chase,
In the tavern or the hall,
At the justice bench and the market place,
At the cudgel play or brawl –
                    Rudyard Kipling, 'Edgehill Fight'

'My Dear and loving husband, my king love', Susan Rodway began a
letter of 1644 to Robert, a private in the London Trained Bands, who was
away fighting at the Siege of Basing House. She was desperately worried
about the lack of news from her husband, particularly as her neighbours
had received letters from theirs. Susan was concerned for her child: 'My
little Willie has been sick this fortnight.' She missed her man terribly:
'You do not consider that I am a lone woman', she reproved him, 'I
thought you would never leave me this long together.' But above all Susan
Rodway was terrified her husband would be killed, and she be left a
widow, ending her letter 'So I rest ever praying for your safe return.'[1]

Susan knew only too well something which can be readily forgotten
both by historians as they fight over the causes and nature of the civil
wars, and by enthusiasts as they dress up to re-enact battles on summer
afternoons. Whatever the civil wars which engulfed the British Isles in the
middle of the seventeenth century were – be they a Great Rebellion,
Puritan or Bourgeois Revolutions, crises of liberty or of parliaments, wars
of religion or of three kingdoms – of one thing there can be no doubt.
The truth that Rudyard Kipling expressed with sad resignation, William
T. Sherman put with brutal frankness. 'Men go to war', wrote the American Civil War general, 'to kill and get killed, and should expect no
tenderness.'[2]

Trying to get some idea of the number of dead in any holocaust, and the manner and impact of their deaths, is extremely difficult, even in the modern period when statistics were more carefully kept than in the seventeenth century. The official total of British dead in the First World War, 765,399, does not convey the loss of a whole generation as powerfully as the name-crowded war memorial on some idyllic English village green, or at some remote New Zealand crossroads with hardly a house in sight.

Had the inhabitants of the hamlet of Myddle in Shropshire decided after 1660 to build a memorial to their men who went off to fight in the civil war, they would have carved twenty-one names into the stone, thirteen of whom did not return – a higher proportion than in the First World War.[3] Six of them, including Thomas Formaston, 'a very hopeful young man', disappeared without trace. Richard Chalmer died at Edgehill, while Reece Vaughan and John Arthur perished during the storm of Hopton Castle, and could well have been among the members of the garrison who were brutally murdered after surrendering. Thomas Taylor was killed at Oswestry. After being shot by a comrade during a dispute over plunder, Nat Owen could not move and was burned alive when the parliamentary army set fire to Bridgwater. Thomas and William Preece died fighting at Ercall, while their brother perished at the end of a rope, hanged for horse stealing. All but one of the men from Myddle fought for the king. Thomas Mould, 'a pretty little fellow, and a stout adventurous soldier', was shot whilst fighting in the roundhead cavalry. 'His leg healed,' recalled a neighbour, 'but was very crooked as long as he lived.'[4]

Other small samples reveal a similarly high level of participation in the war. Joseph Lane wrote in 1645 that his native Cornwall contained a 'large number of poor soldiers maimed and hurt', adding that 'The slain were certainly a considerable number to that poor country.' Of the 312 members of the gentry from Lancashire who fought for the king during the civil wars, 42 (13.5 per cent) lost their lives. A slightly higher percentage, 16 per cent, of the 126 colonels of the King's Northern Army perished as a result of the war: 17 were killed in combat, 3 were executed. The losses for Yorkshire baronets were even higher: of the 27 who fought for the king, and 7 for parliament, 7 (20.6 per cent) perished. The rate was even higher for the 57 royalists from Lancashire who reached the rank of major or above: 17 (29.8 per cent) of them died, including the Earl of Derby who was beheaded for his services to the crown. Twenty-three (30.3 per cent) of a sample of 76 senior military leaders directly or indirectly lost their lives as a result of the war: 8 (22.9 per cent) of the parliamentarians and 25 (36.6 per cent) of the royalists perished.[5]

Modern estimates put a soldier's chances of losing his life directly or indirectly from war at about one in five. Roughly 20 per cent of the participants at Marston and Naseby lost their lives, a proportion, Clarendon admitted, that was unusually high. On the other hand, soldiers often took part in more than one battle, and had to face the scourge of war-related disease.[6]

Seeing all the killing about them, and being all too aware of the deaths of relatives, friends, neighbours and acquaintances, contemporaries tried to estimate the total loss. Hugh Peters preached that in 1645 parliament had captured nearly thirty thousand prisoners (table 2 shows half that amount). John Greene, a London royalist, reckoned that by January 1643, '10,000 men in one place or another hath fallen by the sword' (an estimate three times larger than in table 2).[7] After the war was over Thomas Hobbes reckoned that some hundred thousand people had perished during the fighting and from war-related disease, while Sir William Petty put the English casualties at three hundred thousand.[8]

All these estimates are, of course, inspired guesses. At the best of times early-modern British statistics were rudimentary. Even had there been mechanisms to collect and report them, statistics were rarely seen as the basis for decision making: unlike ours, theirs was not a data-driven society. War made the collection of quantitative information even more difficult. For one thing combat is an inherently chaotic event, in which survival has priority over the careful recording of what happened. After the Siege of Bristol ended a note was made in the St Nicholas Parish records explaining why the deaths of the clerk and sexton had been omitted: 'not only they but many others are left out of this register'. There were no entries in Colchester's parish registers for burials during the extremely brutal siege of 1648 when thousands lost their lives.[9] During the civil wars people were far more concerned with *who*, rather than *how many*, had died. Printed reports of combat gave only the names of the quality who had perished or had been taken prisoner.

Tricks of memory, as well as the ploys of propagandists, produced wildly different estimates. For instance in the nineteen contemporary accounts of the assault of 15 June 1644 on St Mary's Tower during the Siege of York, casualty estimates range from over three hundred to about twenty. The modern authority on that 'Great and Close Siege' leans towards the higher figures.[10] Other evidence supports the view that contemporary accounts were not wild exaggeration. For instance, a nineteenth-century road-widening near Aylesbury dug up a mass grave with two hundred skeletons, which agrees with the numbers of dead given by current newsletters.[11]

Notwithstanding the immense problems of obtaining raw data, and making estimates from biased and confused sources, an attempt may be made to reckon the casualties sustained in the British Isles during the three civil wars. For England and Wales, reports of some 645 incidents – ranging from Marston Moor, the wars' bloodiest battle, to a fracas in Doncaster, where one man was stabbed – have been collated and analysed using a computer.[12] Estimates of casualties are based on contemporary figures, as well as an appreciation of the intensity of the fighting. While such 'number crunching' enables ratios to be calculated, and broken down into geographical and chronological categories, the mathematical precision of the results can be extremely misleading. The most that can be said in defence of these far from perfect figures is that they may be the optimum possible.

Table 2: Parliament and royalists killed and prisoner in England per annum (English and Scots combined)[13]

Year	Incidents	Parliament killed	Parliament prisoner	Ratio killed/ prisoner	Royalist killed	Royalist prisoner	Ratio killed/ prisoner
1642	45	1,225	1,780	1.45	1,308	917	0.70
1643	156	10,829	11,999	1.11	12,152	18,039	1.48
1644	191	9,599	5,507	0.57	12,379	13,822	1.12
1645	109	4,178	1,885	0.45	5,100	15,774	3.09
1646	54	2,141	20	0	3,013	7,815	2.59
1647	3	540	1,500	27.8	240	70	0.29
1648	54	2,045	700	0.29	3,909	10,830	2.77
1649	1	5	0	0	5	0	0
1651	8	710	0	0	3,430	7,400	2.16
1655	2	20	0	0	50	250	5.00
1660	1	5	15	3.00	5	0	0
no date	21	2,883	9,417	2.96	9,109	8,550	0.94
Total	645	34,130	32,823	0.96	50,700	83,467	1.65

Total killed – 84,830
Total prisoner 116,290

The figures in table 2 contain no great surprises. They do not include figures for the two Bishops' Wars in which perhaps a thousand lost their lives. In terms of incidents the war started fairly quickly, reaching a peak of 191 in 1644. There were 563 incidents during the first civil war, which would support the claim made in a parliamentary pamphlet of August 1646 that they had won 304 victories since the king tried to seize Hull four years earlier.[14] In contrast there were only 58 incidents in the second civil war and 8 in the third.

Casualties show a similar pattern, rising sharply in the war's second and third years, to drop off in the fourth. The casualties for 1646, when most of the royalists had surrendered by early summer, were unexpectedly high, which suggests that a fairly spirited resistance continued even after the defeat of Naseby and surrender of Bristol. The figure for 1648 and 1651 rspectively show the greater ferocity of the fighting during the second and third civil wars.

Of the 84,830 people who died in combat in the three civil wars in

England and Wales, 34,130 were parliamentarians and 50,700 were royalists, a ratio of 1.47. In other words, for every two roundheads who died, three cavaliers lost their lives. Over the course of the war, however, this ratio changed.[15] In the war's first two years it was 1.06 and 1.12. By 1644 it had risen to 1.29, suggesting that this was the decisive year. After a slight drop in 1645 to 1.22 it rose to 1.47 in 1646, implying that parliament was fairly effective in mopping up. The ratios for the second and third civil wars, 1.90 and 4.99, show how overwhelming were the army's victories.

The ratio of killed to prisoners, which is an indication of success or defeat, since winning armies rarely lost men captured, shows the change in the relative fortunes of each side. While at the start of the war they favoured the crown 1.45 to 0.70, they quickly changed direction, reaching 0.45 to 3.09 in 1645. During the course of the war 32,823 parliamentarians were taken prisoner, compared to 83,467 cavaliers – a 2.5 ratio.

Of a sample of 76 senior leaders, 42 (55.3 per cent) were taken prisoner at least once. There was a marked difference between the experiences of the two sides. Only 10 (28.6 per cent) of the roundheads, compared to 32 (78 per cent) of the cavaliers, became prisoners. Many royalists were captured and released several times (Colonel William Legge endured this experience on at least six occasions), especially during the last twelve months of hostilities.

Table 3: Parliament and royalists killed and prisoner in England by region (English and Scots combined)[16]

Region	Parliament killed	Parliament prisoner	Royalist killed	Royalist prisoner	Incidents	Killed (per incident)
Southeast	5,234	3,625	7,740	10,552	79	12,974 (164)
East Anglia	423	300	3,857	775	10	4,280 (428)
West	6,453	14,890	6,690	13,564	116	13,143 (113)
Wales	2,724	1,380	4,295	9,247	83	7,019 (85)
Borders	3,491	2,950	6,554	13,876	79	10,045 (137)
Midlands	6,702	4,528	7,184	15,025	145	13,886 (96)
North	9,103	5,150	14,380	20,428	133	23,483 (177)
Total	34,130	32,823	50,700	83,467	645	

The regional figures (table 3) suggest that geographically the fighting was more widely dispersed than has been thought, especially if we combine Wales and the Borders. East Anglia was the exception, providing parliament with a secure base that saw very little fighting. The king lacked such a luxury. While his strength was concentrated in the West, the North, Wales and its Borders, these regions also saw some of the heaviest fighting.

An analysis of incidents by counties suggests a slightly higher geographical differential. The counties with the most incidents were Yorkshire (46),

Cheshire (36), and Devon (35). In Yorkshire, 19,481 people died, including 5,500 at Marston Moor. Yorkshire also has the highest number killed per incident, at 423, followed by Warwickshire, the site of Edgehill, at 182, and Northamptonshire, where Naseby took place, at 175.[17] At the other end of the scale there were no incidents in Cumberland and Rutland, and only one each in Essex, Breconshire, the Channel Isles and the Isle of Man. There were two incidents in Suffolk, in which only three people died.

The average killed per incident gives an indication of the nature of the fighting within that county. Those counties, such as Yorkshire, Warwickshire and Northamptonshire, which had large incidents, saw major battles, in which mostly outsiders died. On the other hand a low average per incident suggests intensive skirmishing between locally based units. Thus regionally the lowest numbers of killed per incident were in Wales (87) and the Midlands (96). If we exclude the Battle of Worcester in which 3,500 died, then the average loss of life in the Borders per incident was 82, supporting the view that this region saw the most vicious small-scale combat. If we look at this phenomenon on a county-wide basis, a slightly different picture emerges. Of those counties which had at least 4 incidents the average casualties were 22 for Bedfordshire, 31 for Surrey, 35 for Flintshire, 39 for Derbyshire, 40 for Carnarvonshire and 50 for Cambridgeshire.

Usually we think of the civil war in terms of large battles or sieges in which thousands of men perished and crucial territory was lost or gained. In fact most of the lives were not lost in these massive confrontations. A sample of 126 Catholic aristocrats and gentry who died fighting for the king shows that 37 per cent perished in major battles (such as Naseby or Marston Moor), 18 per cent in small battles (such as Taunton and Pontefract), while 45 per cent were killed in skirmishes.[18]

Table 4: Loss of life and prisoners in England and Wales by size of incident

Size of incident by loss of life	Parliament killed	% of total	Parliament prisoner	% of total	Royalist killed	% of total	Royalist prisoner	% of total	No. of incidents
1–249	16,050	47	17,623	54	23,788	47	39,281	47	588
250–999	12,330	36	13,550	41	13,000	26	30,683	37	48
1,000	5,750	17	1,650	5	13,912	27	13,503	15	9
Total	34,130		32,823		50,700		83,467		645

As table 4 shows only 17 per cent of the roundheads and 27 per cent of the cavaliers lost their lives in the war's nine largest confrontations in which over a thousand were killed. Only 15 per cent of the total casualties occurred in major battles, as compared to 24 per cent in sieges. Nearly half the casualties (47 per cent) were suffered in comparatively minor skirmishes (including sieges) in which less than 250 perished.

Much of the civil war consisted of small-scale, localized fighting, of sudden attacks, with minor losses yet all too often fatal results. Such sporadic killing might pass almost unnoticed, and all too often unrecorded. Take, for instance, the burials Guy Carleton, Vicar of Bucklebury, Berkshire, recorded in his parish register:

20 April 1644: William Basset, being slain by a soldier.

29 April 1644: Richard Buxie, a soldier of the King was slain by a parliament soldier.

29 October 1644: Richard Ward, Lieutenant, Parliament.

9 December 1645: Henry Hall, being slain was buried.

Even though Bucklebury lay only 5 miles north-east of Newbury, the site of two major battles, none of the 645 recorded incidents took place close enough in time or distance to be linked to the burials the Reverend Carleton recorded. It seems most likely that they died in some violent clash, so insignificant that it passed unnoted by history, although not, of course, by the loved ones they left behind.

Apart from being deliberately killed in combat, many soldiers died accidentally. Such is not surprising for weapons are inherently dangerous machines, especially in the hands of ill-trained troops or careless conscripts. During an argument with a couple of Oxford undergraduates, Captain Stagger's musket went off – accidentally, he said – hitting a woman who happened to be shopping at the butcher's stall next door.[19] A couple of months later 'the going off of a musket unawares' killed Christopher Berry, a gentleman volunteer in Sir Ralph Hopton's troop. Hopton's men must have been a careless bunch, for two days later Thomas Hollomor, a member of the same troop, was 'killed by the going off of a musket'.[20] Private Thomas Hills was killed in February 1645 by the accidental discharge of his own musket. That same month Lieutenant Vernon died when two pistol bullets fired by Captain Gibbon's groom hit him in the shoulder. A court-martial ruled it an accident.[21] The day-to-day accidental loss of extremities was as great, if not a greater problem. 'We bury more toes and fingers that we do men', complained one royalist officer.[22]

Gunpowder is an extremely dangerous substance, particularly for the ignorant. One night the commander of a fortified manor house who was entertaining his officers to dinner sent a servant girl down to the cellar to fetch more wine. On her return they asked her if she had had any problem finding the best bottles. No, she answered. Wedging the candle in one of the barrels of 'black salt' stored in the cellar had given her plenty of light to find the vintage.[23] One suspects that on hearing of their brush with death the officers lost interest in quality, needing instead a good stiff drink. The Earl of Haddington, and several of his staff officers, were not so fortunate when they called for candles. A servant brought them, setting them down on a conveniently placed barrel full of gunpowder.[24] Edward Morton was also blown to smithereens, while mixing a batch of powder for the royal army that exploded, destroying him, his four children and his house. Only his wife survived, a miracle one parliamentary diarist attributed to the Almighty, who spared Mrs Morton for having tried to stop her husband making explosives for the king.[25]

Puritans were always ready to see divine intent behind any accident. After Captain Starker had captured Hoghton Tower, Lancashire, he and his troops inspected the loot. One cavalier was so impressed with the huge stash of gunpowder that he lit his pipe, blowing up the arsenal, as well as himself, his captain, and sixty of his comrades. 'O that this thundering alarm might ever sound in the ears of our Swearing, Cursing, Drunken, Tobacco-abusing commanders and soldiers', hoped a puritan.[26]

Accidents occurred in the rage of battle. John Hampden died at Chalgrove when his overloaded pistol blew up. Lord Aubigny was murdered in the confusion at Edgehill by a Dutch mercenary whom he had just reprimanded for neglect of duty. Major Bridges, and twenty-three other royalists, drowned in the Avon when a partially demolished bridge collapsed.[27] Captain James Hurcus stepped out of his trench at the Siege of Gloucester to see if the grenade he had just thrown at the roundheads had gone off. It did.[28] Equally droll was the death of 'one Thomas Ringe, a parliamentary', whom the Kidderminster parish register recorded buried on 14 October 1642, after he 'brake his neck falling down the rock towards Courfield'. Sir William Waller and his staff were lucky to survive unhurt when the floor of the house where they were holding a council of war collapsed, tipping them all into the basement.[29]

The Duke of Ormonde had an even closer brush with death. 'For some time', he wrote from Dublin in September 1642, 'I lay (they say) dangerously sick of a disease that rages amongst us, and hath taken away more officers than the sword.'[30] Before the technological advances in medicine, public health and the mass killing of the First World War, more soldiers died of war-related diseases than from combat itself.[31] The reasons were simple. From the crowded royalist base of Oxford, Lady Anne Fanshawe wrote that 'the sad spectacles of war', plague and sickness, came 'by reason of so many people being packed together'. John Taylor, the poet, who was appointed water bailiff for the besieged city, vividly recalled the bestial condition of the River Thames:[32]

Dead hogs, dogs, cats and well flayed carrion horses
Their noisome corpses soiled the water courses;
Both swines' and stable dung, beasts' guts and garbage,
Street dirt, with gardeners' weeds and rotten herbage.

And from this water's filthy *putrefaction*,
Our meat and drink were made, which bred infection.

One explanation for the outbreak of disease in the parliamentary army in 1642 was not, as *The True Informer* sneered, because 'the Justice of God follows them into whatsoever place they come'. Rather the hardships of campaigning left soldiers highly vulnerable to infection. During their victorious campaign at Lostwithiel thirty other ranks and one ensign of Henrietta Maria's bodyguard of roughly a hundred men reported sick.[33] During the summer of 1643, half the six thousand roundheads besieging Reading were too ill for duty.[34] In winter, conditions got worse. 'Diverse of the soldiers do starve before our faces, and very many die of sickness partly through cold for want of clothes and partly for want of wholesome meat', reported an Irish observer in March 1642. The Earl of Cork thought that poor rations made for 'a rich churchyard and weak garrison'. Things could get just as bad in a prosperous English county. 'The winter is already come', wrote Captain Rich in late October 1642, when he was with the Essex parliamentary levies in Lincolnshire, 'and our lying in the field hath lost us more than have been taken away either by the sword or the bullet.'[35]

Tiredness, hunger, dirty food and water, long marches by day and cold disturbed sleep by night, all helped the spread of camp fever. Essex's troops brought the infection with them into Devon during the 1644 campaign. In December, 79 people fell victim to it in Ottery St Mary, the parliamentary headquarters for the Siege of Exeter. Pestilence lingered long after the troops left. In 1646 a contemporary estimated that of Barnstaple's population of between four and five thousand, fifteen hundred fell victims – two hundred and seventy-six were interred in the suburban parish of Pilton alone.

Camp fever was most likely a variant of typhoid. Its symptoms were small spots, and with a 75 per cent fatality rate, it was a truly terrible experience. 'As soon as I felt my disease, I rode the six or seven miles back into the country, and the next morning (with much ado) to Bath', wrote Richard Baxter, who as a Chaplain to Colonel Whalley's regiment caught camp fever in August 1645 during the Siege of Bristol. He saw his physician Dr Venner, and after a fortnight 'the fever ended in a crisis of sweat and urine'. Nonetheless he was still so weak that he was unable to return to duty until the end of the month.

Even more devastating than camp fever was that perennial seventeenth-century scourge, the bubonic plague. It has been estimated that between 1570 and 1670, 660,000 people died of the plague in England and Wales. During the strain of war plague was especially catastrophic. In Banbury between 1643 and 1645 there was an average of 255 burials per annum, compared to 73 a year before the war. Between 22 June 1647 and 20 April

1648, 2,099 people died of the plague in war-torn Chester.[36] War-related plague so devastated Stafford that it took a generation for its population to recover. During the 1646 siege, plague became so serious in Newark that the authorities ordered every infected house to be shut up, with a sentry posted outside. Between July and September 1645 there was not a single christening in Manchester parish church: they were too busy burying 748 corpses, a fortyfold increase over the norm. Indeed so virulent was the plague there that many folk vowed that 'they would rather be hanged at their own door than enter such an infected town'.[37]

The noose provided a comfortable demise compared to the agonies of the plague that Thomas Dekker described:[38]

A Stiff and freezing horror sucks up the river of my blood; my hair stands on end with panting of my brains; my eye balls are ready to stand out being beaten with the billows of my tears.

The playwright was not exaggerating. 'The plague takes them very strangely,' said a contemporary, describing its effects on the besieged city of Chester, it 'strikes them black of one side, and they run mad, some drown themselves, others would kill themselves, they die within a few hours.'[39]

Dekker was not exaggerating when in his *Dialogue Between War, Famine and Pestilence* (1604), Pestilence boasts:

War, I surpass the fury of thy stroke
Say that an army forty thousand strong
Enter the crimson lists, and of that number
Purchance the fourth part falls, marked with Red Death?
Why I slay forty thousand in one battle.

And this was no mere exaggeration on Pestilence's part. Of the four thousand English troops sent to France a dozen years before, only a thousand were on the books twelve months later, most of the rest having perished from disease.

Estimates as to the ratio between the number of people who died from disease and from the direct effects of war vary. Jacques Dupâquier, a French demographer, estimated that during the seventeenth century only 10 per cent of military deaths were due to battle. Geoffrey Parker put this figure at 25 per cent. The proportion of soldiers too sick to work was exceptionally high, and would thus suggest that disease produced an excessive death-rate. A sample of two thousand seven hundred garrison troops in Lough Foyle, Ireland, from 1601 to 1603 shows sickness rates of between 14 per cent and 32 per cent. During the years 1642–5 the death-rate for the Banbury garrisons averaged 10 per cent, while that in more crowded cities such as Oxford, Bristol or Exeter, could well have been twice or even thrice as high.[40]

Disease became extremely lethal during sieges. Joseph Bampfield, the royalist governor of Arundel, attributed the majority of the five hundred deaths of its nine hundred garrison during the siege to 'the blooded flux and spotted fever' – typhoid and diarrhoea. An archaeological finding supports this conclusion. Nine members of the royalist garrison of Sandal Castle, Yorkshire, were buried in the same grave during the siege. Three of them died from metal wounds, such as shrapnel. One had a broken arm (which in itself would not have been enough to kill him). Of the two with blows to the skull, one could have been Major Ward who passed away as a result of falling down some stairs. The remaining four show no skeletal damage. Since all of them were under 40 and because most flesh wounds, which would not have marked bone, were rarely fatal, it seems likely that they died of disease. In other words, less than half of this admittedly small sample succumbed directly from combat.[41]

It has been calculated that of the 11,817 people who died in Devon between 1643 and 1645, 4,193 did so as a result of the war. To put that another way, directly or indirectly the war increased the county's dead by 55 per cent. If we combined this total of 4,193 with the 1,634 listed in the computer database it would appear that during the first civil war 2.57 times more people died in Devon from indirect than from direct causes. The death of 2,845 people from disease during the Siege of Plymouth would support this conclusion.[42]

At a conservative estimate roughly a hundred thousand people – soldiers and civilians – died in England from war-related diseases as opposed to combat itself, during the three civil wars.[43] So if we then add in the total of combat deaths from the computer database, 84,830, and round it off with a thousand for the two Bishops' Wars and 500 for accidents, we get a total of 191,830 – say 190,000 – for England and Wales.

Figures for Scotland (table 5) are more unreliable, and should be treated with greater caution.

Even though the Scots figures are much less comprehensive than the English they show that north of the border casualties tended to occur in large pitched battles, as opposed to small skirmishes. This could be a consequence of three factors. First that in Scotland there were fewer disputed areas, each side being more precisely defined in terms of geography or clan territory. Second, the records are not so complete, so many minor actions could have occurred unnoted. Third, the Scots' reliance on conscription favoured raising large concentrated armies. In 1640 the convenanters had 22,000 men in the field, in 1642 they sent over 11,000 to Ireland, dispatched 30,000 to England in 1644 and 14,000–15,000 again in 1648. Leslie led 23,000 men to defeat at Dunbar in 1650, while estimates of those routed during the Worcester campaign a year later vary from 12,000 to 21,000.[44]

Table 5: Parliamentarians and royalists killed and prisoner in Scotland by region (English and Scots combined)

Region	Parliament killed	Parliament prisoner	Royalist killed	Royalist prisoner	Incidents
Borders	1,220	300	1,290	150	6
Central	695		465		8
Fife	210		2,005	1,500	2
Grampian	2,690		555		7
Highlands	3,465		3,050		6
Lothian	610		3,320		8
Strathclyde	5,205		730	10,000	6
Tayside	2,150	1,110	350		3
Total	16,245	1,400	11,765	11,650	46

Total killed: 27,895
Total prisoner: 13,050

Casualties tended to fall into two periods. First the Montrose campaign of 1644–5, when in six battles, Aberdeen, Inverlochy, Auldearn, Alford, Kilsyth and Phillipaugh, the covenanters lost 12,300 compared to 2,400 royalists. Cromwell's invasion reversed the ratio of 1650–1, when in the two major battles of Dunbar and Inverkeithing, the Scots lost 5,000 men, ten times more than the English.

The paucity of figures can only partially explain the extremely high ratio of killed to prisoners north of the border. Scotland lacked England's extensive press which rushed news reports into print within a few days, listing the names and numbers of those killed. But a far more important reason for the relatively small numbers of Scots prisoners was the brutality of the fighting. Time and time again those who surrendered were put to the sword, particularly if they were Irish or members of a hated clan.

The fate of those captured by the English was hardly better. Some 6,120 Scots died fighting in England, mainly at Marston Moor, Preston and Worcester. In addition ten thousand Scots were taken prisoner at the latter two battles, as well as an equal number at Dunbar. They were treated shamefully, dying like flies. Some were transported to the West Indies, where they were worked to death. Thus at a conservative estimate at least ten thousand prisoners must have failed to make it home. Disease struck both sides. Perhaps four to five thousand died from plague in 1644, while as many may have perished in the famine of 1648–9. During the 1650 invasion of Scotland four thousand five hundred of Cromwell's army died from sickness, which explains why he sought a show-down at Dunbar. Thus if we apply the English ratio of battle to non-battle deaths, it would not be unreasonable to assume that some sixty thousand people lost their lives in Scotland during the three civil wars.[45]

If figures for England are guesses, and those for Scotland inspired guesses, those for Ireland are – it must be admitted – miracles of conjecture.

Certainly the devastation the civil wars inflicted on Ireland was unbelievable. As early as 1642 Owen Roe O'Neil reported that much of County Donegal 'not only looks like a desert, but like Hell'. Having travelled extensively throughout Ireland in 1652 and 1653 Colonel Richard Lawrence stated that 'the plague and famine had swept away whole counties that a man might travel twenty or thirty miles and not see a living creature, either man, beast or bird'. A Gaelic Bard lamented:[46]

> I hear not the Duck's call nor goose there,
> Nor the eagle by the harbour proud,
> Nor Even the bees for their whorl there,
> To give honey and wax to the crown.
> No melodious songs of birds there . . .

The number of British families in County Tyrone was halved during the wars. Estimates as to the number of Protestants killed during the first months of the Irish rebellion in the autumn and winter of 1641 vary wildly. The Reverend Devereux Spratt, a clergyman from Trale, put the figure at a hundred and fifty thousand; Richard Baxter and Lucy Hutchinson thought two hundred thousand; Hugh Peters, that puritan firebrand, was confident that the papists had massacred a million. Clarendon (who was both a better historian and human being than Peters) put the figure at forty thousand, which would accord with the estimate of Sir William Petty, the father of English demography.[47]

Writing in 1672, after the civil wars and the land confiscation and deportations decreed by the draconian Act of Settlement, Petty estimated the loss of life in Ireland between 23 October 1641 and 23 October 1652 as follows:

Protestants dead through plague, war and famine (including 37,000 massacred at the outbreak)	112,000
Roman Catholic dead	504,000
Total	618,000

Although Petty's figures are, according to a leading Irish historian 'the best we have', they nonetheless remain extremely tentative.[48] They do not include those, perhaps as many as 40,000, driven into exile. Some of them served in the Spanish or French armies; others were sold as indentured servants in New England (where many prospered) or in the West Indies (where most were worked to death). While Petty surely exaggerated the

213

numbers massacred in 1641, perhaps by a factor as large as nine or ten, his total does not include the three or more thousand Irishmen whom the English outlawed by name as traitors between 1641 and 1643, or the 39,000 children whom he estimated would have been born had there been no civil war. In sum the loss of life for Ireland, a country of roughly 1.5 million people in the 1630s, was quite staggering, even when compared to the rest of the British Isles.[49]

Table 6: Total of war dead, direct or indirect, for British Isles during the civil wars

	Dead	*Total pre-war population*	*% population loss*
England	190,000	5,000,000	3.7
Scotland	60,000	1,000,000	6
Ireland	618,000	1,500,000	41
Total	868,000	7,500,000	11.6

Even though it must be stressed that the figures in table 6 are very rough estimates, and should be taken with a pinch of caution and pound of scepticism, they do suggest that the loss of life the civil wars inflicted on the British Isles was immense, even when set into context of other wars and catastrophes. During the Second World War the population of the Soviet Union fell by about 15 per cent, while that of Germany declined 20–25 per cent in the Thirty Years' War – both appreciably less than Petty's estimates for Ireland. By comparison, at most the Great Famine of the 1840s killed 16 per cent of Ireland's population. The effects of the Wars of the Roses, England's other great civil war, for instance, have been exaggerated, being nowhere as devastating as Shakespeare would have us believe. Even though the American Civil War was by far the bloodiest confrontation in the nation's history, military deaths represented 2 per cent of the total population, while civilian losses may add another percentage point.[50] During the First World War, out of a total population of the British Isles of thirty-five million, officially 765,399 people lost their lives. If we include as war-connected deaths the 150,000 people who died in 1918–19 from Spanish influenza, then 2.61 per cent of the population died directly or indirectly as a result of the war. By comparison only 0.6 per cent died in the Second World War.

Such statistics cannot convey the experience of death, which as the final passage of our lives must inherently pass all understanding. Death is the last enemy: it opens the door to an undiscovered country from which there is no return. Death is as impossible to understand as it is to avoid.

And herein lies its fascination. Some ages, such as our own, try to ignore death, pretending that it does not exist – just as the Victorians tried to ignore sex – while conversely revelling in morbidity. In normal times death could be peaceful: often it was anticipated; always it should be done well. Thus making one's will was as much a matter of the proper disposition of one's soul as it was of one's property.

Death in battle was a very different matter. In one sense it was the soldier's coin, the gambler's chip which the profession of arms uniquely insists is staked on the roulette wheel of combat. 'Men of our profession ought to be well prepared', admitted Robert Munrow, the convenanter colonel, 'having death ever before their eyes, they ought to be ever ready to embrace it.' Sometimes soldiers mocked death as they resorted to the common ploy of laughing at what frightens us. Thus some seventeenth-century troopers went into battle under a flag bearing the skull and crossbones – as have pirates, modern submarine crews, or units as diverse as the 17th Lancers or the Waffen SS.

Soldiers who have come to terms with death – if such a thing is possible – or who believe that death in battle is an automatic passport to eternal bliss, will fight well. Others must console themselves with the thought that everyone has to die some day or another, and if your number's up there is nothing you can do about it. 'A man can die but once; we owe God a death', says Feeble in *Henry IV, Part 2*, before concluding 'and let it go what way it will.'

But as Shakespeare goes on to point out in *Henry V*, 'there are few die well that die in battle'. Although the young men who form the bulk of armies have always clung to the belief that *they* will not die, they cannot forget that even if it were a fine and private place, the grave was one where few embrace. A contemporary ballad, *The Cavaliers' Prayer*, anticipated Andrew Marvell's poetic finery in a way that the ordinary men who risked their lives would not deny:[51]

> Let the Cannons roar, and the Bullets fly
> King Pym doth swear he'll not come nigh
> He says it's a pitiful thing to die,
> Which nobody can deny.

In the sixteenth and seventeenth centuries people were expected to die well, for the hour of their deaths marked the entry to eternal salvation or damnation, being both a judgment *of* the past life, *for* the next. As a popular couplet put it:[52]

> To be blessed in death, one must learn to live:
> To be blessed in life, one must learn to die.

Sir Thomas Fairfax, the parliamentary general, made the same point in his poem 'Life and Death Compared' (1650):[53]

Such vulgar thoughts the world do fill
To think life good, death only ill.
Then life ill-lived, noe evil's worse
Death (dying well) relieves the curse.
And 'tis for certain truth men tell
He nere dies ill that liveth well.

The perfect death was serene, even beautiful. It took place at home, in one's bed, surrounded by family and friends. It was a placid leave-taking, crowned by sage 'last words'. Even when the ideal was not attained, stories to the contrary were put out. Although James I actually died badly, amid his own sick, sores and diarrhoea, his chaplain, William Laud, promulgated the fable that he 'achieved so strong a death'. It was crucial for the sovereign, above all others, to set an example.[54] Those thousands – perhaps tens of thousands – of his subjects who were publicly executed for the myriad of capital offences in early-modern England, invariably lived up to this ideal. Most of those traitors whose final moments were related by broadsheets, died gamely, retaining their self-respect, as well as the respect of the audience, till the very end.[55]

The nature of their trade has required soldiers to die well. A wounded man who moans and screams before his comrades – or worst still the enemy – is viewed with contempt, or has his stretcher shunted to one side. On the other hand the man who suffers in stoic silence is considered a hero. Thus the Elizabethans held Sir Philip Sidney up as the perfect knight because at the Siege of Zupthen he not only bore the agony of a smashed thigh in silence, but gave the last of his water to a dying comrade, saying 'Thy necessity is greater than mine.'

Few of the two hundred poets, including the queen herself, and hardly any of the seven hundred mourners who marched in his funeral procession, doubted Sir Philip's eventual destination. In early-modern England it was widely held that the state of one's mind at the moment of death (which was best determined by one's last words and deeds) committed one's soul to heaven or hell.[56] Thus the dying moments of civil war soldiers were recorded to console loved ones that their new day had opened as auspiciously as the old one had closed.

Some went gentle into that good night. 'I was the last man that had him by the hand a little time before he died', recalled Dr John Hinton of Sir Bevil Grenville. At the start of the Second Battle of Newbury Gabriel Ludlow was severely wounded by grapeshot. His cousin, Bulstrode, galloped over to see 'his belly broken, and bowels torn, his hip bone broken all to shivers'. The surgeons, practising an earlier form of *triage*, considered Bevil too far gone to warrant their attention, which only added to Bulstrode's anguish. 'In this condition he desired me to kiss him,' Bulstrode recalled, 'and soon after having recommended his brothers, mother and

216

sisters to my care, he died.' Edward Hyde wrote that after having 'his leg shot off by a cannon bullet' at the Siege of Reading, Lieutenant-Colonel D'Ewes 'speedily and very cheerfully died'.[57]

Others died hard. Sir Bernard De Gomme recalled that after a comrade was wounded in the thigh during an assault on Bristol 'it swelled, grew black, stank, whereof he died about midnight'. Richard Wiseman, a surgeon at the Siege of Lyme, treated a private in Colonel Ballard's regiment who had been hit in the head by cannon ball fragments. 'I pulled out the pieces of the bones and lacerated flesh from the brain', he wrote, and dressed the wound. But after seventeen days his patient 'fell into a spasm, and died, howling like a dog; as most of those do who have been so wounded'.[58]

A few died bitter. Sir Abraham Shipman had cause enough for anger because a friend accidentaly shot him, and an incompetent surgeon let the musket wound turn septic. He begged his brother to look after his three children, their mother already being dead. As he expired from over a dozen wounds sustained at Marston Moor, Colonel William Fairfax implored parliament to look after his wife and children. Four years later Colonel Cowell's last request was to ask Cromwell to relay a similar appeal to General Fairfax.[59]

A dying concern for one's family was rather rare – at least in the recorded last words. Such is surprising, for wills, which were usually dictated just before death, showed a growing concern for families. The only dying man recorded talking about his mother was the royalist hero, Captain John Smith, which is again unexpected for modern soldiers frequently do so.

Last words could be banal. 'Oh God! I am hurt' said Sidney Godolphin as he fell dead from his horse, having been hit by a musket ball in an ambush near Chagford, Devon. (Contemporaries considered such brevity to be singularly inappropriate for one of England's most promising young poets.)[60] As he lay dying on the floor of a house near Andover in October 1644 a Scots Captain dragged himself up, saying that 'he would not die like a dog under the table'. Flopping down on a chair, the officer promptly keeled over.[61] Lieutenant-Colonel Wigmore muttered a last prayer, while his relative and company captain simply cursed.[62] Another captain in Lord Grandison's regiment, who was fatally wounded during a night attack at Henley-on-Thames in January 1644, asked to be remembered to his colonel.[63]

The last words of a royalist killed outside Edinburgh in the summer of 1650, 'Dam me, I'll go to my king', are ambiguous, and may refer to the recently executed Charles I.[64] But there was nothing unclear about Captain Walton's at Marston Moor. 'See the rogues run', exalted the ironside as he watched the rout of Rupert's cavalry.[65]

More often dying men praised their own cause – or were at least recorded as doing so by partisan pamphleters. After joking about the bullet that shattered his thigh, Colonel John Trevanion expressed 'his great joy and satisfaction in losing his life in the King's service, to whom he had always dedicated it'. Five years later at the Siege of Colchester in July 1648 a royalist ensign exclaimed, 'Oh! That I had been shot with my colours in my hand that furling myself in them, I might have so died, my friends might have believed that I really loved the king.' Breathing his last from the wounds sustained at Worcester in 1651, the Duke of Hamilton said it was an honour to give his life for his sovereign, and thus atone for his trying to force presbytarianism upon the English.[66]

On wishing the enemy ill, parliamentarians invariably invoked the Almighty's assistance. As Valentine Walton lay dying at Naseby he told Oliver Cromwell that he was grateful that 'God had suffered him to be no more than the executioner of His enemies'. Similarly stricken at another of Cromwell's victories Colonel Thornhaugh said 'I rejoice to die since God hath let me see the overthrow of this perfidious enemy.'[67] The last words of that great parliamentary hero John Hampden, six days after being wounded at the Battle of Chalgrove, were inspiringly enigmatic: 'O Lord! save my country. O Lord! be merciful to . . .'[68]

Some rejoiced at Hampden's death: ''tis well he is slain, thereby he hath escaped a hanging', thought the Reverend Robert Levett, of Cheveley, near Newmarket. Many more were shocked. 'Poor Hampden is dead', mourned Anthony Nichols in a letter to Thomas Barrington, 'I have scarce strength to pronounce that word. Never Kingdom received a greater loss in one subject: never man a truer and faithfuller friend.'[69]

The contrast between the death of brave men and the disposal of their mortal remains was marked. Describing the sight after the storming of Bristol a captain recalled that 'as gallant men as ever drew sword . . . lay upon the ground like rotten sheep'.[70] Descriptions of corpses were fairly common. After the Battle of Worcester bodies were 'strewn from Powick Bridge to the centre of the city, scarcely a street being free of the cadavers'. The stink was so bad that 'a man could hardly abide the town'.[71] When Chaplain John Livingston went to Ireland in 1642 and saw his first corpse he remarked how plump it was. Apparently the covenanter assumed that papist rebels must be poor and skinny.

Only the Irish attempted to recover their dead. Eight rebels died trying to regain two bodies at Irishtown in 1641. Four years later after losing four to five hundred at Dundee, the Scots were amazed to see 'a desperate howling among' the Irish, who 'fought desperately to recover their bodies'.[72]

Sometimes an aristocratic or gentry family would try to recover a corpse for internment in the ancestral plot. After he was slain at Sherborne, Captain John Horsey was interred in the nearby family vault. Although 'trod upon and mangled' Lord Falkland's remains were brought back from

Newbury for burial at Great Tew.[73] Captain Francis St Barbe's troops took his body home to be buried at Romsey after he was mortally wounded at the First Battle of Newbury.[74] Sir Ralph Verney was distraught when the servant he dispatched to Edgehill could not find his father's cadaver to bring it home. Immediately after the battle the king's slain standard bearer had been stripped of his finery and tossed into a mass grave with piles of others.

The reason was obvious. 'The flies had blown maggots upon him', a news-sheet described one of the war's first casualties, a soldier killed on 6 September 1642 at Portsmouth.[75] As public health risks the dead had to be interred as quickly, and preferably as cheaply, as possible. The Corporation of Leicester spent 10 shillings getting rid of fifty carcasses after the king's forces took the city in 1645. The parishioners of St Michael's, Basingstoke were unusually charitable in spending £2 6s 7d to bury in their churchyard some fifty-six soldiers slain at Basing House. According to a local legend East Meon Church tried to deal with the victims of a skirmish by burying six of them standing upright under the church floor, before interring the rest in a pit beside the Barleigh road.[76] As outsiders, civil war dead were rarely buried within the churchyard, with a plot and tombsone of their own. 'There were three strangers buried', was all that a Devon parish register bothered to record.[77]

Occasionally the dead were interred with full military honours. A contemporary described the funeral of a royalist major who died of wounds received at Over, in August 1643:

> Then they buried him in a warlike manner, with his sword upon his coffin, and a drum beating before him to the church, where he was buried . . . men giving two volleys of shot there for him and afterwards the same drum beat before them home again.

After his son was killed at the Siege of Denbigh in May 1646 Edward Wynne requested that his body be returned for burial in the family plot. A party of fellow officers carried it to a stream on the Whitchurch road, where it was handed over to a detail of roundheads, who fired a volley, before bearing it to Llanrhaeadr.[78]

Such rites were rare: indeed it is a sad fact that the final resting place of hardly any of the civil war dead was known to their own kith and kin, and even fewer to posterity. Soldiers did not wear 'dog tags' to facilitate accurate identification. Having invariably been stripped of clothes and possessions, as well as been scarred by fatal wounds, their remains were extremely hard to recognize.

The seemingly callous treatment of the dead should not be taken as a sign that the living did not mourn their passing.[79]

If tears could wash the Ill away,
A pearl for each wet bead I'd pay

So wrote Richard Lovelace about what he admitted was his 'immoderately mourning my Brother's untimely death at Carmarthen'. Margaret Lucas, later the Duchess of Newcastle, took the death of her brother Charles Lucas very hard, perhaps because Fairfax executed him after he surrendered Colchester in 1648:

Dear Blessed soul, though thou art gone
Thy fame on earth, and men thy praises give
But all's too small, for thy heroic mind
Was above the praises of mankind.

Depression haunted Margaret for years. 'Black despair like melancholy night, muffles my thoughts, and makes my soul as blind', she wrote in 1662. Even hardened soldiers could take the death of a comrade badly. 'Indeed we are at this time a crazy company', wrote Oliver Cromwell after Colonel Michael Jones passed away.[80]

Letters of consolation leave no doubt about the void the civil war created in tens of thousands of people's lives.

Fathers comforted children. 'My Dear Doll,' the Earl of Liecester wrote to his daughter Dorothy after her husband was killed at the Second Battle of Newbury,[81]

I know it is no purpose to advise you not to grieve . . . God comfort you, and let us join in Prayer to him, that he will be pleased to give Grace to you, to your mother and to myself . . . your father that loves you dearly.

Friends consoled widows and parents. 'How can I contain myself or longer conceal my sorrow for the death of that excellent man, your most dear husband and my noble friend', wrote John Trevelyan to Lady Grace Grenville. He added that Sir Bevil 'died an Honorable death which all his enemies will envy, fighting with invincible valour and loyalty for his God, his King and Country'.[82] On learning of the death of Colonel John Denton, Sir Ralph Verney wrote to his father, Alexander Denton, a prisoner in the Tower, 'I must account it one of my greatest and particular afflictions to lose the man that you and I did love so well.' He took Christian comfort in the thought that John 'lived and died most gallantly, and questionless is most happy'.[83] Even the king, a man reserved almost to the point of indifference, could mourn the loss of loyal subjects. 'You cannot be more sensible', wrote Charles to the Earl of Lindsey four days after Edgehill, 'of your father's loss than my self, his death confirming the estimation I ever had of him.'[84]

Sometimes the death of an exceptionally promising young man was felt way beyond the circle of his family and immediate friends. Sidney Godolphin was such a golden figure, cut down – like Rupert Brooke – before his metal had chance to shine. Born in 1610 in Cornwall, and educated at Oxford, he was a poet and philosopher whose promise touched all who met him. He fought reluctantly for the king, disliking the 'swordsmen' who adopted the king's cause with brutal enthusiasm, and whom, as the war went on and the queen became more influential, Charles embraced with a growing dependence. On hearing that Godolphin had died in a skirmish at Chagford at dawn on 9 February 1643, Sir Bevil Grenville told his wife, 'One loss we have sustained is incalculable . . . as gallant a gentleman as the world had.' Sir Ralph Hopton agreed, calling Godolphin 'as perfect and as absolute a piece of virtue as ever nation bred'. Thomas Hobbes dedicated his *Leviathan* to Godolphin, mourning the fact that this paragon had been slain 'by an undiscerned and undiscerning hand'.[85]

In modern war far more people are wounded than killed. For the British the ratio in the First World War was 2.23, in the Second 1.03. In the Falklands it was 3.04, the proud boast of the medical services there being that not a single man died once he reached a field ambulance. During the civil war, when very few figures on the wounded were kept, the ratio seems to have been a little above even. A list of casualties of Edgehill, where the few available facilities for treating the wounded broke down, shows that 109 died and 138 were wounded, a ratio of 1.27.[86] Of a sample of 76 senior commanders 30.3 per cent were killed and 36.8 per cent wounded, a 1.21 ratio: the injury rate for cavaliers, 41.4 per cent, was much higher than that of roundheads, 31.4 per cent.

The experience of soldiers on being wounded varied. 'Col Hewson, Governor of Dublin was bruised in the shoulder with a bullet, and then beshitt himself', observed Scoutmaster Henry James in March 1650. While this bodily reaction was more frequent than most would admit (albeit not as common as soldiers' scatological conversations would suggest), many men were wounded in the heat of battle without really noticing. When a cannon ball smashed his leg during the Highland campaign, an Irish infantryman pulled out his knife to cut off the remnants, and cheerfully observed that Montrose 'will make me a trooper now I am no good for the foot'.[87] Captain John Birch was wounded in the belly as he assaulted Arundel Castle. Years later a comrade reminded him how, 'you kept in your guts, stopping the whole with your fingers, until you had slain or drawn prisoner the enemy about you'. Birch's adrenal glands must have released massive amount of endorphins, permitting him to keep on fighting, his massive wounds notwithstanding. Afterwards, when the body's natural anaesthetic wore off, Birch's comrade recalled, 'you were lain with so many others on the floor, grovelling'. Colonel Norton had a similar experience after a musket ball hit him in the foot as he charged at the head of Colonel Ludlow's regiment during the Second Battle of Newbury. Only later was he incapacitated, although he told a friend, 'I hope that I will be on both legs again ere it be too long.'[88]

Sir Thomas Fairfax showed a similar heroism in July 1643 when he led his cavalry troop out of a royalist ambush. Although bleeding copiously from an arm wound, he fought ferociously until, exhausted from twenty hours without sleep, he fell unconscious from his saddle. Patched up by a surgeon, after only fifteen minutes' rest, he rode on for another twenty hours, as he carried his 6-year-old daughter Mary to safety. Looking back Sir Thomas wondered how anyone could have survived such an experience: how was it possible 'to find a body so full of pain, and mind so full of anxiety and trouble?'[89]

After being hit on the head in a brawl at Watlington, Bulstrode White-locke managed to make good his escape with John Hampden's help: later he suffered from headaches and confused speech, clear symptoms of concussion. Perhaps the saddest case of a fighting-mad soldier neglecting his wounds was that of Sir John Digby. Caught in an ambush near Taunton that killed the captain of their infantry escort, Digby managed to lead his cavalry to safety, not realizing that a musket bullet had hit him in the right arm above the elbow. Having ridden 'pleasantly and merrily a good distance', the pain set in. Unable to journey any further he was carried by stretcher to Bridgwater where he 'lay day and night in unspeakable and excessive pain' for thirty-one days before he finally expired. The body's natural secretion of endorphins killed Digby, for had he immediately felt the pain of his wound, it would have been an easy matter to remove the bullet from just underneath the skin.[90]

Most of those who were wounded in battle knew it only too well at the time, and afterwards were amazed how they had managed to survive the ordeal of pain. 'I was unfortunately shot through the right side of my nose under the left ear, through all the jugular veins and mouth, and did bleed extremely,' wrote Colonel John Owen to his wife from the 1643 Siege of Bristol, 'but good God be praised I am in a pretty good state, if it doth not turn into a fever.'[91]

Gangrene, with its high, usually fatal fever was as agonizing as it could be lethal. *Mercurius Rusticus* described how the wound Colonel Sandys suffered at Powick Bridge developed:

> In his thigh the flesh did daily rot and putrefy, and was cut away by degrees even to bearing the bone naked, and stunk in so loathsome a manner that as he was a burden to himself so to his friends, too, and those that were about him were hardly able, for the noisomeness of the smell, either to come near him, or to do the office of necessary attendance, or so much as to endure the room where he lay, so intolerable was the stench, and so offensive.

After a month ranting with pain, Sandys died, as did his son, who caught smallpox when brought to bid his father adieu.

Some soldiers managed to survive the most appalling damage. Private George Robinson, of Colonel Springet's parliamentary regiment, was hit in the legs at the First Battle of Newbury. Eventually evacuated to London, he spent six months at St Bartholomew's Hospital, 'lame and sore diseased', having had some sixty bone splinters taken out of his leg. After eight years being 'almost continually in intolerable pain', he was awarded a 10-shilling cash gratuity, pus a £4 per annum pension.[92] The same year George Jennings, another parliamentary private, received a pension for his wounds, which included a broken skull (patched by a silver plate), a slit ear, a cut cheek, a broken jawbone, a maimed hand, several thigh wounds, and an abdominal cut through which his stomach had herniated.

Others received non-combat wounds. Having fought unscathed through much of the Thirty Years' War abroad and the civil wars at home, the only time James Turner was injured was in 1646. Drunk, he stumbled across Colonel Wren, an old enemy. They drew swords, and Turner was cut between his thumb and forefinger, and, he admitted, 'almost lost the use of both'.[93] Henry Collier's wound was less glorious and far more serious. After producing gunpowder for parliament at Stafford for three and a half years, the heat of the copper boilers infected his foot. It would not heal, and eventually he had to have it amputated, which was, he stated in his petition for a pension, 'to his utter undoing'.[94]

Wounds tended to come in four main categories: cuts, penetration wounds, broken limbs, and burns.

Cuts, usually from swords, tended to be the least serious, particularly if they were kept clean and rapidly bandaged to stop the soil organisms which cause gangrene from entering.

Cleanly broken limbs usually healed if a splint was effectively applied. When bones were shattered, or exposed, the limb was usually amputated, often with success. John Woodhall, author of the widely used manual *The Surgeon's Mate* (1617, 1639), advised that when resorting to 'this great and terrible instrument' the patient be placed on a table 'with one strong man behind him, and another before', and the saw, well oiled and sharpened, hidden, to be produced at the very last moment.

All that Woodhall could prescribe for gunpowder burns was to apply a salve, feed the patient quinces, and bleed. Such flash wounds could be truly horrible. Richard Atkyns described what happened when the morning after the Battle of Lansdown a trooper decided to light his pipe next to an ammunition wagon that was also carrying wounded. 'The hurt men made lamentable screeches', he recalled, adding that a nearby horse was 'singed like parched leather'. Seeing his friend Major Thomas Sheldon with his breeches on fire, Atkyns ripped them off. But it was too late. Without a hair of his fine flaxen hair left, and burnt 'like a blackamoor', Sheldon died a few hours later.[95]

Penetration wounds were usually the worst. If they entered the intestines peritonitis was inevitable. Punctures of the chest cavity normally resulted in the victim asphyxiating, or drowning in his own blood. All too often a penetrating wound, such as a pike or musket ball, introduced foreign matter, such as scraps of clothing, which produced sepsis.[96]

Musket wounds were invariably lethal. When they, or cannon shot, hit pike staffs, they sent jagged wooden splinters flying deep into the nearby bodies. On entering the body, muskets balls also shattered bones, turning the fragments into internal missiles. When travelling at full velocity heavy musket balls made an entry wound about half an inch wide. The exit wound was the size of a dinner plate. Unless face wounds were superficial, albeit disfiguring, damage to the head was usually fatal. Lord Belasyse was extremely lucky not only to survive such a wound he received at the Siege of Bristol, but to live another forty-three years with part of a musket ball in his head. Prince Rupert had a similar experience. The ball trapped in his skull caused him no trouble until a block of rigging fell on his head. A French surgeon successfully operated upon him in 1684.[97]

Medical invoices provide details of the types and locations of wounds. In the summer of 1645 George Belgrade sent parliament a bill for the lacerated soldiers he treated. One was burnt, two had bullet wounds, eight had received cuts – the large proportion of the latter being an indication of the good chances of surviving gashes. Of Belgrade's patients eight were hurt in the arms or shoulders, eight in the head and face, five in the back, and two in the legs. An analysis of some pension petitions from royalist veterans in North Wales shows a slightly different pattern: ten had multiple wounds, seven head and face, and ten apiece were hurt in the arms and legs. Seven had lost an arm or one leg, and three both limbs. Of the types of injuries ten were from shot, one a cut, and in twelve cases the information was not recorded. The only explanation for the relatively high number of shot as opposed to cut wounds is that if the men with shot wounds survived they were so badly incapacitated as to qualify for a pension, whereas those without shot wounds recovered so well that they had no long-term claim on public support.[98]

One sort of wounds conspicuous by their virtual absence during the civil wars were psychiatric ones. Records of psychiatric damage caused by the war are most rare. The most obvious was that of Sir Walter Earle, a skilled sapper and veteran of the Thirty Years' War. He must have been under some mental strain. On returning to England he retired to his garden at Charborough, where he built miniature defence works and decorated his house with siege maps. Recalled to the colours to take part in the Siege of Corfe Castle, a musket ball just missed him, piercing his hat. This last straw snapped the veteran's nerve. Soon afterwards Sir Walter was seen dressed in a bear's skin, walking on all fours in the hope of being mistaken for a large dog.[99] After serving as a chaplain at Marston Moor, Thomas Goad, Vicar of Grinton, Yorkshire, fell ill and became distracted, 'and languished in this condition for at least sixteen years'.[100] Another military chaplain, Richard Baxter, felt the strain of the war after he was demobilized. He had a copious and unquenchable nose-bleed – invariably a sign of intense psychological strain. After losing a quart or two of blood, Baxter had a doctor open his vein, but to no avail, for his illness lasted another three months.[101]

Civilians could also suffer mentally from the stresses of war – as Baxter knew only too well. His mother was in a town that was stormed, much of it being burned, with many men killed before her eyes, and the survivors plundered to their shifts. The experience withered her usual over-timid nature. A maid-servant who witnessed the brutal massacre of the garrison of Hopton Castle, Herefordshire, suffered from mental trauma for the rest of her life. Even though he played a minor part in the 1648 Kent rebellion Edward Benlowes' poetry reflected a sense of guilt at having shed blood. The news of Charles I's execution so depressed Alderman Thomas Heyle of York that he hanged himself in his bedroom. William Summers declared that after she lost her son and all her possessions, when the royalists sacked Leicester in 1645, his 'wife hath been distracted ever since'.[102] Sadder still was the case of Lady Jordan, who was caught in the Siege of Cirencester in February 1643. The bombardment, which included a shelling by a large mortar, as well as the subsequent sack, destroyed her adult faculties. She regressed to behaving like a tiny child, being able to find happiness only by playing with the dolls that were made specially for her.[103]

There may be two reasons for the comparative lack of psychiatric casualties in the civil war. First, men were rarely in combat for the long, sustained period of fighting which tend to produce them. With intervals of rest the average soldier can withstand 200–40 days of combat before breaking down. Secondly, when civil war soldiers did break down it could well have passed unnoticed. Combat fatigue was first medically identified in the American Civil War, when it was called 'nostalgia', the symptoms being an intense desire to go home.[104] Since desertion right up until the moment of battle was fairly common and easy during the civil wars, it could be that psychiatric casualties simply upped stakes and walked home, where they were most likely to receive the finest possible care.

In view of the nature of wounds, and the inadequate medical services to treat them, it is surprising that seventeenth-century soldiers spoke little about the subject, particularly when compared to modern combatants who are often more afraid of disablement than death.[105] In part such concerns are a result of outstanding medical facilities, as well as an emphasis (endemic in the American Army) on dealing with one's own casualties rather than inflicting them on the other side. Many seventeenth-century soldiers ignored the possibility of being wounded or had little idea how ghastly a fate it could be. Once John Vicars, that blood-thirsty puritan propagandist, described some royalist wounded 'most woefully cut and mangled, some having their ears cut off, some the flesh of their heads shied off, some with their very skull hanging down and ready to fall dead'. Blood and guts might inspire civilians. After reading these details in *A Perfect and True Relation of the Grete and Bloody Skirmish fought before the City of Worcester*, the London artisan, Nehemiah Wallington, noted in his diary, 'Remember how marvelous works He hath done.' On the other hand gore could back-fire, reminding the roundheads that they too might readily suffer a similar fate.[106]

Wounds purportedly inflicted by poisoned bullets outraged and frightened soldiers on all sides. Stories of dum-dum rounds contaminated with some germ-ridden substance such as horse hair, were reported at Lacock House, Nantwich, Colchester, Powick Bridge and Crowland. In fact such tales of germ warfare were no more than tales. When a bullet dragged foreign matter, such as dirty clothes, into a deep wound, nature had no problem in working her lethal way.

Surgeons knew only too well how little they could in fact do to mitigate the ravages of war. John Steer, a London surgeon, hoped that his 1643 translation of Fabricius Guilielm's *Experiment's in Chyrurgerie* would be 'Very Necessary and useful for Gentlemen and soldiers . . . especially upon sudden occasions.' 'Death', admitted Edward Coke, a parliamentary surgeon, 'will prevail.'[107]

Yet soldiers wanted the surgeons to do something – anything – to thwart the grim reaper, no matter how remote the odds. As George Monck observed, nothing did more to encourage troops to continue fighting than the provision of the best available medical care. Thus when one of Colonel Arundel's men was shot in the face during the Siege of Taunton, the commanding officer ordered his regimental surgeon Richard Wiseman to attend to the man even though he was 'without Eye, Face, Nose or Mouth'. Wiseman admitted, 'I went, but I did not know where to begin.' All the front of his head was shot away, his brain was oozing out of his cranium, part of his smashed jaw hung down onto his throat, from which the stub of his tongue protruded. Wiseman bandaged the wounds as skilfully as he could, and poured a quart of wine down what remained of the poor fellow's mouth. He seemed grateful enough, and was still alive a week later, when Wiseman had to march away with his regiment.[108]

In theory each regiment had a surgeon, who was assisted by two mates. He had to provide his own chest, containing some £25 worth of instruments and medicines. Surgeons were poorly paid at 4 to 5 shillings a day, and were liable to conscription. Since parliament controlled London, the headquarters of the Barber-Surgeons Company and the Royal College of Physicians, they were better able to provide for their troops than was the king, who, after appointing John Bissell Commissary for the sick and wounded, was more inclined to leave their care to charity and volunteers.[109] Wearing a special badge which (like the red cross) recognized their status as non-combatants, surgeons treated both sides. When captured they were quickly released. For instance, after Benjamin Gill, a surgeon's mate was taken at Kidlington, his master, Henry Jackson, requested the roundheads to free him, promising in return to do all he could to obtain the release of any parliamentary surgeons who fell into royalist hands. Occasionally medical men took part in combat. Trapped at the Second Battle of Newbury, Dr. John Hinton led a squad of some twenty cavalier troopers, who had lost their officer, in the break-out at night between the river and Donnington Castle. When the medical man reached the safety of Oxford, Prince Maurice welcomed him with a clap on the shoulder, 'How dost thou Doctor? You have some hearty cavaliers after you!'[110]

Modern research has proved that the sooner a patient receives treatment after being wounded the greater are his chances of surviving. Thus today operations are performed as close to the front line as is feasible, and soldiers are rushed, preferably by helicopter, to field ambulances. Sir Richard Wiseman, Charles II's Surgeon General, recognized this truth by advising his colleagues to treat wounds as soon as possible.[111]

Of a sample of casualties at Edgehill the ratio of killed to wounded for officers was 1: 2.4 as opposed to 1: 1.2 for other ranks.[112] This difference may be explained by the fact that the officers were more likely to be rescued by retainers and so receive prompt and effective medical treatment. Both Colonel Charles Gerard and Captain Henry Bellingham were wounded in the thigh at Edgehill. The former was quickly treated and survived: 'a slovenly surgeon' attended the latter; he failed to notice a superficial wound that turned septic, killing the unfortunate captain. Captain John Hodgson credited his survival of a royalist ambush near Seacroft, in which he received two bullet wounds and several cuts, to the loyalty of one of his troopers, who dragged him into a nearby wood, and 'with much ado got me to Leeds in the night'. Nonetheless Hodgson had to conclude 'it was a considerable time before I was cured'.[113] Officers were more likely to be able to afford medical attention. An eyewitness described the royalist retreat from Torrington in February 1646: 'there were two considerable persons carried in horse litters, groaning and crying out with pain, but not knowing who they were.'[114]

Usually after a fight the wounded were left behind for the locals to look after as best they could. Following the First Battle of Newbury, Charles wrote to the mayor ordering him to care for the wounded, including the roundheads. 'Though they be rebels and deserve the punishment of traitors', the king piously declared, they deserved the same treatment as his own men. The fact of the matter was that the level of medical care enjoyed by either side was pretty rudimentary. After Edgehill some parliamentary wounded were – all too literally – dumped in Hester White's house where they remained 'in great misery' for three months, as she nursed them day and night without being given a penny.[115]

Some wounded were moved to permanent hospitals usually located in large towns. Sir Thomas Spencer's manor house north of Oxford was a royalist hospital. There were hospitals in Northampton (where Lucy Hutchinson nursed), in Bristol, and in Bath, which with its waters was a centuries-old centre for healing. Most of the time parliament used existing hospitals, such as St Bartholomew's, St Thomas's and Bridewell in London. Once it set up a new military hospital in Savoy House in London with its own regulations. The authorities could fine patients for missing church, pillory or even cashier them for being drunk or for swearing, ban them from 'scolding, brawling or chiding' the medical staff, and expel them both if a patient married a nurse.[116]

London's hospitals seemed to have done a reasonably good job: of the 1,112 patients admitted in 1644 to St Bartholomew's, 152 (or 13.6 per cent) died, as did 116 (or 15.1 per cent) of the 796 patients admitted the following year. The survival rate for St Thomas's was not quite as good: 23 per cent of the 1,063 patients admitted in 1644, and 14.7 per cent of the 825 in 1645, died.[117] Nonetheless, considering that a 10 per cent annual death-rate from non-combat causes was not unusual for a garrison or field army, the figures for the London hospitals were creditable. It could be that if a man survived the battlefield, his immediate treatment, and evacuation on a litter over rutted roads to London, he was strong enough to outlast the worst the medical profession had to offer.

Those who pulled through often took months – years – to recover, and usually bore the scars for the rest of their days. After having his thigh bone broken at the Siege of York, Major John Dobeny had to spend a year in bed. Eventually he became Archbishop of York. Most wounded were not so lucky in their pursuit of a public pension. Even though Oliver Cromwell wrote that Thomas Cave, who having lost both eyes fighting in his regiment at Marston Moor was 'in a very sad and punishing condition', should have a pension, the blind soldier had to fend for himself.

Cave did not need eyes to see how inefficient and parsimonious were the provisions for wounded veterans. The day after Edgehill, parliament passed a declaration promising a pension to all wounded or to the relatives of those killed in its service. Based on the Elizabethan system of poor relief, those claiming pensions, or their widows or orphans, had to obtain a note from their commanding officer to receive a 4 shillings a week allotment from their home parish. Their karma was not a happy one. In Suffolk, a rich county that saw next to no fighting, a contemporary recorded that maimed troopers 'usually met with ill entertainment from their several parishes'.[118] After the war the commonwealth allocated £45,000 for the wounded, widows and orphans, and may have been disbursing some six thousand pensions. Yet by 1659 arrears had become so dire that 2,500 maimed soldiers, and 4,000 widows and orphans, petitioned Lord Fairfax for relief.

Following the Restoration the government naturally paid greater attention to royalists, who had been short-changed during the war and scandalously neglected by the commonwealth. In May 1643 Charles I had issued a proclamation that he very much wanted to pay all his wounded soldiers a generous pension. In the meanwhile he urged everyone else to do all they could to help maimed soldiers: they should be given priority in admission to those almshouses the king controlled, and parish authorities were to raise the rates to support widows and orphans. Five days later the king ordered a collection to be taken in every church the following Sunday for maimed soldiers. Such efforts did little: for instance a collection taken the following June raised but £35.[119] After 1660 the cavalier parliament could be more generous with the tax-payers' money. In 1662 they voted pensions up to £20 a year for maimed cavaliers, and established a £60,000 relief fund to 'loyal and indigent officers'. Within a year over a thousand of them had applied for help.

Most of the war's victims had to get by as best they could on their own resources and with a little help from their family and friends. Even though the war bequeathed them terrible problems – endless pain from wounds, missing limbs, loss of sight, or loss of husbands, fathers or brothers – few of the victims left records. Take the case of Susan Rodway, the wife who wrote frantically begging her husband Robert not to get himself killed during the Siege of Basing House, but to come home safe to her and their 'little Willie'. Almost certainly she waited in vain. Robert's company took very heavy casualties, and Susan learned all too well the lesson that is so oft forgot – that men go to war to kill and be killed and rarely receive any tenderness there.[120]

10

WHEN THE HURLYBURLY'S DONE

First Witch. When shall we three meet again?
  In thunder, lightning or in rain?
Second Witch. When the hurlyburly's done,
  When the battle's lost and won.
Third Witch. That will be ere the set of sun.
                                    Macbeth, I. i.1–5

Looking back on his experiences during the civil wars Richard Baxter, the Protestant divine, remembered that wherever you went, whatever the time, virtually the first question anyone asked someone else was, 'do you have the news?'[1] In wartime, as in all moments of crisis, people thirst for news. Today communities group around television sets, or huddle about short-wave radios to hear the latest. In the seventeenth century they avidly wrote to each other, or read news-sheets (invariably entitled *A True Report* . . . etc.) to learn what battles had been lost and won. 'Buy me all the latest news books and send them to me', wrote Henry Oxinden to his cousin Elizabeth in London.

Even before the formal declaration of war printers realized that they could make a profit from practically any news report. 'If the State be extreme sick', admitted a pamphlet writer in August 1643, 'penny pamphlets make us pound foolish.' An eagerness to toss over a copper or two for the latest intelligence sprang less from idle curiosity and more out of diligent necessity: victory or defeat could affect every man, woman and child in the land, as well as the outcome of the war itself. Thus Edward Hyde told Sir Francis Ottley, a county magnate, to bruit news of the king's conquests throughout the highways and byways of Shropshire.[2]

In October 1642 a pamphleteer described the widespread thirst for news that nothing, not even fast and accurate reporting, or even time itself could quench:[3]

Each hour is a herald of homicides, each day a messenger of mischiefs, each week a Diurnall of dangers, each month a Motto of misery, this whole year but a march, and no language amongst us but war.

230

The attempts to disseminate information about the first major confrontation illustrate this quandary. In a letter dated London, 20 October 1643 Stephen Charlton reported that the king and parliament had fought a great battle in which some said that Charles had been taken prisoner and Rupert killed, and others that the Earl of Essex had been slain. Charlton spent the whole morning at the Houses of Parliament to find out more, but had to confess that 'no man could tell me the certainty of it'.[4]

The paucity of clairvoyants at Westminster should not be surprising, for Edgehill was in fact fought three days later on 23 October. During that afternoon people in Alveston, 10 miles north-west of Edgehill, could hear the noise of cannon fire. Soon afterwards terrified parliamentary deserters streamed through the village with lurid stories of a rout. By early the next day renegades arrived in Oxford with similar reports. They exaggerated the extent of the defeat either from genuine fear or else to excuse their cowardice. The inhabitants of Alveston managed to get a more accurate account of the battle by visiting Edgehill on the 24th, while in Oxford parliamentary scouts blazoned that Essex's army had totally routed the enemy, killing and capturing many of them – news which was, a contemporary noted, 'far more welcome' but just as erroneous as the original reports.[5]

The first coverage of Edgehill was published in London on 25 October. A hastily printed quarto, with ink smudges and typos, purporting to be a letter from 'A Gentleman of Quality', described a parliamentary triumph capped by Rupert's capture. The following day another broadsheet, supposedly composed by a soldier who took part in the battle, repeated the story. With far less confidence, it concluded, 'how true it is I dare not affirm'. The next day *A letter from a Worthy Divine* came off the press, but added nothing new to the wildly circulating rumours. The first hard news, *An Exact and True relation of the dangerous and bloody fight . . . near Kineton*, written by a group of parliamentary officers including Denzil Holles, did not appear until the 29th, six days after the battle had been fought about 70 miles from London. As its title suggests this report was far more realistic. By 2 November royalist accounts of Edgehill, such as *A Prayer of Thanksgiving*, had been smuggled from Oxford into London.[6]

Over time news reporting improved greatly, notably on the parliamentary side, which used chaplains as rudimentary war correspondents. In one of the war's most enigmatic headlines 'Shrewsbury yet untaken, but shrewdly strained', *The Kingdome's Weekly Intelligencer* for 7–14 November 1643 put the best possible gloss on dispatches from the Welsh Marches. Two years later, in 1644, a fairly accurate report of Marston Moor appeared in London six days after the battle took place 200 miles to the north. Four more accurate accounts were printed in the following four days. By 1646 excellent dispatches on the activities of the roundhead forces in the West Country appeared in London within three or even two days.

Victory, as the Chinese proverb notes, has a thousand fathers, unlike defeat which is an orphan. Indeed with the exception of becoming a father, men know few forms of joy sweeter than victory on the field of battle. For those who have never felt such ecstasy in person, words cannot convey it as well as a more abstract medium, such as the music of Tchaikovsky's *1812 Overture*. After the drums had stilled, and the cannons fell silent, Francis Barret wrote from Truro to his wife on 18 March 1643 following a royalist triumph:[7]

> Dearest Soul – Oh Dearest soul, praise God everlastingly. Read the enclosed, ring out the bells, raise bonfires, publish these joyful tidings. Believe these truths, excuse my writing longer, I have no time. We march on to meet our victorious friends, and to seize all the rebels left if we can find any living.

Victories were marked by public celebrations: bonfires were lit, toasts drunk, services of thanksgiving held, church bells rung. Many believed that the Almighty was behind their triumph. Seeing the cavaliers break and run at the Battle of Langport in July 1645, Colonel Thomas Harrison 'broke forth into the Praises of God with fluent expression, as if he had been in a Rapture'. Oliver Cromwell, an observer, asked, 'to see this is it not to see the face of God?'[8] After the roundheads captured Preston in March 1643, one of their chaplains, John Tilsley, Vicar of Beane, near Bolton, exulted 'we sung praises to God in the Streets (Sir, it was wonderful to see it), the sun broke forth and shined brightly and hot at the time of the exercise, as if it had been midsummer.'[9]

For centuries men have given God credit for their victories (although rarely the blame for defeat). It was He who blew and scattered the Armada. The official *Forme of Prayer necessary to be used in these dangerous times of Warre* declared in 1624 that 'Victory is absolute in the will and power of God.'[10] Sometimes soldiers gave Him partial credit. 'By God's providence and the courage of the Kentish regiment and that of the Hamlets', wrote Richard Coe of the fighting at Basing, 'we . . . staved them off.'[11] Victors attributed their victories to God – and to God alone – so frequently that to modern secular ears it sounds like a cliché. One of the Earl of Denbigh's officers declared that their capture of Shrewsbury with the loss of only five dead and six wounded had been 'miraculously gained by God's free love'. Sir John Henderson wrote to a friend that 'God hath so blessed us that yesternight we put to flight eight companies of their horse.'[12] For the victory at Nantwich 'God is to have the glory', Sir Thomas Fairfax told his wife.[13]

Three hundred years later, another equally distinguished general, Field Marshal Montgomery, observed that 'The best way to achieve a high morale in wartime is by success in battle.' Sir Henry Slingsby agreed, writing that the royalist capture of Bradford 'gave new strength, courage and health to every soldier'.[14] It made recruiting easier: men flocked to join the parliamentary forces during their successful campaign in the West Country in 1645–6, when an observer reported 'Truly our soldiers march with that cheerfulness as I never seen them before.'[15]

Success bred success. Victory reduced casualties while increasing the opportunities for booty. Describing the pursuit of the king's forces Chaplain Joshua Sprigge asked 'But the Enemy fleeing, what was the army to do but follow? And so they did . . . Notwithstanding the weary march [they] leapt for joy.' Sometimes the victors jumped for the joy of good sport. In the spring of 1646, as the first civil war was drawing to an end, a parliamentary officer described ambushing patrols from the Oxford garrison; 'We had a gallant hunting of them from place to place over the hills.'[16]

Victory could change the victorious. 'When I came to the army, among Cromwell's soldiers, I found a new face of things', noted Richard Baxter after Naseby.[17] The troops had become much more radical. Having ventured their lives for the parliamentary cause, they were determined to see that England became a Godly Nation. Indeed why had God saved them when a thousand fell at their side and tens of thousands at their right, if it were not to do His work? Thus William Dell preached to the New Model Army at their headquarters in June 1646,[18]

> I have seen more of the presence of God in that Army, than in amongst any people that I have ever conversed with in my life . . . for he hath dwelt amongst us, and marched in the head of us, and counselled us, and led us, and hath gone along with us step by step from Naseby.

The wormwood of defeat was far more bitter than victory was sweet. For one thing defeated troops were more likely to be killed or wounded, and invariably were captured or had to flee. For another the survivors were far more liable to pillage, and commit atrocities. After being routed at Cheriton the royalists raged through Alresford screaming 'The Kingdom's lost! The Kingdom's lost!', setting fire to several houses in the town in their panic.[19]

Defeat is as hard to explain as it is to accept, especially by soldiers who believe that God is on their side. After the surrender of Berkeley Castle in September 1645 a royalist officer remarked to the captain in command of the prison detail that 'he thought God was turned Roundhead, the King's forces prospered so ill'.[20] After Montrose had beaten the covenanters on five occasions in a row, Dr Robert Baillie wrote to his cousin, General William Baillie, the leader of the vanquished forces, 'We are amazed that it should be the pleasure of God to make us fall thus the fifth time.'[21] But only one case has been found when defeat caused men to doubt their faith. J. Corbet, vicar of St Mary Crypt, Gloucester, observed during the great siege of 1644 that the news that the enemy had taken Bristol 'made most men infidels, or at least question all things'.[22] A much more common reaction to defeat was dissension within the ranks, and disillusionment with one's cause and leadership.

Explanations of reverses varied. One of Captain Nathaniel Fiennes' troop blamed the rout at Powick Bridge in September 1642 on poor intelligence, tiredness, and the dust which blew from a nearby fallow field into the soldiers' eyes.[23] At the same time the Marquis of Hertford – acting on the adage that there are no bad aristocrats, only bad soldiers – attributed 'our disastrous fortune at Minehead' to the 'evil dispositions and cowardly behaviour' of his enlisted men.[24]

Individuals found it very hard to come to terms with their own losses. Charles was unusually sanguine, telling Sir George Goring that 'we must expect disasters in war, so we hope you not be disheartened by them.'[25] Sir George was less restrained, his sovereign remedy being the bottle, not his king. 'He gave himself his usual license of drinking', Clarendon tartly observed.[26] Even though Charles begged the Earl of Newcastle to stay, following his defeat at Marston Moor he left England to go into exile on the continent, vowing 'I will not endure the laughter of the court.' The half-hearted attack by Lord Arthur Capel and his men on Wem, Shropshire, in October 1643 gave the roundheads something else to laugh about. A poetaster sneered:[27]

> The Women of Wem and a few Musketeers
> Beat the Lord Capel and his cavaliers.

To be fair, however, Capel responded to this humiliation with courage. To encourage his men he strolled about the trenches under fire, treating enemy snipers with lordly disdain: he calmly pulled out and lit his pipe as 'they made many desperate shots at him'. Sir William Waller's only solace after his defeat at Cropredy was his wife. 'I had nearly sunk under that affliction,' he confessed, 'but that I had a dear and sweet comforter.'[28]

The collective impact of defeat was just as devastating. When news of the loss of Reading reached Oxford the royalist garrison was stunned. Not a single drum beat, not a horse's hoofs were heard in the streets, which were usually a cacophany of military preparations: everything instead was silent.[29] When John Vaughan heard in March 1644 that Tenby had fallen he lamented, 'we are all ruined'. The royalist captain continued that his men's morale had virtually collapsed, and without effective action from Prince Rupert (which he thought unlikely), the situation was irretrievable.[30] Defeat made it even harder to recruit soldiers, as Rupert discovered after Marston Moor, when it was observed, 'the Country people tell him that he should rather cut their throats at home than carry them abroad to be slain.'[31] Survivors who stayed with the colours were more likely to mutiny. Cropredy Bridge broke Waller's army. Mutineers attacked and wounded their commander. Troops demonstrated that they wanted to go home. Four hundred from the Whitecoats regiment deserted, being soon followed by sizeable contingents from the Southwark, Tower Hamlets, and Westminster regiments – normally elite units.[32] Two years later roundhead victories turned Sir Richard Grenville's forces into what the Prince of Wales's Council had to admit was a 'dissolute, undisciplined, weakened, beaten army'.[33]

Rest and retraining were the most effective ways to rebuild shattered units. In this regard parliament had an advantage, especially as the war continued. It had more troops, so it could give broken regiments time to sit out a battle or two to recover, and in East Anglia had a secure base in which they could do so. When Lord General Essex commissioned Edmund Ludlow to raise a new regiment of foot in March 1644, he let him recruit 'the choicest of my old soldiers', while taking the rest – all hard cases – 'into his own company'.[34]

Initially the crown had similar advantages. After they broke and ran at the Battle of Horncastle in October 1643, many royalist units were dispersed to backwaters to regain their effectiveness.[35] As the war continued, the situation changed. At Naseby Thomas Howard's brigade of 880 men consisted of seven regiments, his own being reduced to 80 men. Since they were all grossly under-mustered and over-officered, they could barely co-operate with each other.

Individual cavaliers used sardonic humour to help wash down the bitter pill of defeat. The king provided a classic example of this when Cornet Joyce kidnapped him at Holdenby House on 3 June 1647.[36] Charles walked out of the house at six that morning to a flat piece of land (now a delightful lawn), around which five hundred heavily armed roundhead cavalry were drawn up, their horses impatiently stamping in the cold early morning light. The monarch asked the cornet what commission – what authority – had he to arrest him? After some vacillation Joyce answered, 'Here is my commission.'

'Where?'

'Behind me', explained the ensign, pointing to his regiment of desperadoes.

'It is as fair a commission, and as well written as I have seen a commission written in my life', the king sardonically observed.

Alexander Brome handled defeat with the same bitter humour as his sovereign. 'Why should we not laugh and be jolly?' he asked, 'Since all the world now is grown mad.' The royalist poet took mock consolation in the thought that he and his comrades need no longer lock their doors – the enemy had plundered them of everything worth stealing. Samuel Butler was more caustic:[37]

> Virtue is its own reward
> And Fortune is a whore . . .
> Whilst we that fight for love,

> May in the war of honour prove
> That they who make sport of us
> May come short of us.

Fortune was not the only whore in cavalier drinking songs: all women were. The king's followers became maudlinely misogynistic, blaming defeat on 'the rebel sex'. One of their drunken ditties made a crude pun on the word 'breach', equating the female sexual organ first with a breach of faith, then the breach in a wall which proved the undoing of those brave defenders who tried to 'stout it out', a penile pun. Theirs, concludes the song, is a sorrow that 'only deposed kings can know'.[38]

Many cavaliers took comfort by vicariously sharing the king's sufferings – and each other's bottles. Brome wrote in 1646:[39]

> Come pass about the Gourd to me
> A health to our destroyed King.

Richard Lovelace agreed:[40]

> When, linnet like, confined I
> With shriller voice shall sing
> The mercy, sweetness, majesty
> And glories of my king.

In several ways Lovelace epitomized the depth of cavalier despair. Defeat taught the young man who had so gaily gone off to the wars that the face of battle was not as pretty as he would have his Lucasta believe. Lovelace was imprisoned, freed on bond, lost his brother, and fought for the king in the war's closing stages. Bitterly disillusioned, he emerged into a world in which 'the dragon hath vanquished St. George'.[41] The poet wrote:

> Now the Sun is unarmed,
> And the moon lies as charmed
> And the stars dissolved to a jelly,
> Now the thighs of the Crown,
> And the arms are lopped down,
> And the body is all but a belly.

The reaction of the king's commanders was less dramatic but more consequential than that of his poets. As it became clearer that the crown was losing the war, the rifts between them were exacerbated. The quarrel between Sir George Digby and Prince Rupert flared into the open, while in the West Country the Prince of Wales's advisers fought each other with ill-concealed venom.

While the swordsmen, who had come to dominate the royalist officer corps, wanted to continue the war – if only to keep themselves in a job – after Naseby Prince Rupert had sense enough to realize that his uncle's cause was lost. At the end of July 1645 he told the Duke of Richmond that the king had no alternative but start negotiations. 'I believe it be a more prudent way to retain something than lose all', was Rupert's professional judgment.[42] Charles disagreed vehemently. 'Speaking either as a mere soldier or statesman, I must say that there is no probability but of my ruin', he replied, 'yet, as a Christian, I must tell you that God will not suffer rebels or traitors to prosper, or the cause to be overthrown.'[43]

Such a fundamental disagreement between the two leading cavalier commanders was a recipe for disaster. In September 1645 Rupert surrendered Bristol, the last great royalist stronghold. In his professional judgment the city was untenable. Charles stripped his nephew of his command, ordering him out of the country. Outraged, Rupert and his retinue rode to see the king at Newark to demand a court-martial to judge the prince's behaviour. Unable to resist this request – which is almost a right due to all who hold the king's commission, especially when they have a hundred heavily armed and excitable friends with them – Charles agreed. On 21 October the court-martial acquitted Rupert of 'the least want of courage or Fidelity', but added that he should have held Bristol for a little longer since relief was on its way.[44]

The split verdict pleased no one. Rupert went into exile. His followers went off in high dudgeon. Defeat, as is so often the case, led to further ruination. Within nine months the king's cause was lost, and Charles became a prisoner of the Scots.

Becoming a prisoner of war was an experience that the king shared with very many of his subjects. In chapter 9 it was suggested that some 32,823 parliamentarians and 83,467 royalists, a total of 116,290 people, were taken prisoner in England and Wales during the three civil wars.

Surrendering in the heat of battle is the most fraught-ridden transaction a soldier can undertake. In an instant he attempts to turn himself from a dangerous armed enemy into a defenceless fellow creature, throwing his life onto the mercy of people whom, moments before, he had been trying to kill. On the other hand, while the victor has not experienced this metamorphosis, he may still be angry at the death of friends, or gripped by the blood lust that has helped him win the fray. All fighting animals – including man – have instinctively learned that a submissive posture is the safest way to initiate this transaction. Animals lie on their backs, exposing their most vulnerable parts to show that they are no longer a threat. Soldiers wave white flags, the western symbol of innocence, or submissively raise their hands above their heads to prove that they are no longer holding weapons. Sailors strike their colours. Airmen lower the under-carriage of their planes so they can no longer fly fast enough to be dangerous.

While, for obvious reasons, armies do not teach their soldiers the proper way to surrender (although they do instruct them how to behave after the surrender has been accepted), all soldiers develop *ad hoc* rules. During the Second World War, for instance, the British Army unofficially developed the 'sorry chum, too late' rubric by which enemy were shot if they tried to give up after continued resistance was unreasonable. Indeed during a fire-fight in the European theatre a soldier had a fifty/fifty chance of having his offer to surrender accepted.[45] In the civil wars his chances were far better. Since seventeenth-century weapons had far less firepower the consequences of accepting a surrender when none had been offered, were not as fatal. The shorter range of those weapons meant that communication was easier, particularly when both sides spoke the same language.

On the other hand, lack of uniforms could confuse a surrender transaction. At Northallerton, Yorkshire, one of Sir Henry Foulis's troopers was captured when he approached the enemy 'thinking they had been his friends'.[46] Sometimes the two sides distinguished themselves by placing white pieces of cloth or paper in their hats, or wearing different coloured scarves. In the heat of battle, when acrid powder smoke burned eyes and reduced visibility, such minor distinctions could pass unnoticed. Even when they were recognized they could have fatal results. At Edgehill, for instance, the seventeen men from Sir Faithful Forstescue's troop who went over to the crown forgot to remove their orange scarves, and were killed by the cavaliers.[47]

Uniform coats would have lessened the chances of men being killed by mistake. Most of the time – especially at the start of the war – uniforms were confined to a specific regiment. Thus you could have two regiments wearing similar, although not identical white coats, fighting against each other in the same battle. The traditional red coat was not introduced as an all-army uniform until the establishment of the New Model Army in the spring of 1645.

Nonetheless civil war combat – like all combat – was an extremely chaotic affair in which a successful capture was far from easy. Thrice during the Battle of Chalgrove Field the royalists took Sir Samuel Luke prisoner, and on each occasion his comrades rescued him. 'I was twice prisoner in half an hour, but I am a free man', James Audely wrote to Lady Dyer describing the attack on Lichfield in March 1643. Like a true gallant, the cavalier made the most of this opportunity, boasting, 'Bonds cannot hold me: only your noble favours have power to bind me in perpetual service.'[48]

Offers of surrender could be misunderstood, or rejected. At Chewton Mendip on 10 June 1643, a battle which was made even more confusing by a summer mist that suddenly covered the field, Captain Atkyns recorded that 'I gave one Captain Edward Kelly quarter twice, and at last he was killed.'[49] In a skirmish outside Gloucester the Marquis of Vieuville was hit on the head by a pole-axe. Offered quarter he replied, 'Vous voyez ici un grand Marquis poussant.' Unable to understand French (or insufficiently awed by the presence of a great and powerful French aristo-crat), the parliamentary troopers slew him on the spot.[50] Even though he spoke English a royalist officer (most likely a Captain Bynnes) had the same problem during the Siege of Bradford. After leading his infantry in an assault he was separated from his company. Two townsmen sallied out to cut him down. Bynnes begged for quarter, but the townsmen did not understand. Remarking 'Aye they would quarter him', the numskulls hacked the royalist to pieces.[51] At the Siege of Portsmouth, one of the war's first, some defenders opened fire on a herald bearing a white flag and sounding a trumpet, unaware that this was the customary way of requesting a parley. Anyone slow to accept an offer to surrender might be killed. For instance, at Nantwich in 1642 the royalists shot a trooper from Ratcliffe in the arms and shoulders because he did not immediately throw his musket down.[52]

Even those who had been well and truly taken, ran the risk of revenge from some shell-shocked trooper. One such soldier, a Scot, shot Thomas Sandys some time after he had been captured at Roundway Down. After surrendering Gainsborough in July 1643 and having been stripped of his armour and coat, Colonel Francis Thornhagh came across a royalist major whom he happened to have slightly wounded during the siege. Outraged the officer drew his sword and rushed the disarmed colonel, wounding him so badly that he was left for dead. Thornhagh managed to crawl to a nearby house, which fortunately belonged to a tenant who nursed him back to health.[53]

Such incidents taught soldiers the difficulty of having a surrender accepted, and that abject submission was their best chance of survival. Once the second attack on Farnham Castle succeeded on 1 December 1642, 'the Cavaliers within threw their arms over the wall, fell down upon their knees, crying for quarter'. None was killed. After being marched to Windsor Castle they were released a few days later. The victorious parliamentarians moved on to capture Winchester Castle on 17 December; the defenders proffered handfuls of gold coins to persuade the attackers to accept their surrender.[54]

The authorities tried to prevent the killing of prisoners in hot blood. Contemporaries were horrified when the defenders of Barthomley Church had their throats slit after being granted quarter, and wondered how decent Englishmen could 'thus degenerate into such odious inhumanities'.[55] The only excuse the victors offered was that they were 'desperate villains' who richly deserved their fate.[56] Preachers condemned the murder of prisoners. Generals issued orders against it. Armies published ordinances forbidding it.[57] Yet hardly anyone was actually punished for war crimes. Although the *Lawes and Ordinances* Lord General Essex promulgated to his army in 1642 listed death as the penalty for some forty offences none was specified for killing prisoners of war.

It should not, however, be thought that murdering prisoners was common. Apart from captured Irish troops, it was the exception rather than the rule. The victors realized that murdering prisoners was not in their own best interests: someday it could well be their turn to surrender. Thus when an officer ordered that they grant no quarter at the Battle of Braddock Down, the Cornish foot refused, saying 'they could not find in their hearts to hurt men who had nothing in their arms'.[58]

Surrendering was easier when it took place by pre-arrangement, or even during an accidental contact when neither side's blood was on the boil.

For instance, during the night of 7 December 1643 Colonel Edward Apsley, of Warminghurst, Sussex, and Colonel Herbert Morley were making a reconnaissance on horseback near Parnham.[59] They had left their escort behind in a cow barn where they had found some hay for the horses. A cavalry patrol approached. A shot ran out. Apsley and Morley returned to their escort, before approaching the patrol.

'Who are you?' came the challenge from out of the dark.

'A friend.'

'Who are you for?'

'What, do you not know me,' Apsley replied, giving the password, 'God with us.'

'Who are you for?'

He repeated the password. One of the enemy grabbed his horse, another his sword, as Apsley struggled to tell them 'for the king and parliament'.

It was not enough. A royalist threw the roundhead colonel's coat over his head, another pinioned his arms behind him, and Apsley had the good sense not to resist. He was well and truly in the bag.

The concept of being taken a prisoner of war, with rights, duties and obligations, is a modern one that is still being defined. Until the passage of the Hague Convention in 1899 prisoners had few legal rights, although they claimed protection according to vaguely defined laws and customs of war. Thus in 1646 a group of royalist gentlemen held in the Tower petitioned 'We . . . are for the most part of us Prisoners of war, who in all ages, by the Laws of Nature, both Jews, Christians and Barbarians, have and ought to be treated civilly and with humanity, and to be maintained according to our quality.'[60]

This petition is the only instance in which the phrase 'prisoner of war' has been found. Invariably captives were simply described as 'prisoners'. Many of the more prominent, such as the octogenarian, Edward, Lord Montagu, and the Cambridge College heads, Edward Martin, Richard Beale and Richard Sterne, were arrested for their political beliefs rather than their military activities.[61] Because their status was vaguely defined, such prisoners could be released, held indefinitely, or like debtors confined until they had discharged some financial obligation.

At the start of the war the king wanted to treat all captives as rebels, denying them even the vague status that prisoners of war traditionally enjoyed. When he first raised the royal standard in August 1642 one of his men's battle-cries was 'God Save King Charles and hang the round-heads.'[62] After Colonel Viver and Captains Catesby and Lilburne were taken at Brentford three months later, the king was only too willing to oblige his partisans. Lord Chief Justice Sir Robert Heath tried the three on a writ of Oyer and Terminer as common traitors. John Lilburne was outraged, less because of the charge, and more because it described him as a mere 'Yeoman' rather than a 'Gent'. When Lilburne offered to fight any two members of the court (except Prince Rupert) in a trial by combat to decide the matter, the judges sent him back to prison declaring that 'the fellow is mad'. Had Lilburne not been able to smuggle a letter out to his wife he could well have suffered the traitor's punishment, hanging, castration, drawing and quartering. But Elizabeth Lilburne, who was heavy with child, persuaded parliament to threaten similar reprisals on royalist prisoners.[63]

Even this threat did not completely end the execution of parliamentary prisoners as rebels. Twelve months after Chief Justice Heath condemned Captain Turner to death for blockade running, the royalists hanged the sea captain. Parliament retaliated by impeaching Heath, who had to flee to Calais.[64] George Wither, the poet who became a parliamentary cavalry captain, fared better. Captured in late 1642 he was brought before the king, who might well have had him strung up had not Sir John Denham, a fellow poet, persuaded Charles to spare him, with the argument that 'while Wither lives, Denham will not be the worst poet in England'.[65]

On being captured men were usually roughed up and plundered. 'We stripped and sent them away', Cornet John Sterly wrote about some roundheads he took. On the other side Sir Henry Slingsby recalled that when he was marched off in a column of prisoners from Marston Moor, 'We were forced to endure affronts by some of the enemies that came amongst us, and would snatch the soldiers hats from their heads, and their swords from their sides.' Slingsby continued that 'though we complained of it to the officers, yet could we have no remedy'.[66] Rank provided little protection. At the surrender of Chichester in June 1643, the royalists plundered General Sir William Waller of everything except the clothes on his back. 'Myself was stripped unto my shirt', Captain Hodgson recalled of his capture at Bradford.[67] Indeed he was quite lucky to keep his shirt. The only way that the parliamentary garrison of Pinnel House, Wiltshire, managed to persuade their royalist captors 'they not be stripped naked' was to convince them how much better the winner's clothing was compared to their own dirty, vermin-ridden rags.[68] Victors considered plundering pris-oners a perfectly proper perquisite. Parliamentary officers ignored Sir Henry protests about the plundering of his men after Marston Moor. Apart from a brief mention in Humphrey Peake's sermon, *Meditations upon a Siege* (Oxford, 1646, P966B), the morality of this practice was not even discussed.

Being stripped and plundered was part of the violation that all prisoners experienced. 'He that doth not feel it wanteth sense', noted Sir William Waller.[69] A royalist officer described the roundheads taken at Lostwithiel as 'sheep'. Then and now prisoners who cannot control their anger and do not adopt a sufficiently docile stance are likely to be killed. The Scots lieutenant 'who cursed and railed for half an hour' after being taken by parliamentary forces at Newcastle in February 1644 was lucky to escape with his life. Perhaps he did so because once his anger at being captured evaporated (like Japanese prisoners in the Second World War) he was more than co-operative, telling his captors all they wanted to know.[70]

Unlike today, formal and immediate interrogation of prisoners for tactical intelligence – and conversely training to resist such a process – were rare during the civil war, even though contemporaries understood and used techniques which have been refined in our own century.[71]

During the seventeenth century torture was used as rarely in war as it had been in peace – and then only in extremities to discover information. During the Sieges of Limerick and Wardour Castle the defenders tortured boys suspected of smuggling intelligence to traitors within. In the summer of 1644 Colonel John Hutchinson suspected a lad of carrying messages into the besieged garrison of Northampton. Burned with slow match the boy confessed that he had brought letters to a soldier, whom he identified as one Griffith. After being suspended by the neck so that he stood on tip-toes, and having lighted matches placed between his bound fingers, Griffith admitted to plotting with Brimsley, a local butcher and a royalist deserter, who had taken the covenant. Although tortured, Brimsley revealed nothing. Meanwhile the lad whose arrest had started the whole brutal process managed to escape while his captors were celebrating their victory at Marston Moor.[72]

After having their battlefield surrenders accepted the victors usually rounded up prisoners and marched them off to an immediate holding area. This was usually a church, although the rebels taken at Nottingham in 1643 had to suffer the indignity of being held in sheep pens in the market square as the cavaliers plundered the town.[73] After recovering from the ordeal of fighting (and the toils of plunder), the victors escorted their captives to some more permanent place of incarceration. The royalists often sent their prisoners to be held in Coventry – hence the expression.

The ordeal of the nine hundred roundheads who surrendered at Cirencester in February 1643 was extremely harrowing. Capitulation did not end the killing. Still fighting mad, Rupert's men murdered two citizens, before leading the terrified survivors out to a field half a mile outside town, where senior officers inspected them, threatening to hang them. After that hazing, being pillaged by cavalier troops might almost have come as a relief. Anyway, the prisoners were returned to Cirencester and crammed into the church. Here they remained for two days, without food or water, until given a small piece of bread and cheese. Bound with match cord, many lacking hats, shoes and stockings, some having even been robbed of their breeches, they 'were driven like cattle to Oxford'. At Burford they lined up in the snow for an issue of bread. When a woman tried to give them food the cavaliers beat her up. At Witney the prisoners spent the night jammed in the church. Many were barefoot, having to tie rags about their bleeding feet. About a mile outside Oxford the king and his two sons waited, gloating 'to see us drove along more like dogs or horses than men'. Small wonder once they reached Oxford all but sixteen of the prisoners accepted an invitation to join His Majesty's Forces.[74]

Captives were often publicly humiliated, particularly at the start of the war, when the concept of being a prisoner had not fully developed. According to a propaganda sheet the cavaliers tethered the prisoners they took at Brentford, head to toe, and tossed them into cattle pens to spend the night.[75] The next day they marched them across Hounslow Heath where the burrs and thistles ripped bare feet open. Some unfortunates were tied up, before being forced to stand up to their necks in the Thames, where they had not only to combat fatigue and cold but also the cavaliers who prodded them with their swords, forcing them into deeper water. On 7 December 1642 the mob jeered those roundheads captured at Malborough as they were dragged at rope's end through the streets of Oxford. This could have been in retaliation for the treatment five days earlier of ten cart-loads of prisoners who, bound head and foot, were driven through London to the catcalls of hooligans.[76] Sir John Digby recalled that when he and his men were similarly humiliated, some Londoners 'reviled them, others seemed to pity their present distressed condition'.[77] Four thousand royalists taken at Naseby were paraded through the streets of the capital. According to the French ambassador they seemed in reasonable spirits, hardly any of them being wounded. The army jammed six hundred and eighty of them into Lambeth Palace, and caged the rest in the open on Tothill Fields, where they suffered the further indignity of having to listen to puritan sermons – in Welsh.

The war's most spectacular surrender took place at Lostwithiel on 2 September 1644. Charles had forced Essex's army west into the Devon and Cornwall peninsula, bottling them up on the west bank of the River Fowey. The fighting had been long and hard. Many men had hardly slept for eight days, being continuously in combat in the thick hedgerow country, where one side was often within shouting distance of the other. 'Sometimes we argued together, sometimes we scolded together like Fishwomen of Cheapside, and sometimes we fought very hot', recalled a member of Lord General Essex's lifeguard. He went on that the fighting became so confused that 'sometimes the king's men would leap over the hedge into the midst of us, taking us for their own men.'[78]

'It was the greatest blow we ever suffered', Essex admitted of the surrender of six thousand men, thirty-six cannon, ten thousand weapons and several cart-loads of powder at Lostwithiel.[79] The capitulation details had been worked out carefully. At 11 a.m. the rebels were to parade outside Fowey Castle to lay down their weapons, those above the rank of corporal being permitted to keep their swords. Later they were to march to Lostwithiel, with trumpets and drums playing, colours flying.

Immediately after they had given up their weapons, the agreement broke down. A survivor related,

> Then came our misery. For when we had laid down our Arms, and came to march through the enemy's army, we were inhumanly dealt with; abused, reviled, scorned, torn, kicked, pillaged, and many stripped of all they had, quite contrary to the articles . . . in the presence of the king.

A cavalry officer described his ordeal to a friend, 'Sir, no tongue can express the barbarous usage of our men by the Enemy. They stripped many stark naked, and pillaged most of their money, coats and hats.' Two brothers serving the king saw their third sibling who had been fighting on the other side. One grabbed him, and would have killed him, had not the second intervened. At Lostwithiel the townsfolk were even more vicious. 'I saw them strip a woman', an eyewitness wrote, 'she had lain in but three days before. They took her by the hair of her head and threw her into the river, and there almost drowned her. The woman died within twelve hours.' So horrible was this last incident, that Charles ordered the murderers to be hanged.[80]

Richard Symonds, a captain in the King's Life Guard, recalled the surrender from the other side. 'It rained extremely as the varlets marched away', he wrote in his diary, describing how the king and other officers did their best to stop the plunder, even beating their men with the flat of their swords. But to no avail. The contrast between the vicious enemy against whom they had fought for many a day and night, and the broken helpless prisoners, was too much for many of the victors. The rebels 'were stricken with such a dismal fear. . . . So dirty and dejected as was rare to see', Symonds remembered, 'None of them, except some few of their officers did look any of us in the face.'[81]

Prisoners were especially vulnerable to revenge. Take the case of Captain George Sharples who was captured with two hundred Lancashire roundheads in May 1644. Paraded barefoot, and almost naked, he was spotted by Cuthbert, the son of Thomas Clifton, who had been Sharples' landlord at Lytham St Anne's. The sight of his father's old tenant, who had obviously defied his landlord by siding with the rebels, and – worse still

– had risen above his station to become an officer, outraged Cuthbert. He forced Sharples to stand in the mud up to his knees, gave him a psalter, and jeeringly asked if he could sing a verse or two. After Cuthbert and the rest of the ruffians had had their fun, Sharples was locked up with the other prisoners in a church, from which he promptly escaped by stealing a pair of clogs and a musket, walking out disguised as a common soldier.[82]

Being a prisoner could be an emotional strain. After he was taken at Hillesden House in March 1644 Thomas Verney was marched with over two hundred comrades to Padbury, 'where they passed the night in great discomfort'. Verney eventually ended up in St John's College, Cambridge – architecturally one of the better stalags. Yet his family was very worried for his safety. 'God knows what is become of my unhappy brother that was taken', wrote Ralph Verney, 'I know that all sides hate him, and that he will fear the might of their displeasure.'[83] Others tried to turn the ordeal of their captivity to their own advantage. John Bonwick left Christ's College, Cambridge, in 1643 to fight for the king. A year later he was captured at the Second Battle of Newbury, stripped, and almost starved to death on the forced march to a prison in London. At the Restoration seventeen years later, Bonwick, by now the Rector of Newdigate, Surrey, petitioned the Privy Council that they order Cambridge University to grant him a doctor's degree even though he had not completed all the requirements. Apparently he felt that he had endured enough as a parliamentary prisoner, and thus needed to suffer no more as a graduate student.[84]

Practically everyone held captive during the civil wars – and for that matter ever since – would have vehemently disagreed with the cavalier's sanguine contentions.[85] Under sentence of death for taking part in the Norfolk Rising, Sir Roger Estrange wrote 'Loyalty Confined':[86]

> That which the World miscalls a Gaol
> A Private Closet is to me,
> Which in good conscience is my bail
> And innocence my liberty.

Richard Lovelace put it better:

> Stone Walls do not a Prison Make
> Nor Iron Bars a cage.

In an age when conditions for civilian prisoners were deplorable it is not surprising that those for prisoners of war were just as bad, especially when they were held for long periods of time. John Bastwick had a high regard for the royalist soldiers who captured him, calling them 'brave gentlemen'. But he despised the king's gaolers at York Castle, where he 'for a year and half underwent great inhumanity, was cruelly used, uncivilly and most unnecessary abused by a professed Protestant'. Only his belief in God enabled Bastwick to survive the ordeal. Sir Wingfield Bedeham spent at least three years in the Tower. Sir Lewis Dyve was interned there, and in the Fleet Prison, for two and a half years before escaping. He managed to squeeze through a jakes, built overhanging the Thames, and swam to a waiting boat.[87]

Perhaps the most terrible conditions were to be found on the hulks, moored on the Thames, which parliament commissioned to hold military and political captives. Jammed below decks in the cold and damp, with bad water and worse food, many died. Sir Roger Twysden recorded that life incarcerated on the inappropriately named *Prosperous Sarah* was very crowded, filthy and unhealthy. He was outraged when he was charged 20 shillings for four days of such hellish lodging, before being allowed to transfer to a more salubrious confinement in Lambeth Palace. Conditions for royalist prisoners taken at Derby, and held in a dungeon known as the Lion's Den, were just as bad. Captain Palmer, and a puritan minister, 'having nothing else to do', delighted in beating up new arrivals. When Lucy Hutchinson went to dress their wounds, Palmer tried to stop her, saying 'his soul abhorr'd to see this favour to the enemies of God'. Rarely were gaolers punished for abusing prisoners: the only instance found was that of Provost Marshall Thomas Williams, of William Waller's army. A court-martial sentenced him to be hanged by handcuffs for fifteen minutes, and then cashiered.[88]

Unless they could get food sent in from outside, prisoners were invariably hungry. During the twenty-three months he was held 'in the infamous gaol of Newcastle', being 'used worse than a slave in Turkey', John Baynes, a cavalier captain, claimed that 'sometimes a piece of raw liver' was all he had to eat.[89] The only victuals the defenders of Gloucester could spare for the royalists they took during the siege were turnips and cabbage leaves. They spent £18 19s 0d feeding 1,594 Welsh prisoners held in St Mary's and Trinity Church for ten days in March 1643, which works out at roughly a farthing a day. In comparison sixpence was the standard parliamentary daily ration scale. That is what the garrison of Derby enjoyed in the summer of 1645, compared to the penny three farthings they spent feeding the royalists they held.[90]

Confinement left its mark on men. After being held for a winter in a dungeon at Worcester John Wright, a labourer from Hoton, Staffordshire, was so wracked with rheumatism that he could no longer work. William Chillingworth, the Anglican divine and royalist sapper, died from the chill he caught as a result of being locked up in Arundel Castle during January 1644.[91]

Understandably men did all they could to be freed as quickly as possible, while their captors were nearly as eager to save the expense of holding them.

The forty parliamentary soldiers who broke out of Liskeard gaol in August 1644 were unusual, for most captives escaped whilst being escorted into captivity.[92] Henry Taylor, a weaver from Myddle, Shropshire, was a pikeman in Captain Corbet's company, which Sir William Brereton's roundheads caught quite literally napping during a night attack on Nantwich. Taylor had wit enough to discard his pike for a harrow, and walk gaily past the enemy pretending to be a yokel off for a day's work in the fields. Once out of sight he dropped his harrow, grabbed a horse and galloped to safety. One Jubbe, a parliamentary trooper taken during the Siege of Pontefract in April 1645, pretended to be an idiot. When his captors tried to get him drunk, he had wit enough to go along with them. As a result the escort who took him away for further interrogation was 'not too vigilant', enabling Jubbe to make a successful break.[93] Legend has it that Bishop Walter Curll of Winchester escaped by hiding in a cart under a load of dung. After the Battle of Stourton Down on 25 April 1645, Sheriff Carey of Devon managed to escape dressed as a woman.[94] Even though he was only 15, and 'little of statue', Captain Wray was 'a spiritly gallant youth' who commanded a company in Lord Mohun's regiment. Captured at Stourton he was marched to Oakhampton where he persuaded the roundheads to release him as being a mere drummer boy.

William Lister's experiences after the capture of Bradford were fairly typical of those trying to avoid apprehension. Like the rest of his fellow citizens the apprentice lad expected the worst. 'Oh what a night and morning was that in which Bradford was taken!' he recalled, 'What weeping and wringing of hands.' All expected the cavaliers to massacre them. Thus when no more than half a dozen were killed Lister was both relieved and bewildered. With his mother and sister he wandered about the streets 'not knowing what to do, or which way to take'. Eventually Lister stumbled across David Clarkson, Fellow of Clare College, Cambridge, whom he agreed to guide through the enemy's lines to parliament's forces. They managed to slip past a cavalier company by wading a river, and escaped another by lying down in a corn field. As it got dark they walked west to Clayton taking cover behind the hedgerows. After joining ranks with two dismounted roundheads who were trying to rejoin their regiments, they over-confidently congratulated themselves that 'we had escaped all danger'. Then suddenly out of the night a horseman appeared. They ran. He shot and wounded one of the fugitives. Lister hid in a holly tree, while the rest tamely surrendered to the solitary cavalier. 'I have often thought since how easily we might have knocked him down, had we but had courage: but alas! We had none.'

People used all the influence they could to arrange exchanges. 'I pray you give me your help to get an exchange for me', Sir Samuel Luke asked Sir William Brereton, seeking his aid in arranging the parole of his friend, a Mr Church, held in Shrewsbury gaol. Even the remotest connection was worth pursuing. Anne Neile wrote to George Rigby offering to use her influence to get his brother-in-law, Captain Hilton, exchanged for one Browne. Her late husband had been a friend of Rigby's while she was still a tenant of Mrs Hilton's. Presumably Anne was repaying her landlady for a past obligation, or creating one for the future.[95]

On each side local commanders tried to negotiate carefully balanced exchanges in which so many lieutenants counted for a lesser number of captains, and even fewer majors or colonels. In the winter of 1643/4 Sir William Waller began a proposal to Sir George Goring that they open discussions for the exchange of prisoners, 'Noble Lord, God's blessing be upon your heart, you are the jolliest Neighbour I ever met with.' Goring received the letter while dining with his staff, and was so tickled by this 'good pleasant droll' that he immediately accepted. After fifteen days of talks the two sides swopped a sizeable number of prisoners.[96]

When exchange could not be arranged, or the enemy held no one of equivalent rank, captives could be paroled on the promise never to fight again.[97] Sir Hugh Pollard had to write an especially grovelling apology (which parliament published) before they paroled him from London to see his dying father.[98] Officers were frequently paroled. 'I was sent prisoner upon my parole to London, without guards', recalled Joseph Bampfield, who was one of the two hundred out of the original nine hundred garrison able to walk out of Arundel Castle at its surrender. 'I was committed to the Tower, remaining there about six months', continued the royalist company commander, until the Earl of Essex granted him a parole for twenty-eight days so he could arrange to be exchanged for Sir Ellis Layton or a Captain White. Immediately after Bampfield's arrival at Oxford the king approved the transfer, giving him plenty of time to visit relatives in Exeter. Unfortunately on his way back to London some parliamentary stragglers captured Bampfield, wounding him in the left eye. Notwithstanding the Lord General's pass they returned him to London, where two days later Essex ordered his release.[99]

Wounded officers had a good chance of being paroled. They were a particular burden on their gaolers. As gentlemen they could be relied upon to keep their word. Opinion was outraged when Colonels Sheffield and Beckly exaggerated the wounds they had received at Chalgrove, so that they were paroled to an adjacent nearby country house, and then arranged to be rescued by a cavalry patrol.[100] Parliament captured Sir William Vasavour, a veteran of the Scots and Irish Wars, at Edgehill. Freed on parole, he promptly took up arms again for the king. 'Having thus violated his faith given', declared a roundhead pamphlet, Vasavour 'demonstrates himself to the world to be unworthy of the name of a gentleman'.[101]

Far more creditable was the behaviour of Lieutenant Thomas Sandys, whom a deranged parliamentarian soldier had shot after surrendering at

Chewton Mendip. Angry at this flagrant breach of the rules of war, Sir William Waller personally visited the officer, who had two pistol bullets in his chest, ordered his surgeon to attend him, paid for his lodging at an inn at Bath, left him £10, and freed him on the promise to give himself up to the parliamentary authorities at Bristol once he had recovered. Since the parole touched on his word of honour as a gentleman, the capture of Bath by the king's forces six weeks later put Sandys into something of a dilemma. His friend, Captain Richard Atkyns, assured him that his promise was no longer valid. Unsure, Sandys referred the point to Lord Caernarvon, who ruled that he was still obliged to give himself up to the parliamentary garrison at Bristol. Fortunately for Sandys soon afterwards the royalists took England's second city, rendering his parole moot.[102]

Although common soldiers were released on parole it was harder to get them to keep their word by appealing to the officers' code that decreed that a gentleman's word was his bond. Hanging recaptured parole violators may have deterred some other ranks, while still more must have been only too delighted to use their promise never to fight again as an excuse to sit out the rest of the hostilities at home. Towards the end of the first civil war, as it became clear that there was little conflict left to endure, a parliamentarian reported that 'every hour more Gentlemen of Quality do come in'. So many gave themselves up, that lest their own troops be swamped, roundhead commanders had to issue them with blanket paroles, food, and as much as 20 shillings to make their own way home.[103]

At the start of the war prisoners were not handled with such efficiency and humanity. In late 1642 reports that 'that monster of iniquity, Smith, the Provost Marshall' was abusing internees in Oxford Castle 'with Turkish cruelty', started to circulate, profoundly shocking those innocent of the horrors of war.[104]

Oxford Castle held three categories of prisoners. The first consisted of gentlemen, about forty of whom were jammed in a small room and allowed little exercise. Their latrine was an adjacent courtyard, devoid of drainage. Captain Wingate, who was taken at Edgehill, wrote that they were 'beaten, burned with Match, set in a place called Bridewell up to their ankles in their own excrements'.

The second group, composed of puritan ministers, fared no better. Smith delighted in calling them 'Cobblers, Tinkers and Tub Preachers', and taunting 'Where is now your God?' When the divines refused to renounce parliament, the provost forced them to sleep on the cold floor.

Conditions for the third class of prisoners, common soldiers, were even worse. Having been plundered of their clothes, and forced-marched to Oxford, they were in poor shape even before their confinement began. Smith allowed them only a penny farthing a day for food. When they requested medical attention he refused, shouting 'Hang them! Damned Rogues Villain Traitors! The devil take them!' A hundred and eighty men were packed in one black hole, which was so crowded that they had to sleep on top of each other.

In February 1642 Smith forced forty of the most obdurate roundheads into a dungeon where they had to wallow in their 'piss and filth'. Even though their cells were damp, and a river flowed near by, Smith did not give them enough water to drink, let alone wash. Once the captives had to lap the water left after Sir James Peniman's Regiment had completed their ablutions. On another occasion a prisoner recalled that they became so thirsty that they had 'to drink their own urine'.

There were many instances of individual abuse. Smith refused a trooper taken at Banbury medical attention for a head wound: as a result he died. When Private Ockdon asked for water, Sergeant Waller beat him with his cane forty times, clapped him in irons that weighed 28 pounds, and threw him in a dungeon without food or water for two days. Smith chained Mr Freeman, a constable from Banbury, to a cell floor during the winter, as a result of which he perished. With match-cord the provost burned Richard Cowdle's and Robert Neale's fingers to the bone for trying to escape. He chucked the corpse of one Blage, who had been hanged, into Captain Wingate's cell, and only after several days, and a large bribe, would he remove the putrefying remains. Every day two or three of Smith's charges died. Nine captains taken at Edgehill did not survive. One of the provost's victims, the Reverend Edward Wirley, concluded, 'we saw nothing but death before our eyes'.

Wirley was one of forty prisoners who broke out of Oxford Castle in March 1643 and made it via the River Cherwell back to the royalist garrison at Aylesbury. He and Wingate wasted no time in letting people know how horrible conditions were in Provost Smith's hell-hole. Parliament debated the matter in February and May 1643. The commissioners they sent to Oxford that spring visited the captives, cheering them greatly to know that they had not been forgotten.[105]

Smith tried to rebuff this bad publicity by explaining that he was desperately short of men, his best troops having been transferred to the front, and that he was given only £80 a month to feed seventy-five soldiers, twenty-eight horses and a large number of prisoners.[106] A royalist pamphlet, A Warning Piece to all His Majesty's Subjects of England (1643, W932), argued that as rebels the prisoners were getting no more than their just deserts – the fact that many of them were innocents duped by wicked subversives being no excuse.

Few roundheads accepted this argument. Smith became the royalist rogue. Sir Samuel Luke called him 'that bloody Marshall Smith, by whose savage dealings many of our friends did perish'.[107] Many were delighted to learn that the Oxford parliament had ordered him committed a 'close prisoner', and even happier to read that Smith had been made to stand for three market days running in the pillory at Oxford. Since Sir John

Berkenhead, the leading royalist propagandist, concocted this story it would appear that Gaoler Smith had become such a liability that his own side disowned him.[108]

Royalist propaganda also tried to turn Colonel John Venn, the Governor of Windsor Castle, into another Smith.[109] The comparison was inapt. This does not mean that Windsor Castle was some holiday camp. Venn, who was a past warden of the Merchant Tailors' Company, a member of the Long Parliament and a regicide, ran Windsor Castle much like a civilian prison, charging fees for anything above the bare necessities, and selling luxuries to any who could afford them. Thus poor common soldiers had to sleep on straw on the bottom floor of the Curfew Tower. He jammed as many as a hundred and thirty of them in at one time, doling them threepence worth of bread, butter and cheese a day. At least thirty of the common soldiers died. In contrast only one of the hundred and eighty prominent – and thus richer – prisoners held in Windsor Castle during the first civil war succumbed. Six even managed to escape.[110]

After being captured in Devonshire Sir Edmund Fortescue was shipped by boat and barge to Windsor, where he spent his idle hours carving his family coat of arms, and 'Pour le Roy C', on his cell walls. Edward Pitt, Teller of the Exchequer, was held in Windsor Castle after his son joined the royal army. His son and wife died. Parliament confiscated his property, and forbade his tenants to pay him the rent. 'I am here', wrote the desperate captive, 'under the hand and custody of the most unchristian and uncharitable wretch that breathes.' Eventually Pitt was released, but died a week later from his ordeal.[111]

Thomas Knyvett, a Norfolk gentleman, was incarcerated in Windsor for three months for his part in the abortive royalist rising at Great Yarmouth in March 1643.[112] After being held in Norwich for a couple of days, he was moved to the Rose Tavern in Cambridge. Thanks to his connections with Oliver Cromwell's aunt, Elizabeth Hampden, he had enough money to spent 1s 6d for dinner each day. He hoped to be moved to Jesus College, where, he sardonically promised his wife, he would study very hard. By now Cambridge had become a garrison rather than university town with 'nothing but drums and trumpets all day long'. After two weeks locked in the Rose Inn, having to listen to the martial cacophany from Market Hill, Knyvett dryly noted, 'I was never so weary of a Tavern in my life.'

The move to Windsor did not improve things. The journey was an ordeal. The prisoners spent their first night in the Castle like pigs, seven to a bed. Even though the next day they were given two rooms, and eventually permitted to hear Dr Edward Young, Prebend of Norwich, preach 'wonderful sermons', Knyvett found it all very trying. He resented the crudeness of the common soldiers' language, a frequent symptom of the anguish prominent prisoners feel at their loss of status. 'We are at their mercy and therefore must be patient', he painfully concluded. In July Knyvett was paroled to return home to try to prevent the sequestration of his estates.

Being held prisoner is a terrible emotional strain, particularly for those who in peacetime were more used to ordering miscreants to be locked up rather than sharing a cell with them. 'He that is in prison is like him that is at the bottom of a well', wrote John Maxwell, Bishop of Killala, from personal experience, 'he seeth no more of heaven than that which is over their mouth.'[113] The Reverend Hinson, Rector of Battle, Sussex, suffered such a loss of status after Colonel Morley arrested him in July 1643. Taken to the local lock-up he was put in a loathsome cell with a tinker, 'and he none of the jolliest'. Claiming seniority of tenure over his social superior, the ragamuffin refused to share the cell's single bench, forcing the Anglican divine to walk up and down all night to keep warm, the stone floor being too cold to sleep on.[114]

No one expressed the emotions felt by a civil war prisoner better than James Howell. Born in 1594 in Breckonshire, the son of an Anglican minister, Howell attended Jesus College, Oxford, becoming a Fellow. A brilliant linguist and letter writer, Howell travelled widely, earning his keep with his pen. In August 1642 Charles appointed him clerk of the Privy Council. Early the next year, on a brief visit to London, parliament had him arrested. For the next seven years he remained a prisoner, some said for his debts, while Howell maintained it was for his loyalty to the crown.

In prison Howell suffered from acute depression. 'Melancholy is a black noxious humour', he wrote. He confessed to a deep loathing of the Pied Piper who had been able to lead those children out of the walls of Hamelin. It wasn't fair! Why should he still be confined behind walls in 'this unlucky hole'? A few months later, convinced he was dying of melancholy, he started to bequeath the few goods he had left, and confessed to be subject to 'confused troops of wandering cogitations'. By 1645 he was angry that so many of his fellow prisoners had been released, leaving him behind. 'I do not know why I am here, unless it be for my sins', he raged. Sometimes he sounded hopeful, describing the Fleet Prison, with all its time for reading, as 'A College of Instruction'. Mostly, however, he saw himself as one 'buried before death'. After three years confinement he begged to 'breath free air'. He admitted to having conversations with the dead, which he justified by arguing that having been buried alive in prison he was in just as moribund a state as they. Howell realized how utterly dependent he was on his friends, whose help was the only thing that enabled him to survive until his release in 1651.[115]

If the typical prisoner's fate had been half as onerous as was Howell's, it might explain why so many of them turned their coats. But this was not the case. In fact after the humiliation of being captured, roughed up, and plundered, most prisoners were given the choice of being paroled home or volunteering to change sides. Almost all the rebels captured at Banbury in October 1642 went over to fight for the king, as did most of the 1,600 men taken the following February at Cirencester. The next July a thousand of Bristol's defenders joined His Majesty's Forces. Not fully trusting them the king dispersed them throughout his army. But he need not have worried. According to the Duchess of Newcastle, after her husband captured Rotherham most of the rank and file 'took arms for his Majesty's service, and proved very faithful and loyal subjects and good soldiers'.[116]

Men turned their coats in both directions, and often more than once. At the start of the war roundheads tended to go over to the king: towards the end, as it seemed parliament was winning, the flow was in the other direction.

Most of the one hundred and sixty garrison who surrendered Cawood Castle, Yorkshire in October 1642 took the covenant and fought against the king. Five to six hundred of the 875 men captured at Farnham a year later followed suit, as did 300–600 cavaliers taken at Alton. Two-thirds of the five hundred royalists taken at Bridgewater in July 1646 volunteered to join the enemy army, saying, according to one parliamentary news-sheet, how proud they were to have been captured by such fine troops.[117] A month later 450 of the royalists captured at Colby Moor, Pembroke-shire, took the covenant, and volunteered to fight the Irish. More than half the 1,572 troops Fairfax took at Nantwich turned their coats to become, he admitted, some of his best soldiers.[118] Cromwell agreed that many of his finest Ironsides had once been cavaliers.

Why then did soldiers change sides with such ease and such apparent enthusiasm?

Certainly it was not due to coercion. The story of three royalist soldiers who were starved to death at Windsor Castle 'because they refused to serve under the rebel colours' sounds like cavalier propaganda. The parliamentary explanation that two hundred out of three hundred and forty members of the London Red Regiment taken at Brentford went over to Charles after he had paraded them before a smith with orders to brand the recalcitrant on the cheeks, is equally unreliable. Later someone surely would have noticed a hundred and forty stigmatized citizens wandering about the capital.[119] The Earl of Stamford's suggestion that royalist pris-oners who refused to join parliament's forces be sold as slaves to the Barbary pirates never got off the ground.[120] The prisoners from Banbury and Cirencester who suffered under Provost Smith during the war's first winter were the small minority who had already refused to go over to the king, whilst the others were political rather than military captives. It does seem that the majority who changed sides had been reluctant rebels in the first place, who had been shanghaied into the army or dragged at pistol point from their homes or their ploughs.[121]

Those whose ideological commitment was strong in the first place were able to resist pressures to turn their coats.

After Essex surrendered his army at Lostwithiel the crown promised Richard Bulstrode command of a regiment if he was able to persuade his cousin Thomas to switch allegiance. He spent two days with Thomas, treating him with the utmost kindness, trying to convince his cousin to leave the parliamentary army. 'But he was so besotted and seduced by the Zealots of that army, that I could not prevail with him', admitted Richard, 'and so I left him as I found him, willful, stubborn and full of rebellious Principles.'[122]

Edmund Ludlow was a steadfast parliamentarian long before he surrendered Wardour Castle in March 1644. Initially he was pleasantly surprised by the way the royalists treated him, but within a couple of days was outraged when they court-martialled and shot two of his Irish soldiers as deserters, even though they had promised the garrison 'quarter without distinction'. On his way to the royalist headquarters at Oxford, he was billeted one night at Chalk in the house of Richard Aubrey, the historian's father, before being marched to Salisbury. Here he was held in an inn, where he had to debate 'the justice of my cause in the presence of some forty or fifty of the town'. The next night at Winchester several royalist officers came to persuade him to join them. He reached Oxford on the morrow, where he was held in a house near Christ Church, where a couple of Irish Catholics tried to convert him to the king's cause – which reinforced his conviction that Charles had become a papist pawn. After being tricked out of all his personal possessions, Ludlow refused parole, for that would have prevented him from visiting parliamentary troopers held in Oxford Castle. In May 1645 he was exchanged as part of a package of senior officers, being led blindfolded out through the city's defences to the parliamentary lines, his honour and ideology intact.[123]

Changing sides could be far more dangerous than being paroled, especially if you were recaptured. Major Sadler, a deserter from the parliamentary forces, was re-taken at Tiverton in October 1645. A court-martial rejected his defence that during the siege he had tried to betray Tiverton to parliament, and sentenced him to death. Unfortunately for Sadler, the royalists believed his story, for after he escaped parliamentary custody and made it back to the king's forces at Exeter he was once again court-martialled, and this time suffered the capital sentence.[124]

One reason for changing sides was a gut-hatred of papists and the Irish. Four hundred and forty of the seven hundred men he had taken at Haverfordwest, reported William Batten, 'have all taken the Covenant, and express great forwardness to serve against the Irish'. Many of the royalists taken in the West Country in 1646 became angry when they learned how Romanish were 'the ways of the court at Oxford', and promptly volunteered to fight the Irish.[125]

Aside from a visceral hatred of Irish papists, the most persuasive explanation for the ease with which most soldiers changed sides was that they had little ideological commitment to either side in the first place. Sir John Price did so four times, being well rewarded on each occasion in which he carefully calculated what was in his, and his new master's, best interests. Describing the New Model Army – ideologically the most committed group of troopers ever to don the red coat – Richard Baxter, that astute puritan divine, hit the nail on the head:[126]

> For the greatest part of the common soldiers, especially of the Foot, were ignorant men, of little religion, the abundance of them such as had been taken Prisoners, or turned out of Garrisons under the King, and had been soldiers in his army. And these would do anything to please their officers.

Historians have long debated the nature of the civil war and its causes. Some have suggested that it was fought for a love of freedom, that it was the first great crisis of liberty in the history of the west. Others have seen it as the first major bourgeois revolution in which class considerations were paramount. In the last century it was seen as a puritan revolution, a view that scholars have revived recently with talk about England's Wars of Religion. Be all these theories as they may. One thing is inescapable: that as far as the vast majority of ordinary soldiers and even officers who fought and died in the war, and changed sides whenever necessary, were concerned, ideology counted for far less than it has for historians. The war – like most wars – was a war with its own internal dynamics. Soldiers were there because they were there, and they were determined to make the best of the bad job of being there. War provided employment, the opportunity for plunder and excitement. Ultimately most soldiers thought of themselves not as saints in arms but labourers, worthy of whoever happened at the time to have hired them.[127]

The comparative absence of an ideological commitment meant that the civil war was fought in England between Englishmen, at least, with remarkably few atrocities on either side. Propagandists made the most of the abuses they could discover, and were not above inventing more when none could be found. The report that the king and Prince Rupert had ordered a gentleman to be strung up from a tree at Hounslow on 12 November 1642 'for speaking in honour of the parliament', is highly suspect.[128] Equally dubious was the story that Colonel Essex angrily shot one of his privates through the head when the roundhead politely asked for arrears of pay. So too was the yarn that the cavaliers had tied together twenty rebels and thrown them into the Thames. Parliamentary hacks answered this canard by alleging that Colonel Sir Arthur Aston, Governor

255

of Reading, had ordered one Master Boys, a citizen of London, to be hanged, supposedly for spying. Convinced of Boy's innocence the Provost-Marshal refused to carry out the sentence, which was executed by a common soldier for a piece of silver (far less than was earned by Judas). Admittedly Aston had a shabby reputation. Clarendon described him as 'having the good fortune to be much esteemed when he is not known and very much detested where he was'. Yet the tale of Boy's death does not sound credible.[129] The complaint that two of Rupert's men copulated with three women in the chancel of Kingston-upon-Thames Church in front of a portrait of the Blessed Virgin Mary should also be treated with equal scepticism – if only because it shows an atypical puritan solicitude for papist icons.[130]

Often each side put out their own version of an especially brutal event. For instance, after forces nominally under Henrietta Maria captured Burton-upon-Trent in April 1643, the garrisons having refused to surrender, *Mercurius Aulicus* maintained that the queen 'forbade any violence to be offered to the town'. One of Sir Samuel Luke's parliamentary spies reported a very different story: 'Having taken the town the cavaliers drove at least thirty civilians into the church, had cut all their throats, doing great spoil in the town, ravishing the women, forcing many of them to take to the river, where they drowned.' It is difficult to say where the truth lies. Since Henrietta later complained to her husband that her soldiers could hardly march, being overburdened with plunder, the roundhead version would appear to be closer to reality.[131]

The long list of rebel atrocities Bruno Ryves described in *Mercurius Rusticus: or the countries complaint of the outrages committed with a brief chronology of the war* (1685, R2449) should be handled with great scepticism. Appearing some forty years after the events they claim to describe, Ryves focuses on puritan plundering of houses and cathedrals, and their abuse of Anglican divines. Plenty of detail lends credence to his stories. For instance, Ryves asserts that as the roundheads were marching through Chipping Norton a woman called out 'God bless the Cavaliers.' They tied her to one of their carts, stripped her to the waist, scourging her back to the bone with horse whips. Then they dragged her through the mud still tied to the wagon, the stones cutting her bare feet, and as a result she died a few days later. Horrible as this story sounds, lacking names and dates it should be treated with more than a pinch of salt.[132]

Yet at the time many believed such tales. For one thing they were perfectly possible. The abuse of women, particularly by soldiers, has always been far too common. Stories of rape frightened the 'The Virgins of Norwich' into raising money to equip a troop of horse, known as 'the maiden's troop' to protect their hymens from cavalier lusts.[133] Nehemiah Wallington, the London artisan, recorded numerous atrocity stories in his commonplace book. 'Women and Children put before the cannon', 'plundering and firing at Oakington', 'savage cruelty at Bristol', he noted with credulous horror. On the other hand he copied out reports of the massacre of the royalist camp-followers after Naseby with obvious satisfaction.[134]

Such tales brought home man's inhumanity to man. 'It is impossible to avoid doing very unhandsome things in war', John Evelyn admitted to his diary. An eyewitness to the massacre at Bolton, where many perished 'in a bitter shower of blood', concluded with the hope 'that England may see and be ashamed that she hath not long since spewed out such monsters, as are bred in her own bowels'.[135]

There were, to be sure, atrocities. Some were small, spontaneous killings, such as the two or three royalists whom Sergeant Henry Foster's regiment killed on 15 September 1643 when they heard that the enemy had shot one of their own men after he had surrendered.[136] Other outrages were more deliberate acts of spite. Captain Stiles arrested Robert Ram, Rector of Spalding, as a parliamentary propagandist on 25 March 1643, and took him to Crowland, where he was badly treated, notably after the round-heads invested the town. During an artillery bombardment the royalists tied him up above the North Bulwark in plain view, where he remained for three hours until he was recognized and the firing stopped. The incident says as much about the animosity that puritan preachers could engender, as it does about the quality of parliamentary marksmanship.

More serious were the larger massacres carried out on the orders, or at least with the connivance, of superiors. On Christmas Day 1643, after they refused to surrender, the royalists smoked twenty villagers and some of Brereton's troopers out of Barthomley Church, Cheshire, with burning rushes. Granted quarter, they were stripped, before having their throats slit. 'I put them all to the sword', Lord Byron boasted, 'which I find the best way to proceed with these kind of people, for mercy to them is cruelty.' Sir Francis Dodington, another royalist, had an equally bloody reputation. He hanged Irish prisoners after he captured Wardour Castle in 1643. On 19 July 1644 he strung up fourteen of the defenders of Woodhouse, a garrison near Longleat, and beat in another victim's brains. Once Dodington shot a priest dead in the road outside Taunton when the divine responded to his challenge 'Who are you for priest?' by replying 'for God and the Gospel'.[137]

The royalist sack of Bolton in May 1644 was the most serious authorized massacre. It started when the puritan defenders of the 'Geneva of the North' hanged an Irish soldier from their walls to celebrate beating back an assault in which John Russell's regiment had lost some three hundred men. Outraged, Rupert ordered Colonel Broughton's regiment to take the city, which they did, killing as many of the enemy as they could find. It was so widely believed that the Earl of Derby had run Captain Bootle through with his sword, on discovering his former servant fighting against the king, that half a dozen years later Derby was executed, *inter alia* for this crime. Estimates of Bolton's dead range from between two hundred and eighteen hundred. The parish registers record seventy-eight burials, including two women, while John Tilsley, Vicar of Deane, thought at least sixty wives had lost their husbands. Certainly an increase in marriages and remarriages, as well as a drop in the age of marriage in the next couple of years suggests a fairly considerable loss of life.[138]

Two of the first civil war's most cold-blooded massacres occurred in the Welsh Marches in the spring of 1644.

After Colonel Samuel Moor agreed to surrender Holt Castle, Denbyshire, in February, he and his men marched out to line up in parade-order to hand over their weapons. The colonel suspected nothing after he was marched off to be interrogated. A little later a Lieutenant Aldersey told him that thirteen of the garrison had been murdered, their bodies tossed into the moat. Moor could not believe Aldersey's news: 'I could eat but little: then he let me lie on his own bed, where I lay until day break.'[139]

A week after a parliamentary garrison took over Hopton Castle, Herefordshire, a royalist force appeared and demanded their surrender. It was refused, as was another a fortnight later. The five hundred roundheads attacked but were repulsed with heavy losses. Two more parleys took place in which the rebels were warned that if they held out any longer they would be denied quarter. On 13 March a mine destroyed much of the walls. The defenders offered to surrender if they were allowed to march away with their arms and ammunition. This was rejected. So they asked for quarter. It too was spurned. When the castle was taken everyone but the governor and his seond in charge, a Major Phillips, were stripped, hog-tied back to back, and like slaughtered animals had their throats cut, the bodies being thrown into a ditch. Two maidservants, who had to watch this atrocity, were beaten up (one of them going mad as a result of the trauma). The royalists tied a man of 80 who emerged from the cellars after the other survivors had been murdered, to a chair – for he was too old, ill or frightened to stand – and slashed his throat, tossing him into the ditch to join his comrades.

The reasons for this blood-bath – which was as notorious as it was comparatively rare – are complex. At one level the royalists were perfectly within their rights to put to the sword a garrison which had refused several offers to surrender. The fact that they used the method normally employed for slaughtering sheep was a sign of hatred more than sadism. Merely following the laws of war to the last brutal letter does not explain their barbarity.

The fighting at Hopton was extremely bitter, even by the ferocious standards of the Welsh Borders. The royalists took considerable casualties during the assault. The defenders overestimated their chances of holding out, or getting quarter. In addition the royalists were convinced that the rebels were using poisoned bullets, and had murdered wounded cavaliers in cold blood. Many of the king's men were Irish troops, who had few compunctions about meting out to roundhead prisoners the fate that would doubtless be theirs on capture. Finally Colonel Woodhouse, the cavalier commander, relinquished control of his men by deliberately staying outside the castle for at least three hours once they had taken it. If he did so to let them plunder unhindered, the result was one of the worst atrocities in a war that was not notorious for its brutality.

One sign of the comparative lack of gratuitous violence was a remarkable absence of rape in the British civil wars – as was the case before the outbreak of hostilities.[140] Admittedly rape is – and surely was – a crime which far too often goes unreported, largely because of male attitudes towards women. Yet during the civil war male prejudices could have worked in the opposite direction. Propagandists were all too keen to brand the other side's troops as rapists, while commanders have traditionally condemned rape not for the hurt it inflicts on the victims, but the damage it does to military discipline and civilian relations. While both sides attributed all too many atrocities to each other during the Irish massacres of 1641, violation of women was conspicuous by its infrequency.[141] Even though the fighting during Montrose's campaigns was extremely brutal, cases of rape were rare. When his troops captured Aberdeen they 'spoiled the houses and deflowered the women. Such', Robert Douglas somberly notes in his diary, 'was the wickedness of the villains.' A 1644 pamphlet described the many outrages committed by recently demobilized troopers. It gave copious details of gangs operating in Hull, Berwick, Cambridgeshire, Hyde Park, Southwark, Cheapside, Watford and Islington. It even described how at Barwick Trooper John Hawkins and 'his Irish accomplish' held up half a dozen young ladies 'and robbed them of all but of what? Their Maidenheads'.[142]

Rape is not so much a crime of sexual passion as it is one of hatred and violence. As the Russian Army demonstrated in 1945 the ultimate act of aggression and humiliation of an enemy was the systematic violation of their women.

According to Bruno Ryves some roundheads propositioned a couple of chambermaids at the Swan Inn, Wellingborough.[143] When they refused, the soldiers shot one woman and wounded the other. *The Scourge of Civil Warre: the Blessings of Peace* (1645, S2108) reported how a mother was forced 'to behold the Ravishment of her own daughters'. William Trumbull, a gentleman from Berkshire, alleged that troops billeted in his house snatched a servant from her bed and assaulted her.[144] In 1648 the parliamentary newspaper, *Colchester's Tears*, claimed that during the desperate siege of that town the Earl of Norwich stopped Sir Charles Lucas as he was about to ravish a woman. Since the deed was never used to justify Sir

Charles's execution after surrendering Colchester, the story seems fabricated.

Far more credible are three reports of rape. The first came in a letter from Fairfax to Speaker Lenthall which described how three royalists violated a farmer's wife in front of him at Otley, Yorkshire. The general explained this abnormal abomination by adding that the soldiers were French.[145] On 24 May 1645 Captain Richard Symonds watched every carter in the army's baggage train give a soldier, who was tied to a tree naked from the waist up, a lash for ravishing two women. Sir Samuel Luke, who as a scout master ran a spy network, reported that during the spring of 1645 Sir Marmaduke Langdale's men plundered and raped without mercy in Northamptonshire. They tied men neck and heels, before taking their wives and daughters before them. They raped a pregnant wench, and, worse still, violated a gentlewoman and her daughter. Angry because his pocket had been picked of loot, a royalist soldier siezed a girl, stripped her, and scattered gunpowder over her breasts, setting them alight.[146]

Notwithstanding such sickening stories, the fighting in England, at least, was remarkably free from atrocities, largely because of the lack of ethnic or ideological differences. Conversely the presence of such distinctions helps explain the appalling treatment of Irish prisoners captured in England and Scotland.

Hatred of the Irish went back to at least the reformation and the brutal Elizabethan conquest of that unhappy isle. Grossly exaggerated tales of Irish pogroms during the 1641 rebellion further inflamed English antipathies. Yet it took a couple of years fighting before the killing of Irish prisoners became routine. A participant at the Battle of Cheriton described 'most of the Irish' there as 'neither giving or taking quarter'.[147] Even though the London newspapers demanded that the hundred and twenty Irish camp-followers taken at Nantwich in January 1644 'be put to the sword' because they had knives designed 'not only to stab but to tear the flesh from the very bone' hidden in their petticoats, Lord Fairfax sent them home.[148] He was not so generous to Colonel Hawkins and a couple of Irish privates, whom on being recaptured he had shot and hanged respectively, for deserting parliament's forces to serve the crown.[149]

The first major murders of Irish troops started when the king brought over large numbers of them to fight for him in England. While both Charles and parliament exaggerated the impact Irish soldiers would have on the outcome of the war at home, many Englishmen were petrified that they would bring with them the brutality that characterized fighting in their native land. Thus in 1644 when Captain Swanley, a parliamentary naval officer, captured a transport off the Pembroke coast sailing from Dublin to Bristol carrying seventy Irish soldiers and two women, he threw them overboard. Delighted, the *Parliamentary Weekly Intelligencer* crowed that Swanley 'caused them to be tied back to back, and to drink their belly of salt water', while *The Perfect Diurnal* rejoiced that the good captain 'make water rats' of papist vermin 'and cast them into the sea'. Parliament formally voted Swanley both their thanks, as well as a gold chain worth £200. (While receiving just as much parliamentary gratitude, his second in command, Captain Smith, got a chain worth half as much.) The drownings were highly effective, making Irish soldiers, admitted the Marquis of Ormonde, loath to sail to fight in England.[150]

During 1644 the murder of Irish prisoners escalated. After being thrashed at the Battle of Cheriton in March some panic-stricken cavaliers set fire to the town. For this senseless act of vandalism the roundheads retaliated against the hundred and twenty royalist prisoners they had taken. 'We gave none of them any quarter', Robert Harley wrote to his brother, adding the excuse that 'Very many Irishmen were slain.'[151] The defenders of Lyme were in an equally rabid mood after the royalists gave up their siege in June, leaving behind an old Irish woman. Some say that the sailors drove her through the town with slashing swords into the sea: others report that a mob tore her to pieces or else rolled her around inside a nail-studded barrel.[152]

Such abuses fed upon each other. The following month Sir Francis Dodington hanged fourteen of the parliamentary garrison of Woodhouse, Somerset, after they had surrendered on quarter, in retaliation for the hanging of six Irish prisoners by Colonel Sydenham. On hearing the news the Venetian Secretary commented 'This will give great occasion of revenge, so it is to be feared that the war will become more and more cruel.' Alas he was only too right. Soon after, Essex summarily hanged a royalist officer, allegedly for desertion, prompting Prince Maurice to string up a captured parliamentary sea captain. Realizing that being a prisoner of parliament was not a very healthy state of affairs, two Irishmen escaped from the Tower and hid in the house where the French resident had his lodging. Brushing aside claims of diplomatic immunity, parliament sent 'a large force of guards' who broke into the house and beat up the resident's landlord. 'Much incensed', the French ambassador rushed to Oxford to lodge a formal protest with the crown.[153]

By now such diplomatic niceties were irrelevant, especially as far as the Irish were concerned. On 24 October 1644 parliament passed an ordinance that 'no quarter shall henceforth be given to any Irishman, or papist born in Ireland' captured on land or at sea. Although some officers such as the Earl of Denbigh were reluctant to obey this infamous order, most were not.[154] On 11 January 1645 Prince Charles's regiment of horse raided Abingdon, but were beaten back with the loss of a major and lieutenant. 'Five of this regiment were Irish by their own confession,' reported General Richard Browne, 'whom I presently cause to be hanged in the Market place according to an ordinance of parliament.' A few days later Colonel Hawkins was shot against the chancel wall of Nantwich Church 'for that he was an Irishman', and soon after the roundheads hanged two Irish soldiers 20 miles away at Christleton.[155]

Perhaps the most notorious murder of prisoners took place after Colonel Thomas Mytton captured Shrewsbury in a pre-dawn attack in February 1645. After their governor was killed the Welsh troops promptly surrendered, leaving fifty of their Irish comrades to their fate. Mytton selected a dozen by lot, whom he hanged. In retaliation Prince Rupert used a similar means to chose thirteen victims from a cavalry troop his men had just ambushed near Oswestry (since they had surrendered after a single shot had been fired, they were clearly confident that their fellow countrymen would treat them well: Mytton had sense enough to escape, slashing the fellow who tried to grab his bridle across the arm). As the condemned roundheads were paraded before Rupert's troopers, one of them, Philip Littleton, spotted Sir Vincent Corbett ride past. Since he had been his father's park-keeper, Littleton persuaded a cavalier to gallop after Sir Vincent, who returned and on his knees successfully persuaded Rupert to spare the retainer. Less fortunate, the remaining dozen were swung on a crab-apple tree. When Rupert sent one of their comrades to tell parliament what he had done, and that he was determined to hang two of their men for every cavalier executed, the Commons were outraged. They ordered the Earl of Essex to explain to Rupert – who after all as a foreigner could well be ignorant of the nuances of English lynching – that 'there was a very great difference between Englishmen and Irishmen'.[156]

Rupert's threat – which he never carried out – did nothing to reduce the murder of Irish prisoners. When Thomas Middleton took seventy-five Irish troops at Conway Castle they 'were commanded to be tied back to back, and to be cast overboard, and sent by water to their own country'.[157] When Fairfax captured an Irish ship carrying royalist dispatches he hanged the crew – much to the delight of the parliamentary padre, Hugh Peters, who preached that papists were a bunch of cut-throats in the first place.[158] All too many agreed with the bloodthirsty puritan. Turning the victim into the villain, Sir Trevor Williams argued that during the fighting at Ragland in May 1646 three of his soldiers had been shot by the Irish. Sir William Brereton explained that Irish soldiers deserved the noose because they were guilty of 'great spoils and cruelties . . . horrid rapes and insolencies'. With brutal brevity Oliver Cromwell concluded that hanging the Irish was 'a righteous judgment of God upon these barbarous wretches'.[159]

These poor wretches were treated just as barbarously North of the Border. In December 1645 the Scots parliament ordered that all Irish prisoners taken during the Montrose campaign be 'execut without any assyse or process'. The resolution was mostly academic for by now few Irish prisoners were left alive. Just to be sure, the following month parliament decreed that granting them quarter was contrary to the covenant, and was thus a sin.[160]

While killing prisoners went against the unwritten laws of wars, hanging spies did not. Spies have always been treated harshly. To their enemy they pose a threat way beyond the capability of an individual soldier: to their employers that are as great a hazard because their duplicity contradicts the principle of honest loyalty that is the backbone of all fighting forces.

Because they were such a danger spies were executed as publicly as possible. Richard Symonds remembered when the royalist army was marched under a gallows so they could see the body of a spy dangling above. Prince Rupert sent Tobias Beasely, a corporal in his regiment, to spy in London, where before the war he had been a porter at the Ram Inn, Smithfield. Captured, parliament hanged him at Smithfield (the site of many a public execution in Bloody Mary's reign). Corporal Beasely died badly. As the Reverend Quarterman (who doubled as chaplain as well as the provost marshal in charge of the execution) prayed incessantly in his ear, an eyewitness noted that 'the porter showed much unwillingness to go off the ladder'. David Kniverton, another royalist spy, was not given the option of launching himself off into oblivion. Hanged outside the Royal Exchange, his body was draped with copies of parliamentary ordinances forbidding civilians on pain of death to travel about the land without their express permission.

When the other side allegedly executed civilians for travelling without the proper documentation, parliamentary journalists made the most of it. In 1643, for instance, a Mrs Phillips sent her servant William Needle on an errand to Banbury without a pass. The royalists arrested and hanged him as a spy. They also sentenced his mistress to death, and stood the mother of ten children, the youngest of whom she was still nursing, under the gallows with a noose about her neck for several minutes, before reprieving her.[161]

Passes were usually notes signed by a senior official. 'This is to request you and everyone of you to permit the bearer, Mr James Scudamore . . . to pass . . . To Oxford', ran one issued by General William Waller in November 1644.[162]

Yet they were no guarantee of a safe passage. Even though John Taylor had a pass signed by a roundhead major permitting him to go from London to Oxford in 1643, he was robbed of his coat and bag in a wood near Windsor, by a bunch of ruffians who then had the gall to drag him into a pub and make him pay for several rounds of drinks. Actually Taylor counted himself lucky, for all this while the major who had first issued the pass was trying to arrest him as a royalist spy.[163]

Because spies could be so damaging to the other side, and often had such a short life expectancy, as John Cruso explained in his *Treatise of Modern War* (1640), while you cannot have too many of them, 'you must always be suspicious of spies'.[164] Both sides developed intelligence networks. From his base at Newport Pagnell Sir Samuel Luke ran one for parliament. Oxford was the centre of the king's fairly effective spy system which included such assets as 'safe houses' and 'letter boxes', the latter were usually ditches outside the walls where messages were left and picked up.[165]

News of the bloodbaths in Scotland and Ireland, as well as the killing of prisoners in England itself, hardened surviving soldiers as they went about making a war that was dragging on to an ever more bitter end. The king's army was in an especially vicious mood when they marched out of Oxford for the last time in May 1645. Gratuitously they burned Camden House, valued at £30,000, to the ground. After taking Hawkesley House, Worcestershire, 'our soldiers were let in to plunder, and having taken out what they would, they set fire to the rest'.[166] The other side could be just as bad. Chaplain Sprigge recalled that after his roundheads had captured Sherborne in August 1645, 'the soldiers spoil lasted all that day, and most part of that night'.[167]

The violence of the first civil war, in England at least, was directed less against persons than it was against property. From its very start one – if not the – main goal of those who took part in all the hurly-burly of battles lost and won was not religion, liberty or class antagonisms. More than anything else, it was, quite simply, the acquisition of loot and plunder.

11

MORE TO SPOIL THAN TO SERVE

> The common sort of our countrymen that go to war,
> of purpose more to spoil than to serve.
> > Geoffrey Gates, *The Defence of the
> > Military Profession* (1579), 43

By definition all civil wars involve compatriots fighting each other. During the 1640s Englishmen, Scotsmen, Welshmen and Irishmen (and women), killed each other in battles, sieges, skirmishes and ambushes. Yet for most of them death in combat was a remote and random possibility. Their surviving letters, diaries and memoirs show that they were just as – if not more – concerned about losing their property in some almost accidental episode of violence. Most common was the attitude of Sir William Brereton. After reviewing the problems facing Cheshire after a year of civil war he concluded that 'Our greatest care being to preserve the county from plundering.'[1] Parliament justified an assessment to Norfolk, Suffolk and Cambridgeshire to raise soldiers by explaining that it was 'the better to prevent the spoiling of the said counties'.[2] The English language reflected this important change. Although the word plunder was first used in a fairly rare Swedish newsletter of 1632, far more people became aware of it ten years later when *A Relation of the King's Army* described how after capturing Brentford 'they plundered it without any respect of persons'. By the following year the word plunder, brought over from the Thirty Years' Wars by Prince Rupert and his henchmen, had become so familiar that William Prynne used it thrice in a single sentence.[3]

Frequently wars have been financed by the violent seizure of the other side's property, be that through prize money, rapine, looting, spoilage, piracy, privateering, sequestration, 'liberation', reparations, or – to sum them all up – plunder. Indeed the number of words in the language indicates the prevalence of this practice.

In ancient times prisoners were slaughtered, sold into slavery, and their women seized. During the middle ages a sophisticated system of ransom was used to pay the victors and spare the vanquished. During the sixteenth century privateering was used to finance the founding of the British Empire. For instance, only 2 of the 25 ships Sir Francis Drake took to the West Indies in 1585 were Royal Naval vessels, as were 34 of the 197 English ships which defeated the Armada three years later. Through plunder the Swedes were able to field a huge army of 150,000 men in the Thirty Years' War. Thus by the start of the civil war the violent seizure of property had for centuries been an integral part of a soldier's life. 'They were as good fighters and as great plunderers as ever went to a field', Captain John Hodgson wrote approvingly about the Lancashire infantry he had the honour to command.

For armies plunder could be both a blessing and a curse. It could erode military discipline, while alienating civil support. Thus initially commanders were determined to do all they could to stamp it out. In the Bishops' Wars, for instance, Sir Jacob Astley punished some of his troops for rustling Sir Nicholas Tempest's cattle near South Shields. One miscreant revenged himself by setting fire to Tempest's straw, destroying some £20 worth, which must have made a spectacular blaze. Surrounded by burnt timbers, he was hanged with a sign proclaiming his offence, which the whole army could read as they were marched past, because, as Astley noted, 'base minds [are] only awed by fear of punishment'.[4]

On the other hand soldiers often had to plunder to stay alive. It could be an inducement to fight, a reward for victory as well as salve for defeat. Just as unchecked cavalry actions had their civilian origins in the pell-mell excitement of the hunt, so plunder was akin to poaching. It was a popular peacetime substitute for war. Its organized armed gangs purloined game to which they had no claim, and afterwards they would feast on the loot, reinforcing their own sense of group loyalty.[5] Indeed during the war poaching became a very common form of plunder: within a couple of years nearly all of the 2,500 royal deer from Windsor Park had ended up in the bellies of Essex's soldiers.[6]

Plunder provided a psychological satisfaction, being a concrete example of the power a soldier enjoys over unarmed civilians. By the same token, the victims feel violated. Being forced to hand over their goods to fellow countrymen, they increasingly grew tired of the war until, as David Underdown so neatly put it, 'the real enemy was the plunderer' (plate 6).[7]

For Nehemiah Wharton the civil war began in August 1642 with an orgy of plunder.[8] The London apprentice left his master, George Willingham, merchant of St Swithin's Street, on the 16th of that month, most likely as a sergeant, to fight with Denzil Holles's regiment of the city's Trained Bands. Almost immediately he and his comrades started to plunder. Wharton was annoyed to be detached from his unit to fetch some ammunition, because it delayed his arrival in Oxford and meant that he missed all that was worth liberating. The only loot left was a few surplices that he tore up for bandages. At Wendover Sergeant Wharton's regiment chopped up the altar rails for firewood. After hearing a sermon from a Godly minister whom 'the cavaliers had pillaged to the skin', they did the same to the Rector of Southam, Warwickshire, 'a very malignant town'. Even though Lord Brooke threatened to court-martial anyone caught looting, the practice did not stop. The soldiers poached so much deer from the parks of great houses that Wharton boasted to his master 'venison is almost as common with us as beef is with you'. A couple of weeks later looting became so much of a problem that not even drill parades at six in the morning and six at night could control it: so Lord General Essex swore to hang anyone found guilty.

There was something casually cruel about the looting by Wharton and his comrades, who cynically maintained that 'all rich men are Roundheads'. They plundered the house of John Penruddock, a catholic from Ealing, taking all his furniture, leaving him not even a chair or bed, before maliciously vandalizing his garden, ripping up all his fruit trees. At Castlemorton, Worcestershire, they looted Rowland Bartlett's house. Even though a week earlier Captain Scriven's royalists had plundered him of nearly a thousand pounds, they had so much beef, bacon, pots and pans that the Londoners had to steal his carts to carry the loot away. Even so, poor Bartlett's problems were not over. A few days later other parliamentary soldiers from Gloucester returned to steal his clothes, drink his wine and perry, and smash his linen press with their musket buts.[9]

Far from expressing any remorse, Wharton, a religious young man, described this campaign of plunder in Bunyanesque terms as his 'pilgrimage'. Having presumably been well brought up to respect property, he pillaged with the brutal enthusiasm of a godless veteran of the Thirty Years' War. And if the troopers did feel any guilt about stealing the goods of their fellow countrymen they soon assuaged it by listening to 'a famous sermon' or two.

The victims were not able to overcome the experience so easily. The author of *A Relation of the Rare Exploits of the London Soldiers* (1642, R862) wondered how 'these strange inhumanities' were possible, particularly when 'they are practiced amongst Christians against Christians'. The excuse that the prey were papists rang hollow. 'Were they Jews or Atheists it is a stain', the pamphlet indignantly maintained. Anyway religion was all too often an excuse for vandalism and greed. During the sack of Winchester 'our unruly soldiers' looted all the houses, and then 'found a great store of Popish books, pictures and crucifixes', which they triumphantly carried through the streets to the market-place with an enthusiasm apparently enhanced by the copious use of liberated alcohol.[10]

Marauding rapidly became so serious a problem that in September 1642 John Hampden admitted that his troops had 'grown so outrageous that they plunder everyplace', having pillaged in one morning alone five or six houses, selected after asking the locals to discover which malignants' properties offered the richest pickings. Hampden and five fellow round-head regimental commanders warned that unless they started making an example of notorious looters by stringing them up on the nearest tree, their army would become as odious to ordinary folk as was the king's. 'We are all the most abominable plunderers,' Colonel Arthur Goodwin, the parliamentary governor of Aylesbury, confessed to his son-in-law, 'I am ashamed to look an honest man in the face.'[11] Thus on 9 November parliament ordered Lord General Essex to show looters no mercy.

Of course, stories about rapine could – and did – grow with each telling. Lady Scudamore complained to General Waller that his troops had badly ravaged her house. The general had a local alderman look into the matter, but he found only minor damage to the chapel roof, and a few trees cut for kindling.[12]

Even before the formal declaration of war, the royalists had become enthusiastic plunderers. On 11 August 1642 the king's garrison at Portsmouth rustled some three hundred and fifty cattle and sheep from Portsea Island. Three days later a cavalier troop raided Knowle House in Kent. In the course of requisitioning five wagon loads of weapons, they smashed open forty locks, and stripped £40 worth of gold leaf from a coach.[13] One eyewitness alleged that the only reason why the locals cheered as Charles raised his standard at Nottingham was from trepidation that 'the cavaliers would come and ransack their houses'.[14]

The king's soldiers quickly gained an unsavoury reputation for fulfilling such fears. In November the Mayor and Corporation of Sandwich complained that 'the cavaliers are extremely outrageous in plundering when they come, putting no difference at all between friends and supposed enemies'.[15] After spending the night at an inn, rather than paying they would rip up the feather beds, and 'for sport' smash in all the barrels of wine and beer they had not drunk.[16] They massacred a flock of a thousand sheep, wasting the meat they could not eat or take away. Things in Cheshire were even worse. A victim recalled that at Nantwich Lord Grandison's men 'set a pistol at our throats and swear God damn them they will make us swallow a bullet' unless we told them where we had hidden their valuables.[17] At Welverham, they rounded up all the elders, tied them to a cart and dragged them through the mud to a dungeon, in which they spent the night without food or light, to persuade them to reveal where they had stashed their goods. On the following day – a sabbath, puritans noted with added horror – the royalists plundered the village without let or hindrance.[18]

The king issued two proclamations in 1642 and a couple the following year forbidding such outrages. The first, dated 27 August 1642 (less than a week after the declaration of war), stated that many soldiers had broken into the homes of loyal subjects on the spurious grounds that they were 'papists' houses, or houses of persons disaffected'. Quite clearly this was a piece of propaganda aimed at the abuses committed by Sergeant Wharton and his comrades from the London Trained Bands. At first Charles did little to control his own men. He stood idly by watching them loot Wolverhampton in October 1642 because he believed he had no friends in that city. The second proclamation of 25 November was a more serious attempt to counter the adverse effect the plunder of Brentford had had on public opinion. After admitting to 'unjust and unlawful actions done by divers soldiers of Our Army', Charles ordered all taking property without his express permission to be executed without mercy.[19]

Had the proclamation been enforced the king's hangman could have ended the lives of more of his soldiers in a few months than did the roundheads in five years. The crown not only lost the crusade against looting – if indeed it ever really bothered to fight it – but forfeited the propaganda campaign against looters. The sack of Brentford so terrified Londoners that they stood their ground at Turnham Green, the war's critical confrontation, and afterwards fortified the city so well that the crown lost all chance of taking the capital, and thus winning the war. Prince Rupert's sack of Birmingham the following year further alienated public opinion by establishing the indelible image of the cavaliers as avid plunderers.

Even though this view has been challenged with regard to the extent of royalist plundering in Leicester, the activities of Lord Thomas Wentworth's men in Buckinghamshire lend it credence.[20] On 15 May 1643 they raided Winslow for arms. They found a cache, and killed a few enemy stragglers. Heartened by their success, the next day they rode to Great Horwood, where the villagers agreed to fork out over £100 rather than be pillaged. Moving on, they threatened to burn Swanbourne to the ground unless the inhabitants gave up their weapons. When they refused the cavaliers torched Swanbourne, but had to leave at the approach of some three to four hundred armed country folk. Wentworth concluded that although 'we have gotten the king but little by our plundering', the raid had taught the locals a lesson they would not forget.[21]

There is no doubt that the victims learned a lesson: the problem was that it was not the one the plunderers wanted taught.

The first – and quite literally vital – lesson the victims of plunderers then (like those of muggers today) had to learn was not to resist. When Mr Rellisone tried to use his bow and arrow to prevent Sir Francis Wortley's men from pillaging Bakewell House, Warwickshire in October 1642, they killed him. The following year a foraging party shot and killed Edward Morgan when he tried to prevent them requisiting two of his master's oxen from Brampton Park. In 1644, just outside Leicester, a hapless carter met the same fate trying to stop a patrol of Lord Hastings' royalists from seizing his load of plums and spices.[22] That June a cavalier raiding party shot dead the landlord of the Red Lion Inn, Dunstable, when he protested against the seizure of his horses. The following year Andrew Pottinger, a substantial freeholder and parliamentary partisan, with a wife and six young children, died from being hit on the head as he attempted to prevent roundhead troops from the Newbury garrison rustling his sheep. After the inhabitants killed two parliamentary soldiers who were plundering Nuthurst, Sussex, troops from the local garrison retaliated by imprisoning several of them in Arundel Castle.[23]

Most people learned how to survive being plundered. Bereft of their goods, they were at least left their lives – as well as a vivid sense of being violated.

Near Acton on 27 August 1642 the London Trained Bands (of whom Sergeant Wharton was a member) robbed an old man of all his clothes, and his house of all its furniture and fittings down to the bare walls. 'I found him sitting on his only stool, with tears flowing down his hoary beard', reported a bystander.

William Harvey, the physician who discovered the circulation of blood, frequently declared that of all the losses he sustained at the hands of the roundheads during the civil wars 'none was so crucifying to him' than the malicious destruction of his papers, including the only manuscript of his book *De Insectis*.

Bulstrode Whitelocke described how in November 1642 Rupert's troops plundered his house, Fawley Court:[24]

> There was no insolence or outrage usually committed by common soldiers on a reputed enemy which was omitted by these brutish fellows at my house. They had their whores with them, they spent and consumed a £200 load of corn and hay, littered their horses with sheaves of good wheat and gave them all sorts of corn in the straw. Divers writing of consequence and books which were left in my study, some of them they tore in pieces, others they burnt to light their tobacco, and some they carried away with them.

The royalists ate all his food, killed his deer, presented his prize hounds to Prince Rupert, broke open his trunks and chests, slashed up his beds strewing feathers all over the place, and stole his coach and horses. When William Cooke, a long-standing tenant, suggested that they use faggots for firewood, instead of fine timber being seasoned for ploughs, the troops threatened to toss him into the bonfire.

Even though Bulstrode Whitelocke was writing years after the event, it is clear that the pain of being plundered still smarted. The experience left scars that might last a lifetime. Take the Reverend Ralph Josselin, minister of Earls Colne. When the royalists entered the Essex village on 12 June 1648 they plundered promiscuously and started looking for roundheads. Fearing arrest, Josselin, who had served as a parliamentary chaplain, escaped to the neighbouring village of Coggeshall. The next day he returned. The royalists spotted him when his baby daughter cried out for her father. Josselin ran, trying to take refuge in a neighbour's house. But she refused him sanctuary for fear of being further plundered. 'It cut my heart to see my life no more regarded by her, and it was the greatest damper and trouble to my spirit for present that I ever met with', wrote Josselin.[25] One wonders how, over the years, for the minister lived in Earls Colne until his death in 1683, he and his unnamed neighbour felt as they met on the street, raised a glass in the inn, or worshipped together at Divine Service.

This sense of being ravaged by foe and fair-weather friend alike was not confined to parliamentarians. Having his horse stolen by roundhead troops so upset Alexander Brome that he wrote a poem trying to sort out his feelings, which ranged from a violent desire to see the thief hanged, to the philosophical resignation 'that all worldly goods are frail'. Soon after having to surrender Hereford, the royalist magnate, Barnabus Scudamore, told a friend how the enemy had stolen the hangings, linen, pewter, brass, and all movables from his house in Gloucester. They smashed every window, bolt and lock, defaced the ceiling mouldings, ripped out doors, and chopped up the stairs and floor boards for firewood. After draining his barrels of wine and beer the enemy used the precious staves for kindling, even though there was plenty of coal and firewood available. They ripped the lead from his roof, felled the trees in his park, and scared his poor wife almost to death. Mindlessly they slaughtered the cattle he had specially imported from Flanders to develop a breed stock. (Had they not been replaced after the war the very popular breed of white-faced Herefordshire cattle might have never been developed.)[26]

The prospect of being plundered terrified some men almost out of their wits. Nehemiah Wallington bought and read news reports of royalist sackings with a morbid fascination. In the first three months of the war he noted ten such atrocities: at Shrewsbury 'they spare no one', at Salford 'much hurt', noted the London artisan, before concluding 'our condition here is miserable'.[27] Compared to those who sat trembling in London the condition of those who were actually plundered was far worse. 'To hear the pitiful shrieking, weeping and howling of the women and children', wrote a survivor of the sack of Nantwich by Lord Grandison's cavaliers, 'did trouble me more than anything else: God grant I never heard the like.' Another survivor of the same incident voiced the frustration felt by all victims: 'if we stay at home we are now their slaves. Being naked they will have of us what they list.'[28]

Some tried to avoid being plundered by moving away. In late September 1643 Mrs Joyce Jeffries shut up her house in Hereford, which she believed was vulnerable, to move to her country home in Kilkinton. It did not work, for the following month Captain Hammon 'and his barbarous company spoiled her of her goods, coaches linen and money'. Desperate, the widow paid a neighbour to hide her few remaining valuables. The tactic backfired. When the troopers returned the following March they were so angry to find the cupboard bare that they smashed in all the locks to her house. Most folk soon learned how to conceal their valuables. Lady Sussex put them in the turret room over her bedroom which she walled up. As she ostentatiously dined off pewter, she told inquirers that she had sold all her silver. The owner of Dimsdale Farm near Edgehill hung his plate down the well, while Abel Barker, a gentleman from Hambleton, Rutland, kept no cash on his person lest it be stolen.[29]

The trouble with running away from plunderers was that they also plied their trade upon the way. Eight highwaymen relieved Lady Lambert of £8 on the road near Alton.[30] Colonel Hastings' troops based in Ashby-de-la-Zouch became so notorious that they were known as the 'Rob-carriers' because they plundered so many pack trains. One of their victims was Daniel Gittins, a farm manager from Blackwell Hall, who was travelling on business when they robbed him of his horse, saddle bag, cane and buckskin coat at the Wheatsheaf Inn, Daventry. When their efforts to use soap and water to prise off his wedding ring failed, the troopers threatened to smash his brains out and trample him under their horses' hooves. Only the intervention of the serving girls from the inn saved Gittins's life.[31] Abraham Haynes, who was travelling from London to visit his daughter in Shropshire had an equally unfortunate encounter outside an inn just 8 miles short of her house. Suspecting him to be a malignant, the landlord and his cronies searched Haynes for secret messages. Discovering none, they nonetheless kept the £14 they found about him, and for good measure had him arrested and sent back to London, where he languished in jail for six months before being freed without being charged.[32]

All too often the victims of plunder were the most vulnerable. Soon after her husband died a cavalry troop ransacked Lady Elizabeth Wiseman's house, and even though their captain was very polite the widow admitted that the whole affair 'added great affrightment to my late griefs'.[33] In Kent the roundheads searched and pillaged Lady Filmer's house ten times during her husband's painful and dangerous bout of bladder stones. As a young boy Anthony Wood lost the silver plate his godparents had given him at his christening, while the men who spoiled John Wolstenholme's house in Nostel, Yorkshire, wounded two serving maids, calling one 'a Romanish whore' as they stole her purse and gold ring. 'I live in fear of my life with all my family', Wolstenholme concluded.[34]

Sometimes plunderers showed compassion. Billeted in the house of a heavily pregnant gentlewoman near Appleby, during the 1648 invasion, Sir James Turner discovered a cache of gold coins hidden under the floor boards. In tears the lady explained that her husband was a spendthrift so, unnoticed, she had to skim money off from her allowance to save it for a rainy day, such as her impending confinement. Turner returned the money.[35]

Most victims were not so lucky. Perhaps the most heart-rending story concerned Margery Royston, a widow from Warwickshire, who was robbed of the money she had painstakingly saved to reclaim her 9-year-old daughter who had been shipped as an indentured servant to Virginia.[36]

As she mourned for the child she would never see again so that a few troopers could enjoy an evening's carousing, Mrs Royston must have pondered the capriciousness of her fate. Innocent and guilty, friend and foe, honest men and crooks seemed to suffer equally from the whims of plunder. When the royalists took Cirencester in 1643 they freed John Plot, a lawyer of unspotted reputation, whom parliament had imprisoned for his loyalty to the crown. He walked home from his cell only to find his house full of the king's soldiers who stole £1,200 which he never recovered.[37] Plunder could destroy a lifetime's work. After watching the royalists rustle cattle in Worcester in 1646 a diarist noted, 'and so a poor honest man ruined in a one night what he hath laboured for all his days'.[38] A doggerel verse summed up the pain of being plundered by both sides without rhyme, reason or mercy:

> I had six oxen the other day
> And them the Roundheads got away.
> A mischief on them speed.
> I had six horses in the hole
> And them the Cavaliers stole.
> I think in this they are agreed.

The implicit violence and irrationality of plunder made many lose faith in a rational orderly world. After some cavaliers stole his possessions, John Jones, a royalist from Flint, complained that their action was 'against the Laws of this Land, the Covenant of this State, and the Oath of a King'.[39] Interestingly enough, the perpetrators accepted a similar argument. Thomas Chadwick suggested to Hugh Kidd that they should break into Beresford Hall because, 'there was no other law now'.[40] And to prove the point that the rule of the gun had replaced that of the law, Chadwick was shot and killed during the robbery. Captain Antonio Vernatti used the same rationale to excuse the protection racket he and his troops set up at Hatfield Close, Yorkshire. Having escaped from a debtor's prison in London, Vernatti broke into Herbert Le Roy's home, stealing £10. He threatened to burn down Charles Weterlow's house if he did not hand over his livestock and plough, and spurned the orders of the Earl of Newcastle, the royalist theatre commander, to stop by explaining that there was no longer any law in force forbidding his extortions.[41]

Plunder could reduce some victims to despair. In late 1643 a Mrs Harrison wrote to a friend in France that she was afraid that England was

rapidly becoming like Germany which was being ravaged by the Thirty
Years' War. William Davenport found the contradictory signals his tor-
mentors gave him especially confusing. After losing seventeen of his
horses in January 1644, whilst out riding on the following 20 May some
of Captain Standley's troopers seized his mare. Bitter protests did not
save him from having to walk home. Three days later Standley's men
requisitioned three more of his horses. Much to his surprise on 8 June he
received a letter from the captain 'containing many kind expressions of
friendship', saying his men had taken the mare without permission and
promising to return her. A few hours later Standley's troop arrived at
Davenport's house, but instead of giving back his mare as promised,
they seized his remaining seventeen horses, leaving him without a single
mount.[42]

Protestations of amity might explain why Edmund Jodrell, a Cheshire
gentleman, refused the assessment the parliamentary army sent him in
1643. Admittedly he did cough up £20 towards the first demand for £100
which was signed 'Your faithful friends'. But he refused to pay any of
the second assessment for £300 which arrived seven weeks later, signed
'Your very faithful friends'. So the roundheads immediately plundered
him of £150 worth of goods, and threw him into Nantwich jail, where
he languished for several months before being released on the payment of
a further £50. Jodrell – like so many in those lawless days – learned that
the line between assessment and outright plunder was a narrow one, best
not crossed. Between 1642 and 1645 he paid the parliamentary authorities
a total of £423 2s 6d, in addition to the fine and goods seized for non-
payment of taxes. Jodrell claimed that the goods were worth £150. An
inventory valued them, however, at £97 18s 2d, which suggests that victims
of plunder – like those claiming against their burglary insurance policies
today – might have been inclined to exaggerate their losses.[43]

After losing all his goods worth several hundred pounds Silvester
Warner of Marston, Warwickshire prayed 'God will either take him out
of this world or make him more able to undergo these burdens.'[44] In the
spring of 1644 Randolph Crewe wrote to Sir Richard Browne, the king's
agent in Paris, that 'I mourn and groan to think' of the coming campaign
season, with its 'devastation and impoverishment'. Having been sorely
plundered on several occasions of practically everything he owned, including his son's and grandson's inheritance, Crewe added that he had nothing
left in life to lose.[45] Henry Townsend, of Gloucester, summed up many
people's feelings when he suggested that a new verse should be added to
the church's Litany:[46]

> From the plundering of soldiers, their insolence, cruelty, atheism,
> blasphemy, and rule over us, Lord Deliver us.

Soldiers and armies plundered for a number of reasons. For some it was simply a matter of staying alive. The garrison of Newbury, who stole Andrew Pottinger's sheep, killing him in the process, were 'half starved and . . . very desperate'.[47] Sir Samuel Luke, whose parliamentary garrison at Newport Pagnell was so poorly supplied that a couple of fellows had but a pair of breeches between them, was relieved to be able to seize some wagon loads of barley on their way to a brewer, and planned to kill the oxen which pulled them for meat.[48]

Horses (as William Davenport learned only too well), were an extremely attractive item of booty. The largest category of cases (30 per cent) heard after the war by the Indemnity Commission, set up to hear cases of alleged military violence against civilians, involved horses.[49] Cavalry and carters needed them. Stolen horses were highly mobile, hard to identify and almost impossible to recover. Sir Samuel Luke had to tell his cousin, Katherine Barker, that she had little chance of ever seeing her stolen mount again. Richard Napier, who had lost a horse to the royalists at Shrewsbury, begged Colonel Mytton that 'the next time you beat up the enemy's quarters, and take any of their horses, I pray take one for me'.[50]

Both sides regarded loot as a proper reward for a job well done. 'They deserved such encouragement by their excellent service and brave adventures', is how Chaplain Ashe defended the spoilage by his round-heads after Marston Moor.[51] 'The soldiers had the whole plundering of this rich Castle', wrote a parliamentary newspaper about the sack of Sherbourne, 'and to speak the truth they deserve it right well, for they carried themselves most resolutely.' Royalists agreed that the spoils of war were 'the soldiers' right for their hard service'. Commanders promised their men so many hours or even days of pillage if they successfully took a town. Afterwards many took French leave home with their loot, or if denied their due would desert or mutiny in protest. Thus the promise of plunder could become a two-edged sword. It could persuade men to fight, or (as Rupert's cavalry demonstrated at Edgehill and Naseby, and as numerous military commentators warned) it could seduce them into letting victory slip through their sticky fingers.[52]

Celtic troops had an infamous reputation for plundering in England. They were from lands where ethnic, religious and clan difference made fighting more violent. Being relatively poor and ill-equipped they made the most of the opportunities proffered by the wealth of England. Often unable to speak the victims' language they were more likely violently to grab what they wanted, rather than demand it, albeit with drawn sword in hand.

Soon after the civil war started parliamentary scribblers played on English fears. Their first diatribe, *The Welsh Plunder*, sold badly, probably because it was poorly written even by the abysmal standard of the propaganda of that day. Just as terrible was *The True Copy of a Welsh Sermon preached . . . by Shon ap Owen, priest*, a forgery in which a royalist chaplain urges the Welsh soldiers to invade England 'to spoil and plunder, burn and deface whole Towns and Villages'.

Some roundhead propagandists accused the royalists of crimes which their own soldiers were more likely to commit. *A True Declaration of Kingston's entertainment of the Cavaliers* (1642, T2668) claimed that the 'barbarous Behaviour' of the king's Irish and Welsh soldiers was worse than anything known on the Continent. Not only did they stable their horses in churches, and chop up the pews for firewood, but they and their horses used God's house – as well as those of His people – as a jakes.[53]

The reputation of the Scots as avid plunderers was far worse, and far more deserved. In a couple of days in 1645 some Caledonian troopers relieved Richard Richardson, a farmer from Bramshall, Staffordshire, of £6 worth of corn, peas and hay. That same year, during a six-week occupation, the covenanting army plundered Hereford of goods valued at £31,743 5s 2d, and the adjacent parishes of some £30,000 worth. They did so with such an enthusiasm and efficiency – which account books can never properly measure – that a hundred and eighty years later the townsfolk still told stories of the trauma: of how the Scots would prise rings from women's fingers: of how they would stop at nothing to find even the most carefully hidden booty. Captain Thomas Wathen of Hereford concealed his pack-horses in a pit dug in the ground. When the soldiers entered his house, Mere Court, one of them saw Wathen's son rocking his baby brother in a cradle. Picking up the infant, playing with and kissing it, the trooper soon won the boy's confidence. When he asked where was his father, the lad replied that he had gone to hide the horses.[54] It is no wonder that the inhabitants of Cleveland complained in 1646 that whereas the cavaliers had 'only sucked some of our "blood"' the Scots Army 'has devoured our flesh, and are now picking over our bones'.

By the following year the Scots reputation for rapacity was so odious that General David Leslie published two open letters maintaining that 'Never did Army live more peacefully and soberly than we have done.' He even got some forty-seven gentlemen from Nottinghamshire to sign a testimonial to this effect. It did no good.[55]

Sometimes troops plundered for political reasons. Thomas Bradley, a royalist soldier from Wolverhampton, took the opportunity of destroying his landlord's title-deeds when his comrades came across them as they were pillaging the parish chest.[56] Colonel Birch, who started life as a lowly carter, proudly wore the sword the high-born royalist Colonel Arundel surrendered to him in January 1645.

The symbolic significance of vandalizing cathedrals is obvious. At Canterbury Colonel Sande's troops used a statue of Christ for musket practice, cheering every time someone scored a bull's eye by hitting Our Saviour's head or heart. They smashed up the cathedral as one trooper played the current hit song 'The Zealous Soldier' on the organ:[57]

1 'And when did you last see your father?', painting by W. F. Yeames

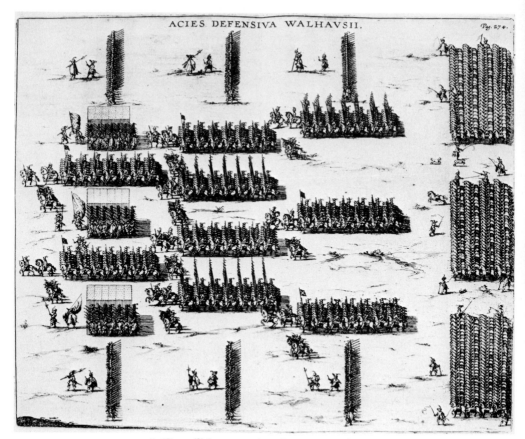

ACIES DEFENSIVA WALHAVSII.

2 'De militia equestri antiqua et nova', 1630

Fig: 7.
Par: 4.
Cap: 6.

3 'Militarie instructions for the cavallrie', 1632

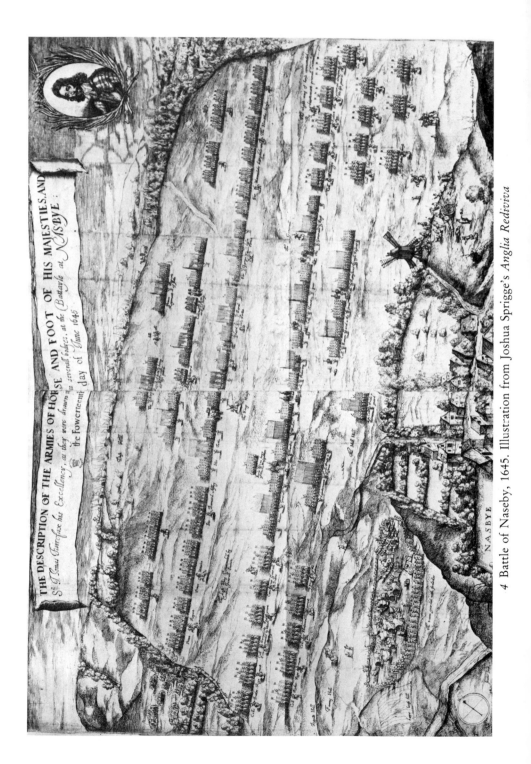

4 Battle of Naseby, 1645. Illustration from Joshua Sprigge's *Anglia Rediviva*

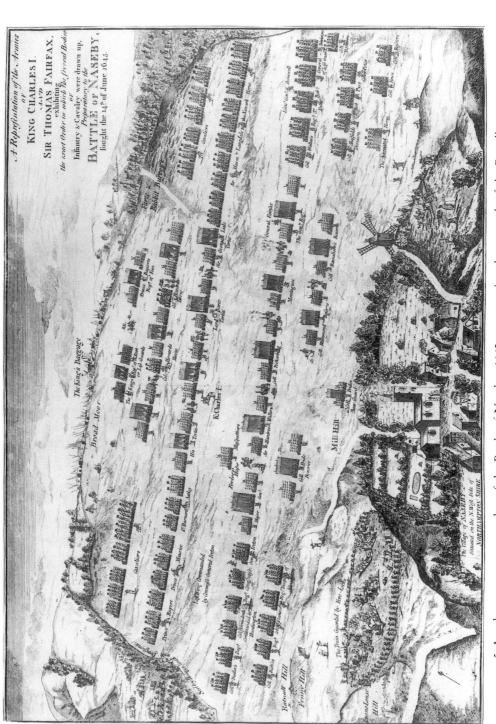

5 Another contemporary plan of the Battle of Naseby, 1645, exaggerating the strength of the Royalist army

THE ENGLISH IRISH SOVLDIER

With his new Difcipline, new Armes, Old Stomacke, and new taken pillage : who had rather Eate than Fight.   30

IF any Souldate
   think I do appeare,
In this ftrange Armes
   and pofture,as a jeere,
Let him advance up to me
   he fhall fee,
Ile ftop his mouth,
   and we wil bothagree.

Our Skirmifh ended,
   our Enemies fled or flain
Pillage wee cry then,
   for the Souldiers gaine,
And this compleat Artillery
   I have got,
The beft of Souldiers,
   I think, hateth not.

My Martiall Armes
   dealt I amongft my foes,
With this I charged ftand
   'gainft hungers blowes ;
This is Munition
   if a Souldier lacke,
He fights like *Iohn a dreams*,
   or Lents thin *Jacke*.

All fafe and cleare,
   my true Arms reft a while,
And welcome pillage,
   you have foes to foile ;
This Pot, my Helmet,
   muft not be forfaken,
For loe I feiz'd it
   full of Hens and Bacon.

Rebels for Rebels dreft it,
   but our hot roft,
Made them to flye,
   and now they kiffe the poft
And better that to kiffe,
   then ftay for Pullits,
And have their bellies
   cram'd with leaden bullets.

This fowle my Feather is,
   who wins moft fame,
To weare a pretty Duck,
   he need not fhame :
This Spit my well charg'd
   Musket, with a Goofe,
Now cryes come eate me,
   let your ftomacks loofe.

This Dripping pan's my
   target,and this Hartichoke
My Basket-hilted blade,
   can make 'em fmoake,
And make them flafh & cut,
   who moft Home puts,
Ile moft my fury
   fheatb into his guts.

This Forke my Reft is,
   and my Bandaleers
Canary Bottles,
   that can quell bafe feares,
And make us quaffe downe
   danger, if this not doe,
What is it then?can raife
   a fpirit into fearfull men.

This Match are links
   to light down to my belly
Wherin are darkfom chinks
   as I may tell yee,
Or Saffages, or Puddings,
   choofe you which,
An excellent Needle ,
   Hungers wounds to ftitch.

Thefe my Supporters,
   garter'd with black pots,
Can fteele the nofe ,
   & purg the brain of plots;
Thefe tofts my fhooeftrings,
   fteept in this ftrong fog,
Is abl of themfelves
   to foxe a Dog.

Thefe Armes being vanifht,
   once againe appeare
A true and faithful Souldier
   As you were ;
But if this wants,
   and that we have no biting
In our beft Armours
   we make forry fighting.

FINIS.

Printed at *London* for R. *Wood*,
   and *A. Cot.* 1642.

6 A 1642 caricature of a pillaging soldier

THE
Parliament of VVomen.

With the merrie Lawes by them newly
Enacted. To live in more Eafe, Pompe, Pride,
and wantonneffe : but efpecially that they might have fu-
periority and domineere over their husbands ; with a new way
found out by them to cure any old or new Cuckolds, and
how both parties may recover their credit
and honefty againe

London, Printed for *W. Wilfon* and are to be fold by him in
Will-yard in Little Saint *Bartholomewes*. 1646.

Aug: 14 London 1646

7 'The Parliament of Women', 1646

8 Prince Rupert's dog Boy, painted by his sister
Princess Louise

9 'A dog's elegy', from a contemporary satirical pamphlet, 1644, on the death
of the dog (right)

A
DOGS ELEGY,
OR
RVPERT'S TEARS,

For the late Defeat given him at *Marston-moore*, neer *York*, by the Three Renowned Generalls; *Alexander Earl of* Leven, *Generall of the Scottish Forces*, Fardinando *Lord* Fairefax, *and the Earle of* Manchester *Generalls of the English Forces in the North.*

Where his beloved Dog, named *B O Y*, was killed by a Valliant Souldier, who had skill in *Necromancy.*

Likewise the strange breed of this Shagg'd Cavalier, whelp'd of a Malignant Water-witch; With all his Tricks, and Feats.

york

Sad Cavaliers, *Rupert* invites you all   } Close-mourners are the Witch, Pope, & devill,
That doe survive, to his Dogs Funerall. } That much lament yo'r late befallen evill.

Printed at *London*, for G. B. July 27. 1644.

10 Hugh Peters, parliamentary army chaplain

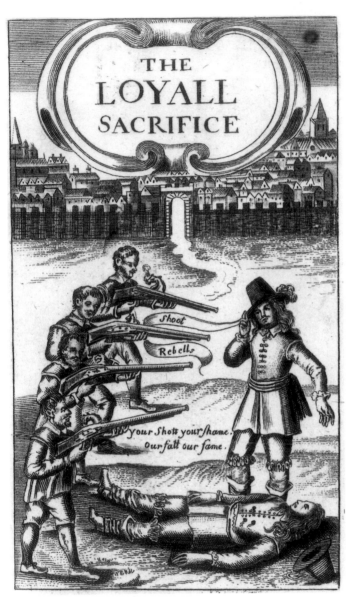

11 'The Loyall Sacrifice'

12 Scene from 'Les Misères et les malheurs de la guerre', showing the hanging of thieves. Etching by Jacques Callot, 1633

THE SIEGE OF BAZINGE HOUSE

A. THE OLDE HOVSE. B. THE NEW. C. THE TOWER THAT IS HALFE BATTERED DOWNE. D. THE KINGES BREAST WORKS. E. THE PARLIAMENTS BREAST WORKS.

13 The Siege of Basing House, 1645, in its final stages, with the principal tower destroyed

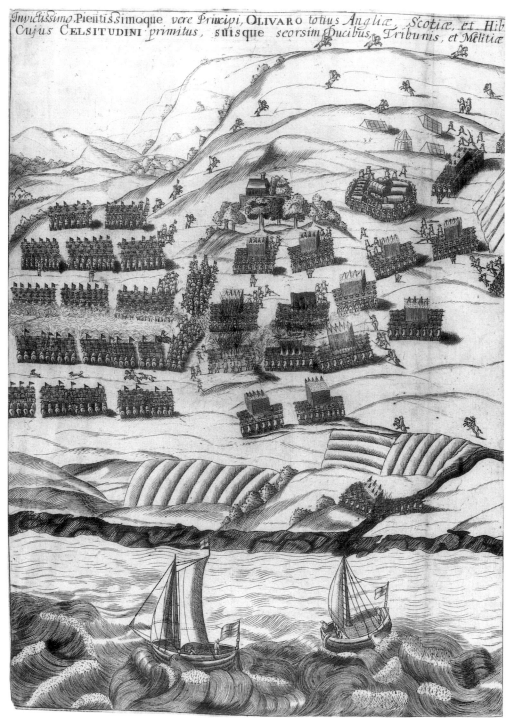

14 An engraving of the Battle of Dunbar, commissioned by Parliament in 1651

ternii PROTECTORI præpotentisimo F.F Fælicitatem, victorias, Triumphos
uiris Primipilaribus, hanc calcographicam Prælij Dunbarrensis Iconim DDD
Sold by Pet. Stent

Groote Tiraney bedreuen den Sr hy. syn vrau en kinderen
Groot Tiranny done agst Sr his wife antchilderen.

15 Atrocities in Ireland, 1641

16 Irish massacre scenes (right)

The Lord Blany force, to ride 14 miles with
out Bridle or Sadell, saue his life, his Lady
lodged in Straw being allowed 2d a day
to releue her & her Children, slew a kinsman
of hers and hanged him up before her face
2 dayes telling her she must expect the
same to terrifie her the moore.

I

Mr Dauenant and his Wife bound in their
Chaires Striped the 2 Eldest Children of 7
yeares old rosted upon Spittes before their
Parents faces Cutt their throte and after
murdred him.

K

5

Arthur Robinsons daughter 14 yeares old the
Rebells bound her armes a broad, deflowered
her one after an other, tell they spoyled her then
pulled the haire from her head and cut out her
tongue that she might not tell of their Cruelty,
but she declared it by writing.

L

A Minister and his wife came to Dublin Ian: 30
1641 left behinde him some goods with a sup:
posed frend sent for them but could not be de:
liuered unlesse he or his Wife came for them
she came and presently they hanged her upe.

M

6

A Woman mangled in so horred a maner that it
was not possible shee should be knowne &
after the Villaine washed his handes in her
bloode: was taken by the Troopers adiudged
to be hanged leaped of the lader & hanged
Himselfe like a Bloodey Tiger.

W

Companyes of the Rebells meeting with the
English stringe for their liues falling downe
before them cryinge for mercy thrust theire
into their Childrens bellyes & threw them into
the water.

X

11

George Forde hanged on a tree in his owne ground
Cut his flesh, a peaces, carying it up & downe,
sayinge this is the flesh of one of the traitors against
our Holy Father the Pope.

Y

a Proclamation that nether English nor Irish should
either sell or keepe in their houses any Powder upon
the losse of goods & life nether any Armes whatsoeuer.
exept with a licence & then but fiue pound at
most at 2 Shill ye pound

12

Front.
C
m m m m
m m m m S 4.
m m m m
D 2
m m m m
m m m m
m m m m
m m m m
m m m m
E.
p p p p
p p p p
p p p p
D 1
p p p p
p p p p
p p p p
p p p p
p p p p
S 1
p p p p
p p p p
p p p p
D 4
p p p p
p p p p
p p p p
p p p p
p p p p
S 2
m m m m
m m m m
m m m m
D 3
m m m m
m m m m
m m m m
m m m m
3 S m m m m
L
Reere.

CHAP. VII.

*Of Marching the Company in Divisions, with the order
and places of the Officers.*

Vr *Souldiers* now being somwhat *expert* in
their *distances*, we will next draw them
forth into a *deep March.* Wherefore note,
that our *files* must be at *order*, and our *Ranks*
at *open order :* the *Muskettiers* of the *right
flank,* are to make the *Van* , and to *march* next after the
Captain; The *Pikes* are to make the *battell*, and to *march*
after the *Ensigne*, either in one or two *divisions*, according
to their number. The *Muskettiers* of the *left flank* (sometimes called the *second division of Muskets*) make the *Reere
Guard*, which is *led* commonly by the *second Serjeant*.
Howbeit if there be but one *division* of *Pikes*, then the
eldest (or *chiefest*) *Serjeant* leads the *second division of
Muskettiers*. If the *Company* be but *small*, then it is best
to make but two *Divisions*, one of the *Muskettiers,* another of the *Pikes;* For the *placing* of the rest of the *Officers*, you may perceive by the *figure* in the Margent :
Wherefore note that M. stands for *Muskets*, p. for *Pikes*,
D. for *Drummes,* S. for *Serjeants,* E. for *Ensigne,* L. for
Livetenant, and C. for *Captaine.*

Note, if you have but three *Drummes*, then let the
Drumme in the second *division* of *Pikes* be wanting : If
onely two, then upon a *March* , the first between the
third and fourth *ranke* of the *front division* of *Muskettiers.*
The second between the third and fourth *ranke* of the
second *division of Pikes.*

Note that between each *Division* in *March,* there ought
to be 12. *foot distance;* 6. *foot* before the *Officer,* and 6. *foot*
behinde him.

CHAP.

17 A page from William Barriffe's Drill Book, 1639

A great and bloudy

FIGHT

AT

COLCHESTER,

AND

The storming of the Town by the Lord Generals Forces, with
the manner how they were repulsed and beaten off, and forced to retreat from the Walls, and a great and terrible
blow given at the said storm, by Granadoes and Gunpowder. Likewise their hanging out the Flag of Defiance, and
their sallying out upon Tuesday last, all the chief Officers
ingaging in the said Fight, and Sir *Charles Lucas* giving the
first onset in the Van, with the number killed and taken, and
Sir *Charles Lucas* his Declaration.

London, Printed for G. Beal, and are to be sold in the Old
Bayley, and neer Temple Bar, 1648.

18 'A great and bloody fight at Colchester', 1648

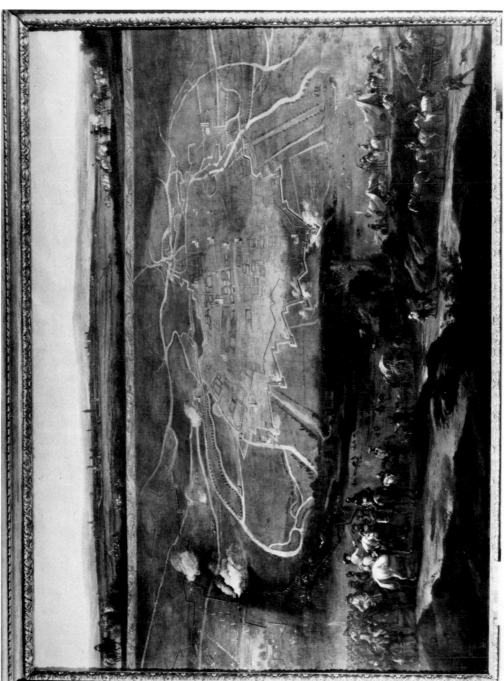

19 The Siege of Oxford by Ian de Wyck

20 Sir Edward Walker with Charles I by unknown artist

21 Portrait of John 1st Lord Byron by William Dobson

22 Colonel Thomas St Aubyn, by Popham

For God and His cause I'll count it gain
To lose my life. I can none happier die
Than to fall in battle to maintain
God's worship, truth, extirpate Papacy.

Their singing done, the troopers splintered the organ pipes as a result the instrument, although repaired, never sounded as sweet again.

When the roundheads captured Chichester in December 1642 they ran up and down the cathedral slashing the cushions with their swords, as their officers cheered them on. They ripped pages out of the prayer books, defaced pictures of the king and queen, smashed statues, ground down the chalice, broke the organ pipes with their halbards, and kneaded pieces of coal into the Bible. Being told that the silver plate had been hidden behind the panelling in the chapter house, the soldiers ripped it out as their commander, Sir Arthur Haselrig, urged them on: 'There boys! There boys! Hack it! Hack it! It rattles! It rattles!'[58]

Lichfield cathedral suffered badly after its capture in March 1643. Apart from smashing the organ, ripping the copes and surplices, and tearing down the tapestries, the troops uses dogs to hunt cats in the cathedral, thinking the echo of the barks and feline hisses off the vaulted cathedral roof great fun. For an encore they brought in a calf wrapped in linen, carried it to the font, and sprinkled it with water in a blasphemous parody of baptism.[59]

Many puritan troopers found the sacrament of baptism especially galling. The following year some rebel soldiers came across a baptism under way in Yaxley, Huntingdonshire. Barring entry into the church, they urinated into the font, in which they baptised a horse.[60] Beauty outraged them as much as holiness. Roundhead vandals trashed the Queen's Chapel in St James', throwing a Rubens into the Thames. At Winchester they broke into the muniment room, tossed some of the records into the river, and used others to make kites.[61]

How then are such incidents to be explained without recourse to postulations such as mindless violence, or anti-episcopal high jinks? One way of doing so is to set them within a military context.

Take Sir Thomas Myddleton's roundheads who kicked in Wrexham's church organ to melt down the metal pipes for musket bullets. At one level the explanation is simple. Short of ammunition they needed the lead to make a very different sort of music. Yet this unit had a reputation for dirty tricks. For instance during a siege, a few weeks earlier in December 1645, they had called out from the walls pretending to be old friends, and promising not to shoot. When the royalists emerged from cover they opened fire, killing six. Harry Brych, a cavalier officer, thought that Myddleton's men were as 'contemptible an enemy as ever we had in Ireland'. A few days later he was outraged to find what they had done to Hawarden parish church – the prayer books torn up and scattered all over the nave, the communion rails torn out and the altar dragged into the centre. 'Some of our soldiers came, and swore it was not right', concluded Brych.[62]

To give another example, the roundheads who hunted cats and baptized a calf in Lichfield cathedral did not do so for unthinking fun: they had just survived some very bitter fighting, in which prisoners had been executed.

In sum, plunder could be a practical way of obtaining military necessities, such as bullets (while providing the added bonus of smashing organs that produced music that most puritans thought papist). Plunder was also a way to demonstrate the power that the armed have over the unarmed. Finally, it could be a satisfying outlet for relieving the ecstasy of victory and the despair of defeat, particularly after an especially vicious fight.

At its least harmful plunder could be a way to vent high spirits. Captain John Hodgson remembered that during the Scots campaign of 1650 someone found a large barrel full of cream which he brought to the officers' mess. They drank it by the dishful, some filling their hats with cream. When the churn was nearly empty two officers turned it upside down over a third's head, so he could lick the inside as the cream dribbled down all over his clothes. Everyone thought it hilarious, including Oliver Cromwell who paused to watch the fun.[63]

Food – which is a great comforter in times of trouble – played an important role in plundering, even in the heat of battle. When the London Trained Bands assaulted Basing House in 1643 they came across an outhouse full of food, which they promptly started to eat, musket fire, cannon balls and a burning roof notwithstanding. A year later, after the Scots had broken through the defences of Newcastle, a company chanced upon a christening feast. As some thirty guests were about to toast the infant, the convenanters burst in, collapsing the banquet table, sending meat and drink flying. The Scots promptly grabbed the vittles, before relieving their hosts of their clothes, money and furniture. In the latter instance a sense of grievance could have augmented the need to eat in order to assuage fear and control elation, because after the sack of Newcastle many common soldiers were outraged that their officers seemed to have got the pick of the loot.[64]

When defeated troops plundered to assuage their sense of shame the consequences could be frightful. After putting up a poor show at Edgehill, Colonel Mostyn's Flintshire regiment was sent to do garrison duty at Chester. The royalists got out of hand and sacked St Mary's Nunner, the town house of Sir William Brereton, the local rebel leader. After being beaten in Cheshire, Ashton's cavaliers brutally plundered Droitwich and Bromsgrove, taking goods from their own county. In Lancashire Prince Rupert's men plundered from friend and foe alike, seizing cattle, sheep and chickens, and killing all who tried to stop them, in a blind rage at having just been defeated at Marston Moor.[65]

Men pillaged through thick and thin. Nehemiah Wharton greatly enjoyed plundering. As a soldier in the London Trained Bands he was free of the restrictions of civilian life, which the erstwhile apprentice may have found most irksome. Even decent family men such as the Reverend Ralph Josselin relished using other people's possessions. At Grantham on 11 September 1644, the parliamentary chaplain noted in his diary, 'We quartered at Mr. Wolph's, a grand malignant. We had a good lodging and diet.' A survivor described how the soldiers lorded it over the country folk of Shropshire: 'They ride up and down, with swords, muskets and dragoons, to the great terror of the people.'

Quite simply plunder was great fun. John Ward, a parliamentary trooper who took part in the capture and sack of Worcester, promptly wrote a poetic paean on the ecstasy. A Devonshire ditty (here modernized, for the dialect is hard to comprehend) described the joys of rapine in a coarser fashion:[66]

> I will work no more
> Do you think I will labour to be poor
> I will sell my cart and also my plough.
> And get a sword if I know how.
> For if I mean to be right
> First I will learn to swear and roar.
>
> But first a warrant it is fit
> From Mr. Captain that I get . . .
> For then I have power in my place
> To steal a horse without disgrace,
> And beat the wives too.

Another street ballad, *The Mercenary Soldier*, repeated this theme in 1646:

> I come not forth to do my country good,
> I come to rob and take my fill of pleasure.

As the war continued, plunder – like so many other activities – became institutionalized in order to limit its damage and enhance its profitability. In 1643 some Staffordshire villagers paid Captain Corbet's troops 13s 4d not to purloin when they spent the night in the parish church. At the same time the churchwardens of St Michael's, Bedwardine, Worcestershire, paid 3 shillings less to some troopers 'for preserving our church goods and writings'. Sixteen leading royalists from Gloucester offered the king a large sum of money in the spring of that year if his forces would spoil only parliamentarians after they had taken the city. Two years later, during the successful Siege of Bristol, Fairfax promised his men two weeks' pay if they gave up the traditional perquisite of a sack. The city fathers were only too happy to contribute to the cost of being spared, while the soldiers were pleased not to have to auction off their loot in a buyer's market.[67]

Because the troops could not carry their swag on the march, markets were often organized to dispose of the proceeds of a successful pillage. After a whole day stripping Weaverham, Cheshire, the royalists held a special fair at Timperley to hawk off the results. On the other side the local county committee might organize such a sale. Following the capture of Chichester they organized a special market, at which, one committee member vouched to a friend, there would be plenty of bargains because 'the soldiers do usually sell cheap'.[68]

By 1644, Ireland, a poor country, had been so badly ravaged that the Council of War had to issue a set of orders how shares of plunder were to be distributed according to rank. It is unlikely, however, that these were followed, for by now conditions had become so decayed, and the war so vicious, that men needed to loot all they could simply to stay alive.[69]

Private enterprise was sometimes used to circumvent the open market. Joyce Hammon managed to buy back for 21s 6d from Captain Gammon some gold and two beaver hats that his men had plundered from her house in Hereford. During William ffarington's absence fighting for the king, the roundheads plundered his house of goods valued at £428 9s 4d. His wife, Margaret, petitioned the local parliamentary commander for their return, saying that they included several family heirlooms. When he offered to let her have them for a bargain price of £350 she balked, and sought the help of her cousin, admittedly a distant one, Ralph Asherton. After Asherton, a parliamentary officer, had arranged for the goods to be transferred to the custody of his company, he advised Margaret that if she would not pay the £350, he could not stop his men from selling her husband's goods for what they would fetch, and that she would never see them again. The fact that he had the gall to sign this thinly veiled blackmail note 'your very loving cousin' could have done nothing to relieve Mrs ffarington's distress.[70]

Sometimes relatives were no protection. Abraham Curtis of Wrexhall, Warwickshire, had three boys, all serving in the parliamentary army. Yet in March 1644 troops from one of his son's companies pillaged him.[71] The terrifying thing about plunder is that soldiers could turn upon their masters. In 1649 a company of roundheads burst into the house of William Prynne, a radical who had been an obdurate enemy of Charles I's for over two decades, having had his ears sliced off and his face branded for his opposition. They roughed up his servants, drank up his beer, smashed up the crockery, took all his money. In all, Prynne recalled, they 'hallowed, roared, stamped, beat the tables with their swords and muskets like so many bedlams, swearing, cursing, blaspheming at everyword.'

One stage removed from plunder was the officially sanctioned practice of free quarter, which as William Hill, a yeoman for Newent, Gloucester painfully learned, was demanded under duress. When in April 1644 Colonel Mynne's regiment of Irish troops moved into the village, Sir Edward Clark, the leading local royalist, ordered the householders to provide them with food and lodging. When Hill demurred 'with sword in hand' Sir Edward went to the yeoman's cottage, and 'said that if he knew anyone in the Town that would not open his doors to let in Colonel Mynne's soldiers, he would break it open'.[72]

The threat of violence lurked behind every encounter between soldiers and civilians, causing resentments which festered for years. During the war neighbours assessed and collected your taxes. Captains did, often with a squad of musketeers behind them, and always demanding and receiving far more than they had in the halcyon days of peace.[73]

The war was less than two months old when the city fathers of Gloucester learned that sad lesson. Eighty-seven rebel troopers arrived on 21 October 1642 to guard the bridge over the River Severn. Straightaway they demanded that the city authorities pay them. Mayor Dennis Wise tried to buy them off with what he optimistically called loans, as he wrote warning parliament that their troops would turn vicious unless they received their arrears very soon. The Mayor and city officers of Preston tried to placate Prince Rupert and his senior officers with a sumptuous feast. 'Banquets were not fit for soldiers' declared the king's nephew as he threw the worthies into jail.[74]

The probability of violence if they refused to billet and feed soldiers, was nearly as certain as the chances of being paid if they complied were remote. Householders were expected to furnish their enforced guests with food and lodging at a set rate in return for an IOU signed by an officer or NCO promising to redeem their expenses at some later date, the costs being met from the soldiers' pay. Because soldiers were rarely and tardily paid, little remained to discharge such tickets, particularly those issued by the king's army.

Financially the cost of free quarter and plunder was immense. A 1645 petition from Bedfordshire, a county which saw comparatively little fighting, claimed that such exactions had cost £50,000. Dr Morrill has estimated that in Cheshire soldiers extorted £120,000 in free quarter, far more than the amount the county raised in taxes, while villages claimed to have lost plundered goods worth an additional £190,000.[75]

Psychologically free quarter could be as painful as plunder, for it involved extending the very personal act of hospitality in one's own home to someone you had not invited, whom you might not like, indeed could well hate, and who might behave in an abominable fashion about which you could do nothing. Knowing they had scant chance of redeeming the chits they had been given for providing free quarter, many householders tried to serve their uninvited guests the worst possible food, which further exacerbated the relations between forced host and reluctant guest.

During the summer of 1643 the royalists troopers who were billeted on the puritan minister of Wrington, Somerset, were encouraged to be on their worst behaviour until he returned to using the Laudian forms of worship. On the other side of the coin, as Sir James Turner, the Thirty Years' War veteran who invaded England with the convenanters in 1644, explained, it was very hard to get a soldier who had endured the hunger, danger, and hardships of a campaign to settle down and behave himself in someone else's home. Such unwanted guests could vent the anger they felt towards the soft life of 'civvie street', by demanding the finest food and accommodation and violently expressing their displeasure when it was not forthcoming. Even when officers strictly supervised free quarter, Turner admitted the abuse of the system 'continues heavy and great'.

John Nicholas could not have agreed more. After being plundered thrice in one week of May 1643 the royalist gentleman was forced to hide amid the insalubrious droppings of his pigeon loft. The following May he was relieved of a further £500 and had to provide free quarter for five captains and fifty other ranks 'so that my house hath been in worse case than an inn'. Another royalist, the poet John Taylor, sardonically noted how quickly every rogue learned to help himself to whatever he wanted by uttering the phrase 'free quarter'. 'We call it free quarter. What a grief!' fulminated John Hacket,[76]

> to be made servile to provide for such guests, and when the family knew it was Judas that dipped his hand with him in the dish, what an expense it was to bring out all the stores, laid up for a year, and to waste it in a week.

In some ways wartime taxation, assessments and sequestration can be regarded as a form of officially sanctioned plunder. They were often extracted with the threat of violence, especially in disputed areas. When the Worcestershire parliamentary committee sent a tax demand for £10 a month to Elmley Lovett they warned the villagers that if they did not start paying within three days 'you will answer the contrary at your peril of pillaging and plundering, and your houses fired, and your persons imprisoned'.[77] Even the mild-mannered poet William Phylip of Hendre Fechan had to threaten his neighbours with violence after being appointed a tax collector. The fact that the bard did so in Welsh verse with the grace of an Eistedfodd champion and the determination of one of Her Majesty's Inspectors of Revenue, did little to hide the implied threat of force:[78]

> Here is the sealed demand of a saint – pray
> Pay without delay.

Lest the saint (his lust he concedes not),
Becomes an angry Devil.

Each side tried to get the other to pay for the war. Defeated loyalists had
their estates sequestered, and had to negotiate to buy them back. The
degree of their involvement in the king's causes determined the price,
while none of the proceedings afforded them anything like due process.[79]
And if they were squeezed dry until the pips squeaked, few victors
minded.

The war was immensely expensive. In terms of the gross national product
its cost may not have been exceeded until the world wars of the twentieth
century.[80] To support the fighting it has been estimated that Oxfordshire
paid £60,000 a year, seventeen times more than it had to fork out in ship
money. At the other end of the scale the expenses of the village constables
of Belton, Leicester rose from £9 7s. 1d. in 1638 to £32 16s. 7d. in 1644.[81]
Exeter spent £18,479 12s. 10d. in ten weeks during the summer of 1643
rebuilding its defences. Sieges cost Gloucester £28,740 and Chester £72,826
12s. 6d. War damaged incomes. The Duchess of Newcastle estimated that
the war had cost her husband £941,300. The war not only ruined Worcester's economy and tax base, but increased the proportion of its population
on poor relief from the peacetime average of 4–5 per cent to 23 per cent
in 1623. Sleaford Grammar School could not collect a penny from its
endowments between 1644 and 1646 because 'these times were so confused
in respect of the wars'.[82]

After the war contemporaries remarked on the damage all around them.
'there is scarce a house in the town that is not flattened, and scarce a
room is not into which shot hath not been made', observed William Jessop
of the ruins of Lyme after the siege.[83] The villagers of Marston complained
that their houses had been destroyed, their fruit trees chopped down, and
their fields so ruined by the construction of earthworks during the Siege
of Oxford that they could no longer farm them. Troops blew up Chipping
Campden, they razed Basing House, they demolished Corfe Castle's walls,
and turned Pembroke Castle into a shell. They smashed in Canterbury
cathedral's stained glass, burned Winchester's record office, toppled the
central spire at Lichfield cathedral, and melted down every piece of silver
plate they could lay their hands upon. Over a hundred and forty towns
in England, and heaven knows how many in Scotland and Ireland, suffered
significant war damage. Sometimes it was direct destruction, such as the
loss of 286 buildings in Gloucester during the siege. More often it resulted
from the decision to level houses, particularly outside city walls, to provide
defenders with clear fields of fire. Defenders blew up 241 houses at
Leicester; 400, valued at £40,000, at Worcester; and 200 worth £49,330 at
Farringdon.[84]

In 1649 John Taylor, poet, water bailiff and ardent scribbler, went on a 600-mile journey in the west of England 'to see', he explained to all who would buy his travelogue, 'the wonders of the West'. He began:

> It's a mad world (My masters) and in sadness
> I travelled widely in these days of madness,
> Eight years a frenzy did this land molest,
> The ninth year seemed to be like the rest.

Farringdon he described as 'a good handsome town, turned into ashes and Rubbish'. The front of Wells cathedral he reported as badly defaced. All over Devon and Cornwall there was considerable damage, while Exeter was 'turned all to ruins, rubbish, cinders ashes and fume'. Two years later in a second travel book, Taylor reported that Lichfield 'is so spoiled', Harlech was 'almost inhabitable', while the lead roof of St David's cathedral had been stripped for bullets.[85]

The overall picture of Wales that Taylor paints is one of relative prosperity. Landlords' rentals very quickly returned to their pre-war level. Although there is no doubt that the war did immense damage, the nature of warfare limited its effects. Battlefields were not turned into the devastated landscapes of, say, the Somme or Caen. Artillery wiped out few buildings, even though many castles were slighted, they were militarily obsolete, and had not to be replaced. Unlike a modern economy, that of pre-industrial England lacked a vulnerable and crucial infrastructure. Few bridges were destroyed, and even though that at Upton-upon-Severn was not repaired until 1830, there were plenty of alternative ways of crossing the river nearby. The pace of restoration could be slow. It took Exeter thirty years to completely rebuild its suburbs, while at York and Gloucester the job was not complete until the eighteenth century. Of a sample of 39 destroyed churches, 4 were rebuilt by the Restoration, 10 by 1700, 7 by 1800, and 7 remained in ruins. Yet there is no evidence that such delays damaged either the local or national economies.[86]

As the war went on and the killing increased, each side seemed to care less about the other, and plunder became more common, brutal and organized. Just as the parliamentarians vented their frustrations on Irish prisoners so the royalists increasingly went in for plunder. For them – unlike the roundheads – it grew into a necessity, with the decline of their supply lines: unable to control plunder the royalists lost the first civil war. On the other side the Committee of Both Kingdoms in Westminster, as well as roundhead commanders in the field, issued strict orders for the exemplary punishment of plunderers. While the royalist Captain Richard Coe recorded the hanging of plunderers without comment in his diary, the puritan Chaplain Sprigge thought that the execution in October 1645 of a trooper chosen by lot from four condemned to death for pillaging Winchester 'made a good impression on the soldiery'.[87]

Unlike many royalist commanders (whom both the brutality of the Thirty Years' War, as well as a desire to punish the rebels, had hardened), most parliamentary leaders realized that plunder was inherently counter-productive. 'I know that the soldier's plunder is but a bottomless bag', Sir William Brereton told the House of Commons in April 1645, 'the state loses by it: the soldier does not account it for pay . . . our reputation is extremely lost thereby with the common people.' In a strikingly modern phrase he concluded that by controlling plunder, particularly when compared to the excessive pillage wreaked by the enemy, 'we then gained their hearts'.[88] The other side agreed. In March 1645 Sir Edward Nicholas wrote in the king's name to Sir William Campion that if he could stop his garrison from plundering he would win 'hearts to his majesty and affections to his Service'.[89]

A classic example of the effectiveness of controlling plunder in winning the hearts, if not the minds, of seventeenth-century Englishmen and women can be seen in the Western Campaign of 1645. Not only were parliamentary soldiers encouraged to fight by being told that they were saving their fellow countrymen from cavalier rapine, but they were strictly and effectively forbidden to maraud. Not even Chaplain Hugh Peters was allowed to destroy Stonehenge, which he thought was a 'monument of heathenness', as his regiment marched past.[90] In May 1645 General Edward Massey justified his order to spare Malmesbury by telling his men that 'he could not judge any part of England to be an Enemy's country, nor an English town capable of devastation by English soldiers'.[91] In addition the New Model Army won friends by promptly paying off the chits it issued for taking free quarter. Such magnanimity brought an immediate military dividend. Civilians supported the invaders with food, lodging and, most precious of all, intelligence. As a consequence the enemy surrendered in droves.[92]

In contrast Charles's inability and reluctance to control the rapacity of his men cost him dear. As defeat loomed and supplies shrank, the cavaliers proved the Duke of Wellington's adage that 'a starving army is worse than none'. Admittedly the crown executed a few looters: the army marched past two swinging corpses at Badminton on 13 July 1644, and a couple more at Stratton Down thirteen days later. Such examples had little effect. William Maurice, a royalist gentleman from Flintshire, complained that the cavaliers were 'plundering and impoverishing the country extremely'.[93] Sir Edward Walker agreed that the behaviour of his own side was enough to turn anyone into a rebel. 'If they would fight more and plunder less', sighed Sir John Colepeper about the king's soldiers. When they took Huntingdon in August 1645 the few royalists in Oliver Cromwell's home town welcomed them with much bowing and scraping. Grovelling made not a jot of difference. After drinking 'by the pailful', the soldiers plundered friend and foe alike, seizing all the horses they could find, and driving off seven hundred cattle which they ransomed back to their owners. Even the king, who was notoriously tolerant of such abuses, was outraged. He ordered two men to be hanged, one for plundering a tradesman and the other for robbing a church.[94]

In early 1645 the villagers of Brent Knoll discovered what it was like to be plundered by desperate and defeated troops.[95] On 25 March some sixty royalist cavalry were billeted on the village. They were a scratch lot, mostly from Colonel Ascough's and Colonel John Tynte's regiments with a few from Lord Hawley's, which helps explain their outrageous behaviour. Certainly their officers did nothing to restrain them. Lieutenant Henry Tynte announced that in his opinion all country folk 'were fools and . . . were good for nothing but to be made idiots'.

In one regard, at least, no one could accuse the soldiers of disobeying their officer's inclinations. They broke into John Jones's house to steal 25 shillings, and took 12 bushels of malt and 6 yards of cloth from William Weakes's home. Three troopers, Francis Swift, Richard Hutchings and John Parsons, who were billeted on Henry Simons, stole his 'fat Bullock', which they gave to a servant. When Simons tried to reclaim it they beat him up, and threatened to run his wife through with their swords if she did not fetch a rope to hang her husband. Discretion proved the better part of matrimony. Having placed the noose about Simons's neck, with many foul oaths the soldiers swore to string him up. Only the immediate offer of 20 shillings assuaged their anger and saved his life.

Simons was lucky to survive (although one wonders whether his marriage did as well). Having stolen thirty horses some troops murdered a labourer on the Axminster road. A private threatened to despoil Mr. Tythingham if he did not hand over three quarters of beans or oats. When Tythingham proffered only six bushels, the brute snarled that he would string him up if he did not give him 40 shillings.

Outrage followed outrage. While drinking at the King's Head pub, two soldiers, Abraham Williams and John Rogers, fell out. Williams drew his sword, slashed at Rogers, cutting his staff in half. It must have been made of strong wood (or else the sword of the softest metal), for Williams's weapon broke. Incensed, he leapt down from his horse to slice open Roger's face with the shattered end.

Within eleven days (that included an Easter Sunday) the royalists plundered £687 worth of goods from eighty-five inhabitants of Brent Knoll. (In the same time they took £850 from the smaller adjacent hamlet of Berrow, after threatening to burn every house there to the ground.) Losses suffered in Brent Knoll ranged from Thomas Coulbroke's 4 shillings to John Somerset's £100.

Thus it is no surprise that John Somerset – who had once served the crown as a captain – became the village-Hampden. On 4 April he led a spontaneous attack against the soldiers. Armed only with pikes, staves and muskets they caught the troopers napping. Although no one was killed, several were wounded, including an officer who was shot in the thigh. When he banged at Thomas Gilling's door demanding sanctuary from the pursuing mob, Gilling told him to 'begone, begone'.

Once reinforcements arrived from Bristol the villagers did not have a chance. They were harshly fined. Colonel Ascough had Somerset and Gilling arrested on the general charge of leading an 'insurrection' against His Majesty's forces, and specifically for ordering Private Abraham Williams to be beaten up. The latter charge sounds most spurious, since Williams was the thug who slashed John Roger's face with his broken sword. Ascough could well have trumped it up to justify his men's plunder. Nonetheless their lawyer, William Morgan, advised Somerset and Gilling that if they went before a court-martial they had not a prayer of proving either their innocence or the soldiers' crimes. From Bristol gaol the pair petitioned Sir Ralph Hopton and the Prince of Wales to be released, and after five weeks they were freed on bail. Never brought to trial, and having forfeited their bail money, they returned home to survive as best they could. Somerset, the erstwhile royalist captain who defied the king's troops, had his estate sequestered by parliament in 1651, and survived by four years to see the Restoration, unlike Gilling, who died in 1658, the same year as Oliver Cromwell.

For its victims plunder involved the blatant seizure of their property without the customary reticence of theft. It was an outrageous violation whose scars could last a lifetime. On the other hand plunder became a way of life for the perpetrators that gave some meaning to otherwise meaningless lives as soldiers in the civil war. Indeed at the local level fighting between garrisons all too frequently became little more than a gangland contest to control protection rackets. A few grew resigned to the abuse. Alexander Broome sang:[96]

> Now our lives,
> Children, wives,
> And estate
> Are a prey to the lust and plunder
> To the rage
> Of our age.

Some men joined the military to avoid being continually plundered: others did so to be better able to 'rob and plunder without control'.[97] Robert Wilson, the isolate of that most beautiful Hertfordshire village of Ashwell, threatened to have the cavaliers plunder any farmer who refused to pay him the high wages he demanded as a day labourer. Lucy Hutchinson condemned plunderers as 'the scum of mankind'. A pamphleteer declared that the good folk of Lancashire had 'resolved to fight it out rather than their Beef and fat bacon shall be taken from them'. The latter response, as the growth of the Clubmen movement showed, was to become the most common reaction to this scourge, which, more than anything else, forced the mass – perhaps the majority of people – who wanted to remain safely neutral, into facing the full horrors of civil war.[98]

12

I DON'T WANT TO GO TO WAR

> I don't want to be a soldier,
> I don't want to go to war.
> I'd sooner hang around
> Piccadilly Underground,
> Living off the earnings of a high born lady.
> Martin Page (ed.), *The Songs and Ballads*
> *of World War II* (1975), 21

In August 1643 a crowd of women gathered outside parliament to demand peace. Estimates of their number ranged from six thousand to three hundred. Reports as to their quality varied equally wildly. One described them as the respectable wives of sober citizens, many suckling their babes: another called them 'Whores, Bawds, Oyster-Women, Kitchen-Stuffe women, Beggar women and the very scum of the scum of the suburbs, besides an abundance of Irish women.' But whatever their number and social status, of one thing there can be no doubt: they and their families wanted peace, and didn't want to go to war.[1] Anticipating the reluctant Tommies of the Second World War, many a seventeenth-century soldier sang:[2]

> I cannot act a soldier's part
> Nor freezing lie in trenches.
> But wish myself with all my heart
> At Chelsea with my wenches.

Historians have often been surprised by the small proportion of the population of the British Isles who took part in the civil wars. Even though these wars were relatively the bloodiest in the islands' history, nonetheless only a small percentage of the adult male population served in the armed forces and even fewer saw action. Children, women, the old, the sick and infirm, all played little direct part in the civil wars, as did many active males who would rather hang around at home living off their own civilian earnings.

The English civil war was not yet a year old when Sir Robert Poyntz described the attitude to fighting in the West Country:[3]

> The Gentry come in apace, but the commons not so heartily, not in any considerable number. The true reason is . . . my countrymen love their pudding at home better than musket and pike abroad, and if they could have peace, care not what side had the better.

During the 1640s most people in the British Isles were more concerned about the mundane happenings within their own orbits than with the earth-shattering events outside. If politics attracted more of their attention than it had before – and would after – most folk were nonetheless far more concerned with buying and selling, making love, money and marriages, having and bringing up children, seeing friends, and paying bills. Although Catholics fought for the king in disproportionately high numbers, as a whole most tried to stay out of the war. 'The most remarkable fact that emerges', writes K. J. Lindley, 'is the extent of Catholic Neutralism during the war. In every county studied the great majority of Catholics were neutral throughout the hostilities.'[4]

For Catholics, as for all religious groups, participation in the war increased with social and economic status. For only 48 per cent of the Warwickshire gentry has evidence been found of some active commitment to either side, be that of a high level, such as fighting, or a marginal one, such as collecting a tax or levy, or spreading propaganda. Of Cheshire's 200 gentry, 40 (20 per cent) took action for the king, 56 (28 per cent) for parliament, leaving 52 per cent neutral. Participation rates for the gentry of other counties vary, ranging from 14 per cent in Suffolk, 38 per cent in Lancashire, 65 per cent in Yorkshire, to an astounding 90 per cent for a group of 38 gentlemen in south-east Berkshire. Merchants tended to be far less active. Of about 200 in Bristol, a city which suffered from some of the war's heaviest fighting, only 30 (15 per cent) showed a minimal commitment to either side, of whom about 20 inclined towards the king.[5]

Unfortunately we lack similar figures for common folk, and have to rely on general impressions.

Looking back on the war, Thomas Hobbes agreed with Poyntz's diagnosis. 'There were very few of the common people that cared much for either of the causes', wrote the political philosopher, who added that when conscripted common soldiers 'had not much mind to fight, but were glad of any occasion to make haste home'.[6] This lack of an ideological motivation also made it easier for troops to change sides once taken prisoner. Modern historians agree that 'a majority had no deep-seated convictions behind their choice of sides'.[7] One of 'the most striking features' of the civil war, writes Lawrence Stone, was the 'almost total passivity of the rural masses'. The war in Somerset, at least, it has been argued, was fought between two minorities who became mere cannon fodder as they struggled to swim against a tide of neutralism and apathy, that developed an increasingly dangerous rip the more it ebbed down the social scale. 'Most of the inhabitants of West Sussex', we are told, 'were sullen and apathetic about the war.'⁸ Such a lack of interest was voiced by the yokel who (according to a story that is as unreliable as it is worth telling) was ploughing Marston Moor the morning before the battle. Told to get the hell out, since king and parliament needed his fields for another purpose, the surprised rustic asked, 'What! Has them two buggers fallen out?'⁹

Before the formal declaration of war the fear of what might happen if them two ever did fall out was widespread. On 30 July 1642 the Earl of Kingston vowed to stay neutral. 'When, said he, if I take arms with the king against parliament, or with the parliament against the king, let a common bullet decide between them.' (In fact a cannon ball rather than a common bullet made the decision. Being taken a parliamentary prisoner to Hull aboard a pinnace that came under friendly fire, he stood up to persuade the royalist artillery to cease: unhappily a ball cut him in half.)¹⁰ Fear of such an end could well have persuaded a Birmingham gentleman to vow 'I never had any intention, nor yet have, of taking up arms on either side.'¹¹

The committed were contemptuous of their fellow countrymen's reluctance to get involved. 'They care not what government they live under', fulminated Sir Arthur Haselrig, 'so long as they may plough and go for market.'¹² But the horns of the dilemma that impaled many people were far more pointed than the parliamentary commander was willing to concede. As thirty-three of William Davenport's Cheshire tenants put it in a petition: 'we would not for the world harbour a disloyal thought against His Majesty, yet we dare not lift up our hands against that honourable assembly parliament'. Sir James Vaughan of Trawscoed shared the same dilemma. When the war started the distinguished lawyer agonized with a friend what he should do 'to keep even with the world, and to secure himself from trouble, at the same time doing no harm to the king and country, but as much good as he could to both'. Countless others agreed. 'I never had any intention, nor yet have, of taking up arms of neither side, my Reason', explained Jonathan Langley, a Shropshire gentleman, 'leads me to both King and Parliament.' After being released from prison at Windsor Castle for taking part in a royalist rising at Great Yarmouth, Thomas Knyvett thought it 'wonderful strange' that men preferred to fight each other rather than find 'a middle way of accommodation'.¹³

Popular songs and verses indicate the widespread desire to stay out of the war.¹⁴

> From Extempore prayers and Godly ditty.
> From the churlish government of a city.

From the power of a country committee.
Libera Nos Domine.

John Rous copied into his diary another rhyme that encapsulated the dilemma neutrals faced:[15]

> For if by force of arms the king prevails,
> He is invited to a tyranny.
> But if, by strength of Parliament, he fails,
> We heap continual wars upon posterity.
> Then he that is not for accommodation
> Loves neither God, nor Church, nor King, nor Nation.

The snag was that on both sides those who were setting the pace remained firmly opposed to any accommodation. Thomas Barrow, a linen draper from Kent, stranded in London, recognized as much. 'If I might but stand as a neutral I should be well, but follow my own and not look after another's business,' he wrote to Henry Oxinden, 'but if I must show myself to one side, I must go according to my conscience, though I suffer from it.'[16] Henry Oxinden could well sympathize with his friend's dilemma. Two years earlier, in July 1642, the king had appointed him to the commission of array, while parliament had made him a county commissioner, hoping to force him off the fence on to their side. 'Caught between Scylla and Charybdis', Oxinden lamented, 'Nothing but Omnipotence can bring me clearly and reputably off.'[17]

Charles had no doubts as to what subjects such as Henry Oxinden should do. 'The time is now come for my faithful friends to show themselves', wrote the king time and time again.[18] 'No neutrality is admitted', agreed Sir Arthur Roe a couple of months afterwards, 'Both parties resolve that those who are not with them are against them.'[19] Convinced that when forced off the fence more gentleman would land on his side than on parliament's turf, the king tried to shift waverers by promiscuously sending them commissions of array, ordering them to raise troops for the crown. Thus in the North Midlands 42 per cent of those who received commission of array remained neutral, compared to only 26 per cent of the parliamentary county commissioners.[20]

This does not, however, mean that the parliamentarians were more tolerant of trimmers. As General William Waller declared, 'We shall take them for nothing more than enemies to the State and men accordingly to be proceeded against.' After staying neutral for the first three years of the war, Richard Baxter became a roundhead chaplain, and with a convert's zeal declared it 'to be a great sin for Men . . . to be Neuters'.[21]

Those who wished to stay sitting on the fence in spite of intense pressure to come down, had a number of options: they could maintain a low profile, they could remove themselves from the scene, they could try to placate both sides, or else they could organize with fellow neutrals to force king and parliament to leave them alone.

Many people managed to avoid being caught up in the war. In the Dacre household at Herstmonceux in East Sussex (which unlike the west of the county saw little fighting), family life continued much as before. The Dacres cut the grain, slaughtered cattle, bought new chamber pots for the bedrooms and coal buckets for the kitchen stoves. The tinker called, and there were fresh cherries to be picked. Two hundred miles away to the north at Elmswell, Yorkshire, Henry Best continued farming as usual with hardly an interruption. The only real indication that there was a war going on found in Best's memorandum book was a note that he had transferred the payment of the fee farm from the king to parliament in 1644. Best was lucky to be left unmolested, especially after parliament imprisoned his brother as a radical unitarian, for when they suspected John Alford's son of royalism, the Sussex gentleman disavowed him, telling a friend that the lad 'must stand and fall by his own affections, the misery of the times is such as what was black yesterday is white today'.[22] Years after the conflict was over a Midlands rector wrote in the parish register his recipe for successful trimming: 'when an uncivil war was being waged most fiercely between King and Parliament throughout the greater part of England, I lived well because I lay low.'[23]

To avoid choosing sides others had to run, and – as often as not – lived badly. After his son was severely wounded fighting for the king at the Second Battle of Newbury, Sir Humphrey Mildmay escaped from London to what he assumed would be the safety of his country estate. The approach of Fairfax's army dashed all hopes of a quiet and comfortable life. 'I removed in fear' he wrote in his diary for 13 July 1645, adding a week later, 'all grow worse'.[24] Two years earlier Nicholas Guise fled from Gloucester to London to avoid having to 'engage myself in some party which I did not like'. Many Englishmen, such as John Bargrave, Fellow of St Peter's Cambridge, Sir Roger Pratt, Thomas and Lady Catherine Whitehall, left England to escape the fighting, and (added Pratt) to 'give myself some convenient education'. Horrified by the vulgarity of the cavalier army, and loathe to choose sides, John Evelyn bolted from Oxford in 1642. He first hid in his country estate where quite literally he cultivated his garden, before going abroad with the king's permission on the Grand Tour.[25]

Unable to flee, and unwilling to chose sides, other neutrals, known as ambidexters, tried to please both. 'For King *and* parliament', replied a gentleman from Grantham on being asked by a radical neighbour whom he really supported.[26] He, and his ilk, attempted a difficult, indeed dangerous balancing act, which, observed a Shropshire parliamentarian, gave them 'much to do to keep their throats from being cut'.[27] Faced by the intense pressure of placating both sides without alienating one or the other, a

Wiltshire village constable made a note to himself, 'Woe is me, poor Bastard.'[28]

In at least twenty-two counties, and in several towns, participants and neutrals tried to reach pacts limiting the effect of hostilities. Towards the end of 1642, for instance, the gentry of Lincolnshire agreed to raise a cavalry troop to maintain peace within the county, and promised not to recruit soldiers to be dispatched out of the county to either side, but rather co-operate for a negotiated peace. That year at Heworth Moor, Yorkshire, a crowd estimated at forty thousand petitioned the king for neutrality.[29] Early the next year Devon royalist and roundhead gentry agreed to oppose 'all forces whatsoever that shall enter that county'.[30] Such agreements were part of the live and let live attitude which is far more common in war than generals would like either their own men or posterity to think. Informally reached and backed by little force and even less legitimacy, these agreements tended to break down as the strains of war increased.[31]

'Alas My Lord, there is such a universal wariness of the war', George Digby admitted to Henry Jermyn in August 1645.[32] Ten months later William Sancroft (later the Archibishop of Canterbury), told his father 'The truth is, men begin to grow weary.'[33] Poets agreed. Andrew Marvell compared the tired land to a neglected garden:[34]

> Shall we never more
> That sweet militia restore,
> When gardens only had their towers,
> And all the garrisons were flowers?

Writers of anonymous doggerel repeated this widespread war-weariness:[35]

> There dwells a people on this Earth
> That reckons true Religion Treason,
> That makes sad War a Holy mirth,
> Counts madness real, and nonsense reason.

Perhaps the most dramatic demonstration of the widespread desire for neutralism was the clubmen movement. As one of their banners pithily put it:[36]

> If you offer to plunder or take our Cattle,
> Be assured we will bid you battle.

Far from being a return to pre-war values, risings of clubmen were essentially spontaneous *jacqueries* – revolts of desperate peasants. In the first three months of 1645 they took place in the bitterly contested border counties of Shropshire, Worcestershire and Herefordshire. Between May and June they broke out in the western counties of Wiltshire, Dorset and Somerset. On 30–31 July ten thousand clubmen assembled at Cefn Oun, and Llantristant, Glamorganshire, to proclaim themselves the 'Peaceable Army'.[37] From September to November there were clubmen risings in Berkshire, Sussex, Hampshire, South Wales and the Welsh Borders. Clubmen movements broke out in parts of the country that, as one of their leaders put it, had 'more deeply . . . tasted the Misery of this unnatural intestine War'. Notwithstanding the taunts of their opponents that they were nothing but a 'vulgar multitude ignorant of manners', all but the highest ranks of rural society joined the clubmen. Quantity, admittedly, exceeded the quality. Twenty thousand clubmen were reported in Wiltshire and Devon, and sixteen thousand in Berkshire.

Perhaps as many as six hundred clubmen were killed in the war, and about seven hundred briefly detained as prisoners, which would suggest that they were not as significant a force in the war as recent research might imply.

While clubmen occasionally voiced fairly sophisticated ideas, such as those drawn up on 24 June 1645 in 'The Desires and Resolutions of the clubmen of the Counties of Dorset and Wiltshire', the movement remained a disorganized gut reaction against the war and 'the outrages and violence of the soldiers'.[38]

Since by now the king was losing, he was obliged to take more notice of them than did the parliamentary forces, who – after initial negotiations – scattered the clubmen with brutal ease. Oliver Cromwell described the ten thousand protesters, whom he dispersed from Hambledon Hill on 2 August 1645, killing a dozen, 'but cut very many', and capturing four hundred, as 'poor silly creatures, whom if you please to let me send home, they promise to be very dutiful'.[39]

Women, most seventeenth-century Englishmen agreed, were also silly creatures whose chief virtue lay in staying at home and being very dutiful to their fathers and husbands. Yet the war presented these weaker vessels with challenges and problems which, as Sir Hugh Cholmley wrote about his wife, with whom he endured the Siege of Scarborough Castle, made them show 'a courage even above her sex'. Captain Priamus Davies, who served under Brilliana Harley at the Siege of Brampton praised the parliamentary heroine for her 'masculine bravery'. And by the end of the war such courageous women made more than one chauvinist think twice. Edward Foord wondered in 1646:[40]

> Women they say the Weaker Vessels are,
> If so, it is a paradox to men
> That those were never trained up in war
> So often should obtain the victory.

For most women – like men – the war was a time of intense highs and lows. After Lady Anne Fanshawe's father, a royalist MP, escaped from parliamentary custody he summoned her and her sister to join him in Oxford. Anne recalled that never had they to endure such hardships.

> From as good a house as any gentleman in England had, we came to a baker's house in an obscure street, and from rooms well furnished, to lie in a very bad bed in a garret, to one dish of meat and that not the best.

In such straits Anne likened herself and her family to 'fishes out of water'. The only way she could adjust to the ordeal was through obedience to those men such as her husband, father, and king, who exercised authority over females.

On the other hand, for a young impressionable woman the university town was still a most exciting place, right in the centre of things. 'We had the perpetual discourse of the losing and gaining of towns and men,' Anne recalled, 'and most bore it with martyr-like cheerfulness.'[41]

If not the weaker vessel, seventeenth-century women were at least the more vulnerable one, particularly to the violence of civil war. Lady Filmer did not go outside for five months in 1643 for fear of rebel marauders, who had already requisitioned her coach and five horses, and searched her house ten times. Lady Anne Clifford, a royalist trapped in London, spent most of nearly seven years 'in my own Chamber without removing . . . The Civil Wars being then very hot'. Margaret Eure recognized the dangers war posed to women, writing that 'it is an ill time with them of all creatures for they are exposed to all villainies'.[42]

At best threats of violence increased the dependence of already dependent females. Even though Joyce Jeffries was fairly well off, having five servants, a steward and £800 a year, she was still susceptible to military pressure. Her diary is replete with demands to help pay for the war. She had to cough up cash for carters to take her goods to be stored in the countryside where she hoped they would be less exposed to plunder. It did not work: armies stole her possessions, and she got so worried that in December 1642 she became ill. Eventually she went to live with her cousin and learned to pay protection money, forking out, for instance, 5 shillings worth of refreshments to a party of king's soldiers, who stopped by the house having just been defeated by Sir William Waller. Luckily assuaging their thirst also satisfied their appetite for plunder.[43]

At worst women could be killed and raped. Surprisingly, very few were violated (see chapter 10). A few, however, lost their lives, many their husbands or sons, while still more had to bring up families, and run businesses alone.

There is no doubt that there is something erotic about war, with its handsome uniforms, romantic trappings, macho-values, opportunities for casual couplings with fit young men a long way from home. 'The young women conversed without any circumspection or modesty', remembered

Clarendon about the way the war loosed ties of parental authority. Lonely and frightened soldiers have always sought the security – no matter how brief and impersonal – of a woman's embrace.[44]

How effective they were in finding such solace remains difficult to say. Of course, in a society where in peacetime neighbours pried into each other's beds, and called upon the church and its courts to uphold morality, it would be remarkable if many illicit relations passed unnoticed. Parish registers do not indicate the baptism of a bumper crop of bastards.

So the evidence is impressionistic. In Somersetshire soldiers from outside the county seem to have had no problem finding compliant females. Like the GIs over here during the Second World War, many county folk thought the troopers over-sexed and over-paid. The soldiers had a swaggering self-confidence that the local lads interpreted as arrogance and some of the local lasses found irresistible. With looted coins jangling in their pockets, troopers might offer a simple village girl excitements undreamed of in her usual rural round. Such goings on outraged village worthies – not to mention the fathers of daughters, as well as girls who said no, or else had never been propositioned in the first place. When a sanctimonious householder espied a girl dallying under a hedge with a soldier he drew his sword and stabbed the man. On another occasion, after watching her servant girl traipse into a barn with a trooper, a mistress peeped around the door, and saw 'the soldier lying upon her and her clothing up so that she saw her naked skin'. Outraged, the mistress called a posse of local lads, who threw the slut into a mill stream.[45]

Moral outrage could, however, all too easily become hypocrisy that turned victims into scapegoats. When in late 1645 some of Goring's defeated royalists arrived in the village of Doulting, Somerset, 'they were very rude and beat up most of the people'. Demanding a woman to 'dress their meat', the villagers offered them Joan Easton, who spent 'all the day and night with them', apparently doing more than preparing a joint or two of the roast beef of Merry England. Afterwards Joan became an outcast. Even though she had no previous record of promiscuity, the villagers circulated stories about her sexual licence, presumably to mitigate their own cupidity and cowardice.[46]

On the other hand troops could genuinely fall for local girls. Captain Innes, the commander of a Scots company billeted in Hipswell, Yorkshire, was smitten by Alice Townsend. Unused to sassenach civility the sawney offered £3,000 and then £4,000 for the 17-year-old's hand: it did his wooing no good. The captain 'was so wild a blood looking man,' Alice recalled, 'that I trembled all the time he was in the house'. So she ran away from home. When Innes threatened to have his men smash up her mother's cottage unless she told him where her daughter was hiding, Mrs Townsend complained to General Leslie, who told Innes to stop, allowing Alice to return home. She must have been an attractive girl for soon afterwards Captain Jermyn Smith asked her to marry him. She refused. Luckily one of his troopers, Private Thomas Binke, told her, as she was bandaging his wounded hand, that Jermyn was planning to abduct her during her usual walk to Lowes, 'and force me on horseback away with them, and God knows what end he would make of me'.[47]

A few women liked such a rough wooing. Sir John Gell hated his royalist rival Sir John Stanhope so bitterly that after his death he plundered his house, and broke the nose and fingers from his stone monument in the parish church. He even dug up the flower beds that were Lady Stanhope's pride and joy. Far from loathing him, the widow allowed Gell to court her, and accepted his marriage proposal.[48] Even more surprising was the behaviour of Susan Denton, a middle-aged spinster long past making a good match. The roundheads captured her after storming Hillesden House, Buckinghamshire. 'We were not shamefully used in any way by the soldiers', wrote Pen Verney, a fellow prisoner, 'but they took everything, and I was scarce left the clothes on my back.' As the captives were being marched off to be penned for the night in the local church, Susan caught the eye of Captain Jeremiah Abercromby, the Scotch-Irish commander of the guard detail. It was a case of love at first sight – the slightly desperate spinster, and the rugged Ulster officer. 'I think few of her friends like it a bit, but if she had not him she would not have any', an aunt sniffily concluded. The couple were quickly married, since Abercromby had to march on with his regiment. Sadly he was killed near Bristol a few months later.[49]

Abercromby at least behaved like a gentleman – which is more than can be said for some. In the village of Myddle an army captain courted 'a lonely handsome woman' who had married a local landowner more to please her father than herself. Falling for the captain's blandishments to take her away from all that to Ireland, where no one cared about previous marriage vows, she left her spouse and child. Her officer was no gentleman. He deserted her at Chester, and she had to return home to her husband, who only took her back on the receipt of a second dowry. Sometimes it was the wronged husband who suffered the most. Worried sick by his wife's affair with Lieutenant Thomas Corneby, an officer from the parliamentary garrison, an apothecary from Newport Pagnell slit his throat in three places.[50]

Women were, however, less likely to be troubled by romantic strangers then persistent neighbours, particularly when their husbands were away at the war. Convinced that Nat Owen, a parliamentary deserter and horse thief, was sleeping with his wife, Richard Manning led a patrol from the roundhead garrison at Moreton Corbet to Myddle, to have him arrested. In fact they ran into a cavalier party, killing its officer.[51] Troopers in Newport Pagnell assured local girls that sleeping with them was not really adultery since there was a war on. A yeoman from Clutton, Somerset, tried to persuade the wife of a labourer who had been away with the army in Ireland for two years, to go to bed with him, by explaining that 'her husband used the company and lay with women in Ireland and had the carnal knowledge of their bodies, and he would wish her to do the like with men here in England'.[52] Civilians were not above such spurious arguments. J. Bostock, clerk to the local council of war, was found guilty of committing adultery with Alice Chetwood. Since they did so in a minister's house, on the Sabbath, and – worse still – during the hours of divine worship, the pair were lucky to get off with having to stand in Nantwich market-place with a sign describing their crimes about their necks.[53]

Amidst the dislocation and partings of civil war, most husbands and wives remained faithful, as they desperately missed each other. 'In my absence', noted Chaplain Ralph Josselin, '[my wife] was wondrous sad and discontented.'[54] 'It was the first time we had parted since we had married', Lady Anne Fanshawe recalled of the day in March 1645 when her husband left Oxford to go to the wars: 'He was extremely affected, even to tears, though passion was against his nature.' Two days later their infant child died, victim of the fevers that ravaged the garrison town. The following May, Anne joined Richard to share the adventures of campaigning. After he was captured at Worcester and marched to London, she loyally followed him to the capital, where every morning at four, even in the rain, she stood in the street outside Richard's cell window to talk to him.

In contrast to Anne Fanshawe's unalloyed joy, Mary Monro's relief on learning that her husband had not been killed after his major deserted him in the face of the enemy was most highly restrained. 'My dear heart', she wrote to Colonel John Monro, 'I have received two packets from you which is no little comfort, for you were absolutely reported to be dead.' Jonathan Rosleigh, a royalist from Cornwall, suffered dearly during the war. His house was plundered to the tune of £8,130, several of his ships were lost, and he was unable to collect debts worth £1,325. After spending a year imprisoned in St Mawes Castle, an ordeal for a 69-year-old man, he wrote to his wife, 'My dearest love, thy kind letters do much to comfort my troubles', signing himself (perhaps with that sardonic humour that keeps men going in time of war), 'thy overburdened friend'.[55]

Most couples had to communicate by letters, in which they shared their best hopes and worst fears. Wives begged their husbands to write. 'It is a great grief to be without you, and it is more because you do not write to me', Lady Elizabeth Denbigh wrote, 'I beseech you, for God's sake, let me hear oftener from you.'

Soldiers were just as desperate for news. 'My Dear, let me hear often from thee', scribbled Sir Simon Harcourt, 'for thy loving lines must & ever shall be the most welcome and acceptable present that can be sent unto thy most faithful and affectionate husband.'[56] In 1643 Lord Henry Spencer told his wife how their friend Sir William Croft had been given home leave: 'I envy him, and all others that can go to their houses.' Writing to her on 25 August, when the fighting at the Siege of Gloucester was at its fiercest, Spencer graphically expressed how much a fighting soldier needed a good wife:[57]

> My Dearest Heart:
> Just as I was coming out of the trenches, on Wednesday, I received your Letter of the 20th of this instant, which gave me so much satisfaction that it put all the inconveniences of this Siege out of my thoughts ... writing to you and hearing from you being the most pleasant entertainment that I am capable of in any Place; but especially here, where, but when I am in the Trenches (which place is seldom without my company) I am more solitary than I ever was in my life.

A month later Spencer was dead, killed at the First Battle of Newbury.

Husbands often downplayed the risks they ran on active service. 'I know your fears for me are great, considering the times here', wrote Sir Simon Harcourt, 'which I believe are made more dangerous by report than in truth they are.' He concluded 'I am of the opinion that the great dangers of this rebellion are past.' Eleven months later at the Siege of Kilgobbin Castle a sniper fatally shot Sir Simon: he left behind a widow who eight years later was still grateful 'that God gave me an honest and kind husband'.[58]

Wives were petrified of being widowed. 'What can be more doleful, or greater terror', asked *The Widowes' Lamentation* (1643, W2093), than that 'our husbands should be taken from us by violent deaths.' Naturally they begged them to be careful. A year after they were married Basil Fielding went off to fight for the king. His wife Elizabeth sent him a stream of nigh-hysterical letters. 'You cannot imagine what I would give to see you again', she wrote in one, adding in another 'Oh dear God, what I would give to see you, for God's sake write to me, and come as soon may be.' Quite obviously Elizabeth wanted her husband physically. So too did Kate Lloyd, who wrote to her husband serving with the parliamentary army in London, that she desired nothing 'but thyself, which is more prized than all the rest, and I hope ere long to enjoy'.[59]

Elizabeth Bourchier poured out her innermost hopes and fears in her letters to her husband, the Earl of Rutland, who was away hazarding his life for the king.

> Oh my heart, so you were safe I did not care if I were dead, it is a grief to me that you would leave me, you can imagine what I would give to see you again.... For God's sake write to me and come as

soon as you can. Stay not from your dutiful and obedient wife and humble servant.

Apart from the ending this letter from a worried wife transcends both time and class. Susan Rodway, the common soldier's wife who wrote telling her husband when he was fighting with the London Trained Bands at Basing House how worried she was for his safety and for their child, would have whole-heartedly endorsed the sentiments Lady Bourchier expressed in another letter to the Earl: 'I am in perpetual fear for you', she wrote in August 1644, 'I would rather live with you with bread and water than from you with all the plenty in the world.'[60]

During the seventeenth century birth and infancy were at best dangerous times for both mother and child. The civil war made them even more hazardous. 'Poor child, I pray God bless him and make him a happy man, for he hath but troublesome beginning', Mary Verney wrote to her husband Ralph soon after the birth of their son.[61]

War forced pregnant women to make arduous journeys. Travelling from Oxford to inspect her property in London, Captain Richard Atkyns's pregnant wife was arrested.[62] Eventually released, she made it to London to find her house on the Strand full of soldiers. The sight of them smashing her furniture so upset Mrs Atkyns that she became ill, miscarried, and nearly died. An enemy patrol surprised the parliamentary fugitives, Anne and John Hutchinson, in a Leicestershire village in the autumn of 1642. John made a dash for it, his pregnant wife being 'somewhat afflicted to be so left alone in a strange place'. Fortunately the commander of the royalist troop was her brother, Sir Allen Apsley. Even so Anne attributed the sickly constitution of the daughter she bore a few weeks later (to die at the age of 3) to the 'griefs and frights in those troublesome times'.[63] Heavy with child Anne Fanshawe escaped with her husband first to the Scilly Islands and then the Isle of Jersey, where she arrived 'almost dead'. The war forced her to move constantly and to go into exile. Thus Anne buried children in Lisbon, Madrid, Paris, Oxford, Yorkshire, Hertfordshire and Kent.

When Thomas Springate, a member of the parliamentary garrison of Arundel Castle, fell dangerously ill in 1644, his pregnant wife Mary had to travel through terrible winter weather to join him. Her coach skidded into a ditch, she had to take a boat through flooded countryside and walk many miles across wet cold ground to reach her husband, who was delirious by the time she arrived. Having sat up with him for forty-eight hours until he passed away, Mary Springate survived to give birth to his posthumous child.[64] Lady Anne Saville, who was trapped in the Siege of York, suffered a similar ordeal. Having just lost her husband, and denied a midwife by the parliamentary attackers, she gave birth the day after

York fell.[65] After marrying Edward Heath when she was only 13, and enduring much of the war in disease-ridden Oxford, where three of her babies died, Lucy Heath was given permission to return to her home near Oakham. Unfortunately another son died when he was only 2. Parliament sequestered much of her husband's estates, while bandits from Rockingham Castle took most of the rest. Distraught, Lucy wrote to a friend that the parliamentarians had denied her:

> So much as might bury my dear babe I have now newly lost; and to this is added this time when I need them, being big with child, the taking away of my linen even to my baby clothes and mantles, all which I confess I much more prize *in regard* they were the gift of my dear mother.

Six months later Lucy had her child. Six months after that the baby died. And half a year later its 27-year-old mother passed away, worn out by war, worry and pregnancies.[66]

The wars' most famous pregnant refugee was Henrietta Maria. Seven months in her term, the queen left her husband (whom she never again saw) in Oxford in April 1644 for the safety of the West Country. Desperately worried, the king begged Sir Thomas Mayerne, the royal family physician 'for the love of me go to my wife, C.R.' On 14 June Henrietta had a daughter in Exeter. The painful labour left the baby with one shoulder permanently lower than the other, and the mother exceedingly debilitated. 'Here is the woefullest spectacle my eyes yet ever looked upon,' an attendant wrote home, 'the most and weak pitiful creature in the world, the poor Queen.' Yet Fairfax refused to grant Her Majesty a safe conduct to travel to take the healing waters at Bath. Thus less than a month after a painful confinement the sick, helpless and hated queen had to take ship at Falmouth, and after being fired upon by a parliamentary vessel she landed at Brest, so ill that the doctors concurred that 'her days will not be many'.[67]

The queen and her daughter, Henrietta-Anne, were fortunate to survive this ordeal. Frightened by the sudden appearance of a cavalier patrol near Plymouth, Colonel Robert Bennett's wife went into premature labour, and died, losing the child.[68] Simple war-weariness, and excessive childbearing, killed Lady Dudley. In the absence of her husband on royal service, she had to manage the estate, and put up with 'the horrid rudeness of the soldiers and Scots' billeted upon her. 'The troubles and destruction of those sad times did much affect and grieve' the poor woman, her sister recalled, that as a result she expired giving birth to her sixteenth child.[69].

War made bringing up children even more difficult than it was in peace. 'She looks like a slattern' wrote Mary Verney about the only woman she could find to wet-nurse her son.[70] During the Siege of Rathbury Castle, Ireland, the wife of the governor, Arthur Freke, offered to buy a pint of milk for her child from John Barry in return for forgiving a £14 debt. 'Yet this base, ungrateful rebel, and perjured papist devil', wrote the governor in his diary, 'would not give us one drop, but called us parliamentary dogs, rogues, and rebels, hourly.'[71]

The social dislocation of combat may have discouraged well-off mothers from farming babies out to other women, prompting them into the far safer practice of breast feeding for themselves – which may have been the only way in which the war actually saved lives. When Samuel Luke, the parliamentary governor of Newport Pagnell, heard from his wife that their son, Oliver, would not do his homework, he reprimanded the lad, telling him that if he caught the fever that was going around it would be a sign of God's displeasure. The admonition worked, for a month later Luke wrote to Oliver saying how glad he was to learn that he had turned over a new leaf.[72] In preparation for the Siege of Scarborough, which lasted for twelve bitter months, Lady Elizabeth Cholmley sent her two children to Holland: 'whom I parted with not without great trouble, for I was fond of them', explained the royalist governor's wife. Mothers found losing grown-up children to the wars equally painful. 'My Dear Ned,' wrote Brilliana Harley to her son in London, 'I never was in such sorrow, as I have been since you left me.'[73]

War, and the fratricidal conflict of civil war, could be quite terrifying for children. Although a work of Victorian fiction, W. F. Yeames' famous painting 'And when did you last see your father?' (plate 1), conveys the terror innocents must have felt when caught up in the brutal struggles of grown-ups. Even Sir Thomas Byron, the commander of the roundheads who sacked Bulstrode Whitelocke's house in November 1642, and according to the painter sternly interrogated his children as to when they had last seen Bulstrode, found it all distasteful. 'It was a barbarous thing to hurt those innocent children', he said as he tried to hug and kiss and make much of them.[74]

At the happiest of times bringing up children in the seventeenth century was hard enough. There was the problem of disease, the scourge of infant mortality, and worries about families and friends. War compounded these difficulties. A letter by Elizabeth Moore, who lived on the borders of Hertfordshire and Bedfordshire, illustrates in a moving way how one woman tried to hold her family together:[75]

2 June 1644.

Good Sister:

I had written to you before this time, but that I have had an extreme sore eye, and is not very perfect. Little Will hath been much set back with the breeching of his teeth. . . . He grows very much in length though not in breadth. We ask for your company here many times.

Here are great fears at this time for it is reported that the enemy is at Bedford, and that they have plundered Hatch in Hertfordshire. The countys are all in arms. Beside eight horse which are sent in, we hear that they are drive back, but we cannot know for any certainty. . . . There is no place free from distraction and trouble, I pray God fit us all for what he please to impose on us, for these are bad times. I should go to my sister Needham's next week, but I cannot resolve by reason of this ill news. My uncle in Lincolnshire is ill done by the Cavaliers, they have taken all his writing and books. Hevencoate hath been very sick. He is in Norfolk at my cousins. Thus we see how uncertain the world is. I pray God set an end to all these troubles that we may have a happy putting upon again, for which I pray and ever remain your loving sister, Eliz Moore.

Whatever happened to Elizabeth Moore, whether she found the happiness for which she prayed, or else had her hopes, home, and family destroyed, we do not know. Nonetheless her letter is worth quoting in full because it conveys the anguish and uncertainty, the courage and determination ordinary women showed as they faced the reality of war. And most families pulled through to become a source of quiet pride and warm solace. Sir John Gibson of Wilburn, Yorkshire, wrote in his *Autobiography*:[76]

> When uncivil civil wars withall
> Did bloodshed bring and strife
> Twelve sons my wife Penelope
> And three fair daughters had,
> Which then a comfort was to me
> And made my heart full glad.

War divided families politically as well as geographically. ''tis most unseemly done, and it grieves my heart', Edmund Verney told his elder brother Ralph for not siding with the king.[77] Sometimes the bonds of kinship survived the divisions of war. Lord Stamford ended a proposal to his 'Worthy Cousin', Colonel Edward Seymour, Governor of Dartmouth, that they exchange prisoners, with the hope that 'let these times be what they will, I shall never alter from being yours.'[78] At other times political allegiance overcame kinship. 'Sir John, you are my kinsman, and one I have much honoured', Colonel Boynton told Governor Hotham as he grabbed his cousin's horse as he was deserting parliament for Charles, 'but I must now waive all that, and arrest you as a traitor to the kingdom.'[79] Soon afterwards parliament shot Hotham and his son for treason.

The sword divided hundreds of families. At Edgehill, to take but one example, William Feilding, Earl of Denbigh, and Henry Carey, Earl of Dover, charged against their sons, Basil and John, while Sir Edmund Verney was killed trying to save the royal standard from the parliamentary army in which his son Ralph was an officer. Three of the cousins of Denzil Holles, who commanded a roundhead regiment, were royalists, as were at least six members of Cromwell's family. Sir Thomas Maulever's son fought and was imprisoned for the king his father voted to execute.[80] Divisions permeated all levels of society. Peter and Christina Daniels of Over Tably, Cheshire had four sons and four daughters. Two of the boys, Peter and Thomas, served the king, being killed at Gloucester and Brentford. Their two brothers John and William sided with parliament, both surviving to become colonels. Three daughters married royalists, and one a roundhead.[81]

Family members not only fought on different sides, but, most worrying of all, could actually kill each other. 'My dear heart, my dear life, my sweet joy', wrote Elizabeth Bourchier to her husband (who was fighting for parliament as his father served the crown), 'I hope God will preserve you from your father's and everybody's hurt.' Only one case has been found when a family member personally killed another. As he lay dying from musket wounds sustained in an unsuccessful storm of Wardour Castle, Private Hillsdeane, a roundhead, affirmed that his royalist brother had fired the fatal shot. He forgave him, saying he had only been doing his duty. The pain of a death in a divided family was even more intense. Lady Denbigh's son Basil was a roundhead while her husband William was a royalist, the two taking part on opposite sides at Edgehill. The following April the Earl was mortally wounded storming Nottingham while serving in Prince Rupert's regiment. 'O my dear Jesus, put it into my dear son's heart to leave their merciless company that was the death of his father', prayed his widow.[82]

Statistics bear out the prevalence of divided families. Of the gentry who participated in hostilities 6 per cent in both Lancashire and south-east Berkshire, 7 per cent in Suffolk, and 16 per cent in Yorkshire were divided, as compared to 15 per cent of the aristocracy, and 20 per cent of the 159 families listed in the *Dictionary of National Biography*.[83]

The most painful division a family could suffer during the war was, of course, that inflicted by death. Although roughly a third of families in early-modern England lost at least one parent before all children came of age, and public opinion could treat widows as pathetic figures of fun, there was something particularly sad about the fate of a young woman who lost a husband in war, especially at the hands of her fellow countrymen.[84]

It was, wrote Margaret Eure, whose second husband, Colonel William Eure, perished in 1644, 'the greatest misfortune that could ever happen to me in this world . . . the death of the gallantest man that I ever knew in my Life'.[85] Uncertain if her husband had survived the rout of Charles II forces at Worcester in 1650, 'for three days it was inexpressible what affliction I was in', remembered Anne Fanshawe, 'I neither eat, nor slept,

305

but trembled at every motion I heard, expecting the fatal news.' She was exceedingly relieved to learn that Sir Richard had been taken prisoner.[86]

Officers' ladies might learn such news from the pamphlets which were rushed into print after most battles, giving details of the fighting with an appended casualty list. Common soldiers' women did not even have this solace. In the absence of any formal system of notification, or accurate muster records, particularly for defeated units which tended to suffer the most casualties, they had to rely on informal networks, usually of comrades who survived. All too often women never learned the fate of their men who went to the wars not to return. Desperate for news, some even consulted astrologers such as William Lilly, whose files are full of enquiries from women such as the butcher's wife who learned in 1649 that her husband had died five years before.[87]

Two days after hearing that her husband Lord Charles Moore had been killed in a skirmish near Meath in September 1643, Lady Alice described herself as 'a wretched woman, desolate and distressed . . . I am not capable of receiving comfort myself in this dreadful extremity.'[88] Typical of the trauma of losing a husband to the war was that experienced by Cary Verney. She was only 16, 'as sweet a creature as any living', when she married Thomas Gardiner, the son of the prominent lawyer and Recorder of London. Three months after their wedding day he joined the army, leaving her pregnant. At first Captain Gardiner was lucky: taken prisoner near Windsor he was released within three days. But in July 1645 his number came up: he was killed in a skirmish near Oxford, leaving 'a sad disconsolate widow, great with child', and 'not a penny in the house'. Cary tried to get the £80 her brother-in-law Harry Gardiner owed her, but he too was killed. Her own brother was in France, unable to help. Her in-laws were cruelly indifferent, even after she gave birth to a weak, sickly, almost blind baby. So Cary Verney returned to her family's house in Claydon. Two years later, most folk thought her lucky to marry John Stewkeley, a widower with several children.[89]

All too often the sad fate of widows became grist for propaganda mills, or, sadder still, fodder for callous comedians. At the start of hostilities one pamphlet maintained that 'there was not a widow amongst us, from old crocked beldames of four score and fifteen to the young buxom widow of twenty' who could now hope to find a 'young lusty husband'.[90] The following year *The Virgins' Complaint for the Loss of their Sweethearts* argued that war had deprived them of their rightful role of being 'a helper for man in his necessities'. The death of so many young swains, the virgins complained, forced them to 'betroth ourselves to frosty bearded usurers, that are as cold in their constitutions and performances as they are in their charities'. At times this pamphlet became comic, with its images of ancient 'bumbling fumblers' trying to satisfy young females, as they tottered on their crutches. Beneath the pamphlet's bawdy was a message serious enough to sell five editions between 1643 and 1646: 'To shed human blood is against all divine and human laws, and barbarous it is for men, handsome young men, with their weapons.' Of course, the reference to men's weapons was a crude pun, yet it touched on an important issue for a society that believed that the female sexual urge was far stronger than the male, and if aroused and then not satisfied within marriage was a threat to social stability:[91]

> No fleety potion
> Not other notion
> Of Physic for our sickness can be found
> Only one thing makes us this consold
> The oil of man can ease us in this hold.

At the end of the first civil war, *Hey-Hoe for a Husband, or the Parliament of Maids* – allegedly written by a gaggle of virgins that included a Miss Priscilla Prick-Story – proposed legislation that would forbid old widows from marrying young men, and force every tenth man in each parish to wed every tenth woman, regardless of their looks.[92] Of course, all these pamphlets were written tongue in cheek, yet one suspects that their humour was wasted on the hosts of women widowed by the civil wars.

Certainly it did not amuse 'The many thousand Wives and Matrons' who in February 1643 purportedly petitioned for peace. They explained that 'each of us has a loving and kind husband as ever lay a leg over a woman', yet now they were 'poor distressed wives this cold weather lying alone in our beds without the warm touches and embraces of any man to comfort us'.[93]

Behind such misogyny lay some deep-rooted male fears.[94] First there was the real, and usually unvoiced fear that they would be killed. Men wanted – they needed – their wives to help them, either to run businesses when they were away fighting, solace them in prison, or help compound for their estates. But afterwards, men worried, those heroines might become harridans unwilling to accept traditional male authority after the war ended (see plate 7). When a group of women petitioned parliament in 1649 for the release of John Lilburne, men shouted at them to go home and wash their dishes – in other words to return to their traditional duties.[95] The transition from heroine to harpy that terrified males was apparent in the two editions of *Joanereidos: or Feminine Valour Eminently discovered in Western Women*. It first appeared in 1645. When reissued in 1647 the author included a savage satire on women, 'for', he explained, 'the satisfaction of his Friends'. *The City Dames Petition in the behalfe of the long afflicted, but well-affected Cavaliers* (1647, C4350), hinted at male fears in the choice of the names of the purported petitioners. Women were either uppity, as evidenced by Mrs Snatchall and Mrs Troublesome, or over-sexed, as suggested by Mrs Stradling and Mrs Hornee, or both as hinted at by Mrs Overdoe.

It is tempting to dismiss such broadsheets as no more than cruel male jests. *The Virgins Complaint*, to name but one of the many lampoons, sold five editions, not just because it was written by virgins, and was crudely comic, but purportedly because it was believable. *The Mid-wive's Just Complaint* (1646, M2004), a satirical petition against war because it was bad for the birthing business, had a point – albeit one laboriously put. So too had John Denton, a sober fellow if ever there was. When he wrote to his Great Aunt Isham in August 1644 'I think if these times hold there will be no men left for women', he was voicing a thought so forlorn that most folk could swallow it only if sugared with a dusting of humour.[96]

In addition to losing sons and husbands in the conflagration, women could lose their own lives. Sometimes they did so accidentally. On 25 May 1645 the parish register for Romsey, Hampshire, noted the burial of 'Frances Nash, daughter of Francis, mortally wounded by a soldier *per infortuniam*.'[97] She almost surely fell victim to Goring's troops who at the time were in the area. Muskets discharged while being cleaned, or when a soldier tripped. Powder wagons exploded, killing innocent bystanders. At the Siege of Pontefract in April 1644 a stray round hit Alderman Tayton's maidservant as she was hanging out the washing. She died that evening, being given a full military funeral.

Of the women who risked their lives hiding escaped prisoners, the most famous was Jane Lane who helped Charles II get away after Worcester. Many women went to the wars as camp-followers – some were whores, most were wives or women who cooked for and nursed their man.[98]

A few women even dressed as men in order to remain with their husbands or lovers or else for the excitement of army life. The story that the two thousand royalists Fairfax captured at Acton Church, Cheshire in January 1644 included 'a female regiment' of about one and twenty well-armed, bloodthirsty Amazons is incredible: most likely the women were camp-followers.[99] Jane Ingleby, the daughter of a Yorkshire yeoman, is said to have charged with the king's cavalry at Marston Moor and, wounded, escaped back to the security of her father's farm.[100] A newspaper reported the capture of a woman dressed as one of General Lindsay's cavaliers in 1642. Oliver Cromwell surprised a small raiding party under Lord Henry Percy, Baron Alnwick, at Andover, in March 1645, which included 'a youth of so fair a countenance'. Suspicious, he ordered the youth to sing, 'which he did with such a daintiness', that Oliver took the matter up with Lord Percy, who 'in some confusion did acknowledge she was a damsel'.[101] Eight months later Poyntz's men captured a cavalier corporal who turned out to be a woman. Charles thought the cross-dressing of women as soldiers so pernicious and common that in July

1643 he issued a proclamation forbidding the practice (*inter alia*) as 'a thing which nature and Religion forbid, and our Soul abhors'.[102]

Reports of 'she-soldiers' were rife if only because they made excellent copy. 'Molly', the landlady of the Mad Dog pub at Blackheath, supposedly fought dressed as a man. In 1655 the popular ballad *The Gallant She-Soldier* described the career of a heroine who served in the army under the alias of 'Mr Clarke':

> Her Husband was a soldier, and to the wars did go,
> And she would be his comrade, the truth of all is so,
> She put on man's apparel, and bore him company
> As many in the army for truth can testify.

Finding the thought that women could fight and die in combat difficult to accept, men sometimes turned them into scapegoats. Take, for instance, the destruction of the frigate *Duncannon* by rebel fire as it entered Youghal Harbour. A lucky cannon ball hit the woman who was serving the magazine, smashed her to pulp, and her lantern into the barrels of powder, thus exploding the ship with the loss of eighteen lives.[103] This anyway is the story the Earl of Inchiquin told the House of Lords. Yet there is no way that his Lordship could have possibly known that the female gunner's mate was to blame for the loss of a major ship, for the blast obliterated all the evidence. His readiness to blame a woman was symptomatic of the chauvinism that men felt towards women, particularly when they got caught up in war, the most masculine of all human activities. Thus as they marched towards battle civil war soldiers often ducked suspected harlots, or else vented their frustrations by treating crones as witches.

Women (as we have seen in chapter 7), got trapped in sieges, where they collected intelligence, smuggled messages, loaded weapons, carried food and ammunition, even sniped at the enemy, and had to endure all the horrors of that most horrid form of war. Some brave females defended their husband's castles: Blanche Arundel at Wardour Castle; Charlotte, Countess of Derby at Lathom House; Lady Mary Bankes at Corfe; Lady Brilliana Harley at Brampton Bryan; Lady Lettice Digby at Geashill; and the Countess of Portland at Carisbrooke. And thus in battles and sieges, skirmishes and ambushes, plundering and pillage, all over the land, men and women who did not want to go to war got trapped. Some died, others were destroyed, while for many of those – both men and women – who overcame their ordeals, as James Strong put it in *Joanereidos* (1645) 'the weaker vessels are the stronger grown'.[104]

13

THEN WE STARTED ALL OVER AGAIN

And how well I remember that terrible day
How our blood stained the sand and the water,
And how in that hell they called Sulva Bay
We were butchered like lambs to the slaughter.
　But the band played 'Waltzing Matilda'.
When we stopped to bury our slain
We buried ours, and the Turks buried theirs,
　Then we started all over again.
　　'And the Band Played Waltzing Matilda',
(Australian folk song about the Gallipoli Campaign,
　　popular during the Vietnam war)

On 21 March 1646 Lord Jacob Astley surrendered the remnants of the king's field army at Stow-on-the-Wold. Even though Charles did not personally capitulate to the Scots until 5 May, when he still retained garrisons in the West Country and Wales (the last of which, Harlech, held out until the following March) for the cavalier army the first civil war was over. As Astley sat on the ground, contemplating his future, with a veteran's sardonic sense of realism he told his captors, 'You have done your work boys, you can now go and play, unless you fall out amongst yourselves.'[1]

In one sense Astley's prognosis proved right. The victors did fall out. Parliament broke with its army, radical regiments struggled with more conservative commanders, the Scots and their erstwhile English allies became obdurate enemies. In another way Astley was wrong, for the roundheads' work was not done. Although beaten in battle, and having surrendered, the royalists rose again, and again, to be smashed down in a second and then a third civil war.

The experience of these two civil wars was different from that of the first in two main ways. They were fought with a much greater degree of ferocity. Unlike those of the first civil war, the pamphlets which described the battles of the second and third invariably included the word 'bloody' in their title. *Colchester's tears . . . dropping from the sad face of a new war* (31 July 1648, C5018) recognized implicitly that this second struggle was very different from the first. When Lady Carlisle was interrogated in 1649 about royalist plots she was taken to the Tower and shown the rack, presumably to jog her memory.[2] Corpses were desecrated. Tit-for-tat murders took place. Prisoners were frequently killed in the heat of combat, or during the cold blood of revenge. As one parliamentary veteran ruefully observed, the English were now treating their captured compatriots as if they were Irish prisoners of war. After watching the Battle of Maidstone in June 1648 George Thomson concluded that 'the old quarrel is revived by the same parties with more violence than formerly'.[3] Looking back at the first civil war George Wither wrote in 1646:

> For these four years of discord have so changed
> The gentleness, already of this Nation.
> And men and women are so far estranged
> From civil to barbarous inclination.
> They are so prone to mutinous disorders,
> So forward in all mischievous projections
> So little moved with robberies and murders.

Some found all these murders and mutinies, rapacity and robberies hard to explain. Writing in 1650 John Canne blamed it all on drugs, asserting that the combatants must have snuffed ground-up 'Cobabba' (tobacco?), which makes one 'straightways run mad and be ready to do any bad thing'.[4]

One reason for this viciousness of the second and third civil wars was that the sides which waged them were very different from those who fought the first. They were less wars between the same ethnic groups, such as Englishmen fighting Englishmen, or Scots against fellow Caledonians, and more ethnic conflicts between the nations of an utterly disunited kingdom. Just as the first civil war started with the collapse of central authority in London, initially with the Prayer Book Rebellion and then the Irish Revolt, so in the second and third civil wars the centre, under Cromwell, succeeded in restoring its authority over the fringes. Thus the War *of* the Three Kingdoms became the War *between* the Three Kingdoms.

Historians agree that after the first civil war there was 'widespread and serious economic and social dislocation' in England. Wracked with plague, food shortages and high prices, the country was on the verge of anarchy by the summer of 1647. During the past two years there had been serious disorders in thirty-six of England's forty counties. Oliver Cromwell sardonically remarked to a friend, 'Sir, this is a quarrelsome age.'[5]

Even though the war was over, soldiers continued to plunder and extract free quarter. For instance a party from Colonel Jones's regiment turned up in 1647 at Penrhyn, the home of Humphrey Jones, a rich Welsh royalist. Since it was Halloween, they demanded money. So Jones took them to his cellar and plied them with drink, as some forty of his neighbours joined in the festivities. Well liquored, the soldiers drew their swords, killing one man. Even though the civilians managed to arrest thirty-one troopers (who must have been too plastered to put up much resistance), and sent them to be locked up in Caernavon Castle, the governor, Captain Glyn, released them without even attempting to find the murderers. That September in Faversham, a party of roundhead soldiers, having had their fill of plundering royalists, decided to teach a barber and tapster a lesson for speaking disrespectfully of parliament. So they bound them back to back, put them on a horse, rode them to the gallows, placed nooses around their necks, until, at the very last moment, someone blew a trumpet to announce a 'reprieve'.[6]

Many civilians found puritan ministers as much, if not more of a burden. William ffarington complained to a friend in 1648 that the English people 'are fallen under the harrows and saws of impertinent, pragmatical and ignorant preachers'. Attempts to abolish the traditional Christmas were especially resented. Those who rioted at Canterbury on 25 December 1647 wanted a return to the good old days of roast goose and plum pudding, not revelling recusants and plump prelates, as they sang the latest version of the war's most popular ballad, *The World Turned Upside Down*:

> To conclude I'll tell you news that's right
> Christmas was killed at Naseby Fight.

No wonder Robert Baillie, the Scottish minister, concluded that the land was 'in a most pitiful condition, no corner of it free from the evils of a cruel war. . . . Every shire, every city, many families divided in this quarrel, much blood and universal spoil made by both armies.' Major General Peter Egerton agreed that 'the whole country is exhausted'. Lancashire was in especially bad shape, with hardly a horse to plough or cow to graze the fields. Much of the land was unfarmed because parliament had sequestered it from the royalist owners. At the other end of the land, things were just as bad in Cornwall: Penzance was reported so 'exquisitely plundered' that 'the inhabitants are utterly undone'. In Bath (which had not been the scene of particularly intense fighting) the authorities replaced the broken windows in the Alms Houses, got the school a new door, gave the Market House and Guildhall face-lifts that included new roofs and gutters, resoldered the water pipes, restored the masonry around the Roman baths, and patched up the city's streets with thirty-two wagon-loads of stone. Rent rolls fell during the war, those of a sample of 31 Cheshire estates by 50 per cent, as had those from some 27 estates in Gloucestershire. Half a dozen years of bad harvests increased food prices:

meat went up 50 per cent, corn doubled. While this helped restore rental incomes, it also added to a general sense of post-war misery that the failure to find a political solution exacerbated. 'I hear all things are in England in a very great confusion still', wrote Secretary Nichols, an exile in France,[7]

> As the King at first called a Parliament he could not rule, and afterwards the parliament raised an army it could not rule, so the army had made agitators they cannot rule. What will in the end be the conclusion of this, God only knows.

In times of trouble many people turned for a solution to the conclusion they best knew – those halcyon days of peace. 'Oh Sir', a correspondent from Chatham wrote to a friend in May 1648, 'that God would move all men's hearts to peace.'[8] That same month a cavalier reported that 'The kingdom generally desires the King, and the people grows to be unquiet, but they are afraid of a new war.'[9] A fortnight later, on 16 May 1648, sporting white ribbons, petitioners from Surrey marched on parliament demanding peace. At Whitehall they insulted a group of soldiers, calling them rogues. They disarmed a couple of sentries outside the parliament house, and slew a third with his own sword as they chanted, 'A King! A King!'. At this point the soldiers opened fire, killing one of the peace marchers.[10]

The Surrey mob showed how readily a longing for peace became translated into a longing for the old ways, and the restoration of an unfettered monarchy. As a contemporary ballad put it:[11]

> If now you know what remedy
> There may for all these mischieves be,
> Then may King Charles Alone,
> Be sat upon the throne.

Charles recognized his main chance. 'You cannot be without me', he told the army commanders in August 1647, 'You will fall to ruin if I do not sustain you.'[12] Some royalists were motivated by a simple loyalty towards the king, albeit less as a man and more as a symbol. 'Last night we drank the King's health in abundant manner, being his coronation day, and much celebrated it with ringing of bells and bonfires' wrote a cavalier from West Wales in March 1648. Other royalists were concerned about the growth of radicalism in the army as well as the interference of the Presbyterians in English affairs. Sir Thomas Knyvett told his friend John Hobart that he feared that 'A marriage between the Presbyterian Incubus and the Independent Succubus' would 'beget a new generation of devils'.[13]

Perhaps the best example of rank-and-file royalist attitudes in the second civil war is to be found in an anonymous diary written during the Siege of Colchester in the summer of 1648. The diarist blamed the crown's defeat in the first civil war on 'our luxuries and remiss in discipline', as well as 'our laziness which was called moderation and indifference to the cause'. The other side did not have these problems 'for their officers being mechanics, and the meanest trades, understood no pleasure'. Such cavalier snobbery – which was a form of class consciousness unaffected by reading Marx – led to the diarist's second main explanations for fighting: 'an Honourable striving of gentlemen for their birthrights – I mean their properties limited and protected by the laws – against need and barbarous murderers.' This sense of social superiority carried over into the author's view of the enemy, whose bravery he refused to accept:[14]

> The madness among the vulgar is more admired than true valour, and the reason is manifest, for they judge only by the appearance without considering the cause, so that the extreme, thus it forms the vice, yet it renders the action more conspicuous. But the wise distinguish better . . .

The changes in roundhead attitudes between the first and the second and third civil wars are far harder to chart. They were not a simple reaction that things will never be the same until the king enjoys his own again. On the other hand the roundheads clearly felt that once the royalists had surrendered they had no right to take up arms again, and thus condemn the land to an endless series of civil wars. In his poem 'To the Lord General Fairfax' John Milton asked:[15]

> For what can war but endless wars still breed?
> Till truth and right from violence be freed,
> And public faith cleared from the shameful brand
> Of Public Fraud. In vain doth valour bleed,
> Where avarice and rapine share the land.

As the winners, the roundheads had more opportunity to develop and explain their ideas, and were in the unusual and (for many) painful position of being in charge. Yet their attitudes during the second and third civil wars were logical developments of the mentalities (discussed in chapter 3) that had helped them fight the first – the view of life as a struggle and the conviction that they enjoyed a special covenant with God, which, as fighting intensified, combined to persuade them that the war was a crusade. For this reason they were able to explain victory as well as their own bravery in terms of the Almighty's special favour. In addition an enhanced belief in God was one way of handling the mixed feelings of both guilt and an intense, almost climactic elation, which follows successful combat.[16]

During the first civil war many soldiers recognized the effect combat was having upon them. 'An Army is a harsh, cruel world, a brutal self-seeking power', wrote Chaplain William Sedgwick in his memoirs, adding that 'Many are wholly taken off from wars by the great experience we had of the beastly deceits, the horrible cruelty and corruption that attended it.' Preaching in 1646 Hugh Peters reminded the victorious roundheads that in the army they had found a way to exercise their talents as human beings, sink their differences and unite to achieve common goals. That year, in another sermon, Peters told the troops that in the army 'Men are not in their proper work, which eccentric motions produce many things uncouched.' And then, as if the effects of combat were as obvious to those who had endured it as they had been painful, Peters concluded, 'I need not particularize.'[17]

Right after combat survivors' emotions came to the surface. Time and time again roundheads gave God full credit for their victory and preservation. 'Thus the Lord of Hosts hath done great things for us, to whose name be ascribed all glory', wrote Fairfax after capturing Nantwich in 1644. 'Sir, this is nothing but the hand of God, and to Him belongs all the Glory', exulted Cromwell after Naseby. That same day Colonel John Okey, whose regiment of dragoons had taken heavy casualties, wrote to a friend, 'Now what remains but that you and we should magnify the name of our God that did remember a handful of despised men, who they had thought to have swallowed us up before them.' Okey embellished God's victory by portraying His soldiers as the underdogs, even though in fact they outnumbered the royalists: 'And I desire you that you would, on our behalf, bless God That hath made us instruments for our kingdom's good.' Cromwell did much the same, telling parliament that at Naseby 'honest men served you in this action'.[18]

Combat changed the way in which many troopers thought of themselves. 'I speak not now of our Army of soldiers', wrote William Erberry, 'but our army of saints.'[19] In *Orders from the Lord of Hosts*, a sermon first given to Colonel Edward Rossiter's regiment, E. Reynolds described this process:[20]

> Because there is death in the camp soldiers carry their lives in the hand, and look death in the face daily. . . . Soldiers stand in most need to be very holy men because they may be taken away very suddenly . . . a holy army is victorious and successful . . . Yea, is this not to be clearly seen . . . in our new model?

This view that victory had somehow sanctified the survivors was not merely something preachers handed down like medals of approval. It was a conviction that the rank and file accepted and in many ways originated. 'Sir, you may speak against the preaching of Soldiers in the Army', a young trooper told Chaplain Thomas Edwards, 'but I assure you that if they may not have leave to preach, they will not fight.'[21] Indeed had not 'God blessed' His soldiers so bountifully 'within these four months to rout the enemy twice in the field?'

These new-found saints did not want to become suckers. They were adamant that the army's 'harvest should not end in chaff, and what it had won in the field should not be thrown away in the Council Chamber'. In their songs soldiers voiced the fear that they would be betrayed: that having won the war they would somehow lose the peace:[22]

> That if our Armies lay down Arms
> Before the work is at an end,
> We may expect worse Harms
> More precious lives and States to spend.

'Do you not think', demanded Edward Sexby, during the Putney Debates of 1647, 'that we fought all this times for nothing? All here, both great and small, do think that we fought for something.' Within a couple of years after the first civil war many radical soldiers were certain that the thing for which they had been fighting was a new concept of self:

> I think that the poorest he that is in England hath a life to live, as the greatest he: and therefore truly, Sir, I think it's clear that every man that is to live under a government ought first by his own consent put himself under that government.

Colonel Thomas Rainsborough's words still come ringing down over the centuries as an inspiring declaration of the rights of man, the rule of law, the consent of the governed, even of democracy. Yet their majesty should not lead us into exaggerating either the contemporary importance of the Putney Debates or the extent of such radical sentiments within the army.

The New Model Army which won the war for parliament should not be thought of as a radical collection of saints. For one thing winning wars – unlike losing them – is not a very saintly activity. The New Model was basically nothing more than a highly polished version of the old.[23] Promotion was by seniority, not sanctity, while many of the troops, particularly the infantry, were captured royalists or conscripts, who at war's end saw themselves as labourers who had been more than worthy of their hire.

'We', petitioned the troopers of Whalley's Regiment in May 1646, 'who have adventured our estates and Lives, yea all that was near and dear to us' did not want pie in the sky in the next world, but cash on the barrel in this – preferably within the next few days.[24] Over the next few months in some thirty-four English counties and most Welsh ones soldiers disobeyed orders and demanded the pay that was their due.[25] Although their officers described these actions as mutiny, the army mutinies of 1646 and 1647 were more akin to unofficial strikes in which the rank and file elected shop-stewards (known as 'agitators') to press for their demands. Like most refusals to obey orders they took place outside combat over economic grievances.[26] 'Money! Money!' chanted the Wiltshire levies who mutinied

THEN WE STARTED ALL OVER AGAIN

THEN WE STARTED ALL OVER AGAIN

in Devon. 'Many of the soldiers', acknowledged the Commissioners of Disbandment, 'profess that money is the only thing that they insist on.'[27]

By February 1647 the soldiers were owed some £2,800,800 – the infantry being due eighteen weeks' arrears, the cavalry forty-three. In addition the latter, who were both paid more and were more radical, were ordered to hand back their horses, even though many of them had bought the animals with their own money.[28] The refusal of many to pay the new excise taxes that parliament had enacted to raise money for the soldiers, raised the possibility that money would be taken away from even more deserving folk, prompting the question:[29]

> Is nothing left to pay arrears
> But widows' rights and orphans' tears?

Even after many of the troops had received some, if not all their due, and some twenty thousand soldiers were demobbed in early 1648, the New Model Army remained far more concerned with material grievances, and the apprehension that they might be prosecuted for acts committed during the war, than with radical ideologies.[30]

There were, to be sure, the Levellers. This radical movement came out of the City of London: its civilian origins are obvious from the title of its first manifesto, *A Remonstrance of Many thousand Citizens*, which had been written by William Walwyn, a prosperous Merchant Taylor, and Richard Overton, a jobbing printer. Its demands, the abolition of the monarchy, reform of the House of Commons, annual elections, the end of imprisonment for debt and of conscription, were not intended to appeal primarily to soldiers – especially to pressed men who resented the soft life of civvy street. Thus it is not surprising that the Levellers could not find any genuine troopers to introduce their declaration, *The Case of the Army Truly Stated*, and had to get five bogus agitators to adopt it in October 1647.

At the end of that month representatives of the army – officers and other ranks, agitators and grandees – met in Putney Church to debate the Levellers' demands. Their discussions proved inconclusive. The torch of liberty – or, if you prefer the arson of anarchy – was to flare but for a moment. If it has shed light on the aspirations of modern socialists it provided seventeenth-century common men with very little warmth. Military discipline quickly reasserted itself. In November Generals Fairfax and Cromwell crushed a mutiny at Ware, Hertfordshire, shooting a ringleader in front of his comrades.

But by now, having fallen out among itself, the army could no longer go out and play: there was work to be done fighting a second civil war.

Charles had ended the first in May 1646 by surrendering to the Scots. After being 'barbarously baited' by Presbyterian preachers, who tried to force him to adopt their faith, the Scots handed the king over to parliament in February 1647.[31] The following June, Cornet James Joyce abducted Charles from Holdenby House, taking him into army custody, from which he escaped in November, fleeing Hampton Court for the Isle of Wight. Here on Boxing Day the king signed a secret *Engagement* with the Scots promising to accept Presbyterianism for three years if they invaded England and restored him to the throne. Thus with the stroke of his pen 'Charles R' began the second civil war and in effect signed his own death warrant.

Although deliberately hatched, the second civil war began in a sporadic, haphazard way. In January 1648 Sir Marmaduke Langdale seized Berwick, and Sir Philip Musgrave took Carlisle for the crown. There were widespread royalist riots on 23 March, the anniversary of the king's accession. On 9 April Cromwell had to use force against a London mob. Shooting a demonstrator only made things worse, for the following day 'many evil disposed persons' shot up the Lord Mayor's house forcing His Worship to seek refuge in the Tower.[32]

All over the land spontaneous acts of protest against the army erupted. 'You would not imagine to what a great height we are grown unto here', wrote the author of *An Exact Relation of another Great Fight in . . . Cambridge* (1648). After various student factions started brawling amongst each other, and royalist tradesmen weighed in, the authorities called on Captain Pickering's cavalry troop to restore order. The fracas later that month in Norwich was far more serious. When parliament tried to arrest the mayor a riot broke out, in the course of which shops were plundered and weapons seized. Troops from Fleetwood's regiment were rushed in to restore order, but in the mayhem some ninety-four barrels of gunpowder exploded. 'Not many that were killed as yet found, or can be found,' reported Colonel Charles Fleetwod, 'for many are torn to pieces and carried limb from limb, several arms, legs, etc., being found in the streets.' In all a hundred and twenty persons lost their lives, and another hundred and eight were brought to trial, several of whom being executed in the Castle Ditch.

All over the land, too, ordinary folk discussed these events and wondered about what they should do. For instance, in May, in Exning, Suffolk, Oliver Bridgeman asked his neighbour William Gibson, a husbandman aged 37, if 'he would go to Bury to take up arms for the king?'

'What reward shall he have?' Gibson wanted to know.

'With a horse he should have four pounds, with fire-arms three pounds, and if without arms twenty shillings.'

Gibson asked 'what he and such as he was should have if the country [i.e. parliament] were overthrown?'

They would, Bridgeman replied, 'be well rewarded'.

Thomas Poulter, another villager, asked Bridgeman if he intended fighting?

'If he liked the business he would', came the reply.

Poulter then inquired if 'he should take up arms to beat down the troopers that were for the parliament', and Gibson chipped in by demanding if they could be beaten in the first place. Suddenly waxing confident Poulter assured his friends that the whole of Suffolk would be under arms for the king within three days and wagered £5 that parliament would not last another week.

What then, inquired Gibson, would happen to all those who supported parliament?

'They must either run away,' answered Poulter, assuring his neighbours that he 'had a warrant in his house this month that he who would not take up arms for the King would be hanged'. Mrs Poulter agreed that within three days there would not be a roundhead left alive in England.

Such spontaneous optimism (fuelled one suspects by a jug or two of ale) helped produce the English risings of the early summer of 1648.

The Welsh rising, however, resulted mostly from discontent about arrears of pay. Angry that his men had not got their due, Colonel John Poyer seized Pembroke Castle, prompting other disgruntled roundheads to commandeer Tenby and Chepstow. By March the situation in South Wales was out of hand. 'We long to see our king' became the message that many royalists openly sported in their hat bands.

So on 1 May parliament ordered Cromwell to take eight thousand troops and crush the Welsh royalists, and on 13 June, 'all able men from Sixteen to Sixty' were told to rendezvous at Cowbridge with weapons and horse ready to fight for parliament.[33] Even though 'we had a sharp dispute', reported Colonel Thomas Horton, and 'wholey routed' eight thousand royalists at St Fagans on 8 May, it took Cromwell until 11 July to capture Pembroke Castle. To be sure he was unlucky: his siege artillery accidentally sank in the River Severn, the weather was bad, the food terrible and the terrain atrocious. 'Many tedious, hungry and wet marches over the steep and craggy mountains', Horton summed up campaigning in Wales.[34] The English soldiers thought the Welsh 'spiteful and mischievous people' who, having denuded their land of all food and goods, refused to come out and fight like real men. No wonder Cromwell exacted a terrible revenge on the defenders of Pembroke Castle.

In May a rising also broke out in Kent, where resentment had festered for several months over the efforts to court-martial the civilians involved in the riots protesting against the abolition of Christmas. By the 29th some ten thousand men assembled at Burham Heath where they elected the Earl of Holland their leader, and vowed to march on London. Parliamentary propagandists were terrified. 'In a word their rage is against all Godly men', alleged one hack, adding that many cavaliers had assured him that their main objective was to rape the citizens' wives as their husbands were forced to watch.[35]

319

It is unlikely that it was this prospect which stimulated General Fairfax and his seven thousand men into prompt and resolute action. Having captured a thousand rebels at Blackheath on 30 May, two days later they drove the remnants back from Burham Heath into Rochester. At first the battle went badly for the roundheads. Attacking at about seven in the morning Fairfax made little progress. He underestimated the enemy as 'no more than a number of men huddled together'.[36] Even though they had only been together for ten or so days, many royalist units fought like veterans in the small fields outside the town where thick hedges provided plenty of cover. At the head of his reserves Fairfax managed to push the royalists into the town where they fought, a cavalier recalled, 'from street to street, porch to porch, often falling upon the enemy's horse with only their swords'. Foot by foot, house by house, alley by alley, the royalists were thrust back until they reached St Faith's Church on the High Street. There, without warning, resistance suddenly collapsed and the survivors, 'huddled into a crowd of confused destruction', an eyewitness recalled, 'were overwhelmed'.

A few, including the Earl of Holland, escaped and rode towards London (where Skippon's militia slammed the gates in their face). After being turned back at Surbiton, they moved east, crossed the Thames, and eventually ended up, completely exhausted, at St Neots.[37] Here Colonel Adrian Scrope's men attacked them at dawn on 30 July. The end was brief and brutal. Driven into an inn, with his back to the River Ouse, Holland surrendered, crying out 'Gentlemen Soldiers, I am a gentleman, and desire you that I may be used as a gentleman. I pray you let me have quarter for my life.' Colonel John Dulbier, the parliamentary Quarter Master General in the first civil war who had changed sides, was not treated so gently. 'To express their detestation of his treachery', the roundhead troopers 'hewed him to pieces'.

Such atrocities were all too common on both sides in the localized fighting which exploded all over the land in 1648. Even though Captain Bee, a woollen draper, surrendered the parliamentary garrison at the Bishop's Palace in Lincoln on 30 June on the promise that their lives and goods would be spared, the royalists plundered him and his men without mercy before throwing them in gaol. Although he was wounded in several places the cavaliers refused William Lloyd, Sheriff of Merionethshire, medical attention for several days. Instead Sir John Owen carted him around North Wales for thirty hours (some say on a stretcher, others bleeding on horseback) until he died of neglect. When he heard the news Lloyd's son slew three royalist prisoners in cold blood.[38]

Michael Hudson fared as badly. A quiet, plain-spoken man, Hudson studied at Oxford, where he graduated as a Doctor of Divinity before becoming a royal chaplain. After helping the king escape from Oxford in April 1646, Hudson went into hiding, was arrested by the army, escaped, and was re-arrested. He escaped a second time disguised as a porter by balancing a barrel of apples on his head. The second civil war enabled this divine costermonger to show his true colours. At Woodcroft House, Northamptonshire, he staged a royalist rising which two companies under Colonel Thomas Waite easily put down. Since one of Waite's kinsmen had been killed in the fighting, the colonel denied 'that rogue Hudson' quarter, driving him up to the roof where he was pushed off the edge, clinging for dear life to a battlement. So the roundheads hacked his hands off at the wrist. Hudson fell to the moat, and as he tried to use his stumps to swim to the bank they smashed in his head. Afterwards Trooper Wood, a grocer from Stamford, bragged that he had cut out the reverend doctor's tongue for a souvenir.[39]

Horrible as such incidents were, they pall beside the brutality of the Siege of Colchester.[40]

It started in June when some of the survivors of the Kent rebellion holed up in the Essex market town on the River Colne. On the 6th they beat the drum for volunteers and according to an eyewitness managed to recruit 'a good number of poor Bay-Weavers, and such-like people, wanting employment'. The royalists sent foraging parties out into the surrounding countryside. 'They plundered us, and me in particular', wrote Ralph Josselin, the minister of Earls Colne, 'of all that was portable.'[41]

The parliamentary troops were equally rapacious. When Whalley's regiment arrived at the Earl of Warwick's house at Leigh, they requisitioned some horse, two brass guns, most of the pikes and muskets, four barrels of powder and some match and bullets. 'And after the drinking of some twenty hogsheads of beer, one hogshead of sack, and eating up all our meat, and killing at least one hundred deer,' the earl's steward ruefully reported, 'we were rid of our guests.'

Admittedly by now civilians had become resigned to such manners, but the behaviour of the parliamentary soldiers four days later after the capture of Sir Charles Lucas's house, a few hundred yards south of Colchester's walls, went way beyond the pale. The victorious roundheads ran amok. They burst into the family vault, tearing open Lady Lucas's and Lady Killigrew's coffins, and dismembered the corpses of Sir Charles's mother and sister, throwing arms and legs about the vault, and cutting off their hair to wear as favours in their hats. 'This was beyond what had ever been known of before, among the most inhuman and barbarous monsters', a royalist defender of Colchester, who could have easily seen the atrocities from the walls, wrote in his diary.

Although indefensible their behaviour is explicable. In taking the house the roundheads killed only four or five defenders, letting the rest slip away, and had taken heavy casualties, many of whom were veterans, depriving the raw, terrified recruits of a steadying presence. In addition to losing their small-unit leaders, and having been badly frightened, the survivors were disappointed not to find the rich booty they had been led to expect (Sir Charles Lucas's house having been well and truly plundered on several previous occasions). So they vented their rage on the closest objects – the dead. Last, and far from least, the troopers' behaviour was part of the general viciousness that characterized the second and third civil wars, and which was to all too apparent during the Siege of Colchester.

Fighting started at 3 p.m. on 13 June, when Colonel Simon Needham's Tower Regiment attacked the Headgate, where the London road entered the city wall. The contest went on until midnight. 'Here you might see the limbs of men, horses, fire, dust confused together in one horrid Chaos', an eyewitness reported.[42] Having lost their colonel, two captains, and a hundred other ranks, Needham's men went beserk, slashing and killing like lunatics, taking no prisoners. But it did them no good, for by failing to capture the city's main gate, the roundheads condemned themselves to a long and bloody siege. Its pattern readily became obvious. The following day a soldier wrote in his diary 'Nothing of importance happened, but three of Captain Cannon's men killed with a cannon bullet.'

The parliamentary reverse at Headgate heartened the king's men. 'I earnestly desire you not to be dismayed, for we trust in God', Robert Vesey wrote home to his wife the next day, asking her to send him some clean linen.[43] On 6 July Sir Charles Lucas and Sir George Lisle led a large raiding party across a narrow footbridge over the River Colne to recapture the parliamentary stronghold at East Mill. It was as neat a piece of action the war had ever seen. One observer noted that the royalists sallied out 'as if it had been a sporting skirmish amongst tame soldiers in a general muster', killing nineteen enemy, and pitching their cannon into the river, before making a dignified withdrawal. In return Fairfax paid three grenadiers 3 shillings, and twenty assault troops half a crown, to storm the gatehouse, which they did, a chance grenade exploding a magazine, persuading ninety royalists to give up.

They were lucky to have their surrenders accepted, for attitudes towards the enemy very quickly hardened at the Siege of Colchester. By 18 June a parliamentary pamphlet was arguing that after the city capitulated, one out of every thirteen bachelors, one out of ten married men (who presumably should have known better) and a fifth of the Londoners should be shot, and the rest transported.[44]

A week later stories that the defenders were using poisoned bullets started to circulate: it was widely believed that General Goring had ordered his men to chew the bullets and roll them in sand so that they would inflict gangrenous wounds: indeed the parliamentarians claimed that several prisoners had given them affidavits to that effect. 'Our soldiers', observed a parliamentary officer, 'were exasperated with the loss of blood of their fellow soldiers, many being slain with chewed or poisoned bullets.'[45] Although these slugs were in fact crude castings made from lead water-pipes, the roundheads continued to believe that the enemy was using dum-dum rounds: in cold blood they executed some twenty prisoners taken with roughly hewed musket balls on them. John Rushworth, the parliamentary war correspondent, agreed that the enemy were getting no more than their just deserts. He reported – and thus promulgated – the tale that the royalists had amputated the fingers of several wounded officers, including a colonel, to loot their rings. Even more unreliable was the story that the cavaliers were using scythes to cut off the enemy's feet, since one unit adopted the sobriquet 'the Shavers'.[46]

Terrible cold, wet weather made the siege worse for all involved. 'The season sad and threatening', was how one diarist described August, when there were two floods within a week.[47]

Hunger – and then starvation – added to the defenders' woes. Although at first they had boasted that 'Before they yield the town they would drink their own Urine and gnaw their fingers to the bone', by August the garrison were driven close to doing so. Between July and August the black-market price of butter and cheese rose fivefold to 5 shillings a pound. Hungry troopers hunted down dogs, smashing their heads in with their musket butts, for even the mangiest of beasts would fetch 12 shillings.[48] During the siege the garrison slaughtered and ate some eight hundred horses, once roasting one whole nag in public to raise morale. By the end of the siege the daily ration consisted of 7 ounces of bread made from malt, oats and salt water. 'It was not only distasteful', noted a royalist, 'but such unwholesome food, that many chose to eat their horse and dogs' flesh without it.' The rancid horse meat was no better. John Rushworth gloated, 'Let them eat horse meat and Maggots till the flux (already among them) increases their disease.' But what else could the desperate royalists do, for as one of them explained, 'there is no death more terrible than starving'.

As appalling as the siege was for the soldiers, it was even worse for the hapless civilians trapped in Colchester. When it began the royalists threatened to place the Essex Committee, who had run the county for parliament, as hostages in the thick of the fighting. In retaliation some members of parliament suggested that they do the same to the wives of the royalist commanders. Although they did not molest Lady Norwich and Lady Capel (who was pregnant), parliament arrested and mistreated Sir Arthur Capel's 16-year-old son.

Colchester's inhabitants, who had been staunch parliamentarians in the first civil war, had little love for their uninvited guests during the second, deposing their mayor, William Cooke, 'an ignorant wretch', for admitting the cavaliers in the first place. Women and children thronged Lord Norwich's headquarters begging him to let them leave the town. When he gave five hundred of them permission to do so, Fairfax ordered his men to fire blanks to drive them back, and, when that did not work, seized four females, whom they stripped naked, driving them and the rest back whence they came. The troopers trapped within the city were not sympathetic. According to one story, seeing a woman begging for food for her starving infant, a soldier exclaimed, 'God damn me! That child would make a good deal of meat well boiled.'

After a last desperate attempt to break out of the city (which failed largely because the common soldiers believed their officers were scheming to desert them), the 3,531 garrison of Colchester surrendered on 28 August. Only a barrel and a half of powder were left, and the last dog, cat and most of the horses had been devoured. 'It was a sad spectacle to see', wrote John Rushworth, 'so many fine houses burnt to ashes, and so many inhabitants sick and weak.' Even though there was little loot to be had from the vanquished cavaliers, 'Our troops could not without much difficulty and slashing be kept from falling upon them', wrote William Osborne to his wife, 'so greedy they were for new clothes and of the spoil of the enemy.' One hundred and eighty houses had been burned in the siege, the city was fined £14,000, while the number of dead was nigh incalculable – burials having passed unrecorded in the parish registers with the collapse of local government.[49]

Colchester's defenders held out for as long and as bravely as they did because they hoped that the invading Scots would beat Cromwell's troops and triumphantly relieve them. At the time this was a perfectly reasonable aspiration because the forces that crossed the border on 8 July, 'bringing', complained a parliamentary newspaper, 'their lice and their Presbytery', were – on paper at least – impressive enough to make royalists gloat:[50]

> For Cromwell's Army's not so great
> As men here do suppose.
> The Scots can at breakfast eat
> All but his fiery nose.

Acting from national – rather than nasal – considerations, parliament prepared to defend England. Among the troops they raised was Captain Samuel Birch's company which was mustered 'after much money spent and pains taken' in Manchester on 15 May.[51] It was a fairly typical territorial unit of 137 men including a captain, lieutenant, ensign, two sergeants, a couple of drummers and three corporals. After a few days' training they marched to the Siege of Beetham House, Cumberland, where they were lucky not to lose a single man. During their first six or seven weeks the new company lived well, almost entirely on free quarter, and moved nearly every day.

After Beetham House surrendered on 20 June, Captain Birch's men marched to Carlisle 'in extremity of wet and foul weather', finding the occasional night's shelter in barns. 'A miserable time for the soldiers as I have ever seen', concluded their commanding officer. They were employed guarding the border before trekking back to Carlisle, the weather having got even worse. 'Such a wet time', noted Birch at Penrith on 8–9 July, 'hath not been seen in the memory of man. The soldiers in great want of provisions.' A week later the Scots ambushed his men at Appleby, killing four or five of them and wounding several more. The survivors must have panicked for they retreated for two days without pausing to eat. In August the company was at Knaresborough, where the arrival of reinforcements under Cromwell so inflated the cost of food that Birch's men could hardly buy a thing with the sixpence a day they were issued. As part of the field army they moved west, across the Pennines, where on 17 August they fought in the climactic Battle of Preston. 'Diver's soldiers shot or hurt, some very dangerously, most performed well', was their CO's laconic summary.

Unlike Naseby, Marston Moor or Edgehill, Preston was a long drawn out, dispersed and extremely confused confrontation. On its first day Cromwell's forces fought Langdale's English royalists among the hedgerows and narrow lanes of Ribbleton Moor. Captain John Hodgson recalled that initial resistance was slight. The first enemy his Lancashire company encountered were huddling in a ditch, from which they shot irresolutely above his men's heads. This so encouraged Hodgson's troops that they readily followed him behind a hedgerow to outflank the enemy, who promptly threw down their weapons. Soon, however, the going got rough. 'There was nothing but fire and smoke', Hodgson remembered, 'The bullets flew freely: then was the heat of the battle that day.'[52]

Gradually the royalists were pushed west into Preston, where around the bridge across the River Ribble fighting lasted until nightfall. That evening the Duke of Hamilton decided to withdraw south towards Warrington where he hoped to take up a strong defensive position behind the River Mersey.

Quickly the retreat turned into a rout. At Wigan Sir James Turner ordered his Scots rearguard to make a stand in the market-place. Standing shoulder to shoulder the pikemen waited. It was – for once – not raining. In the moonlight a regiment of Scots cavalry appeared. Turner ordered his infantry to open ranks to let them through. 'But my pikemen being demented (as I think we were all) would not hear me, and two of them ran full tilt at me' with their pikes, one of which just missed his belly, while the other pierced the inside of his right thigh. 'This was an unseasonable wound', the veteran dryly commentated. Outraged by the craven behaviour of his Scots infantry, all of whom were by now chanting that they were 'Cromwell's men', Turner ordered the cavalry to charge. When they refused, he shouted that the roundheads were attacking, which terrified the horsemen into breaking through the foot, trampling many under hoof. Turner managed to gather up some of the survivors, and marched for two more days before a surgeon tossed him a bandage, telling him to

325

dress his wounds for himself. By now the invaders' morale had collapsed. When Trooper Patrick Grey shot his captain, whether deliberately or by accident, he was executed on the spot. But that did not deter the soldiers from mutinying to stop the débâcle from continuing.[53]

Apart from the 'most tempestuous, windy and rainy weather', as well as an unbearable fatigue, the most serious problem facing the roundheads after Preston was dealing with the thousands of Scots prisoners of war. Many civilians simply murdered the stragglers in revenge for their terrible plundering. The rest were easily rounded up, too shattered to escape. 'Two men will keep a thousand from running away', Cromwell told Speaker William Lenthall, 'Surely, Sir, this is nothing but the hand of God.'[54]

After spending a few days mopping up after the battle, and guarding prisoners, more to protect them from irate civilians than to prevent them running away, Captain Birch and his company were given five days' rest and recuperation 'not far from the sea side'. Next they marched to Waddington before moving north in September to Kendal and Penrith 'still miserably distresed for want of meat'. On 9 October they took part in the surrender of Appleby Castle, of which Birch was appointed governor. With the end of the campaign season half his company were given leave to visit home, their commander boasting that not a single one of his men had mutinied, unlike those of so many other captains he might mention. Birch was even prouder when all the furloughed men reported back to Appleby Castle, which they demolished on 10 December, before moving up to guard the border. During the winter, stuck amidst the bleak countryside, morale plummeted, and Birch's boasts proved premature: there was a mutiny in his company, for which two of his men were cashiered. The company patrolled the border until March, when they returned to Manchester, where on 29 March 'we lodged our colours, lay down our arms, and disbanded'.

In ten and a half months Birch's company had moved at least 84 times, took part in one major battle, two sieges and one ambush. For 300 days' service they had received 138 days' pay, mostly getting by on free quarter. During this time 178 men served in the company, 38 of whom deserted, 3 were discharged sick, 7 with permission, 2 were cashiered for mutiny, 2 for stealing, 1 was transferred to another unit, and perhaps a dozen were killed or died of wounds or sickness. Of the original 137 members recruited in May 1648, 99 stayed with the company until it was disbanded in the following March. Perhaps because they were mainly from Manchester the original cadre were far less likely to desert than replacements drawn from other areas. All but 7 of the 122 members of the company who fought at the Battle of Preston were from the original group. Of the 38 men who deserted from Birch's company, 14 did so before Preston, and 24 afterwards. Combat played little part in their decision to run; only

3 men deserted between 17 and 20 August, compared to the 12 who ran between 18 and 20 September after receiving three weeks' pay.

The experiences of the Scots troopers who surrendered after Preston were far less pleasant than those of the victorious roundheads. They were so many, and so demoralized, that through indifference and pure hatred thousands of them died like flies. For instance, of the fifteen hundred prisoners who were jammed into St Thomas's Church, Chapel-en-le-Frith, between 14 and 30 September, forty-four died, and fifteen more succumbed during the 50-mile march to Chester. Parliament set up a committee to try to deal with the five thousand prisoners taken after Preston. It recommended that all conscripts be sent home on the promise never again to invade England, while all volunteers were to be shipped as slaves to the Barbados.

Sir James Turner was marched to Hull where he was held in the common gaol.[55] Conditions were severe. His captors threatened to clap him in irons if he did not take the covenant, and – adding insult to injury – charged him Ritz-rates of 1s 6d a day for food, 1s 0d for bedding and a groat for candles. In December his wife arrived. 'I was extremely glad to see her, though very sorry that she should have made so long a journey in so bad a time of year.' Lady Turner managed to get her husband moved to a better prison in Newcastle, where she stayed with him for a month before returning home. After she had left, and he learned that his estates had been confiscated, and that the king and the Duke of Hamilton (his old CO), had been executed, Turner became extremely depressed, gaining little pleasure from the solitary walks he was permitted with an escort of two guards. At last, in November 1649, after fourteen months in captivity he was released on paying his gaolers £45 and promising to go overseas for at least a year. So delighted was Turner to be free (and scared lest the army change their minds) that he took the first ship out of port, not caring where it was headed.

Compared to other senior officers Turner was lucky to escape with his life: the army was determined to make an example of the leaders of the second civil war.

At Cardiff in May 1648 Cromwell shot two of the prisoners he had taken during the Welsh campaign, and sold 240 of the bachelors for a shilling apiece to be transported to Barbados.[56] After the surrender of Tenby Castle two months later, he shipped the three leaders of the Welsh revolt, Colonels John Poyer, Rowland Laugharne and Rice Power, to the Tower, where they were court-martialled and sentenced to death. At General Fairfax's command, only Poyer, chosen by lot, faced the firing squad in the Piazza at Covent Garden.

The defenders of Colchester met a similar fate. After surrendering the town the rank and file were mercilessly pillaged, before being marched off. Those who were too ill and faint to keep up, the guards 'pistolled in the highways'. The survivors were shipped to the Barbados or else to prisons throughout the land. In an attempt to try to discredit stories about their mistreatment, parliamentary hacks wrote about how grateful the prisoners held at Woodstock were for the many kindnesses of their gaoler, Captain John Grimes:[57]

> The Little birds in praise of him shall sing
> In honour of his name the bells shall ring,
> The woods shall echo for his resounding fame
> And everything shall honour Grimes his name.

It is unlikely that such verses either charmed or convinced, especially after the executions of Sir Charles Lucas and Sir George Lisle. Immediately following the army's entry into Colchester on 28 August, Fairfax arrested Lisle, Lucas and Sir Bernard Gascoigne (a Tuscan mercenary). By two the next afternoon a court-martial condemned them to death for breaking the paroles they had given in the first civil war. At about seven that evening the three were marched out to the Castle Keep. Lucas was first. As his shattered body fell, Lisle ran forward catching it, tenderly kissing the face. Then, standing to receive the volley, he told the firing squad to come closer, lest they miss.

'I'll warrant you sir,' replied a trooper, 'we'll hit you.'

'Friends, I have been nearer you when you have missed me', Lisle sardonically replied. But for once their aim was true (plate 11).

Having taken off his coat to meet the fate of his comrades Gascoigne was reprieved. Because he was a foreigner, Fairfax did not want to upset public opinion abroad.

There is no doubt, however, that by shooting Lisle and Lucas the general inflamed opinion at home. Very quickly the pair became martyrs: it was said that the grass never again grew on the spot where they fell. Within a few days eight pamphlets appeared condemning this 'most barbarous unsoldierly murder'. Edmund Verney, who was himself to be murdered a year later at Drogheda, called it 'an act so horrid and barbarous'.[58] Even though Fairfax explained that Lisle and Lucas had been shot as a warning, as well as 'for some satisfaction of military justice, and in part to avenge the innocent blood they had caused to be spilt, and the trouble, damage and mischief that they have brought', hardly a royalist was convinced, particularly after the execution of the most famous of the victims of the second civil war.

When the army council had met in a tear-filled session at Windsor Castle five months earlier at the start of the second civil war they enunciated this theme of spilled blood. 'It was the duty of this day to go out and fight,' the council declared in April 1648, and 'to call Charles Stuart, that man of blood, to account for the blood he had shed, and mischief that he had done.'[59] Of course, the reasons for the king's death are many and complicated. Yet for the soldiers who chopped off his head one stood out: that having once surrendered, Charles had reneged, and was no longer entitled to the protection accorded prisoners of war. In other words – like the garrison of a town who held out beyond all reasonable hope of relief – the king and his crew were not entitled to quarter, since their stubborn malignancy had caused 'the needless loss of much blood'. The indictment against the king listed specific battles – Edgehill, Caversham, Gloucester, Newbury, Cropredy, Bodmin, Leicester, Naseby, at which he had been present, and at which consequently 'much innocent blood of the free people of this nation has been spilt, many families undone . . . '.[60]

If, as S. R. Gardiner has alleged, the king's trial and execution was 'the work of military violence cloaked in the mere tatters of legality', for the soldiers who brought him to justice it possessed a legitimacy that fitted their code.[61] While there is no doubt that the news of the king's execution caused that sort of cosmic shock that comes at most once in a generation, many a roundhead who fought in many a battle against the king welcomed it with a fervent amen! 'That the king is executed is good news to us: only some few honest men and a few cavaliers bemoan him', wrote Cornet John Baynes to his brother Adam, from Pontefract, where he was besieging the last royalist hold-out. Baynes thought that chopping off Charles Stuart's head would persuade Pontrefract to surrender, make other royalists see sense, and lead to the execution of 'justice upon Hamilton, Goring, etc.'[62]

The cornet did not have long to wait. On 28 March 1649 the Duke of Hamilton, leader of the Scots invasion, the Earl of Holland, leader of the Kentish rising, and Arthur Lord Capel, a commander at Colchester, who had escaped from jail and been recaptured, were publicly beheaded in front of the parliament house in Westminster on a scaffold the army had specially erected for the occasion.

Having punished its enemies at home, the army turned to deal with those abroad. And there were none, they agreed, more worthy of chastisement than those who had first shed innocent English blood – the foul papist rebels of Ireland.

When fighting resumed in Ireland in 1646 it was conducted with that unmitigated savagery which had been the norm for centuries. After helplessly watching the Irish kill parliamentary prisoners at the Battle of Knockanoss in 1647, an English officer cheerfully noted how his troops made the rebels 'pay the price of their insolent attempt by putting the greatest part of them to the sword'. Day after day the slaughter continued. 'We were killing till night as fast as we could', the officer concluded. An English diarist recorded that at Clontarfe the 'soldiers got very good pillage, and so left the town burning'. The following summer Roger Boyle, later Earl of Orrery, reported that at Limerick 'We had a fair execution [i.e. massacre] for about three miles, and indeed it was bloody, for I gave order to kill all, although some prisoners of good quality were saved.'[63] Colonel Michael Jones, the parliamentary commander in Ireland, ordered some six hundred prisoners killed in cold blood, on the grounds that they were deserters: indeed after he captured his own nephew, Elliot, who had gone over to the crown, he had him hanged.

Cromwell, who succeeded Jones, was in an equally merciless mood even before he sailed for Ireland. He assured his senior officers that God wanted them to crush these barbarians, and told the rank and file to think of themselves as Israelites ordained to extirpate idolatry from Canaan. Crossing the Irish Sea was a far more turbulent going-over than that of Jordan, for according to Chaplain Hugh Peters (who prided himself as something as an expert both on maritime as well as mortal transitions), Cromwell was sicker than any man he had ever seen. In Dublin the general announced that 'God hath brought him thither . . . for the carrying out of the great work against the barbarous and bloodthirsty Irish.'[64]

Cromwell wasted no time in beginning His great work, although he did so in a most barbarous and bloodthirsty manner. Marching north on 10 September the parliamentary army arrived at Drogheda, the strategic town that controlled the mouth of the River Boyne.[65] Well protected by a wall 1½ miles long, 20 feet high, 6 feet thick at the base and 4 at the top, dotted with some 29 guard towers, and defended by 319 cavalry and 2,221 infantry, Drogheda was a tough nut to crack. 'He who could take Drogheda could take Hell', boasted its governor, Sir Arthur Aston, the veteran soldier.

Never loath to engage the devil (or at least Irish papists whom he thought just as bad, if not worse), Cromwell called upon Aston to surrender, warning that 'If this be refused you will have no cause to blame me.' When the Irish spurned this offer the English opened up with their siege cannon, firing five hundred rounds that made at least two breaches in the wall south of the River Boyne. The following day the first two assaults were repulsed with heavy loss of life, including Colonels Close and Nicholas Wall. It was a Promethean struggle. When a cannon ball struck off his legs, Lieutenant-Colonel Warren continued fighting on his stumps, until the English hacked him down. Going so often into the breach that it became too crammed with English dead – not to mention the corpses of some fifty Irish prisoners murdered in hot blood – that they could no longer return, the English fell back. It seemed as if the Irish had won.

So in person Cromwell led one last desperate throw, which 'after a very hot dispute' broke through the barricade of bodies. Several thousand roundheads poured through the breach, chasing the enemy the hundred yards or so up to St Michael's Mount, a man-made hill. It appears that the English van granted the Irish quarter, but Cromwell, white with fighting fury, countermanded that no prisoners be taken. The English beat Sir Arthur Aston to death with his wooden leg, convinced that it held his stash of gold coins (they were eventually found in his money belt). The terrified survivors retreated across the river to St Peter's church, where a thousand more were murdered. Some took refuge in the steeple, where they got no sanctuary from this Army of Saints. Cromwell ordered the pews to be dragged underneath and set alight to smoke them out. One rebel was heard screaming 'God damn me, God confound me. I burn, I burn.' Smouldering bodies dropped from the tower. One brave man jumped, and having broken only a leg was spared. Other defenders escaped to the walls, from which they sniped down at the English. So Cromwell ordered all the officer prisoners to be knocked on the head, every tenth man shot, and the rest sent to the Barbados. His chaplain gloated that over 3,500 Irish perished at Drogheda for the loss of only 64 English. On the other side the Earl of Inchiquin lamented, 'There was never so cruel a fight'.[66]

Nearly as many perished the following month in the even crueller massacre at Wexford, where on 11 October, after a traitor opened the gates, Cromwell's men poured into the town. Even though they had been spared the horrors of a storm their blood lust was unmitigated. In the mêlée two boat-loads of refugees sank, drowning some 330 folk, many of them civilians. Priests and friars were dispatched without mercy, as they foolishly approached the puritans brandishing crucifixes in the misguided hope that this would save them. Two hundred women were butchered at the Market Cross as they begged for quarter. 'Seeing thus the righteous hand of God upon such a town and people', explained Cromwell, 'we thought it not good nor just to restrain our soldiers from right of pillage nor doing execution upon the enemy.'[67]

The bloodletting continued. In October Cromwell routed the Irish in a very vicious skirmish on the beach at Arklow, 7 miles north of Wexford. After the Irish cavalry had driven his horse back into his infantry, the general ordered them to fire at point-blank range. 'Whereby some of them begun to tumble, the rest running off in great disorder.' Seeing this panic fear, 'our horse took encouragement . . . the enemy was in great confusion and disorder. . . . It pleased God to give our men courage: they advanced and, falling upon the enemy, totally routed them.'[68]

Ten days later four hundred men were killed at Carrick, where the defenders hurled stones down from the walls. Tired and ill, Cromwell's army continued to campaign through the winter. 'I tell you,' its commander wrote to parliament, 'a considerable part of your army is fitter for a hospital than the field.'[69] In February 1650 the army massacred the two hundred defenders of Callan who refused to surrender. After taking the small outpost of Thomastown in October Cromwell hanged the sergeant and corporal since they were the most senior officers left alive. Even though a couple of days later on 20 March Gowran Castle surrendered 'at mercy', Cromwell reported 'all but one officer shot & a priest hanged'.[70]

The fighting did not always go Cromwell's way. Arriving at Clonmel in County Tipperary on 27 April he immediately ordered the garrison to surrender. Even though desperately short of supplies, Hugh Duff O'Neill refused, enduring a twelve-day artillery bombardment that breached the wall. But behind the breach O'Neill built a corral of stones, timber, and even dung, in front of which he dug a 6-foot trench. So when over a thousand roundheads charged through the breach at eight on the morning of 9 May they were trapped. An eyewitness recalled that the enclosure

> was crammed full with horsemen armed with helmets, back breast swords, muskets and pistol. On which those in the front, seeing themselves in a pound, and could not make their way further, cried out 'Halt! Halt!' on which those entering behind at the breach thought by those words that those of the garrison were running away, and cried out 'Advance! Advance!'

After the Irish closed the gap with their pikes, Hugh Duff O'Neill's men shot down into the heaving mass with muskets and grapeshot, stabbing them with pikes, slashing them with scythes, until 'in less than an hour's time about a thousand men were killed, being atop one another'. Cromwell was as angry 'as ever he was since he first put on a helmet against the king,' observed an officer in Clotworthy's regiment, 'for he was not used to being thus repulsed'.[71]

Even though Cromwell never returned to Ireland after sailing home from Youghall to Bristol on 28 May 1650, the legacy of his expedition has remained ever since. During the 1650s the English confiscated the land (roughly 55 per cent of the whole) of some six thousand Irishmen, forcing untold thousands more on pain of death to move to the barren west. 'To Hell or Connaught' were the alternatives the English offered papists whom they could not imagine going anywhere but down in the next life. And the Irish have never forgotten the brutality of Cromwell's conquest. In 1972 a best-selling record (which topped the pops in Dublin) protested against the introduction of internment without trial in Northern Ireland:[72]

> Through the streets of Belfast
> In the dark of early morn,
> British soldiers come marauding
> Wrecking homes with scorn . . .
> Round the world the truth will echo
> Cromwell's men are here again.

When Cromwell's men went to Scotland in 1650 they did not make such a lasting impression.

As the Montrose campaign demonstrated, fighting in Scotland was far more vicious than that in England (although less so than in Ireland).

Towards the end of the first civil war General David Leslie besieged Dunaverty Castle on the Mull of Kintyre. Even though the garrison of three to four hundred men under Archibald Mor Macdonald was short of supplies, it refused to surrender, prompting Leslie's troops to attack, with the loss of forty men, including a popular major. When force failed, Leslie resorted to guile: by cutting off its water supply he made the garrison surrender. All but one of them (a young man who was allowed to enter the French Army), he either had shot or tossed over a cliff roped together. 'Should we not deny here was cruelty enough', thought a veteran of the Thirty Years' War, 'for to kill men in cold blood, when they had submitted to service, hath no generosity at all in it.'[73]

The cruelty of Cromwell's invasion of Scotland came less from deliberate brutality, and more from arrogance compounded by unbridled success. The Ironsides who marched north across the border in the summer of 1650 did not think much of the Scots. Their streets were empty, their women were 'pitiful sorry creatures': poorly dressed, they constantly whined how the lairds had drafted their menfolk.[74] The roundheads found the noise of the pipes hideously archaic, since English soldiers had given up trying to march to that din years ago.

Gradually the weather worsened. Morale fell. In spite of the rain and cold the troops were too exhausted to carry their tents, and surplus rations, so threw them away. For looting some curtain material a soldier in Colonel Coxe's regiment was hanged on a specially built gibbet, the country being so bare that there were no trees available. Realizing that his army was falling apart Cromwell manoeuvred for days outside Edinburgh desperately trying to bring the enemy to battle.

He managed to do so at Dunbar in September. On the morning of the 2nd Captain Hodgson recalled that the English army was 'shattered, hungry and discouraged'. In addition the Scots outnumbered them, 22,000 to under 12,000. Leslie drew up his forces on Doon Hill, blocking the English retreat south to Berwick. Less than six thousand of the Scots were adequately trained, their officers had been chosen more for their loyalty to the kirk than to their men, hardly any of whom they had bothered to get to know. One royalist dismissed them as 'ministers' sons, clerks and sanctified creatures'.[75]

The quality of Cromwell's officers and men was markedly higher, most of them being veterans of many a scrap. On the eve of the battle the Scots captured an English trooper, an old sweat, who had lost an arm fighting in the first civil war. General Leslie asked if the Ironsides intended fighting. 'What', he retorted, 'do you think we came here for?' So impressed was the Scots commander that he released the fellow, who promptly reported the conversation back to Cromwell, adding that the enemy had plundered him of 20 shillings. And so impressed was Cromwell that he personally gave the veteran £2.[76]

Cromwell took advantage of his men's pugnacity at four on the morning of 3 September by unleashing his infantry against the centre of the Scots lines. 'I never beheld a more terrible charge of foot than was given by our army', reported a veteran correspondent. As a cold wet dawn broke, and a thin moon waned, they caught the enemy unawares: many Scots officers had left their units to bed down in more comfortable billets; more soldiers lacked lighted match to fire their weapons. So when Cromwell outflanked the Scots' right, pinning them between Doon Hill and the English infantry to their front, a panic fear set in. Dawn revealed a ghastly sight (plate 14). After pushing back some Scots cavalry, Captain Hodgson and his company moved forward to the crest of a hill, where they saw the terrified horse trying to crash through the ranks of confused foot, hacking and slashing their own men, trampling many of them to death. Those who survived dropped their arms, begging for quarter or else running mindlessly about, seeking safety. Few found it. An observer wrote:[77]

> The Foot threw down there Arms, and both Horse and Foot Ran several ways. . . . We pursued them as far as Hoddington, killing, wounding them all the way, there were about 4,000 slain in this place, and in the pursuit about 10,000 taken Prisoners, most of them wounded. . . . We lost not forty men.

Faced with this huge bag of prisoners Cromwell ordered the sick and wounded to be sent home, on condition that they left their weapons behind, and dispatched the remaining 5,100 south to Newcastle, with instructions to its governor, Sir Arthur Haselrig, to 'let humanity be exercised towards them'.

It was not. At Morpeth the captives were jammed into a walled garden. Since many had not eaten for eight days they dug up and gobbled raw cabbages which gave them dysentery. Most of the survivors were herded into Durham Cathedral, where in one of England's loveliest buildings took place an atrocity as ugly as that of the Burma Railway. Even though they received some oatmeal, beef, more cabbages, coal for heat, plus straw to lie upon, the 'flux' ravaged the Scots. They 'were so unruly, sluttish and nasty', Haselrig reported, 'they acted rather like Beasts than men'. Within this holy hell-hole all discipline broke down. Underneath the high Gothic ceiling and stained-glass windows men lay dying in their own blood and excrement, their moans echoing like some ghastly plainchant in the cathedral's superlative acoustics. Some men simply gave up. Those with money were robbed and murdered: those with warm clothes were strangled and stripped. By the end of October only six hundred Scots were left alive. 'They do still die daily', Haselrig concluded, 'and so doubtless so they will, so long as any remain in any prison.'[78]

Some of the survivors were shipped as indentured servants to New

England. Many, such as John Stewart, a veteran of all five of Montrose's victories, were sold as indentured servants to the Lynn iron works. Most were treated decently, being given medical attention, housing and land. Two thousand five hundred more were transported to fight in Ireland. Some were sent to Virginia, while a few unfortunates ended up in that purgatory, Barbados. In October 1651 those still alive at Durham were sent to King's Lynn to work as forced labour draining the Fens.[79]

How many of the Scots who were marched south from Dunbar ever made it home one cannot say, but it would not be unreasonable to estimate that half died as a result of their experiences – twice as high a proportion than those who perished on the Burma Railway.

In many ways, down even to the date of its climactic confrontation, the Worcester campaign was a replay of Dunbar. In 1650, the year after his father's execution, Charles II went to Scotland where he took the covenant with ill grace. Positive that the English would flock to join his standard, on 3 August 1651 he crossed the border at the head of 16,000 Scots troops. They were a ramshackle lot: the soldiers plundered with the enthusiasm that their senior commanders reserved for quarrelling amongst each other, or for making pessimistic prognostications. General Leslie was convinced that his army 'would not fight', while the second Duke of Hamilton considered the invasion 'very desperate'.

Even though the Scots won a skirmish at Warrington (prompting the English royalist, Sir Humphrey Mildmay, to brag 'the news grows hot and good'), fewer than two thousand recruits had joined the king by the time he arrived at Worcester on 23 August.[80] It was a strategic town located on the River Severn in rich farmland that provided ample supplies for the royalists, who were exhausted from marching 300 miles in twenty days. They had less than a week to rest and rebuild the city's crumbling walls, before Cromwell arrived with 28,000 men.

At five in the morning of 3 September the roundheads attacked, moving north on both sides of the Severn towards Worcester. On the west bank Fleetwood's men advanced across the River Teme at Powick Bridge, while the bulk of the fighting between Charles and Cromwell took place east of the River Severn. After about two hours royalist resistance collapsed. The defeat was worse than ever, as the royalists were driven back into Worcester, where the slaughter was appalling. 'What with the dead Bodies of the Men and the Dead Horses of the Enemy filling the streets, there was such a nastiness that a man could hardly abide the town', remembered Bulstrode Whitelocke.[81]

Two thousand, perhaps three thousand, royalists perished in the carnage. Some of the fugitives were so exhausted that country folk simply cudgelled in their skulls. Others stood and fought – at least for a while. A hundred royalist horse galloped to Kidderminster where in the market place they were ambushed by thirty roundheads. 'And till Midnight the Bullets flying towards my Door and Windows, and the sorrowful fugitives hastening for their Lives', wrote Richard Baxter, 'did tell me the Calamitousness of War.'[82]

The victors, who claimed to have lost only two hundred men, had no doubt whom to thank. 'We are the people that the Lord hath done all this for', exulted a parliamentary journalist. 'The Lord of Hosts was wonderfully with us', thought Sir Robert Stapleton. Oliver Cromwell agreed that 'the Lord appeared so wonderfully in His mercies'.[83]

The victors were equally sure whom to blame. Although they failed to apprehend and execute Charles II, who after several narrow escapes made it back to the Continent, they wreaked vengeance on his minions. Parliament ordered the Council of State to make an example of those taken at Worcester, and in its turn the Council instructed the governors of Liverpool, Chester, Stafford, Worcester and Shrewsbury to send all captives in their hands to Bristol for transportation. Public opinion seemed to support revenge. In Bromsgrove a blacksmith told the fugitive king that Charles Stuart deserved to hang 'more than all the rest for bringing in the Scots'. Doubtless relieved that the fellow had not seen through his disguise, His Majesty tactfully agreed.[84] Only the surgeon's incompetent treatment of Hamilton's shattered leg, which became fatally gangrenous, saved the Duke from the axe. The Earl of Derby, Captain John Benbow and Sir Timothy Fetherstonaugh were executed, as were five other ranks captured at Chester.

Initially the ten thousand prisoners taken at Worcester were herded into the cathedral, from whence they were marched to London. The lucky ones were fed on tuppence ha'penny a day, and were lodged in churches along the way. Henry Newcombe, minister of Sandback, Cheshire, remembered that the prisoners 'were miserably used', and in a sincere, if misguided attempt to cheer them up, gave them a brace of sermons.[85]

A few Scots, such as the indefatigable Sir James Turner, managed to escape. Taken to Oxford he cut his way through the roof of the house in which he was incarcerated. Climbing out through an empty building next door, he slipped past the sentries, to hide for two days in a house under construction, before meeting up with some other fugitives. They were not the best of company. While his companions did carry him a couple of miles after his ill-fitting shoes turned his feet bloody raw having walked in them for three leagues, they insisted on stopping at every tavern they passed for several rounds of ale which Turner had to stand. 'I thank God they would drink no wine', recalled the thrifty Scot. At Mortlake he hired a decrepit nag from an extremely rude old man. So low had he sunk, thought Turner, that no 'man could ever have conceived that I had been an officer in any army in the world'. Eventually he made it to the capital, where he hid for several weeks, before finding a ship that took him to the Continent.[86]

Even though the Council of State ordered that all the officers and every tenth other rank be court-martialled, the army lacked the resources to try so many prisoners. Instead parliament sent the bulk home on parole to a war-torn Scotland, where many of them found it desperately hard to make an honest living. On 2 December 1651 Robert Bell, a survivor of the Worcester campaign, was sentenced to be hanged for robbing an English soldier of £10.

The army sent the rest of the captives, about 1,300 English and some foreign mercenaries, as virtual slaves to Barbados. Since it cost no more than £5 to ship these wretches to the West Indies where they were sold for £10 to £30 depending on their skills, the trade was almost as lucrative as it was cruel. Heinrich Von Uchteritz, a German soldier of fortune, transported with nineteen compatriots captured at Worcester, recalled how he had 'a miserable life' in Barbados. He mucked out pig houses and swept the slave quarters. Other captives toiled in the grinding room or sugar mills. Up at 6 a.m. they were worked, with but an hour's break for a meal of boiled maize mush, for twelve hours a day under the relentless sun. They were treated abominably. 'I have seen an Overseer beat a servant with a cane about the head till the blood flowed for an offence which was not worth the speaking of', noted a traveller. Von Uchteritz was lucky that some German merchants ransomed him for 800 lb of sugar after only eighteen weeks of servitude. He went back to his family convinced that 'no one, but myself, as far as I know, came out again'.[87]

A few others did. After fourteen years in Barbados Thomas Jackson returned to England where he was arrested in April 1665 for speaking 'treasonable words' against Charles II. Caribbean slavery seems to have addled Jackson's mind, for the Kendall magistrates excused his behaviour saying that, 'The fellow seemeth but simple.'[88]

A similar judgment might have been made on anyone who prophesied that less than nine years after his last and in many ways his greatest victory at Worcester, Cromwell's rule would have collapsed, and the rump of his army would have restored Charles II to the throne. Although royalist resistance did not end after the Battle of Worcester, by September 1651 to all extents and purposes the civil wars were over.[89] Indeed during the second and third civil wars the totality of the army's victories at Colchester and Preston, in Ireland, at Dunbar and outside Worcester made the royalist risings during the commonwealth even more pathetic. The original Sealed Knot had about as much chance of overthrowing the government as does its namesake today. Penruddock's rising in Salisbury began as a farce and ended as a tragedy: its leaders were executed, and their dupes transported. Of course, the tensions that helped produce the civil wars did not die away after hostilities ended. The hatreds that engendered the Irish massacres of 1641 may still be seen on the streets of Belfast today. And yet the Battle of Worcester in 1651 marked the 'stand down'

337

of the wars to which a decade before so many young gaily went, and from which too many did not return.

Preaching to the victorious, battle-bloody Ironsides at Worcester, drawn up in their tired but Godly ranks, some having received their baptism of fire a decade earlier at Powick Bridge, a couple of miles away, and the site of the wars' first main skirmish of 23 September 1642, Hugh Peters declared:[90]

> When your wives and children shall ask you where you have been, and what news: say you have been in Worcester, where England's sorrows began, where they were happily ended.

And thus sounded 'the last post', and Britain finally started to come home again from its civil wars.

14

DOES IT MATTER?

Does it matter? – losing your legs? . . .
For people will always be kind,
And you need not show that you mind
When others come in after hunting
To gobble their muffins and eggs.

Does it matter? – losing your sight? . . .
There's such splendid work for the blind,
And people will always be kind,
As you sit on the terrace remembering
and turning your face to the light.
                Siegfried Sassoon, 'Does it matter?'
                    Poems (New York, 1949), 76

For William Blundell of course it mattered. The war mattered for every
minute of each day from the second on 18 March 1643 when 'my thigh
was broken with a shot in the king's service', until the moment of his
death forty-five years later. For the rest of his life, the royalist captain
recalled, 'I was lying in great pain of my broken leg', which made walking
agony. Sometimes the anguish became unbearable. 'I may beg to God to
assist my soul when my body lies in torment, and by the extreme anguish
thereof hath stupefied or perverted my reason.' At other times he tried
to handle the distress, depression and disillusion with a mocking sense of
humour. In 1651 he wrote to Margaret Haggerston, his sister-in-law, a
bitterly whimsical letter recalling how he used to be able to walk dressed
in his soldier's uniform to see her in the halcyon days before being
wounded, and wondered if he would ever do so again:

> For you will remember what a pretty straight young thing, all dashing
> in scarlet I came into Haggerston [Hall] when you saw me last. But
> now, if you chance to hear a thing come – Thump – Thump – up
> your stairs like a knocker, God bless us, at midnight, look out confi-
> dently: a gross full body of an ell [45 inches] or more in the waist. . . .

339

The thing is no goblin, but the very party that we talk on. 'By my truly,' you will say, 'and that was a great pity.' And by my troth, sister, it is so.

Even though Blundell admitted that *'Affliction gives great understanding'*, underlining the words in his commonplace book, there is no doubt that the civil war did make a difference, and that no matter how kind people were, he could never again fully turn his face to the light.

While the violence of the war killed many hundreds of thousands of people, destroying families, widowing women, orphaning children, and forcing individuals to endure some of the most horrible experiences we can know, the impact of the war – as a war – was surprisingly limited. That is not to say the civil wars were unimportant. In terms of British history there was no more significant happening. But the residue of war was not a lost generation, not one which swore 'Hell Never', not even a generation which wanted to say Goodbye to all that, as it appeased its enemies. What terrified posterity was less the war, and more the social dislocation it caused. The Commonwealth turned their world upside down: the Restoration tried as best it could to return it right side up.[1]

And here lies a paradox: that collectively the effects of the civil wars, as military experiences, were, particularly in England, far less than one might anticipate.

To be sure, directly or indirectly a very large number of people lost their lives in the civil wars. As has been suggested in chapter 9 casualties amounted to 190,000 (or 3.7 per cent of the total population) in England, 60,000 (6 per cent) in Scotland, and perhaps as many as 660,000 (41 per cent) in Ireland, making a total for the British Isles of 868,000 (11.6 per cent). Using the number of prisoners taken in England as a base it would not be too hazardous to conjecture that one out of every four adult males served at some time in some capacity in the armed forces. General Robert Venables, a parliamentary commander, thought that the wars 'were so general that almost every man was in action or affection engaged in them in one part or another'.[2]

In England, at least, the loss of life was replaced fairly rapidly. The war deaths represented a short-term phenomenon which does not really show up all that much in the decade-based demographic data. During the century from 1570 to 1670, 660,000 people died of the plague in England and Wales, three and a half times more than from the civil war: yet during this whole period the population of the country continued its healthy growth.[3]

Women might lose husbands, and children their fathers, but orphanage was a sadly familiar fact of family life in early-modern England. Some women remarried, many children found stepfathers or uncles to help them grow to maturity. While the pain of bereavement lasted a lifetime, families rarely carried losses, either of members or of wealth, from one generation to another. The Fifth Baronet Clarke's claim that he had been forced into highway robbery by the financial losses sustained by his predecessor, Sir Simon, a Warwickshire gentlemen, during the civil war sound like special pleading. It worked. The baronet escaped the gallows: he was transported to Jamaica instead.[4]

The fact that the vast majority of loved ones had been killed fair and square, or had died from disease, an act of God, muted the desire for revenge, and hatred of the enemy. A father killed by the Nazis in his tank is just as dead as one murdered in their gas chambers: yet the legitimacy of one death as opposed to the crime of a holocaust helps the scars of war heal far sooner.

Yet during the civil wars, when a relative was killed illegitimately, there was little the survivors could do about it. What most upset Adam Martindale was not his being drafted into the parliamentary army, or the bankrupting of his father's grain business, or the fact that his royalist sister had been plundered time and time again. Adam was bitter about the way in which Lord Derby had dragooned his brother to fight at Edgehill, by threatening to shoot him if he refused. It was not fair, Adam concluded.[5] John Harvey's son would have agreed. In 1646 a soldier from Tutbury Castle robbed and shot John Harvey as he was riding to Uttoxeter Market. Although his son tried to find out who had killed him he was unable to do so. Years later Humphrey Hill, who had been a member of the Tutbury garrison, approached the son and offered to tell him the murderer's name. At the last moment, however, he changed his mind, and there was nothing that the Harvey family could do about it – except hate.[6]

After the fighting ended most folk, however, wanted to put animosities behind them and get on with the rest of their lives. Sir Aston Cokayne wrote to his friend, Sir Henry Hastings, with a degree of sincerity that – he admitted – exceeded his literary skills:[7]

> What tumults we have seen and dangers past
> Such as in graves many thousand cast!
> And though I am no poet, I confess
> I am enamored of quietness.

William Osborne, a soldier in the parliamentary forces, agreed with these sentiments. After surviving the Siege of Colchester, and describing the destruction and looting of the city, as well as the shooting of Lisle and Lucas, he ended a letter to his wife by saying how much he wanted to return home to his normal, sane, safe, boring routine:[8]

> My thoughts are now (dear heart) inclining homeward, and I shall follow my letter at the heels and return to my former condition,

which I think not on without much perplexity to my spirit, but the will of God be done.

When Englishmen returned home to live with their families, to take wives, bring up children, and marry them off, sometimes they did so with erstwhile enemies. After the war ended the sister of Sir Henry Vane, a prominent parliamentarian, married the ardent royalist, Sir Thomas Riddel. The death of her husband, John Meldrum, a parliamentary colonel, in battle did not stop his widow Jane from marrying his kinsman, George Meldrum, a royalist major. Perhaps the most famous roundhead/royalist marriage was of Sir Thomas Fairfax's daughter, Mary, to George Villiers, second Duke of Buckingham. Admittedly Cromwell tried to stop it, sending a cavalry patrol to Yorkshire, but the family approved. Parental attitudes to such marriages were on traditional lines: he was not good enough for her; her dowry was not large enough for him. Although after the Restoration Colonel John Hutchinson fulminated when he heard that his son had secretly married Sir Alexander Ratcliffe's girl, that he 'was so discontent that he at once resolved to have banished them together', he soon becme reconciled to being linked with a prominent cavalier family.[9]

Physical wounds did not heal so quickly: indeed wounds that heal are nothing more than temporary annoyances. Even though Stephen Winthrop, a Colonel in the New Model Army blamed his sciatica on 'my much lying in wet fields' he was still able to live a reasonable life. The badly wounded became dependent on the charity of others. During his three and a half years' service in the king's forces Robert Davies was wounded seventeen times, having suffered a cracked skull, lost the use of both feet and of one eye, and had thus to petition for a 40-shilling pension.[10]

Damaged property tended to be repaired far more quickly than broken bodies. For one thing it was easier to restore the former: for another there was money to be made in doing so.

In once sense the civil wars were immensely costly. Professor Aylmer has suggested that in terms of Gross National Product the cost of the civil war for the British Isles was not exceeded until the world wars of the twentieth century.[11] Buildings were destroyed: yet seventeenth-century fighting did not damage the environment as does modern war with all its high explosives. Cities were sacked, but most were rebuilt. Many were burned, yet fire, like London's Great Fire of 1666, was all too common a catastrophe. People lost goods: yet plunder still remained in circulation. Even though Elizabeth Coole almost certainly never got back her husband's boat, valued at £6, which was requisitioned in 1644 for the crossing of the River Ouse, perhaps someone else made good use of it, if only for a quiet afternoon's fishing.[12] The royalist blockade of Newcastle cut off

London's coal supply, forcing the city to cut down all its trees for fuel. Yet they soon grew back again.

The war was a – if not the – high point in many men's lives. In his diary Richard Wood, Vicar of Fremington, called 1 July 1644, the date of the royalist assault on Barnstaple, as 'a day never to be forgotten by the inhabitants'. On 14 January, 'Holly-Holy Day', for over a century the townsfolk celebrated the parliamentary victory at Nantwich in 1644, by wearing sprigs of holly. At the height of the first civil war the *Weekly Accompt* declared 'we have seen the fury of the sword, and we fear the horror of the want of bread'. An eyewitness of the explosion of eighty-four barrels of powder at Torrington, that in a flash wiped out the church and two hundred prisoners penned therein, called it 'The most terriblest sight that I ever saw.' Roger Boyle explained that seeing the extermination of an English regiment near Kildare due to a lack of military knowledge had made such an impression on him that he decided to write his *Treatise on the Art of War*.[13]

There is no doubt that soldiers remembered such terrible sights till their dying day. In 1659 a miller from Barwick, Somerset, boasted that 'he was a cavalier, and he would be a cavalier, and the devil should take all them that were not cavaliers'.[14] The king's men were especially proud of their military service. On his tombstone Sir John Gibson commemorated himself as 'Kt. Of Welbourne, Captain of the North-Riding Horse under King Charles the Martyr'. John Pitt, who died in Kidderminster in 1694 aged 76 described himself as 'a loyal subject and servant of King Charles the Martyr'. Others saw being a soldier a crucial part of the pilgrimage that is life. After the parliamentarian George Pearl died in 1644 his family erected a memorial in Barnstaple parish church describing him as 'a soldier of Christ under whose banner he fought'. Captain Daniel Blackford's tablet in Oxhill Church waxed lyrical:[15]

> When I was young I ventured my life and blood,
> Both for my king and for my country's good,
> In elder years my aim was chief to be,
> Soldier to him who shed his blood for me.

In view of the richness of the literature and art of the early seventeenth century the relative absence of war poetry, plays or painting is remarkable. Those who wrote trying to make sense of the war, tended to be ordinary folk scribbling in diaries and letters for private reading.[16] Thomas Wither's *Campo Musae* (1643), a rambling epic seventy pages long, is perhaps the best description of combat by a soldier-poet. Thomas Fuller's explanation that he was too busy and too frightened to write during the wars does not ring true. Inigo Jones, who survived the storm of Basing House, and had to be carried out naked in a blanket, all his clothes having been plundered, never sketched the civil war. The thesis of the *Leviathan*, the greatest piece of political thought to come of the period, that war is the natural state of humankind, was not based on Thomas Hobbes's own direct experience of fighting. Neither was Abraham Cowley's *The Civil War*, an epic-length description of the hostilities. Having never taken part in combat, the poet based his work largely on the newspaper *Mercurius Aulicus*. Poets who did fight, and tried to describe their experience, often ended up writing appalling drivel:[17]

> In July Last, the second day or more
> One thousand six hundred forty and four,
> On Marston Moor two awful armies met
> Opposed they stood, against another set.

And so droned on William Lithgow's attempt to describe his part in the wars' bloodiest battle.

After the wars, participants developed almost a form of amnesia. They seemed not to have wanted to remember them. Very rarely did Thomas Fuller, who became a best-selling divine, allude to his military experiences, that included being chaplain to Basing House. His definition of Gunpowder as 'the emblem of political revenge', was surely a droll reference to the fighting. But most of the time he was trying to forget in order to forgive. 'Lord, since these woeful wars began', he prayed in *Good Thoughts for Bad Times* (1659), 'one, formerly my intimate acquaintance, is now turned a stranger, yea an enemy. Teach me how to behave myself towards him.' Another popular theologian, Jeremy Taylor, exhibited a similar reticence. In 1645 he was captured at Cardigan Castle in a very brutal storm in which well over half the 350 defenders were killed. Only once did Taylor allude to this trauma in his extensive writings, and but obliquely. He compared the military storm to one at sea, in which he was cast afloat off the coast of West Wales in a little boat, and when he tried to find some safe harbour the cable broke and he lost his anchor.[18] In his *Divine Meditation up Several Occasion* (1680), General William Waller made no reference to his war services.

Soldiers who wrote military manuals after the civil wars hardly mentioned them in their texts. When Sir Balthazar Gerbier gave a public lecture in London on military fortification he did not give a single example from the recent fighting.[19] Neither did Robert Boyle in his *Treatise on the Art of War* (1673). While Sir James Turner's *Pallas Armata, Military Essays* (1683) was jammed packed with practical examples – including 156 pages from Greece and Rome alone – the Scots veteran hardly drew upon his own wartime experiences in Germany, Scotland, Ireland and England.

Such omissions might not be surprising if ex-servicemen had been able to return to civilian life as easily as they could discard a buff coat for a ploughman's smock. The parliamentary ordinance guaranteeing apprentices their old jobs back after being demobilized seems to have worked fairly well. There were exceptions. William Harrison, a felt-maker of Newcastle-under-Lyme, refused in 1646 both to re-employ his old apprentice, Thomas Parry, a four-year veteran in Colonel Bowyers's roundhead regiment, and to discharge him from his articles, explaining 'that he not cared a straw for any ordinances of parliament'.[20] Thomas Reade, a cavalier veteran, found getting work equally difficult. After the king's defeat he returned to Hereford, but finding no employment there went to London. Saying nothing about his previous service (which included acting as Colonel George Monck's secretary) he managed to find work as an accountant for a roundhead officer, who dismissed him without paying the £400 he claimed in fees, on learning of his previous service. So Reade returned to Scotland after a decade away, a bitter man. Colonel John Rosworme, the mercenary who built Manchester's defences, returned home to Germany in much the same frame of mind, because the city authorities never paid him the £60 annuity they had promised for saving them.[21]

Some old soldiers were quite literally reduced to the gutter. Captain Richard Atkyns recalled how a groom gave him a fresh horse when his had been killed under him at the Battle of Cheriton. After the battle Atkyns personally thanked the fellow and gave him £10 – a huge sum which almost certainly persuaded him to desert that evening. Fifteen years later Atkyns recalled, 'I saw him begging in the streets of London, with a muffler about his face, and [he] spoke inwardly as if he had been eaten up with a foul disease.'

Such sights were comparatively rare. 'Of all the old [i.e. New Model] army you cannot see a man begging about the street', wrote Samuel Pepys in 1663, 'You shall see this captain turned a shoemaker, this lieutenant, a baker, that a haberdasher, this common soldier a porter, and every man in his apron and frock, etc., as if they had never done anything else.' The cavalier ex-servicemen were very different from the roundheads, 'running with their belts and swords, swearing and cursing'.[22]

The transition from soldier to baker, haberdasher or porter was, as Pepys suggested, complicated for it took place in two waves which affected both sides in different ways and at different times. This process limited the wars' long-term impact.

After the end of the first civil war there was not a mass demobilization of the victorious army. True, some soldiers were paid off, but many remained with the colours, demanding their rights, and striking for arrears of pay. In the second and third civil wars these soldiers put down royalist risings and crushed the Scots and Irish. Some left the service, perhaps for their old lives, or for new ones as settlers in Ireland. Many stayed with the large standing army that averaged 40,000 men during the Commonwealth, reaching a peak of 53,065 in December 1649. With the Navy, which was transformed from a local defence force into a fleet of 217 vessels able to project British power across oceans, defence spending rose to 90 per cent of the budget.[23] Those who remained in the service obviously liked the life: it was well paid and secure. Thus on the parliamentary side there were few forcibly discharged old soldiers who could not settle down in civilian life after the traumas of the war.

For cavaliers things were different – although not as different as one might expect. Many royalists who wanted to remain soldiers were absorbed into the roundhead army as they surrendered during the closing phase of the first civil war. Those who surrendered during the second and third civil wars were lucky not to be transported to Barbados. Seeing what could happen to them most royalists laid low, or went into exile.

Admittedly a few cavalier veterans, left without a pension, and with only their pistols and a horse, turned to highway robbery. In 1647 the Sheriff of Oxfordshire claimed to have arrested a hundred such villains. Perhaps the most romantic highwayman was Captain James Hinde, who had fought at Worcester, and was hanged at Oxford with two other royalist officers, Hussey and Peck. Yet the admittedly rudimentary statistics do not indicate a postwar crime wave.[24] If Sir Anthony Ashley Cooper and his fellow magistrates at the August 1646 Wiltshire Assizes were typical, ex-soldiers condemned to death were often reprieved for having 'been a faithful servant of the state'.[25]

If during the 1650s roundheads stayed with the colours, and cavaliers kept a low profile, or lurked abroad in exile, after the Restoration the whole order changed. Roundhead officers such as John Hodgson tried to avoid cavaliers, such as Daniel Lyster, anxious to settle old scores. 'I told him that the business was over', wrote Hodgson, 'and that it was not reasonable to rip into old troubles.'[26] Charles II was able to restrain his followers. Unlike most exiles he had not grown more ultra abroad. If they were determined on revenge, Charles gave it to them in symbol terms. Cromwell's corpse was dug up and vilified. The regicides were hunted down and executed. But there was no massive punishment, or return of lost lands. Even though some died bravely, such as the regicide John Okey, pledging his faith in 'that Good old cause', Charles II created no martyrs as did Bloody Queen Mary Tudor.

The new king was content to let bygones be bygones. The City of London quite literally scratched out its history of co-operation with Cromwell by drawing lines through the appropriate pages of its record books. William Morris, a royalist gentleman from North Wales, went through the diary he wrote during the war changing 'the rebels' to 'the parliamentarians'. Instead of altering the record the Reverend Whitehead of Swinsehead, Hampshire, hid it. He boarded the copy of the covenant that he and fifty of his flock had signed behind the ceiling of his study, where it remained undiscovered until 1846.[27]

The assistance the king proffered to his old soldiers tended to turn them into dependants. At the Restoration many cavalier officers hoped to be revenged for their sufferings:[28]

> We have ventured our estates,
> And our liberties and lives,
> For our Master and his mates
> And have been tossed by cruel fates,
> When the rebellious Devil Drives
> So that one out of ten survives . . .
> We have fought, we have paid
> We've been sold and betray'd.

Alexander Brome's estimates that only a tenth of the cavalier officers had survived seems hard to accept since nearly seven thousand of them applied for the £60,000 that Charles set aside for their relief in 1663. Doing so co-opted them into the system, which was why, Richard Oxinden explained, he was not asking for help from the new regime.[29]

When old wounded soldiers appeared before local magistrates petitioning for assistance, they had to do so deferentially, for a pension was no right. Sergeant William Stoakes, of Shepton Mallet, was wounded at the war's first battle, Babylon Hill, fought at Edgehill, Brentford, took part in the capture of Bristol and the Siege of Gloucester, stormed Bolton, 'received many dangerous hurts' at Marston Moor, and was taken prisoner at Naseby. In 1662 he petitioned the Somersetshire magistrates saying how much he had suffered from 'the usurped and tyrannical power' of parliament, 'and since it had pleased God to restore his sacred majesty', Sergeant Stoakes hoped that the magistrates would grant him a pension. They did.[30] Forty shillings a year was enough to keep him quiet and loyal to the new regime.

William Mercer endorsed this view. A veteran of the king's service at Gloucester, Lostwithiel and Ireland, he published *The Moderate Cavalier* in 1675:

> From Gloucester's Siege till Arms laid down
> In Trewoe fields, I for the Crown,
> Under St. George Marched up and Down,
>   And then Sir
> For Ireland came, and had my share
> Of Blows, not lands, gained in that war.
> But God defend me from such fare.
>   Again Sir.

The king's old soldiers were not incendiaries, he argued, but honest men who should be rewarded, not, however, by pensions, charity, or doles, but by their betters giving them honest work.[31] Their betters agreed.

When asked if the ex-servicemen surely deserved some benefits for having ventured their lives, Sir Thomas Wroth, a Somersetshire gentleman, curtly observed, 'they were well paid for it'.

The war had scared many Englishmen. It was not the loss of life, or even the property damage which had frightened them. It was their dislike of soldiers, and more, their fear of seeing their world turned upside down again. The king got his own again at the Restoration so that England would never again be twirled topsy-turvy.

Having had troopers plunder them, insult them, wound them, and kill their family and friends, most Englishmen wanted as little as possible to do with the army. 'As for soldiers', wrote Sir Roger Burgoyne in 1645 'I could never trust them.' In celebration of the wars' end, William Blundell wrote, 'The husbandman may now enjoy his own/And look the armed soldier in the face.' Anthony Wood described those undergraduates who went down from the university to become soldiers as having 'been *debauched* by bearing arms'.[32] Of course, killing left men with a deep distrust of the army. As ambassador to Sweden Bulstrode Whitelock described to his hosts the horrors of civil war: 'brother against brother, sons against father, fathers against sons'. But what petrified him the most was having the social order turned head over heels. The English people, declared the ambassador, were sick and tired of seeing 'servants riding on horseback & Masters in great want'.[33]

Letters, pamphlets and ballads show how widespread were these sentiments. The thing which most upset the royalists about the trial and execution of Robert Yeomen and George Bowyer, two citizens of Bristol, for plotting to betray the city to Prince Rupert's forces, was the social composition of the members of the court-martial. William Bowels was 'a Pedant, and from whipping of Boys was made an unrighteous judge'. Robert Baught was 'a sheep skin dresser', who in better times would have stood hatless in Alderman Yeoman's presence, but now leapt up from his chair and snatched the cap from the accused's head.[34]

> Beggars are Lords and Lords are beggars made
> The Holy war hath had a gallant trade,
> Knaves are ennobled, good men undone we see,
> Can a more thorough reformation be?

So asked William Dugdale in 1649.[35]

The Restoration provided an answer. No standing army was its slogan. A fear of soldiers, not because they killed people, but because they turned society head over heels, became its keyword. Perhaps the abuses of Cromwell's major generals were exaggerated, but the fear of a standing army turned the revolution of 1688 into one as bloodless as that of 1640 had been bloody. This unconscious memory of the war has remained within the Anglo-American tradition long after William Walker, the last surviving civil war soldier, died in Chelsea Hospital in 1736.[36] The ghost of Oliver Cromwell sat with the Founding Fathers as they wrote the Constitution in 1787. In England the system of purchasing commissions remained in force until 1871 to make sure that no russet-coated captain who knew what he fought for and loved what he knew should lead British soldiers into battle – lest he might be tempted to do so against his betters.

The English experience was very different from that in Ireland and Scotland. For one thing the civil war in England was less the product of long-term forces building up over the decades, even centuries, and more the result of short-term events, as well as miscalculations on the part of the king. Even though the war came to be fought over the central issue of religion it did not start as a war of religion. Indeed many of the causes of the first English civil war, particularly the immediate ones, are to be found outside England in Scotland and Ireland.

This helps explain why Scottish and Irish fighting was very different and far bloodier.

The fighting in Scotland began with a deep-seated religious confrontation, the rejection of an English Prayer Book. It soon became more a complex clan feud with roots dating back centuries, as well as a religion-based Highland/Lowland struggle. 'Throughout Argyll we left neither house nor hold unburned, nor corn, nor cattle, that belonged to the whole name of Campbell', boasted Colonel James MacDonald, an Irish officer in Montrose's service. The loss of Scots lives was appalling, especially during the second and third civil wars, when ten thousand Scots may have died in captivity or exile. Seven hundred of the thousand clansmen Sir Hector MacLean of Duart had raised, died at Inverlocky in 1651. Twenty-three years later thirty-two of a hundred and forty holdings in the clan's estates were still vacant. The war destroyed Scottish self-confidence. If anything, violence got worse, especially as the growth of the cattle trade provided rich pickings for rustlers. The 1707 Act of Union did not solve the problem. That came after the defeat at Culloden Moor in 1745, and the ensuing Scots Diaspora.

The civil wars in Ireland were part of a centuries-old struggle. After the Tudor conquest the English had two options, conciliation or extermination. Religious and ethnic differences made the first impossible: some Irish nationalists would suggest that the English tried the latter with the Cromwellian settlement of the 1650s and the famine of the 1840s. Be that as it may. There is no doubt that the Irish Revolt of 1641 and the ensuing horrors were one more chapter in the sad story of Anglo-Irish relations. This seventeenth-century war is not over. It seems likely that it will continue to fester in the tawdry streets of Derry or Belfast well into the twenty-first century.

From one thought, however, we can take some comfort. No matter for how many years Ulster's seventeenth-century war may last, it will not produce the nuclear Armageddon of a world war. In times of tension and détente the threat of war will always remain. So will its legacy. In spite of the commanders and conquests, the change of governments and destruction of tyrants, the development of destructive technologies and ideologies, war remains an individual act. And so too is coming to terms with war, understanding it, even, perhaps, overcoming it. War, be it ancient or modern, is perhaps best understood by letting the survivors tell their stories. Such is not an easy process. After all they found war hard enough to comprehend. 'Thou wouldst think it strange', wrote Sir John Oglander, the cavalier, to his posterity, 'if I should tell you that there was a time in England when brothers killed brothers, cousins cousins, and friends their friends. . . . When thou went to bed at night, thou knewest not whether thou should be murdered afore day.'[37]

Many – even most – of the men, women and children who lived in the British Isles in the middle of the seventeenth century went in some way or another to the wars. Some did so gaily, others were forced. Some left innocently, others knowingly. The wars were an adventure to some, an opportunity for others, and a catastrophe to many more. Richard Lovelace was one of the uncountable victims. Like many a young man who went off to the wars, he discovered that the face of battle was not as pretty as he would have his fair Lucasta believe. He was imprisoned, freed on bond, lost his brother. Lovelace fought for the king in the war's closing stages. Having become utterly disillusioned, he emerged into a post-war world where he believed 'the dragon hath vanquished St George'. Lovelace wrote:[38]

> Now the Sun is unarmed,
> And the moon lies as charmed
> And the stars dissolved to a jelly,
> Now the thighs of the Crown,
> And the arms are lopped down,
> And the body is all but a belly.

And what happened to his Lucasta? Well they say she married Mr Dinnent, a nobody from Leicester: for no matter how many folk war kills, she knew that life must somehow go on.

NOTES

ABBREVIATIONS

All dates are old style, with the year starting on 1 January. References to correspondence in the Notes normally take the form: date, sender, addressee, source. Manuscripts are cited by the call number. Place of publication is not given if London. To save space, references occurring in close proximity in the text have been grouped under one note number, with a full stop between each. Books published between 1641 and 1700 have often been identified by their number from Donald G. Wing, *Short Title Catalogue of Books Printed in England, Scotland, Ireland, Wales and British Americas and British Books Printed in Other Countries*, 1641–1700 (New York, 1945–51).

BIHR	*Bulletin of the Institute of Historical Research.*
BL	British Library
Bodleian	Bodleian Library, Oxford
CSPD	*Calendar of State Papers Domestic.*
CSPV	*Calendar of State Papers, Venetian.*
CUL	Cambridge University Library.
Clarendon, *History*	Edward Hyde, Earl of Clarendon, *The History of the Rebellion and Civil Wars in England*, 6 vols (Oxford, 1888).
CUL	Cambridge University Library.
DNB	*Dictionary of National Biography*, ed. L. Stephens and S. Lee, 63 vols (1885–1900).
Folger MSS	manuscripts in Folger Shakespeare Library, Washington, DC.
Gardiner, *Civil War*	S. R. Gardiner, *The History of the Great Civil War*, 4 vols (1893).
Gardiner, *Commonwealth*	S. R. Gardiner, *History of the Commonwealth and Protectorate*, 3 vols (1894–1901).
Gardiner, *History*	S. R. Gardiner, *History of England, 1603–42*, 10 vols (1893).

HMC	Historical Manuscripts Commission.
JSAHR	*Journal of the Society for Army Historical Research.*
n.pa.	no pagination.
n.d.	no date.
Rushworth, *Collections*	John Rushworth, *Historical Collections of Private Passages of State*, 6 vols (1680-1701).
SP 16	State Papers, Charles I, in Public Record Office, London.
STC	A. W. Pollard and G. R. Redgrave, *A Short Title Catalogue of Books Printed in England, Scotland and Ireland and of English Books Printed Abroad 1475–1640* (1969), followed by citation number.
TRHS	*Transactions of the Royal Historical Society.*
TT	Thomason Tracts: in British Library.
Warburton, *Cavaliers*	E. G. B. Warburton, *Memoirs of Prince Rupert and the Cavaliers*, 3 vols (1849).

1 THE ACTUALITIES OF WAR

1 Anthony Wood, *Athenae Oxoniensis* (Oxford, 1813), 460. John Aubrey remembered him as 'an extraordinary handsome man, but proud. He wrote a poem called *Lucasta*', *Brief Lives* (Harmondsworth, 1982), 265.
2 John Morrill, 'The Religious Context of the Civil War', *Transactions of the Royal Historical Society*, 5th series, XXXIV (1984), 155–78. Historiographical surveys can be found in P. A. M. Taylor, *The Origins of the English Civil War* (Boston, 1960), and R. C. Richardson, *The Debate on the English Revolution* (1967). M. Kishlansky, 'Saye What?', *Historical Journal*, 38 (1990), 917–37. J. S. A. Adamson, 'Politics and the Nobility in Pre-Civil War England', *Historical Journal*, 39 (1991), 231–55.
3 See for instance, Steven Ellis, '"Not mere English": the British Perspective, 1400–1650', *History Today*, XXXVIII (December 1988), 4–49.
4 In using 'British' in a geographical, rather than a political or cultural sense, my intention is not to offend Irish susceptibilities. The fact that there is no clear word to define the relationship between the various parts of the United Kingdom may help explain its lack of unity over the centuries.
5 *The Widowes Lamentation for the Absence of their Dear Children and Suitors and for divers of their deaths in these fatal civil wars* (1643, W2093).
6 There are no shortages of description of individual battles. By one reckoning some 386 accounts of Naseby have been written, Sir Charles Rowe, *The Battle of Naseby* (1988), n.pa. I am grateful to the author for sending me a copy of this pamphlet.
7 Mary Coate, *Cornwall in the Great Civil War* (Oxford, 1933). R. W. Ketton-Cremer, *Norfolk in the Civil War: a Portrait of a Society in Conflict* (Hamden, Conn., 1970). A. C. Wood, *Nottinghamshire in the Civil War* (Oxford, 1937). David Underdown, *Somerset in the Civil War and Interregnum* (Newton Abbot, 1973). A. J. Fletcher, *A Country Community in Peace and War: Sussex,*

1600–1660 (1975). Alan Everitt, *The Community of Kent and the Great Rebellion* (Leicester, 1973). Valerie Pearl, *London and the Outbreak of the Puritan Revolution* (Oxford, 1960).

8 C. H. Firth, *Cromwell's Army* (1962), and C. H. Firth and G. Davies, *The Regimental History of Cromwell's Army* (2 vols, Oxford, 1940).

9 Ronald Hutton, *The Royalist War Effort, 1642–46* (1983). Ian Roy, 'The Royalist Army in the First Civil War', Oxford D.Phil., 1963. P. R. Newman, 'The Royalist Army in the North of England', York, Ph.D., 1978. Joyce Malcolm, *Caesar's Due: Loyalty and King Charles, 1642–1646* (1983).

10 J. H. Hexter, *The Reign of King Pym* (Cambridge, 1941). Blair Worden, *The Rump Parliament* (Cambridge, 1974). Brian Manning, *The English People and the English Revolution* (1976).

11 Richard Holmes, *Acts of War: The Behaviour of Men in Battle* (New York, 1985), 7–8, forms the basis of this passage.

12 Leo Tolstoy, *War and Peace* (Harmondsworth, 1971), 921. Karl von Clausewitz, *On War* (Harmondsworth, 1968), 102.

13 Norman Dixon, *On the Psychology of Military Incompetence*, quoted Holmes, *op. cit.*, 4. W. T. Divale and M. Harris, 'Population Warfare and the Male Supremacist Complex', *American Anthropologist* 18 (1976), 521–33. *Boswell's Life of Samuel Johnson*, ed. Anne and Irvin Ehrenpreis (New York, 1966), 307. J. Keegan and R. Holmes, *Soldiers: A History of Men in Battle* (New York, 1986), 261. For an unsympathetic view of the relationship between masculinity and violence see Betty A. Reardon, *Sexism and the War System* (New York, 1985).

14 Bulstrode Whitelocke, *Memorials of the English Affairs* (Oxford, 1853), I, 215.

15 Dedicatory verse to Lt.-Colonel Richard Elton, *Complete Body of the Art Military* (1650, E653).

16 Holmes, *op. cit.*, 58.

17 Clarendon, *History*, V, 464.

18 B. Liddell Hart, *Strategy: the Indirect Approach* (1964), 23–4.

19 G. Ward, Ric Burns and Ken Burns, *The Civil War: An Illustrated History* (New York, 1990), 394. William H. Davenport (ed.), *Biography Past and Present: Selections and Critical Essays* (New York, 1965).

20 Gwynne Dyer, *War* (1986), 4. R. J. Lifton, *Home from the War: Vietnam Veterans: Neither Victims nor Executioners* (New York, 1973), 191.

2 THE DRUM'S DISCORDANT SOUND

1 C. H. Firth, *Cromwell's Army: A History of the English Soldier during the Civil Wars, the Commonwealth and the Protectorate* (1962), 6.

2 R. Lockyer, *Buckingham* (1981), 251.

3 R. Johnson, *Relations of the Most Famous Kingdomes and Commonwealths* (1630), 28, quoted L. Boynton, *The Elizabethan Militia* (1967), 262.

4 *CSPD, 1638–9*, 448.

5 *CSPD, 1637–8*, 594.

6 Robert Baillie, *Letters and Journals* (Edinburgh, 1841–2), I, 41.

7 H. P. Kendal, 'Local Incidents in the Civil War', *Halifax Antiquarian Society Reports* (1909–10), 3.

8 Geoffrey Parker, *The Military Revolution* (Cambridge, 1988), 1. M. Roberts, *The Military Revolution, 1560–1660* (Belfast, 1956).

9 G. N. Clark, *War and Society in the Seventeenth Century* (1958), 9–10.

10 Karl von Clausewitz, *On War* (Harmondsworth, 1968), 119.
11 L. Schwoerer, *'No Standing Armies!'* (Baltimore, 1973). J. Brewer, *Sinews of Power* (New York, 1989).
12 G. R. Elton, *Policy and Police* (Cambridge, 1972), 4–5.
13 Alan MacFarlane, *The Justice and the Mare's Ale* (New York, 1981), 11–22.
14 *Certaine Sermons Appointed by the Queen's Majesty to be Declared and Read by all Parsons, Vicars and Curates Every Sunday and Holiday* (1623), 89–98.
15 L. Stone, *The Crisis of the Aristocracy 1558–1641* (Oxford, 1965), 770.
16 J. A. Sharpe, *Crime in the Seventeenth Century: A County Study* (Cambridge, 1983), 131–3. The rates for Sussex appear to have been a little higher: C. B. Herrup, *The Common Peace: Participation and the Criminal Law in Seventeenth-Century England* (Cambridge, 1987), 26.
17 Macfarlane, *op. cit.*, 191.
18 0.88 riots per annum as compared to 2.83: figures calculated from Buchanan Sharp, *In Contempt of All Authority* (Berkeley, 1980), 10.
19 Macfarlane, *op. cit.*, 190ff.
20 For more on the problems of crime statistics see: Lawrence Stone. 'Interpersonal Violence in English Society, 1300–1980', *Past and Present*, 101 (1983), 22–37; J. A. Sharpe, 'History of Violence in England', and L. Stone, 'A Rejoinder', *Past and Present*, 107 (1985), 205–24; J. S. Cockburn, 'Patterns of Violence in English Society: Homicide in Kent, 1560–1985', *Past and Present*, 130 (1991), 70–107.
21 Oliver Millar, *Rubens and the Whitehall Ceiling* (1958), 18.
22 P. Bjurstrom, 'Rubens' "St George and the Dragon" ', *Art Quarterly* (Spring 1955), 27–42.
23 Abraham Cowley, *Writings*, ed. A. R. Waller (1905–6), I, 22–3.
24 Thomas Carew, *Poems* (1640), 29–30, quoted by W. Schumaker, 'Vox Populi: The Thirty Years' War in English Pamphlets and Newspapers', Princeton Ph.D. (1975), 29–30.
25 D. Stevenson, *Alisadair MacColla and the Highland Problem in the Seventeenth Century* (Edinburgh, 1980), 16–19. G. Parker, *The Military Revolution* (Cambridge, 1988), 29.
26 Parker, *op. cit.*, 29. A. Macfarlane, *The Justice and the Mare's Ale* (Cambridge, 1981), 191.
27 John Gillingham, *The Wars of the Roses* (Baton Rouge, 1981), 4–5.
28 I am grateful to my colleague Larry Champion for the point about the printing of *Richard II*.
29 Mervyn James, *English Politics and the Concept of Honour* (1978), 33.
30 The only aristocrat to be executed was Lord Audley, for rape and sodomy in 1631. Charles personally signed the warrant that John Archer, the ringleader of the 1640 attack on Archbishop Laud's palace, be racked to find out the names of his accomplices, SP 16/465/50.
31 L. Stone, *Crisis of the Aristocracy* (Oxford, 1965), 266.
32 J. Nichols (ed.), *The Progresses, Processions and Magnificent Festivities of King James the First* (1828), 971.
33 2/3/25, Cromwell to Carleton, SP 84/126/3.
34 Anthony Weldon, *The Court of King Charles* (1811), II, 27.
35 John Glanville, *The Voyage to Cadiz*, ed. Alexander Grant (Camden Society, 1883), 3–4.
36 8/11/25, Wimbledon to Buckingham, SP 16/9/30.
37 8/11/22 and 2/11/25, Delaware to Edmondes, BL: Stowe MSS, 176, 268.
38 *A Journal of all the Proceedings of the Duke of Buckingham* (1627). A Con-

tinued Journal of all the Proceedings of the Duke of Buckingham (1623), and *A True Report of all the Special Passages of Note Lately Happened in the Island of Ré* (1623).

39 Sir Edward Conway to his father, the Secretary of State, SP 16/78/71.

40 Firth, *op. cit.*, 2–3.

41 J. R. Kent, *The English Village Constable, 1580–1642* (Oxford, 1986), 277.

42 William Hunt, *The Puritan Moment* (Cambridge, Mass., 1983), 183–4.

43 S. J. Stearns, 'Conscription and English Society in the 1620s', *Journal of British Studies*, XI, 2 (May 1972), 1–23.

44 John Rous, *Diary*, ed. M. A. E. Green (Camden Society, 1856), 1 and 13.

45 16/11/27, ? To Mead, Thomas Birch, *Court and Times of Charles I*, ed. R. F. Williams (1848), I, 285.

46 *CSPD, 1628–29*, 240.

47 Schumaker, *op. cit.*

48 Stearns, *op. cit.*, 5.

49 C. V. Wedgwood, *The Thirty Years' War* (New York, 1961), 493. G. Parker, *The Thirty Years' War* (1984), 211.

50 Schumaker, *op. cit.*, 248. Barbara Donagan, 'Codes and Conduct in the English Civil War', *Past and Present*, 118 (1988), 68–9.

51 Folger MSS, V. A. 436, fol. 26v.

52 Sydenham Poyntz, *The Relations of Sydenham Poyntz, 1624–36* (Camden Society, 1990), 80.

53 W. C. and C. E. Trevelyan, *Trevelyan Papers* (Camden Society, 1872–3), 80.

54 R. D. Fitzsimon, 'Irish Swordsmen in the Imperial Service in the Thirty Years' War', *Irish Sword*, IX (1969), 22–31. Jane H. Ohlmeyer, 'The Wars of Religion, 1603–66', 19–21. E. M. Furgol, 'Scotland turned Sweden: the Scots Covenanters and the Military Revolution, 1638–1651', 5–6. I am most grateful to Dr Ohlmeyer and to Dr Furgol for sending me a copy of their unpublished papers.

55 Sir James Turner, *Memoirs of his Life and Times, 1630–72* (Edinburgh, 1829), 6–10. Thomas Raymond, *Autobiography* (Camden Society, 1917), 38.

56 *CSPD, 1640–41*, 212.

57 *A Worthy Speech of the Rt. Honourable the Lord Brooke* (1643, B495), n.pa. HMC, *Twelfth Report*, appendix, pt IX, 56–63.

58 J. P. Kenyon, *The Civil Wars of England* (New York, 1988), 44.

59 Rushworth, *Collections*, V, 145. M. Toynbee, *Cropredy Bridge: 1644, the Campaign and the Battle* (Kineton, 1970), 18–21.

60 These figures are based on an analysis of G. Smith and M. Toynbee, *Leaders of the Civil Wars, 1642–1648* (Kineton, 1977).

61 John Rosworme, *Good Service Hereunto Ill Rewarded, or an historical relation of eight years service . . . done in and around Manchester* (1649, R1996). W. G. Ross, *Military Engineering during the Great Civil War* (1984), 30–2. Kenyon, *op. cit.*, 49. P. R. Newman, *Companion to the English Civil Wars* (New York, 1990), 53.

62 S. Reid, *Scots Armies of the 17th Century: Army of the Covenant, 1639–51* (Leigh-on-Sea, 1988), 12–13.

63 Joyce Malcolm, *Caesar's Due: Loyalty and King Charles, 1642–1646* (1983), 234–5.

64 J. Corbet, *A True and Impartial History of the Militarie Government of the Citie of Gloucester* (1647, C6249), 11.

65 W. Barriffe, *Military Discipline for the Young Artilleryman* (1643, B917), chapter 1.

66 Firth, *op. cit.*, 9.
67 J. Adair, 'The Court Martial Papers of Sir William Waller's Army, 1644', *JSAHR*, 44 (1966), 214–15.
68 H. Oakes-Jones, 'The Old March of the English Army', *JSAHR*, 6 (1927), 5–8. M. C. Fissell, 'Tradition and Invention in the Early Stuart Art of War', *JSAHR*, 65 (1987), 133–47.
69 A. J. Fletcher, *A Country Community in Peace and War: Sussex, 1600–1660* (1975), 187.
70 G. Markham, 'The Muster Master', ed. C. L. Hamilton, *Camden Miscellany*, 4th series, 14 (1975), 49–75. T. G. Barnes, *Somerset, 1625–1642* (1961). Fletcher, *op. cit.*.
71 D. P. Carter, 'The Exact Militia in Lancashire, 1625–1649', *Northern History*, 11 (1975), 87–108.
72 Boynton, *op. cit.*, 269.
73 P. Haythornthwaite, *The English Civil War* (Poole, 1983), 17.
74 T. S. Scanlon, 'Citizen Soldiers: The Role of the London Trained Bands in the Puritan Revolution', Harvard Ph.D. (1974). Boynton, *op. cit.*, 262.
75 A. A. Garner, *Boston in the Great Civil War* (Boston, 1972), 1. A. L. Leach, *The History of the Civil War (1642–49), in Pembrokeshire* (1937), 30.
76 David Stevenson, *The Scottish Revolution, 1637–44* (Newton Abbot, 1973), 140–5. M. C. Fissell, 'Bellum Episcopale: The Bishops' Wars and the End of the Personal Rule in England, 1638–1640', California at Berkeley Ph.D. (1983), 61, 85–7.
77 *CSPV, 1640–42*, 16.
78 Ross Lee, *Law and Local Society in the Time of Charles I: Bedfordshire and the Civil War* (Bedford, 1986), 67.
79 D. Gardiner, *The Oxinden and Peyton Letters, 1642–70* (1937), 174.
80 John Aston, 'The Journal of John Aston', in J. C. Hodgson (ed.), *North Country Diaries* (Surtees Society, CXVIII, 1890), 5.
81 Rushworth, *Collections*, III, 1237.
82 Alexander C. Dow, *Ministers to the Soldiers of Scotland: A History of the Military Chaplains of Scotland Prior to the Crimean War* (Edinburgh, 1962), 83.
83 J. Lanes, *Reign of King Covenant* (1956), 77.
84 James Howell, *Epistolae-Ho-Elianae* (1903), I, 344.
85 SP 16/412/102–3.
86 John Livingston, *A Brief Historical Relation of the Life of John Livingston* (1736), 104–5.
87 Edward Waller, *Poems* (1893), I, 75–6.
88 Quoted in Anon., *Falklands* (1897), 98.
89 Fissell, *op. cit.*, 76.
90 C. H. Firth, 'The Reign of King Charles I', *TRHS*, 3rd series, VI (1921), 41.
91 C. R. Russell, 'Parliament and the King's Finances', *Origins of the English Civil War* (1973), 91–116. 22/1/35, Charles to Wentworth, J. O. Halliwell (ed.), *Letters of the Kings of England* (1846), II, 287.
92 C. H. Firth, 'Ballads of the Bishops' Wars, 1638–40', *Scottish Historical Review*, III, 11 (April 1906), 260.
93 Malcolm, *op. cit.*, 12–13. C. Holmes, *Seventeenth Century Lincolnshire* (1983), 137. W. Knowler (ed.), *The Earl of Strafford's Letters and Dispatches* (1739), II, 371.
94 Clarendon, *History*, I, 150.
95 Earl of Hardwicke, *Miscellaneous State Papers, 1501–1726* (1778), II, 113–21.

96 SP 16/423/29.

97 A. H. Dodd, 'Wales and the Second Bishops' War', *Transactions of the Honourable Society of Cymmrodorion*, XII (1948), 95.

98 HMC, *Twelfth Report*, appendix, pt IV, p. 552. Fissell, *op. cit.*, 63. J. Bruce (ed.), *Letters and Papers of the Verney Family* (Camden Society, 1853), 228. SP 16/455/no. 38.

99 O. Ogle, W. H. Bliss and W. D. MacGray (eds), *Calendar of Clarendon State Papers* (Oxford, 1867–76), II, 101.

100 G. Wrottesley, 'The Stafford Muster of AD 1640', *Collections for a History of Staffordshire*, XV (1894), 201–10.

101 *CSPD, 1640*, 477. *CSPD, 1639*, 59. Fissell, *op. cit.*, 182–3, 308. Bodleian: Rawlinson MSS, B210, 36.

3 A SIGHT – THE SADDEST THAT EYES CAN SEE

1 Robert E. Bell, *Memorials of the Civil War . . . The Fairfax Correspondence* (1849), I, 11.

2 William Beamont, *A Discourse on the War in Lancashire* (Chetham Society, 1864), iii.

3 W. C. and C. E. Trevelyan, *Trelawny Papers* (Camden Society, 1875), 200.

4 *Ibid.*, 210.

5 Rushworth, *Collections*, I, 297.

6 Clarendon, *History*, I, 434–5.

7 Quoted by T. L. Coonan, *The Irish Catholic Confederacy and the Puritan Revolution* (New York, 1954), 49.

8 13/8/37, Wentworth to Charles, John Nalson (ed.), *An Impartial Collection of the Great Affairs of State* (1682–3), I, 11–12.

9 A. Clarke, 'The Breakdown of Authority', in T. W. Moody, F. X. Martin and F. J. Byrne (eds), *A New History of Ireland, 1534–1691* (Oxford, 1976), 170–88. A. Clarke, *The Old English in Ireland, 1625–42* (1966), 228–9. A. Clarke, 'The Genesis of the Ulster Rising of 1641', in *Plantation to Partition*, ed. P. Roebuck (Belfast, 1981), 29–41.

10 12/12/41, *Calendar of State Papers, Ireland, 1633–47*, 344, 354. James Hogan (ed.), *Letters and Papers Relating to the Irish Rebellion* (Dublin, 1936), 1.

11 *The Autobiography of the Rev. Devereux Spratt*, ed. T. Spratt (1886), 10.

12 Thomas Fitzpatrick, *The Bloody Bridge and Other Papers Relating to the Insurrections of 1641* (Dublin, 1903, reprinted Port Washington, NY, 1970), 22, 75–7. *A Bloody Battell, or the Rebell's Overthrow* (1641, B3228), n.pa.

13 Spratt, *op. cit.*, 10. R. Baxter, *Reliquiae Baxterianae* (1696, B1370), 40. L. Hutchinson, *Memoirs of the Life of Colonel John Hutchinson* (1906), I, 173.

14 K. Lindley, 'The Impact of the 1641 Rebellion upon England and Wales, 1641–45', *Irish Historical Studies* XVIII (1972), 143–76.

15 J. L. Malcolm, *Caesar's Due: Loyalty and King Charles, 1624–46* (1983), 16, note 40.

16 Joseph Lister, *Autobiography*, ed. T. White (London, 1842), 6.

17 Richard Baxter, *Reliquiae Baxterianae*, (1696), 29–33.

18 *A Bloody Plot Practiced by some Papists in Darbyshire* (1642, F2080), n.pa. *Bloody Newes From Norwich* (1641, B3274).

19 Michael M'Enery, 'A Diary of the Siege of Limerick Castle, 1642', *Journal of the Royal Society of Antiquarians of Ireland*, XXXIV (1905), 163.

20 Thomas Carte, *Ormonde Papers* (1739), II, 53, III, 59–63. 4/6/42, Conway

to Crawford, J. T. Gilbert, *A Contemporary History of the Affairs of Ireland from 1641 to 1652* (Dublin, 1879–80), II, 138.

21 *True Relation of the ... Relieving of Tredagh* (1642, T2904), 1. *A True Relation of Diverse Great Defeats given against the Rebels of Ireland* (1642, T2903), 12.

22 Deposition of Grany ny Mullen of 25/5/53 in M. Hickson, *Ireland in the Seventeenth Century* (1884), I, 152.

23 Gilbert, *op. cit.*, I, xxxii, 35–9. For another example of similar brutality see *A Full Relation, not only our Good Successe* (1642, F2356).

24 C. I., *A New Remonstrance from Ireland* (1642, I3), 2. James Turner, *Memoirs of his Life and Times, 1630–70* (Edinburgh, 1829), 14–20. Clanricade made the warning in at least two letters: ?/7/42, Clanricade to Lord Justices, 19/5/42, Clanricade to Ormonde, Carte, *op. cit.*, III, 74, 98.

25 John Hooker, 'The Chronicles of Ireland', in Ralph Holinshed, *Holinshed's Chronicles of England, Scotland and Ireland* (1808), reprinted in Charles Carlton, *Bigotry and Blood* (Chicago, 1977), 8–12.

26 Gilbert, *op. cit.*, II, 199.

27 J. A. Atkinson (ed.), *Tracts Relating to the Civil War in Cheshire, 1641–59* (Manchester, 1909), 2–3.

28 Martin Van Creveld, *Technology and War* (New York, 1988), 110.

29 BL: Harleian MSS, 2135, 72. Robert Ram, *The Soldier's Catechism: Composed for the Parliamentary Army* (7th edn, 1645), 1–2.

30 *A Declaration of the Commons Concerning ... The Grand Rebellion in Ireland* (1643), 62.

31 Rushworth, *Collections*, V, 43.

32 Rushworth, *Collections* IV, 477ff.

33 SP 16/488/21.

34 10/1/42, Alfred Kingston, *Hertfordshire in the Great Civil War* (1894), 11. John Morrill, *The Revolt of the Provinces* (1976), 139. Bulstrode Whitelocke, *Diary* I (1990), 131.

35 Clarendon, *History* I, 589.

36 A. H. Dodd, 'Caernarvonshire in the Civil War', *Caernarvonshire Historical Society Transactions*, XIV (1953), 7.

37 Brian Manning, 'Neutrals and Neutralism in the English Civil War, 1642–46', Oxford D.Phil. (1957), 214–15.

38 HMC, *Fifth Report*, appendix, 148.

39 Morrill, *op. cit.*, 41 and 142.

40 Robert Sidney, Earl of Leicester, *Sydney Papers*, ed. R. W. Blencowe (1825), xxi. *Two Speeches made in the House of Peers* (1642), 4, quoted in J. T. Zaller, 'Anti-War Sentiment During the English Civil War', Minnesota Ph.D. (1974), 28.

41 Norman Tucker, 'Denbigh's Loyal Governors', *Denbighshire Historical Society Transactions*, V (1956), 12.

42 Ruth Spaulding, *The Improbable Puritan: A Life of Bulstrode Whitelocke* (1975), 95. W. A. Day, *Pythouse Papers* (1879), xvii.

43 HMC, *Fifth Report*, appendix, 161.

44 *The Parliamentary History ... of England* (1763), 167–8.

45 TT: 669 f8 (21).

46 Warburton, *Cavaliers*, I, 226.

47 *A True Relation of the Late Victory* (1644, T2992), 1.

48 Edward Chisenhall, *A Brief Journal of the Siege of Latham Hall, 1644* (1823), 9.

49 T. Raymond, *Autobiography* (Camden Society, 1917), 46.

50 Spaulding, *op. cit.*, 95.

51 *Reply to the Nineteen Propositions*, Rushworth, *Collections*, IV, 711.

52 Christopher Hill, *Change and Continuity in Seventeenth-Century England* (Cambridge, Mass., 1975), 181.

53 R. Ashton, *The English Civil War* (1978), 256. J. R. Phillips, *Memoirs of the Civil Wars in Wales* (1878), 111.

54 Quoted by A. C. Dow, *Ministers to the Soldiers of Scotland* (Edinburgh, 1962).

55 John Bond, *A Sermon Preached in Exon before the ... Military Officers and Souldiers of the County* (1643). Stephen Marshall, *Meroz Cursed* (1642, M762). *A Warning Peice to Warre* (1642, W937), made the same argument as did Bond, but from the parliamentary side.

56 Ashmolean MSS 830, 293. I am grateful to Dr John Morrill for bringing this reference to my attention.

57 HMC, *Portland*, I, 90.

58 J. Keegan and Richard Holmes, *Soldiers: A History of Men in Battle* (New York, 1986), 279.

59 H. J. Webb, *Elizabethan Military Science* (Madison, Wisconsin, 1965), 193, note 3.

60 W. H. Blaauw, 'Passages of the Civil War in Sussex from 1642 to 1660', *Sussex Archaeological Collections*, V (1855), 81.

61 Hudibras, iii, C2, v, iv.

62 The tradition of defending the soldiers' profession went back to the previous century with the publication of books such as Barnaby Rich, *A Right Excelent and Pleasant Dialogue Betwene Mercury and an English Soldier* (1574), Geoffrey Gates, *The Defence of Militarie Profession* (1579), and William Blandy, *The Castle* (1581).

63 Paul A. Jorgensen, *Shakespeare's Military World* (Berkeley, 1956), 74–5.

64 *A True Relation of the Passages Which Happened at Portsmouth* (21 September 1642, T3015).

65 Hutchinson, *op. cit.*, 9.

66 Keegan and Holmes, *op. cit.*, 49.

67 *A True and Exact Relation of the Secret Passages at the Siege of Manchester* (24 September 1642, T2462), 1.

68 Baxter, *op. cit.*, 40, 51.

69 D. Parker, *Familiar to All: William Lilly and Astrology in the Seventeenth Century* (1975), 132.

70 Keith Thomas, *Religion and the Decline of Magic* (1973), 313. John Hodgson, *Autobiography* (1883), 21. A. J. Fletcher, *A County Community in Peace and War: Sussex, 1600–1660* (1975), 286.

71 Turner, *op. cit.*, 14–20. D. Stevenson, *The Scottish Revolution, 1637–44* (Newton Abbot, 1973), 131. Clarendon, *History*, IV, 75–6.

72 S. Freud, *Civilization and its Discontents* (New York, 1963). K. Lorenz, *On Aggression* (New York, 1970). R. Ardrey, *The Territorial Imperative* (New York, 1970). D. Morris, *The Human Zoo* (New York, 1972).

73 Glenn Grey, *The Warriors* (New York, 1970), 28–51.

74 P. Haythornthwaite, *The English Civil War, 1642–1651* (Poole, 1983), 143.

75 S. Poyntz, *The Relations of Sydenham Poyntz, 1624–36* (Camden Society, 1908), 45.

76 R. Miles, *Ben Jonson: His Life and Work* (1985), 21. Jonson makes the same

point in his *Works*, ed. C. H. Hertford and P. E. Simpson (1947), VIII, 213–14.

77 Betty A. Reardon, *Sexism and the War System* (New York, 1985), 52.

78 Public Record Office: LC5/180.

79 S. Ashe, *Good Courage Discovered and Encouraged* (1642, A3956), 2. W. Bridge, *A Sermon Preached unto the Volunteers of the City of Norwich and Yarmouth* (1643, B4466), 10–18.

80 Field Marshal Montgomery made the same point, although less pithily: J. Ellis, *The Sharp End of War* (1980), 7. Gardiner, *Commonwealth*, II, 46.

81 In one study 75 per cent of those convicted of assaults claimed they had done so in self-defence, even if in the vast majority of cases they had landed the first blow. Hans Toch, *Violent Men: An Inquiry into the Psychology of Violence* (Chicago, 1969), 248.

82 Hogan, *op. cit.*, 6. Robert Orr, *Reason and Authority: The Thought of William Chillingworth* (Oxford, 1967), 193.

83 G. H. Tupling, 'The Causes of the Civil War in Lancashire', *Lancashire and Cheshire Antiquarian Society Transactions*, 65 (1955), 1. E. Brockbank, *Richard Hubberthorne of Yealand* (1929), 43.

84 Anthony Kellett, *Combat Motivation: The Behaviour of Soldiers in Battle* (Boston, 1982), 152. A. Fletcher and J. Stevenson, *Order and Disorder in Early Modern England* (Cambridge, 1985), 2–4.

85 W. Hussey, *The Magistrates Charge for the Peoples' Safety* (1647, H3818), 22.

86 *Certain Sermons or Homilies* (1547, reprinted with introduction by R. B. Bond, Toronto, 1987), 162–7. This theme was reinforced in *The Second Tome of Homilies* (1623), 275–322.

87 J. Bruce, *Charles I in 1646* (Camden Society, 1856), 79.

88 Sidney, *op. cit.*, xxi–xxiv. B. Schofield (ed.), *The Knyvett Letters (1620–44)* (1949), 50, 101–3. R. W. Ketton-Cremer, *Norfolk in the Civil War: A Portrait of a Society in Conflict* (Hamden, Conn., 1970), 180–9.

89 Gardiner, *History*, I, 4.

90 Warburton, *Cavaliers* I, 121. J. G. Marston, 'Gentry, Honour and Royalism in Early Stuart England', *Journal of British Studies* XIII (1973–4), 21–43. Vane to Windebanke, SP 16/465/60.

91 Quoted by John Buchan, *Oliver Cromwell* (1941), 99.

92 N. Tucker, 'Colonel Sir Roger Mostyn, First Baronet, 1624–1690', *Flintshire Historical Society Publications*, XVII (1957), 42–54.

93 S. ffarington, *The ffarington Papers* (Chetham Society, 1856), 57.

94 W. C. and C. E. Trevelyan, *op. cit.*, 240.

95 Folger MSS, V.b.2 (1).

96 Whitelocke, *op cit.*, I, 182.

97 G. Parker, *The Military Revolution* (Cambridge, 1988), 173 n. 11.

98 Edmund Ludlow, *Memoirs* (Oxford, 1894), I, 114.

99 H. Slingsby, *Original Memoirs Written During the Great Civil War*, ed. Sir Walter Scott (1806), 28. Clarendon, *History* II, 341. Baxter, *op. cit.*, 43.

100 Arnold Boate, *A Remonstrance of Divers Remarkable Passages. . . . from Ireland* (1642, B3371), n.pa.

101 Quoted by R. E. Sherwood, *Civil Strife in the Midlands, 1642–51* (1974), 180.

102 G. R. Aylmer, 'Collective Mentalities in Mid-seventeenth Century England, II: the Royalists', *TRHS*, 5 series 37 (1987), 23. A. J. Fletcher, 'Honour, Reputation and Local Office Holding in Elizabethan and Stuart England', in

A. Fletcher and J. Stevenson, *Order and Disorder in Early Modern England* (Cambridge, 1985), 92–115.

103 F. and P. Verney, *Memoirs of the Verney Family*, I, 282–3.

104 T. Barnes, *Somerset, 1625–1640: A County's Government during the 'Personal Rule'* (Cambridge, Mass., 1961), 341.

105 R. Symonds, 'Diary of the Marches of the Royal Army 1644–5' (Camden Society, 1859), 21.

106 S. A. H. Burne, 'The Battle of Hopton Heath, 1643: Transcribed from the Sutherland Papers', *Collection for a History of Staffordshire* (1936), 183.

107 *CSPD, 1644*, xxxvi, 261.

108 William Beamont, *A Discourse of the War in Lancashire* (Chetham Society, 1864), 82.

109 Sir Richard Bulstrode, *Memoirs and Reflections upon the Reign and Government of King Charles I and King Charles II* (1721), 2. John Guy, 'William Beau, Bishop and Secret Agent', *History Today*, 26, 12 (1976), 297.

110 Quoted by J. S. Scanlon, 'Citizen Soldiers: The Role of the London Trained Bands in the Puritan Revolution', Harvard Ph.D. (1974), 100.

111 J. Taylor, *Mad Verse, Sad Verse, Glad Verse and Bad Verse* (Oxford, 1644, T479).

112 Turner, *op. cit.*, 76. Rushworth, *Collections*, V, 726. C. V. Wedgwood, *The King's War* (1971), 381.

113 R. Atkyns, *Vindication of Richard Atkins* (1968), 12. Richard Holmes, *Acts of War: The Behavior of Men in Battle* (New York, 1985), 20–1, 50–1.

114 C. Carlton, *Charles the First: The Personal Monarch* (1983), 241, 261–3, 275, 280–4, 288, 290, 295, 299–302.

115 The fact that the author served in the Welch Regiment, now the Royal Regiment of Wales, may possibly have influenced his judgment on this point.

116 G. Nugent, *Some Memorials of John Hampden, his Party and his Time* (1832), I, 308.

117 J. R. Phillips, *Memoirs of the Civil War in Wales and the Marches, 1642–49* (1874), I, 199.

118 This seems to be a fairly common process. To give but two examples: the parliamentarians who surrendered at Lostwithiel fought bravely at the Second Battle of Newbury two months later, while the 51st Highland Division, after surrendering in France in 1940, and then being reconstituted, led the invasion of France four years later.

119 David Williams, *History of Modern Wales* (1951), 95–101. C. Russell, *Crisis of Parliaments* (1971), 385. A. H. Dodd, *Studies in Stuart Wales* (1952), 62. John Corbet, 'An Historical Relation of the Military Government of Gloucester', *Somers' Tracts* V, 304.

120 Carte, *op. cit.*, I, 89. N. Tucker, *North Wales in the Civil War* (Denbigh, 1958), 1.

121 Charles MacKay (ed.), *The Cavalier Songs and Ballads of England from 1642 to 1684* (1863), 86.

122 John Stallworthy, *The Oxford Book of War Poetry* (Oxford, 1988), 50.

123 A. Brome, *Poems*, ed. R. R. Dubinski (Toronto, 1982), I, 94.

124 Marston, *op. cit.*, 4, 27.

125 Thomas Venn, *Military and Maritime Discipline* (1672, V192), 3.

126 Chisenhall, *op. cit.*, 10.

127 C. V. Wedgwood, *Velvet Studies* (1949), 32.

128 M. James, *English Politics and the Concept of Honour* (1978), 4–12, 73.

129 J. Bampfield, *Apologia* (The Hague, 1685, B618), 4.

130 *Othello*, III. iii. 158–64.

131 In the First World War some 385 British soldiers were shot for cowardice, most of whom were veterans suffering from shell-shock, and thus incapable of making a rational decision. In the Second World War no British soldiers, and only one American, suffered a similar fate. Anthony Babington, *For the Sake of Example* (1983). General Sir John Hackett, *The Profession of Arms* (New York, 1983), 221, argues that the best way to manage fear is through 'the exclusion of the alternative'.

132 Ashe, *op. cit.*, 25. Esther Cope, *The Life of a Public Man: Edward, First Baron Montagu of Boughton, 1562–1644* (Philadelphia, 1981), 195.

133 Norman Dixon, *On the Psychology of Military Incompetence* (New York, 1986), 197.

134 12/6/43, Agostini to Doge, *CSPV, 1642–43*, 283. Clarendon, *History*, IV, 47, 346. Warburton, *Cavaliers*, II, 181.

135 M. Weidhorn, *Richard Lovelace* (New York, 1970), 107–60.

136 E. B. Jorgens, 'Politics and Women in Cavalier Song: A Report from a Collection of Secular Song Manuscripts', *Explorations in Renaissance Culture*, XV (1989), 25–48.

137 Rushworth, *Collections*, VI, 93.

138 *The Soldiers' Language* (1644, S4426), A4.

139 S. J. Greenburg, 'Cavalier Propaganda Stereotypes in Seventeenth Century England', Fordham University Ph.D. (1983), 152.

140 Warburton, *Cavaliers*, III, 316.

141 N. Wallington, *Historical Notes* (1869), II, 175. Orr, *op. cit.*, 189.

142 Sir Philip Warwick, *Memoirs of the Reign of King Charles I* (Edinburgh, 1825), 253.

143 S. Luke, *Letter Books* (1963), 97. *A Great Victory obtained by Colonel Norton and his horse* (1644, G1771), n.pa.

144 'A Model of Christian Charity', *The Puritans*, eds Perry Miller and T. H. Johnson (New York, 1963), 195.

145 18/10/42, Sir Bevil Grenville to wife, in John Stucley, *Sir Bevil Grenville and his Times* (Chichester, 1983), 117. V. Snow, *Essex the Rebel* (Lincoln, Nebraska, 1970), 343. Street ballads called the Earl's house 'Cuckold's Hall', Alex Broome, *A Collection of Loyal Songs Written against the Rump Parliament* (1731), I, 196.

146 B. R., *The Cambridge Royalist Imprisoned* (1643, B160), n.pa.

147 See for example *Corn-u-copia, or Roome for a Ram-Head* (1642, G6328, reprinted 1976).

148 James, *op. cit.*, 81–5.

149 Thomas Carlyle (ed.), *Oliver Cromwell's Letters and Speeches* (1904), III, 64–5.

150 P. Heylyn, *A Letter from an Officer in His Majesty's Army* (1643, H1724a), 6.

151 W. Cartwright, 'On the Queen's Return from the Low Countries', *Poems and Plays* (Madison, 1951), 351.

152 SP 16/503/561X.

153 R. H. Bainton, 'Congregationalism from the Just War to the Crusade in the Puritan Revolution', *Studies in the Reformation* (Boston, 1963), 249–58. Michael Carver, *Velvet Glove: The Decline and Fall of Moderation in War* (1982), 12–18.

154 J. B. Sanderson. *Who would Kill in 1642?* (Glasgow, 1983), 2–18.

155 L. Lloyd, *The Stratagems of Jerusalem* (1602), cited by J. R. Hale, 'Incitement

to Violence? English Divines on the Themes of War, 1578–1631', *Renaissance War Studies* (1983), 487–511.

156 Calybute Downing, *A Sermon Preached before the Renouned Company of Artillery* (1641, D2105), n.pa. Ashe, *op. cit.*, 2–6. M. Walzer, *The Revolution of the Saints: A Study in the Origins of Radical Politics* (Cambridge, Mass., 1965), 63, 282–3.

157 Sheffield Public Library, Strafford papers: 40/60. William Haller, *The Rise of Puritanism* (New York, 1957), 142–58.

158 Webb, *op. cit.*, 190ff.

159 Walzer, *op. cit.*, 278–9.

160 Robert Ram, *A Sermon Preached at Balderton March 27, 1646, Being a Day of Humiliation Throughout the Whole Army before Newark* (1646, R195), 3.

161 Baxter, *op. cit.*, 51.

162 *Ibid.*, 53.

163 Raymond, *op. cit.*, 36.

164 Day, *op. cit.*, xvii.

165 Blaauw, *op. cit.*, 31.

166 Hutchinson, *op. cit.*, 174. Sir Thomas Fairfax, *The Fairfax Correspondence*, ed. G. W. Johnson (1848), I, 441.

167 *A True Relation of the Barbarous Crueltie . . . of the Bloudy Cavaleers* (1642, T2931). A description of the same event from the other side may be found in Peter Young, *Edgehill, 1642: The Campaign and Battle* (Kineton, 1967), 296.

168 Atkinson, *op. cit.*, 62–3.

169 Malcolm, *op. cit.*, 72.

170 B. Manning, *The English People and the English Revolution* (1976), 170–2. G. A. Harrison, 'Royalist Organizations in Gloucester and Bristol', Manchester, MA (1961), 38.

171 Day, *op. cit.*, xxxiv.

172 Ralph Hopton, *Bellum Civile* (Leigh-on-Sea, 1988), 4–7. David Underdown, *Somerset in the Civil War and Interregnum* (Newton Abbot, 1973), 34–6.

4 NAMING OF PARTS

1 G. Nugent, *Some Memorials of John Hampden, his Party and his Time* (1832), II, 194–7.

2 E. W. Harcourt, *The Harcourt Papers* (Oxford, 1880–1905), I, 116.

3 The fine was remitted: see M. A. E. Green, *Calendar of the Proceedings of the Committee for Compounding, 1643–56* (1888), 1098. *Lord's Journals*, V, 81. J. Webb, *Memorials of the Civil War . . . As it Affected Hertfordshire* (1879), II, 85.

4 *The Western Husbandman's Lamentation* (1644, W1412), dialect modernized, quoted by Brian Manning, *Neutrals and Neutralism in the English Civil Wars, 1642–46* (Oxford D.Phil., 1957), 403.

5 H. P. Kendall, *Local Incidents in the Civil War* (Halifax Antiquarian Society Reports, 1909 and 1910), 8.

6 Adam Martindale, *The Life of Adam Martindale as Written by Himself* (Chetham Society, 1845), 35.

7 Charles Kerry, 'The Autobiography of Leonard Wheatcroft', *Journal of the Derbyshire Archaeological and Natural History Society*, XXI (1899), 27.

8 Sir Henry Slingsby, *Original Memoirs Written in the Great Civil War* (1806), 42–3. Richard Gough, *The History of Myddle* (Harmondsworth, 1983), 73–4.

9 William Beaumont, *A Discourse of the War in Lancashire* (Chetham Society, 1864), 19–20.
10 J. Stucley, *Sir Bevil Grenville and his Times* (Chichester, 1983), 25.
11 Brian Manning, 'The Peasantry and the English Revolution', *Journal of Peasant Studies*, II (1975), 150.
12 C. Holmes, *The Eastern Association in the English Civil War* (1975), 165.
13 It was later reduced to £60. A. A. Garner, *Boston in the Great Civil War* (Boston, 1972), 50.
14 24/8/43 and 29/4/44, Agostini to Doge, *CSPV, 1643–45*, 13 and 95. Ian Roy, 'The Royalist Army in the First Civil War', Oxford D.Phil. (1963), 184–8. J. P. Kenyon, *The Civil Wars of England* (New York, 1988), 140.
15 J. and T. W. Webb (eds), *Military Memoir of Colonel John Birch, written by his secretary* (Camden Society, 1873), 197.
16 William Barriffe, *Militarie Instructions for the Cavallrie* (Cambridge, 1632), 1.
17 T. Venn, *Military Observations, or the Tacticks Put into Practice* (1672, V192A), 3. J. Corbet, *Historical Relation of the Military Government of Gloucester* (1645, C6249), 16. T. Fairfax, *Short Memorials* (1877–90), 360. M. D. G. Wanklyn, 'The King's Armies in the West', Manchester MA (1966), 29. *A True Relation of the Late Victory . . . At Plymouth* (1644, T2992), 3.
18 Edward Cook's *The Prospective Glasse of War, Shewing You a Glimpse of War's Mysteries* (1628, STC 5669), B2.
19 28/5/40, Conway to Countess of Devonshire, M. H. Nicolson (ed.), *The Conway Letters: The Correspondence of Anne, Viscount Conway, Henry Moor and their Friends, 1642–84* (New Haven, 1930), 18. D. Johnson and D. G. Vaisey, *Staffordshire in the Great Rebellion* (Stafford, 1964), 52.
20 Sir Hugh Cholmley, *Memoirs* (1870), 59. 22/1/43, Aston to Prince Rupert, W. A. Day, *Pythouse Papers* (1879), 13.
21 *True News from Oxford* (1642, T2845), n.pa.
22 A. Wood, *Life and Times* (Oxford, 1891), 55.
23 John Adair, *By the Sword Divided: Eyewitness Accounts of the English Civil War* (1983), 74–84.
24 J. R. Hale, *Renaissance War Studies* (1983), 507.
25 W. Emberton, *Skippon's Brave Boys: The Origins, Development, and Civil War Service of London's Trained Bands* (Buckingham, 1984), 29. 21/12/42, Roe to Elizabeth of Bohemia, J. Webb, *Memorials of the Civil war . . . As it affected Hertfordshire* (1879), II, 356.
26 Rushworth, *Collections*, V, 53. B. Manning, *The English People and the English Revolution* (1976), 241–2.
27 H. A. Dillon, 'On a MS list of officers in the London Trained Bands', *Archaeologia* (1890), 129–66.
28 M. J. D. Cockle, *A Bibliography of Military Books up to 1642* (1900, 2nd edn 1957).
29 F. Varley, *Cambridge during the Civil War* (Cambridge, 1935), 125.
30 Derby Museum, *Derby and the Great Civil War: Catalogue of Exhibition, 2–23 October 1971* (1971), item 59.
31 M. J. D. Cockle, *A Bibliography of Military Books* (1900), 95, identifies Cruso as the Don: John Fassnidge, *Military Skills* (1984), 15, argues that the college fellow was too old to be a writer on war.
32 John Cruso, *The Complete Captain, or an Abridgement of Caesars Warre by Henri* (1640, STC 6099).
33 William Garrard, *The Art of Warre* (1591), 169.

34 P. Young and W. Emberton, *The Cavalier Army: Its Organization and Everyday Life* (1974), 73.

35 J. Turner, *Pallas Armata: Military Essays* (1683, T3292), 217. *Military Orders and Articles Established by his Majesty* (n.d., CUL Sel.4.25.4). See also *Instructions for Musters* (1623, STC 7683).

36 *The Grounds of Military Discipline* (1642, G2139).

37 Barriffe, *op. cit.*, 299ff.

38 T. Esper, 'The Replacement of the Longbow by Firearms in the English Army', *Technology and Culture* VI (1965), 382–93. M. Creveld, *Technology and War* (New York, 1988), 89. W. G. Ross, *Military Engineering in the Great Civil War* (1887, reprinted 1984), 45. Anthony Wood, *Life and Times* (Oxford, 1891), I, 59.

39 R. N. Dore, *The Civil Wars in Cheshire* (Chester, 1966), 65.

40 G. Dyer, *War* (1986), 12–13. W. McNeill, *The Pursuit of Power* (Chicago, 1982), 128–30. A. Kellett, *Combat Motivation: The Behavior of Soldiers in Battle* (Boston, 1982), 81. T. N. Dupuy, *The Evolution of Weapons and Warfare* (Fairfax, VA, 1984), 133. 31/7/43, Meldrum to Speaker, quoted by C. H. Firth, 'The Raising of the Ironsides', *TRHS*, XIV (1900), 69.

41 Keith Thomas, 'Numeracy in Early Modern England', *TRHS*, 5th series, 37 (1987), 109.

42 'Military Diary, May–June 1642, the Siege of Limerick', *Journal of the Royal Society of Antiquaries of Ireland*, 5th series, XIV (1904), 180.

43 Kellet, *op. cit.*, 23.

44 S. L. A. Marshall, *Men against Fire* (New York, 1947), 42. Robert Monro, *Expedition with the Worthy Scotch Regiment* (1637), II, 75. G. F. Nuttal, *Richard Baxter* (1965), 38–9.

45 Adair, *op. cit.*, 159.

46 W. C. and C. E. Trevelyan, *Trelawny Papers* (Camden Society, 1872), 80–4.

47 Holmes, *op. cit.*, 165.

48 Wanklyn, *op. cit.*, 25–6.

49 R. Hutton, *The Royalist War Effort* (1983), 22.

50 Robert Bennet, 'An Original Diary of Colonel Robert Bennet of Hexworthy, 1642–43', *Devon and Cornwall Notes and Queries*, 18 (1935), 256.

51 Figures calculated from Young, *Marston Moor*, 54, and M. Toynbee and P. Young, *Cropredy Bridge* (Kineton, 1970), 141–3.

52 Figures from muster roll in BL: Harleian MSS 427.

53 P. W. Thomas, *Sir John Birkenhead* (1969), 145–6.

54 *An Exact Description of Prince Rupert's Malignant She-Monkey* (1643, E3639), n.pa. J. Vicars, *Jehovah Jirah* (1644, V313), I, 430–1. *A Declaration of a Strange and Wonderful Monster born in Kirkham Parish* (1646, D602), n.pa.

55 For a similar piece of nonsense see George Lawrence's *The Debauched Cavalier* (1642, L656).

56 A. Gladstone, 'The Conception of the Enemy', *Journal of Conflict Resolution*, 3 (1959), 132–7. W. Brereton, *The Successes of our Cheshire Forces* (1644, B4372), 6. L. Hutchinson, *Memoirs* (1906), 95.

57 M. B. Pickel, *Charles I as a Patron of Poetry and Drama* (1936), 9.

58 Lois Potter, *Secret Rites and Secret Writing: Royalist Literature, 1641–1660* (Cambridge, 1989) 26. W. G. Grant, *Margaret the First: A Biography of Margaret Cavendish, Duchess of Newcastle, 1623–1673* (1957), 47. R. A. Anselment, 'Clarendon and the Caroline Myth of Peace', *Journal of British Studies*, 23, 2 (1984), 37–55. H. Erskine-Hill and Graham Story, *Revolutionary Prose of the English Civil War* (Cambridge, 1983), 3. J. M. Carter, *The*

Military and Social Significance of Ballad Singing in the English Civil War (Manhattan, Kansas, 1980), 5.

59 *A True and Faithful Relation of the Besieging of the Town of Manchester* (1642, T2462). J. Livingstone, *A Brief Historical Relation of the Life of John Livingstone* (1848), 106.

60 *A Relation of the Actions of the Parliament's Forces* (1642, R811), n.pa. H. Townsend, *Diary* (1915–20), I, 125. J. Eales, *Puritans and Roundheads: The Harley's of Brampton Brayn and the Outbreak of the English Civil War* (Cambridge, 1990), 176.

61 *A True Relation of the Great and Glorious Victory through God's Providence obtained by Sir William Waller* (1643, T2958). *The Soldiers' Language* (1644, S4426), n.pa.

62 A. Kingston, *Hertfordshire in the Great Civil War* (1894), 124.

63 Young, *op. cit.*, 246–9.

64 *A True Relation of the Late Fight between the Parliamentary Forces and Prince Rupert* (1644, T2980), 4.

65 W. Beech, *More Sulphur for Basing* (1645, B1680), 4–32.

66 Elton, *op. cit.*, 2.

67 B. Donagan, 'Codes and Conduct in the English Civil War', *Past and Present* 118 (1988), 84. For examples of such articles see: 'Articles of War – 1642', *JSAHR*, 9, (1930), 117–23; *Military Orders and Articles Established by His Majesty for the Better Ordering and Governing of his Army* (York, 1642, C2493.8); *Military Orders and Articles Established by His Majesty for the Better Governing of his Majesty's Army* (1643); and *Orders Established the 14th of January by . . . Sir Thomas Fairfax for regulating the army* (1646, E740).

68 'Articles of War – 1642', *JSAHR* 9 (1930), 117–23. Robert, Earl of Essex, *Lawes and Ordinances of Warre* (1642, E3314). *Lawes and Ordinances of War* (1642, L695a). *Military Orders and Articles* (28 August 1642).

69 George Monck, Duke of Albermarle, *Observations on Political and Military Affairs* (1671, A864).

70 J. Keegan and R. Holmes, *Soldiers* (New York, 1986), 18. J. Aston, 'The Diary of John Aston', in J. C. Hodgson, *North Country Diaries* (Surtees Society, CXVIII, 1890), 12–13. Young, *op. cit.*, 39. 18/9/44, Robartes to CBK, J. R. Powell and E. K. Timings, *Documents Relating to the Civil War* (Naval Records Society, 1963), 172.

71 P. Young, *Marston Moor* (Kineton, 1970), 5.

72 Joshua Sprigge, *Anglia Rediviva* (Oxford, 1854), 95.

73 D. Underdown, *Revel, Riot and Rebellion: Popular Politics and Culture in England, 1603–1660* (New York, 1985), 187.

74 J. H. Mayo, *Medals and Decorations of the British Army and Navy* (1897), 6.

75 10/3/43, Staynings to John Willoughby, Trevelyan, *op. cit.*, III, 233.

76 P. Hardacre, *The Royalists during the Puritan Revolution* (1956), 13–14.

77 Young and Emberton, *op. cit.*, 147.

78 M. Foster, *Sir Troilius Turbeville* (1980), 18. F. J. Varley, *The Siege of Oxford* (1932), 24.

79 P. Young, *Naseby* (1985), 198.

80 H. Townsend, *Diary* (1915–20), I, 125.

81 *A true relation of . . . Gell*, reprinted in S. Glover, *History . . . Of the Country of Derby* (1829), I, appendix, 69. Clarendon, *History*, IV, 225.

82 R. Symonds, *Diary* (Camden Society, 1859), 63. G. N. Godwin, *The Civil*

War in Hampshire (1904), 295. J. Hodgson, *Memoirs* (Bradford, 1902), 151. *A Large Relation of the Fight at Leith*, ed. Sir W. Scott (1806), 1–3.

83 *A True and Exact Relation of the Manner of his Majesteis Setting up of His Standard at Nottingham* (1642, T2452). William Lilly, *The Life and Death of Charles I* (1774), 242.

84 J. L. Malcolm, *Caesar's Due* (1983), 150ff.

85 BL: Harleian MSS, 986.

86 *An Account of Powick Bridge by a Trooper in Captain Nathaniel Fienes Troop* (1642), 2. Vicars, *op. cit.*, III, 281.

87 J. Vicars, *God's Arke* (1646, V309), 45.

88 Carter, *op. cit.*, 21. Kendall, *op. cit.*, 19.

89 Edward Cooke, *The Character of Warre* (1626, reissued 1640), C3. John Raynsford, *The Young Soldier* (1642, R419D), n.pa., P. Young, *Edgehill* (Kineton, 1967), 14.

90 J. Taylor, *Works* (Manchester, 1877), 5. Donald Lupton, *A Warre-like Treatise of the Pike* (1642, L3496), 87.

91 Dedicatory verse to Elton, *op. cit.*, frontispiece.

92 J. Turner, *Memoirs* (Edinburgh, 1829), 32.

93 Marshal St Cyr estimated that half the infantry casualties in the Napoleonic wars were caused by soldiers being accidentally shot by comrades in the ranks behind them, Keegan and Holmes, *op. cit.*, 66–7. J. Gwynne, *Military Memoirs of the Great Civil War* (Edinburgh, 1822), 25. W. Emberton, *'Loves Loyalty': The Story of the Close and Perilous Siege of Basing House* (Basingstoke, 1972), 44.

94 A death slide, which is made to sound more dangerous than it really is, is a wire, usually over water to cushion a fall, down which a soldier slides holding a toggle. Kellett, *op. cit.*, 85–7, 219–29.

95 G. F. Linderman, *Embattled Courage: The Experience of Combat in the American Civil War* (1988), 19ff, is very interesting in dealing with attitudes to fear.

96 H. G. Tibbutt, *The Life and Letters of Sir Lewis Dyve, 1599–1669* (Streatly, 1948), 109. Nugent, *op. cit.*, II, 441.

97 T. Raymond, *Autobiography* (Camden Society, 1917), 38.

98 Sprigge, *op. cit.*, 70. J. Sedgwick, *England's Conditioned Parrelled* (1642, S2360), printed in J. R. Phillips, *Memoirs of the Civil War in Wales and the Marches* (1874), I, 182–4.

99 Townsend, *op. cit.*, 173.

100 Monck, *op. cit.*, 23.

5 A SOLDIER'S LIFE IS TERRIBLE HARD

1 10/7/31, Steynings to John Willoughby, W. C. and C. E. Trevelyan, *Trelawny Papers, Part III* (Camden Society, 1872), 80–4.

2 Q. Wright, *A Study of War* (Chicago, 1965), 223–4.

3 T. Carte, *Original Letters . . . found among the Duke of Ormonde's Papers* (1739), I, 23. *Mercurius Britannicus* (23 October 1947).

4 BL: Harleian MSS, 6804, 73.

5 Figures calculated from Ann Hughes, *Politics, Society and Civil War in Warwickshire, 1620–1660* (Cambridge, 1987), 201–2.

6 C. Holmes, *The Eastern Association in the English Civil War* (1975), 239.

7 C. H. Firth, 'The Raising of the Ironsides', *TRHS*, 13 (1900), 19–52.

8 Sir Henry Slingsby, *Original Memoirs written in the Great Civil War* (1806),

70. Richard Gough, *The History of Myddle* (Harmondsworth, 1983), 13. Joshua Moore, 'A brief relation of the life and memoirs of John, Lord Belasyse', Folger MSS, Va., 216.

9 E. A. Lawrence, 'Parliamentary Army Chaplains, 1642–45', Oxford D.Phil. (1982), 75.

10 M. Toynbee and P. Young, *Strangers in Oxford* (1973).

11 Quoted by Martin Hazell, *Fidelity and Fortitude; Lord Capel, his Regiments and the Civil War* (Leigh-on-Sea, 1987), 34.

12 Anthony Wood, *Life and Times* (Oxford, 1891), I, 69.

13 Frank Larkin (ed.), *Stuart Royal Proclamations* (Oxford, 1983), 910.

14 Rushworth, *Collections* V, 666–7

15 G. A. Harrison, 'Royalist Organization in Gloucester and Bristol', Manchester MA (1961), 221.

16 Ruth Spaulding, *The Improbable Puritan: The Life of Bulstrode Whitelocke* (1975), 91–2. Bulstrode Whitelocke, *Diary* (1990), 144–5.

17 Henry G. Tibbutt (ed.), *The Letter Book of Sir Samuel Luke* (Bedford, 1963), 122–3. P. Young, *Edgehill* (Kineton, 1967), 45. J. P. Kenyon, *The Civil Wars of England* (New York, 1988), 126.

18 Clarendon, *History* III, 267. Mary Coate (ed.), 'An Original Diary of Colonel Robert Bennet of Hexworthy, 1642–1643', *Devon and Cornwall Notes and Queries*, XVIII (1935), 251–9.

19 Richard Holmes, *Acts of War: the Behavior of Men in Battle* (New York, 1985), 126. E. Archer, *A True Relation of the Red Trained-bands* (1643, A360), 7.

20 Folger MSS, Xd 483 (11).

21 Larkin, *op. cit.*, 859.

22 Stuart Peachey, *Civil War and Salt Fish: Military and Civilian Diet in the Mid-seventeenth Century* (Leigh-on-Sea, 1988), 1-7.

23 This supposition is based on the experience of the US Civil War, cf. G. F. Linderman, *Embattled Courage: The Experience of Combat in the American Civil War* (1987).

24 R. Coe, *Exact Dyarie of the Progress of Sir William Waller's Army* (1644, C4881), 1. James Coleman, 'A Royalist Account of the Withdrawal of the King's Forces from Taunton, 13 December 1644', *English Historical Review*, 13 (1898), 308.

25 *A True Relation of the Sad Passages between the Two Armies in the West* (1644, T3043), n.pa.

26 Archer, *op. cit.*, 4.

27 C. Holmes, *op. cit.*, 167.

28 5/9/43, William Harlakenden to Sir Thomas Barrington, *Cambridge During the Civil War* (Cambridge, 1935), 107. 20/10/44, Waller to Committee of Both Kingdoms, G. N. Goodwin, *The Civil War in Hampshire* (1904), 271–2.

29 Alfred Kingston, *East Anglia in the Great Civil Wars* (1897), 191.

30 M. Spufford, *The Great Reclothing of Rural England* (1984), 120–6. J. Thompson, *The Other Army: Camp Followers in the English Civil War* (Leigh-on-Sea, n.d.), 15.

31 For instance Sir Ralph Monckton had three horses shot from under him at Naseby, and one at Marston Moor and Rowton, yet he never expressed the least regret or appreciation: *The Monckton Papers*, ed. Edward Peacock (1884), 17–21. P. Edwards, *The Horse Trade in Tudor and Stuart England* (Cambridge, 1988), 15. 23/9/44, Arthur Trevor, to Ormonde, Carte, *op. cit.*, I, 64.

32 Folger MSS, Xd 483 (11).

33 J. Lilburne, *Innocency and Truth Justified* (1645, L2118), 25.

34 J. Malcolm, *Caesar's Due: Loyalty and King Charles, 1643–1646* (London, 1983), 101ff. G. Dyer, *War* (1986), 48.

35 Based on an analysis of R. R. Temple, 'The Original Officer List of the New Model Army', *Bulletin of the Institute of Historical Research*, 59 (May 1986), 50–77.

36 Peter Young, *Naseby* (1985), 270.

37 George Monck, Duke of Albemarle, *Observations on Military and Political Affairs* (1671, A864), 23. Sir George Gresley, 'A true account of the imploying of me raising a foot regiment under Sir John Gell', S. Glover, *History of Derby* (Derby, 1829), 70.

38 D. Lupton, *A Warre-like Treatise of the Pike* (1642, L3496).

39 Roger Boyle, Earl of Orrery, *Treatise of the Art of War* (1677, 0499), 24. Robert Monro, *The Scotch Military Discipline Learned from the Valiant Swedes* (1644, M2454a), 192. C. H. Firth, *Cromwell's Army* (1905), 73.

40 Stuart Peachey and Alan Turton, *Old Robin's Foot: the Equipment and Compaigns of Essex's infantry, 1642–45* (Leigh-on-Sea, 1987), 46.

41 William Reinking, *A More Exact and Particular Relation of the Taking of Shrewsbury* (1646, R768), 3–4.

42 J. Hodgson, *Autobiography* (1882), 32.

43 For examples see: *A True and Exact Relation of the Several Passages at the Siege of Manchester* (1642, T2462), 4; H. Foster, *A True and Exact Relation of the Marching . . . for the relief of the City of Gloucester*, reprinted in J. Washbourn, *Bibliotheca Gloucesterensis* (Gloucester, 1828), I, 253; and A. J. Fletcher, *A County Community at Peace and War: Sussex, 1600–1660* (1975), 270.

44 E. Ludlow, *Memoirs* (Oxford, 1894), I, 72.

45 C. H. Firth, 'The Siege and Capture of Bristol by the Royalist Forces in 1643', *JSAHR*, IV (1925), 193.

46 10/4/44, Roe to Sir Richard Browne, R. E. Bell, *Memorials of the Civil War* (1849), I, 98. 14/4/43, Roe to Boswell, J. Webb, *Memorials of the Civil War . . . As it affected Herefordshire* (1879), II, 2, 357. 16/2/43, Agostini to Doge, *CSPV, 1642–43*, 246.

47 B. Blackwood, *The Lancashire Gentry and the Great Rebellion, 1640–1660* (Manchester, 1978), 51.

48 A. Miller, 'Joseph Jane's Account of Cornwall during the Civil War', *English Historical Revue* (1975), 101. C. H. Firth, 'The Raising of the Ironsides', *TRHS*, 13 (1900), 71.

49 Abraham Cowley, *The Civil War* (Toronto, 1973), 108.

50 H. G. Farmer, 'Sixteenth–Seventeenth Century Military Marches', *JSAHR*, XXVIII (1950), 49–52, and *The Rise of Military Music* (1912), 25–39.

51 D. Underdown, *Somerset in the Civil War and Interregnum* (Newton Abbot, 1973), 78.

52 J. Turner, *Memoirs* (Edinburgh, 1829), 22.

53 Edward Robinson, *A Discourse of the War in Lancashire* (Chetham Society, 1864), 57.

54 For an example of regulations on camp-followers see *A True Description of the Discipline of War . . . Used in His Majesty's Army* (1642, T2677), n.pa. J. Cruso, *Treatise on Modern War* (1640), 157.

55 J. W. Bund, *The Civil War in Worcester* (1905), 10–11.

56 Coe, *op. cit.*, 5. Ian Roy, 'The English Civil War and English Society', *War and Society* (1975), 23.

57 HMC, *Fifth Report*, appendix, pt I, 72.
58 12/4/43, R. Harley to Edward Harley, HMC, *Portland*, III, 107. 'The Journal of John Aston', in J. C. Hodgson (ed.), *North Country Diaries* (Surtees Society, 1890), 7, 28.
59 R. Symmonds, *Diary of the Marches of the Royal Army during the Great Civil War* (Camden Society, 1859), 40, 74.
60 5/12/44, Agostini to Doge, *CSPV, 1643–45*, 162. P. L. Ralph, *Humphrey Mildmay: Royalist Gentleman* (New Brunswick, NJ, 1947), 155. Coe, *op. cit.*, 5.
61 *The Soldiers Report Concerning Sir William Waller's Fight against Basing House* (1643, S4431), 3–4. *A True relation of the storming of Bristol . . . By Sir Thomas Fairfax's army, 11 September 1645* (1645, R144), 16.
62 Clarendon, *History*, IV, 453
63 J. Gwynne, *Military Memoirs of the Great Civil War* (Edinburgh, 1822), 34–7.
64 *Ibid.*
65 R. Atkyns, *Vindications* (1967), 22.
66 J. R. Phillips, *Memoirs of the Civil War in Wales* (1874), II, 229.
67 *Intelligence from the Armie* (June 1643, I261), n.pa.
68 HMC, *Beaufort*, 39.
69 Edward Burchall, 'Diary', in T. W. Barlow, *Cheshire: Its Historical and Literary Associations* (Manchester, 1855), 164.
70 J. R. Powell and E. K. Timmings, *Documents Relating to the Civil War* (Naval Records Society, 1963), 133.
71 *Memoirs of Colonel John Birch*, ed. J. and T. W. Birch (Camden Society, 1873), 92. J. Gwynne, *op. cit.*, 39.
72 Turner, *op. cit.*, 32.
73 Phillips, *op. cit.*, 253.
74 J. Birch, *Military Memoir* (Camden Society, 1873), 17ff.
75 *His Highness Prince Rupert's Late Beating up of the Rebels Quarters at Portcome and Chinnor* (Oxford, 1643, H2076g), 16.
76 Foster, *op. cit.*, I, 253–71. Phillips, *op. cit.*, I, 197–8.
77 HMC, *Fourteenth Report*, IV, 63.
78 *A True Relation of what Service . . . Sir John Gell*, reprinted in Stephen Glover, *History of the County of Derby* (1829), I, appendix, 68.
79 R. Bulstrode, *Memoirs* (1721), 74. J. Hodgson, *Memoirs* (Bradford, 1902), 23.
80 'Iter Carolinum: Journal of the King's Marches', *Somers' Tracts*, ed. Sir Walter Scott (1811), 263–75.
81 C. H. Firth, 'Prince Rupert's Journal in England for September 5, 1642 to July 4, 1646', *English Historical Review*, III (1898), 729–41.
82 BL: Harleian MSS, 986. 6. T. Ellis, *An Exact and Full Relation of the Last Fight* (1644, E605), n.pa.
83 Robert Douglas, 'Civil War Diary', in James Madiment (ed.), *Historical Fragments Relating to Scottish Affairs* (Edinburgh, 1832), 51–89. *CSPD, 1644*, 519.
84 Archer, *op. cit.*, 1–17
85 Young, *Marston Moor* (1970), 6.
86 Young, *Naseby*, 221–2.
87 N. Wharton, *Letters*, ed. H. Ellis, *Archaeologia*, XXXV (1853), 310–34, and ed. S. L. Ede-Borrett (Leigh-on-Sea, 1983).
88 J. Vicars, *Jehovah Jireh* (1643, V313), 200.
89 Foster, *op. cit.*, 253–71.

90 Such accidents were very common. For another example see *A True and Exact Relation . . . Manchester* (London, 1642, Wing T2462), 4.

6 THE EPITOME OF WAR

1 R. Boyle, Earl of Orrery, *Treatise on the Art of War* (1677), n.pa. Cruso, *Treatise on Modern War* (1640), 123.
2 Edward Luttark, 'With the Boring Parts Left Out?', *New York Times Book Review* (23 March 1986), 13. J. Morrill, *The Revolt of the Provinces* (1976), 51. R. Hutton, *The Royalist War Effort* (1983), 175–8. J. Malcolm, *Caesar's Due* (1983), 176. I. Roy, 'The Royalist Army in the First Civil War', Oxford D.Phil. (1963), 350. M. D. G. Wanklyn, 'Landed Society and Allegiance in Cheshire and Shropshire in the First Civil War', Manchester Ph.D. (1976), 271–2. M. Bennett, 'The Royalist War Effort in the North Midlands, 1642–46', Loughborough Ph.D. (1986), 267.
3 J. Keegan and R. Holmes, *Soldiers* (New York, 1986), 265.
4 Bodleian: Banks MSS, 63/39.
5 Karl von Clausewitz, *On War* (Harmondsworth, 1968), 140.
6 14/6/45, Cromwell to Lenthall, W. C. Abbott, *The Writings and Speeches of Oliver Cromwell* (New York, 1937), I, 360. 14/6/45 John Rushworth to Samuel Luke, C. and W. Whetham, *A History of the Life of Colonel Nathaniel Whetham* (1907), 102.
7 J. Keegan and J. Darracott, *The Nature of War* (New York, 1981), 167–8.
8 Quoted by G. Dyer, *War* (1986), 13.
9 Hugo Grotius, *De jure Belli* (1625), quoted by J. R. Hale, *Renaissance War Studies* (1983), 341.
10 R. E. Maddison, 'The King's Cabinet Opened: a case study in pamphlet history', *Notes and Queries*, 2142 (1966), 2–9.
11 Sir Ralph Hopton, *Bellum Civile*, ed. Alan Wicks (Leigh-on-Sea, 1988), 15–19.
12 *Account of Powicke Bridge by a Trooper in Captain Nathaniel Fiennes's Troop* (1642), 10.
13 Richard Baxter, *Reliquiae Baxterianae* (1696, B1370), 40-2.
14 Figures from P. Young, *Edgehill* (Kineton, 1967), 105.
15 Edward Benlowes, 'Canto XII', in George Saintsbury (ed.), *Minor Poets of the Caroline Period* (Oxford, 1905), 450.
16 Bodleian: Ashmolean MSS, 830, 292.
17 *Parliamentary History* XII, 38. Clarendon, *History*, II, 316.
18 The king's order 'If York be lost, I shall esteem my crown a little less', is in *The Letters, Speeches and Proclamations of King Charles I*, ed. C. Petrie (1935), 144–5. This description of Marston Moor is mainly based on P. Young, *Marston Moor* (Kineton, 1970), Austin Woolrych, *Battles of the English Civil War* (1961), 66–80, and William Seymour, *Battles in Britain* (1975), II, 83–103.
19 Lion Watson, *A More Exact Relation of the Late Battell Fought near York* (1644, W1082), 6.
20 T. Carlyle, *On Heroes and Hero-worship* (1908), 453.
21 4/1/45, Charles to Ormonde, T. Carte, *Ormonde Letters* (1739), III, 367. W. D. Cooper (ed.), *The Trelawny Papers* (Camden Society, 1855) 18.
22 John Spalding, *Memorials of the Troubles in Scotland* (Aberdeen, 1835), II, 452.
23 D. Stevenson, *Alasdair MacColla and the Highland Problem in the Seventeenth Century* (Edinburgh, 1980), 128–35, 156–7, 188, 218–19. James M. Hill, *Celtic Warfare* (Edinburgh, 1986), 1–3, 45–8, 58–9.

24 E. M. Furgol, *A Regimental History of the Covenanting Armies, 1639–1651* (Edinburgh, 1988), 196. P. Gaunt, *The Cromwellian Gazetteer* (1987), 209.
25 25/5/45, Charles to Henrietta Maria, *Reliquiae Sacrae Carolinas* (The Hague, 1649), 262–3.
26 Panic caused by confused orders is fairly common in battle. For instance they prompted the Royal Welsh Fusiliers to run at Alma, cf. Holmes *op. cit.*, 225.
27 Clarendon, *History*, V, 179.
28 13/7/44, Luke Lloyd to wife, HMC, *Fourteenth Report* IV, 64. Gardiner, *Civil War*, I, 362.
29 N. Fiennes, *A Most True and Exact Relation of the Battel Fought . . . near Edge Hill* (1642, F875), 2.
30 19/6/45, Charles to wife, *Reliquiae Sacrae Carolinas* (The Hague, 1649), 256–7. 25/5/45, Digby to Jermyn, SP 16/10/2. Robert Herrick, *Poetical Works* (Oxford, 1956), 271. Sir George Wharton, *An Astrological Judgment* (1645, W1540).
31 Simeon Ashe, *A Continuation of True Intelligence . . . of the Earl of Manchester's Army* (1644), 3–7. *A True Relation of the Great Fight and Routing of the King's Forces at Rowton Heath*, printed in Rupert Morris, *The Siege of Chester* (Chester, 1925), 114–15. P. Young, *Naseby* (1985), 337. J. E. Adair, *Cheriton, 1644: The Campaign and the Battle* (Kineton, 1973), 125. 12/4/43, Robert Harley to Edmund Harley, HMC, *Portland*, III, 108.
32 M. Rowe, *Exact and Full Relation of the Great Victory Obtained Against the Rebels at Dungon's Hill* (1647, R2068), n.pa. *An Exact and True Relation of a Bloody Fight . . . before Tadcastle and Selby* (1642, W3611), 6. *A True Relation of the Great and Glorious Victory* (1643, T2958), 4.
33 Clarendon, *History*, III, 631.
34 Gardiner, *Civil War*, I, 377.
35 J. Adair, *Life of John Hampden* (1976), 219.
36 Simeon Ashe, *A True Relation of the most Chief Occurrence at . . . Newbury* (1644, A3968.2), 8. A. Kingston, *East Anglia in the Great Civil War* (1897), 105.
37 *A True Relation of a Good and Happy Victory . . . to . . . the Earl of Essex* (1642, T2878), 5. R. P. Stearns, *The Strenuous Puritan: Hugh Peters, 1598–1660* (Urbana, 1954), 249.
38 J. Barratt, 'A Royalist Account of the Relief of Pontefract', *JSARH*, 53 (1975), 158–69.
39 12/4/43, Robert Harley to Edmund Harley, HMC, *Portland*, III, 107.
40 P. R. Newman, *The Battle of Marston Moor, 1644* (Chichester, 1981), 112–13.
41 Keegan and Holmes, *op. cit.*, 259–66.
42 Bulstrode Whitelocke, *Diary* (1990), 140–1.
43 Boyle, *op. cit.*, 186. Clarendon, *op. cit.*, IV, 585.
44 Ashe, *op. cit.*, 5.
45 J. Keegan, *The Face of Battle* (New York, 1976), 20.
46 *Ibid.*, 117.
47 R. Bulstrode, *Memoirs* (1721), 84.
48 12/4/43, R. Harley to Edmund Harley, HMC, *Portland*, III, 110.
49 Lion Watson, *op. cit.* Sir Hugh Cholmley, *Memoirs* (1870). Lady Margaret Newcastle, *Life of William Cavendish, Duke of Newcastle* (1886).
50 Morris, *op. cit.*, 73.
51 12/4/44, Robert Harley to Edward Harley, HMC, *Portland*, III, 106.
52 R. Atkyns, *Vindications* (1967), 19.
53 P. Young, *Marston Moor*, 84ff.

54 P. Young, *Naseby*, 318.
55 That between Major General Crawford's Foot and Cromwell's Horse at Marston Moor was unusual. Cf. Newman, *op. cit.*, 112–13.
56 For Cropredy see R. Symonds, *Diary of the Royalist Army during the Great Civil War* (Camden Society, 1859), 22–4. Fiennes, *op. cit.*, 3.
57 17/12/42, Foulis to T. Chaloner, H. Foulis, *An Exact and True Relation of a Bloody Fight . . . before . . . Tadcastle and Selby* (1642, F1639.5), n.pa.
58 C. V. Wedgwood, *The King's War, 1641–47* (1971), 309.
59 Gardiner, *op. cit.* I, 215. C. H. Firth, *Cromwell's Army* (1962), 174.
60 William Gerrard, *The Art of Warre* (1591), 269. James Audley, Earl of Castlehaven, *Memoirs* (1680), 133.
61 *The King's Forces Totally Routed by the Parliament's Army* (1645, K595), 8.
62 See for instance Sir Charles Rowley, *The Battle of Naseby* (n.d.), n.pa, and R. R. Newman, *Marston Moor, 2 July 1644: The Sources and the Site* (York, 1978).
63 This ratio would of course increase as the war continued, and the ratio of musketeers grew, and with better training misfires declined. On the other hand better-trained troops would move faster, and so reduce the number of volleys fired. M. Van Creveld, *Technology and War* (New York, 1980), 110.
64 Folger MSS, Va. 216, n.pa.
65 S. Glover, *History of the County of Derby* (Derby, 1829), 80.
66 Stuart, *Gunpowder Triumphant* (Leigh-on-Sea, 1987), 24–7, 32. Adair, *op. cit.*, 131.
67 Hill, *op. cit.*, 1–3, 45–8. Stevenson, *op. cit.*, 81–3. D. Stevenson, 'The Highland Charge', *History Today*, 32 (August 1982), 3–5. S. Reid, *Scots Armies of the Seventeenth Century, 3, The Royalist Army, 1639–46* (Leigh-on-Sea, 1989), 43–5, questions the importance of the Highland charge.
68 A. V. B. Norman and D. Pottinger, *English Weapons and Warfare, 449–1660* (New York, 1979), 211.
69 30/1/44, Byron to Ormonde, T. Carte, *Original Letters . . . among the Duke of Ormonde's papers* (1739), I, 54.
70 Young, *Edgehill*, 28.
71 Abbot, *op. cit.*, I, 230. For a similar description see *ibid.*, I, 243–5.
72 Newman, *op. cit.*, 79.
73 Edmund Ludlow, *Memoirs* (Oxford, 1894), I, 98–100. J. A. Atkinson, *Tracts Relating to the Civil War in Cheshire, 1641-59* (Chetham Society, 1909), 144. *A Fuller Narrative of the Late Victory obtained by Col: General Poyntz* (1645, F2488), 4.
74 Quoted by P. R. Newman, 'The Royalist Army in the North of England', York Ph.D (1978), 95.
75 *Battaile on Hopton-heath* (1643, B1162), 4–5.
76 Young, *Marston Moor*, 222.
77 J. Adair, *By the Sword Divided* (1983), 97.
78 Captain P. A. Chamber, 'Cavalry in Battle: Marston Moor', *Cavalry Journal*, I (1906), 185–90.
79 Richard Pearse, 'The Use of the Matchlock when Mounted', *JSAHR*, 180 (December 1966), 201–6.
80 Atkyns, *op. cit.*, 9ff.
81 Fiennes, *op. cit.*, 5. D. Holles, *An Exact and True Relation of the Dangerous and Bloody Fight . . . near Kineton* (1642, E3617-8), 55, expresses a similar view.
82 See, for instance, W. Eldred, *The Gunners' Glass* (1647, E332), 22v.

83 Royal Commission on Historical Monuments, *Newark on Trent: The Civil War Siegeworks* (1964), 19.
84 R. E. Sherwood, *Civil Strife of the Midlands, 1642–51* (1974), 30. Hale, *op. cit.*, 395–6, 402.
85 William E. Phillips, 'Sir Francis Ottley's Papers', *Shropshire Archaeological and Natural Historical History Society* (1894–6), 203.
86 Sherwood, *op. cit.*, 52.
87 Adair, *op. cit.*, 92.
88 *Ibid.*, 108.
89 J. T. Gilbert, *The History of the Irish Confederation and War in Ireland, 1641–43* (Dublin, 1882–91), II, 258.
90 Fiennes, *op. cit.*, 6.
91 G. Ormerod, *The History of the County Palatine and the City of Chester* (1875–82), I, lxi.
92 W. Brereton, *A letter . . . of the Great Victory Obtained . . . at Middlewich* (1643, B4368.A), 4.
93 M. Howard, *War in European History* (1976), 31.
94 Baxter, *op. cit.*, (1696), 54. HMC, *Portland*, III, 108.
95 R. Holmes, *Acts of War* (New York, 1985), 66.
96 *A True and Perfect Relation of the Barbarous and Cruel Passages of the King's Army at Old Brainceford* (1642, T2551), 1.
97 E. I. Hogan, *The History of the War in Ireland from 1641 to 1653 by a British Officer in the Regiment of Sir John Clotworthy* (Dublin, 1873), 18.
98 9/7/42, Grenville to wife, G. Nugent, *Some Memorials of John Hampden* (1832), II, 370.
99 Rushworth, *Collections*, V, 35.
100 Young, *Marston Moor*, 124.
101 Ludlow, *op. cit.*, 41.
102 *A Full Relation, not only of our good successe* (1642, F2356), 8–9.
103 Folger MSS, Va. 216, n.pa.
104 Foster, *A True and Exact Relation of the Marchings . . . for the relief of Gloucester* (1643), reprinted in J. Washbourn, *Bibliotheca Gloucesterensis* (Gloucester, 1828), I, 253–71.
105 Field Marshal Slim and General S. L. A. Marshall record similar incidents involving the Essex Regiment in Eritrea in 1940 and US infantry in Normandy in 1944, cf. Holmes, *op. cit.* (New York, 1985) 224–5. W. C., *A Continued Success of his Excellency, Sir Thomas Fairfax, at and since the routing of the Enemies Forces at Torrington* (1646). *A Fuller Relation of Sir Thomas Fairfaxes Routing of all the King's Armies in the West* (1645, F2491), 9.
106 Boyle, *op. cit.*, 164, 187.
107 Nugent, *op. cit.*, II, 370. Watson, *op. cit.*, 7.
108 R. Douglas, 'Civil War Diary, January–November, 1644', in James Maidment (ed.), *Historical Fragments Relating to Scottish Affairs* (1832), 65. Carte, *op. cit.*, I, 55–8.
109 C. R. Markham, *The Life of the Great Lord Fairfax* (1870), 225.
110 Sherwood, *op. cit.*, 201.
111 Clarendon, *History*, III, 283.
112 Newman, *op. cit.*, 102.
113 Warburton, *Cavaliers*, III, 137.
114 Clarendon, *History*, IV, 218.
115 *A Full Relation, not only of our good successe* (1642, F2356), 9.
116 Clarendon, *History*, III, 281.

117 W. Money, *The First and Second Battles of Newbury* (1884), 63.
118 *A True Relation of the Late Battle near Newbury* (1643, T2977), 5.
119 Warburton, *Cavaliers*, III, 111. Simeon Ashe, *A Continuation of True Intelligence . . . of the Earl of Manchester's Army* (1644), 7.
120 Young, *op. cit.*, 141.
121 Clarendon, *History*, III, 283ff.
122 Denzil Holles, *An Exact and True Relation of the Dangerous and Bloody Fight . . . near Kineton* (1642, E3618), 7.
123 For instance a Gurkha officer reported in the Burma campaign that the first thing he noticed about soldiers who had been in combat for a sustained period was their jaws. 'They had been clenched for hours, and when they eventually relax mouths drop open, giving men an almost idiot appearance.' S. L. A. Marshall noticed the same phenomena with US troops in Normandy. John Ellis, *The Sharp End of War: The Fighting Man of World War II* (1982), 115.
124 J. P. Kenyon, *The Civil Wars of England* (New York, 1988), 147.
125 For instance depression and the need to return to mundane jobs was reported by survivors of the US Civil War, concentration camps, Vietnam and Hiroshima. See A. Kellet, *Combat Motivation* (Boston, 1982), 313; R. J. Lifton, *Death in Life: Survivors of Hiroshima* (New York, 1967), 28; Miklos Nyiszli, *Auschwitz* (Greenwich, Conn., 1961); Victor Frankl, *Man's Search for Meaning* (New York, 1985); Bruno Bettelheim, *The Informed Heart* (New York, 1963); and P. Caputo, *A Rumor of War* (New York, 1986).
126 Richard Coe, *An Exact Dyarie* (1644, C4881), 6.
127 30/6/44, Waller to Committee of Both Kingdoms, *CSPD, 1644*, 293. R. Symmonds, *Diary* (Camden Society, 1859), 147. Gardiner, *op. cit.*, II, 56.
128 *An Exact and True Relation of the Dangerous and Bloody Fight . . . near Kineton* (1642, E3618), 7.
129 W. Stewart, *A Full Relation of the Late Victory . . . on Marstam Moor* (1644, S5530).
130 Michael J. M'Enery, 'A Diary of the Siege of Limerick Castle', *Journal of the Royal Society of Antiquarians of Ireland*, 34 (1905), 178.
131 *A True and Exact Relation of the Several Passages at the Siege of Manchester* (1642, T2462), 5.
132 *The Battaile on Hopton-heath in Staffordshire* (1643, B1162), n.pa.
133 T. Ellis, *An Exact and Full Relation of the Last Fight between the King's Forces and Sir William Waller* (1644, E605), n.pa.
134 Abbot, *op. cit.*, I, 360.
135 C. H. Cooper, *Annals of Cambridge* (Cambridge, 1904), II, 303. *A Great Wonder in Heaven* (1643, G1787). *Signes from Heaven* (1646, 53778), 4, cxxxviii. E. M. Symonds, 'The Diary of John Green, 1635–37', *English Historical Review*, XLIII (1928), 39. C. Durston, 'Signs and Wonders and the English Civil War', *History Today* (October 1987), 22–7. Ghosts have reportedly been sighted at several US Civil War battlefields, including Bentonville, NC, Fort Macon, NC, Sailor's Creek, Antietam and Chickamauga: my thanks to John Goode for this point.
136 B. Denton, *Naseby Fight* (Leigh-on-Sea, 1988), 52. John Milton, *Paradise Lost*, Book II, lines 533–6. Immediately after the execution of Archbishop William Laud in 1645, *A Charme for Canterburian Spirits* reported that his ghost had appeared in several guises and places in London, C. Carlton, *Archbishop William Laud* (1987), 228.

7 THE MISERABLE EFFECTS OF WAR

1 G. Parker, *The Military Revolution* (Cambridge, 1988), 40.
2 N. M. Bennett, 'The Royalist War Effort in the North Midlands, 1642–46', Loughborough Ph.D. (1986), 216. John Webb, *Memorials of the Civil War . . . Herefordshire* (1878), II, 131.
3 This estimate is based on the data in P. Young, *Naseby* (1985), 284–8. It is certainly too high for some troops must have surrendered at more than one place.
4 9/2/43, Walter Littleton to Colonel Henry Hastings, HMC, *Hastings*, II, 91.
5 *A Letter: being a full Relation of the Siege of Banbury Castle* (1644, L1347), 2.
6 C. H. Firth, *Cromwell's Army* (1905), 29.
7 J. Greene, 'The Diary of John Greene', *English Historical Review*, XLIII (1928), 602.
8 J. H. Pafford, *Accounts of the Parliamentary Garrison at Chalfield and Malmesbury* (Devizes, 1940), 13–16.
9 H. G. Tibbutt (ed.), *The Letter Book, 1644–45, of Sir Samuel Luke, Parliamentary Governor of Newport Pagnell* (Bedford, 1963), no. 404. C. Hill, *A Tinker and a Poor Man: John Bunyan and his Church, 1628–1688* (New York, 1989), 45–61.
10 Edmund Ludlow, *Memoirs* (1894), I, 53.
11 5/5/43, Crawford to Prince Rupert, Warburton, *Cavaliers*, II, 8.
12 Warburton, *Cavaliers*, II, 85.
13 J. Birch, *Military Memoirs* (Camden Society, 1873), 111. Pafford, *op. cit.*, 28–9.
14 S. Porter, 'Property Damage in the English Civil War', London Ph.D. (1984), 150ff.
15 Historical Monuments Commission, *Newark on Trent: The Civil War Siegeworks* (1964), 20.
16 Richard Gough, *The History of Myddle* (Harmondsworth, 1981), 73–4.
17 Webb, *op. cit.*, II, 175.
18 A. M. Auden, 'Clun and its Neighbourhood in the First Civil War', *Transactions of the Shropshire Archaeological and Natural History Society*, VIII (1908), 312.
19 Sir Ralph Hopton, *Bellum Civile* (1988), 67. J. W. Bund, *The Civil War in Worcestershire* (Birmingham, 1905), 145.
20 Lucy Hutchinson, *Memoirs of the Life of Colonel John Hutchinson* (1906), II, 373–4. Tibbett, *op. cit.*, no. 7332.
21 T. Malbon, *Memorials of the Civil War in Cheshire* (Manchester, 1889), 47.
22 Analysis of the sieges described by P. Young and W. Emberton, *Sieges of the Great Civil War* (1978).
23 Roger Boyle, Earl of Orrery, *A Treatise of the Art of War* (1675, 0699), 15.
24 Gardiner, *Civil War*, I, 206.
25 Sun-Tzu, *The Art of War* (1971), 41, 78. Siege data derived from the sample in Young and Emberton, *op. cit.*, less Shipton and Chester, which were besieged intermittently for 1,095 and 957 days respectively. If they are included the average increases to 130 days. R. R. K. Temple, 'The Original Officer List of the New Model Army', *BIHR*, 59 (1986), 58–61.
26 Simeon Ashe, *A Continuation of the True Intelligence* (1644), 2.
27 Rushworth, *Collections*, V, 679–80.
28 M. Cuffe, *The Siege of Ballyally* (Camden Society, 1841), 17. M. J. M'Enery,

'A Diary of the Siege of Limerick, 1642', *Journal of the Royal Society of Antiquaries of Ireland*, 34 (1905), 181.

29 Ludlow, *op. cit.*, I, 60, 73–74.

30 William Lithgow, *Experimental and Exact Relation upon that Famous and Renowned Siege of Newcastle* (1645), reprinted in *Somer's Tracts* (1809–15), V, 289.

31 Barnabus Scudamore, *A Letter Sent to . . . Lord Digby . . . Concerning the Siege of Hereford* (Oxford, 1645), n.pa.

32 Firth, *op. cit.*, 168.

33 William Robinson, *Staffordshire's Misery Set Forth in the True Relation of the Barbarous Cruelty of the Forces Raised Against the Parliament* (1643, R1723), endpiece.

34 *A True and Exact Relation of the Several Passages at the Siege of Manchester* (1642, T2462), 9.

35 C. Duffy, *Siege Warfare: the Fortress in the Early Modern World, 1494–1660* (1979), 254.

36 *Perfect Occurrences*, 3–10 April 1646, quoted by Historical Monuments Commission, *op. cit.*, 48. William Beamont, *A Discourse on the War in Lancashire* (Chetham Society, 1864), 62.

37 HMC, *Bath*, I, 37.

38 Ludlow, *op. cit.*, I, 63. BL: Harleian MSS, 6798, 364.

39 Sir Hugh Cholmley, 'Narrative of the Siege of Scarborough', *English Historical Review*, XXXII (1917), 586–7. *An Exact Relation of the Surrender of Scarborough Castle* (1645, E3698), 4.

40 J. Wroughton, *The Civil War in Bath and North Somerset* (Bath, 1973), 88. Paul Slack, *The Impact of Plague in Tudor and Stuart England* (1985), 98–9, 121–2.

41 John Washbourne, *Bibliotheca Gloucesterensis* (Gloucester, 1823–25), 465.

42 John Adair, *Cheriton, 1644: The Campaign and the Battle* (Kineton, 1973), 86–7.

43 J. R. Powell and E. K. Timmings, *Documents Relating to the Civil War, 1642–48* (Naval Records Society, 1963), 155.

44 Clarendon, *History*, V, 190. Porter, *op. cit.*, 171. P. Wenham, *The Great and Close Siege of York, 1644* (Kineton, 1970), 42.

45 T. Burrow, 'The Town Defences of Exeter', *Transactions of the Devonshire Association*, 109 (1977), 36. C. Carlton, *The Court of Orphans* (Leicester, 1974), 88–9. *Good and True News from Reading* (1643, W1037).

46 W. G. Ross, *Military Engineering in the Great Civil War, 1642–49* (1984), 30.

47 *A True and Exact Relation of the Several Passages at the Siege of Manchester* (1642, T2462), 2. J. Rosworme, *Good Service Hitherto Ill Rewarded* (1649, R1996), 4.

48 David Sturdy, 'The Civil War Defences of London', *London Archaeologist*, VII, 13 (1975), 334–8.

49 William Lithgow, 'The Present Survey of London', *Somers Tracts*, ed. Sir Walter Scott (Edinburgh, 1809–15), IV, 536.

50 Samuel Butler, *Hubridas*, pt 2, canto 2.

51 HMC, *Bath*, I, 1–8.

52 R. Holmes, *The Sieges of Pontefract Castle, 1644–48* (Pontefract, 1887), 45. Cholmley, *op. cit.*, 587.

53 Stephen Bull, *Granadoe! Mortars in the Civil War* (Leigh-on-Sea, n.d.), 2. *A Letter: Being a Full Relation of the Siege of Banbury Castle* (1644, L1347),

8. M. A. E. Green, *The Letters of Queen Henrietta Maria* (1857), 167. T. R. S. Whiting, *Gloucester Besieged, 1640–1660* (Gloucester, 1984), 12–13. Porter, *op. cit.*, 128.

54 Edward Chisenhall, *A Brief Journal of the Siege against Lathom Hall, 1644* (1823), 42.

55 George Ormerod, *Tracts Relating to the Military Proceedings in Lancashire during the Great Civil War* (Chetham Society, 1844), 184.

56 Beaumont, *op. cit.*, viii.

57 Gardiner, *Civil War*, I, 98.

58 H. W. Gillman, 'The Siege of Rathbury Castle, 1642', *Journal of the Cork Historical Society*, I, (1895), 16.

59 I. Tullie, *A Narrative of the Siege of Carlisle in 1644–45* (Carlisle, 1840), 14. R. Holmes, *op. cit.*, 107.

60 C. Holmes, *Seventeenth Century Lincolnshire* (1980), 178.

61 *Diary of Henry Townsend of Elmley Lovett*, ed. J. W. Bund (1915–20), I, xxxiv.

62 Hopton, *op. cit.*, 75.

63 P. Gaunt, *A Cromwell Gazetteer* (1987), 148.

64 Philip Nelson, *The Obsidional Money of the Great Rebellion, 1642–47* (1976).

65 Folger MSS, Va. 216, n.pa.

66 M'Enery, *op. cit.*, 181–4.

67 Whiting, *op. cit.*, 8.

68 R. Holmes, *op. cit.*, 70.

69 Ormerod, *op. cit.*, 177.

70 Wenham, *op. cit.*, 69–70. D. Pinto, 'William Lawes at the Siege of York', *Musical Times*, 127 (October 1986), 579–83.

71 M'Enery, *op. cit.*, 178.

72 P. Warwick, *Memoirs of the Reign of Charles I* (Edinburgh, 1813), 295. 31/12/42, Trevor to Ormonde, Carte, *op. cit.*, I, 15. Sir John Oglander, *A Royalist's Notebook* (1936), 117.

73 Washbourn, *op. cit.*, 281.

74 Gillman, *op. cit.*, 12.

75 Tullie, *op. cit.*, 15.

76 J. W. Bund, *The Civil War in Worcestershire* (Birmingham, 1903), 297. Tullie, *op. cit.*, 28.

77 Gough, *op. cit.*, 272.

78 A. Bayley, *The Great Civil War in Dorset* (Taunton, 1910), 87.

79 *A True Relation of... Sir John Gell* (1646), reprinted in S. Glover, *History of Derby* (1829), appendix I, 69.

80 Bund, *op. cit.*, 310–11. Townsend, *op. cit.*, 126.

81 P. McGrath, *Bristol and the Civil War* (Bristol, 1981), 46. L. Hutchinson, *Memoirs of the Life of Colonel Hutchinson* (1968), 126. *A Declaration of all the Passages of the Taking of Portsmouth* (1642, D604), 3.

82 O. Ogle, W. H. Bliss and W. D. MacGray (eds), *Calendar of Clarendon State Papers* (Oxford, 1867), I, 24.

83 Townsend, *op. cit.*, xxx, 133, 255. Bund, *op. cit.*, 305.

84 Edward Robinson, *A Discourse on the Warr in Lancashire* (Chetham Society, 1864), xii. W. Dugdale, *Heraldic Miscellanies* (1793), 11.

85 R. Holmes, *op. cit.*, 98.

86 R. E. Sherwood, *Civil Strife in the Midlands, 1642–51* (1974), 145.

87 Bund, *op. cit.* 96.

88 C. H. Firth, 'The Siege and Capture of Bristol by the Royalist Forces in 1643', *JSAHR*, 4 (1925), 203. R. Holmes, *op. cit.*, 105.

89 Gaunt, *op. cit.*, 144. R. H. Morris, *The Siege of Chester, 1643–46* (Chester, 1923), 229. J. Wilshire and S. Green, *The Siege of Leicester, 1645* (Leicester, 1970), 16.

90 Eyewitness account by the Earl of Warwick in Powell, *op. cit.*, 147. Antonia Fraser, *The Weaker Vessel* (1985), 204–7. *An Exact and True Relation in Relieving the Resolute Garrison of Lyme* (1644, E3611), 5.

91 *Ibid.*, 184–90.

92 J. T. Gilbert, *The History of the Irish Confederation and war in Ireland, 1641–43* (Dublin, 1882–91), I, xlv.

93 Cuffe, *op. cit.*, viii.

94 *Ibid.*, 192–5.

95 9/5/45, Helen Neale to William Neale, Morris, *op. cit.*, 85.

96 *Ibid.*, 197–203. J. Eales, *Puritans and Roundheads: The Harleys of Brampton and the Outbreak of the English Civil War* (Cambridge, 199), 3, 150–70.

97 Chisenhall, *op. cit.*, 17–47. C. Petrie (ed.), *Prince Charles, Prince Rupert and the Civil War* (1974), 27–34.

98 F. T. Varley, *The Siege of Oxford* (1932), 127–30. 3/6/45, Digby to Legge, HMC, *First Report*, appendix, 116.

99 Ludlow, *op. cit.*, I, 69.

100 Eales, *op. cit.* Gillman, *op. cit.*, 20.

101 W. Phillips (ed.), 'Sir Francis Ottley's Papers', *Transactions of the Shropshire Archaeological and Natural History Society*, 2nd series, VIII (1896), 218.

102 *An Exact and True Relation of the Taking of Arundel* (1644, E3624), n.pa. *A True and Exact Relation of the Several Passages at the Siege of Manchester* (1642, T2462), n.pa. G. Monck, Earl of Albemarle, *Observations upon Military and Political Affairs* (1671, A864), 119.

103 Sir Barnabus Scudamore, *A Letter . . . Concerning the Late Siege of Hereford* (1645, S2130), 1.

104 T. Malbon, *op. cit.*, 91, 117–18.

105 *The Earle of Essex His Letter to Master Speaker, July 9, 1643* (1643, E3322), 6.

106 The same was true for the American Army, Lee Kennett, *G.I.: The American Soldier in World War II* (New York, 1987), 160.

107 HMC, *Bath*, I, 30–7.

108 M'Enery, *op. cit.*, 186.

109 Powell, *op. cit.*, 192.

110 Ludlow, *op. cit.*, I, 54. Rushworth, *Collections*, V, 301. *The Victorious and Fortunate Proceedings of Sir William Waller and his Forces* (1643, V344), 7. J. Malcolm, *Caesar's Due* (1983), 93. James A. Atkinson (ed.), *Tracts relating to the Civil War in Cheshire 1641–59* (Chetham Society, 1909), 103–4.

111 J. Dorney, *A Brief and Exact relation of the . . . Siege of . . . Gloucester* (1643), reprinted in Washbourn, *op. cit.*, I, 224–5.

112 Auden, *op. cit.*, 309.

113 W. H. Blaauw, 'Passages of the Civil Wars in Sussex from 1642 to 1660', *Sussex Archaeological Society Collections*, V (1852), 63.

114 Warburton, *Cavaliers*, II, 261.

115 28/2/45, William Batten to ?, Powell, *op. cit.*, 190. 18/5/43, Fiennes to Earl of Forth, *Two State Martyrs, of the Murder of Master Robert Yeomans and*

Master George Bowcher (1643, T3535), 17. T. Carte, *Original Letters* (1739), I, 23.

116 Wenham, *op. cit.*, 57–74. Robert Baillie, *Letters and Journals* (Edinburgh, 1841), I, 193.

117 Ludlow, *op. cit.*, I, 72. Scudamore, *op. cit.*, 11.

118 *A True Relation of the Taking of Bristol ... by an eyewitness* (Oxford, 1645, T3049), 14. *An Exact and Perfect Relation of the Proceedings in Yorkshire* (1643, E3606), 2.

119 R. Atkyns, *Vindications* (1967), 9. *An Exact Relation of the Bloody and Barbarous massacre at Bolton by an Eyewitness* (1644, E3683), n.pa.

120 *An Exact Relation of the Siege Before York* (1644, E3697), n.pa. Warburton, *Cavaliers*, II, 166.

121 *An Exact and True Relation in Relieving the Resolute Garrison of Lyme* (1644, E3611), 4.

122 Hutchinson, *op. cit.*, 239.

123 *Ibid.*, II, 377. S. Poyntz, *Letter to William Lenthal* (1645, P3136), 3–5.

124 E. Green, 'The Siege and Defence of Taunton, 1644–45', *Somersetshire Archaeological and Historical Society Publications*, XXV, 2 (1897), 45. Edward Drake, 'Civil War Diary', in A. R. Bayley, *The Great Civil War in Dorset* (Taunton, 1910), 168–9.

125 W. D. Christie, *Life of the First Earl of Shaftsbury* (1871), I, 97–100.

126 *A Perfect Relation of the Taking of the Town of Preston* (1643, P1519), 3. Clarendon, *History*, 342.

127 Hutchinson, *op. cit.*, 299ff.

128 B. G. Blackwood, *The Lancashire Gentry and the Great Rebellion, 1640–60* (Manchester, 1978), 3 and 30.

129 John Corbet, *An Historical Relation of the Military Government of Gloucester* (1645, C6248), 21.

130 J. R. Phillips, *Memoirs of the Civil Wars in Wales* (1874), II, 7.

131 Lithgow, *op. cit.*, V, 290.

132 J. Sprigge, *Anglia Rediva* (1854), 120. *A True Relation of the Taking of ... Lincoln* (1644, T3056), 3.

133 Ormerod, *op. cit.*, 82.

134 Rushworth, *op. cit.*, 137–8.

135 This has been used to partially explain the viciousness of the island fighting in the South Pacific in the Second World War, Robert O'Connell, *Of Arms and Men: a History of War, Weapons and Aggression* (New York, 1989), 290–2.

136 *A Relation of the Taking of Cirencester* (1642, R875), *Several and Remarkable Passages expanded to both Houses of Parliament* (1642), *Prince Rupert his Declaration* (1643), from Warburton, *Cavaliers*, 108–22.

137 *A True Relation of Prince Rupert's Barbarous Cruelty against the Town of Birmingham* (1643, P3489), 16–17. *Prince Rupert's Burning Love to England Discovered in Birmingham's Flames* (1643), 25–9. *A Letter from Walshall by a Worthy Gentleman to his Friend in Oxford Concerning Birmingham* (1643). All reprinted in 1933.

138 *True Relation ... Sir John Gell* (1646), in Glover, *op. cit.*, I, 68.

139 Bayley, *op. cit.*, 286–8.

140 Joseph Lister, *Autobiography*, ed. T. Wright (1842), 19–25.

141 *A Perfect Diurnal* (no. 97, 1645). Rushworth, *Collections*, IV, 1411. Clarendon, *History* (1876), V, 175. R. Symonds, *Diary* (Camden Society, 1859), 180–1. Wilshire, *op. cit.*, 17–18.

142 Gilbert, *op. cit.*, IV, xi.
143 Gardiner, *op. cit.*, II, 365. G. N. Godwin, *The Civil War in Hampshire, and the Story of Basing House* (1904). John Adair, *They Saw it Happen: Contemporary Accounts of the Siege of Basing House* (1961).
144 H. Peters, *The Full and Last Relation of all Things Concerning Basing-House* (1645, P1702), 2. Abbott, *op. cit.*, I, 387.

8 TRADESMEN OF KILLING ... MANAGERS OF VIOLENCE

1 J. Hackett, *The Profession of Arms* (New York, 1983), 219. Roger Boyle, Earl of Orrery, *Treatise of the Art of War* (1677, 0699), 185.
2 J. R. E. Bliese, 'Battle Orations in Medieval Europe', *Historian*, 53 (Spring 1991), 449–504.
3 He used the same rhetorical device to the regiments at Andover on 12 May 1649: W. C. Abbot, *The Writings and Speeches of Oliver Cromwell* (Cambridge, Mass., 1937), I, 608, II, 68.
4 J. Keegan, *The Mask of Command* (New York, 1988).
5 Matthew Carter, *A Most True and Exact Relation of that ... Unfortunate Expedition of Kent, Essex and Colchester* (1650, C662), 109.
6 *The Souldier's Report* (1643, S4431), n.pa.
7 *CSPD, 1644–45*, 307.
8 Figures for leaders based on sample of 76 listed in G. Smith and M. Toynbee, *Leaders of the Civil Wars, 1642–1648* (Kineton, 1977). I am grateful to Sandra Moore for assembling the data. For more on the rank and file see chapter 9.
9 C. Holmes, *The Eastern Association in the English Civil War* (1975), 39–40.
10 Clarendon, *History*, IV, 589. C. H. Firth, *Cromwell's Army* (1905), 46. 11/8/45, Fairfax to Father, R. E. Bell, *Memorials of the Civil War* (1849), I, 246.
11 *Great Victorie Obtained by the Earl of Denbigh* (1644, G1760), n.pa. S. Ashe, *A Continuation of True Intelligence* (1644), 4.
12 P. R. Newman, 'The Royalist Army in the North of England', York Ph.D. (1978), 40. B. G. Blackwood, *The Lancashire Gentry and the Great Rebellion* (Manchester, 1978), 55. The sample of 76 is based on an analysis of the entries in Smith and Toynbee, *op. cit.*
13 C. Holmes, *op. cit.*, 164.
14 I. Tullie, *A Narrative of the Siege of Carlisle in 1644–45* (Carlisle, 1840), 11.
15 J. L. Malcolm, *Caesar's Due* (1983), 96. Warburton, *Cavaliers*, III, 71.
16 J. Cruso, *Militarie Instructions for the Cavallrie* (Cambridge, 1632), 2–12. H. J. Webb, *Elizabethan Military Science* (Madison, Wisc., 1965), 36. Boyle, *op. cit.*, 12.
17 W. Brereton, *The Success of Our Cheshire Forces* (1644, B4372), 5. E. M. Furgol, *A Regimental History of the Covenanting Armies, 1639–1651* (Edinburgh, 1990), 365.
18 J. Adair, *By the Sword Divided: Eyewitness Accounts of the English Civil War* (1983), 120–1. B. Lyndon, 'Parliament's Army in Essex, 1648', *JSAHR*, LIX (1981), 152. J. A. Atkinson (ed.), *Tracts Relating to the Great Civil War in Cheshire* (Chetham Society, 1909), 126.
19 E. W. Harcourt, *The Harcourt Papers* (Oxford, 1880–1905), I, 113.
20 S. Luke, *The Letter Books, 1644–1645, of Sir Samuel Luke, Parliamentary Governor of Newport Pagnell*, ed. H. G. Tibbutt (Bedford, 1963), 160.
21 L. Hutchinson, *Memoirs of the Life of Colonel John Hutchinson* (1906), I, 318–19.
22 P. Young, *Marston Moor* (Kineton, 1970), 18. Folger MSS, Xd, 483 (11).

23 William Starbucke, *A Spiritual Song of Comfort . . . to the soldiers that are now gone for the cause of Christ* (1644, S5268a).

24 J. Adair, *The Life of John Hampden* (1976), 199.

25 L. P. Wenham, *The Great and Close Siege of York* (Kineton, 1970), 118–19.

26 Edmund Ludlow, *Memoirs* (Oxford, 1894), 93. Sir Edward Walker, *Historical Discourses* (1705–7), 34.

27 SP 16/503/56, IX.

28 I. Roy, 'The Royalist Council of War', *Bulletin of the Institute of Historical Research*, 35 (1962), 150–69. Charles Carlton, *Charles I: The Personal Monarch* (1983), 250–77.

29 Clarendon, *op. cit.*, III, 353.

30 Peter Heylyn, *Short View of the Life and Reign of King Charles* (1658, H1735), 63–4.

31 P. Warwick, *Memoirs of the Reign of King Charles I* (1815), 262. H. Slingsby, *Original Memoirs written during the Great Civil War* (1806), 66–7.

32 Adair, *op. cit.*, 63.

33 John Washbourne (ed.), *Bibliotheca Gloucesterensis* (Gloucester, 1823–5), cxlviii. P. Young, *Naseby* (1985), 309.

34 C. H. Firth, 'The Siege and Capture of Bristol by the Royalists forces, 1643', *JSARH*, 4 (1925), 194. *His Highness Prince Rupert's Late Beating up* (1643, H2076G), 10.

35 *A Declaration and Manifestation of the Proceedings of Both Armies* (1642, D531), 5.

36 Warburton, *Cavaliers*, II, 141.

37 HMC, *Fourth Report*, appendix, 269.

38 Clarendon, *History*, IV, 212.

39 J. W. Bund, 'The Siege of Worcester', *Transactions of the Worcestershire Naturalists Club*, VI (1917), 86.

40 Warburton, *Cavaliers*, II, 118. BL: Harleian MSS, 164, 233.

41 *Prince Rupert's Disguises* (1642, P3488).

42 *Observations upon Prince Rupert's White Dogge called Boye* (1643, TT F.245, 33), 4–9. *A Dog's Elegy* (1644, D1830).

43 Sir Thomas Fairfax, *Short Memorials* (1877–90), 420. Young, *op. cit.*, 269. G. Markham, *The Life of the Great Lord Fairfax* (1870). J. W. Wilson, *Fairfax: General of Parliament's Forces in the Civil War* (1985). A. H. Burne, 'Generalship in the First Civil War', *History Today*, VI (1951), 63–9.

44 T. S. Baldock, *Cromwell as a Soldier* (1899). A. Woolrych, 'Cromwell as a Soldier', in J. S. Morrill, *Oliver Cromwell and the English Revolution* (1990), 119–48.

45 Abbott, *op. cit.*, I, 190–1, 334, 634.

46 *Ibid.*, I, 204, 236, 256.

47 *Special Passages*, 9–16 May 1643, quoted in Abbott, *op. cit.*, I, 231.

48 *Ibid.*, I, 218.

49 *Ibid.*, I, 258, 377.

50 A. Fraser, *Cromwell: Our Chief of Men* (1973), 370. D. Little, 'Some Justification for Violence in the Puritan Revolution', *Harvard Theological Review*, 65 (October 1972), 577–89.

51 This is based on an analysis of the entries in G. Smith and M. Toynbee, *op. cit.*

52 In March 1944 a group of US troops were asked what qualities made a good leader. 31 per cent replied courage and example, 26 per cent keeping them informed, 23 per cent concern for men's welfare, 5 per cent friendliness. My hunch is that if such a survey were possible for the seventeenth century the

figures for courage and example would be even higher. Anthony Kellet, *Combat Motivation: The Behaviour of Soldiers in Battle* (Boston, 1982), 152–3, 298.

53 Jeremy Taylor, *Works* (1822), V, 293.
54 Sir Edward Lake, 'Account of an interview with Charles I', *Camden Society Miscellany, IV* (1859), 1–19.
55 D. Henry, a practising psychiatrist, argues that Falkland became so depressed that he committed suicide at Newbury, 'The Death of Lord Falkland', *History Today*, XXI, 12 (1971), 842–7. Clarendon, *History*, IV, 253–4. Bulstrode Whitelocke, *Memorials of the English Civil War* (1853), I, 215.
56 HMC, *Beaumont*, 41.
57 Miriam Slater, *Family Life in the Seventeenth Century: The Verneys of Claydon* (1984), 11.
58 *Diary of Henry Townsend*, ed. J. W. Bund (1915–20), I, 126.
59 *A True Relation of the Barbarous Cruelty . . . of the Bloudy Cavaliers* (1642, T2931).
60 E. Walsingham, *Brittaniae Virtutis imago: or the Life of Major General Smith* (Oxford, 1644, W649), 18–23.
61 J. Gwynne, *Military Memoirs* (1822), 30–7.
62 W. Reinking, *A More Exact and Particular Relation of the Taking of Shrewsbury* (1645), 4. HMC, *Bath*, I, 7. L. Winstock, *Songs and Music of the Redcoats; A History of War Music of the British Army, 1642–1900* (Harrisburg, PA, 1970), 5–13.
63 R. Ram, *The Soldiers Catechism* (1645), 22–3. G. N. Godwin, *The Civil War in Hampshire and the Story of Basing House* (1904), 240. R. Atkyns, *Vindications* (1967), 11.
64 I am grateful to Don Higinbotham for a useful discussion about General S. L. A. Marshall's conclusions about the reluctance to fire weapons. While they have been challenged recently, they profoundly affected US tactics in Korea and Vietnam. See R. Holmes, *Acts of War* (New York, 1985), 58.
65 Drummond was also suspected of collusion with the enemy. David Stephenson, *Alasdair MaCiolla and the Highland Problems of the Seventeenth Century* (Edinburgh, 1980), 185.
66 Whitelocke, *op. cit.*, II, 287.
67 Clarendon, *History*, IX, 135. Gardiner, *Civil War*, II, 6.
68 23/9/44, Trevor to Ormonde, T. Carte, *Original Letters . . . from the . . . Ormonde Papers* (1739), I, 65. P. Young, *Edgehill* (Kineton, 1967), 131.
69 During the Second War the desertion rate in the British Army was 4.48 per thousand. It peaked at 10.05 in 1940–1. In the US Army in Vietnam in 1971 it was 73.4, while 176.9 were absent for less than twenty-four hours without leave. R. Holmes, *op. cit.*, 85–7.
70 Godwin, *op. cit.*, 24.
71 *Ibid.*, 167.
72 *The Civil War Papers of Sir William Boteler*, ed. G. H. Fowler, (Bedford, 1936), 28.
73 C. Holmes, *op. cit.*, 171.
74 M. Toynbee and P. Young, *Cropredy Bridge* (Kineton, 1970), 42. A. Fletcher, *A County Community in Peace and War: Sussex 1600–1660* (1975), 341.
75 R. H. Morris, *The Siege of Chester* (Chester, 1923), 23.
76 D. Underdown, *Revel, Riot and Rebellion* (New York, 1985), 159.
77 F. Larkin, *Stuart Royal Proclamations* (Oxford, 1983), II, 824, 1019.
78 Clarendon, *History*, IV, 264.

79 J. Chudleigh, *His Declaration to his Countrymen* (Oxford, 1643), 1–3. Rushworth, *Collections*, V, 272.
80 Godwin, *op. cit.*, 169.
81 A. Wood, *Life and Times of Anthony Wood* (Oxford, 1891), I, 90.
82 A. M. Auden, 'Clun and its neighborhood in the First Civil War', *Transactions of the Shropshire Archaeological and Natural History Society*, VIII (1908), 333.
83 R. W. Cotton, *Barnstaple and the Northern Part of Devon in the Great Civil War* (1889), 275–9.
84 Godwin, *op. cit.*, 130.
85 Bruno Ryves, *Mercurius Rusticus* (1685), 129.
86 J. Adair, 'The Court Martial papers of Sir William Waller's Army, 1644', *JSAHR*, 44 (1966), 205–26. G. Davies, 'Dundee Court Martial Record, 1651', *Miscellany of the Scottish Historical Society*, III, 2nd series, XIX (1919), 9–66.
87 C. Coates, *History of the Antiquities of Reading* (1802), 229.
88 This was a fairly high number. The average given to convicts in Australia, for example, being thirty.
89 A. MacFarlane, *Justice and the Mare's Ale* (New York, 1981), 195.
90 Godwin, *op. cit.*, E. Archer, *A True Relation of the Red Trained-Bands of Westminster* (1643), 2. Malbon, *op. cit.*

9 TO SLAY AND TO BE SLAIN

1 The royalist newspaper *Mercurius Aulicus* printed Susan's letter: John Adair, *By the Sword Divided, Eyewitness Accounts of the English Civil War* (1983), 118.
2 Quoted by G. E. Linderman, *Embattled Courage: The Experience of Combat in the American Civil War* (New York, 1987), 211.
3 R. Hutton, *The Royalist War Effort, 1642–46* (1983), 28.
4 R. Gough, *History of Myddle* (Harmondsworth, 1981), 72ff.
5 M. Coate, *Cornwall in the Great Civil War* (1933), 191. B. G. Blackwood, *The Lancashire Gentry and the Great Rebellion, 1640–60* (Manchester, Chetham Society, 1978), 112. P. R. Newman, 'The Royalist Army in the North of England', University of York Ph.D. (1978), 38. P. Roebuck, *Yorkshire Baronets* (Oxford, 1980), 43–5. P. R. Newman, 'Aspects of the Civil War in Lancashire', *Transactions of the Lancashire and Cheshire Antiquarian Society* (1983), 119–20. Sample based on analysis of G. Smith and M. Toynbee, *Leaders of the Civil Wars, 1642–1648* (Kineton, 1977).
6 G. Parker, *The Military Revolution* (Cambridge, 1988), 55. Gardiner, *Civil War*, II, 251. Clarendon, *History*, IV, 140, was referring to a skirmish near Thame of July 1643.
7 John Greene, 'The Diary of John Greene, 1635–57', ed. E. M. Symmonds, *English Historical Review*, XLIII (1928), 390.
8 H. Peters, *God's Doings and Man's Duty* (1646, P1703). T. Hobbes, *Behemoth* (1969), 95.
9 I. Roy, 'England Turned Germany? The Aftermath of the Civil War in its European Context', *TRHS*, 5th series, XXVIII (1978), 142. David Clarke, *The Siege of Colchester* (Colchester, 1975), 26.
10 P. Wenham, *The Great and Close Siege of York* (Kineton, 1970), 57–74.
11 I have tried to be cautious in my estimates, which is a reflection of my military training. Care is needed both to compensate for the optimistic claims of excited soldiers, and to avoid the embarrassment of being attacked by many more enemy than you thought you had left alive!

12 Figures for England include Wales.
13 I am grateful to Paul Peterson and Fran Haga for their help in entering this data, and for helping crunch numbers. Scots have been defined as parliamentarians or royalists depending on whose side they were fighting. Thus at Marston Moor they were the former, at Preston or Worcester the latter.
14 *A Perfect Table of the . . . Victories Obtained . . . By the Earl of Essex and Sir Thomas Fairfax* (August 1649).
15 All ratios are of course expressed in terms of one.
16 Regions are as follows: *Southeast*: Bedfordshire, Surrey, Hampshire, Kent, Middlesex, Buckinghamshire, Sussex. *East Anglia*: Norfolk, Suffolk, Cambridgeshire, Essex, Huntingdonshire. *West*: Cornwall, Devonshire, Somersetshire, Channel Isles, Scilly Isles, Wiltshire. *Wales* includes Monmouthshire. *Borders*: Worcestershire, Herefordshire, Shropshire, Gloucestershire. *Midlands*: Northamptonshire, Derbyshire, Oxfordshire, Staffordshire, Warwickshire, Leicestershire, Lincolnshire, Nottinghamshire. *North*: Northumberland, Durham, Lancashire, Yorkshire, Cheshire, Isle of Man.
17 Essex has not been counted, since only one incident took place there, the Siege of Colchester, in which 800 lost their lives.
18 Based on analysis of lists in Roger Palmer, Earl of Castlemaine, *The Catholique Apology* (1674, C1240), 574–80. Those who died of wounds, in sieges and were executed have been excluded. A recent analysis of the peerage as a whole argues that the civil war does not appear to have killed many of them: T. H. Hollingsworth, 'The Demography of the British Peerage', *Population Studies*, XVII, 2, (1965), 64.
19 A. Wood, *Life and Times of Anthony Wood* (Oxford, 1891), I, 62.
20 R. W. Cotton, *Barnstaple and the Northern Part of Devonshire during the Great Civil War* (1889), 105–6.
21 G. N. Godwin, *The Great Civil War in Hampshire* (1904), 164–6.
22 BL: Harleian MSS, 6904, 122.
23 Donald Reid, *English Civil War Firearms* (Leigh-on-Sea, 1989), 57.
24 E. Furgol, *A Regimental History of the Covenanting Armies, 1639–1651* (Edinburgh, 1988), 54.
25 E. Burghall, 'The Diary of Edward Burghall,' in T. W. Barlow, *Cheshire: Its Historical and Literary Associations* (Manchester, 1855), 166.
26 E. Broxap, *The Great Civil War in Lancashire, 1642–51* (Manchester, 1642–51), 68–9.
27 Clarendon, *History*, III, 289 IV, 487.
28 Rushworth, *Collections*, V, 288.
29 J. W. Bund, *The Civil War in Worcestershire, 1642–46* (Birmingham, 1905), 54. W. Waller, 'Recollections', in *The Poetry of Anne Matilda* (1788), 107.
30 T. Carte, *Ormonde Letters* (1739), III, 106.
31 J. Keegan and J. Durracott, *The Nature of War* (1981), 206.
32 P. Slack, *The Impact of Plague in Tudor and Stuart England* (1985), 73. R. and T. Kelly, *A City at War: Oxford, 1642–46* (Cheltenham, 1987), 25–6.
33 BL: Harleian MSS, 6804, 109.
34 *The Parliamentary or Constitutional History of England* (1763), XII, 349–51.
35 P. Logan, 'Medical Services in the Armies of the Confederate Wars', *Irish Sword*, IV (1960), 221. A. Kingston, *East Anglia in the Great Civil War* (1897), 147.
36 Slack, *op. cit.*, 151, 180ff. S. Porter, 'Property Damage in the English Civil War,' London Ph.D. (1984), 198. R. H. Morris, *The Siege of Chester* (Chester, 1923), 210.

37 Historical Monuments Commission, *Newark on Trent: The Civil War Siege-works* (1964), 23. E. Broxap, *The Great Civil War in Lancashire* (Manchester, 1910), 154.

38 *The Plague Pamphlets of Thomas Dekker*, ed. F. P. Wilson (Oxford, 1925), 25–6.

39 Morris, *op. cit.*, 210.

40 Parker, *op. cit.* D. Stewart, 'Sickness and Mortality Rates in the English Army until the Twentieth Century', *Journal of the Royal Army Medical Corps*, 91 (1948), 22–35. I. Roy, 'The English Civil War and English Society', *War and Society*, I, (1977), 31.

41 K. Manchester, 'Paleopathology of a Royalist Garrison', V, *OSSA: the Journal of the Oestological Research Laboratory, University of Solna, Sweden* (1979), 25–33.

42 Oswald, *op. cit.*, 73–116. R. N. Worth, *The Siege of Plymouth* (Plymouth, 1873), 51, claims that during the siege some eight thousand people died as a result of fighting and disease.

43 In the American Civil War, when weapons were far more damaging and medical attention a little better than during the British, for every soldier who died in combat, two died from disease and one civilian perished from a war-related cause. This supports the assertion that my ratio of 1 to 1.1 combat to non-combat death for Britain is conservative.

44 Edward M. Furgol, 'Scotland turned Sweden: The Scottish Covenanters and the Military Revolution, 1638–1651', 14–15. I am most grateful to Dr Furgol for sending me a copy of this unpublished paper.

45 Dr Furgol gives the covenanter military losses as follows (letter to author, 1 March 1990):

Year	Killed	Prisoners
1644	3,000	800
1645	7,200	
1646	2,000	
1648	1,000	4,600
1650	4,000	10,000
1651	4,800	10,000
Total	22,000	25,400

46 Jane H. Ohlmeyer, 'The Wars of Religion, 1603–1660'. I am grateful to the author for sending me a copy of her forthcoming paper. R. Bagwell, *Ireland under the Stuarts* (1906–16), II, 301. T. L. Coonan, *The Irish Catholic Confederacy and the Puritan Revolution* (Dublin, 1954), 328.

47 W. Macafee and V. Morgan, 'Population in Ulster, 1660–1760', *Plantation to Partition*, ed. P. Roebuck (Belfast, 1941) 47. *The Autobiography of the Rev. Devereux Spratt*, ed. T. Spratt (1886), 10. R. Baxter, *Reliquiae Baxterianae* (1696, B1370), 40. L. Hutchinson, *Memoirs of the Life of Colonel John Hutchinson* (1906), I, 173. H. Peters, *A True Relation of the Passages of God's Providence in a Voyage for Ireland* (1642, P1722), 22. Clarendon, *History* (1876), II, 20. M. Hickson, *Ireland in the Seventeenth Century* (1884), I, 167.

48 P. J. Corish, 'The Rising of 1641', and 'The Cromwellian Regime', in T. W. Moody, *et al.* (eds), *A New History of Ireland* (Oxford, 1976), II, 292 and 357.

49 J. T. Gilbert, *A Contemporary History of Affairs in Ireland from 1641 to 1652* (Dublin, 1879–80), III, 340–80.

50 C. V. Wedgwood, *The Thirty Years' War* (New York, 1961), 493. G. Parker, *The Thirty Years' War* (1984), 211. I am grateful to my colleague Bill Harris for the figures on the US Civil War.

51 'The Cavaliers' Prayer', Alex Broome, *A Collection of Royal Songs written against the Rump parliament between the Years 1639–1661* (1731), I, 96.

52 Philippe Aries, *Hour of our Death* (New York, 1981), 300.

53 C. R. Markham, *The Life of the Great Lord Fairfax* (1870), 425.

54 Rushworth, *Collections*, I, 156.

55 C. Carlton. 'The Rhetoric of Death: Scaffold Confessions in Early Modern England', *Southern Speech Communications Journal*, XLIX (Fall 1983), 66–79. R. Holmes, *Acts of War* (New York, 1985), 30.

56 Richard Wunderle and Gerald Broce, 'The Final Moment before Death in Early Modern England', *Sixteenth Century Journal*, XX (1989), 260.

57 Sir John Hinton, *Memoirs of Sir John Hinton, Physician in Ordinary to His Majesties Person* (1697). Edmund Ludlow, *Memoirs*, I, 82. Clarendon, *History*, IV, 27.

58 Sir T. Longmore, *Richard Wiseman: Surgeon General to Charles II* (1891), 45.

59 14/10/44, Sir Abraham Shipman to ?, HMC, *Fourth Report*, appendix, 271. P. Young, *Marston Moor* (1970), 174. 11/9/48, Cromwell to Fairfax, Abbott, *op. cit.*, II, 649.

60 Irene Coltman, *Private Men and Public Causes: Philosophy and Politics in the English Civil War* (1962), 135.

61 R. Symonds, *Diary* (Camden Society, 1859), 141.

62 John Webb, *Military Memoirs of Colonel John Birch* (Camden Society, 1873), 179.

63 Samuel Turner, *A True Relation of the late Skirmish at Henley-upon-Thames Whereon a Great Defeat was Given to the Redding Cavaliers* (1643, T3334), 4.

64 *A True Relation of the Proceeding of the English Army now in Scotland* (1650, T3023), 16. *A Large Relation of the Fight at Leith*, ed. Sir Walter Scott (London, 1806, originally 1650).

65 W. C. Abbot (ed.), *The Writings and Speeches of Oliver Cromwell* (Cambridge, Mass., 1937–47), II, 287. Antonia Fraser, *Cromwell, Our Chief of Men* (1973), 174.

66 Mary Coate, *Cornwall in the Great Civil War and Interregnum, 1642–1660* (Oxford, 1932), 100. Matthew Carter, *A Most True and Exact Relation of that . . . Unfortunate Expedition of Kent, Essex and Colchester* (1650, C662), 143. Clarendon, *History* (1876), VI, 513.

67 Fraser, *op. cit.*, 252.

68 Warburton, *Cavaliers*, II, 208.

69 A. Kingston, *East Anglia in the Civil War* (1897), 114.

70 R. Atkyns, *Vindication* (1968, originally 1669), 28.

71 J. W. Bund, *The Civil War in Worcestershire, 1642–46* (Birmingham, 1905), 251, 258.

72 J. Livingstone, *A Brief Historical Relation of the Life of John Livingstone* (1736), 111. *True Relation of . . . the Army in Dublin* (1642, T2922). Charles McNeil (ed.), *The Tanner Letters: Documents of Irish Affairs in the Sixteenth and Seventeenth Centuries Extracted for the Tanner Collection* (Dublin, 1943), 186.

73 R. Temple, 'The Original Officer List of the New Model Army', *BIHR*, 59 (May 1986), 58–63. Clarendon, *History*, III, 46.

74 Derek Hall and Norman Barber, *Colonel Richard Norton's Regiment of Horse* (Leigh-on-Sea, 1989), 17.

75 *A True Relation of the Passages which Happened at Portsmouth* (1642, T3015), 11.

76 G. N. Godwin, *The Civil War in Hampshire and the Story of Basing House* (1904), 169.

77 Helen Stokes (ed.), *Records of the Borough of Leicester, 1603–88* (Cambridge, 1923), 343. R. W. Cotton, *Barnstaple and the Northern Part of Devonshire during the Great Civil War* (1889), 127.

78 N. F. Tucker, 'Denbigh's Local Garrisons', *Transactions of the Denbighshire Historical Society*, V (1956), 26.

79 C. H. Wilkinson, *The Poems of Richard Lovelace* (Oxford, 1930), 86.

80 W. D. Grant, *Margaret the First: A Biography of Margaret Cavendish, Duchess of Newcastle, 1623–1673* (1957), 101. K. Jones, *A Glorious Fame: The Life of Margaret Cavendish, Duchess of Newcastle* (1988), 68–70. Gardiner, *Commonwealth*, I, 143.

81 A. Collins (ed.), *Letters and Memorials of State . . . From the Originals at Penshurst* (1746), 671–3.

82 G. Nugent, *Some Memorials of John Hampden* (1832), II, 383–5.

83 F. P. and M. M. Verney, *Memoirs of the Verney Family during the Civil War and Commonwealth* (1892–9), II, 202.

84 W. D. Fellowes, *Historical Sketches of Charles I, Cromwell, Charles II and the Principal Persons of that Period, including the King's Trial and Execution* (1824), 321.

85 Coltman, *op. cit.*, 135–8, 169.

86 BL: Harleian MSS, 6804, 92.

87 Henry Jones, 'Diary, 1605–82', *Journal of the Royal Society of Antiquaries of Ireland*, V (1893), 44–59. J. M. Hill, *Celtic Warfare* (Edinburgh, 1986), 48–9.

88 29/10/44, Norton to Richard Major, John Birch, *Military Memoirs* (Camden Society, 1873), 215.

89 T. Fairfax, *Memorials*, ed. C. H. Firth (1870), 426–31.

90 T. Fairfax, *Short Memorials* (1699), 385. R. Spaulding, *The Improbable Puritan: A Life of Bulstrode Whitelocke* (1975), 84. Bulstrode Whitelocke, *Diary* (1990), 133–4. Sir John Digby, 'The Life of Sir John Digby', *Camden Miscellany* (1910), 111.

91 W. E. Wynne (ed.), 'Correspondence during the Great Rebellion', *Archaeologia Cantiana* (1875), 205–6.

92 E. Melling, *Kent in the Civil War* (Maidstone, 1960), 23.

93 Sir James Turner, *Memoirs* (Edinburgh, 1829), 43.

94 D. A. Johnson and D. G. Vaisey, *Staffordshire in the Great Rebellion* (Stafford, 1964), 38.

95 R. Atkyns, *Vindication* (1968), 20.

96 P. Logan, 'Medical Services in the Armies of the Confederate Army', *Irish Sword*, IV (1960), 217.

97 Folger MSS, V.A. 216 n.pa. G. Martin, 'Inside Prince Rupert's Head', *History Today*, 40 (December 1990), 38–43.

98 C. H. Firth, *Cromwell's Army* (1962), 256. N. Tucker, *North Wales in the Civil War* (Denbigh, 1958), 171–3.

99 C. Duffy, *Siege Warfare, The Fortress in the Early Modern World* (1979), 146.

100 *CSPD, 1660–61*, 205.
101 Baxter, *op. cit.*, 59.
102 John Shawe, 'The Life of Master John Shawe', *Yorkshire Diaries*, ed. Charles Jackson (Surtees Society, 1877), 136. Helen Stocks (ed.), *Records of the Borough of Leicester, 1603–88* (Leicester, 1923), 359.
103 Aubrey, *op. cit.*, 19.
104 R. Holmes, *Acts of War* (New York, 1985), 257. A. Kellet, *Combat Motivation*, 273–6.
105 G. Grey, *The Warriors* (1970), 104–6.
106 N. Wallington, *Historical Notices* (1869), 105.
107 H. A. L. Howell, 'The Story of the Army Surgeon and the Care of Sick and Wounded during the Great Civil War', *Journal of the Royal Army Medical Corps*, III (1904), 430.
108 George Monck, Duke of Albermarle, *Observation of Political and Military Affairs* (1671), 78. Longmore, *op. cit.*, 46–7.
109 W. J. Birkin, 'The Royal College of Physicians of London and its Support of the Parliamentary Cause in the English Civil War', *Journal of British Studies*, 23, 1 (Fall 1983), 47–63. M. Toynbee, *The Papers of Captain Henry Stevens, Wagon-Master to Charles I* (Oxford Record Society, 1961), 18–19.
110 S. Luke, *The Letter Book, 1644–45, of Sir Samuel Luke, Parliamentary Governor of Newport Pagnell*, ed. H. G. Tibbutt (Bedford, 1963), nos 1040, 1242. Hinton, *op. cit.*, 18.
111 W. B. Richardson, 'Richard Wiseman and the Surgery of the Commonwealth', *The Asclepiad*, III (1889), 231–55.
112 BL: Harleian MSS, 6804, 92.
113 Clarendon, *History*, II, 373. J. Hodgson, *Memoirs of Captain Jon Hodgson* (Bradford, 1903), 142.
114 W. C., *A More Full Relation of the Continued Success of His Excellency Sir Thomas Fairfax* (1646, C159), 5.
115 21/9/43, Charles to Mayor of Newbury, J. O. Halliwell, *Letters of the Kings of England* (1846), II, 344. *CSPD, 1625–49*, 693.
116 Firth, *op. cit.*, 253–63, 294. C. H. Firth, 'The Sick and Wounded in the Great Civil War', *Cornhill Magazine*, X (1901), 289–99. Howell, *op cit.*, 304. Logan, *op. cit.*, 220.
117 *A True Report of the Great Cost and Charge of Four Hospitals in this City of London* (1646, T3091). G. Robinson, 'Wounded Soldiers in London during the First Dutch War', *History Today*, XVI, 1 (1966), 38–45.
118 *Another Order for Maimed and diseased Souldiers* (1643, A3272). A. Everitt (ed.), *Suffolk and the Great Rebellion* (Ipswich, 1960), 13.
119 F. Larkin, *Stuart Royal Proclamations* (Oxford, 1983), II, 893. 930.
120 I am most grateful to Stephen Freeth, Keeper of the Manuscripts, Guildhall Library, and to James R. Sewell, City Archivist, Corporation of London, for searching the index to the testamentary records of the Archdeaconary and Commissary Courts (c. 1630–65), at the Guildhall Library, as well as the miscellaneous index and index to the Hustings deeds at the Corporation of London Record Office. A Robert Rodway was listed as a member of the Tallow Chandlers' company in 1668–9; and was a master of an apprentice in that year, but this could well be too late for the Basing House veteran. He would have been in his fifties, rather old to be admitted to a company. While the Court of Orphans records for this period are missing, considering that Robert's company was not a regular trained band unit, it seems probable that he was not a citizen.

10 WHEN THE HURLYBURLY'S DONE

1 J. Adair, *By the Sword Divided* (1983), 163.
2 2/5/42, Henry Oxinden to Elizabeth Dallison, D. Gardiner, *The Oxinden and Peton Letters, 1642–70* (1937), 3. W. Phillips, 'Sir Francis Ottley's Papers', *Transactions of the Archaeological and Natural History Society of Shropshire* (1894–96), 47. In *The Experience of Defeat: Milton and Some of His Contemporaries* (1984), Christopher Hill deals with long-term political as opposed to short-term military defeat.
3 *England's Divison and Ireland's Distraction* (1642, E2961), quoted by J. T. Zeller, 'Anti-War Sentiment during the English Civil War', Minnesota Ph.D. (1974), 61.
4 HMC, *Fifth Report*, appendix, 160–1.
5 R. Baxter, *Reliquiae Baxterianae* (1696, B1370), 43. B. Whitelocke, *Memorials* (Oxford, 1853), I, 188. Sir Humphrey Mildmay's diary shows a similar reaction to news of Marston Moor, P. L. Ralph, *Humphrey Mildmay: Royalist Gentleman* (New Brunswick, 1947), 175.
6 S. J. Greenberg, 'Dating Civil War Pamphlets, 1641–1644', *Albion*, 20, 3 (1988), 396–7.
7 R. W. Cotton, *Barnstaple and the Northern Part of Devon in the Great Civil War* (1889), 180.
8 Baxter, *op. cit.*, 54. C. V. Wedgwood, *The King's War* (1971), 439.
9 J. Tilsley, *A True Relation of the Taking of the Town of Preston* (1643, T1275), in E. Broxap, *The Great Civil War in Lancashire, 1642–51* (Manchester, 1910), 64.
10 J. R. Hale, *Renaissance War Studies* (1983), 498.
11 R. Coe, *An Exact Dyarie of the Progress of Sir William Waller's Army* (1644, C4881), n.pa.
12 *Great Victories obtained by the Earl of Denbigh* (1644, G1760), n.pa 11/10/43, Henderson to Colonel-General Henry Hastings, HMC, *Hastings*, II, 104–5.
13 28/1/44, Fairfax to wife, R. E. Bell (ed.), *Memorials of the Civil War . . . the Fairfax Correspondence* (1849), I, 74–5.
14 B. Montgomery, *Memoirs* (1960), 83. Sir Henry Slingsby, *Diary* (1836), 97–9.
15 J. Rushworth, *True Relation of the Fight at Bovey Tracy between Sir Thomas Fairfax and Three Regiments of the King's Horse* (1646, R2336), n.pa.
16 Wedgwood, *op cit.*, 514.
17 Adair, *op. cit.*, 210.
18 W. Dell, *The Building and Glory of the Truly Christian and Spiritual Church* (1646, D918), 15.
19 Eliot A. Cohen and John Gooch, *Military Misfortunes:The Anatomy of Failure in War* (New York, 1990). *A Fuller Relation of the Great Victory Obtained . . . At Alsford* (1644, A3B), n.pa.
20 J. Sprigge, *Anglia Rediviva* (1854), 126.
21 Wedgwood, *op cit.*, 449.
22 Whiting, *op cit.*, 8.
23 *Account of Powick Bridge by a Trooper in Captain Nathaniel Fienne's Troop* (1642), 11.
24 R. Hopton, *Bellum Civile* (1988), 19.
25 BL: Sloane MSS, 1519, 25.
26 Clarendon, *History*, V, 209.
27 W. J. Farrow, *The Great Civil War in Shropshire* (Shrewsbury, 1926), 54.

28 HMC, *Beaumont*, 41. Sir William Waller, 'Recollections', in *The Poetry of Anne Matilda* (1788), 123.

29 A. Wood, *Life and Times* (1891), I, 99.

30 William Maurice, 'An Account of the Civil War in North Wales', *Archaeologia Cambrensis*, I (1846), 43.

31 14/7/44. Report of Captain Robert Clarke, in C. H. Firth, 'Marston Moor', *TRHS*, XII (1898), 76–9.

32 *CSPD, 1644*, 309.

33 Wedgwood, *op. cit.*, 504.

34 E. Ludlow, *Memoirs*, I, 90.

35 Rushworth, *Collections*, V, 282.

36 Rushworth, *Collections*, VI, 515–17. Thomas Herbert, *Memoirs of the Last Years of the Reign of King Charles* (1959), 25–40.

37 Charles MacKay, *The Cavalier Songs and Ballads of England from 1642 to 1684* (1863), 29. A. Brome, *A Collection of Loyal Songs written against the Rump Parliament between the Years 1639–1661* (1731), I, 199–200.

38 E. B. Jorgens, 'Politics and Women in Cavalier Song: a report from a collection of secular song manuscripts', *Explorations in Renaissance Culture*, XV (1989), 25–48.

39 *Ibid.*, 10.

40 J. Webb, *Memorials of the Civil War . . . Herefordshire* (1879), I, 271–2.

41 Philip Lindsay, *For King and Parliament* (1949), 197.

42 Warburton, *Cavaliers*, III, 149.

43 31/7/45, Charles to Rupert, J. O. Halliwell (ed.), *Letters of the Kings of England* (1846), II, 383–5.

44 C. Carlton, *Charles I: the Personal Monarch* (1983), 292–5.

45 A Canadian private described this process: 'We began the house and barn clearing on the edge of the town. Not many prisoners were taken, as if they did not surrender before we started on a house, they never had the opportunity afterwards.' J. Ellis, *The Sharp End of War* (1980), 100–1. J. Keegan and R. Holmes, *Soldiers: a History of Men in Battle* (New York, 1986), 271.

46 Sir Henry Foulis, *An Exact and True Relation of a Bloody Fight . . . before Tadcastle and Selby* (1642, F1639.5).

47 C. H. Firth, *Cromwell's Army* (1905), 231–2.

48 S. Glover, *History . . . of the County of Derby* (Derby, 1829), 79.

49 R. Atkyns, *Vindications* (1968), 15.

50 Washbourne, *op. cit.*, II, 292.

51 J. Lister, *Autobiography* (1842), 17.

52 J. A. Atkinson, *Tracts Relating to the Civil War in Cheshire* (Chetham Society, 1909), 62.

53 Atkyns, *op. cit.*, 27–9. L. Hutchinson, *Memoirs of the Life of Colonel Hutchinson* (1906), II, 236.

54 G. N. Godwin, *The Civil War in Hampshire* (1904), 46.

55 Atkinson, *op. cit.*, 101. Thomas Malbon, *Memorials of the Civil War in Cheshire* (Manchester, 1889), 94–5.

56 E. Archer, *A True Relation of the Red Trained-Bands of Westminster* (1643), 13.

57 E. Symmonds, *A Military Sermon Preached at Shrewsbury, March 3, 1643 to His Majesty's Army* (1644, S6346), 34.

58 Clarendon, *History*, III, 429.

59 J. Adair, *Cheriton, 1644: The Campaign and the Battle* (1973), 58–9.

60 *A True Relation of the Cruel and Unparalleled Oppression . . . Upon the Gentlemen Prisoners in the Tower* (1647, T2938), 2.

61 Esther Cope, *The Life of A Public Man: Edward, First Baron Montagu of Boughton* (Philadelphia, 1981).

62 A. Fraser, *Cromwell our Chief of Men* (1973), 85.

63 Rushworth, *Collections*, V, 83. P. Gregg, *Free-Born John: A Biography of John Lilburne* (1961), 101–4. M. George, *Women in the First Capitalist Society* (1990), 77.

64 R. W. Cotton, *Barnstaple and the Northern Part of Devon in the Great Civil War* (1889), 275–9.

65 G. Nugent, *Some Memorials of John Hampden, his Party and his Times* (1832), II, 346. It is a good story, but probably apocryphal.

66 17/12/42, Stery to Sergeant Major Alexander, H. Foulis, *op. cit.*, 9. Henry Slingsby, *Diary* (1836), 54.

67 J. Hodgson, *Memoirs* (Bradford, 1902), 25.

68 *Mercurius Aulicus* (3 January 1645).

69 Quoted by B. Donagan, 'Prisoners in the English Civil War', *History Today*, 41 (1991), 31.

70 *A True Relation of the Late Proceedings of the Scottish Army* (1643, T2990), 6.

71 See, for instance, C. Carlton, 'Thomas Cromwell: A Study in Interrogation', *Albion*, V, 2 (Summer 1973), 116–28. The interrogation reports of prisoners taken at Penzance deal with political attitudes: Folger MSS, Xd, 483 (21).

72 J. Langbein, *Torture and the Law of Proof* (Chicago, 1977), M. J. M'Enery, 'A Diary of the Siege of Limerick, 1642', *Journal of the Royal Society of Antiquaries of Ireland*, 34 (1905), 181. Ludlow, *op. cit.*, I, 60. Hutchinson, *op. cit.*, II, 369–70.

73 Hutchinson, *op. cit.*, 257.

74 *An Exact Relation of the Proceedings of the Cavaliers at Cirencester* (1643, E3695a), n.pa.

75 *A True and Perfect Relation of the Barbarous and Cruel passage of the King's Army at Old Brainceford* (1642, T2551), 10.

76 William Laud, *The Works of the Most Reverend Father in God, William Laud* (Oxford, 1847–60), III, diary entry for 2 December 1642.

77 Sir John Digby, *Life* (Camden Society, 1910), 90–110.

78 *A Second Gunpowder Plot* (1644, S2328), 4.

79 Rushworth, *Collections*, V, 303.

80 G. S., *A True Relation of the Sad Passages between the Two Armies* (1644, S28), 6–11. B. Donagan, 'Codes and Conduct in the English Civil War', *Past and Present* (1988), 89–91.

81 R. Symonds, *Diary* (Camden Society, 1859), 66.

82 Edward Robinson, *A Discourse of the Warr in Lancashire* (Chetham Society, 1864), 51.

83 F. P. and M. M. Verney, *Memoirs of the Verney Family* (1892–9), I, 195–7.

84 4/12/60, *CSPD, 1660–61*, 403.

85 P. Lindsay, *For King and Parliament* (1949), 172.

86 M. Hussey, *Jonson and the Cavaliers* (1964), 124.

87 J. Bastwick, *Utter Routing of the Whole Army of the Independents and Sectaries* (1646, B1072), 653–4. H. G. Tibbutt, *The Tower of London Letter Book of Sir Lewis Dyvie, 1646–47* (Bedford, 1958), 52.

88 Roger Twysden, 'Journal', *Archaeologia Cantiana*, III, (1860), 153. Hutchin-

son, *op. cit.*, (1968), 144–5. J. Adair, 'The Court Martial Papers of Sir William Waller's Army', 1644, *JSAHR*, 44 (1966), 217.

89 R. Holmes, *The Sieges of Pontefract Castle, 1644–48* (Pontefract, 1887), 395.

90 J. R. S. Whiting, *Gloucester Besieged 1640–1660* (Gloucester, 1981), 9. Derby Museum, *Derby and the Civil War: Catalogue of the Exhibition, October 1971* (Derby, 1971), Item no. 95.

91 D. Johnson and D. G. Vaisey, *Staffordshire in the Great Rebellion* (Stafford, 1964), 37. R. Orr, *Reason and Authority: The Thought of William Chillingworth* (Oxford, 1967), 196–7.

92 Symonds, *op. cit.*, 55.

93 R. Gough, *History of Myddle* (Harmondsworth, 1981), 232. N. Drake, 'A Journal of the First and Second Sieges of Pontefract Castle, 1644–45', *Surtees Society Miscellany*, 37 (1861), 45.

94 Hopton, *op. cit.*, 40–1.

95 6/3/45, Luke to Brereton, *The Letter Book, 1644–45, of Sir Samuel Luke*, ed. H. G. Tibbutt (Bedford, 1963), 182. 11/9/47, Trelany to Semour, HMC, *Fifteenth Report*, pt VII, 66. 13/1/44, Neile to Rigby, HMC, *Fourteenth Report*, pt IV, 61.

96 Warburton, *Cavaliers*, III, 39.

97 Contained in *Military Orders . . . established by His Majesty*, n.d., and *Commons' Journals* for 9 February 1643.

98 Sir Hugh Pollard, *To The Right Honourable House of Commons, the Humble petition of Sir Hugh Pollard* (1642, P2773).

99 J. Bampfield, *Apology* (The Hague, 1685, B628A), 5–7.

100 Clarendon, *History*, IV, 89–90.

101 J. W. W. Bund, *The Civil War in Worcestershire* (Birmingham, 1905), 26.

102 Atkyns, *op. cit.*, 27–9.

103 J. Rushworth, *A More Full and Exact Relation of the Several Treaties between Sir Thomas Fairfax and Sir Ralph Hopton* (1646, R2327), 4–5.

104 This section based on *A True and Most Sad Relation of the Hard Usage and of the Extreme Cruelty used on Captain Wingate with others of the Parliamentary Souldiers, etc. at Oxford* (1642, T2512), *An Exact Relation of the Proceedings of the Cavaliers at Leicester Containing a True Declaration of the Bloody Cruelties* (1644, E3695.5), Edmund Chillenden, *The Inhumanity of the King's Prison-Keeper at Oxford* (1643, C3876), 2–22, and Edward Wirely, *The Prisoner's Report* (1643, W3099). *Intelligence from the Armie with a Relation of Captain Wingates Escape from Oxford and the Conditions of the Prisoners there* (8 June 1643, I261).

105 Whitelocke, *op. cit.*, I, 194, and *Diary* (1990), 145.

106 BL: Harleian MSS, 6804, 51.

107 12/6/45, Luke to Richard Knightley, S. Luke, *The Letter Book, 1644–45, of Sir Samuel Luke*, Parliamentary Governor of Newport Pagnell, ed. H. G. Tibbutt (Bedford, 1963), no. 1374.

108 17/3/44, Sir Edward Nicholas to Lord Ruthven, *CSPD, 1644*, 57. Sir John Birkenhead, *Newes from Smith, The Oxford Jaylor . . . who is sentenced to stand in the pillory for three market days for his notorious libelling against state and kingdom* (1645, B2969).

109 Bruno Ryves, *Mercurius Rusticus, or the countries complaint of the barbarous outrages committed* (1685, R2449), 101.

110 O. Morshead, 'Royalist Prisoners in Windsor Castle', *Berkshire Archaeological Journal*, 56 (1958), 26. R. South, *Royal Castle: Rebel Town* (Buckingham, 1986), 36.

111 R. W. Cotton, *Barnstaple and the Northern Parts of Devon during the Great Civil War* (1889), 99. Morshead, *op. cit.*, 7.
112 B. Schofield, *The Knyvett Letters, 1620–44* (1949), 33–5, 109–15.
113 10/5/44, Maxwell to Denbigh, HMC, *Fourth Report*, appendix, 266.
114 W. H. Blaauw, 'Passages of the Civil War in Sussex from 1642 to 1660', *Sussex Archaeological Collection*, V (1852), 64.
115 J. Howell, *Epistolae Ho-Elianae* (1892), 357–59, 368–9, 421–6, 485.
116 P. R. Newman, 'The Royalist Army in the North of England', York Ph.D. (1978), 167.
117 E. Green, 'The Siege of Bridgwater', *Somerset Archaeological and Natural History Society Proceedings*, XXII, 3, (1877), 18.
118 Gardiner, *Civil War*, I, 295.
119 Morshead, *op. cit.*, 12. Blaauw, *op. cit.*, 66.
120 *CSPV, 1643–45*, 241.
121 Washbourne, *op. cit.*, 173.
122 R. Bulstrode, *Memoirs and Reflections upon the Reign and Government of King Charles I and King Charles II* (1721), 111.
123 Ludlow, *op. cit.*, I, 79–83.
124 Sprigge, *op. cit.*, 144–6.
125 J. R. Powell and E. K. Timings, *Documents Relating to the Civil War* (Naval Records Society, 1963), 210. Rushworth, *op. cit.*, 4–5.
126 Baxter, *op. cit.*, 53.
127 Changing sides was common during the American Revolution. 'We fought with British soldiers and they fought them with those of America', commented General Nathan Greene. M. Glover, *The Velvet Glove: The Decline and Fall of Moderation in War* (1982), 163.
128 *True Relation of Two Merchants of London who were taken prisoners by the Cavaliers* (1642, T3075). John Webb (ed.), *Military Memoir of Colonel John Birch, Governor of Hereford in the Civil War* (Camden Society, 1873), xi.
129 *A True and Perfect Relation of the Barbarous and Cruel Passage of the King's Army at Old Brainceford* (1642, T2551), 10. *A True Relation of the Putting to Death of one Master Boys, a Citizen of London, by the Bloody Minded Person, Colonel Aston, a Known and Professed Papist* (1642, T3029). Clarendon, *History*, VIII, 38.
130 Warburton, *Cavaliers*, III, 126.
131 R. E. Sherwood, *Civil Strife in the Midlands* (1974), 69.
132 Ryves, *op. cit.*, 167–8.
133 N. Wallington, *Historical Notices of Events Occurring Chiefly in the Reign of Charles I* (1869), II, 171.
134 Folger MSS, Vol. 436, 89. G. R. Aylmer, 'Collective Mentalities in Mid-seventeenth Century England; I: The Puritan Outlook', *Transactions of the Royal Historical Society*, 5th series, 36 (1986), 23.
135 J. Evelyn, *Diary* (1955), I, 43. *An Exact Relation of the Bloody and Barbarous Massacre at Bolton . . . by an Eyewitness* (1644, E3683), 1.
136 Washbourne, *op. cit.*, 262–3.
137 Gardiner, *Civil War*, I, 292. D. Underdown, *Somerset in the Civil War and Interregnum* (Newton Abbot, 1973), 75. The Reverend Praph, Vicar of Terrington, Herefordshire, suffered a similar fate at the hands of Colonel Massey's troops when he responded to their challenge that he was for God and the King.
138 G. Pendlebury, *Aspects of the Civil War in Bolton and its Neighbourhood, 1640–1660* (Manchester, 1983), 12. Warburton, *Cavaliers*, II, 430.

139 HMC, *Bath* I, 38–9.

140 Between 1592 and 1640 there were only three cases of reported rape in East Sussex, an area with a population of about 40,000: C. B. Herrup, *The Common Peace: Participation and the Criminal Law in Seventeenth-Century England* (Cambridge, 1987), 27.

141 Carver, *op. cit.*, 115. Fraser, *op. cit.*, 331. This conclusion does not support the view of feminist writers that rape 'is a conscious tactic of warfare': see Betty A. Reardon, *Sexism and the War System* (New York, 1985), 40, and S. Brownmiller, *Against our Will, Men, Women and Rape* (New York, 1976), 31–113. Brownmiller's work has sparked a long debate which L. Ellis, *Theories of Rape* (New York, 1989), summarizes.

142 Robert Douglas, 'Civil War Diary', in James Maidment (ed.), *Historical Fragments Relative to Scottish Affairs* (Edinburgh, 1832), 67. *A Discovery of Many Great and Bloudy Robberies Committed by the Late Disbanded Troopers Chiefly about the City of London since the Disbanding of the Army of the North* (1644, D1642), 1–3.

143 Ryves, *op. cit.*, 97.

144 C. Durston, *The Family in the English Revolution* (Oxford, 1988), 147. I cannot accept the conclusion of this excellent book that rape was fairly common during the English civil war.

145 *A Fuller Relation of that Miraculous Victory Obtained by . . . Fairfax . . . at Wakefield* (1643, F2491A), 1–3.

146 Symonds, *op. cit.*, 17. Luke, *op. cit.*, no. 664.

147 *A Fuller Relation of the Great Victory Obtained (Through God's Providence) at Alsford* (1644, A3B), n.pa.

148 Gardiner, *Civil War*, I, 296.

149 'The Diary of Edward Burghall', in T. Worthington Barlow (ed.), *Cheshire: Its Historical and Literary Associations* (Manchester, 1855), 182.

150 Godwin, *op cit.*, 106. J. R. Powell, *Documents Relating to the Civil War* (Naval Records Society, 1963), 141. T. Carte, *Original Letters . . . Among the Duke of Ormonde's Papers* (1739), I, 48.

151 HMC, *Portland* III, 109.

152 Edward Drake, 'Civil War Diary', in A. R. Bayley, *The Great Civil War in Dorset* (Taunton, 1910), 188.

153 1/8/44 and 26/9/44, Agostini to Doge and Senate, *CSPV, 1643–45*, 126 and 143. Sir Edward Walker, *Historical Discourse upon Several Occasions* (1705–7), 39–40. Ludlow, *op. cit.*, I, 95.

154 Auden, *op. cit.*, 57–8.

155 Sir Richard Browne, *A Letter . . . Containing a True Relation of a Great Victory . . . near Abingdon* (1645, B5144), 5. Malbon, *op cit.*, 158.

156 J. E. Auden, 'The Anglo-Irish troops in Shropshire', *Transactions of the Shropshire Archaeological Society*, 50 (1939–40), 59–60. Gough, *op. cit.*, 75. Warburton, *Cavaliers*, III, 73, 391.

157 J. R. Phillips, *Memoirs of the Civil Wars in Wales and the Marches* (1874), II, 326.

158 Wedgwood, *King's War*, 506.

159 23/5/46, Sir Trevor Williams to Sir John Trevor, H. Cary, *Memorials of the Great Civil War in England* (1842), I, 64. R. Holmes, *Acts of War* (New York, 1985), 367. J. Malcolm, *Caesar's Due* (1983), 121.

160 J. R. N. McPhail, 'Documents Relating to the Massacre at Dunvarty', *Highland Papers*, II (1916), 254.

161 *A Perfect Relation of the Cause and Manner of the Apprehending William Needle and Mistress Phillips* (1643, P1509), n.pa.
162 Folger MSS, V 62 (19).
163 J. Taylor, *Mad Verse, Sad Verse, Glad Verse, Bad Verse* (Oxford, 1644, T479), 5.
164 J. Cruso, *Treatise on Modern War* (1640), 161.
165 Sir Samuel Luke, *Journal of Sir Samuel Luke, Scoutmaster to the Earl of Essex, 1643–44* (Oxford, 1950–3), and *The Letter Books, 1644–45, of Sir Samuel Luke, Parliamentary Governor of Newport Pagnell,* ed. H. G. Tibbutt (Bedford, 1963). W. Lilly, *History of His Life and Times* (1774), 119ff.
166 Slingsby, *op cit.*, 145.
167 Sprigge, *op. cit.*, 86–7.

11 MORE TO SPOIL THAN TO SERVE

1 James A. Atkinson, *Tracts Relating to the Civil Wars in Cheshire, 1641–59* (Chetham Society, 1909), 29.
2 Rushworth, *Collections* II, 3, 95–8.
3 Entry on 'Plunder' in *Oxford English Dictionary*.
4 J. Ashton, 'The Journal of John Ashton', in J. C. Hodgson (ed.), *North Country Diaries* (Surtees Society, 1890), 13.
5 R. B. Manning, 'Plunder as a Symbolic Substitute for War in Tudor and Early Stuart England'. I am most grateful to Dr Manning for letting me have a copy of this unpublished paper.
6 R. South, *Royal Castle: Rebel Town* (Buckingham, 1981), 43.
7 D. Underdown, *Somerset in the Civil War and Interregnum* (Newton Abbot, 1973), 86.
8 N. Wharton, 'The Letters of Sergeant Nehemiah Wharton', *Archaeologia*, XXXV (1853), 311–13.
9 J. W. Bund, *The Civil War in Winchester* (Birmingham, 1905), 56. R. Sherwood, *Civil Strife in the Midlands* (1974), 17.
10 H. Foulis, *An Exact and True Relation of a Bloody Fight . . . before Tadcastle and Selby* (1642, F1639.5), 9.
11 J. Adair, *The Life of John Hampden* (1976), 186–7. Bodleian: Carte MSS, 103, 91.
12 4/6/43, Waller to Lady Scudamore, Folger MSS, V.B. 2 (1).
13 *A True Relation of the Passages Which Happened at Portsmouth* (1642, T3015), 2. Elizabeth Melling, *Kentish Sources, II, Kent and the Civil War* (Maidstone, 1960), 16.
14 *His Majesty's Proceedings in Northamptonshire, Gloucestershire, Wiltshire and Warwickshire* (1642, H2086), 4.
15 Melling, *op. cit.*, 17.
16 *Ibid.*, 17.
17 R. Morris, *The Siege of Chester, 1643–46* (Chester, 1923), 28.
18 G. Ormerod, *The History of the County Palatine and the City of Chester* (1872), I, lxii.
19 *A Relation of the Rare Exploits of the London Soldiers* (1642, R862), 6–8. F. Larkin, *Stuart Royal Proclamations* (Oxford, 1983), II, 820.
20 M. Bennett, 'Leicester royalist officers and the war effort in the county, 1642–46', *Leicestershire Archaeological and Historical Society Transactions*, 59 (1984–5), 50.
21 Warburton, *Cavaliers*, II, 191–3.

22 J. Eales, *Puritans and Roundheads: The Harleys of Brampton Bryan and the Outbreak of the English Civil War* (Cambridge, 1990), 166. Sherwood, *op. cit.*, 164–5.

23 W. Money, *The First and Second Battle of Newbury* (1884), 226. A. J. Fletcher, *A County Community in Peace and War: Sussex, 1600–1660* (1975), 275.

24 C. V. Wedgwood, 'The Scientists and the English Civil War', in *The Logic of Personal Knowledge: Essays presented to Michael Polanyi* (1961), 62–3. B. Whitelocke, *Memorials of English Affairs* (1853), I, 188–9, and *Diary* (1990), 138–9.

25 R. Josselin, *The Diary of Ralph Josselin* (1976), 128–9.

26 A. Brome, *Poems*, ed. R. R. Dubinski (Toronto, 1982), I, 274. B. Whelen, 'Hereford and the Civil War: some Original Papers', *Dublin Review*, 179 (1926), 68–9.

27 N. Wallington, *Historical Notices of Events Occurring Chiefly during the Reign of King Charles I* (1869), II, 87–90.

28 J. Malcolm, *Caesar's Due: Loyalty and King Charles, 1642–1646* (1983), 85.

29 HMC, *Fifth Report*, appendix, 402.

30 18/9/43, Robert Lambert to Charles, Lord Lambert, *CSPD, 1641–43*, 487.

31 J. R. Phillips, *Memoirs of the Civil War in Wales and the Marches, 1642–49* (1874), I, 243.

32 Bruno Ryves, *Mercurius Rusticus* (1685, R2450), 57–8.

33 A. Kingston, *East Anglia in the Great Civil War* (1897), 372.

34 Melling, *op. cit.*, 21. A. Wood, *Life and Times* (Oxford, 1891), 94–5. R. E. Bell, *Memorials of the Civil Wars . . . the Fairfax Correspondence* (1849), I, 135–6.

35 J. Turner, *Memoirs* (Edinburgh, 1829), 59–62.

36 There seems to be no trace of the daughter in colonial records. I am grateful to Christa Howerton for checking this point. HMC, *Fourth Report*, appendix, 272.

37 Clarendon, *History*, III, 417.

38 Henry Townsend, *Diary* (1915), 128.

39 M. Hazell, *Fidelity and Fortitude, Lord Capel and his Regiment and the English Civil War* (Leigh-on-Sea, 1987), 25.

40 D. A. Johnson and D. G. Vaisey, *Staffordshire in the Great Rebellion* (Stafford, 1964), 31.

41 *CSPD, 1641–43*, 481.

42 28/12/43, Mrs Harrison to John Bradley, *CSPD, 1641–43*, 508. William Davenport, 'Civil War Diary', printed in J. P. Earwacker, *East Cheshire* (1977), I, 430.

43 T. Malbon, *Memorials of the Civil War in Cheshire* (Manchester, 1889), 242–6.

44 HMC, *Fourth Report*, appendix, 264.

45 10/4/44, Ranulph Crewe to Sir Richard Browne, Robert E. Bell, *Memorials of the Civil Wars . . . the Fairfax Correspondence* (1894), I, 98.

46 Townsend, *op. cit.*, I, lxxx.

47 Money, *op. cit.*, 226.

48 S. Luke, *The Letter Book, 1644–45, of Sir Samuel Luke, Parliamentary Governor of Newport Pagnell*, ed. H. G. Tibbutt (Bedford, 1963), 168–9. Alfred Kingston, *East Anglia in the Great Civil Wars* (1897), 191.

49 I. Gentles, 'Military–civilian Conflict in the English Revolution, 1643–1655: the evidence of the Indemnity Papers', 10–11. I am most grateful to Dr Gentles for sending me a copy of this unpublished paper.

50 Luke, *op. cit.*, 159. S. Leighton, 'Mytton Manuscripts: Letters and papers of Thomas Mytton of Halson', *Montgomeryshire Collections*, VIII (1874–5), 153.

51 S. Ashe, *A Continuation of the True Intelligence . . . of the Earl of Manchester's Army* (1644), 8. Gardiner, *Civil War*, I, 367.

52 Roger Boyle, Earl of Orrery, *Treatise of the Art of War* (1677), 164. James Audley, Earl of Castlehaven, *Memoirs* (Waterford, 1680), 133. R. Ward, *Animadversions of Warre* (1639), 28 and 65.

53 J. Webb, *Memorials of the Civil War . . . Herefordshire* (1879), I, 288; II, 395–9.

54 D. A. Johnson and D. G. Varsey, *Staffordshire in the Great Rebellion* (Stafford, 1964), 34. Webb, *op. cit.*, 395. *A Declaration Concerning the Miserable Sufferings of the County under the Scots forces* (1646, D574), n.pa.

55 David Leslie, *Two Letters from Lt. General David Leslie* (1646, N843), 5–7.

56 Sherwood, *op. cit.*, 31.

57 R. Ashton, *The English Civil War* (1978), 193. L. S. Winstock, *Songs and Music of the Redcoats: A History of the War Music of the British Army, 1642–1902* (Harrisburg, Penn., 1970), 15.

58 W. H. Blaauw, 'Passages of the Civil War in Sussex from 1642 to 1660', *Sussex Archaeological Collection*, V (1852), 51. *Military Memoirs of Colonel John Birch* (Camden Society, 1873), 162–3.

59 Sherwood, *op. cit.*, 54.

60 T. George, 'War and Peace in the Puritan Tradition', *Church History*, 53 (1984), 499.

61 D. Underdown, 'The Problem of Popular Allegiance in the English Civil War', *TRHS*, 31, 5th series (1981), 97.

62 12/12/45, Harry Brych to Ormonde, T. Carte, *Original Letters . . . Found among the Duke of Ormonde's Papers* (1739), I, 30.

63 J. Hodgson, *Memoirs* (1883), 37.

64 William Lithgow, *Experimental and Exact Relation upon that Famous and Renowned Siege of Newcastle* (1645), reprinted in *Somer's Tracts*, V, 291–3.

65 N. Tucker, 'Colonel Sir Robert Mostyn, First Baronet, 1624–1690', *Flintshire Historical Society Publications*, XVII (1952), 44. E. Robinson, *A Discourse on the Warr in Lancashire* (Chetham Society, 1864), 156.

66 John War, *The Taking of Winchester* (1643, W777), n.pa. *Military Memoirs of Colonel John Birch*, 209.

67 D. A. Johnson, *Staffordshire in the Great Rebellion* (Stafford 1964), 44. P. Styles, 'The Royalist Government of Worcester during the Civil War, 1642–46', *Transactions of the Worcestershire Archaeological Society*, V (1976), 26. C. H. Firth, *Cromwell's Army* (1905), 193.

68 9/43, F. Cheynell to Lt.-Col. Baynes, HMC, *Seventh Report*, appendix II, 680. Ormerod, *op. cit.*, I, lxii.

69 Ian Ryder, *An English Army for Ireland* (Leigh-on-Sea, 1987), 26.

70 S. ffarington, *The ffarington Papers* (Chetham Society, 1856), 97, 108.

71 D. F. Mosler, 'A Social and Religious History of the English Civil War in the County of Warwick', Stanford Ph.D. (1975), 173. Gardiner, *Commonwealth*, I, 96.

72 G. A. Harrison, 'Royalist Organisation in Gloucester and Bristol', Manchester MA (1961).

73 M. Bennet, 'Contributions and Assessment: Financial Exactions in the English Civil War', *War and Society* (1981), 8–9, does not accept the view that military–civilian relations were especially violent. I am inclined to the views of S. Porter, 'The Fire Raid in the English Civil War', *War and Society* (1984), 37, and Gentles, *op. cit.*, that they were.

74 G. A. Harrison, 'Royalist Organizations in Gloucester and Bristol', Manchester MA (1961), 45. Robinson, *op. cit.*, 54.

75 H. G. Tibbutt, *Bedfordshire in the First Civil War* (Elstow, 1956), 15. J. Morrill, *The Revolt of the Provinces* (1976), 86.

76 Sir Edward Nicholas, *The Nicholas Papers* (Camden Society, 1886), I, 62. J. Taylor, *Ad Populum, or a Lecture to the People* (1644). John Hacket, *Scrinia Reserata* (1692), II, 206.

77 Townsend, *op. cit.*, III, 239.

78 J. Lloyd, 'Colonel John Jones of Maesygarnedd', *Merionethshire Historical and Record Society*, II (1953–4), 98.

79 Barry M. Rosenburg, 'The Parliamentary Policy and Practice of the Composition, Sequestration and the Sale of Royalist Lands, 1642–1660 in Durham and Northumberland', Virginia Ph.D. (1978).

80 G. E. Aylmer, *Rebellion or Revolution?* (1985), 71.

81 Ian Roy, 'The English Civil War and English Society', *War and Society* (1975), 29. M. Bennet, 'Leicester Royalist Officers and the War Effort in the County', *Leicestershire Archaeological and Historical Society Transactions*, 69 (1984–5), 49. M. Coate, 'Exeter in the Civil War and Interregnum', *Devon and Cornwall Notes and Queries*, 18 (1935), 343.

82 Margaret Cavendish, Duchess of Newcastle, *The Life of William Cavendish, Duke of Newcastle* (1886), I, 150. P. Slack, *Poverty and Policy in Tudor and Stuart England* (1988), 72. Ian S. Beckwirth, *Gainsborough during the Great Civil War* (Gainsborough, 1969), 23.

83 J. R. Powell and E. K. Timmings, *Documents relating to the Civil War, 1642–48* (Naval Records Society, 1963), 155.

84 S. Porter, 'Property Damage in the English Civil War', London Ph.D. (1984), 85 and 237. R. and T. Kelly, *A City at War: Oxford, 1642–46* (Cheltenham, 1987), 46. C. V. Wedgwood, 'The Common Man in the Civil War', *Truth and Opinion* (1960), 229. J. Washbourne, *Bibliotheca Glousterensis* (Gloucester, 1823–5), 465. R. H. Morris, *The Siege of Chester, 1643–46* (Chester, 1923), 200–5.

85 'John Taylor's Wanderings to see the Wonders of the West (1849)', in John Taylor, *Works* (Manchester, 1870–8), I, 1.

86 Porter, *op. cit.*, 189–218.

87 R. Coe, *Exact Diarie* (1644, C4881), 3. J. Sprigge, *Anglia Rediviva* (1854), 133.

88 Malbon, *op. cit.*, 253–4.

89 I. Roy, 'The English Civil War and English Society', *War and Society*, I, (1975), 32.

90 G. N. Godwin, *The Civil War in Hampshire* (1904), 315.

91 Rushworth, *Collections* V, 739.

92 J. Rushworth, *Letter sent to . . . William Lenthal . . . Concerning Sir Thomas Fairfax's Gallant Proceedings in Cornwall* (1646, R275), 4–5. D. Underdown, *Somerset in the Civil War and Interregnum* (Newton Abbot, 173), 106.

93 R. Symonds, *Diary* (Camden Society, 1859), 30. W. Maurice, 'An Account of the Civil War in North Wales', *Archaeologia Cambrensis*, I (1846), 39.

94 C. V. Wedgwood, *The King's War* (1971), 454, 497.

95 H. Symmons, 'A By-Path of the Civil War', *Somersetshire Archaeological and Natural History Society Proceedings*, LXV (1919), 48–75. Underdown, *op. cit.*, 90–1.

96 C. MacKay, *The Cavalier Songs and Ballads or England from 1642 to 1684* (1863), 9.

97 HMC, *Ninth Report*, appendix II, 387.

98 D. Underdown, *Revel, Riot and Rebellion* (New York, 1985), 218. L. Hutchinson, *Memoirs* (1906), I, 221. E. Broxap, *The Great Civil War in Lancashire* (Manchester, 1910), 60.

12 I DON'T WANT TO GO TO WAR

1 A. Fraser, *The Weaker Vessel* (1985), 256.
2 J. S. Gillingham, *Cromwell: Portrait of a Soldier* (1976), 21.
3 1/6/43, Poyntz to Ormonde, T. Carte, *Original Letters . . . Found Among the Duke of Ormonde's Papers* (1739), I, 21.
4 Alan Everitt, *Change in the Provinces* (Leicester, 1969), 10. K. J. Lindley, 'The Part Played by Catholics in the English Civil War', Manchester Ph.D. (1968), iv–v, and 'The Part Played by Catholics', in B. Manning (ed.), *Politics, Religion and the Civil War* (1973), 126–70. For a different view see D. F. Mosler, 'Warwickshire Catholics in the Civil War', *Recusant History*, XV (1973), 126–73, and P. R. Newman, 'Catholic Royalist Activists in the North, 1642–46', *Recusant History*, XIV (1977), 26–38, and 'Roman Catholic Royalists: Papist Command under Charles I and Charles II, 1642–60', *Recusant History*, XVI (1981), 396–405.
5 Anne Hughes, *Politics, Society and Civil War in Warwickshire, 1620–1660* (Cambridge, 1987), 161. R. N. Dore, *The Civil War in Cheshire* (Chester, 1966), 16. B. G. Blackwood, *The Lancashire Gentry and the Great Rebellion, 1640–1660* (Manchester, 1978), 47. P. McGrath, *Bristol and the Civil War* (Bristol, 1981), 46. C. Durston, *The Family and the English Revolution* (Oxford, 1988), 45–6.
6 B.Manning, 'Neutrals and Neutralism in the English Civil War', Oxford D.Phil. (1957), 397.
7 J. Morrill, *The Revolt of the Provinces* (1976), 74.
8 L. Stone, *The Causes of the English Revolution, 1529-1642* (New York, 1972), 54. D. Underdown, *Somerset in the Civil War and Interregnum* (Newton Abbot, 1973), 117–18. A. J. Fletcher, *A County Community in Peace and War: Sussex, 1600–1660* (1975), 271.
9 J. L. Sanford, *Studies and Illustrations of the Great Rebellion* (1858), 590.
10 L. Hutchinson, *Memoirs of the Life of Colonel John Hutchinson* (1906), I, 217.
11 J. Birch, *Military Memoirs* (Camden Society, 1873), 217–18.
12 J. Buchan, *Oliver Cromwell* (1941), 78–9.
13 William Davenport, 'Civil War Diary, 1643–45', in J. P. Earwacker, *East Cheshire* (1977), I, 430. Hugh Thomas, *A History of Wales, 1485–1660* (Cardiff, 1972), 204. 22/2/43, Langley to Sir Francis Otterly and Henry Bromley, HMC, *Fourth Report*, 218, 265. 16/7/43, Thomas Knyvett to Katherine Knyvett, B. Schofield (ed.), *The Knyvett Letters, 1620–44* (1949), 18.
14 Morrill, *op. cit.*, 76.
15 J. Rous, *The Diary of John Rous*, ed. M. A. E. Green (Camden Society, 1856), 124.
16 D. Gardiner, *The Oxinden and Peyton Letters, 1642–1670* (1937), 41.
17 *Ibid.*, 311–12.
18 8/42, Charles to Traquair, HMC, *Ninth Report*, appendix II, 243. See a similar letter from the king to Argyle of 9/5/42 in HMC, *Argyle*, 612.
19 Gardiner, *Civil War* I, 38–9.
20 M. Bennett, 'The Royalist War Effort in the North Midlands, 1642–46', Loughborough Ph.D. (1986), 216.

21 *Sir William Waller's Warrant Against Neutrality*, in Birch, *op.cit.*, 217.
22 Fletcher, *op. cit.*, 270, 287.
23 Morrill, *op. cit.*, 89–90.
24 P. L. Ralph, *Sir Humphrey Mildmay: Royalist Gentleman* (New Brunswick, 1947), 181. For another example of the economic plight of refugees, see 24/1/42, Nicholas Willoughby to his brother John, W. C. Trevelyan, *Trevelyan Papers* (Camden Society, 1872), 215.
25 D. Underdown, *Riot, Revel and Rebellion: Popular Politics and Culture in England, 1603–1660* (New York, 1985), 153. Edward Cheney, *The Grand Tour and the Great Rebellion* (Geneva, 1988), 60. J. Evelyn, *Diary* (1955), II, 82.
26 C. Holmes, *Seventeenth Century Lincolnshire* (1983), 149.
27 H. Johnstone, 'Two Governors of Shrewsbury during the Civil War and Interregnum', *English Historical Review* XXVI (1918), 267.
28 I. Roy, 'The English Civil War and English Society', in Brian Bond and Ian Roy (eds), *War and Society* (1975), 29.
29 Morrill, *op. cit.*, 37.A. Woolrych, 'Yorkshire's Treaty of Neutrality', *History Today*, VI (October 1956), 696–706.
30 Underdown, *Revel, Riot and Rebellion*, 154.
31 For instance troops on both sides made the unofficial Christmas truce in the opening year of the First World War. Tony Ashworth, *Trench Warfare, 1914–18: The Live and Let Live System* (1980).
32 Warburton, *Cavaliers*, III, 160.
33 H. E. Cary, *Memorials of the Great Civil War in England, 1646-52* (1842), I, 64.
34 A. H. Burne and P. Young, *The Great Civil War* (1959), 223.
35 H. Townsend, *Diary* (1915–20), II, 267.
36 J. Sprigge, *Anglia Rediviva* (1854), 80.
37 C. M. Thomas, 'The Civil War in Glamorgan', in G. Williams (ed.), *Glamorgan County History* (Cardiff, 1974), IV, 269.
38 Quote from petition adopted by some thousand clubmen at Woodbury Hill, Worcester, 5 March 1645, in *The Diary of Henry Townsend*, ed. J. W. Bund (1915–20), II, 221–2. B. Manning, 'Neutrals and Neutralism in the English Civil War', Oxford D.Phil. (1957) and J. T. Zeller, 'Anti-War Sentiment during the English Civil War', Minnesota Ph.D. (1974) stress the importance of economics as opposed to violence in motivating the clubmen. See also Oliver Warner, 'The Clubmen and the English Civil War', *Army Quarterly*, XXXVIII (1936), 287–91, Morrill, *op. cit.*, 98–9, 109–10, 196–8, Roy, *op. cit.*, 26, R. Hutton, *The Royalist War Effort* (1983), 162, and Fletcher, *op. cit.*, 272.
39 4/8/45, Cromwell to Fairfax, W. C. Abbott, *The Writings and Speeches of Oliver Cromwell* (New York, 1937), I, 369.
40 J. Eales, *Puritans and Roundheads: The Harleys of Brampton Brayn and the Outbreak of the English Civil War* (Cambridge, 1990), 173. E. Foord, *Wine and Women* (1646, F1462), 27.
41 A. Fanshawe, *Memoirs* (1905), 56.
42 Lady Filmer to Anthony Weldon, E.Melling, *Kent and the Civil War* (Maidstone, 1960), 20. *The Diaries of Lady Anne Clifford*, ed. D. J. H. Clifford (Stroud, 1990), 139. Fraser, *op. cit.*, 208.
43 J. Jeffries, 'Diary of Joyce Jeffries', *Woolhope Naturalists' Field Club Transactions* (1921–3), lv.
44 E. Hyde, *The Life of Edward, Earl of Clarendon* (Oxford, 1857), 358–9.

G. Grey, *The Warriors* (New York, 1970), 62ff. R. Holmes, *Acts of War* (New York, 1985), 93–108.
45 G. R. Quaife, *Wanton Wenches and Waywood Wives* (New Brunswick, 1979), 49–50.
46 *Ibid.*, 50.
47 A. Thornton, *Autobiography of Mrs. Alice Thornton of East Newton, Co. York*, (Surtees Society, 1875), 44–7.
48 Hutchinson, *op. cit.*, (1968), 101.
49 F. P. and M. M. Verney, *Memoirs of the Verney Family during the Civil War and Commonwealth* (1892–9), II, 200.
50 21/5/45, Luke to Lt.-Col. Richard Cokayn, S. Luke, *The Letter Books, 1644–45, of Sir Samuel Luke* (Bedford, 1963), 285.
51 Richard Gough, *The History of Myddle* (Harmondsworth, 1981), 73–4.
52 Quaife, *op. cit.*, 133.
53 T. W. Barlow, *Cheshire: Its History and Literary Associations* (Manchester, 1855), 165.
54 R. Josselin, *Diary* (Oxford, 1976), 51.
55 M. Coate, *Cornwall in the Great Civil War* (Oxford, 1933), 235. HMC, *Sixteenth Report*, appendix iv, 97.
56 25/5/44, Elizabeth Deny to Earl of Denby, HMC, *Fourth Report*, appendix, 261. E. W. Harcourt, *The Harcourt Papers* (Oxford, 1880–1905), I, 147.
57 A. Collins (ed.), *Letters and Memorials of State . . . from the originals at Penshurst* (1746), II, 669. J. Webb, *Memorials of the Civil War . . . as it affected Herefordshire* (1878), I, 313.
58 Harcourt, *op. cit.*, II, 148, 170.
59 HMC, *Fourteenth Report*, IV, 62.
60 HMC, *Fourth Report*, appendix, 261.
61 Verney, *op. cit.*, I, 380.
62 R. Atkyns, *Vindications* (1968), 30.
63 Fanshawe, *op. cit.*, 110–12. Hutchinson, *op. cit.*, I, 174.
64 H. Dixon (ed.), 'An Original Account of the Springett Family', *Gentleman's Magazine*, XXXVI, (1851), 369–71.
65 *Ibid.*, 113.
66 R. and T. Kelly, *A City at War: Oxford, 1642–46* (Cheltenham, 1987), 39.
67 3/7/44, Francis Basset to wife, R. Polwhele, *Traditions and Recollections* (1826), I, 17.
68 R. Bennett, 'An Original Diary of Colonel Robert Bennett of Hexworthy, 1642–1643', ed. Mary Coate, *Devon and Cornwall Notes and Queries*, XVIII (1935), 253.
69 Sir Hugh Cholmley, *Memoirs* (1870), 71. Thornton, *op. cit.*, 48–50.
70 Verney, *op. cit.*, 124.
71 H. W. Gillman, 'The Siege of Rathbury Catle', *Journal of the Cork Historical Society*, I (1895), 19.
72 3/2/45 and 23/3/45, Luke, *op. cit.*, 126, 203.
73 Webb, *op. cit.*, I, 317.
74 B. Whitelocke, *Diary* (1990), 139.
75 Folger MSS, L.6. 701.
76 Durston, *op. cit.*, 140.
77 Verney, *op. cit.*, II, 136.
78 Folger MSS, Vb, 265, 38.
79 G. Nugent, *Some Memorials of John Hampden* (1832), II, 423.
80 Durston, *op. cit.*, 50ff.

81 R. N. Dore, *The Great Civil War in Cheshire* (1966), 17.
82 E. Ludlow, *Memoirs* (Oxford, 1894), I, 75. HMC, *Fourth Report* (1874), 259, 261.
83 Durston, *op. cit.*, 45–6.
84 C. Carlton, *The Court of Orphans* (Leicester, 1974), and 'The Widow's Tale: Male Myths and Female Reality in Sixteenth and Seventeenth Century England', *Albion*, X, 2 (Summer 1978), 95–103.
85 Verney, *op. cit.*, I, 297.
86 Fanshawe, *op. cit.*, 105.
87 K. Thomas, *Religion and the Decline of Magic* (1973), 308.
88 J. T. Gilbert, *A Contemporary History of Affairs in Ireland from 1641 to 1652* (Dublin, 1879–1880), lxi.
89 Verney, *op. cit.*, I, 60–78.
90 *The Widowes' Lamentation for the Absence of the Dear Children and Suitors and for Divers of their Deaths in these Fatal Civil Wars* (1643, W2093), 3–4.
91 *The Virgins' Complaint for the Loss of their Sweethearts* (1643, V640), 1–4.
92 *Hey-Hoe for a Husband, or the Parliament of Maids* (1647, H1659), n.pa.
93 *The Humble Petition of the Many Thousands Wives and Matrons of the City of London and Other Parts of this Kingdom* (1643, H3475), 7.
94 I am grateful to my daughters for pointing this out to me on more than one occasion.
95 Gardiner, *Commonwealth*, I, 44.
96 Gardiner, *Civil War*, III, 207.
97 G. N. Godwin, *The Civil War in Hampshire* (1908), 309.
98 R. Holmes, *The Siege of Pontefract Castle* (Pontefract, 1887), 53. H. A. L. Howell, 'The Army Surgeon and the Care of the Sick and Wounded in the Tudor and Stuart Period', *Journal of the Royal Army Medical Corps*, II (1904), 606–15, 737–45.
99 J. A. Atkinson, *Tracts Relating to the Civil War in Cheshire* (Chetham Society, 1909), 120.
100 Fraser, *op. cit.*, 221.
101 W. C. Abbott, *Writings and Speeches of Oliver Cromwell* (New York, 1937), I, 333.
102 Fraser, *op. cit.*, 220–1.
103 J. Thompson, *The Other Army, Camp Followers of the English Civil War* (Leigh-on-Sea, n.d.), 6. 19/7/45, Inchiquin to Lords, Charles McNeil (ed.), *The Tanner Letters: Documents on Irish Affairs in the Sixteenth and Seventeenth Centuries Extracted from the Tanner Collection* (Dublin, 1943), 191.
104 Durston, *op. cit.*, 90ff.

13 THEN WE STARTED ALL OVER AGAIN

1 Rushworth, *Collections* VI, 140.
2 Gardiner, *Commonwealth*, I, 60.
3 R. K. G. Temple, 'Discovery of a Manuscript Account of the Battle of Maidstone', *Archaeologia Cantiana*, 97 (1981), 211. G. Wither, *Vox Pacifica*, quoted by J. T. Zeller, 'Neutrals and Neutralism in the English Civil War', Minnesota Ph.D (1974), 47.
4 John Canne, *Emanuel or God With us* (1650, C439), 17.
5 27/7/91, Cromwell to Thomas Knyvett, W. C. Abbot, *The Writings and Speeches of Oliver Cromwell* (New York, 1937), I, 408.
6 H. F. Abell, *Kent and the Great Civil War* (1901), 73.

7 R. Baillie, *The Letters and Papers of Robert Baillie* (1841–2), II, 57. R. Scrope and T. Monkhouse (eds), *State Papers Collected by Edward, Earl of Clarendon* (Oxford, 1767–86), II, 382.
8 *Sad News out of Kent* (1648, S259), 5.
9 Gardiner, *Civil War*, IV, 122.
10 *A True Narrative of the Late Skirmish between the Soldiers of Colonel Barkstead's Regiment and the Petitioners* (1648, T2794).
11 H. Rollins, *Cavaliers and Puritans* (New York, 1923), 28.
12 Sir John Berkeley, 'Memoirs,' in John Ashburnham, *A Narrative . . . Of his Attendance on King Charles* (1830), cliv.
13 11/2/48, Knyvett to John Hobart, Bodleian: Tanner MSS, 58, 695.
14 In this regard one is reminded of western explanations for the suicidal bravery of Japanese, Chinese or Vietnamese troops – that life does not mean so much to them. 'Diary of the Siege of Colchester', in HMC, *Twelfth Report*, appendix, pt 9, 26.
15 *Poetical Works of John Milton*, ed. H. Darbishire (Oxford, 1955), 153.
16 R. J. Lifton, *Home from the War: Vietnam Veterans* (New York, 1973), 108–10, uses the work of Freud and Wilfred Owen's poetry to make these points.
17 C. Hill, *The Experience of Defeat* (1984), 115. W. Haller, *Liberty and Reformation in the Puritan Revolution* (New York, 1955), 209. Hugh Peters, *Mr. Peters' Last Report on the English Wars* (1646, P1707).
18 J. A. Atkinson, *Tracts Relating . . . to the Civil War in Cheshire, 1641-59* (Chetham Society, 1909), 109. Abbot, *op. cit.*, I, 360. P. Young, *Naseby* (1985), 339.
19 Quoted by Hill, *op. cit.*, 86.
20 E. Reynolds, *Orders from the Lord of Hosts* (1646, R1222), 8-9.
21 Thomas Edwards, *Gangraena* (1646, G228), I, 111.
22 Lifton, *op. cit.*, 126–30, describes this process with Vietnam veterans, while Christopher Hill, in *A Tinker and a Poor Man: John Bunyan and his Church* (New York, 1989), discusses it with regard to a soldier who almost certainly never saw action. O. G. Body, 'The New Model Army under Sir Thomas Fairfax', *Journal of the Royal Artillery*, 65 (1938), 215. *The Watchman's Warning Piece, Or, Parliament Soldiers Prediction* (1646, W1041), n.pa.
23 P. R. Newman, *Companion to the English Civil Wars* (New York, 1990), xv.
24 Quoted by A. Woolwych, *Soldiers and Statesmen: The General Council of the Army and its Debates, 1647–1648* 1987, 77.
25 *Ibid.*, 3. J. Morrill and J. D. Walter, 'Order and Disorder in the English Revolution', in A. Fletcher and J. Stevenson, *Order and Disorder in Early Modern England* (Cambridge, 1985), 143.
26 Of nine mutinies in the covenanting armies, five were over pay, one about replacing an unpopular CO, one unknown, and only one combat-related. Analysis based on E. M. Furgol, *Regimental History of the Covenanting Armies, 1639–1651* (1988).
27 R. Holmes, *Acts of War* (New York, 1985), 330. J. Morrill, 'Mutiny and Discontent in English Provincial Armies, 1645–47', *Past and Present*, 56 (1972), 49–74. Gardiner, *Civil War*, III, 263.
28 H. Shaw, *The Levellers* (1968), 26, 49–53. Ian Roy, 'Arrears of Pay and Ideology in the Army Revolt of 1647', in Brian Bond and Ian Roy (eds), *War and Society* (1975), 61. I. Gentles, 'The Arrears of Pay in the Parliamentary Army at the End of the First Civil War', *BIHR*, 18 (1975), 59.
29 *Mercurius Melancholius* (30 October 1647). CUL: Syn 7.64 123 and 5.
30 M. Kishlansky, 'The Army and the Levellers: The Road to Putney', *Historical*

Journal, 23 (1979), 795–824. R. Ashton, 'The Problems of Indemnity, 1647–1648', in C. Jones *et al.* (eds), *Politics and Religion in Revolutionary England* (Oxford, 1986), 117–40.

31 10/6/46, Charles to Henrietta Maria, J. Bruce, *Charles I in 1646* (Camden Society, 1856), 45.

32 *A Full Narrative of the Late Riotous Tumult with the City of London* (1648, F2349), 1–2. A. E. Everitt, *Suffolk and the Great Rebellion*, 1640–1660 (Ipswich, 1960), 99.

33 *A Full Relation of the Whole Proceedings of the Late Rising and Commotion in Wales* (1647, F2374), 11.

34 8/5/48, Horton to Fairfax, *A Declaration of Major Gen: Lawton and His Forces* (1648), n.pa. *A Fuller Relation of the Great Victory Obtained Against the Welsh Forces* (1648, F2490), 1.

35 *Newes From Kent* (1648, N977), 4–6.

36 Abell, *op. cit.*, 217–19.

37 R. J. Millward, 'The Battle of Surbiton', *History Today*, 20 (October 1970), 716–24.

38 *Perfect Occurences*, 14 March 1649. *A Narrative of Letters* (1648), 4. N. F. Tucker, *North Wales in the Civil War* (Denbigh, 1955), 155.

39 *DNB*. A. Kingston, *East Anglia in the Great Civil War* (1897), 264. R. W. Ketton-Cremer, *Norfolk in the Civil War* (1970), 325.

40 Descriptions of the Siege of Colchester from *A Diary or Account of the Siege . . . of Colchester*, in Daniel Defoe, *A Tour . . . of Great Britain* (1927), 18–31; 'Diary of the Siege of Colchester,' in HMC, *Twelfth Report*, appendix pt 9, 24–9; *Diary of the Siege of Colchester by the Forces under the Command of General Fairfax* (1650, D1378.2); Matthew Carter, *A Most True and Exact Relation of the . . . Unfortunate Expedition of Kent, Essex, and Colchester* (1650, C662), 136–7, 166; D. C. Woodward and C. Cockerill, *The Siege of Colchester, 1648: A History and a Bibliography* (Chelmsford, 1979), 7–21; *The Siege of Colchester, 1648* (Colchester, n.d.), 9–18.

41 D. C. Woodward and C. Cockerill, *The Siege of Colchester* (Chelmsford, 1979), 6. 12/6/48, R. Josselin, *Diary* (Oxford, 1974), 128.

42 B. P. Lyndon, 'Parliament's Army in Essex, 1648', *JSAHR*, LIX, (1981), 152.

43 *The Earl of Norwich, Lord Capel, and Sir Charles Lucas, their Peremptory Answer on Refusing to Surrender Colchester* (1648), 7.

44 *An Exact Narrative of Every Dayes Proceeding since the Insurrection of Essex* (1648, E3663), 7.

45 T. S., *A True and Exact Relation of the Taking of Colchester Sent in a Letter from an Officer in the Army who was Present during the Siege* (1648, S186), 1–2.

46 J. Rushworth, *A Letter . . . before Colchester* (1648, R2321), 6. *Another Fight at Colchester and the Storming of the Town by the Parliamentary Forces* (1648, A3260), 2–3.

47 16/8/48 and 24/8/48, Ralph Josselin, *Diary* (1976), 1301.

48 *From the Leaguer at Colchester More Certain News* (1648, F2242), 5. C. L. Markham, *The Life of the Great Lord Fairfax* (1870), 325.

49 29/8/48, Osborne to wife, Henry Ellis, *Original Letters Illustrative of English History*, 3rd series, IV (1846), 272. Stephen Porter, 'Property Damage in the English Civil War', London Ph.D. (1984), 109.

50 *Mercurius Fidelicus* (17 August 1648), quoted by Elizabeth Brockbank, *Richard Hubberthorne of Yealand: Gentleman, Soldier and Quaker, 1628–1662* (1929), 44.

51 Samuel Birch, 'Civil War Diary', HMC, *Portland MSS*, III, (1894), 173–80.
52 J. Hodgson, *Memoirs* (Bradford, 1902), 120.
53 Sir James Turner, *Memoirs of his Life and Times* (Edinburgh, 1829), 66–70.
54 20/8/48, Cromwell to Lenthall, Abbott, *op. cit.*, I, 633-8.
55 Turner, *op. cit.*, 82.
56 Abbot, *op. cit.*, I, 609.
57 *The Piteous Moans, Pious Wishes and Constant Resolutions of the Prisoners taken at Colchester* (1648, P2297), 7.
58 G. K. Fortescue, *Catalogue of the Pamphlets ... Collected by George Thomason* (1908), I, 168. 20/9/48, Edmund Verney to Ralph Verney, F. P. and M. M. Verney, *Memoirs of the Verney Family during the Civil War and Commonwealth* (1892–9), II, 340.
59 Gardiner, *Civil War*, IV, 120. P. Crawford, 'Charles Stuart, that Man of Blood', *Journal of British Studies* XVI, 2 (Spring 1977), 54.
60 S. R. Gardiner, *Constitutional Documents of the Puritan Revolution* (1968), 373–5.
61 Gardiner, *Commonwealth*, I, 1.
62 R. Holmes, *The Siege of Pontefract Castle, 1644–48* (Pontefract, 1887), 210.
63 *A Perfect Narrative of the Battle of Knocknones by an Officer in the Parliament's Army Present and Acting at the Fight* (1648, P1501). John T. Gilbert, *A Contemporary History of Affairs in Ireland from 1641 to 1652* (Dublin, 1879–80), xxxiv. *A letter from Lord Broghill ... Concerning ... Defeating the Rebels in Ireland* (1651, O486), 5.
64 I. Roots, *The Speeches of Oliver Cromwell* (1989), 5. Abbot, *op. cit.*, II, 107, 326-7. A. Fraser, *Cromwell* (1973), 5.
65 Abbot, *op. cit.*, II, 120–5, J. G. Simms, 'Cromwell at Drogheda', *The Irish Sword*, XI, (1973–4), 217–20. Fraser, *op. cit.*, 332–4.
66 Scrope and Monkhouse (eds), *op. cit.*, II, 22.
67 Gardiner, *Commonwealth*, I, 13. Abbot, *op. cit.*, II, 139. Fraser, *op. cit.*, 344–6.
68 Abbot, *op. cit.*, II, 164.
69 25/11/91, Cromwell to Lenthall, Abbot, *op. cit.*, II, 173.
70 Abbot, *op. cit.*, II, 172, 214, 222, 223, 234.
71 J. Hewitt (ed.), *Eye-Witness Accounts to Ireland in Revolt* (Reading, 1974), 28. E. I. Hogan (ed.), *The History of the War in Ireland from 1641 to 1653 by a British Officer in Sir James Clotworthy's Regiment* (Dublin, 1873), 107.
72 'The Men behind the Wire', in C. Carlton, *Bigotry and Blood: Documents on the Ulster Troubles* (Chicago, 1976), 111.
73 J. R. N. McPhail, 'Documents relating to the Massacre at Dunaverty', *Highland Papers, Scottish Historical Society, 1916*, II, 248–50. D. Stevenson, *Alisdair Macolla* (1980), 236–7. Turner, *op. cit.*, 48.
74 *A Large Relation of the Fight at Leith*, ed. Sir W. Scott (1806), 207–8.
75 Hodgson, *op. cit.*, 143. Gardiner, *Commonwealth*, I, 292.
76 Gardiner, *Commonwealth*, I, 284.
77 3/9/50, Rushworth to Speaker Lenthal, *Parliamentary History of England* (1752–61), XIV, 341–2. *A True Relation of the Routing of the Scots near Dunbar* (1950, T3040), 4–5. C. H. Firth, 'The Battle of Dunbar', *TRHS*, 2nd series, XIV (1900), 19–52.
78 Sir Arthur Haselrigg, *A Letter from Sir Arthur Hesilrige to the ... Council of State* (1650, H1122), 1–3. *CSPD, 1649–50*, 105, 334, 397, 402, 419. Abbott, *op. cit.*, 321.
79 C. E. Bank, 'Scottish Prisoners Deported to New England', *Massachusetts Historical Society Publication*, 41 (1927–8), 13. I. C. C. Graham, *Colonists from*

Scotland, Emigrants to North America, 1710–1783 (Ithaca, 1956), 10. M. Tepper, *Passengers to America* (Baltimore, 1977), 146–9.

80 P. L. Ralph, *Sir Humphrey Mildmay* (1947), 195.

81 B. Whitelocke, *Memoirs* (1860), 507.

82 R. Baxter, *Reliquiae* (1696, B1371), 69. Clarendon, *History*, 78.

83 *An Exact and Perfect Relation of Every Particular of the Fight at Worcester* (1651, E3603), 1–2. 3/9/51, Stapleton to Lenthall, J. W. Bund, *The Civil War in Worcestershire* (1905), 249. 8/9/51, Cromwell to Lenthall, Abbott, *op. cit.*, II, 467.

84 D. Underdown, *Royalist Conspiracy in England, 1649–1660* (New Haven, 1960), 52.

85 Gardiner, *Commonwealth*, I, 11. Henry Newcombe, *Autobiography* (1852), 33.

86 Turner, *op. cit.*, 96.

87 C. Bridenbaugh, *No Peace Beyond the Lines: The English in the Caribbean, 1624–1690* (New York, 1973), 110–11. V. T. Harlow, *A History of the Barbados, 1625–85* (Oxford, 1926), 302. H. Beckles, *White Servitude and Black Slavery in Barbados, 1627–1715* (Knoxville, 1989), 53.

88 A. C. Dow, *Cromwellian Scotland* (Edinburgh, 1979), 20. HMC, *Twelfth Report*, appendix pt 7, 35.

89 The idea that 1688/9 was a fourth civil war has been raised in J. G. A. Pocock, 'The Fourth Civil War: Dissolution, Desertion and Alternative Histories of the Glorious Revolution', *Government and Opposition*, XXIII (Spring 1988), 151–66. I am grateful to Dr Pocock for giving me a copy of his article. In *Three British Revolutions* (Princeton, 1980), I raised the idea that the revolutions of 1640, 1688 and 1776 were a continuum.

90 Gardiner, *Commonwealth*, II, 46.

14 DOES IT MATTER

1 William Blundell, *Cavalier: Letters of William Blundell to his Friends* (1933), 10 and 39. *Crosby Record: A Cavalier's Note Book* (1880), 93.

2 C. H. Firth, *Narrative of General Venables* (Camden Society, 1900), 1.

3 P. Slack, *The Impact of Plague in Tudor and Stuart England* (1985), 151 and 180ff. E. A. Wrigley and Roger Schofield, *The Population History of England* (1981). I am grateful to Dr Schofield for his advice in this matter.

4 D. F. Mosler, 'A Social and Religious History of the English Civil War in the County of Warwick', Stanford Ph.D. (1975), 223.

5 Adam Martindale, *The Life of Adam Martindale as written by himself* (Chetham Society, 1845), 35. Edward Robinson made the same complaint about Colonel Tildsley, E. Robinson, *A Discourse of the Warr in Lancashire*, ed. W. Beaumont (Manchester, 1864), 20.

6 D. A. Johnson and D. G. Vaisey, *Staffordshire in the Great Rebellion* (Stafford, 1964), 30.

7 D. Fleming, 'Faction and Civil War in Lancashire', *Transactions of the Lancashire Archaeological and Historical Society* (1981–2), 32.

8 29/8/48, William Osborne to wife, Henry Ellis, *Original Letters Illustrative of English History* (1846), IV, 272.

9 C. Durston, *The Family and the English Revolution* (Oxford, 1988), 53–5.

10 P. Young, *Naseby, 1645: The Campaign and the Battle* (1985), 1657, and *Edgehill, 1642: The Campaign and the Battle* (Kineton, 1967), 229.

11 Ian S. Beckwirth, *Gainsborough during the Great Civil War* (Gainsborough, 1969), 23. G. E. Aylmer, *Rebellion or Revolution?* (1985), 71.

12 L. P. Wenham, *The Great and Close Siege of York* (Kineton, 1970), 36.

13 John Lowe, 'The Campaigns of the Irish Royalists Army in Cheshire, November 1643 to January 1644', *Transactions of the Lancashire and Cheshire Historical Society*, CXI (1959), 72. J. R. Chanter, *Literary History of Barnstaple* (Barnstaple, 1866), 120. *Weekly Accompt*, quoted by J. Webb, *Memorials of the Civil War . . . Herefordshire* (1897), II, 3. *A Fuller Relation of Sir Thomas Fairfax's Routing of all the King's Army's in the West* (1645, F2491), 9. K. M. Lynch, *Roger Boyle, First Earl of Orrery* (Knoxville, 1965), 221.

14 D. Underdown, *Somerset in the Civil War and Interregnum* (Newton Abbot, 1973), 191.

15 J. C. Hodgson, *North Country Diaries* (Durham, 1910–15), II, 53. Robinson, *op. cit.*, xxi. Chanter, *op. cit.*, 25.

16 P. W. Thomas, 'The Impact on Literature', in J. Morrill (ed.), *The Impact of the English Civil War* (1991), 129–37, lists nineteen poets active during the civil war years.

17 J. L. Milne, *The Age of Inigo Jones* (1953), 51 and 96. T. O. Calhoun, L. Heyworth and A. Pritchard (eds), *The Collected Works of Abraham Cowley* (Newark, NJ, 1989), I, 363–7. William Lithgow, 'Experimental and Exact Relation upon that famous and renowned Siege of Newcastle', *Somers Tracts*, ed. Sir W. Scott (1809–15), 279.

18 T. Fuller, *Good Thoughts for Bad Times* (1659, F2432), 3. William Addison, *Worthy Doctor Fuller* (1965), 124, 284. C. J. Stranks, *The Life and Writings of Jeremy Taylor* (1952), 65.

19 Sir Balthazar Gerbier, *The First Public Lecture Read at Sir Balthazar Gerbier his Academy Concerning Military Architecture and Fortifications* (1649, G561).

20 D. A. Johnson and D. G. Vaisey, *Staffordshire in the Great Rebellion* (Stafford, 1964), 54.

21 Firth, *op. cit.*, 301. J. Rosworme, *Good Service Hitherto Ill Rewarded* (1649, R1996).

22 9/11/63, S. Pepys, *Diary*, ed. R. C. Latham and W. Matthews (Berkeley, 1970–83), IV, 373–4.

23 H. M. Reece, 'The Military Presence in England, 1649–1660', Oxford ·D.Phil. (1981), 50–2, 286. J. Brewer, *Sinews of Power: War Money and the English State, 1688–1783* (New York, 1989), 11. G. Parker, *The Military Revolution* (Cambridge, 1988), 62 and 81.

24 J. Mather, 'The Moral Code of the English Civil War and Interregnum', *Historian*, 44 (1982), 223. J. A. Shape, *Crime in Seventeenth Century England: A County Study* (Cambridge, 1983), 106, 206–9. W. A. Speck, *Reluctant Revolutionaries: Englishmen and the Revolution of 1688* (1988), 197. C. V. Wedgwood, 'Captain Hinde, the Highwayman', *Truth and Opinion* (1961), 249–51.

25 W. D. Christie, *Life of The First Earl of Shaftesbury* (1871), I, 62.

26 J. Hodgson, *Memoirs of Captain John Hodgson* (Bradford, 1902), 169.

27 It now hangs in Trinity College Library, Cambridge. A. Kingston, *East Anglia in the Great Civil War* (1897), 367.

28 A. Brome, *Poems* (Toronto, 1982), I, 111.

29 20/5/60, R. Oxinden to Henry Oxinden, D. Gardiner, *The Oxinden Letters, 16-7-42* (1933), 233.

30 Young, *op. cit.*, 22–1.

31 William Mercer, *The Moderate Cavalier* (1675, M1739), 1 and 12. Underdown, *op. cit.*, 189.

32 F. P. and M. M. Verney, *Memoirs of the Verney Family during the Civil War*

and Commonwealth (1892–9), II, 205. Blundell, *op. cit.*, 28. R. and T. Kelly, *A City at War: Oxford, 1642–46* (Cheltenham, 1987), 45.

33 B. Whitelocke, *Diary* (1990), 132.

34 *Two State Martyrs* (1643), 14.

35 William Dugdale, *The Holy Reformation* (1649), quoted by A. Hughes, *Politics, Society and Civil War in Warwickshire, 1620–1660* (Cambridge, 1987), 300.

36 L. G. Schwoerer, '*No Standing Armies!*': *The Anti-army Ideology in Seventeenth Century England* (Baltimore, 1974). P. Young and W. Emberton, *The Cavalier Army: Its Organization and Everyday Life* (1974), 144.

37 Quoted by M. Ashley, *The Greatness of Oliver Cromwell* (1957), 93. E. Robinson, *A Discourse of the Warr in Lancashire*, tries to explain the war in his own county to 'the generations to come'.

38 Philip Lindsay, *For King and Parliament* (London, 1949), 197.

INDEX

Abbotsbury, assault on 172–3
Abercromby, Captain Jeremiah 298
Act of Settlement 213
Act of Union (1707) 349
Aldersey, Lieutenant 258
Alford, John, disavows son 293
Allen, Richard, a surgeon 199
Alvechurch, vicar of 103
America, Civil War 214, 225;
  Revolution 5; violence in 10
Antrim, Randall MacDonnell, Earl of
  122
Appleby Castle, surrender 326
Apsley, Colonel Edward, captured 240
Apsley, Sir Allen 301
Archer, Elias 95, 96, 109, 200
archers 74
Argyll, Archibald Campbell, Earl of
  122
aristocrats, in war 13
Arklow beach, skirmish at 331
army/ies, chance encounters 106–8;
  changes in 8; composition of 20–2;
  conditions 89, 102; distrust of 348–9;
  dodging the draft 14; incompetence
  14–17; on the march 102–4, 109–12;
  organization 97–8; poorly equipped
  27, 28; quality 22–4; recruitment 29;
  ritual 82–4; standing 8; training
  23–4; volunteers in 19; as weekend
  warriors 22, 24; winter quarters
  89–91, 94, 95, 96; 'you can go and
  play' 310, 317
Arthur, John, death of 202
artillery 139–40, 171, 284, 291; training
  in 75; trains 98; use of 171–3
Arundel, Blanche, bravery 309
Arundel, Thomas Howard, Earl of 28

Arundel (place), property damage
  157–8; Siege of 160, 170, 270
Ascough, Colonel 286, 287
Ashe, Reverend Simeon 47, 48, 49, 57,
  62, 125, 126, 127, 129, 147, 158, 182,
  275
Asherton, Ralph 280
Ashley, Sir Bernard 106
Ashurst, Captain 173
Asiog Castle, garrison butchered in 123
Astley, Sir Jacob 29, 77, 106, 117, 127,
  266, 310
Aston, John 81, 104
Aston, Sir Arthur 69, 255, 330–1
astrologers 125, 306
Atkinson, Colonel 136
Atkyns, Captain Richard 54, 70, 105,
  130, 137, 138, 171, 194–5, 223, 249,
  301, 345
atrocities 34–6, 123, 256–63, 320–2
Aubigny, Lord Georg Stuart, murdered
  208
Aubrey, John 75
Aubrey, Richard 254
Audley, James 238
Auldearn, Battle of 195
Ayle, Captain Edmund 29
Aylesbury, mass grave at 203
Aylmer, G.E. 342

Babylon Hill, skirmish at 116, 347
baggage trains 102–3, 107, 144, 260
Baillie, Robert 171, 233, 312
Baillie, William 122, 233
Baker, Colonel 22
Balfour, Sir William 121
ballads 78, 79, 136, 215, 279, 312, 348
Ballard, Sir Thomas 141, 196

Balle, John 51
Ballylally Castle 165
Bampfield, Ann 32
Bampfield, Joseph 57, 210–11, 248
Banbury, as 'Den of Thieves' 151; siege of castle 159
Bankes, Lady Mary 166, 309
Banqueting Hall, Whitehall 12
Barefoot, Henry 65, 193
Barriffe, William, training manual 69
Barker, Abel 272
Barker, Katherine 275
Barret, Francis 232
Barret, Robert, *The Theorike and Practike of Modern Warres* 63
Barriffe, William 22; *Military discipline* 72–3
Barrington, Thomas 218
Barrow, Maurice 190
Barrow, Thomas, linen draper, as neutral 292
Barry, John 303
Bartlett, Rowland, plundered 267
Basing House 80, 86, 104, 109; sacked 177–9; Siege of 95, 96, 164, 194, 195
Bastwick, John, as prisoner 245–6
Bates, Private 52
Bath, Henry Bourchier, Earl of 65
Bath (place), restored 312
Batten, William 254
battles 113–49; aftermath 143–9; close-order combat 134, 136, 142; command communications 131–2; course of 129–43; as deliberate events 125; loud noises 132; peripheral 119; preliminaries 125–9; visibility in 132–4
Baught, Robert 348
Baven, Robert, thief 199
Baxter, Richard 34, 45, 51, 63, 76, 87, 104, 116, 140, 213, 230, 233, 255; at Worcester 335–6; from neutral to roundhead 292; illness 209, 225
Bayle, Matthew, a 'veriest knave' 67
Baynes, Captain John, as prisoner 246
Baynes, Cornet John 329
Beale, Richard, arrested 240
Beasley, Tobias 263
Beaumont, Francis and John Fletcher, *The Knight of the Burning Pestle* 23
Beckly, Colonel, on parole 248
Bedeham, Sir Wingfield, as prisoner 246

Bee, Captain, plundered 320
Beech, Master Gunner 75
Beech, William, preacher 80
Beeston Castle 169, 193
Beetham House, surrender 324
Behre, Hans 21
Belasyse, Lord John 91, 134, 142, 157; wounded 224
Belgrade, George, surgeon 224
Bell, Robert 337
Bellingham, Captain Henry, wounded 227
Belvoir Castle 163, 172
Benbow, Captain John, executed 336
Benburb, Battle of 99
Benlowes, Edward 118
Bennet, Colonel Robert 77, 94, 95, 97, 185, 302
Bennet, Sir Humphrey 94
Berkeley, Sir John 198
Berkeley, Sir Thomas 170
Berkeley Castle 174, 233
Berkenhead, Sir John, editor of *Mercurius Aulicus* 77, 251
Bernard, Lord 135
Bernard, Richard, *The Bible-Battal or the Sacred Art Military* 62
Berners, Lord 94
Berry, Christopher, death 207
Bertie, Robert, Earl of Lindsay 16
Best, Henry, avoidance of war 293
Binke, Private Thomas 298
Birch, Colonel John 107, 152, 184, 221, 276
Birch, Samuel, company movements 324–7
Birmingham, sacked 175–6
Bishe, John 23
Bishops' Wars 1, 24–30, 43, 50, 51, 69, 104
Bissell, John, Commissary for the sick and wounded 227
Blackford, Captain Daniel 343
Blackhole Heath 141, 144
Blaketon, Sir William 120
Bletchingdon House 168
Blundell, William 339–40, 348
Boate, Arnold 52
Bolle, Captain 76
Bolton, attacked 171–2; sacked 257–8
Bond, Reverend John 42
Bonwick, John, as prisoner 245

Bootle, Captain, killed 257
Borlase, Sir John 33
Bostock, J., as adulterer 299
Both, Captain 173
Bouchier, George, Bristol merchant 170
Bourchier, Elizabeth 300–1, 305
Bowels, William 348
Bowle, Reverend 86
Bowyer, George 348
Boyle, Roger, Earl of Orrery 113, 128, 142, 155, 329–30; *Treatise on the Art of War* 343, 344
Boyne, Philibert de 21
Boynton, Colonel 304
Boys, Master, hanged 256
Braddock Down, Battle of 129, 141, 142, 240
Bradford, Siege of 239
Bradley, Thomas 276
Bramham Moor, training at 8
Brampton Castle 159, 166
Brecon 164
Brent Knoll village, plundered 286
Brentford, Battle of 54–5, 85; sacked 158, 175, 269
Brereton, Sir William 53, 65, 67, 74, 123, 130, 134, 140, 170, 184, 247, 262, 265; comment on plunder 285; house plundered 278
Bretby House, plundered 176
Bridenbaugh, Carl 9
Bridge, Reverend William 47, 48, 49
Bridgeman, Oliver, indecision 318–19
Bridges, Major, drowned 208
Bridgwater, Siege of 165; surrender 159–60
Bristol, capture 119, 233–4; merchants of 163; Siege of 155, 161, 165, 203; surrender 124
Bristol, Earl of, see Digby, Sir George
broadsheets 231, 307–8
Brome, Alexander, defeated 235, 287; 'His Mistress Affrighted in the Wars' 56; poem on plunder 271
Brooke, Robert Greville, Second Baron 20, 54, 60, 83, 110, 160
Broome, Thomas, Warden of Clun Hospital 154
Broughton, Colonel 257
Browne, Christopher 31, 32
Browne, Sir Richard 261, 274
Browne, Thomas 68

Brych, Harry 277
Bryon, Sir John 172
Buckingham, George Villiers, 1st Duke of 15; assassinated 16, 17
Buckingham, George Villiers, 2nd Duke of 342
Bulstrode, Sir Richard 53, 108, 129, 254
Bulstrode, Thomas 254
Bunyan, John 152
Burghall, Edward 200
Burgoyne, Sir Roger 348
Bushell, Thomas, Master of the Oxford mint 81, 193
Butler, Samuel 236
Bynnes, Captain 239
Byron, General (Lord) John 135, 169, 170, 171, 257
Byron, Sir Richard, governor of Newark Castle 108
Byron, Sir Thomas 303

Cadiz, attacked 12, 14–15; English failure at 16, 17
Callan, massacre at 331
Cambridge University, as prison 245, 251
camp fever 209
camp-followers 103, 110, 161, 257
Campion, Sir William 46, 285
Canne, John 311
Canterbury, riot in 312
Capel, Arthur, Lord 50, 93, 192; comment on bed 105–6; executed 329; humiliation 234
Capel, Lady, son molested 323
Capel, Mary (daughter) 192
Cardigan Castle 174, 344
Carew, Thomas 11, 25
Carey, Henry, First Earl of Dover 304
Carey, Sheriff, escape 247
Carisbrook Castle 166
Carleton, Guy, Vicar of Bucklebury 207
Carlisle, Lucy, Countess of 39, 311
Carlisle, James Hay, Third Earl of 27
Carlisle, Siege of 157, 163
Carlyle, Thomas 122
Carnarvon, Robert Dormer, First Earl of 83
Carne, Captain 23
Carnwath, Robert Dalzell, First Earl of 124

Carrick, massacre at 331
Carter, Sergeant-Major Matthew 181
Cartwright, William 61
Case of the Army Truly Stated, The 317
Castle, Major James 90
Castlemain, Roger Palmer, First Earl of 195
casualties *see* deaths
Catesby, Captain, captured 241
catholics, as neutrals 290
cavaliers 53, 117, 206, 235–6, 346; in Oxford 93; as plunderers 278; propensity for drink 59; romantic ethos 58; self-image 79; as 'Shavers' 323
Cavalier's Prayer, The 215
cavalry 97–8, 124, 126, 135–9, 140, 144; at Edgehill 117; formations 135; Irish 331; Scots 325; success and failure 145; training 8, 75
Cave, Thomas, wounded 228
Cavendish, Margaret, *see* Newcastle, Duchess of
Caversham, Battle of 194–5
Cecil, Sir Edward, Viscount Wimbledon 7, 14–15
Chadwick, Thomas 273
Chalfield, garrison at 151–2
Chalmer, Richard, death 202
Chaloner, Allen 153
Chandos, George Brydges, Sixth Baron 65
Charles I 115; at Bristol 119; at Edgehill 147; at Lostwithiel 243, 244; at Naseby 141; at Oxford 92; campaigns 109; capitulation 310, 317; captured 235; on care of the wounded 227–8, 229; commitment to peace 12; counter-coup 37–8; and deserters 197; in disguise 124–5; entry to London 31–2; and Ireland 35; as leader 186–7; letter of consolation 220; as needed 313; on neutrality 292; plans for army 22–3; prisoner of the Scots 237; trial and execution 328–9; war against Scots 24–6, 28
Charles II 261, 287, 305, 346; escape 336; in Scotland 335; treatment of soldiers 347
Charlton, Stephen 40, 231

Chatfield House, Wiltshire, parliamentary garrison at 95
Cheriton, Battle of 83, 125, 128, 129, 130, 134, 261
Chester, Siege of 65, 123, 124, 130, 159
Chesterfield, Lady Catherine 176
Chetwood, Alice, as adulterer 299
Chewton Mendip, Battle of 238
Chichester 241, 280
children 34, 340; survival 301–4
Chiles, Mary 164
Chillingworth, William 48, 59, 158, 246
China 10
Chisenhall, Captain Edward 41, 161, 193
Cholmley, Lady Elizabeth, sends children to Holland 303
Cholmley, Sir Henry 196
Cholmley, Sir Hugh 42, 69, 130, 157, 165, 295
Christmas 312
Chudleigh, Sergeant-Major James, changed sides 197–8; *His Declaration to His Countrymen* 198
churches/cathedrals, desecrated 29–30, 87, 110, 276–8
Cicero 61
Cirencester, stormed and plundered 174, 175
City Dames Petition . . . 307
City of London, records scratched out 346
Civil Wars, aftermath 339–50; books on 2–3; causes/reasons 2, 8, 45–52; choosing sides 44–6, 53–6; confusion 115–16; costly 342; as crusade 61–4, 63; damage 283–4; early warnings 37–40; enjoyment of 66–7; as erotic 296–7; experience 5–6; fears concerning 40–3; first skirmishes 64–5, 116; formal declaration 82–3; four influences 9; how regarded 4–5; ideology 255; leadership 180–200; memories 12–13; records 4, 6; reluctant participation in 290–309; run-up 31–2; second and third 310–38; sporting idioms 145
Clanricarde, Ulick Bourke, Fourth Earl of 36
Clark, Captain William 80
Clark, Richard 161
Clark, Sir George 8

Clarke, Fifth Baronet, as robber 341
Clarkson, David 247
Clausewitz, Karl von 4, 8, 114
Cleland, James, *Propaideia, or the Institution of Young Nobleman* 57
Clifford, Lady Anne, in London 296
Clifton, Cuthbert 244–5
Close, Colonel, death 330
clothes 96–7, 241; uniforms 5, 132, 238
Clotworthy, Sir John 140–1
Clubmen movement 288, 294–5
Coe, Richard 96, 102, 104, 232, 284
Cokayne, Sir Aston 341
Coke, Edward 226
Colchester, aftermath 327–8; Siege of 181, 259, 313, 321–4
Colchester's Tears . . . 259, 311
Colepeper, Sir John 285
Coles, Henry 51
Collier, Henry, injured 223
Collins, Cornet 153
combat fatigue 225
Commissioners of Disbandment 317
Commonwealth 8, 340
Conway, Sir Edward 26, 29, 35, 69
Cooke, Edward 84; *The Character of Warre* 72; *The Perspective Glasse of War . . .* 69, 72, 94
Cooke, William, mayor of Colchester, deposed 323
Cooke, William, a tenant 270
Coole, Elizabeth 342
Cooper, Sir Anthony Ashley 172, 346
Corbet, J., vicar of St Mary Crypt, Gloucester 161, 233–4
Corbet, John, governor of Gloucester 22, 55, 69–70
Corbett, Sir Vincent 262
Corfe Castle 163, 166
Cork, Richard Boyle, Second Earl of 209
Corneby, Lieutenant Thomas 298
Coulbroke, Thomas, robbed 286
court-martial 90, 198–200, 207, 236–7, 327
Courtnay, Captain 169
covenanters 122–3
Cowdle, Richard, tortured 250
Cowell, Colonel William 217
Cowley, Abraham 11, 27, 101; *The Civil War* 344
Cowper, Anthony 70

Coxe, Colonel 333
Craffaud, Major, killed 178
Craig, Thomas 13
Cranage, George 163
Crawford, General Lawrence 35, 120, 152
Crediton Down, Siege of 157
Creighton, George 139
Crew, Thomas 79
Crewe, Randolph 101, 274
Crewkerne 132
crime 9–10, 29, 346
Croft, Sir William 300
Cromwell, Oliver 45, 60, 61, 63, 68, 76, 102, 114, 126, 140, 168, 220, 232; 'a quarrelsome age' 311; at Marston Moor 120–1; and barrel of cream 278; comment on horses 147; corpse dug up 346; description of cavalry 135–6; dispersal of protesters 295; and female 'soldier' 308; in Ireland 330–2; as leader 180, 190–1; praises God 315, 326, 336; in Scotland 332–4; shot prisoners 327; view of Irish 262
Cropredy Bridge, Battle of 21, 77, 109, 121, 125, 131, 197, 234; aftermath 147
Crowland, Siege of 127
Cruso, John 103, 183; *Militarie instructions for the cavallrie* 72; *The Complete Captain* 72–3; *Treatise of Modern War* 80–1, 100, 263–4
Cuffe, Elizabeth 165
Culloden Moor, Battle of 54, 349
Curll, Bishop Walter, escape 247
Curtis, Abraham 280

Dacre household, avoidance of war 293
Daniels, Peter and Christina 305
Darbridgecourt, Thomas 55
Dave, William 32
D'Avenant, Sir William 92; 'The Soldier going to the Field' 56
Davenport, John 62, 70
Davenport, Sir William 68, 274, 291
Davies, Norman, comment on war 4–5
Davies, Priamus, in praise of women 295
Davies, Robert 342
De Gomme, Sir Bernard, death 217
deaths 14, 17, 182, 184, 186, 226, 315,

340–1; as accident 208; in battle 215; of children 301–2; disposal of corpses 218–19; due to disease 208–12; last words 217–18; numbers of 202– 7; perfect 216–17; in sieges 211–12

Declaration of the valiant . . . Famous apprentices of London 71

defeat, results 233–7

Dekker, Thomas, *Dialogue Between War, Famine and Pestilence* 210

Delaware, Lord 15

Dell, William 233

Denbigh, William Feilding, First Earl of 140, 163, 232, 304, 305

Denbigh, Lady Susan, death of husband and son 305

Denbigh, Lady Elizabeth 299, 300

Denham, Sir John 241

Denton, Alexander 220

Denton, Colonel John 220, 308

Denton, Susan, marriage 298

Derby, Charlotte Tremoille, Countess of 56, 164, 166; bravery 309

Derby, James Stanley, Seventh Earl of 67, 257

desertions 196, 225, 235

Devereux, Robert, Second Earl of Essex 13

Devereux, Robert, Third Earl of Essex 21, 32, 57 8, 68, 73, 83, 94, 96, 111, 117, 142, 147, 235; *Lawes and Ordinances* 239; and propaganda 255; 'Ramhead' 60; surrender of Lostwithiel 242–3

D'Ewes, Lieutenant-Colonel 76, 217

Digby, Lady Lettice, bravery 309

Digby, Sir George Second Earl of Bristol 125, 167, 236, 294

Digby, Sir John 144, 222, 243

Digges, Thomas 140

disease 157, 209–12, 303, 311, 340

Dobeny, Major John 228

Dobson, William 92

Dod, John 37

Dodington, Sir Francis 257, 261

Dolland, John 45

Donovan, 'The Universal Soldier' 6

Douglas, Robert, a covenanter 109, 142

Dowdell, Lady Elizabeth 165

Downame, John, *The Christian Warfare*, pamphlet 62

Downing, Calybute, Vicar of Hackney 62

D'Oyley, Colonel Charles 190

Drake, Francis 159

Drake, Sir Francis 12–13

drink 10, 59, 82, 93, 111, 162, 163, 193, 195, 286, 312

Drogheda, Siege of 330–1

drugs 82, 311

Drummond, Captain 195

Drummond, William, poet 26

Dryden, John 22

Dudley, Lady, death 302

Dudley, Sir Gamuel 127

Dugdale, William 348; *Baronage of England* 164

Dulbier, Colonel John, hewn to pieces 320

Duncannon, frigate 309

Duncannon, Siege of 177

Dungon's Hill, Battle of 126

Dupaquier, Jacques, French demographer 210

Durham Cathedral, holocaust in 334

Dyer, Thomas, pick-pocket 199

Dymb Dyott, a deaf-mute 160

Dyve, Sir Lewis 86, 246

Earle, Sir Walter, as mad 224–5

Earls Colne, Essex 10

Easton, Joan, as outcast 297

Edgehill, Battle of 21, 54, 77, 81, 98, 100, 111, 114, 115, 117– 18, 125, 126–7, 135, 140, 141, 142; aftermath ▸146–7, 148; casualties 227; desertions from 196; news of 231

Edwards, Chaplain Thomas 315

Egerton, Major General Peter 312

Eisenhower, Dwight D., *Crusade in Europe* 63

Eldred, Thomas, *The Gunner's Glass* 75

Elizabeth of Bohemia 12, 18, 187

Elizabeth I 180

Elliot, Bartholomew 198

Ellis, Thomas 148

Elton, Colonel Richard, *The Compleat Body of the Art Military* 74

Elton, Geoffrey 3, 9

Emitee, Thomas, *A New Remonstrance from Ireland* 36

England, ill-prepared for war 7–8; invaded by Scots 119–20

English, as effeminate 7
Erberry, William 315
Erwyn, John 35
Esmonde, Baron Lawrence 169
Essex, Earl of see Devereux, Robert
Eugaine, Captain de 23
Eure, Colonel William, death 305
Eure, Margaret 39, 296
Eures, Lieutenant 30
Europe, as warlike 8
Evelyn, John 9, 31, 257; fled England 293
Exact Relation of another Great Fight . . . in Cambridge, An 318
Exeter 65

Fairfax, Mary, marriage 342
Fairfax, Sir Thomas 69, 81, 120, 123, 140, 167, 181, 189–90, 232, 262; at Colchester 323–4; at Rochester 320; attitude to queen 302; 'Life and Death Compared' 215; and plunder 279–80; praises God 315; treatment of prisoners 328; wounded 222
Falkland, Lucius Cary, Second Viscount 27, 79, 192, 218–19
Falklands War 5, 221
families, divided loyalties 304–5; life disrupted 340–2
Fanshawe, Lady Anne 92, 299, 305–6; death of children 301; in Oxford 296
Fanshawe, Richard 299, 306
Farnham Castle, attacked 239
Farnham Church, attacked 184
Farr, Henry 182
Farringdon, Siege of 161
Felton, John 16, 17
Fetherstonaugh, Sir Timothy, executed 336
ffarington, Margaret 280
ffarington, William 51, 280, 312
Fielding, Sir Richard 58, 168, 194, 197
Fiennes, Colonel Nathaniel 58, 108, 116, 125, 132, 140, 170, 234; court-martialled 168
Filmer, Lady Anne, ransacked 272
First World War 214, 221
Fisher, Captain John 71
Fisher, Thomas, *The Warlike Directions* 72
Fleet prison 246, 252
Fleetwood, Colonel Charles 318

food 94, 95–6, 110, 157, 160–1, 167, 209, 278, 282, 285, 287; prices 312–13; shortages 311, 323
Foord, Edward, comment on women 295
Forbes, Sergeant-Major 84
Formaston, Thomas 202
Fortescue, Sir Edmund, as prisoner 251
Fortescue, Sir Faithful 238
Forth, Earl of, see Ruthven, Patrick
Foster, Colonel Thomas 51
Foster, Sergeant Henry 110, 111, 112, 142, 257
Fouche, Henry 126
Foulis, Sir Henry 129, 132
Francis, Captain John 110
Frederick V, Elector Palatine 12, 18, 187
Freeman, Mr, as prisoner 250
Freke, Arthur 160, 167, 302–3
Freud, Sigmund 5
Fromm, Erich 54, 55
Fuller, Thomas 343; *Good Thoughts for Bad Times* 344; *History of Worthies of England* 164

Gallant She-Soldier, The 309
Gammon, Captain 280
Gandy, John, schoolboy 67
gangrene 222
Gardiner, Harry, killed 306
Gardiner, S.R. 2, 329
Garrard, Colonel 27
garrison/s 89, 95, 163; growth 150–1; life 150; raids from 153–4; towns 151–2; treatment of villages 152–4
Gascoigne, Sir Bernard, set free 328
Gell, Sir John 53, 67, 71, 82, 98, 108, 163; unusual courtship 298
Gerard, Colonel Charles, wounded 227
germ warfare 226
Gheyn, John de, *The Exercise of Armes* 72
Gibbs, Captain 126
Gibson, Sir John 343; *Autobiography* 304
Gibson, William, indecision 318–19
Gill, Benjamin, surgeon's mate 227
Gilling, Thomas 287
Gittins, Daniel, robbed 272
Gloucester, property damage 157; Siege

of 82, 86, 105, 112, 158, 159, 169, 233

Gloucester Regiment, 69–70

Glyn, Captain 312

Goad, Thomas, as mad 225

God Fighting for Us in Ireland, pamphlet 37

Godolphin, Sidney, death 221; last words 217

Gomme, Sir Bernard de 21, 188

Goodwin, Colonel Arthur 268

Goring, Sir George 40, 44, 53, 120, 123, 124, 132, 137, 140, 144, 234, 248, 323; fondness for drink 195; orders soldiers to chew bullets 322

Gouge, William 62

Gough, Richard 10, 153

Gowran Castle, surrender 331

Graves, Robert 45

Great Rebellion 1, 201

Greaves, Dr Edward 157

Greene, John 148, 151, 203

Grenville, Lady Grace 220

Grenville, Sir Bevil 66, 76, 128, 141, 142; death 216–17, 220; decision to enlist 50; as tyrant 68

Grenville, Sir Richard 67, 198, 235

Greseley, Sir George 98

Grey, Trooper Patrick, executed 326

Griffith, Dr, daughter killed 178

Grimes, Captain John, gaoler 328

Grossmede, Dr 87

Grotius, Hugo 64, 115

Guilielm, Fabricius, *Experiments in Chyrurgerie* 226

Guise, Nicholas, avoidance of war 293

Gulf War 145

gunpowder 207–8, 223, 344

Gustavus Adolphus 18, 150, 181

Gwynne, Captain John 85, 105, 139, 194

Gwynne, Richard 161

Hacket, John 282

Hackett, General Sir John 6

Hagerston, Margaret 339

Hague Convention (1899) 240

'Halcyon days', use of phrase 79

Hallden, 'a stubborn fellow' 69

Hamilton, James, First Duke of 19, 24, 28, 29, 325, 335, 336; executed 327, 329; last words 218

Hammon, Captain, as plunderer 271–2

Hammon, Joyce 280

Hammond, Lieutenant 23

Hampden, John 60, 86, 128, 184, 186; death 208; last words 218; on plunder 267–8

Hancock, George, company clerk 109

Harcourt, Sir Simon 66, 184; letters to wife 299–300

Harlakenden, William 96

Harley, Captain Edward 71

Harley, Lady Brilliana 166, 167; bravery 295, 309; letter to son 303

Harley, Sir Robert 104, 125, 126, 129, 130, 140, 261

Harrington, William, propaganda against wife 77–8

Harris, Sir Paul 67

Harrison, Mrs, comment on England 274

Harrison, Thomas, regicide 178, 232

Harrison, William 345

Hart, Captain, governor of Tamworth 157

Hartford, William Seymour, Eleventh Earl of 32

Harvey, Captain 90, 194

Harvey, John, shot 341

Harvey, William 177; destruction of papers 270

Haselrig, Sir Arthur 277, 291, 334

Hastings, Sir Henry 65, 341; troops known as Rob-carriers 272

Hausted, Peter, Oxford don 78–9

Hawarden Castle 166

Hawkins, Colonel 262

Hawkins, Trooper John 259

Hawley, Lord 286

Haydon, Sir John 7

Haynes, Abraham, jailed 272

Hazard, Dorothy 165

Heath, Edward and Lucy 302

Heath, Sir Robert, Lord Chief Justice 241

Henderson, Sir John 232

Henrietta Maria, Queen 159, 256; birth of daughter 302; in Oxford 92

Herbert, Captain 29

Hereford, Siege of 157

Herr, Michael, comment on Vietnam 86

Hertford, William Seymour, First Marquis of 32, 234

Hewson, Colonel, Governor of Dublin, wounded 221

Hexham, Captain Henry, *The Principles of the Art Militarie* 72

Hey-Hoe for a Husband . . . 307

Heyle, Alderman Thomas, hanged himself 225

Heylyn, Peter, royalist divine 60

Highland Charge 134–5

Hill, Humphrey 341

Hill, William 281

Hills, Private Thomas, death 207

Hillsdeane, Private, killed by brother 305

Hilton, Captain 248

Hinde, Captain James, hanged 346

Hinson, Reverend, as prisoner 252

Hinton, Dr John 216, 227

HMS Reformation, ship 170

Hobart, John 90, 313

Hobbes, Thomas 203, 290; *Leviathan* 221, 343–4

Hodgkins, Captain (Wicked Will) 163, 193

Hodgson, Captain John 46, 82, 100, 109, 278, 333, 334; at Preston 325; plundered 241; wounded 227

Hoghton Tower, captured 208

Holland, Captain 173

Holland, Henry Rich, First Earl of 24, 25, 28; elected leader 319; executed 329; surrender of 320

Hollar, Wenceslaus, *The Kingdom of England and Principality of Wales* . . . 103

Holles, Denzil 71, 110, 141, 146, 182, 231, 305

Hollomor, Thomas, death 207

Holmes, Cornet 137

Holmes, Oliver Wendell 6

Honourable Artillery Company 102; oldest regiment 70–1

Hook, Captain 71

Hooker, John 36

Hopton, Sir Ralph 42, 65, 69, 81, 104–5, 121, 154, 198, 221, 287

Hopton Castle 168–9; massacre at 225; sacked 258; Siege of 157

Hopton Heath, Battle of 53, 83, 136

Horncastle, Battle of 235

horses, comment on 147; eaten 157, 161, 323; forage for 90; stolen 274, 275

Horsey, Captain John, burial 218

Horton, Colonel Thomas 319

hospitals 228

Hotham, Sir John 39, 304

Howard, Captain Arnold 198

Howard, Richard 152

Howard, Thomas 235

Howell, James, as prisoner 252

Hubberthorn, Richard 48

Hudson, Michael, bravery and death 320–1

humour 58–9, 77, 106, 108–9, 194, 235; in sieges 162

Hurcus, Captain James, death 208

Hurry, Sir John 107, 122, 144, 195

Hussey, Captain, hanged 346

Hussy, William 49

Hutchings, Richard, as robber 286

Hutchinson, Anne 301

Hutchinson, John 35, 45, 100, 152, 154, 163, 242, 301; marriage of son 342

Hutchinson, Lucy 34, 35, 45, 165, 173, 213, 287; as nurse 228

Hyde, Edward, First Earl of Clarendon 1, 5, 34–5, 51, 79, 117, 125, 126, 181, 195, 197, 202, 213, 230; comment on women 296–7; *History of the Rebellion and Civil Wars in England* 28

Inchiquin, Murough O'Brien, First Earl of 309, 331

infantry 97–8, 131, 137–9; 'to push of pike' 134

Ingleby, Jane, as soldier 308

Innes, Captain, tries to buy girl 297

Instructions for Musters and Armes and their use 22

Inverlochy, Battle of 123

Ireland 12, 30, 51–2, 103, 134, 177, 218, 349–50; atrocities in 34–6; cause of trouble 32–3; deaths 213–14; Elizabethan campaigns 12, 13; fighting resumed 329–32; hatred of Irish 160–2; massacres 259, 337; plunderered 280; Rebellion 33–8, 311

Ireton, Henry 124

Ironsides 140, 338; in Scotland 333

Isle of Ré 15, 17

Jackson, Henry 227

Jackson, Thomas, return from slavery 337
James, Henry 221
James I (VI of Scotland) 12; death 216
Jane, Joseph 101
Jeffries, Joyce, plundered 271–2, 296
Jennings, George, wounded 223
Jermyn, Henry 294
Jervis, Captain Sam 85
Jessop, William 283
Jodrell, Edmund, plundered 274
Johnson, Dr Samuel 5, 47
Johnson, Richard 7
Jones, Humphrey, house plundered 312
Jones, Inigo 179, 343
Jones, John, robbed 273, 286
Jones, Michael 153, 220, 312
Jonson, Ben 11, 47, 71, 140
Jordan, Lady, as mad 225
Jordan, Thomas, *The Christian Soldier in Preparation for Battle* 49
Josselin, Reverend Ralph 76, 96, 270–1, 279, 299, 321
Joyce, Cornet James, abducts Charles I 235, 318
Joyful Newes From the Sea 188
Jubbe, a parliamentary trooper, escape 247

Kelly, Captain Edward, killed 238
Kelso, Battle of 25, 27
Kettel, Dr Ralph 93
Kidd, Hugh 273
Kilgobbin, Siege of 300
Killigrew, Lady, corpse dismembered 321
Kilsby, skirmish in 64–5
Kingston, Robert Pierrepont, First Earl of 291
Kipling, Rudyard 201
Kniverton, David 263
Knockanoss, Battle of 135, 329
Knyvett, Henry 39
Knyvett, Sir Thomas 49–50, 251–2, 291, 313

La Rochelle, English expedition to 15–16, 17
Lake, Sir Edward 81, 190
Lambert, Lady, robbed 272
Lambeth Palace, as prison 246
Lane, Joseph 202
Lane, Jane, helped Charles I 308

Langdale, Sir Marmaduke 124, 260, 318
Langley, Jonathan, Shropshire gentleman 291
Langley, Major, a royalist 60
Langport, Battle of 104, 144, 232
Lansdown, Battle of 126, 130, 142
Lathom House, attack from 161–2; Siege of 160, 166–7, 175
Laud, William, Archbishop of Canterbury 29, 32, 82, 216
Lauder, George, *The Scottish Soldier* 139
Laugharne, Colonel Rowland, court-martial 327
Lawrence, Colonel Richard 213
Le Roy, Herbert, robbed 273
Leaguer Ladies 103, 161
Legge, William 167
Legh, Gerald 57
Leicester, Robert Sydney, Sixteenth Earl of 39, 49; letter of consolation 220
Leicester (place), sacked 177
Leighton, Alexander 62
Leighton, Major 139
Lenthall, William 114, 326
Leslie, Alexander, First Earl of Leven 20, 25, 144; *Articles and Ordinances of War for the . . . Army of . . . Scotland* 80
Leslie, Sir David 120, 122, 123, 182, 212, 276, 333, 335
L'Estrange, Roger 170; 'Loyalty Confined' 245
letters 161, 201, 230–1, 303–4, 348; between husbands and wives 299–301; of consolation 220
Levellers 82, 317
Levett, Reverend Robert 218
Lewis, William 162
Lewson, Sir Richard 39
Lichfield Cathedral 83–4, 160
Liddell-Hart, Sir Basil 3, 5
Lilburne, Elizabeth 241
Lilburne, John 55, 241, 307
Lilly, William 52, 306; *A Prophesy of the White King* 45
Limerick, Siege of 35, 156, 157, 161, 163, 242
Lincoln 174
Lindley, K.J. 290

Lindsey, Montague Bertie, Second Earl of 220
Liskeard gaol 247
Lisle, Sir George, at Colchester 322; executed 328
Lister, Joseph 34, 176
Lister, William, escape 247
literature 343–4
Lithgow, William 344
Littleton, Philip 262
Liverpool 171
Livingston, Chaplain John 27, 79, 218
Lloyd, Kate, letter to husband 300
Lloyd, Ludovick 62, 145
Lloyd, Luke 108
Lloyd, William, Sheriff of Merionethshire 320
London, defences 158–9; mobs in 318; trees cut down in 343
'London Cuckold . . .', ballad 53
London Red Regiment 253
London Trained Bands 96, 101, 104, 108, 109, 110, 111, 118, 178, 195–6, 201, 278, 279; as plunderers 266–7, 269, 270
Long, Colonel 151
Lostwithiel 109, 121, 242, 243–4
Louis XIII 15
Lovat, Lord 113
Lovelace, Richard 220; on defeat 236; described 1; 'Stone Walls do not a prison make . . .' 245; 'To Lucasta from Prison' 55–6, 58, 350
Lucas, Lady, corpse dismembered 321
Lucas, Sir Charles 133, 174, 259–60; at Colchester 322; executed 220, 328; house captured 321–2
Ludlow, Edmund 42–3, 51, 100, 136, 146, 152, 156, 169, 171 186, 235; as possible turncoat 254
Ludlow, Gabriel 216
Luke, Sir Samuel, governor of Newport Pagnell 60, 94, 97, 152, 184, 247, 250, 256, 260, 264, 275; reprimands son 303; thrice captured 238
Lumsden, James 141
Lunsford, Colonel Thomas, cruelty 43–4
Lunsford, Henry 116
Lupton, Donald 134; A Warre-Like Treatise of the Pike 47, 84–5
Lupton Heath 108

Luther, Martin 61
Lutzen, Battle of 18
Lyme 165; Siege of 158
Lyster, Daniel 346

MacColla, Alasdair 123
Macdonald, Archibald Mor 333
MacDonald, Colonel James 349
MacDonald, Ian Lom 123
MacDonald clan 195
McDonnell, James 48
Mace, Thomas 162
Machiavelli 61
Magdeburg, Siege of 175
Maidstone, Battle of 311
Malcolm, Zachary 122
Malmesbury, garrison at 153
Manchester, Edward Montagu, Second Earl of 57–8, 61, 76, 107, 117, 186, 240
Manchester, William 115
Manchester (place), Siege of 148, 158, 168
Mandeville, Lord, see Manchester, Second Earl of
Manifold Miseries of Civil War, The 20
Manners, Captain 139
Manning, Richard 298
Mansfield, Count Ernest von, militarily useless 14, 16–17
maps, shortage 103–4
Markham, Gervase 23; The Souldier's Exercise 71–2
marriage 342
Marriot, Thomas 64
Marshal, General S.L.A. 75, 113, 140
Marshal, William 148
Marshall, Reverend Samuel 148
Marshall, Stephen 42
Marshall's Elm, skirmish at 116, 141
Marston Moor, Battle of 47, 77, 81, 98, 114, 115, 119–20, 127, 128, 136, 141, 142; aftermath 146; deaths at 202; news of 231
Martin, Edward, arrested 240
Martindale, Adam 67, 341
Marvell, Andrew 215, 294
Marx, Karl 2
Mary Tudor 13
masques 11
massacres 12, 32, 34, 257–8, 259, 337
Massey, Edward 46, 285

Massey, Sir George 119
Massie, Captain 154
Maulever, Sir Thomas 305
Maurice, Prince 121, 150, 227, 261
Maurice, William 285
Maxwell, John, Bishop of Killala 252
Mayerne, Sir Thomas 302
Meldrum, George, marriage 342
Meldrum, Sir John 75, 140, 151, 184;
  re-marriage of wife 342
mercenaries 20–1, 46
Mercer, William, *The Moderate
  Cavalier* 347
Mercurius Aulicus, royalist newspaper
  54, 77, 79, 82, 256, 344
Mercurius Rusticus 222
Meyrick, Sir John 128
Mid-wive's Just Complaint, The 308
Middleton, Thomas 104
Mildmay, Sir Humphrey 293, 335
military engineering 158
militia units, Boston 24; Isle of Wight
  23; London 71, 85, 86, 87;
  Pembrokeshire 24; Tower Hamlets
  22, 71 *see also under* regiments; and
  named regiments
Milton, John 140, 188; *Paradise Lost*
  149; 'To the Lord General Fairfax'
  314
Mollineux, Captain 106
Molyneux, Colonel Caryll 83
Monck, George 81, 88, 98, 132, 168,
  226
Monckton, Colonel Sir Philip 137, 144
Monro, Mary and John 299
Monro, Richard 76
Montgomery, Battle of 194
Montgomery, Field Marshal Sir
  Bernard 232
Montrose, James Graham, Fifth Earl of
  54; campaign 122, 212, 233, 262,
  332–3, 334–5
Moore, Colonel Samuel 157, 258
Moore, Elizabeth, letter to sister 303–4
Moore, Joshua 98
Moore, Lord Charles and Lady Alice
  306
Moore, Robert, a 'veriest knave' 67
More, Sir Thomas 13
Morgan, Edward, killed 269
Morgan, William 287
Morley, Colonel Herbert 240, 252

Morrill, John 2
Morris, William 346; hanged 198
Morton, Thomas, *Englands Warning-
  Piece* 20
*Most true and exact Relation of a Great
  Overthrow given to the Cavaliers,*
  pamphlet 37
Mostyn, Sir Roger 51, 278
Mould, Thomas, death 202
Moyle, Colonel 101
Mullen, Mary 35
Munrow, Robert 215
music 102, 162
mutinies 29, 82, 316–17
Myddle, Shropshire 9–10, 153, 202, 298
Myddleton, Sir Thomas 277
Myn, Colonel 167
Mytton, Colonel Thomas 188, 262

Nairn, plunder of 122
Nantwich 106, 135, 169, 232, 239; jail
  274; plundered 268
Napier, Archibald, First Baron 56
Napier, Richard, horse stolen 275
Napoleon Bonaparte 95
Naseby, Battle of 98, 109, 114, 115,
  123–5, 125, 126, 131, 140, 141, 144,
  145, 189–90, 235; aftermath 146;
  deaths at 202
Nash, Francis, killed 308
navy 25, 46, 345–6
Neale, Lady Helen 166
Neale, Robert, tortured 250
Neale, William 42
Needham, Colonel Simon 184, 322
Needle, William, hanged 263
Neile, Anne 248
neutrals 290
Neve, Sir William Le 147
New Model Army 77, 86, 98, 107,
  123–4, 132, 160, 182, 233, 255, 285,
  345; described 316; material
  grievances 317
Newark, sieges 63, 155, 160
Newburn, Battle of 26
Newbury, First Battle 5, 132, 139, 192,
  227; Second Battle 84, 109, 128, 133,
  145, 147, 227
Newcastle, William Cavendish, First
  Earl of 53, 58, 81, 119–20, 130, 150,
  234

Newcastle, Margaret Cavendish, Duchess of 78, 220, 253
Newcastle (place), gaol at 246; Siege of 156
Newcombe, Henry 336
Newport, Sir Francis 28, 39
Newport Pagnell 152; garrison at 275
news, dissemination 178, 230–1, 232, 233
Newton, Sir Henry 192
Nicholas, Sir Edward 285, 313
Nichols, Anthony 218
Nichols, John 282
Northampton, Spencer Compton, Eleventh Earl of 53, 136–7, 148
Norton, Richard 136, 178, 221–2
Norwich, Lady, at Colchester 323
Norwich, Lord, see Goring, George
Nottingham Castle 172

Ockdon, Private, as prisoner 250
Okey, Sir John 82, 124, 144, 315, 346
O'Neil, Owen Roe 213
O'Neill, Hugh Duff 332
ordnance 3–4
Ordnance Office, state of 7
Ormonde, James Butler, Twelfth Earl of 33, 35, 139, 208, 261
Orrey, Earl of, see Boyle, Roger
Osborne, William, letter to wife 324, 341–2
Oswestry Castle 163
Ottley, Sir Francis 230
Overton, Richard, printer 317
Owen, Nat 153, 298
Owen, Sir John 222, 320
Oxford, as garrison town 91–4, 234; Siege of 157, 161, 167
Oxford University, abuse of system 81–2; royalist supporter 70; students 74
Oxinden, Henry 26, 28, 230, 292
Oxinden, Ralph 38
Oyer and Terminer, writ of 241

Paget, Sir William, Fifth Baron 50, 76
painting 11
pamphlets 40–1, 61, 62–3, 71, 78, 140, 151, 188, 189, 230, 250, 287, 306–7, 310–11, 328, 348; and Irish Rebellion 34, 35, 37
papists, hatred of 254–5
parish registers 203, 207

Parker, Geoffrey 210
Parker, Henry 61
Parker, Matthew 78
parliament 8, 26, 115, 319; Long 30, 31–2; Short 25, 28, 30
Parliamentary Weekly Intelligencer 261
Parsons, John, as robber 286
Parsons, Sir William 33, 34, 136
Patton, General 48
peace, demanded 289; petitioners for 313; return of 45–6; talks 93–4, 101
Peake, Humphrey, *Meditations upon a Siege* 241–2
Pearl, George 343
Peck, Captain, hanged 346
Pembroke, Philip Herbert, Twenty-Fifth Earl of 39
Pembroke Castle, seized 319
Peniman, Sir James 250
Penruddock, John, house plundered 267
Penruddock's rising 337
pensions 224, 228–9, 347
Penzance, plundered 312
Pepys, Samuel 345
Percy, Henry, Baron Alnwick 308
Perfect Diurnal, The 261
Peters, Reverend Hugh 86, 127, 157, 178, 203, 213, 262, 285, 315, 330, 338
Petition of Right, (1628) 17
Petty, Sir William 203, 213–14
Peyton, Sir Thomas 25–6, 56
Phelips, Sir Robert 24
Phillips, Mrs 263
Phillips, Sir Thomas 82, 258
Phylip, William, of Hendre Fechan 282
Pickering, Captain 318
Pickery, Colonel 178
Pilgrimage of Grace (1536) 13
Pinkney, Major, death 184
Pinnel House, garrison saved from plunder 242
Pitt, Edward, as prisoner 251
Pitt, John 343
Place, Captain Edward 186
plague 157, 209–10, 311, 340
Plumtree, Dr 163
plunder 265–6, 320; by royalists 286; of cathedrals 276–8; consequences 278–9; control 285–8; and free quarter 281–2, 311–12; institutionalized 279–80; reasons for

274–5; Scots reputation for 276; victims 266–75, 287
Pollard, Sir Hugh 248
Pontefract, Siege of 160, 164
Popham, Colonel 96
population 173, 214, 340
Porter, Endymion 53
Porter, Robert 175
Portland, Countess of 166, 309
Portsmouth, morale in 163; Siege of 239
Pottinger, Andrew, killed 270, 275
Poulet, Lord 29
Poulter, Thomas, indecision 318–19
Power, Colonel Rice, court-martial 327
Powick Bridge 103, 108, 116, 141; skirmish at 83, 188, 234
Poyer, Colonel John 319; court-martial 327; fondness for drink 195
Poyntz, Sir Robert, comment on war 290
Poyntz, Sydenham 19, 47, 158
Prater, Colonel Richard, governor of Nunney Castle 160
Pratt, Dr 199
Pratt, Sir Roger, fled England 293
Prayer Book Rebellion 33, 311
prayer manuals 87
Preece, Sergeant William 91, 202
Preston 173, 174–5, 281, 325
Priestley, Samuel 67
printers 230
prisoners 291; conditions 249–52; deported 212, 213–14; escape 247, 250, 251; exchanged 247–8; killed 36, 239–40, 257, 311, 323, 330; parole 248–9; plundered 241–2; ransomed 265; rights and conventions 240–3; sent to Coventry 242; treatment 242–3, 245–6, 327, 334–5, 336–7; vulnerable to revenge 244–5
propaganda 11, 77–80, 255–7, 259, 306, 319; against plunder 268–9; roundhead 78–80, 275–6; royalist 60, 78, 251
Prosperous Sarah, as prison ship 246
Protestants 61
Prynne, William 61, 265, 280
puritans 60, 63, 148; concept of war 62
Putney Debates (1647) 316, 317
Pyle, Ernie 86
Pym, John 24, 32
Pyne, John 116

Rainsborough, Colonel Thomas 316
Rallingson, Richard 81
Ram, Robert 194, 257; *Soldiers' Catechism* 63
Ramsay, Sir James 37
rape 256, 259, 260, 296, 319
Ratcliffe, Sir Alexander, marriage of daughter 342
Rathbury Castle, Siege of 160, 162, 167, 302
Raymond, Thomas 20, 64
Raynford, John, *Military Observations* 84
Raynor, Mr, hanged 177
Raynsford, John, *The Young Soldier* 72
Reade, Thomas 345
Reading 168, 173; betrayed by Sir Richard Fielding 194; loss of 234
regiments, desertion from 235; tradition 77 *see also under* militia units; named regiments
Reinking, William 100, 194
Relation of the Rare Exploits of the London Soldiers, A 267
religion 61–4, 80, 86, 93, 127, 255, 315–16
Rellisone, Mr, killed 269
Restoration 8, 348
Reynolds, E., *Orders from the Lord of Hosts* 315
Reynolds, Lieutenant 163
Rich, Captain 209
Richardson, Richard 276
Riddel, Sir Thomas, marriage 342
Rigby, Colonel Alexander 167
Rigby, George 248
Ringe, Thomas, death 208
Ripon, Treaty to 26
roads and bridges 103
Robartes, Sir John, First Earl of Radnor 81
Roberts, Reverend 176
Robinson, Major, killed 178
Robinson, Private George, wounded 223
Roche, Leca, engineer 21
Rochester, Battle of 320
Rodway, Susan 201, 229; letter to husband 301
Roe, Owen 99
Roe, Quartermaster 107
Roe, Sir Arthur 292

Roe, Sir Thomas 101
Rogers, David, thief 199
Rogers, John, in fight 286
Rolle, Sir William 77
Roseworme, John 21, 158, 345
Rosgill, Christopher 162
Rosleigh, Johnathan 299
Ross, Battle of 139
Round-Head's Remembrancer, The,
    pamphlet 61
roundheads 55, 59–61, 108, 117, 127,
    132, 144, 153–4, 166, 168, 170, 172,
    242; changes in attitude 314; as
    church plunderers 276–8; deaths 206;
    treatment of deserters 198–9
Rous, John 292
Rowse, A.L. 9
Rowton Heath, Battle of 109, 124, 125,
    133, 134, 136, 139
royalism 52, 53–4
royalists 125, 144, 151–2, 184, 242,
    254–5, 286, 312; at Worcester 335; as
    plunderers 268; treatment of
    deserters 196–8
Royston, Margery, robbed 273
Rubens, Peter Paul, 'Saint George and
    the Dragon' 11
Rudge, Barnaby 183
Rudyerd, Sir Benjamin 40, 64
Rupert, Prince 21, 57, 69, 93, 111, 116,
    117, 125, 144, 168, 187–9, 257; at
    Bristol 119, 124; at Marston Moor
    119–20, 127; campaigns 109; court-
    martial and exile 236–7; created Duke
    of Cumberland 188; and defeat 234;
    propaganda against 77; wounded 224
Rushworth, John, 26, 114, 170, 323
Russell, Colonel, governor of Lichfield
    188
Russell, John 257
Russell, Sir William 51
Ruthven, Patrick, Earl of Forth 20, 107,
    121
Rutland, John Manners, Eighth Earl of
    300
Ryves, Bruno 198, 256, 259

Sadler, Major, court-martialled 254
Safety, The, ship 114
St Augustine 61
St Barbe, Captain Francis, burial 219
St Lawrence, William, schoolboy 67

Salisbury, Sir Thomas 39, 54, 55
Sancroft, William, Archbishop of
    Canterbury 294
Sande, Colonel 276
Sandys, Colonel 83, 222–3
Sandys, Richard 172
Sandys, Thomas, shot 239, 248–9
Sanford, Captain Thomas 141, 169, 193
Saville, Lady Anne 301–2
Sawyer, Mr, killed 177
Saye and Sele, William Fiennes, First
    Viscount 32, 128, 136
Scarborough, Siege of 157, 295, 303
Scholefield, Reverend Jonathan 84
Scotland 102, 103, 134, 177, 349;
    bloodbaths in 264; deaths in 212–13;
    fighting resumed 332–4; religious war
    against 24–30; use of new prayer
    book in 7–8; violence in 12; war in
    122–3
*Scourge of Civil Warre: the Blessings of
    Peace, The* 259
Scrope, Colonel Adrian 320
Scudamore, James 263
Scudamore, Lady, house plundered 268
Scudamore, Sir Barnabus 168, 171, 271
Scudamore, Sir John 51
Sealed Knot 337
Second World War 54, 63, 75–6, 78, 86,
    145; population decreases 214;
    prisoners in 242; surrender in 238;
    wounded 221
Sedgwick, Chaplain William 314
Sedgwick, John 87
Sedgwick, Obadiah, preacher 87, 110
Self-Denying Ordinance 123
sermons 47–50, 86–7, 110, 251
sex, perverted 77–8
Sexby, Edward 316
Seymour, Colonel Edward, Governor
    of Dartmouth 304
Shakespeare, William 13, 44, 48, 49, 78
Sharples, Captain George, humiliation
    244–5
Sheffield, Colonel, on parole 248
Sheldon, Major Thomas 223–4
Shelford House 172
Sherborne Castle, sacked 176
Sherman, General William T. 4, 201
Shipman, Sir Abraham, death 217
Shrewsbury, capture of 262
Shuckburgh, Richard 53

Sidney, Sir Philip 216
sieges 154–72, 309; aftermath 172–9;
  and civilians 163–4, 173; cost 283;
  ending 167; morale 162; mortar fire
  159–60; sense of isolation 161; state
  of besiegers 167–8; surrender 168–70
Simons, Henry, robbed 286
Skippon, Sir Philip 71, 86, 118, 121, 180
slaves 253, 327, 337
Slingsby, Sir Henry 8, 51, 67, 91, 131,
  187, 232; captured 241
Slingsby, Sir Walter 134, 139
Smith, Captain Jermyn 298
Smith, Captain William 104, 169
Smith, Miller 164
Smith, Provost Marshall 253; treatment
  of prisoners 249–51
Smith, Sir John 64–5, 81, 217; bravery
  192–4
Smith, Thomas 38
soldiers, 'a panic fear' 140–4, 194–5; age
  182–3; behaviour 28–30, 80; chain of
  command 185; chanting psalms 30,
  83–4; coercion 80–1; defeated 172;
  demobilization 8, 345–6; described
  54, 60; desertion 196–9, 326–7;
  discipline 93, 126; drill 73–5, 92;
  effect of combat 314–15; fatigue 105,
  126; friendship 51, 76; as heroes
  192–4; honour 54–8; leaving/
  returning home 90–1, 101; mental
  attitude 127–9; morale 125–6;
  obedience 50–1, 52; over-sexed, over-
  paid 297–8; pay 28, 77, 81, 94, 255,
  316–17, 322; promotion 81–2;
  punishment 80–1; recruitment 67–8,
  76–7, 232–3, 235; selective memory
  129–31, 343–4; 'stouting it out'
  168–9; training 66–71, 73–5, 76, 77,
  84–6; as turncoats 253–5; wenching
  59, 93
Soldier's Catechism: composed for the
  Parliamentary Army, pamphlet 37
Solemn League and Covenant 62, 119
Somerset, Edward, Marquis of
  Worcester 20
Somerset, John 286–7
Spencer, Henry, First Earl of
  Sunderland, letter to wife 300
Spencer, Sir Thomas 228
spies 260, 263–4, 309

Spiritual Snapsacke for the
  Parliamentary Soldier, A 61
Spratt, Reverend Devereux 34, 213
Sprigge, Chaplain John 86, 109, 174,
  233, 264, 284
Springate, Lady Mary 157–8, 301
Springate, Thomas 301
Springe, Sir William 190
Stagger, Captain 207
Stamford, Henry Grey, First Earl 304
Standley, Captain 274
Stanhope, Lady, unusual courtship 298
Stapleton, Sir Robert, praises God 336
Stawell, Sir John 116, 141
Staynings, John 81
Steele, Captain Thomas 168, 169
Steer, John, London surgeon 226
Stephen, Sir Henry 106
Stephenson, Richard 165
Sterly, Cornet John 241
Sterne, Richard, arrested 240
Stewart, Captain William 148
Stewart, John, First Earl of Traquair 7
Stewart, John, sold 334–5
Stewkeley, John 306
Steyning, Amias 19, 76, 89
Stiles, Captain John 185, 257
Stoakes, Sergeant William 347
Stocker, John, a joiner 177
Stone, Henry, thief 199
Stone, Lawrence 290
Stone, Nicholas, Enchiridion of
  Fortification 105
Strange, Lord 51
Strong, James 165; Joanereidos . . . 307,
  309
Styles, Richard 160
Styward, Thomas, The Pathwaie to
  Martiall Discipline 71
Summers, William 177; wife's madness
  225
Sun-Tzu 155
Sunderland, Henry Spenser, Second
  Earl of 56
supernatural events 148–9
surgeons 226–7
surrender 237–44; as chaotic 238–40
Sussex, Lady Frances 38; walled-up
  valuables 272
Sutton, Thomas, The Good Fight of
  Faith 63
Swadlin, Thomas, The Soldiers

Catechism composed for the King's Army 52, 87
Swanley, Captain 260–1
Swift, Francis, as robber 286
Sydenham, Colonel William 261
Symmons, Edward, *A Militarie Sermon . . . Preached at Shrewsbury . . . To His Majesty's Army* 52
Symonds, Richard 83, 104, 147, 260, 263; on surrender of Lostwithiel 244
Syon's Calamity or England's Misery . . . pamphlet 40

Tantalus, Private 162–3
Tawney, R.H. 128
taxation 282–3
Taylor, Henry, escape 247
Taylor, Jeremy 190, 344
Taylor, John 39, 53–4, 84, 208–9, 263; journey in England 284
Taylor, Thomas, pamphlets by 62
Temple, Sir William 33
Tenby, fall of 234
Thames, filthy condition of 208–9
Thelwell, Captain 23
Thirty Years War 17–20, 214
Thomson, George 311
Thornhaugh, Colonel Francis, last words 218; wounded 239
Tildsley, Colonel 67
Tillam, Mr, a surgeon 176
Tilly, Marshall Johann 175
Tilsley, John, Vicar of Deane 232, 258
Titus, Silius 96
tobacco 30, 160, 162–3, 311
Tolstoy, Leo 3, 4
Torrington, Battle of 181
torture 242
Towenley, Colonel Charles 146
Tower Regiment 322
Townsend, Alice, unusual courtship 297–8
Townsend, Henry 274
training manuals 4, 69, 71–4, 75, 84, 185
transportation 212, 213–14, 327, 334–5, 336, 337
Travers, Jacob 167
Treason in Ireland . . ., pamphlet 34
Trelawny, Sir John 122
Trenchard, Thomas 31
Trevannion, Sir John 76; last words 218

Trevelyan, G.M. 1
Trevelyan, George 51
Trevelyan, John, letter of consolation 220
Trevor, Sir Arthur 55, 69, 89, 93, 97, 143, 196
trimmers 292
troops *see* soldiers
True Copy of a Welsh Sermon preached . . . by Shon ap Owen, a priest 275
True Declaration of Kingston's entertainment of the Cavaliers 276
True Informer, The 209
True Relation of the Bloody Conspiracy of the Papists . . ., pamphlet 37
True Representation of the Miserable Estate of Germany, A, horrific woodcuts in 18–29
Trumbull, William 259
Trussell, Marston 143
Tucker, Captain William 37
Tullie, Isaac 160, 183
Turbeville, Troilus, Lieutenant, created knight 81
Turner, Sir James 36, 46, 54, 73, 85, 94, 102, 106, 282; at Wigan 325–6; campaign recollections 19– 20; as compassionate plunderer 272–3; escape 336; injured 223; *Pallas Armata, Military Essays* 344; as prisoner 327
Turnham Green 118, 128, 175
Turpin, Captain 198
Twysden, Elizabeth 165
Twysden, Sir Roger, as prisoner 246
Tynte, Colonel John 286
Tynte, Lieutenant Henry 286
Tythingham, Mr, robbed 286

Uchteritz, Heinrich Von 337
uniforms *see under* clothes
Upton Bridge, skirmishes at 103
Usury, Sir John 154

Vane, Sir Henry 19, 50; marriage of sister 342
Vasavour, Sir William, on parole 248
Vaughan, John 234
Vaughan, Reece, death 202
Vaughan, Sir James 291
Veil, Marquis de la 112
Venables, General Robert 340

Venetian Secretary 101, 104, 261
Venn, Captain Thomas 56, 83; *Military Observations* 73; *Military and Maritime Discipline* 161
Venn, Colonel John 68, 251
Venner, Dr 209
Vere, Lord 76
Vernatti, Captain Antonio, as plunderer 273
Verney, Cary, fate of 306
Verney, Henry 187
Verney, Mary 302
Verney, Penn 298
Verney, Sir Edmund 29, 50, 52, 192, 304, 328
Verney, Sir Ralph 38, 219, 304; letter of consolation 220
Verney, Thomas, as prisoner 245
Vernon, Lieutenant, death 207
Vicars, John 78, 83–4
victories, effect 231–3
Vieuville, Marquis de, killed 238–9
violence 9–10, 164, 264; due to drugs 311; in Ireland 12; and plunder 281; in Scotland 12
Virgin's Complaint, The 306, 308
Viver, Colonel, captured 241

W.H., a Captain 130–1
Waite, Colonel Thomas 321
Wales, rising in 319; state of 284; troops from 54–5
Walker, Sir Edward 84
Walker, William 349
Wall, Colonel Nicholas, death 330
Waller, Edward 27
Waller, Sir William 42, 67, 79, 94, 96, 97, 104, 107, 109, 121, 125, 167, 169, 178, 181, 194, 196, 197; accident 208; defeat 234; *Divine Meditation up Several Occasion* 344; as negotiator 248; plundered 241; on trimmers 292
Waller Plot 170
Wallington, Nehemiah 59, 78; commonplace book 256–7; fascination for plunder 271
Walsingham, Edward 193
Walton, Captain, last words 217
Walton, Valentine 76; last words 218
Walwyn, William, *A Remonstrance of Many Thousand Citizens* 317
Wandesford, Sir Christopher 33

Warburton, Robert 177
Ward, Colonel 22
Wardour Castle, Siege of 100, 152, 156, 157, 167, 242
Warner, Silvester, plundered 274
Warning piece to warre, A, pamphlet 43
Warren, Lieutenant-Colonel, death 330
Warrington, skirmish at 335
Wars of the Roses 13, 214
Warwick, Sir Philip 59, 182, 187, 321
Warwick Castle, Siege of 60
Washington, Colonel Henry 160, 164
Waterloo, Battle of 113
Wathen, Captain Thomas 106, 276
Watson, Lion 120, 130, 142
Wavell, Field-Marshall 1, 3
Weakes, William, robbed 286
weapons and armour 98–101
weather 102, 104–5
Weekly Accompt, The 101, 343
Weldon, Sir Anthony 67
Wellington, Duke of 129, 145
Welsh Plunder, The 275
Wemyss, James, Master Gunner 7
Wentworth, Thomas, First Earl of Strafford 32–3, 269
West, Sergeant 22
Westminster Trained Bands 85, 86
Westmorland, crime in 10
Weterlow, Charles, robbed 273
Wexford, massacre at 331
Whalley, Colonel Edward 76, 77, 160, 164
Whalley's Regiment 316, 321
Wharton, Nehemiah 110, 111, 266, 267, 269, 270, 279
Whistler, John 92
White, Charles 154
White, Hester 228
White, John 64
Whitecoat Regiment 120–1, 145, 235
Whitehall, Thomas and Catherine, fled England 293
Whitehead, Reverend, hidden covenant 346
Whitelocke, Bulstrode 5, 38, 51, 64, 128, 303; as ambassador 348; at Oxford 94; at Worcester 335; comment on war 39–40, 41; house plundered 270; wounded 222
Whitely, Mr 45

Wicked Resolution of the Cavaliers, The 78

Widowes' Lamentation, The 300

Wigmore, Lieutenant-Colonel, last words 217

Wilde, Oscar 4

Williamham, George, merchant 110

Williams, Abraham, in fight 286

Williams, Provost Marshall Thomas, hanged and cashiered 246

Willingham, George 266

Willoughby, John 32, 45

Wilmot, Henry 117

Wilson, Robert 287

Wiltshire levies 316–17

Winceby, Battle of 84

Winchester, Charles Paulet, Fifth Marquis of 178

Winchester (place), sacked 267

Windebanke, Francis 30, 168

Windsor Castle, as prison 251

Wingate, Captain, as prisoner 249

Winkles, Thomas 64

Winter, Lady Mary 166

Winthrop, Stephen 342

Wise, Mayor Dennis 281

Wiseman, Lady Elizabeth, house ransacked 272

Wiseman, Sir Richard, Surgeon General 217, 226, 227

Withenshaw House, Siege of 160

Wither, Thomas, *Campo Musae* 343

Withers, George 241, 311; 'A Soldier Thinks of Sin' 41–2

Wolph, Mr 279

Wolstenholme, John, house ransacked 272

women 103, 110, 161, 178; bravery 164–7, 308–9; butchered 331; demand peace 289; how viewed 307–8; as immodest 296–7, 298–9; as she-soldiers 308– 9; treatment 78, 244, 256, 259, 323–4; unusual courtships 297–8; in war 295–300

Wood, Anthony 1, 70, 348

Wood, Richard, Vicar of Fremington 343

Wood, Trooper 321

Woodbridge, John 152

Woodcroft House, royalist rising at 321

Woodhall, John, *The Surgeon's Mate* 223

Woodhouse, Colonel 259

Worcester 103; Battle of 335–8; praised 111; Siege of 160, 163, 164, 164–5

World Turned Upside Down, The 312

Worsley, Captain 65

Wortley, Sir Francis 269

wounds 221–3, 339, 342; four categories 223–4; non-combat 223; psychiatric 224–5; treatment 225–9

Wray, Captain, escape 247

Wright, John 246

Wroth, Sir Thomas 347

Wurzburg, capture 19

Wyndham, Hugh 51

Wyndham, Lady 165

Wyndham, Sir Thomas 52

Wynne, Edward, burial 219

Yarmouth militia 23

Yeames, W.F., famous painting 303

Yeomans, Robert, Bristol merchant 170, 348

York, Siege of 105, 156, 158, 162, 203

Yorke, William 68

Young, Dr Edward 251

Young, Ensign Arthur 192